THE INTELLECTUAL WORLD
OF THE ITALIAN RENAISSANCE

Language, Philosophy, and the Search for Meaning

In this book, Christopher Celenza provides an intellectual history of the Italian Renaissance during the long fifteenth century, ca. 1350–1525. His book fills a bibliographic gap between Petrarch and Machiavelli and offers clear case studies of contemporary luminaries, including Leonardo Bruni, Poggio Bracciolini, Lorenzo Valla, Marsilio Ficino, Angelo Poliziano, and Pietro Bembo. Integrating sources in Italian and Latin, Celenza focuses on the linked issues of language and philosophy. He also examines the conditions in which Renaissance intellectuals operated in an era before the invention of printing, analyzing reading strategies and showing how texts were consulted, and how new ideas were generated as a result of conversations, both oral and epistolary. The result is a volume that offers a new view on both the history of philosophy and Italian Renaissance intellectual life. It will serve as a key resource for students and scholars of early modern Italian humanism and culture.

Christopher S. Celenza is Dean of Georgetown College at Georgetown University, where he has a joint appointment as Professor of History and Classics. He is the author of several books including the prize-winning *The Lost Italian Renaissance and Machiavelli: A Portrait*. His work has been featured in Salon, The Huffington Post, and on radio and television. Former Director of the American Academy in Rome, he has held fellowships from the Guggenheim Foundation, the American Council of Learned Societies, the Harvard University Center for the Study of the Italian Renaissance (Villa I Tatti), the American Academy in Rome, and the Fulbright Foundation.

THE INTELLECTUAL WORLD OF THE ITALIAN RENAISSANCE

Language, Philosophy, and the Search for Meaning

CHRISTOPHER S. CELENZA

CAMBRIDGE
UNIVERSITY PRESS

One Liberty Plaza, 20th Floor, New York, NY 10006, USA

Cambridge University Press is part of the University of Cambridge.

It furthers the University's mission by disseminating knowledge in the pursuit of education, learning, and research at the highest international levels of excellence.

www.cambridge.org
Information on this title: www.cambridge.org/9781107003620
DOI: 10.1017/9781139051613

First published 2018

Printed in the United States of America by Sheridan Books, Inc.

A catalogue record for this publication is available from the British Library.

ISBN 978-1-107-00362-0 Hardback

Cambridge University Press has no responsibility for the persistence or accuracy of URLs for external or third-party internet websites referred to in this publication and does not guarantee that any content on such websites is, or will remain, accurate or appropriate.

For Stephen J. Campbell

CONTENTS

PREFACE

This book grew out of three trajectories. The first has to do with a continued interest in Italian Renaissance intellectual life, especially in its Latinate variety.[1] The remarkable *I Tatti Renaissance Library*, under the general editorship of James Hankins, has provided an ever-expanding series of Renaissance Latin texts (with corresponding English translations). The field can be taught and researched now by a much broader constituency than ever before. As that project has grown and come to maturity, there has been a second, more recent scholarly emphasis on what we can call "vernacular classicism." Under this rubric one can include studies of the diffusion, in Italian vernaculars, of thought-worlds identified with the culture of ancient Greece and Rome.[2] But there has as yet been little work attempting to unite the Latinate and vernacular tendencies; to discuss their qualitative differences; and to show, indeed, that they were linked. Finally, the third trajectory has to do with the broad meaning that "philosophy" possessed in the Renaissance. There are historiographic reasons as to why Italy's long fifteenth century has traditionally taken up so little space in the history of Western philosophy.[3] But suffice it to say that, instead of fitting fifteenth-century thinkers

---

[1] The journal *Humanistica lovaniensia* is invaluable on this front, not least its yearly "Instrumentum bibliographicum neolatinum." Much work on Italian Renaissance studies, up to 2003, is discussed in David Rundle and Martin McLaughlin, "Introduction," *Renaissance Studies* 17 (2003), 1–8 (an introduction to a volume of *Renaissance Studies* devoted to the *studia humanitatis*, the five humanities disciplines of grammar, rhetoric, history, poetry, and moral philosophy, that together formed the disciplinary core of Italian Renaissance humanism). Since then, see Christopher S. Celenza, *The Lost Italian Renaissance* (Baltimore: Johns Hopkins University Press, 2004); Jonathan Woolfson, ed., *Palgrave Advances in Renaissance Historiography* (New York: Palgrave, 2004); James Hankins, ed., *The Cambridge Companion to Renaissance Philosophy* (Cambridge: Cambridge University Press, 2007); Michael Wyatt, ed., *The Cambridge Companion to the Italian Renaissance* (Cambridge: Cambridge University Press, 2014).

[2] See David Lines, "Beyond Latin in Renaissance Philosophy: A Plea for New Critical Perspectives," *Intellectual History Review* 25 (2015), 373–89.

[3] See Celenza, *The Lost Italian Renaissance* and idem, "What Counted as Philosophy in the Italian Renaissance? The History of Philosophy, the History of Science, and Styles of Life," *Critical Inquiry* 39 (2013), 367–401.

into Procrustean beds of "philosophy" versus "literature," "Latin" versus "vernacular," the goal here is to let Renaissance thinkers speak on their own, premodern terms.

Premodern: recognizing the differences in the basic conditions under which Renaissance intellectuals operated is paramount.[4] A key precept of this book is that technologies condition, though they do not determine, literary output. Much of fifteenth-century intellectual life occurred before the existence of printing with moveable type, and all of the long fifteenth century is circumscribed within a culture in which the basic circumstances of reading and writing were vastly different from those of today. Importantly, for the Italian Renaissance intellectuals highlighted in this book, reading was social and generational. The material consulted, the reading strategies adopted, and the conclusions reached tended to be the results of conversations both oral and epistolary. And those conversations played themselves out among intellectuals who were parts of discernible generational cohorts.[5]

This book is episodic, rather than synthetic, more a series of soundings than a linear narrative; because of the themes pursued, it circles back chronologically on more than one occasion. Most of all, it is an invitation to future work.

One final note: This is a book about intellectuals in the Italian Renaissance. Simple as that sentence might sound, the terms "intellectual," "Italian," and "Renaissance" all need explanation. It is best to begin with "Italian," since it will give us a sense of place; to have a sense of place make sense, we also need a feeling for time. The time in question is what I will be calling the "long fifteenth century." For now, it is enough to know that the period in question runs from about 1350 to about 1525 – a "long" century indeed. Italy during this period was not a country, the way we think of countries today. It was instead a collection of city-states, small political units bigger than cities and possessed of a powerful sense of independence and cultural identity. Living in one of them, one would have felt patriotism toward the city and a strong belief that it – not "Italy" – was one's real home. Still, there were times during the long fifteenth century when certain intellectuals did refer to Italy as a unity. Usually these instances occurred when the person in question was in exile or when invaders from beyond the Alps found their way into the Italian peninsula. In other words, only threat or absence

[4] See Christopher S. Celenza, "What Did It Mean to Live in the Long Fifteenth Century?" in Rivka Feldhay and F. Jamil Ragep, eds., *Before Copernicus: The Cultures and Contexts of Scientific Learning in the Fifteenth Century* (Montreal: McGill-Queen's University Press, 2017). For a view stressing some of the premodern conditions of Italian Renaissance life, see Guido Ruggiero, *The Renaissance in Italy: A Social and Cultural History of the Rinascimento* (Cambridge: Cambridge University Press, 2015).

[5] Ronald G. Witt's focus on generations and communities of intellectuals evinces the kind of social and interactive reality of premodern intellectual life that is central to my approach: Ronald G. Witt, *In the Footsteps of the Ancients: The Origins of Humanism from Lovato to Bruni* (Leiden: Brill, 2000).

could evoke the idea of Italy as a whole. So there never emerged the kind of national spirit that later arose in, for example, France and England by the sixteenth century. Italy remained fragmented, something to keep in mind when we refer to the "Italian" Renaissance.

As to "Renaissance," this term is much less complicated. Among certain segments of society, a renewed and concentrated interest in the ancient world – in the language, art, and culture of ancient Rome and then ancient Greece – took hold in Italy. This tendency had its origins in a time much earlier than the long fifteenth century and can be documented even in the thirteenth century, in the northern Italian city of Padua.[6] If the term itself is uncomplicated, the questions surrounding it have multiplied over the past three or four decades. Was the Italian Renaissance a phenomenon only for male elites? The answer, more or less, is yes, especially if we are thinking about the long fifteenth century. Accordingly, the question arises: How can it still be relevant and important, given the concerns of scholars in the twenty-first century?

The answer to this third question revolves around, and radiates outward from, the meaning of the third term: intellectual, which conjures up different things for different people. Today "intellectual" can sometimes bear negative connotations. For some, it evokes snobbish elitism or, even worse, a lack of effective participation in the world: the intellectual does not matter and is on the margins. For others, the term can sometimes suggest the classic stereotype of the romantic individual, alone and thinking deep thoughts, who, when ready, puts pen to paper and releases writing into the world.

To get beyond those stereotypes, in any era, one needs to look at intellectuals in a broad fashion, considering how they worked, their stated goals, their unstated assumptions, what sorts of professional positions they filled, how they situated themselves in relation to current institutions, what sort of materials they had at hand when doing their work, and so on. This book reveals Renaissance-era intellectuals as they were: social creatures, immensely learned in a deep but in many respects limited way, and enmeshed in a thoroughly premodern world when it came to everything from living conditions to theories of human rights. Far from Romantic individuals, most of the Renaissance intellectuals we will meet were highly social, whether in the traditional sense (privileging social interactions with others) or through letter writing, reflecting thereby an intellectual's sociability, something that does not require personal contact in the literal sense but that implies a conversation: that the enterprise of reading and writing is something to be shared.

The short version: we are talking primarily about a period that spans the years 1350–1525 in what we now consider Italy, and the primary subject matter will be the lives, careers, and writings of intellectuals.

---

[6] See Witt, *In the Footsteps*.

ACKNOWLEDGEMENTS

I am grateful to editors and publishing houses for permission to use some material drawn from the following: Christopher S. Celenza, "Creating Canons in Fifteenth-Century Ferrara: Angelo Decembrio's *De politia litteraria*, 1.10," in *Renaissance Quarterly*, 57 (2004), 43–98; "Petrarch, Latin, and Italian Renaissance Latinity," *Journal of Medieval and Early Modern Studies*, 35 (2005), 509–36; "End Game: Humanist Latin in the Late Fifteenth Century," in Y. Maes, J. Papy, and W. Verbaal, eds., *Latinitas Perennis II: Appropriation and Latin Literature* (Leiden: Brill, 2009), 201–42; "The Platonic Revival," in J. Hankins, ed., *The Cambridge Companion to Renaissance Philosophy* (Cambridge: Cambridge University Press, 2007), 72–96; "Marsilio Ficino," in the *Stanford Encyclopedia of Philosophy*, 2011 (8000 words), online at http://plato.stanford.edu/entries/ficino/; "Late Antiquity and the Italian Renaissance," in *The Oxford Handbook of Late Antiquity*, ed. S.F. Johnson (Oxford: Oxford University Press, 2012), 1172–99; "Coluccio Salutati's View of the History of the Latin Language," in N. van Deusen, ed., *Cicero Refused to Die: Ciceronian Influence Through the Centuries* (Leiden: Brill, 2013), 5–20; "Introduction: Salvatore Camporeale and Lorenzo Valla," in Salvatore I. Camporeale, *Christianity, Latinity, and Culture*, tr. Patrick Baker, ed. Patrick Baker and Christopher S. Celenza (Leiden: Brill, 2014), 1–15.

To Ronald G. Witt, who before his death read a copy of this manuscript and offered valuable suggestions, my deepest thanks, as ever. My former colleagues at Johns Hopkins University have offered endlessly stimulating conversation and ideas regarding the topics covered in this book. Thanks especially to Shane Butler, Bill Egginton, Earle Havens, Silvia Montiglio, Larry Principe, Eugenio Refini, Matt Roller, and Walter Stephens. To my wife, Anna Harwell Celenza, thanks as always for reading, critiquing, suggesting, and, mostly, for being there all these years. Finally, this book is dedicated to another former Johns Hopkins colleague, Stephen J. Campbell, in admiration of his scholarship and gratitude for his friendship.

ABBREVIATIONS

Bruni, *Ep.* = Leonardo Bruni, *Epistolarum libri VIII*, ed. Lorenzo Mehus, 2 vols. (Florence, 1741; repr. with intro. by James Hankins, Rome: Edizioni di Storia e letteratura, 2007)

Bruni, *The Humanism* = *The Humanism of Leonardo Bruni*, ed. and tr. Gordon Griffiths, James Hankins, and David Thompson (Binghamton: MRTS, 1988)

Bruni, *Opere* = Leonardo Bruni, *Opere letterarie e politiche*, ed. P. Viti (Torino: UTEP, 1996)

Bruni, *Schriften* = Leonardo Bruni, *Humanistisch-philosophische Schriften mit einer Chronologie seiner Werke und Briefe*, ed. Hans Baron, Quellen zur Geistesgeschichte des Mittelalters und der Renaissance, 1 (Leipzig: Teubner, 1928; reprint, Wiesbaden: Sändig, 1969)

Celenza, *Poliziano's Lamia* = Christopher S. Celenza, ed., *Angelo Poliziano's Lamia in Context: Text, Translation, and Introductory Studies* (Leiden: Brill, 2010)

Ficino, *Commentaire / Commentarium* = Marsilio Ficino, *Commentaire sur le Banquet de Platon, De l'amour / Commentarium in convivium Platonis, De amore*, ed. and tr. P. Laurens (Paris: Belles Lettres, 2002)

Ficino, *Op.* = Marsilio Ficino, *Opera Omnia* (Basel, 1576)

Ficino, *Platonic Theology* = Marsilio Ficino, *Platonic Theology*, 6 vols., ed. and tr. Michael J.B. Allen and James Hankins (Cambridge, MA: Harvard University Press, 2001–06)

Garin, *Pros.* = Eugenio Garin, *Prosatori latini del Quattrocento* (Milan: Ricciardi, 1952)

Hankins, *Humanism and Platonism* = James Hankins, *Humanism and Platonism in the Italian Renaissance*, 2 vols. (Rome: Edizioni di storia e letteratura, 2003)

Hankins, *Plato* = James Hankins, *Plato in the Italian Renaissance*, 2 vols. (Leiden: Brill, 1990)

Kristeller, *Studies* = Paul Oskar Kristeller, *Studies in Renaissance Thought and Letters*, 4 vols. (Rome: Edizioni di storia e letteratura, 1956–96)

Kristeller, *Supplementum* = Paul Oskar Kristeller, *Supplementum ficinianum*, 2 vols. (Florence: Olschki, 1938)

McLaughlin, *Literary Imitation* = Martin McLaughlin, *Literary Imitation in the Italian Renaissance* (Oxford and New York: Oxford University Press, 1995)

Patota = Leon Battista Alberti, *Grammatichetta e altri scritti sul volgare*, ed. Giuseppe Patota (Rome: Salerno Editrice, 1996)

Pico, ed. Garin = Pico della Mirandola, *De hominis dignitate, Heptaplus, De ente et uno, e scritti vari*, ed. Eugenio Garin (Florence: Vallecchi, 1942)

Pico, *Op.*, = Pico della Mirandola, *Opera Omnia* (Turin: Bottega d'Erasmo, 1971), a facsimile of Pico della Mirandola, *Opera Omnia* (Basel, 1572), with additional material

Pico, *Oration* = Pico della Mirandola, *Oration on the Dignity of Man: A New Translation and Commentary*, eds. Francesco Borghesi, Michael Papio, and Massimo Riva (Cambridge: Cambridge University Press, 2012)

Poggio, *Lettere* = Poggio Bracciolini, *Lettere*, 3 vols., ed. Helene Harth (Florence: Olschki, 1984–87)

Poggio, *De avaritia*, ed. Germano = Poggio Bracciolini, *Dialogus contra avaritiam (De avaritia)* (Livorno: Belforte, 1994)

Poggio, *De nob.* = Poggio Bracciolini, *La vera nobiltà*, ed. and Italian tr. Davide Canfora (Rome: Salerno, 1999).

Poggio, *Op.* = Poggio Bracciolini, *Opera Omnia*, 4 vols., ed. Riccardo Fubini (Turin: Bottega d'Erasmo, 1964–69).

Poliziano, *Op.* = Angelo Poliziano, *Opera Omnia* (Venice: Aldus Manutius, 1498)

Poliziano, *Silvae* = Angelo Poliziano, *Silvae*, ed. and tr. Charles Fantazzi (Cambridge, MA: Harvard University Press, 2004)

Rizzo, *Lessico* = Silvia Rizzo, *Il lessico filologico degli umanisti* (Rome: Edizioni di storia e letteratura, 1984)

Tavoni = Mirko Tavoni, *Latino, grammatica, volgare: Storia di una questione umanistica* (Padua: Antenore, 1984)

Valla, *De vero* = Lorenzo Valla, *De vero falsoque bono*, ed. and tr. Maristella Lorch (New York: Abaris, 1977)

I

BEGINNINGS

Histor y of any sort involves choices about where to begin. Any cultural development, political movement, or religious evolution can be extended backward almost infinitely. One can find causes, of causes, of causes . . . without end. This dilemma – where to begin – comes into special relief when thinking about Italian Renaissance culture, since the one thing that most of the intellectuals we will meet in this book had in common was that they looked to the distant past, to the epoch of ancient Greece and Rome, to find cultural ideals. Yet in many ways they were all fundamentally connected to the social and material conditions of their day, medieval people looking to distinguish themselves from the culture they saw around them and in which they were embedded. At some point, you simply have to decide that you need a beginning. So we'll begin in the fourteenth century. For in many ways, when it comes to intellectual life, developments that occurred in the fourteenth century shaped the evolution of the Renaissance definitively.

More specifically we'll begin in 1364, with a letter. Intellectuals were and are many different things, but above all they are readers and writers. Listening carefully to what they say by analyzing what they write offers the best entryway into their world. Done right, it can give us context, a sense of the thinker's personality, and an opening to consider the various perspectives from which we can consider the writer. So here is what Petrarch wrote to Boccaccio in 1364. The two were close friends, Boccaccio a little younger and, sometimes, in awe of Petrarch. Petrarch had heard that Boccaccio had burned some of his Italian poetry when he encountered Petrarch's poetry, so in awe was Boccaccio of Petrarch's talent. Petrarch writes that he too had undergone some ambivalence in his career. While now he was devoted primarily to Latin literature, there had been a time when he hoped "to devote most of my time to this enterprise of writing in the vernacular." Latin, he went on, had been cultivated to such an extent and by such great geniuses of antiquity that nothing significant could be added, either by me or by anyone else. On the other hand, the vernacular, having been but recently discovered and still quite rustic owing to recent ravagers and to the fact that few have cultivated it, seemed capable of ornament and augmentation.[1]

Petrarch lived from 1304 to 1374 in a tumultuous century. By 1364, he was immensely famous by the standards of his day, as a vernacular poet and as a learned writer in Latin whose accomplishments were the envy of the educated.

What then does this letter tell us? First, Petrarch reveals an assumption regarding the Latin language that was widespread in his time, something that, considered in its fullness, should stop modern readers in their tracks. Educated people in Petrarch's time and place were bilingual in ways difficult to imagine today, with their education after the elementary level occurring in Latin. To be educated was to be considered *litteratus*, a word that meant not only "literate" the way we consider this status today, which is to say "able to read and write in one's native language." Being *litteratus* also signified fluency as a reader (especially) but also as a writer and to an extent speaker of Latin specifically.

Part of Latin's appeal had to do with permanence and tradition. This was an era before mass transit and well before anything like radio or television, when many people could not hear "standard" versions of native languages in a relatively uniform way. Owing to these factors, vernaculars (native languages, learned by children in the home) seemed inherently unstable. In Italy, the dialect of Tuscany differed substantially from that of Naples, which was very different from that of Milan, and so on. Decade by decade and region by region, people's "mother tongues" proved so variable that they did not seem appropriate for serious writing. Latin, on the other hand, did.

Latin, first, had a long and continuous history by the time the fourteenth century rolled around. Latin itself ceased to be a native language about two centuries after the Roman Empire fell in 478. But it experienced great success as an official language used by the Church in all its dealings, from the Mass to the many theological and administrative writings the Church's growth inspired. The twelfth and thirteenth centuries saw the rise of universities, where new, standardized forms of Latin evolved. Meanwhile, in what are now France, Spain, Portugal, and Italy, the "Romance" languages of French,

---

[1] Francesco Petrarca, *Res Seniles: Libri V-VIII*, ed. Silvia Rizzo (Florence: Le Lettere, 2009), 30–50, at 42–44. My translation.

Spanish, Portuguese, and Italian developed. Yet they did so in unorganized ways, emerging as they did from spoken versions of Latin but developing their own grammars, vocabularies, and, importantly, dialects. This latter aspect, dialects, proves crucially important in understanding why, from the time of the Roman Empire's fall to the fifteenth century, little attention was given to writing and promoting grammars of those languages (one noteworthy exception occurred in the case of Tuscan, as we shall see in Chapter 6). These vernaculars, or commonly spoken languages, did not exist in one fixed form in the European Middle Ages. Instead, even within one broad language group, Italian, for instance, there would be countless local variants, from region to region and, importantly, decade to decade.

Only one language was thought to stand the test of time, to be permanent enough to study, to teach, and to use for official purposes: Latin. Indeed, the word "grammar" – *grammatica* – meant one thing throughout the Middle Ages: Latin. When we observe, as we often do in the Middle Ages and Renaissance, someone saying that he studied *grammatica*, what that meant was he studied Latin. When Petrarch says that at a certain point he believed "nothing significant could be added, either by me or by anyone else" to the store of Latin literature, he reveals an anxiety shared by many when they looked at ancient literary achievements. What could you add to something already perfect?

It is also worth highlighting that Petrarch says that the vernacular was "recently discovered and still quite rustic." "Recently discovered": Petrarch points here to two communities of writers: first, to the "Sicilian school" of poets, who, inspired by medieval French troubadours and their tales of love and heroism, flourished in the thirteenth century and wrote love poetry of great beauty in the vernacular. Elsewhere, in another work of his, Petrarch says that the Sicilian poets "were the first."[2] Certain writers in Tuscany, members of the so-called Sicilian-Tuscan school, joined them in the early canon of recognized and important Italian poets. In other words, relatively recently (from Petrarch's perspective), a group of writers had succeeded in writing literature in the vernacular that was worthy of being read and considered seriously. It was poetry, to be sure, and it dealt with matters of love, predominantly, rather than history, philosophy, or theology. But it was worth taking seriously. If these early poets represented one of the two communities of writers, the other community was, instead, a community of one: Dante Alighieri (1265–1321).

[2] Petrarch, "Triumphus cupidinis," in Francesco Petrarca, *Opere di Francesco Petrarca*, Emilio Bigi, ed. (Milan: Mursia, 1963), 4.35–36: "i ciciliani / che fur già primi."

Absences often tell as much, or more, about a writer's frame of mind than things that are overtly present. The fact that Petrarch could say that the vernacular possessed "that few have cultivated it" is astonishing, since by the time he was writing this letter, Dante's *Comedy* (*Commedia*) was well known. In its three "canticles," *Inferno* (Hell), *Purgatorio* (Purgatory), and *Paradiso* (Paradise), Dante had expressed with beauty and elegance a magnificent journey. Dante, the poet himself, is the *Comedy*'s principal character, and we follow him as he explores the realms of hell, purgatory, and heaven. Along the way we meet notable figures from the ancient world; famous characters from Italian history; and, most importantly, Dante's two main guides, the ancient Latin poet Virgil, who accompanies Dante through purgatory, and then, in paradise, Beatrice, the woman who served as Dante's muse.

Dante wrote, very deliberately, in the Tuscan vernacular, that variety of Italian spoken most purely in Florence, that would later serve as the model for "literary" Italian. The work that we know as *The Divine Comedy* (the adjective "Divine" was added only later) elicited admiration, fascination, and comment, so much so that a bit later, in 1373, the city of Florence asked Boccaccio himself to lecture publicly on Dante's *Comedy*.[3] Another thing, then, that we learn from this letter of Petrarch's is that he had a ghost hanging over his head, the ghost of a writer, Dante, who had so perfectly expressed a vision of the cosmos that his work seemed indeed divine. He had done so not in Latin, but in Italian: a surprising fact, given that many of the themes that pop up in the *Comedy* deal with subjects – philosophy, theology, science – that traditionally would have been addressed in Latin.

Dante himself had early on written a work called *On the Elegance of the Vernacular* (*De vulgari eloquentia*), a work in which he argued that the vernacular should be cultivated as a serious language. Paradoxically, he wrote this text in Latin, in the hopes that it would reach intellectuals, but the arguments he made there were powerful: the vernacular was natural and learned in the home, and matters expressed in the vernacular could reach more than just a small section of the well educated. To be sure, it would need cultivation, rules, and hard work to make it worthy of serious literature, since man was "a most unstable, variable animal" (*instabilissimum et variabilissimum animal*).[4]

---

[3] See Michael Papio, "Introduction: Boccaccio as *Lector Dantis*," in Giovanni Boccaccio, *Boccaccio's* Expositions *on Dante's* Comedy, tr. with introductions and notes by Michael Papio (Toronto: University of Toronto Press, 2009), 3–37, at 7–10.

[4] Dante, *De vulgari eloquentia*, ed. Pier Vincenzo Mengaldo, in Dante, *Opere minori*, 2 vols. (Milan: Ricciardi, 1979), 1.9.6.

As to Petrarch, he informs us in that letter that, if early in his life he too thought one might raise the vernacular to the level of a language of craft and precision, soon thereafter he abandoned that plan. What Petrarch is doing is making a symbolic leap over Dante, shaping and refining a carefully polished persona: Petrarch the serious, pious, scholarly intellectual who has left vernacular poetry behind. He is offering a carefully staged presentation of self.

The truth is that Petrarch worked on his vernacular poetry his entire life: a manuscript in the Vatican Library shows that throughout his life he revised and reordered his poems, called *Rime sparse* in Italian – "Scattered Rhymes" – or, as he would refer to them in Latin, *Rerum vulgarium fragmenta*: "Fragments of things in the vernacular."[5] All of this might sound terribly academic, but for one fact: Petrarch's definitive shifting of gears – moving from the vernacular to Latin, from idealizing love poetry to historical studies, from a more or less secular attitude toward life to one marked by a profoundly religious outlook – effected a definitive change in attitudes toward literature and scholarship in Italy. For the next five generations, the field on which leading Italian intellectuals would play, work, and occasionally battle was a primarily Latinate one. The long fifteenth century saw a lot of attention to the Italian vernacular, increasingly so as the fifteenth century wore on. But Petrarch's powerful presence signaled the beginning of a cultural movement whose main linguistic vehicle was the Latin language.

Backgrounds

When we study the past, we tend to examine it through categories that make the most sense to us. This tendency is natural and unsurprising. But a problem arises: sometimes the categories that make the most sense to us would not have made sense in the same way to the people from the past whom we are studying. The question becomes: should we use the categories that make sense to us or try to understand what categories were operative in the period we are studying? The perspective I am advocating in this book is the latter. Take one example: philosophy. Today, those who study philosophy are disposed to believe that it deals primarily with verbal arguments: that the best philosophy is one in which a thinker makes clear, rationally delineated arguments that cohere with one another into a system. Religion, with all its

---

[5] MS Vatican City, Biblioteca apostolica vaticana, Vat. Lat. 3196; see also Luca Marcozzi, "Making the *Rerum vulgarium fragmenta*," in Albert Russell Ascoli and Unn Falkeid, eds., *The Cambridge Companion to Petrarch* (Cambridge: Cambridge University Press, 2015), 51–62.

ambiguities and its necessity of appealing to a higher power above human reason, has no place in this scheme. But in the thirteenth, fourteenth, and fifteenth centuries things were different.

On the one hand, as we shall see, in universities one could find significant antecedents for the more modern view. The notion was common and widely accepted that philosophy as a discipline was separate from religion, based on human reason alone, and as such could function autonomously within a limited intellectual realm. On the other, when we look at university life as it was situated within intellectual life generally, we can see that this view, though operative, is misleading. Most thinkers would have thought of academic philosophy (considered in this just-sketched way) as the minor partner when it came to religion. And indeed, universities were structured in such a way that philosophy served as basic preparation for the study of theology, seen as something higher and more important. The relationship between the two fields, philosophy and religion, is the reverse today in academic, intellectual circles, with philosophy seen as the higher intellectual discipline. The example of "philosophy" as a discipline is one among many that one could name to make this case: certain categories as we understand them today were different in the past, despite their name, which on the surface might have been the same.

So a word to the wise: looking into the past, we should not fear difference. There is nothing wrong with looking for antecedents to the way we think and live today, to find things that "look like us" in the past. But history would not be history if we did not recognize fundamental differences in outlook (when these are clearly present and can be substantiated by evidence) that shaped thinkers in the past. Since we are dealing with intellectuals, the best place to begin is with education.

Grammatica

Sometime between the years 1369 and 1373, a Neapolitan intellectual, Guglielmo Maramauro, wrote a commentary to Dante's *Inferno* (Dante had died in 1321 and by then his work was considered a classic). In the preface to his commentary, Guglielmo explains that what he was doing involved compiling resources, including prior commentaries on Dante. Of one of these he notes, "it is in *grammatica*" (*el quale è in grammatica*).[6] Maramauro, this otherwise little known figure, notes this fact in passing, simply as a way of

---

[6] Guglielmo Maramauro, *Expositione sopra l' "Inferno" di Dante Alighieri*, ed. Pier Giacomo Pisoni and Saverio Bellomo (Padua: Antenore, 1998), pref.

acknowledging the resources he had consulted when preparing his Dante commentary. It was worth noting for him that one of the resources he had used was in *grammatica*. By this term he means simply Latin. It will serve as a good jumping off point for us, as we try to see what was distinctive about education in Italy's long fifteenth century. It would be impossible here to summarize adequately all the diverse local conditions in which young people were educated, with all their specific differences.[7] But there was one thing all educated children would have had in common after an elementary-level understanding of basic arithmetic and vernacular reading: that much of their education thenceforth proceeded in Latin. Indeed, three characteristics serve to distinguish their education and to highlight its substantial differences from norms in our own era: the presence of Latin, the premium placed on memorization, and the relatively small set of resources people had at their disposal.

Education is a conservative enterprise, in the most literal sense of that word: dedicated to preserving what has gone before and passing it down. In Italy by the fourteenth century, despite local differences, certain tried-and-true methods had been developed to ensure that students could reach their goals, stage by stage in their education. If the word *grammatica* signified "Latin," it also had embedded in it its more literal meaning, "grammar." This is to say, young students needed a method to learn a foreign language that was not spoken in the home anymore but was nonetheless necessary as an instrument. The first things they had to learn were basic vocabulary and basic grammar, and one of the basic texts used was called *Janua*, or "the doorway," so called because it was seen as a gateway to Latin, itself an entryway to all the other liberal arts.

Imagine, today, if your education occurred in a language not only different from your own native language but also in a "dead" language − a language, that is, that was not spoken naturally by anyone. Your teachers would be speaking the language in class, and gradually you would grow used to hearing it spoken, with the accents and pronunciations, in most cases, of the native language of the speakers. But its status would have been unquestioned, and you would have come to think of it, indeed of language in general, in a special way: native languages were for jokes, for basic commerce, and for

---

[7] See Robert Black, *Humanism and Education in Medieval and Renaissance Italy: Tradition and Innovation in Latin Schools from the Twelfth to the Fifteenth Century* (Cambridge: Cambridge University Press, 2001); Paul F. Grendler, *Schooling in Renaissance Italy: Literacy and Learning, 1300–1600* (Baltimore: Johns Hopkins University Press, 1989); Ronald G. Witt, "What Did Giovanni Read and Write? Literacy in Early Renaissance Florence," *I Tatti Studies* 6 (1995), 83–114.

intimate occasions, from those basic ones in the home to those between lovers. Latin, on the other hand, would have been seen as the language appropriate for serious matters, as the official language of religion, as a language of international diplomacy, of learning. Most importantly, these impressions would have been formed at a young age, if you were one of those few people fortunate enough to receive this kind of education.

Given the distinctive status of Latin (as a dead language but also as one that was required for higher matters), it needed special vehicles to be taught and learned. If the presence of Latin serves as the first factor distinguishing the long fifteenth century from our own, the second is the main vehicle: standard texts taught by memorization.

The most notable of these texts was *Janua*, divided into eight parts, which corresponded to the parts of speech: nouns, verbs, participles, pronouns, prepositions, adverbs, interjections, and conjunctions.[8] It assumed little basic knowledge on the part of young students; it was designed to teach them both what the parts of speech were and how they functioned, as well as basic word forms, what grammarians today call "morphology." The first few lines of *Janua*'s poetic preface give us a sense of what it was like:

> *Ianua sum rudibus primam cupientibus artem / Nec prae me quisquam recte peritus erit*: "I am the doorway for the ignorant who desire the first art / And without me no one will be truly learned."

The preface goes on:

> For I teach gender and case, species and number, and formation in their parts, which are inflected. I put method in the remaining parts of speech, explaining what agrees the best. And no use of the word remains that I do not teach. Therefore, unskilled beginner, read and dedicate yourself to study, because you can learn many things with rapid study.[9]

Much of this will ring unfamiliar today, even to students who have studied foreign languages.

The key is the notion that Latin is "inflected." Practically speaking, this means that words have different endings depending on where they appear in a sentence: a noun that is the subject of a sentence will have a different ending if it appears as the direct object, different again if it is the indirect object, and so on. This aspect represents the noun's "case." "Gender" in Latin is three-fold (masculine, feminine, and neuter), and nouns and adjectives will, again,

[8] Federica Ciccolella, *Donati Graeci: Learning Greek in the Renaissance* (Leiden: Brill, 2009), 22.

[9] Cit. in Ciccolella, *Donati Graeci*, 21; tr. in Paul Gehl, *A Moral Art: Grammar, Culture, and Society in Trecento Florence* (Ithaca, NY: Cornell University Press, 1993), 88–89.

have different spellings and will "decline" (meaning move among the cases) differently according to their gender. To put it all more simply, Latin is like a puzzle: the student needs to learn how to match the right words one with the other, to make sense of any text.

To help teach these matters, *Janua* was structured in a question and answer format, a time-honored method then for teaching basic materials of all sorts. *Poeta quae pars est?* "What part of speech is 'poet'?" *Nomen.* "Noun." *Quare est nomen?* "For what reason is it a noun?" *Quia significat substantiam et qualitatem propriam vel communem cum casu.* "Because it signifies a substance and a quality proper to the thing itself or held in common with other things along with case."[10] And so on. A text such as this was learned by oral repetition, over and over, until it was fixed in the student's mind, deeply embedded and giving him (in rare cases "her") a lifelong knowledge of its contents. The use of *Janua* represents one aspect of teaching, and (needless to say) the way it was used and taught would have varied from region to region. But certain aspects of this style of education are worth bringing into relief, since they are so different from what we are used to today.

Take the oral part of this process. We are much more habituated than were premodern people to thinking of literacy in at least two ways: first, as composed of reading and writing together, in roughly equal parts and, second, having to do with texts outside the reader, meaning simply on a printed page or on a screen. For us, at least implicitly, texts inside one's head – memorized – do not necessarily "count" when we think of literacy. Moreover, our notion of literacy is changing radically with the advent of new media, as we free up our memories to accommodate more and more short-term content. The more you can count on having material available online, the less you need to store in your memory. This was another fundamental difference between Petrarch's day and our own. When we think of literacy in the long fifteenth century, we need to adjust the balance a bit, to reflect the fact that they possessed much more knowledge "inside" the reader, meaning that much of what they learned (much more at least than in our own cases) they memorized. This process had consequences, since of course there are limits to what a person can memorize. One of these con- sequences was that thinkers, all throughout the long fifteenth century (much as in the case of their medieval predecessors), fervently believed in the authority of a relatively limited variety of important texts. This mentality emerged also from a simple fact: in an era when books were hand produced, there were far fewer of them than we might intuitively assume today. Not

---

[10] Cit. in Ciccolella, *Donati Graeci*, 22.

only that, but – especially in the fourteenth century – there were no real "public" libraries, such as would come into existence in a limited way in the fifteenth century.[11]

If our hope is to offer some context for Petrarch and the educational world that formed him and his contemporaries up to adolescence, we can highlight these distinctive general features: a lot of Latin, a lot of memorization, and a heavy reliance on a relatively small series of authoritative texts. These factors represented the basic general formation of all educated Italians, however diverse they were when it came to particulars.

Moving on from secondary schooling, universities represented the other major factor influencing thinkers at the outset of the long fifteenth century. Most Italian intellectuals during this period had substantial experience at universities. Though some would criticize universities and position themselves as "outsiders," these powerful medieval institutions had a profound and shaping effect on many people.

Universities had their roots in the twelfth and thirteenth centuries in Europe, and they emerged almost spontaneously, as respected teachers, known as "masters" (*magistri*) developed followings among students.[12] As these masters habitually gravitated to certain parts of major cities, institutions grew up around those gathering places. Some of the earliest such institutions arose in Bologna, Paris, and Oxford. By the middle of the thirteenth century these universities came to be designated with the term *studium generale*, a term that implied that they were places of teaching and learning (*studium*) and that aspects of any given university superseded its local context. For example, a student who earned the title "master" (*magister*) also possessed by virtue of that title a "license to teach anywhere" (*licentia ubique docendi*), which meant that the skills learned were transferable.

Universities were generally divided into four "faculties," sections responsible for teaching certain subject matters: the "lower" faculty of "arts" and the three "higher" faculties of medicine, theology, and law. It was in the arts faculty that the "liberal arts" were taught, which included seven subjects. Three were verbally oriented: grammar, rhetoric, and logic. The other four were more mathematical in nature and included arithmetic, geometry, astronomy, and music. A student proceeded through study of these various subjects and earned the status of Bachelor of Arts (*baccalaureus artium*, the origins of our modern B.A. degree) and Master of Arts (*magister artium*, the

---

[11] See Chapter 11.
[12] See Marsha Colish, *Medieval Foundations of the Western Intellectual Tradition* (New Haven: Yale University Press, 1997), 265–73.

ancestor of our M.A.). Only then did the student have the right to enter one of the three higher faculties of medicine, theology, and law, with the ability to earn a doctoral degree (a long process that lasted in many cases up to nine years).

One scholar has pointed to helpful statistics that can put the rise of universities in Western Europe in context. In the year 1300 there were eighteen of these institutions. By 1378, there were twenty-eight. And by the year 1500 one can count sixty.[13] These numbers tell us, first, that the model was a success. Every university was slightly different, its own individual institution despite commonalities: not all had equal strength in all four faculties; each developed its own set of specialties, and so on.

Still, one can track the rise of common curricula as well as common teaching methods, which made medieval universities uniform enough that they were recognizably similar across different contexts. The most important similarity lay in teaching methods, which consisted of two broad approaches: the "lecture" and the "disputation." The lecture, known as *lectio* or *lectura* in Latin, took its name from the Latin verb from which those two nouns are drawn: *legere* – "to read." At root, reading served precisely as the center of the lecture. A master would read an authoritative text out loud, Aristotle's *Nicomachean Ethics*, say, in a Latin translation, and stop to comment on it and to explain the text's meaning. This process led to one of the two major genres of writing that arose out of medieval university practices: the "commentary." A commentary on Aristotle's *Nicomachean Ethics*, for instance, would highlight a certain section, out of which the author (the master) would quote a word or a short phrase, known as a *lemma*. The *lemma* would be followed by a section explaining it, sometimes being as minimal as a definition of the word, other times offering a lengthy explanation of where it fit in Aristotle's thought, how it pertained to Christian thinking, and so on. The *lemma* and the commentary surrounding it were normally written in different scripts, so that a reader could easily differentiate them.

If the lecture, and its written expression, the commentary, represented one of the two genres of medieval teaching and writing at the university level, the disputation was the other, equally important and equally productive. For here, a master would set forth "questions" (*quaestiones* in Latin) in class.[14] These questions would have to do with matters that came up in the course of

[13] Jacques Verger, "Patterns," in H. De Ridder-Symoens, *A History of the University in Europe*, 2 vols. to date (Cambridge: Cambridge University Press, 1992–96), I: 35–67, at 55–65.

[14] See *Les genres littéraires dans les sources théologiques et philosophiques médiévales: définition, critique, et exploitation*, ed. Institut d'Études Médiévales (Louvain-la-Neuve: Université catholique de Louvain, 1982).

study and were typically structured in a way that allowed objections to be aired and answered. In their written format, they reflected the idea that students could in certain circumstances air these possible objections.

So a question would be posed, such as the one Thomas Aquinas asked in the thirteenth century, in his masterpiece the *Summa theologica*, his great work of theological synthesis, when he began by asking whether "sacred doctrine" is necessary, meaning, was there a need to study theology. This moment occurs right away, in the first "article" of the first "question."[15] The answer, as one can imagine, is "yes," which is to say that in Aquinas's view the discipline of theology is necessary. But it is the way he gets there that is important for us, so much so that it is worth examining in depth.

The standard format for this type of inquiry had five parts. First, one would state the problem in the form of a question. Second, one presented "objections" (points that could be made in favor of a negative answer to the question). Third was the statement that began, in Latin, with the words *sed contra* – "but on the other hand" – whereby a point or points contrary to the objections could be made. Fourth was the statement that began "I respond that" (*respondeo quod*), in which the master answered the question. Fifth were specific responses to the original objections. Aquinas's treatment here represents a perfect example of the form.

The question with which the first article begins is: "Whether, besides the philosophical sciences, any further doctrine is required?" Structurally, the first things to occur are "objections" to the proposition. Here is the first objection:

> It seems that, besides the philosophical sciences, we have no need of any further knowledge. For man should not seek to know what is above reason: "Seek not the things that are too high for thee" (Eccl. 3.22). But whatever is not above reason is sufficiently considered in the philosophical sciences. Therefore, any other knowledge besides the philosophical sciences is superfluous.

The assumption here is that "philosophy" deals with matters that are accessible to human reason and that "doctrine" – the Latin *doctrina* – represents a body of learning that is able to be formalized and taught. The quotation from the Old Testament book Ecclesiasticus (known more commonly as Sirach) urges humility, and it sounds like precisely the sort of thing one might have

---

[15] Thomas Aquinas, *Summa theologiae: Latin Text and English Translation* (New York: McGraw-Hill, 1964), 1a1a, q.1; translation from *The Summa Theologica of St. Thomas Aquinas*, 2nd ed., 22 volumes (London: Burns, Oates, and Washbourne, 1913–42).

heard in a classroom, as students sought to formulate answers to the question at hand.

The second objection enters into touchy territory. Here it is, in full:

> Further, knowledge can be concerned only with being, for nothing can be known, save the true, which is convertible with being. But everything that is, is considered in the philosophical sciences – even God himself; so that there is a part of philosophy called theology, or the divine science, as is clear from Aristotle. Therefore, besides the philosophical sciences, there is no need for any further knowledge.

It is clear to all that God exists. If He exists, he partakes of Being. Anything that partakes of Being is studied under the rubric of philosophy, which is why (the objection asserts) there is a branch of philosophy known as theology. This latter statement is the tricky part. Aristotle, Aquinas's authority, had indeed said in his *Metaphysics* that theology – the study of the divine – was one of the "theoretical" branches of philosophy.[16] The potential problem here occurs in the relationship of the two fields, philosophy and theology, since philosophy was decidedly seen to be subordinate to theology – philosophy was "theology's handmaiden," a phrase whose substance (if not its exact wording) dates to the eleventh century.[17]

It was important to Aquinas that the relationship between the two fields be understood correctly. The *sed contra* section expands on this idea:

> On the contrary it is written (2 Tim. 3.16): "All scripture inspired of God is profitable to teach, to reprove, to correct, to instruct in justice". Now scripture, inspired of God, is not a part of the philosophical sciences discovered by human reason. Therefore, it is useful that beside the philosophical sciences there should be another science, i.e., inspired of God.

"Scripture" here means the Bible, both the Old and the New Testaments, and the point that Aquinas wants to make is that these texts had a divine source, something fundamentally different from the sorts of texts – like those of Aristotle, for example – that arose from the practice of human reason.

Scripture was "revealed," meaning that its messages, its mysteries, and its infinitely interpretable story lines came from God. In other words, one could make the argument that this separate, sacred, divine body of knowledge deserved its own "science," by which Aquinas means a discipline that can lead to knowledge of a specific and focused kind.

---

[16] Aristotle, *Metaphysics*, ed. W.D. Ross (Oxford: Clarendon, 1924), 6.1, 1026a19.
[17] Bernardus Baudoux, "Philosophia 'Ancilla Theologiae,'" *Antonianum* 12 (1937), 292–326.

The stage has been set for the *respondeo quod*, the "response" that the Master would give in the course of classroom discussion, here formalized by Aquinas, as he fixes in writing a spontaneous but brilliantly learned response:

> I answer that, it was necessary for man's salvation that there should be a knowledge revealed by God, besides the philosophical sciences investigated by human reason. First, because man is directed to God as to an end that surpasses the grasp of his reason: "The eye hath not seen, O God, besides Thee, what things Thou hast prepared for them that wait for Thee" (Isaiah, 64.4). But the end must first be known by men who are to direct their thoughts and actions to the end. Hence it was necessary for the salvation of man that certain truths which exceed human reason should be made known to him by divine revelation.

Thus far in Aquinas's final answer to this question, a series of core issues comes into play.

First, we learn that the "philosophical sciences" are grasped by human reason. This means that, on balance, they can be apprehended and understood without divine illumination. Second, an assumption about humanity emerges: "man is directed to God as to an end that surpasses the grasp of his reason." Human beings possess an inborn desire for God. "But the end must first be known": in other words, that inborn desire is manifest, on the surface, to greater and lesser extents in different people. So, for "man" (human beings) to achieve salvation – and there can be no higher goal, Aquinas implies – "certain truths which exceed human reason should be made known to him by divine revelation." Not everything that is worth studying can be subject to proof, whether proof garnered from observation or offered by logical argumentation.

There are also truths about God that can be discovered and investigated with the aid of human reason. Still, divine revelation was necessary:

> For the truth about God, such as reason can know it, would only be known by a few, and that after a long time, along with the admixture of many errors, whereas man's whole salvation, which is in God, depends upon the knowledge of this truth. Therefore, in order that the salvation of men might be brought about more fitly and more surely, it was necessary that, besides the philosophical sciences investigated by reason, there should be a sacred science by way of revelation.

One can sense a tension here.

On the one hand, Aquinas is quite clear that for humanity, salvation represents the ultimate priority. Though a select few might be able to reach conclusions regarding God and salvation by means of human reason alone, most people cannot achieve that objective and need, instead, revelation. There is a side of Aquinas that wants to protect the power and prerogatives of human reason and hence, in disciplinary terms, the power of philosophy. On the other hand, Aquinas would be the first to say that salvation is more important than any conclusions at which human reason might arrive, so that philosophy's reach is limited. Therefore, theology (what he means when he says "a sacred science by way of revelation") must have its own real purpose and reach its own, higher conclusions. And it must do so based on revelation, using scripture and later sacred texts as its point of departure.

Stepping back, what can we learn? First, the two great genres of medieval scholastic writing, the commentary and the question, served important purposes. They were both intimately linked to classroom practice, the commentary to the lecture and the question to the disputation. The many thousands of students trained in medieval universities learned not only content but also ways of thinking, as they made their way through their curricula. Through lectures they learned the art of reading closely, teasing out many levels of meaning in key, authoritative texts. Through the disputation they learned to question received wisdom, to subject stated conclusions to rigorous verbal testing, and to apply logic in the service of discovery.[18] As universities came to maturity in the late thirteenth and early fourteenth centuries, these bedrock techniques of teaching and learning formed generations of students.

But something unsurprising occurred as universities expanded and as more of them arose in late medieval Europe. Curricula grew standardized, and, as often happens in higher education, questions were sometimes asked not because they were relevant to everyday life but simply because they were on the curriculum. Moreover, the two great genres of medieval university writing came to seem too constricting to some. Even within the university world, some scholars called for new genres of writing that could have more immediate relevance to life outside the university. For example, one of the greatest figures in the history of the University of Paris, Jean Gerson (1363–1429) helped revive an old form of writing called the "tractate" – *tractatus*.[19]

---

[18] See Alex J. Novikoff, *The Medieval Culture of Disputation:* (Philadelphia: University of Pennsylvania Press, 2013).

[19] See Daniel Hobbins, "The Schoolman as Public Intellectual: Jean Gerson and the Late Medieval Tract," *The American Historical Review* 108 (2003), 1308–37; and Hobbins, *Authorship and Publicity before Print: Jean Gerson and the Transformation of Late Medieval Learning* (Philadelphia: University of Pennsylvania Press, 2009).

These treatises were written in a form designed to be accessible, rather than in the stylized and standardized question or commentary format, and they were designed to have an application to some issue or problem outside the university context. They were still written in Latin, and more specifically in the medieval Latin of university life, but their relative accessibility made them an important addition to the other two genres of writing.

Gerson, active when he was, when the number of universities was on the rise, signals another noteworthy tendency. If one thinks back to Aquinas's brilliant "question" on the necessity of theology, one is struck by its incisiveness and precision. Yet there are many elements to religious experience, one of which is the spiritual, affective dimension that engages people's emotions. If the formalized style of both the commentary and the question served as one limiting factor, another was that it was difficult in those genres of writing to touch on that more spiritual aspect of religious experience. The highly logical style had its place, but Gerson (like many other figures both inside and outside the university environment) came to believe that one needed to pay more attention to the spiritual element than university practices traditionally afforded.

No one figure exemplifies this tendency more than Petrarch, someone who had spent time in university settings but who came to see them as arid, and who took the stance of an "outsider," even to extremes.

2

DANTE, PETRARCH, BOCCACCIO

PETRARCH (1304–74) REPRESENTS THE CENTRAL FIGURE BEHIND
the Renaissance revival of antiquity, the change in direction when it
came to the language in which intellectuals wrote, and the propensity among
some Renaissance intellectuals to see themselves as outsiders.[1] Yet in all these
respects, he had a background that needs to be explored and that can be
understood as a conversation: with other towering figures, such as his predecessor Dante or his contemporary Boccaccio; with ancient, long dead
luminaries whom he idealized; and finally with the many people and institutions with which he came into contact during the tumultuous fourteenth
century.

First, there was the poet Dante Alighieri (1265–1321). We know Dante
primarily through his most important work, the *Divine Comedy*, whose first
part, *Inferno*, begins with some of the most famous words in Western literature:

> Midway in the journey of our life
> I found myself in a dark forest
> For the straight path was lost
>
> Oh, how hard it is to say what a cruel thing it was
> This wild forest harsh and stark
> Which even to think about renews my fear.[2]

The poet tells an archetypal story: a man, in the middle of his life, finds
himself lost, alienated, and adrift. To emerge from this perilous personal state,

---

[1] See Christopher S. Celenza, *Petrarch: Everywhere a Wanderer* (London: Reaktion, 2017).

[2] Dante Alighieri, *Inferno*, in *The Divine Comedy*, Italian text and translation, with a
commentary by Charles S. Singleton (Princeton: Princeton University Press, 1970–75),
1.1–6: "Nel mezzo del cammin di nostra vita / Mi ritrovai in una selva oscura / Ché la
diritta via era smarrita. / Ahi quanto a dir qual era è cosa dura / Esta selva selvaggia e aspra e
forte / Che nel pensier rinova la paura." My trans.

he must go on a journey in which he encounters many people, places, and things.

What a journey it was. Dante's *Comedy* offered its medieval readers a voyage to the depths of hell and back (the understandable adjective "divine" was added later and not part of Dante's original title). The structure is one of descent, followed by ascent: descent into hell (*inferno* in Italian), ascent into purgatory (*purgatorio*), and finally to paradise (*paradiso*) where, in a final, rapturous moment, the central figure, Dante (standing in for humanity) encounters God. Each book, or "canticle" (*cantica*), as they are known – *Inferno*, *Purgatorio*, and *Paradiso* – consists of thirty-three "cantos" (*canti*), chapter-like episodes describing Dante's voyage. There is also a first introductory canto to the *Inferno*, so that the total number of cantos is one hundred. Along the way Dante introduced readers (and listeners, since the poetic masterpiece was meant to be heard) to historical episodes, notable figures, and memorable adventures that ranged from low to high, described in language that even today can seem in some places astonishingly vulgar, in others mellifluously sublime.

At the outset Dante meets the figure who will guide his journey through hell and most of purgatory: the poet Virgil. Virgil's presence may not strike readers today as particularly momentous. Allowing Dante to tell us of their meeting makes one thing clear: Dante's choice to have Virgil as his guide was full of meaning large and small. On the outskirts of hell, before he enters, Dante sees before his eyes "someone who, because of long silence, seemed faint" (*Inf.* 1.62–3). Tremulous, Dante asks this mysterious man who he might be and receives the reply:

> I was a poet. I sang of that righteous
> Son of Anchises who came from Troy
> When proud Ilium was destroyed by fire.[3]

Soon Dante realizes with whom he is speaking:

> 'Are you that Virgil, that fountain
> That pours forth such a rich stream of speech?'
> I answered him, shame upon my brow.[4]

It is indeed Virgil, author of the *Aeneid*, Roman antiquity's most famous work of epic poetry.

---

[3] Ibid.: "Poeta fui, e cantai di quell giusto / figliuol d'Anchise che venne di Troia, /poi che 'l supervo Ilion fu combusto."
[4] Ibid.: "'Or se' tu quel Virgilio e quella fonte / Che spandi di parlar sì largo fiume?' / Rispuos'io lui con vergognosa fronte."

The *Aeneid* told the tale of Aeneas (the "son of Anchises") who, after fleeing Troy as the Greeks destroyed it, went on an epic journey that ended with the founding of Rome. The *Aeneid* was the principal text of Roman poetry. Studying the *Aeneid* was the way highly educated people in Dante's day would have learned Latin grammar in depth, scrutinizing the poem, dissecting every word, and committing most if not all to memory. Dante the character is in awe:

> You are my master, my author.
> You alone are the one from whom
> I took the noble style that has brought me honor.[5]

"You alone." Dante shows reverence ("master," "author"), even as he allows himself a moment of self-appreciation, if not vanity, unashamed to proclaim that his own noble style has brought him honor as a poet. From this early part of the *Comedy* on, Dante sees himself as participating in a club that has few members: those who would write works of lasting importance.

He succeeded masterfully. The *Divine Comedy* was recognized immediately for its wide-ranging erudition, encompassing both ancient literature and theology. It was "published" per the standards of the day, meaning that Dante made it public when he deemed it finally ready, allowing manuscript copies to be made, finishing its last part, *Paradiso*, only two years before he died in 1321. Dante's life and work made him a signal figure and one whose reputation would haunt Petrarch for his whole career, their similarities contributing as much to that process as their differences.

As to similarities, both shared the theme of exile. For Dante, his exile was literal. Dante was a patriotic and politically active Florentine, who had fought on behalf of his city in battle and participated in the city's complicated political life. He belonged to a political faction known as the "White Guelphs," and it was this factional alliance that led, in the end, to his exile. It is worth opening a parenthesis on this topic, because it illuminates not only Florentine politics but also the political situation in Italy in general.

During Dante's era, Italian city-states had matured greatly in the two centuries prior, with some in central Italy – Florence especially – having gained great wealth and prominence. Florence identified itself as a republic, which signified that it had some traditions of shared governance. But that tradition of shared governance also meant that there were often rival clans

---

[5] Ibid.: "Tu se' lo mio maestro e 'l mio autore, / tu se' solo colui da cu'io tolsi / Lo bello stilo che m'ha fatto onore."

fighting, often literally, for pieces of the pie. Because of these rivalries, which in one form or another existed in all major Italian centers, cities would ally themselves with stronger foreign powers, often doing so in league with other cities. But within the hothouse environment of internal politics, there were frequent disagreements as to how and with whom these alliances should be made. If unstable internal politics represents the first characteristic marking political life in Dante's era, the second emerged from a Europe-wide rivalry, that between "Empire" and papacy, or the "Ghibellines" and "Guelphs."[6]

Since the eleventh century Europe had been riven between supporters of the Holy Roman Empire, whose broad center was what we now know as Germany, and the papacy. Supporters of the Empire were known as Ghibellines (a corruption of the German word "Waiblingen," which referred to a castle important to the Hohenstaufen family, who in the twelfth century represented the Empire). Those who sided with the popes were termed "Guelphs" (a similar corruption of the word "Welf," the family name of the Bavarians who in the twelfth century were opposed to the Hohenstaufens). It seems complicated today, since we are accustomed to thinking of Germany as one unified nation. However, many rival powers existed then, and conflict ensued throughout the Middle Ages. By Dante's day this conflict had escalated to such a point that in his own city of Florence – traditionally a Guelph city and thus a supporter of the papacy – was split into two factions, led by rival families, the White Guelphs and Black Guelphs (the colors having to do with the crests of the two principal competing families). These factions set themselves against each other, and Dante found himself on the losing side (as did Petrarch's father, as it happens).

So, we have factions upon factions and little resembling modern nations, or modern concepts of the rule of law. Clan was the basis of politics, even in Dante's Florence. Though we can find the distant origins of the language of law and rights in the ancient world, in Dante's era, and in Petrarch's, we need to remember that they all lived in a fundamentally premodern world.

The Ghibelline-Guelph split, too, brings into relief two powerful, formational facts about Italian history. First, Italy's city-states, wealthy and powerful though they may have been, were still small and needed to ally, both with one another and with powers outside of Italy – such as, in some cases, a German "emperor" who in truth had little connection to Italy. He was needed often not because of any notional political unity toward which

---

[6] See Philip Jones, *The Italian City-State: From Commune to Signoria* (Oxford: Clarendon, 1997); Lauro Martines, *Power and Imagination: City-States in Renaissance Italy* (Baltimore: Johns Hopkins University Press, 1988); Daniel Waley and Trevor Dean, *The Italian City Republics* (London: Routledge, 2009).

people were aiming but because he was powerful. Second, the presence of the papacy (to which Guelphs were loyal) distinguished Italy, even in its medieval period, as something quite different from other political entities. Later than Petrarch's era, Machiavelli (1469–1527) remarked that popes, unlike other princes, "have states and do not defend them, have subjects and do not govern them."[7] Despite this fact and unlike other princedoms (Machiavelli was pointing out), popes have security and at least some stability.

The presence on Italian soil of Christianity's central and most important institution served as a distinguishing mark for all of Italy: as a point of pride, of contention, and at times a source of anticlerical revulsion, as people close to the institution could see unsavory sides of the papal court not always apparent from far off. The important point in any case is this: the papacy's presence made Italy unique, possessing an institution that made it just a little different from everyone else. One cannot understand Italy without highlighting the papacy's importance.

The same goes for understanding intellectuals, Dante – and Petrarch – included. In his *Comedy*, certain popes for whom Dante had little admiration wound up suffering in hell, such as Nicholas III (pope 1277–80), who had appointed three extended family members as cardinals. He was thus guilty of the sin of simony, a sin named after Simon Magus, who appears in the Acts of the Apostles, attempting there to bribe Saint Peter, to no avail.[8] Arriving in the circle of hell that houses those who committed this sin, the seriousness of the crime emerges from the canto's first lines:

> O Simon Magus! O scum that followed him!
> Those things of God that rightly should be wed
> To holiness, you, rapacious creatures,
>
> For the price of gold and silver, prostitute.
> Now, in your honor, I must sound my trumpet
> For here in the third pouch is where you dwell.[9]

Dante tells us what has gone wrong. The Church is the bride of Christ, and as such it must be kept pure. What those guilty of simony have done is the equivalent of a husband prostituting his bride, selling something for gain in a context where such an act should be forbidden. The punishment fits the crime, for we learn that this *bolgia*, or "pouch," of hell is possessed of a hole in

---

[7] Niccolò Machiavelli, *Il principe*, ed. G. Inglese (Turin: Einaudi, 1995), chap. 11 (pp. 73–77).

[8] Acts, 8: 9–24.

[9] *Inferno*, translated by Mark Musa (New York: Penguin, 1984), 19.1–6.

which the guilty must remain, head first, forever, stacked one on top of another.

Here Dante sees the legs of one of these sinners twitching, and he asks Virgil's help. Virgil, Dante's master and guide, carries Dante down to a point where a spirit, who addresses Dante in a surprising way, greets him. In fact, the spirit believes mistakenly that Dante is Pope Boniface VIII (and he is surprised, since the book of fate predicted a later death for Boniface):

'Is that you here already upright?
Is that you here already upright Boniface?
By many years the book has lied to me.

Are you fed up so soon with all that wealth
For which you did not fear to take by guile
the lovely lady, then tear her asunder?'[10]

Virgil tells Dante to correct the spirit's misperception, which Dante dutifully does, informing the spirit that he is not, in fact, Boniface.

The spirit then reveals that he is instead the shade of Pope Nicholas III, thereafter disclosing the nature of the torment that he suffers:

Beneath my head are pushed down all the others
Who came, sinning in simony, before me,
Squeezed tightly in the fissures of the rock.

I, in my turn, shall join the rest below
As soon as *he* comes, the one I thought you were
When, all too quick, I put my question to you.

But already my feet have baked a longer time
(and I have been stuck upside down like this)
than he will stay here planted with feet aflame:

soon after him shall come one from the West,
a lawless shepherd, one whose fouler deeds
make him a fitting cover for us both.[11]

Beneath the allusive language, what we discover is this: that Dante believed that Pope Nicholas III, Pope Boniface VIII, and (as we learn after Nicholas's speech) Pope Clement V (pope 1305–14) would all wind up in hell, guilty of the sin of simony, condemned accordingly to eternal torment. Dante wastes no time in giving Nicholas a piece of his mind, as he addresses the infernal pope directly:

[10] Ibid., 19.52–57, tr. Musa.
[11] Ibid., 19.73–84, tr. Musa.

> Well, tell me now: what was the sum of money
>
> that Holy Peter had to pay our Lord
> before He gave the keys into his keeping?
> Certainly He asked no more than 'Follow me'.[12]

In other words, popes have a sacred obligation, one that reaches back to the earliest days of Christianity and to Christ's decision to give to Peter the "keys to the kingdom of heaven."[13] Peter was a "rock" on which Christ's Church would be built and his successors (popes, in other words) have an obligation to live up to the sacred standards of their earliest exemplar. Dante has one final reproof for Nicholas:

> You have built yourselves a God of gold and silver!
> How do you differ from the idolator,
> except he worships one, you worship hundreds?

Three popes in a row in hell. What can this mean? By Dante's day that special relationship between Italy and the papacy was already forged. The relationship entailed a kind of closeness that at times bred contempt, even when the papacy moved, as it did, to Avignon, where Petrarch grew up.

If Dante's lines in canto 19 of the *Inferno* offer us insight into his view of the papacy, they also remind us of something else. His masterpiece the *Comedy* achieved that status almost immediately because it had great contemporary value, with names and situations that would have struck chords in his fourteenth-century readers. It held on to its status as a masterpiece because its themes were lasting, compelling, and eternal. What were these themes? Alienation and redemption (as the character Dante, guided by Virgil and then by Beatrice, his eternal love object, journeys from the depths of hell to the heights of paradise); rewards and punishments for conduct meted out accordingly; Christian universalism, as the universe is represented as an interconnected whole, ruled over and pervaded by God: these and other aspects have made the *Comedy* one of Western literature's enduring works of genius.

Imagine wanting to make your mark as a poet and having this towering legacy just in your rearview mirror. This was the situation in which Petrarch came to maturity. And Dante had left behind more than his brilliant *Comedy*. In addition to other literary works in the vernacular, Dante authored two Latin works that, though less famous, make for an interesting point of

---

[12] Ibid., 89–93, tr. Musa.
[13] Mt. 16:19.

departure when considering Petrarch's environment. One, *On Monarchy*, shared some of the same views about the papacy. There, Dante argued that a secular emperor should have a separate sphere of power, rather than being notionally "under" the rule of the pope, as popes were trying to argue. Dante partook in an ample medieval tradition of political writing, attempting, as did many others, to understand what relation Church and state should have.[14]

The other work emerges as more relevant, especially as we begin to situate Petrarch in context. Dante's work *On the Eloquence of the Vernacular (De vulgari eloquentia)* called for the use of the vernacular in high-minded literary works.[15] How strange this all seems to us today. Dante wrote a work in Latin, in which he argued that it was *not* Latin but the vernacular that was a suitable literary language. Not only this, but in another work, his *Convivio*, or *Banquet* – written in Italian – he had claimed that Latin was nobler than the vernacular. Why? Why did Dante so obviously disagree with himself? Dante left both of those works – the Tuscan *Banquet* and the Latin *On the Eloquence of the Vernacular* – incomplete. This fact – coupled with the reality that their author was one of the most brilliant minds to grace Western intellectual life – points us toward a crucial problem: language. It was one that Dante had suggested but left unaddressed and that Petrarch – for the Renaissance – resolved, though in doing so he left behind ghosts, as his own personal ambivalences regarding the primacy of Latin emerged throughout the Renaissance in different ways.

As to Dante, *On the Eloquence of the Vernacular* remained incomplete. Dante began the work soon after he was in exile in around 1302 (as internal evidence reveals). Why he did not finish it is unknown. Though it did not circulate widely in Dante's own day, it has attracted the attention of modern scholars in large part because of Dante's advocacy of the vernacular as a language of high literature. Modern scholars have sometimes exaggerated Dante's goals, however, for reasons having to do more with modern nationalism than with Dante's world. He was not defending the vernacular as an "Italian" patriot. Instead he was suggesting that the vernacular could be made suitable for literature. No more, no less.

Several factors played a role. First, it is anachronistic to think that there was "a" vernacular in late medieval Italy. Instead, there seemed to be a great plurality of vernaculars that varied almost incalculably by region and by decade. Dante had acknowledged as much: in his *Convivio*, he had written that *lo latino*

---

[14] For a Latin text and English translation see Dante, *Monarchia*, ed. and tr. Prue Shaw (Cambridge: Cambridge University Press, 1995).

[15] For a Latin text and English translation see Dante, *De vulgari eloquenti*, ed. and tr. Steven Botterill (Cambridge: Cambridge University Press, 1996).

è perpetuo e non corruttibile – "Latin is perpetual and incorruptible" – as contrasted to the vernacular, which, he went on, is "unstable and corruptible."[16] Dante said there that "the vernacular follows usage, whereas Latin follows art" (*lo volgare seguita uso, e lo latino arte*) by which he meant that Latin was a language of craft ("art," or *ars*, in Latin), unnatural but precisely because of its constructed-ness able to express more than the vernacular.[17] And in his *On the Eloquence of the Vernacular*, he remained consistent: he wrote that all vernaculars are in a state of constant evolution, because "man is a most unstable, variable animal."[18] Dante was concerned with defending Tuscan against other competing vernaculars. What he wanted to do in any case was to standardize it, to create in effect a secondary language that would have its own set of permanent rules.[19] But to a new generation of thinkers beginning with Petrarch, this sense of permanence is exactly what Latin already had. For the next five generations, Petrarch, haunted as he was by Dante's towering presence, set the tone for the Renaissance appreciation of language. Not only that: through force of ego, he also succeeded in harnessing many different energies then in the air, unifying them, and thus becoming the acknowledged center of a newly invigorated cultural movement.

To understand all that Petrarch accomplished, four aspects come to the fore, all interrelated: a new Latin; a renewed emphasis on Christianity; a new philosophy manifested in different genres, not all of them works of philosophy on the surface; and a foundational attitude toward politics.

First, as to the Latin: Petrarch's move to a "new" Latin, one unlike the Latin used in universities and the Church, encompassed not only language, strictly speaking. It also fostered historical and scholarly research, as his attempts to refine his Latin led him to research ancient authors with an eye toward discovering their secrets. It was reciprocal, in other words: the desire to learn more about Latin led inevitably to learning more about history, and vice versa.

Some of these tendencies can be observed in a letter Petrarch wrote late in life to Pope Urban V. Petrarch calls Latin learning "the root of our arts and the foundation of all knowledge."[20] But it is the context in which that statement is uttered that is particularly interesting. First, the letter is written

---

[16] Dante, *Convivio*, ed. Franca Brambilla Agena, 2 vols. (Florence: Le Lettere, 1995), v.2: 1.5.7.

[17] Ibid.

[18] Dante, *De vulgari eloquentia*, ed. Botterill, 1.9.6 (my tr.): "homo sit instabilissimum atque variabilissimum animal."

[19] Ibid., 1.1.3–4.

[20] Petrarch *Epistolae seniles*, 9.1, in Petrarch, *Letters of Old Age*, 2 vols., tr. Aldo Bernardo (New York: Italica, 2005), 312, tr. Bernardo, modified. See Emanuele Casamassima, "L'autografo della seconda lettera del Petrarca a Urbino V (*Senile* IX 1)," *Quaderni petrarcheschi* 3 (1985–86),

to a pope, Urban V, for whom Petrarch has special regard. It might be odd to think that this most Christian of men wrote screeds against the papacy in the form of a series of anonymous but public letters (the letters "Without a name" – *sine nomine*).[21] Like Dante, though, he had seen much of which he disapproved. But Urban V, Petrarch hoped, was different. Urban's choice of name, for example, signaled that he wanted to take the papacy back to the *Urbs* – "the City" – as Rome was known.

And Urban was willing to listen, obviously, to Petrarch as Petrarch defended Italy and Italians against French disdain. The letter makes clear that the king of France, in an effort to have Urban remain in Avignon, sent an ambassador to Urban praising France and denigrating Italy. So Petrarch writes the pope defending Italy, "for spoken words fade away while written words remain."[22] For Petrarch the crux of the matter is as follows: "Tell me, what of the liberal arts, of the natural or historical sciences, wisdom, eloquence, ethics, and is there any part of philosophy in Latin that was not practically all discovered by Italians."[23] Petrarch recalls ancient greatness here, and ancient tradition, and he has time as well for medieval achievements: "Italians established both civil and canon law, and then Italians have so explicated them that nothing, or very little, remains for foreigners."[24] Civil law reaches back to ancient Rome and canon law to the early Church, but renewed study of both kinds of law indeed occurred in medieval Italy at the University of Bologna, beginning in the eleventh century. And then, ultimately: "The root of our arts and the foundation of all knowledge – Latin letters – were invented here; so was the Latin language and the Latin name . . . they all, I repeat, originated here, not elsewhere, and they have grown here."[25] So there are ancient achievements. But Petrarch's highlighting of medieval accomplishments in jurisprudence foregrounds his appreciation of, one might almost say longing for, Italy, the land of his ancestors but not where he grew up. True, he writes, the French might boast of the University of Paris.[26] But that is about it, one institution to set against all these Italian cultural achievements.

103–34, at 116; and Silvia Rizzo, *Ricerche sul latino umanistico* (Rome: Edizioni di storia e letteratura, 2002), 37.

[21] Francesco Petrarca, *Sine nomine*, ed. Ugo Dotti (Turin: Aragno Editore 2010).

[22] *Sen.* 9.1, tr. Aldo Bernardo, modified, in Petrarch, *Letters of Old Age* (New York: Italica Press, 2005), 312.

[23] Ibid.

[24] Ibid.

[25] Ibid.

[26] Ibid., 313.

Finally, here is the key point: "And let no one doubt ... that nowhere is the Church so great, whether you measure her power or the devotion not only of the Italians but of all the people believing in Christ, since here the Church was born, here she matured, and here – with God willing and you, I hope, acting – she will remain forever."[27] For Petrarch, then, learning, Christianity, Italy, and Latin were all bound together in an inextricable fashion. If contemporary society had torn them apart, he suggests, now is the time to put them back together. The Church must move back to Rome. When it comes to language and Latin, this sense – that Latinate imperial majesty could and should be linked to Christianity – was one element that fueled Petrarch's thinking. It would return later in the thinking of Lorenzo Valla.

Another important element was the relation of Latin to the vernacular. In this respect, Petrarch's position is easy to read on the surface, though it becomes more complicated, the deeper one probes. Two letters to Boccaccio serve as a way in to Petrarch's attitudes. Both reveal the relationship of the two men, as they grew ever closer after their first meeting in 1350; both have the ghost of Dante hovering above them; and both show that Petrarch worked out his positions on language and other matters predominantly in a social way: in conversation with others.

The first of these letters arose when Petrarch wanted to quell an opinion he had heard was making the rounds: that he had something against Dante.[28] He is writing in response to a letter by Boccaccio, in which Boccaccio seemed to have apologized for praising Dante, having assured Petrarch that any praise for Dante would redound to Petrarch's glory as well. Petrarch responds and says, defensively, that there was no need for Boccaccio to have done so. After all, he had only seen Dante once, when young and, besides, they were both Florentine in origin, with their families bound together by kinship ties. It is true, however, at least in Petrarch's mind, that he had enemies, people who might stoke those sorts of rumors. One of these rumors was that Petrarch, though known as an avid collector of books, deliberately decided not to acquire Dante's *Comedy*. These rumor-mongers say, in other words, that "I never had his book; and though I was most eager in collecting all the others, indeed seeking some that were almost hopeless to find, with respect to that one, which was indeed new and easy to obtain, I was, in a way that was different for me and not my usual habit, rather indifferent."[29]

---

[27] Ibid., 313, tr. Bernardo, modified.
[28] Petrarch, *Epistolae familiares*, 21.5; Latin text consulted in Francesco Petrarca, *Prose*, ed. Giuseppe Martellotti (Milan: Ricciardi, 1955) 1002–14, at 1002.
[29] Ibid.

The "Dante's ghost" part of all this is clear: Petrarch says, "his book," or in Latin, *librum illius*, "the book of that one," most literally. He was so intent not to name Dante that he needed to find circumlocutions to refer to Dante and his *Comedy*. Yet, Petrarch tells Boccaccio something noteworthy: in this case, those charges are true. But there was a reason. When he was young and enamored of the idea of writing vernacular poetry, he did indeed avoid "the book of that one," because Petrarch feared unwittingly becoming an imitator. Now, however, he has matured and changed his outlook: "Today, these worries are far behind me. Now that I have departed and have put aside that fear by which I was held back, I welcome with my whole mind all others and him above all."[30] What Petrarch is signaling here is that any concerns he may, once, have had about "all others and him above all" (meaning all other vernacular poets and Dante above all) have vanished. He is in a new, more mature phase now, having left behind the desire to write great vernacular poetry. From now on, he will focus his attention on Latin writing: in the realm of poetry, there will be his Latin epic *Africa*; and then, otherwise, his heart and mind will turn to historical and philosophical work.

Another letter fills this picture out, written even later in life, again to his friend Boccaccio, this time in 1364.[31] Here Petrarch is responding to something he had heard regarding Boccaccio, to the effect that Boccaccio, having seen Petrarch's vernacular poetry at a young age, became depressed and resolved to burn his own fledgling efforts, since they could not compare with Petrarch's poetry. Petrarch implores Boccaccio not to go that route; he tells Boccaccio that if he in fact occupies third place after Dante (still unnamed) and Petrarch, then Boccaccio should be satisfied with that ranking; finally, Petrarch relates his own trajectory: "Now it is true that at one time I had indeed had an intention contrary to my current one, hoping to devote most of my time to this enterprise of writing in the vernacular. The reason is that it seemed to me that both of the two more elevated styles of Latin" – he means prose and poetry –

> had been cultivated to such an extent and by such great geniuses of antiquity that nothing significant could be added, either by me or by anyone else. On the other hand, the vernacular, having been but recently discovered and still quite rustic owing to recent ravagers and to the fact that few have cultivated it, seemed capable of ornament and augmentation.[32]

---

[30] Ibid.
[31] Francesco Petrarca, *Res Seniles*, Libri V–VIII, ed. Silvia Rizzo, with Monica Berté (Florence: Le lettere, 2009), 5.2, 30–51.
[32] Ibid., 42.

So much is contained in this short passage. First, there is the anxiety about antiquity and specifically about Latin. Having fallen in love with the ancient Roman world and its literary expression, Petrarch considered himself unequal to the task of writing anything that would measure up to ancient greatness. This seemingly unreachable ancient greatness represented one reason to move to the vernacular. The other, he conveys, is that vernacular was "but recently discovered" – fair enough, one might say – though it was "still quite rustic owing to recent ravagers" and to the relative paucity of writers who had engaged in vernacular writing. Here again the presence of Dante looms large, unnamed though powerfully influential as he is.

However, there is more to Petrarch's disquiet – in the case of Dante – than mere jealousy. There is also the matter of how texts circulated. Petrarch tells Boccaccio about his younger years, when he had begun an important project in the vernacular:

> Urged on by the stimuli of youth, I had begun a great work in that genre, and I had laid down the foundations of the edifice along with the plaster, stone, and wood. But then when I looked at our own age, the mother of pride and indolence, I began with some bitterness to note how great was the "genius" of those who tossed those things around, how "beautiful" was their style of speaking. The result is that you would say writings are not recited but ripped apart.[33]

"Foundations," "plaster," "stone," "wood": Petrarch means that he had written poems in Italian (by "great work" he refers most likely to his *Canzoniere*), poems that were crafted (hence the metaphorical mention of building materials) with great effort and attention to language, tradition, and poetic originality.

But then (as always, it seems, in Petrarch's mind) the age in which he lived disappointed him. For readers today, what he says seems obscure, when he recalls noticing "how great was the 'genius' of those who tossed those things around, how 'beautiful' was their style of speaking," to such an extent that it seems that "writings are not recited but ripped apart." What can this mean? Why should a writer, whose words exist fixed on a page, care all that much how, or even if, his works were being recited? The answers to these questions lie in the fact that Petrarch's writerly world existed in a strange hybrid form (strange to us) between written and oral, fixed and indeterminate, immaterial and material.

---

[33] Ibid.

First, there are those two key verbs: "recite" (*recitari* in Latin) and "rip apart" (*discerpi*). If our primary image of poetry is of it being written down, for Petrarch one main association had to do with the voice, with "recitation." Or rather, he understood that this was how it worked in his day, that things written down had a kind of reciprocal existence, with one part being on the page and another coming to life only when recited. The Latin word translated here as "writings" is *scripta*, which at the most literal level means "things written down." Those who recite *scripta* seem not to be reciting but rather to be "ripping apart." The Latin word translated as "ripping apart" is *discerpi*, a word with a violent connotation. Other possible translations would be "tearing apart" or "plucking to pieces," resonances that Petrarch well understood.

So, a lot is going on in this passage. There is the ghost of Dante, of course, first and foremost. But in some ways more important, since it is less obvious to modern readers, the inherent instability in the ways texts circulated emerges as this letter's defining feature.[34] Petrarch goes on to say: "I heard this [the performances of those reciting poetry] again and again, and as I repeatedly considered all this, I came to the conclusion that, to build on soft mud and sand that was always giving way was work wasted, and that I, and my work as well, would simply be torn apart in the hands of the common herd."[35]

It is a rather grim picture: on the one hand, Petrarch acknowledges that the ancients were the greatest authors and that one cannot add much to them. On the other hand, he says he believed early on that the vernacular, only "recently discovered," could indeed be improved, that even he might add something to it. But seeing and hearing the way people mangled what he wrote in the vernacular when they recited his work, and understanding, one suspects, how texts themselves, handwritten as they were and thus each an individual product, were inevitably a bit different one from the other, Petrarch seems to have sensed despair. He could do nothing original; therefore (the picture he paints here suggests anyway), he retreats into the study of the ancients.

That picture, however, is incomplete. We know in fact that, far from abandoning his vernacular writing, Petrarch persisted, throughout his whole, wandering life, to continue work on the *Canzoniere*, having overseen nine

---

[34] See Justin Steinberg, "Dante *Estravagante*, Petrarca *Disperso*, and the Spectre of the Other Woman," in Zygmunt G. Baranski and Theodore J. Cachey Jr., *Petrarch and Dante: Anti-Dantism, Metaphysics, Tradition* (Notre Dame: University of Notre Dame Press, 2009), 263–89.

[35] Petrarca, *Res Seniles*, Libri V–VIII, 5.2, 42–3.

editorial redactions throughout his peregrinations, with the last completed in the year of his death, 1374. In that same year he wrote his vernacular *Triumph of Eternity*, the sixth and final in a series of poetic "Triumphs" that, coming after Love, Chastity, Death, Fame, and Time, projected the poet into the time after time, when God would choose to render the final judgment, when the wicked would be punished, the just rewarded and when Petrarch himself would, he hoped, come face to face again with his muse Laura, unimaginably beautiful as she will be after the resurrection and after she puts back on her "veil." Even then, even at the end of time, Petrarch is reminded of writing:

> Before all those who are to be remade is the one whom the world, weeping, calls, with my tongue and my tired pen; though heaven too yearns to see her whole. At the bank of a river born in the Cevennes, love bestowed upon me such a long war for her, one that my heart calls to memory even now. What a fortunate stone, that covers that beautiful face. At that time when she will have put back on her veil, if he who saw her on earth was blessed, what will it then be to see her in heaven?[36]

His "tired pen" – *stanca penna*. One of the reasons Petrarch's pen was tired was that, ever conscious of the written word's potential power, instability, and capacity to shape the self, he lived a life marked by a set of contradictions: private but obsessed with public recognition, deeply religious yet critical of the Church of his time, misanthropic yet possessed of a gift for friendship.[37] But there was one polarity that shaped Petrarch his whole career and indeed inflected the rest of the humanist movement after him: that related to language and specifically to the question of Latin versus vernacular.

The letter to Boccaccio, previously noted, where Petrarch discusses his work being "ripped apart" is as good a testimony as any to isolate the public image he wanted to project: that he had, in the course of his growth into real maturity, left behind the frivolities of youthful love poetry in the vernacular and moved instead into the august realm of serious work in Latin.[38] His "Letter to Posterity," a remarkable document of autobiography, addressed to unnamed future readers, tells a similar story. He writes there: "Adolescence deceived me, young manhood corrupted me, old age corrected me."[39] Part of this process of maturation had to do with leaving carnal love behind, but another was linked to his public devotion to scholarship in Latin, seen as more serious and lasting than the vernacular. Yet the fact that he kept

---

[36] *Triumphus Eternitatis*, verses 135–45, in *Opere*, 317.

[37] See Celenza, *Petrarch: Everywhere a Wanderer*.

[38] See Francesco Petrarch, *Lettera ai Posteri*, ed. and tr. Gianni Villani (Rome: Salerno, 1990).

[39] Ibid., 34.

working privately on his vernacular poetry signals something important, something that remained true for the rest of the humanist movement in Italy: Latin and the Tuscan vernacular were richly interdependent. In this case as in others Petrarch represented a model for what came after him, however much future generations might have found him wanting.

Perhaps it was after all the ghost of Dante. About fifty years later, Leonardo Bruni, a leading Florentine thinker whom we shall meet in more detail later, wrote short biographies of Dante and Petrarch as well as a comparison of the two. He had high praise for both. But in the comparison, after listing the many excellent traits of each (Dante wrote a perfected vernacular, for example, and Petrarch had the gift to be able to excel in prose and poetry, a rarity), Bruni says something interesting: "in the vernacular Petrarch is the equal of Dante in the writing of *canzoni* and in sonnets he has the advantage. Yet I confess nonetheless that Dante's major work" – Bruni means the *Divine Comedy* – "takes the lead over any work of Petrarch."[40] By Bruni's day (he died in 1444) Dante's *Comedy* had become an acknowledged classic. In Petrarch's it was well on the way to becoming one.

Comparisons with Dante aside, there was more that Petrarch accomplished. This accomplishment, when all is said and done, entailed the emergence of a new and different view of history. Surprisingly to modern ears, it all took wing because of academic scholarship, scholarship that we can view in two ways: as the product of a social environment and as a result of individual virtuosity.

As to the social environment, Petrarch's relationship with his admirer and friend Giovanni Boccaccio (1313–75) comes to the fore. It was through their letters that the two developed their relationship, as we have seen. Boccaccio, today, is known as the author of the *Decameron*, one of the cornerstones of Italian and indeed of Western literature. Boccaccio's Tuscan prose would be prized as an exemplar of the Tuscan language, later, in the early sixteenth century. A series of one hundred tales set over ten days (hence the fancifully Hellenizing title: *deka*="ten," *hemera*="day"), the *Decameron* is set dramatically outside of Florence, where seven young women and three young men have gone to escape the Black Death of 1348. This bubonic plague afflicted not only Florence but also all of Europe from 1348 to 1352, killing up to one-third of the population. Boccaccio's introduction to the *Decameron* contains one of the most affecting and memorable descriptions of this devastating illness ever recorded:

[40] Bruni, "Lives of Dante and Petrarch," in Bruni, *The Humanism*, 100, tr. slightly modified.

Whether it descended on us mortals through the influence of the heavenly bodies or was sent down by God in His righteous anger to chastise us because of our wickedness, it had begun some years before in the East, where it deprived countless beings of their lives before it headed to the West, spreading ever-greater misery as it moved relentlessly from place to place. Against it all human wisdom and foresight were useless.[41]

Boccaccio describes people's reactions to this terrible and unforeseen affliction, which "caused all sorts of fears and fantasies in those who remained alive, almost all of whom took one utterly cruel precaution, namely to avoid the sick and their belongings."[42] Some went into seclusion in small groups, gathering food and wine and living moderately, away from society. Others "maintained that the surest medicine for such an evil disease was to drink heavily, enjoy life's pleasures, and go about singing and having fun, satisfying their appetites by any means available, while laughing at everything and turning whatever happened into a joke." Respect for law plummeted and "people felt free to behave however they liked." Some abandoned Florence, hoping to escape the plague's reach. In the event, no one had the perfect solution. Some lived; some died. The social fabric frayed to such an extent that though it was difficult to believe, "fathers and mothers refused to tend to their children and take care of them, treating them as if they belonged to someone else." The wealthy died without the usual accompaniment of family and kin, and those of the lower orders fared worse: "Many expired out in the public streets both day and night, and although a great many others died inside their houses, the stench of their decaying bodies announced their deaths to their neighbors well before anything else did ... the city was overwhelmed with corpses."[43]

We have a grim description of death and disease, the almost immediate decay of the social fabric of the city, and a Florence where "there was not enough consecrated ground to bury the enormous number of corpses that were being brought to every church every day at almost every hour."[44] It is hard to believe that a book beginning in this fashion emerged as touchstone of comic, satirical literature. But it did, and the reason has to do with the nature of the author, a person who was known to be sweet natured and who we can tell from his correspondence was occasionally prone to self-doubt.

Take the fourth story on the fifth day, a story that is short and typical both of the sort of humor that the *Decameron* represents and of the values it embeds

---

[41] Giovanni Boccaccio, *Decameron*, tr. Wayne Rebhorn (New York: Norton, 2013), 4.
[42] Ibid., 7.
[43] Ibid., 7–8.
[44] Ibid., 11.

within its pages. A respectable older man, Messer Lizio da Valbona, lived in Romagna (relatively close to Ravenna) with his wife, Giacomina. Messer Lizio had a late-in-life surprise, when his wife gave birth to a baby daughter, whom they named Caterina. She grew up to be beautiful, and the couple "took extraordinary care in guarding her, for they hoped to be able to arrange a great match for her."[45] At the same time a young, relatively well-born man named Ricciardo, also from the region, was a regular guest at Messer Lizio's house, so much so that both Messer Lizio and his wife trusted young Ricciardo completely, as if he were a son of their own. Yet Ricciardo, observing Caterina's beauty and grace, fell passionately in love with her, a passion he tried unsuccessfully to hide from her. Noticing his attention, "she fell for him as well, to Ricciardo's great delight."[46] Both confessed their attraction to each other and a plan was hatched to find a way to meet on the roof, since there would be no other way for them to be alone together, since Caterina was so closely guarded.

Though it was only the end of May, Caterina used the pretext of the heat in her room to convince her parents to allow her to sleep on the roof, so that she might spend the time outside, in the cool air, "listening to the song of the nightingale."[47] The nightingale had a long history as a symbol, reaching back to antiquity, and it had historically evoked many things: loss, the hope of spring, and love among them. Boccaccio's use is much earthier. Sleeping on the balcony, Caterina is visited by Ricciardo, and "after a multitude of kisses, the two of them lay down together, and for virtually the entire night, they took their pleasure of each other, delightedly making the nightingale sing again and again."[48] Exhausted, they fell into a deep sleep, and "Caterina cradled Ricciardo's neck in her right arm, while with her left hand she held him by that thing which you ladies are too embarrassed to name when you are in the presence of men."[49]

Morning arrived, and Lizio, the father of the house, went to the roof to check on his daughter. Seeing them in that state, he called for his wife and said, "Quick, woman, get up. Come see how fond your daughter is of the nightingale, for she's captured it, and she's holding it in her hand."[50] His wife Giacomina came up to see and was startled and made angry by what she saw. But Lizio was prudent and said that now that they had caught Caterina and

[45] Ibid., 417.
[46] Ibid.
[47] Ibid., 418.
[48] Ibid., 419.
[49] Ibid.
[50] Ibid.

Ricciardo in this position, the thing to do was to compel ardent Ricciardo to marry Caterina. So, they woke the young lovers up, and Lizio informed Ricciardi (who by this point was terrified) that he had one choice: "you must take Caterina as your lawful wedded wife."[51] Ricciardo agreed immediately, and right then and there – for the mother, Giacomina, had brought up one of her rings – married Caterina, with the two parents as witnesses. A few days later they undertook a ceremony in public to cement the wedding, and Ricciardo took Caterina home with him. "And for many years after that he lived with her in peace and happiness, catching nightingales both day and night to his heart's content."[52] Nightingales. Get it?

We learn a lot more from this tale, of course, than that Boccaccio was an inveterate comic with a flair for the salty amusing tale. There is in fact a whole social world enfolded in his little story. First, recall that the parents' most fervent hope was to arrange a good marriage for their daughter. This desire, fictional though the tale is, signals an important truth regarding the world in which Boccaccio (not to mention Dante and Petrarch) lived: marriage existed primarily to pass on and consolidate family property. The very fact that, in this episode, something like love at first sight prevails in the end serves by its exceptional nature to highlight this point. There is the telling if brief description of what constituted a real wedding: an agreement between two people in the presence of witnesses. No priest needed to be there, though they were all Catholic. No civic authorities needed to be present, though the participants were all citizens. And even the public ceremony could be left to later.[53] Finally, there is the fact that age brings wisdom, as the older-than-average father, Lizio, does not strike out violently against Ricciardo upon discovering him in bed with his daughter.

In short, this tale, like so many others in Boccaccio's *Decameron*, takes as its main subject matter real, recognizable people and their everyday concerns. In that respect the *Decameron* was and remains a quite revolutionary work: a brilliant piece of comic literature that also, by the variety of its one hundred tales, reflected a society's concerns back onto itself, even as it remains eminently readable today. It was, in other words, a triumph: a triumph for Boccaccio as an author but also a triumph for the enterprise of writing itself.

So it can come as a great surprise to modern readers that, only slightly later in life, Boccaccio had a crisis of conscience, wracked by guilt over the salaciousness of his early work, and that he switched, definitively, to

---

[51] Ibid., 421.

[52] Ibid., 422.

[53] See Gene Brucker, *Giovanni and Lusanna: Love and Marriage in Renaissance Florence* (Berkeley: University of California Press, 1986).

researching and writing works of scholarship in Latin. His friend Petrarch's severe classicism – the shadow he placed over the vernacular, even as he himself continued working on his own vernacular writing – surely played a role.

One other letter from Petrarch to Boccaccio stands out as exemplary, precisely because it was written late in both men's lives.[54] In it, Petrarch writes to inform Boccaccio that he, Petrarch, has gone ahead and translated one of Boccaccio's tales from the *Decameron* into Latin. The letter tells us so much about the tenor of their relationship that it is worth examining in depth. Here is how it begins:

> I have seen your book [*the Decameron*] that you published in our mother tongue some time ago – when you were a young man, I believe. Whence or how it was brought to me I do not know. I would be lying if I told you I read it. It is certainly a big book and one that was written for the common herd, and in prose; and in any case I was busy and time is short.[55]

One old man writing to another, slightly less old perhaps but an ardent admirer. The two had been in touch for decades by this point (the letter is from the early 1370s); one does not need to be a literary critic to read the undertones: "I did not find the time to read your book, Boccaccio, it was written for the common herd," meaning it was written in the vernacular. The exaggerated Latinate bias we have seen in Petrarch must have always loomed large between the two men. By this point in Boccaccio's life he had all but sworn off the vernacular, having dedicated himself for many years to Latin works of scholarship such as would have pleased his grim older friend. Yet the city of Florence also commissioned Boccaccio (in 1373, right around the time of this letter) to offer public lectures on Dante's *Comedy*, an assignment he accepted. Even Boccaccio had to admit that there was a vernacular literature worthy of comment. Just not his own, his *Decameron*, the work for which his name still lives for educated readers today.

Petrarch goes on regarding Boccaccio's *Decameron*:

> I did enjoy reading through it quickly, enjoyed leafing through it; even if I came upon anything rather lewd, your age at the time you were writing excused it, as did the style, the language, and the very levity of the subject matter, along with the levity of those who seemed likely to read such

---

[54] See Petrarch, *De insigni obedientia et fide uxoria: Il Codice Riccardiano 991*, ed. Gabriella Albanese (Alessandria: Edizioni dell'Orso, 1998); there is an English tr. in Petrarch, *Letters of Old Age*, 2 vols., tr. Aldo Bernardo (New York: Italica, 2005), 2: 655–68; I cite from Petrarch, *Opera Latina* (Venice, 1503), CCii–iv.

[55] Petrarch, *Opera Latina* (Venice, 1503), CCii.

things. It matters a great deal for whom you are writing, and variety in morals excuses variety in style. Amid much light-hearted fun, I caught several pious and serious things about which I still have no definitive judgment since nowhere did I get totally absorbed.[56]

If the tone here does not quite evince passive aggression, it comes close enough to something like it that we can once more sense the tenor of the relationship. Words such as "lewd," "levity," and "light-hearted fun" all serve as opposites of the imagined, almost dreamlike identity that Petrarch labored so long to construct for himself, an identity that Boccaccio, too, had finally adopted: sober, serious, and grave. The two were clearly friends, so that we should not have the impression of a hectoring Petrarch and a cowering Boccaccio. Rather, we can imagine Boccaccio as any other junior partner in intellectual relationships of this sort, where the senior figure's arrogance, occasional longwindedness, and egoism come to be tolerated in exchange for the many other pleasant aspects of the association.

The tale in the *Decameron* that caught Petrarch's eye was the last one, which told the story of "Griselda," one of the few stories in Boccaccio's masterpiece almost entirely devoid of humor. To read the tale today is to run smack into the chasm-like difference between our world and that of Boccaccio and Petrarch. To recognize that it was this tale that Petrarch chose to translate allows us insight into Petrarch's mind. The story concerns Gualtieri, the Marquis of Saluzzo (a town near Turin), who as an active young man did not want to take a wife, being more enthused about "hawking and hunting." But his vassals did not like the idea that he should remain unmarried and even suggested that they could help him find the right connection. Eventually, they persuaded him to marry, though the marquis stipulated that he and only he would be the one to pick his prospective bride and that they must accept and celebrate her no matter who she turned out to be. The marquis chose Griselda, a girl of great beauty from a nearby farming village, on whom he had had his eye for a time. He negotiated with her father, they came to terms, and it was agreed that they would marry.

Griselda was told nothing, until one day the marquis decided to visit the humble peasant town. When he arrived, all his vassals in tow and in the presence of her father, the first thing he did was to ask her "whether, if he were to wed her, she would do her best to please him and never get upset at anything he ever said or did, and whether she would be obedient."[57] She replied that she would. Thereafter, "taking her by the hand, he led her outside

[56] Ibid.; and Petrarch, *Letters of Old Age*, tr. Bernardo, 2:655, modified.
[57] Boccaccio, *Decameron*, tr. Rebhorn, 841.

and in the presence of his entire company as well as all the other people living there, he had her stripped naked."[58] The marquis had brought along clothing that he had made for her and had his servants dress her, again, in front of everyone. He then announced to the crowd that this, indeed, was the woman he would take as a wife. His astonished company approved the choice, and the marquis married Griselda (described, understandably, as "stunned and embarrassed") then and there, returning thence to his own magnificent house, "where the wedding was celebrated in as beautiful, festive, and magnificent a style as if he had married the daughter of the king of France."[59]

Thus far, one might imagine, the marquis's treatment of Griselda was bad enough. But more was in store for her. As they settled into married life, Griselda became an admired ornament to the marquis. She became "so charming, so pleasant, and so well-mannered that she did not seem like a shepherdess . . . but like the child of some noble lord." In addition, "she was so obedient and attentive to her husband that he thought himself the happiest, most contented man in the world."[60] Presently she became pregnant, giving birth to a baby girl. It was at this point that something snapped in the marquis. As Boccaccio puts it: "the strange idea popped into his head to test her patience by subjecting her to constant tribulations and generally making life intolerable for her."[61] So, for one thing, the marquis began telling Griselda that all the vassals were upset with her low origin (a manifest untruth). The marquis then informed her that no one liked the little girl to whom she had given birth. Griselda replied that she well knew that she was socially inferior to the vassals and knew as well that she was unworthy of being married to the marquis.

Soon thereafter, the marquis sent a servant to Griselda. The servant said: "My lady, if I don't want to be put to death, I have to do what my lord has commanded, and he has commanded me to take this daughter of yours and to."[62] Overcome by emotion, the servant could say no more. Griselda inferred that the servant had been ordered to put the child to death. Yet again, she acquiesced, and though sick at heart, "she immediately took her daughter from the cradle, and without ever changing her expression, she kissed her and blessed her and placed her in the servant's arms."[63] Then obedient Griselda said to the servant: "do exactly what your lord, who is my

[58] Ibid.
[59] Ibid., 842.
[60] Ibid.
[61] Ibid., 843.
[62] Ibid.
[63] Ibid.

lord as well, has ordered, but don't leave her to be devoured by the beasts and birds unless he told you to do so." The servant took the baby away and conferred with Gualtieri, who "marveled at her constancy."[64] Gualtieri then sent the child to be raised in Bologna, again without informing Griselda.

Then they had a son. And so, Gualtieri, up to his usual tricks, behaved as follows:

> One day, glowering at her with feigned fury, he said: "woman, ever since you gave birth to this boy, I've found it completely impossible to live with my vassals, so bitterly do they complain that one of Giannucole's grand-sons" – Giannucole was Griselda's father – "is to succeed me as their lord. So if I don't want to be deposed by them, I'm afraid that I'll have to do in this case what I did in the other one, and that I'll also eventually have to leave you and find another wife."[65]

Again, Griselda bore this blow with what then seemed like constancy but what today seems like masochism: "My lord" – she said after hearing the news – "you should think about your own happiness and about how to satisfy your desires. Don't waste another thought on me, for nothing is of any value to me unless I see that it gives you pleasure."[66] The same routine ensued, with the boy being spirited away secretly to Bologna.

It should be said that throughout the tale signs of objection crop up, as if Gualtieri's behavior is not only difficult to understand but also crazy, not to put too fine a point on it. After the episode with the son, for instance, Gualtieri's subjects "condemned him, blaming it all on his cruelty, whereas they felt nothing but the most profound pity for his wife."[67]

Gualtieri's final act of cruelty, his ultimate test for his wife, was to follow through, a few years later, on his threat to end their marriage. He said to all and sundry, his poor wife included, that he would gain a papal dispensation, so that he could marry again. He arranged to have fake documents sent to him, which were believed to originate with the papacy. Griselda grieved, but only privately, offering a long speech offering to give back her ring and all her clothes and asking only to keep the simplest of dresses, a request Gualtieri granted. She went back to her father Giannucole.

Meanwhile, Gualtieri convinced all his vassals that he was indeed remarry-ing and then asked none other than Griselda herself to see to the arrange-ments. Griselda was to tidy up the lord's house, take care of the invitations,

---

[64] Ibid.
[65] Ibid.
[66] Ibid.
[67] Ibid., 843.

and so on. Again, she did so uncomplainingly. By this point, his daughter had reached the age of twelve. She was chosen as the fictive bride. When she had arrived, everyone but Gualtieri believing she was to marry him; Griselda, again, was gracious, welcoming the girl, praising her beauty, and even complimenting Gualtieri on his choice.

Finally, after all this, Gualtieri chose to reveal that it had been his plan all along to test Griselda: "I wanted to teach you how to be a wife," he informed her, "to teach them [his subjects] how to manage one, and at the same time to beget for myself perpetual peace and quiet for the rest of my life with you . . . And since I've never seen you deviate from my wishes in either word or deed, and since it seems to me that you will provide me with all the happiness I've desired, I intend to restore to you in an instant that which I took from you over such a long time."[68] He revealed to her that the two children – for the boy had been brought along as well – were theirs, that they had not after all been put to death, and that he loved Griselda more than anything else. Griselda wept for joy, the ladies of the household helped her change into more suitable clothes, her father Giannucole was given deluxe lodgings, and Gualtieri "lived a long, contented life with Griselda, always honoring her in every way he could."[69]

This story, again the last in the *Decameron*, was so extreme that even the *Decameron*'s characters were not united in their appreciation, with some of the ladies who heard the tale criticizing parts of it, others praising parts. Why was this the tale that Petrarch chose to translate into Latin?

On one hand, the answer is relatively simple, as Petrarch himself, at the end of the letter, offers his own reasoning:

> I decided to retell this story in another language not so much to encourage the married women of our day to imitate this wife's patience, which to me seems hardly imitable, as to encourage the readers to imitate at least this woman's constancy, so that what she maintained toward her husband they may maintain toward our God.[70]

In other words, the tale in this Latin version should be taken as allegorical, a way to help human beings understand how to bear up under the difficulties that God in His infinite but not always understandable wisdom throws our way. Think Job. And there is certainly something to Petrarch's explanation: what scholars today call "exemplarity" – the use of historical examples to teach virtue to readers – was always utmost in Petrarch's mind, even if he himself did not use that term.

---

[68] Ibid., 848.
[69] Ibid., 849.
[70] Petrarch, *Opera Latina*, CCiv; Petrarch, *Letters of Old Age*, tr. Bernardo, 2:655.

In a subsequent letter, Petrarch relates to Boccaccio that he had shared this Latinized version of the Griselda story with two friends. One of them wept half way through, so moved was he by the events described therein. The other simply found it unbelievable. About the latter friend, Petrarch says "that there are some who consider whatever is difficult for them, impossible for everyone" – offering thereby a veiled critique of that friend.[71] Yet in the end, the Griselda tale and Petrarch's choice to translate it serve as a reminder that men and women traveled in separate spheres and that the virtues admired in woman included obedience above all.

Later in the letter poignant news emerges: Petrarch has heard that his earlier letter had not reached Boccaccio. And indeed there is no recorded reply from Boccaccio. Petrarch's two letters are not dated specifically, though internal evidence allows us to believe that they were composed in the early 1370s. Both letters appear in Petrarch's *Letters of Old Age*. In fact, Petrarch chose to end his *Letters of Old Age* with four letters to Boccaccio followed by, as the last letter, his *Letter to Posterity*, as if to pass on his legacy, first to Boccaccio, his most ardent admirer, and then to posterity in general. Petrarch died on July 19, 1374, having left Boccaccio 50 florins in his will, a generous sum.[72]

For Petrarch, real literary work was something to be shared: with friends, such as Boccaccio, with his many contemporary readers, and finally with – as he had intimated – posterity. Then, too, there was the virtuosic element to Petrarch, the fact that he had a nose for discovery, the diligence to work through and collate Latin texts, and the will and energy to spread the word of his discoveries. For example, after he discovered Cicero's oration *Pro Archia* (in 1333, in Liège), which showed Cicero defending Archias, a poet, whom Cicero defended precisely because he was a poet, Petrarch made sure that others had copies of this oration.[73] It was a meaningful moment: in defending the poet Archias, Cicero had told his audience that poetry served an important function, since "all the arts which have to do with humanity possess a certain common link, and it is as if they are bound together, one with the other."[74] A bit later in the oration, when Cicero excuses himself for speaking in way that is different from the customary habit in courts of law, he does so

---

[71] Petrarch, *Opera Latina*, CCiv(v); Petrarch, *Letters of Old Age*, tr. Bernardo, 2:670.

[72] Petrarch, "Testament," in Theodore Mommsen, ed., *Petrarch's Testament* (Ithaca, NY: Cornell University Press, 1957), pp. 68–93, at p. 82; for the value see Richard Goldthwaite, *The Economy of Renaissance Florence* (Baltimore: Johns Hopkins University Press, 2009), table A1. For Petrarch's vision see Giuseppe Mazzotta, *The Worlds of Petrarch* (Durham, NC: Duke University Press, 1993).

[73] See Petrarch, *Seniles* 16.1, in Francisci Petrarchae, *Opera Latina* (Venice, 1503), unpaginated; an English translation of the letter can be found in Aldo Bernardo, tr., *Letters of Old Age* (New York, 2005), pp. 599–607.

[74] Cicero, *Pro Archia*, sec. 2.

by suggesting he will be speaking "a bit more freely concerning the study of the humanities," using for the "humanities" the expression *studia humanitatis ac litterarum*.[75] Literally, the words mean "studies of humanity and letters," but more expansively they designated the field (literature, encompassing a broad conception of philosophy) with which Petrarch fell in love and that often has been identified as the core of Renaissance humanism.[76]

Another discovery left Petrarch somewhat shocked. In 1345, when on another research trip (this time to Verona), he found a manuscript of Cicero's letters to his best friend, Titus Pomponius Atticus.[77] With Atticus Cicero was accustomed to discuss family, to reveal his inner emotional states, and to engage in sometimes scurrilous gossip about Roman politics and his own role therein.[78] Petrarch had been accustomed to the stoically virtuous Cicero (the sort of person who would defend a poet who needed his protection); to the Cicero who had written dialogues on friendship, on different schools of philosophy, on rhetoric, and on so much more; and to the Cicero who was a hero of Rome and its republic, with all the gravity that status implied. Finding instead that Cicero was also concerned with run of the mill problems, an overwrought Petrarch went so far as to write Cicero an angry letter, in which he upbraided the ancient sage: "I have heard you saying much, complaining much, wavering much, and though I had long known you in the capacity of advisor to others, now finally I see what you are to yourself."[79] Not wanting to end on a sour note, Petrarch then proceeded to write Cicero a second (and longer) letter, stressing Cicero's positive qualities, though still with a tinge of criticism, suggesting that Cicero did not live up to the way of life that a true philosopher should embody.[80] In short, Petrarch's engagement with Cicero was emotional: it went beyond discovery and textual work and into the realm of affective engagement with exemplary figures of the past.

---

[75] Ibid., sec. 3.

[76] See Paul Oskar Kristeller, *Renaissance Thought and Its Sources* (New York: Columbia University Press, 1979).

[77] See most recently, with ample bibliographies, Martin Eisner, "In the Labyrinth of the Library: Petrarch's Cicero, Dante's Virgil, and the Historiography of the Renaissance," *Renaissance Quarterly* 67 (2014), 755–90; Martin McLaughlin, "Petrarch and Cicero: Adulation and Critical Distance," in William H.F. Altman, ed., *Brill's Companion to the Reception of Cicero* (Leiden: Brill, 2015), 19–38.

[78] On the *Letters*, see D.R. Shackleton Bailey, *Cicero's Letters to Atticus*, with translation and commentary, 7 vols. (Cambridge: Cambridge University Press, 1965–70); Cicero, *Letters to Atticus*, 4 vols., ed. and tr. D.R. Shackleton Bailey (Cambridge, MA: Harvard University Press, 2014).

[79] Petrarch, *Le familiari*, ed. Vittorio Rossi, 4 vols. (Florence: Sansoni, 1933–68; reedition, Florence, Le lettere, 1997), 24.3.1.

[80] Ibid., 24.4.

What did Petrarch leave behind? First and foremost, his attitude toward the Latin language comes to the fore. Petrarch took a somewhat disjointed intellectual movement, with a burgeoning interest in the classics, and oriented it in two important ways: first, though Dante had made a lasting mark with his *Comedy* in the Tuscan vernacular, Petrarch (as we have seen with his interactions with Boccaccio) firmly planted the flag for Latin. This move on his part was not without its ironies: Petrarch himself continued work on his vernacular poetry throughout his life, indeed until the very last year of that storied life. And there is no doubt that some of his embrace of a crowd-shunning, stoic-oriented, virtue-praising embrace of Latin was at least partially induced by the looming shadow of Dante's great achievement in the vernacular, a shadow growing ever-larger in Petrarch's old age.

All of that said, for the next five or so generations, the most prominent Italian intellectuals would work out much of their thinking in Latin. As we shall see, many of these intellectuals were also so firmly committed to what they saw as classical values that they worked hard to have their own Latin work as well as Greek and Roman texts translated into the vernacular. But Latin was seen, until the end of the fifteenth century, as the only medium that could ensure relative permanence; it was and remained the only language with which one could converse across cultures.

Second – and this legacy was less lasting and more in line with the culture of his era – Petrarch steered humanism in the direction of religion. Both elements had profound resonances in the life, work, and thought of the key figure around whom humanism coalesced in the next generation, Coluccio Salutati.

3

THE ITALIAN RENAISSANCE TAKES
ROOT IN FLORENCE

PETRARCH, BY THE TIME OF HIS DEATH, POSSESSED A EUROPE-
wide following. His Italian poetry was on the lips of many, and his
scholarly identity – Latinate, focused on the presumed virtue of the ancients,
and deeply Christian – had become an ideal for many intellectuals. He also
represented one key constituent part of a group of writers who later became
known as the "Three Crowns of Florence," the other two being Dante and
Boccaccio.[1] In other words, by the late fourteenth century, Dante, Petrarch,
and Boccaccio together became a source of Florentine cultural pride, a
"cultural memory" that, like all such memories, elided a lot, even as it
allowed new cultural work to go forward.

What was elided, what elements did that cultural memory leave out? For
one thing, there was the fact that, of the three, only Boccaccio died in
Florentine territory. Dante, as we have seen, wrote most of his notable work
in exile from his home city. Petrarch, though he could claim family connections, grew up in France and spent most of his Italian years elsewhere, often in
places (such as Milan and Padua) with political traditions starkly at odds with
those of Florence. Only Boccaccio, known to be friendly, genial, and constructive, remained, giving lectures toward the end of his life on Dante's
Comedy and, as a dedicated friend, preserving Petrarch's memory by carrying
out the sort of scholarly work that Petrarch had found most meaningful.

They were all dead by the end of 1375, Boccaccio passing away on
December 21 of that year, having arrived in his lectures on Dante only at
the end of canto 16 of the *Inferno*.[2] It was Boccaccio more than anyone else

[1] See Victoria Kirkham, "Le tre corone e l'iconografia di Boccaccio," in Michelangiola
Marchiaro and Stefano Zamponi, eds., *Boccaccio letterato* (Florence: Accademia della Crusca,
2015), 453–84.
[2] For the lectures, see Giovanni Boccaccio, *Esposizioni sopra la Comedia di Dante*, ed. Giorgio
Padoan (Milan: Mondadori, 1965); and Michael Papio, ed. and tr. *Boccaccio's Expositions on*

who wed all three of the "Crowns" together.[3] As Boccaccio neared the end of his life, another figure, one who became a most ardent defender of the city of Florence, emerged as Florence's "chancellor" (a position that entailed high governmental and diplomatic responsibilities): Coluccio Salutati, around whom a vibrant group of intellectuals gathered. It was largely through his agency and powerful persona that the Italian humanist movement took root in Florence.

Before delving into Salutati's life and work, it is worth reflecting both on the humanist movement as such and on the various conditions that made Florence an optimal home for a new intellectual undertaking. As to humanism, the most empirically inclusive (though not necessarily the best) way to describe it is as a turn among intellectuals to a series of predominantly verbal subjects, all of them in Latin and, eventually, in classicizing Latin. These subjects included grammar, rhetoric, poetry, history, and moral philosophy.[4] "Grammar" ranged much more broadly than we might imagine the term today. It included the basics: parts of speech, the structure of sentences, the way one changed and manipulated verbs and nouns to make meaning, and so on. But it had strong links with poetry and indeed had done so since the Middle Ages. One way to learn parts of speech is to "dissect" a lengthy poem, such as Virgil's *Aeneid*, which was quite popular throughout the Middle Ages and acquired new resonances for the Renaissance. Take the opening lines of the *Aeneid*, which we can look at line-by-line, word by word:

> Arma virumque cano, Troiae qui primus ab oris
> Italiam fato profugus Lavinaque venit Litora

> I sing (*cano*) arms and a man (*arma virumque*), who came (*qui . . . venit*) first (*primus*) from (*ab*) the shores (*oris*) of Troy (*Troiae*), exiled (*profugus*) by fate (*fato*), to Italy (*Italiam*) and the Lavine shores (*Lavina . . . litora*).

Dante's Comedy (Toronto: University of Toronto Press, 2009), who offers a splendid introduction at 3–38.

[3] See Martin Eisner, *Boccaccio and the Invention of Italian Literature: Petrarch, Cavalcanti, and the Authority of the Vernacular* (Cambridge: Cambridge University Press, 2013); Celenza, *The Lost Italian Renaissance*; Patrick Baker, *Italian Renaissance Humanism in the Mirror* (Cambridge: Cambridge University Press, 2015); and Brian Maxson, *The Humanist World of Renaissance Florence* (Cambridge: Cambridge University Press, 2013).

[4] Paul Oskar Kristeller argued forcefully for this notion in many of his works and especially in his *Renaissance Thought and Its Sources* (New York: Columbia University Press, 1979). For more recent literature, see D. Rundle and M. McLaughlin, "Introduction," *Renaissance Studies* 17 (2003), 1–8; and Celenza, *The Lost Italian Renaissance*.

Virgil tells first what he was doing, "singing" (for it was understood that poetry was rhythmic and, in a sense, incomplete, if not heard as well as read silently). What was he singing? "Arms" and "a man" – meaning a story of war, together with the story of a man, the hero, Aeneas. At a basic grammatical level, those two nouns, "arms" and "man" are direct objects of the verb "I sing"; therefore they appear in what Latin calls the "accusative" case, which has nothing to do with "accusation" as we understand the term, other than the fact that it indicates something toward which one is pointing. The action of the verb, singing, is, as it were, pointing directly toward a story of war with a central heroic character: "Arms and a man." You will notice, too, that the two words, *arma* and *virum*, are not separated by one of the normal Latin words for "and," which would be *et* or *ac*. Instead, the phrase runs in Latin: *arma virumque*. The word for "man," *virum*, has something tacked on to it at the end, *que*. That small word, which in grammatical terms is called a "particle" (and more specifically an "enclitic"), separates the word to which it is attached from the word that preceded it. As Latin had evolved naturally in the ancient world, that sort of grammatical construction helped in a formal sense, when the language was written down, since in the ancient world for many centuries there was neither punctuation nor word separation. So listeners would have known that the two words were separate, even as the person reciting ("singing") the poem would have been cued to place emphasis where it belonged.

In other words, something as seemingly simple and neutral as grammar (linked to poetry as it was) served as a springboard for humanists to consider details of language, the study of myth, history, and more. The other subjects all shared the same propulsive power. History allowed humanists to encounter the ancient past with which they were enraptured; and more, it offered examples from the ancient past that, they believed, could help shape behavior (especially of the leadership class) in the present. Rhetoric deepened the study of persuasion in a culture that valued oral performance. And moral philosophy became the centerpiece, really, of what the entire movement was all about: how should you live? In what does real friendship consist? In what did true nobility consist? These and many other questions animated humanists, as they had Petrarch. The study of words on the page, combined with a passion for the ancient Roman past, led humanists to discover manuscripts that had been hidden for centuries. These discoveries led them to think differently about history, as we shall see, than had been done in the past. And this spirit of discovery jumped, eventually, off the page and into the outside world, leading to discoveries scientific and otherwise.

But it all began in earnest, in a rooted fashion, in Florence in the late fourteenth and early fifteenth centuries.[5] So the question presents itself: why Florence? Three reasons emerge. The first has to do with wealth, pure and simple. Culture cannot find support if financial resources are lacking. And Florence as a city was quite wealthy, its money having been earned by bankers and cloth merchants who had for at least two centuries been plying these two trades with energy.[6] The second reason is connected to the first. Bankers and merchants travel. The Medici company, to give one example, eventually had branches in Bruges, Geneva, and London, to name just three non-Italian cities, as well as a series of outposts in different cities in Italy.[7] What this meant was that Florence had a leadership class that was, on balance, well traveled and whose members brought a certain cosmopolitanism to their worldviews. Having seen a lot, in other words, they tended to be more open to nontraditional forms of learning and culture.[8]

Finally, one other major factor comes to the fore, one that at first glance will seem paradoxical: Florence's university was quite small and undistinguished. The left bank of the Seine river in Paris, for example, had hosted one of Europe's most thriving universities since the early thirteenth century. Bologna, too, had a large portion of the city marked by the presence of its famous university, with its concentration on the study of civil and canon law. Today, if you visit those two cities or others like them (Oxford, for instance) that had powerful medieval universities, you can still sense the presences of those institutions. Not so in the case of Florence. While lacking a prominent university might not seem an advantage at first glance, in the case of the city's embrace of humanism, it was. The reason is that, though universities were and are productive and efficient centers for preserving the most useful knowledge, they are not always "early adopters" when it comes to embracing new forms of knowledge creation.

And humanism was new. Thinking about the humanist movement only in terms of its verbal disciplinary focus does not allow us to see what, precisely, was new. All of the five verbal disciplines – grammar, rhetoric, poetry, history, and moral philosophy – were studied in the Middle Ages. Indeed,

---

[5] For the most recent general history, see John Najemy, *A History of Florence, 1200–1575* (London: Wiley-Blackwell, 2008).

[6] See Goldthwaite, *The Economy of Renaissance Florence*.

[7] See Raymond De Roover, *The Rise and Decline of the Medici Bank, 1397–1494* (Cambridge, MA: Harvard University Press, 1963).

[8] This was a stance that was deeply rooted in late medieval northern Italy and gained even more traction in Florence owing to the conditions described. See Ronald G. Witt, *The Two Latin Cultures and the Foundation of Renaissance Humanism in Medieval Italy* (Cambridge: Cambridge University Press, 2011).

many times the way they were approached was only slightly different in the Renaissance, a matter of degree, not of kind. Coluccio Salutati (1331–1406) is the perfect person through whom we can see these gradual changes taking place. Ultimately, too, it is through Salutati (and the group that gathered around him) that we can see what, precisely, was new in Italian Renaissance humanism.

Like Dante and Petrarch, Salutati had an early "exile" from Florentine territory in his family background.[9] Though he was born in Stignano (a very small town near Lucca, a Tuscan city within Florentine dominion), his father suffered from a political purge when a Ghibelline faction took power. The family moved to Bologna, where Salutati was educated, proving an apt pupil, in his early adolescence, of a respected teacher, Pietro da Moglio. Pietro da Moglio was well known in Bologna, having had several pupils and eventually becoming acquainted (as letters show) with both Petrarch and Boccaccio. He worked on classical texts, much as Petrarch had done with the text of Livy. Da Moglio focused his attention on the use of the ancient comic writer Terence (among other authors) as a teaching tool.[10] This choice was important, since Terence, one of two of ancient Rome's great comic playwrights, was especially prized for his use of everyday language. If Cicero was, eventually, universally esteemed as the teacher of proper, elegant, indeed perfect Latin, Terence was the author to whom one turned for everyday usage. Salutati learned a lot at the feet of Pietro da Moglio, nothing more than, as he wrote in a poem directed to Pietro, *quid epistola posset* – "how powerful a letter can be."[11]

Letters. We have already seen how Petrarch employed the form: as a means of self-examination, of firming up his relationships, and of offering scholarly comment on matters of importance (as in his letters to Boccaccio). Yet there was another type of letter, and of letter writing, with which Italy was utterly suffused in the late Middle Ages: powerful indeed, as Salutati had averred. These were formal letters that communicated political, diplomatic, and other administrative positions and ideas. Sometimes these matters passed from person to person, in the case, for example, of a real estate transaction or other private legal matter. Sometimes – at the highest levels – these matters were communicated from state to state, in the case of diplomatic

---

[9] See Ronald G. Witt, *Hercules at the Crossroads: The Life, Works, and Thought of Coluccio Salutati* (Durham, NC: Duke University Press, 1983); and Witt, *Footsteps*, 292–337.

[10] Leonardo Quaquarelli, "Moglio, Pietro da," *Dizionario biografico degli italiani* 75 (2011), 267–73.

[11] Ibid. See also Berthold L. Ullman, *Studies in the Italian Renaissance* (Rome: Edizioni di Storia e letteratura, 1973), 298.

negotiations, warfare, and the creations of political alliances. The men who wrote these letters, and Salutati was no exception, were trained as notaries, a category of employment so important that we need to understand its implications.

Notaries played significant roles in the political and cultural life of the northern and central Italian city-states in the high Middle Ages and the Renaissance.[12] Their professional status reached back to the twelfth century, when notaries gained what became known as the *publica fides*, which we can translate as "public trust."[13] Notaries can best be understood as fulfilling the sorts of functions that lawyers often carry out today. Then as now, without public trust in legal documentation, transactions between people would break down.

Beyond these everyday legal functions, notaries also were well positioned to be professional writers. Many studied the "art of letter writing," known in Latin as the *ars dictaminis*, a discipline that allowed those who mastered it to write formal letters for many occasions.[14] By Salutati's era, the University of Bologna offered a two-year course of notarial studies where one could study the *ars dictaminis* and more. Having studied with Pietro da Moglio first, Salutati completed that course in 1350. The next step would have been to take a qualifying exam for the Guild of Notaries in Bologna. But political unrest there meant that Salutati's family moved back to Florentine territory, to a small town called Buggiano, roughly 60 kilometers west of Florence, between Florence and the sea. It was there that he got his start as a young notary.

Salutati's reputation grew to such an extent that in 1374 he was called to Florence to serve a governmental body charged with supervising Florence's elections, which were done by lot. A year later, in 1375, Salutati became Florence's chancellor, an office that, in effect, made him official Florence's chief letter writer, a position of great importance, especially in so far as Florence at that very moment went to war with the papacy. Salutati's letters from that period, which justified Florence's actions against the papal cause and attempted to maintain that Florence still desired to be a loyal Guelf, or pro-papal city, led to his becoming internationally famous. War was not avoided, though in this case it petered out when a settlement was reached.

More important was the way writing grew to become a central element in matters of politics. Later, in the fifteenth century, Enea Silvio Piccolomini (a writer, thinker, and churchman who eventually became Pope Pius II)

---

[12] See Witt, *In the Footsteps*, esp. 90–93.

[13] See Armando Petrucci, *Writers and Readers in Medieval Italy: Studies in the History of Written Culture*, ed. and tr. Charles M. Radding (New Haven: Yale University Press, 1995), 152.

[14] See Witt, *Footsteps*, 1–80.

made a fascinating claim: he said that one of Florence's rivals in Salutati's era, Giangaleazzo Visconti, tyrant of Milan, feared that Salutati's letters could harm him more than a thousand Florentine knights.[15] Piccolomini, in that same passage, wrote that the Florentines were to be praised since, in selecting their chancellors, they looked not so much for candidates who possessed technical knowledge of the law, as did other cities but rather for men who were skilled in oratory and in "those arts called 'the humanities.'"[16] Why then did the humanist movement flourish first and most formidably in Florence? One reason, surely, was the link between verbal, Latinate, classi-cizing humanist eloquence and political power.

Salutati was so respected that he was reelected to the position of chancellor every year thereafter until his death in 1406. This fact is noteworthy – extraordinary, really – given Florence's form of government: a republic. Much later, Machiavelli, in his classic *The Prince*, had this to say about republics: "in republics, there is more life, more hatred, more desire for revenge."[17] The reason for this intense set of experiences, as he would detail elsewhere, was the inevitable existence in republics of factions: groups of citizens at odds with one another. This facet – never-ending competition among citizens in a society in which citizens, at least notionally, had equal rights – represented the downside of republics. Yet Florence proudly remained a republic, long after many Italian city-states surrendered to the siren call of rule by one. To Salutati and those intellectuals who gathered around him, Florence's republicanism remained an important part of the city's and their own identities, on occasion fueling intellectual work, inflect-ing the way intellectuals wrote and thought, and serving as one important factor in the way they approached the world.

As to Salutati, the competition endemic to republics makes it even more remarkable that he was repeatedly elected to what was, on balance, the most important administrative office of the city. It signals something noteworthy about him: that, in addition to his political savvy, he had a magnanimous nature, one especially suited to attracting and encouraging the work of younger intellectuals. Before turning to this circle of followers, it is worth reflecting on Salutati's own work.

[15] "crebro auditus est dicere non tam sibi mille Florentinorum equites quam Colucii scripta nocere." Cit. S. Rizzo, "Il Latino nell'Umanesimo," in A. Asor Rosa, ed., *Letteratura italiana*, vol. 5, *Le Questioni*, pp. 379–408.

[16] "Commendanda est multis in rebus Florentinorum prudentia, tum maxime quod in legendis cancellariis non iuris scientiam, ut pleraque civitates, sed oratoriam spectant et quae vocant *humanitatis studia* [my emphasis]." Cit. Rizzo, ibid., 29–31, at 31.

[17] Niccolò Machiavelli, *Il principe*, ed. Giorgio Inglese (Turin: Einaudi, 1995), chap. 5, pp. 29–31.

Salutati differed from Petrarch in one important, and understandable, respect. Petrarch had been the first major humanist to link the emerging concerns of the Italian Renaissance (a love of classical antiquity and an abiding respect for classical Latin) to religion. Petrarch's moody interiority reflected his bifurcated nature as someone who wanted public acclaim on the one hand but, on the other, believed sincerely that the cultivation of his own soul along Christian lines remained the ultimate priority. Salutati by contrast was first and foremost a public person, most of whose working hours were taken up with the business of government, Florentine diplomacy, and the burdens and delights of citizenship in one of Europe's wealthiest and busiest cities. What this meant was that, without him ever overtly proclaiming this to be so, Salutati's interests verged more toward the secular: he, like Petrarch and other humanists, loved the classical world and classical Latin, but he did not prioritize the merging together of classical and Christian interests, as had Petrarch.

Like many Renaissance thinkers, Salutati prized the letter not only for its power in formal situations, as we have seen, but also as a means of literary expression. Looking at one letter will prove useful since the letter in question led to one signal, albeit modest, scholarly accomplishment, something that in turn demonstrates humanism's historical turn. More than anything the letter reminds us that many scholarly problems and achievements were the results of conversation, whether in person or on the page. In this case, the letter exchange occurs between Salutati and an educator, notary, and diplomat named Giovanni Conversino from Ravenna. Conversino had been a student of Salutati's own beloved mentor, Pietro da Moglio. They had that educational bond in common, as well as a growing friendship, one in which Conversino, being a bit younger than Salutati, clearly believed himself the junior partner, as it were.

Conversino had written a letter to Salutati asking to be included in Salutati's circle of friendship, and in it he addressed Salutati in a way that, in Salutati's view, attributed honors and plaudits to him that seemed excessive. And then there was something else a bit strange. Here is Salutati:

> Among the honors you attributed to me, I was wonder-struck that you had addressed me in the plural. As your writings attest, you have seen much. Tell me, I ask you, whom among the ancients will you cite who did not address in the singular, I will not only say a friend or even equals, but also lords and princes of the world?[18]

---

[18] Coluccio Salutati, *Epistolario*, ed. F. Novati, 4 vols., Fonti per la storia d'Italia, 15–18 (Rome: Istituto storico italiano per il medioevo, 1891–1911), 2.408, cit. in Christopher S. Celenza, "Coluccio Salutati's View of the History of the Latin Language," in N. van Deusen, ed., *Cicero Refused to Die: Ciceronian Influence Through the Centuries* (Leiden: Brill, 2013), 5–20, at 11.

So what does Salutati mean? First, in the letter, Salutati began by assuring Conversino how welcome his letter had been, as if to emphasize that Conversino did not need to subordinate himself to Salutati.

Yet it is the issue of using the plural as an honorific that means the most to Salutati. Those who have studied French, Italian, German, Spanish, and some other modern languages will recognize why Conversino might have done so: the reason is that many languages – and quite unlike English – have two ways of saying "you," one for use among friends and presumed social equals, another that is more formal. At times, as in French, Spanish, and German, that formal form is identical to the plural "you" – "you" as a group of people, rather than "you" as one person. And this, for Salutati, is the rub: in ancient Latin, this usage did not exist. There was no separation. There was a plural "you," of course, used only for cases when someone was addressing a group. But in the singular there was only one "you" – *tu*.

Salutati's next move in the letter is to list several respected ancient authors, both pagan and Christian, none of whom would have endorsed using a plural form of the word "you" as an honorific. Salutati calls Cicero onto the stage. What if, Salutati suggests, Cicero came back to life and said this to Conversino: "My dear Giovanni, what rule of mine, what example moves you that, when you are writing to one man, you address him in the plural as if you were speaking to the senate?"[19]

Conversino's response is telling. He suggests, first (and erroneously), that there were indeed ancient cases in which the plural "you" was used as a marker of honor. Conversino also remarks that there are cases – and here he is quite correct – when Salutati himself had used the plural "you" as an honorific. Conversino also makes quite clear that from then on he will, as per Salutati's wishes, use the singular *tu* when addressing him.

You might ask: why is any of this important? Taking a look at Salutati's next letter (his response to Conversino's response, as it were) can help us better understand. First and foremost, Salutati acknowledges that there may be times when diplomacy, his own included, demands that one use the honorific *vos*. Courtly customs must indeed, in certain political contexts, be respected. So right off the bat we learn that Salutati – and the strain of humanism he represents – does not lean toward the habitual predilection of intellectuals to posit that the everyday world in which we live can be imagined away. In other words, if you are the chancellor of Florence and

---

[19] Ibid., 409: "Quid responderes Ciceroni nostro si diceret: mi Iohannes, qua mea regula quove meo moveris exemplo, ut ad unum scribens, quasi litteras ad senatum dirigas, illum pluraliter alloquaris?"

you are corresponding with, say, the French royal court, the court will be expecting the use of the plural *vos* as an honorific. Salutati was a man of the world, and he knew diplomatic protocols. Which did not mean he liked them: he laments in this letter that the French especially seem inclined to fashion their Latin in this ahistorical fashion.

Then things move in a more interesting direction, because it is at this moment in the letter – like many other moments in the history of Italian Renaissance humanism – when history intrudes, inescapably present precisely as a result of humanists' passion for the past. In discussing, and trying to elucidate for his friend, the question of when this modern, ahistorical custom of using *vos* as an honorific had arisen, Salutati reaches back into the history of the Latin language.

When, then, did the modern habit arise? Salutati does not believe "that this vanity began with Caesar when he became dictator" – this had been Conversino's position, who had followed a medieval misreading of a key ancient text that would have permitted the erroneous interpretation – "but rather many centuries later; when, though, I do not know."[20] Salutati looks into some ancient examples and finds only one author, the relatively late Ennodius (474–521, bishop of Pavia and prolific letter writer) in whose work the honorific *vos* is found. Salutati's and Conversino's exchange continued, their friendship strengthened by their mutual intellectual interests.

Salutati's epistolary network, broad as it was, included many other correspondents, often people with whom he had a relationship in which the delicate balance between the formal and informal was in play. One such instance occurred in 1395 (shortly after his letter exchange with Conversino). Yet again, a personal matter led Salutati into historical territory. Cardinal Bartolommeo Oliari had written Salutati urging him to collect his letters, as many others had done, since in Oliari's view Salutati was the most famous letter writer of his age. Not only that, but Salutati rivaled even admired ancients in this respect, luminaries such as Cassiodorus, a late Roman diplomat, whose life had spanned the tumultuous sixth century CE, and who in his retirement had created *Vivarium*, the early medieval monastery perhaps most important in joining the texts, ideas, and mentalities of the ancient Roman world with those of the then new, emerging Christian order.

Salutati responded at length. First, he returned to the *tu/vos* problem, explaining to the cardinal why, eminent as he was, he was being addressed as *tu* rather than *vos*. Here, Salutati recapitulates the arguments used in the

---

[20] Salutati, *Epistolario*, 2: 418–19: "Non puto quod hec vanitas inceperit cum Cesare dictatore; sed post plura secula; quando tamen ignoro."

earlier letter to Conversino. Again, however, a correspondent's hint – in this case Oliari's mention of Cassiodorus – leads Salutati to an extended discussion of history. Before he arrives at the matter of letter collections by respected predecessors, Salutati believes he must respond to the very idea that he could even be in the same league as Cassiodorus. To get to that point, he gives a brief reflection on the history of the Latin language, a reflection that shows that he has pondered the questions deeply. Despite the depth of his thinking, features of Salutati's thinking can also seem odd to modern scholarly readers.

The first of these elements has to do with dates. It is self-evident today that we can, relatively easily, find more or less precise dates for figures, events, and moments from the historical past. If one wanted to find out the date for, say, a writer from the fifth century, there would be numerous ways to do so, with most people turning first to online resources, themselves derived from the massive reference works created in the nineteenth and twentieth centuries. Not so in Salutati's day. When he responds here to Oliari, his "history" – something that for us first and foremost would be framed around dates – is for him instead something that derives from examples and from categories that resonated for him and, presumably, for his correspondent: "Without doubt that ancient era flourished with every sort of literary study, and it was on that account so strong when it came to eloquence that posterity, however intense its efforts at imitation, could not preserve that majesty of speech and that zenith of eloquence."[21]

So, the first assumption: there was a golden age, when perfection had been achieved, a high point from which matters inevitably declined. Salutati goes on: "now there did remain, in their immediate successors, a certain similarity and a kind of trace of antiquity." A "trace": the Latin word Salutati uses is *vestigium*, which also means "footstep." It is as if giants once walked the earth, leaving behind visible, tangible clues as to what they did, only their examples remaining. And then: "Soon thereafter, as posterity forsook that entire style of writing, and as with the passing of time that early glory, hardly noticeably, passed away, thereafter there was a departure from Cicero, the prince of eloquence, with a dissimilarity that became ever more manifest."[22] The

[21] Salutati, *Epistolario*, 3: 80: "Floruit proculdubio seculum illud priscum omni studio literarum, et adeo in eloquentia valuit, quod non potuerit imitatrix quanvis et studiosa posteritas illam dicendi maiestatem et culmen eloquentie conservare."
[22] Ibid., "Mansit tamen in proximis successoribus similitudo quedam et aliquale vestigium antiquitatis; sed, paulatim ab illa scribendi soliditate discedente posteritate, cum ipso temporis lapsu latenter primum decus illud effluxit, deinde manifestiore dissimilitudine ab eloquentie principe Cicerone discessum est."

assumption, so taken for granted that Salutati need not expound on it, is that Cicero represents the unquestioned high point of ancient Latin style, the best, most exemplary writer, and the model to which all aspire. In the expression "prince of eloquence," the Latin word for "prince" is *princeps*, which can indeed mean "prince," with all its royal connotations. But it also means "first," as in "first in a descending sequence," or as in "first [most important] citizen." So if there is a hierarchy of writers, Cicero stands at the top and is in a way the origin of what comes after him; and if there is an imagined republic of Latin writers, Cicero is the most important citizen of that community. He is, in short, exemplary.

Now from "time to time," Salutati suggests, there may have been a "few who seemed to emerge from among their contemporaries and who consequently seemed to the rather unlearned to attain to that sublime level. If you don't believe me, it behooves you to place the writers themselves before your eyes."[23] It is time, in other words, to begin the history, to commence mentioning and categorizing more Latinists who have appeared throughout history. Some of these names occur in Cicero's correspondence, so Salutati lists those names. He then moves on to successive eras. Modern readers, again, might expect a strict chronological listing. But this is not quite the way Salutati presents things.

Here is Salutati's recounting of Latinists, in the order that he gives it (he did not add dates to their names, but it is helpful here to do so, so that we can get a sense of Salutati's priorities and of how doing history in his era differed so substantially from that enterprise in our own): Seneca (3 BC–AD 65), Valerius Maximus (20 BC–AD 50), and Livy (59 BC–AD 17). These prose writers, though coming after Cicero, at least seem to be in the same league, Salutati suggests. Then there is Tacitus (AD 56–117), who is not in the same rank as these earlier writers. Thereafter come Suetonius (AD 69–140), Pliny the Younger (AD 63–113), Martianus Capella (who was active in the fifth century AD), Apuleius (AD 123/5–80), Macrobius (who was active from 395 to 423). About this latter group Salutati says that, in their writings, "it can be seen ... to what extent that majesty of ancient speech which reached its apex in Cicero had diminished."[24] Again, the high point was Cicero, whose use of language possessed "majesty" or, in Latin, *maiestas*: an attribute reserved for royalty.

[23] Ibid., "Fuerunt pauci tamen per tempora, qui adeo viderentur inter coevos emergere, quod ad illam attingere sublimitatem ab imperitioribus putarentur. Hec non michi credas velim, sed ipsos scriptores ante oculos tibi ponas."

[24] Ibid., 3: 82: "in quorum scriptis percipitur quantum tractu temporis ornatus ille locutionis effloruit quantumque maiestas illa prisci sermonis, que cum Cicerone summum apicem tenuit, imminuta est."

A few of these names resonate today: Livy, the great historian of ancient Rome; Seneca, the Stoic and doomed associate of the decadent Roman Emperor Nero; Tacitus, who wrote about corrupt Roman emperors as well as about the habits of the early Germans; and Suetonius, whose "Lives" of the emperors remain riveting reading today. The others were important in Salutati's day, sufficiently so that he chose to include them here in his list of writers, having gathered them together to make a point: that there was change in ancient Latin, that there was decline.

Next Salutati moves to writers of late antiquity. Once again he uses a chronology that does not respect the order in which we would place these figures. This is not to say that Salutati did not know (or could not have known, had he wanted to do so) what the chronological order was. Rather, it did not seem to matter as much to him as it would to us, if we were composing a history. He mentions (again, it will be useful to see the dates, even though Salutati does not add them himself): Cassiodorus (490–585), Ambrose (340–397), Symmachus (345–402), Jerome (347–420), Augustine (354–430), Ennodius (474–521), and Sidonius Apollinaris (430–485), among some others. Salutati says that all these writers lived in a period when eloquence had revived "in a certain way," part of one larger period in which it was still possible to raise one's style to an appropriate level.[25] He makes no comment as to how Latin evolved, whether it was competing with other local vernaculars, such as those brought by foreign invaders, and so on. And then he moves to the Middle Ages.

In fact, the medieval writers whom he lists are so seemingly unworthy that Salutati lumps them together as "plurals," as it were. For example, Salutati mentions "Peters of Abelard" and "Johns of Salisbury," as if they were representative of the tendency toward decadent Latin without one needing even to specify what they wrote or worked on. Today, Peter Abelard (1079–1142) and John of Salisbury (1120–80) are highly respected as touchstones of medieval thought. Abelard is known for his tumultuous love affair with a young student, Eloise, who had been placed in his charge, an affair that their passionate series of still preserved letters documents even today.[26] And he is credited with creating what would later become a key part of the scholastic method, dividing up important topics into "questions," in his treatise *Yes and No* (*Sic et non*). John of Salisbury, who though English served as bishop of the French city of Chartres, authored a series of works that show an insider's knowledge of then developing

[25] Ibid.
[26] See Michael Clanchy, *Abelard: A Medieval Life* (Oxford: Blackwell, 1999); Jean Jolivet, *Abélard en son temps* (Paris: Les Belles Lettres, 1981); John Marenbon, *The Philosophy of Peter Abelard* (Cambridge: Cambridge University Press, 1997).

educational culture, works that are invaluable today for sources about twelfth-century thought.[27] Indeed, in one of these works, the *Metalogicon*, John satirized some overly picky styles of reasoning with many of the same basic motivations that, later, Petrarch and others would express: they were too particular, not fundamentally connected to the sorts of problems that real life presents, and so on. In short, John of Salisbury at least was in many ways an antecedent, spiritual kin of later humanists. In many ways but one, that is: the way he wrote Latin. So for Salutati, Abelard, John of Salisbury, and many others like them "never worried themselves too much about eloquence."[28]

Yet Salutati sees reason for optimism, since closer to home, "the study of literature has risen somewhat in our day." For "study of literature" Salutati writes, in Latin, *studia litterarum*, by which he means, not so much literature the way we think of that term today, but rather literary and historical disciplines that were now being practiced in line with classical models. This is to say that certain thinkers, such as Albertino Mussato (1261–1329), to name one of Salutati's choices, one whom he terms "the first cultivator of eloquence," have allowed these Latinate, classicizing studies to rise again.[29]

Then Salutati takes his part in the creation of the literary mythology of Florence, naming a sequence of figures who were already touchstones – of debate, wonder, and pride – in the continuing saga of the creation of Italian literature:

> Those Florentine lights have also risen: I will pass over Dante Alighieri, the highest glory of vernacular eloquence, who can be compared to no one who has flourished in our day or even to any of the ancients in his knowledge or intelligence. Petrarch and Boccaccio have also come forth, all of whose works, if I am not mistaken, posterity will celebrate. Even still, I think that no one capable of judging rightly is unaware how much they differ in capacity of speaking from those ancients.[30]

So much is contained in this short statement.

[27] See Michael Wilks, ed., *The World of John of Salisbury* (Oxford: Blackwell, 1984); Hans Liebeschütz, *Medieval Humanism in the Life and Writings of John of Salisbury* (London: University of London, 1950).

[28] Ibid., 3: 83: "inciderint enim licet Ivones, Bernardi, Hildeberti, Petri Blesenses, Petri Abaelardi, Riccardi de Pophis, Iohannes Saberii et alii plures, qui sibi nimis de eloquentia blanditi sunt."

[29] For recent literature on Mussato, see Witt, *Footsteps*, 117–73.

[30] Ibid., 3: 84: "emerserunt et ista lumina florentina; ut summum vulgaris eloquentie decus et nulli scientia vel ingenio comparandum qui nostris temprobus floruit, aut etiam cuipiam antiquorum, Dantem Alligherium, pretermittam; Petrarca scilicet et Bocaccius, quorum opera cuncta, ni fallor, posteritas celebrabit: qui tamen quantum ab illis priscis differant facultate dicendi nullum arbitror qui recte iudicare valeat ignorare."

First, there is Florentine pride: even if both Dante and Petrarch spent most of their productive time outside of Florence, they "counted" as Florentines owing to their heritage. Dante reached the heights of "vernacular eloquence," and he was so learned that he could be compared to the ancients. The subject matter was different of course, but the level of his learning was beyond compare. And, of course, he wrote his masterpiece in the vernacular, not Latin. Then there are Petrarch and Boccaccio, who will live on. And yet, "in capacity of speaking" – meaning in the quality of their Latin – they are not to be placed in the same league as the ancients.

Is this statement of Salutati too restrictive? How can it be that the Three Crowns of Florence, celebrated today precisely for their achievements in Italian literature, can be, if not reprimanded, then at least "cut down to size" because their Latin (not their native language, needless to say) did not sound authentically classical? This question represents the central hinge around which the intellectual history of the Italian Renaissance turned. Salutati, in his brief, almost off-the-cuff response in this letter, encapsulated and expressed both sides of the problem, as it would come to be defined over the next century.

On the one hand was a need for a standard language, one able to be understood and used across cultures. The Italian vernacular would not do if one were communicating with, say, the king of France and his court. And it would not do, in truth, even in universities, where (then as now) the need for a standardized vocabulary often presented itself in specialized research. Moreover, this was the Italian Renaissance, after all. As Petrarch had discovered, the various varieties of Medieval Latin, functional as they were, did not, in their vocabulary and syntax, match ancient Latin. Accordingly, this new Latin (what scholars today call "Neo-Latin") needed to respect classical idiom. It was a project that would take more than a century to realize in full. Even now, at this early phase, Salutati recognized that Petrarch's style was not quite in line with ancient models.

On the other hand, Salutati emphasized Dante's brilliant use of the vernacular. In truth, even though the "official" line of many humanists would remain the same (classicizing Latin was best, all else was barbarism), a taste for the vernacular grew during the fifteenth century. Humanists, some of them Salutati's younger students, would sometimes translate their own Latin works into Italian. The reason was that what we can call "vernacular classicism" grew in the fifteenth century.[31] Merchants and others shared the

---

[31] See Andrea Rizzi and Eva del Soldato, "Latin and Vernacular in Quattrocento Florence and Beyond: An Introduction," *I Tatti Studies*, 16 (2013), 231–42.

taste both for thinking about classical antiquity and for thinking with the models – of behavior, style, and philosophical concerns – it presented. They might not have had the time or the inclination to learn Latin fluently, let alone to do the sort of scholarly work that was often entailed in appreciating newly discovered ancient Latin texts. But they liked reading and hearing about famous ancient examples – about how the ancient Romans in their early heroic phase threw off kingship to foster self-governance, or how Cicero argued for the merits of the Roman republic, and so on. Taste, in other words, is a funny thing. Oftentimes the people we think about as representing "high" culture represent the visible tip of a much larger iceberg, whose bulk lies concealed from view.[32] In this case, we have those who wrote – the humanists – and who thus are our primary sources. But they reflect a broader appreciation of the classical world shared by people for whom writing was not a chief concern.

As to Salutati, his primary professional identity was as a man of action: he was a civil servant who for the whole of his long chancellorship saw his main responsibility as serving the state of Florence. Yet he also wrote works that, though they might not be the easiest reading today, reflect his interests in broad intellectual themes.

Sometimes these works represent the same sort of "conversational" approach apparent in his letters. This is to say that Salutati often wrote things that were targeted to a specific person, rather than (as we have sometimes come to expect from authors) a "final statement" on a topic or idea, an immutable, complete opinion valid in all places and for all time. Salutati's premodern world, instead, was more "local." To give an example, in the years 1381–82 he wrote a treatise called *On the World and Religious Life.*[33] There he presents exhaustive arguments as to why a life of monastic seclusion is better than a life of political action in the world. The ascetic, prayerful, monastic life affords one the ability to come closer to God, to achieve inner peace, and to avoid the falsity and hypocrisy of the world of political action. Salutati wrote all this, of course, when he himself was engaged in a life of political action *par excellence* as Florence's chancellor.

---

[32] For this idea in very different contexts, see Pamela Long, *Openness, Secrecy, Authorship: Technical Arts and the Culture of Knowledge from Antiquity to the Renaissance* (Baltimore: Johns Hopkins University Press, 2001); Pamela Smith, *The Body of the Artisan: Art and Experience in the Scientific Revolution* (Chicago: University of Chicago Press, 2004); Deborah Harkness, *The Jewel House: Elizabethan London and the Scientific Revolution* (New Haven and London: Yale University Press, 2007).

[33] Coluccio Salutati, *On the World and Religious Life*, ed. and tr. Tina Marshall (Cambridge, MA: Harvard University Press, 2014).

The question therefore arises: was he simply a hypocrite, defending something in one treatise that he could not have really believed, or that at the very least the conduct of his own life belied? An earlier generation of scholars wrestled over just this question – indeed over whether many humanists, not just Salutati, could be accused of insincerity, since they often seemed to tailor their messages to their audiences.[34]

Today, this question seems like the wrong one to be asking. Salutati wrote this treatise to a friend, a little-known figure named Niccolò Lapi of Uzzano.[35] Niccolò had been a canon lawyer. At a certain point in his life, he decided to join Santa Maria degli Angeli (Saint Mary of the Angels), a monastery in Florence. Salutati visited Niccolò there, and Niccolò asked Salutati to write something to help him persist in his monastic vows, to stay firm in the life he had chosen. So Salutati complied with *On the World and Religious Life*. This gesture was neither an act of hypocrisy nor a permanent statement of an unshakeable theory about the right sort of life. Rather, it was an act of friendship, one that emerged after an obviously fraught emotional conversation. The conversation, of course, is lost to us, but the evidence for it remains. And keep in mind: Salutati, like all his contemporaries, lived in the world of manuscripts. How could he have guessed that, half a millennium later, scholars would be poring over his treatise searching for an unshakeable commitment to this or that way of life?

Other aspects of his work show that Salutati emerged as Florence's leading voice for the study of the humanities. It is hard to imagine today what a charged matter this type of study was at the time. The reason was that the study of the humanities depended almost entirely on the study of ancient pagan, which is to say non-Christian, authors. Petrarch resolved the problem by turning all his studies inward, using what he read to further his intense self-examination along Christian lines and thus allowing the humanist movement to take a largely Christian tack. But this trajectory was not sustainable.

First, there was the matter of the discovery of ever more "new" ancient texts. Salutati, for example, paralleled his hero Petrarch when he added to his library a manuscript containing Cicero's *Familiar Letters* (Cicero's letters to his friends) just as Petrarch, earlier, had discovered Cicero's *Letters to Atticus*. In both cases the Cicero revealed was a busy, active, sometimes gossipy political figure, rather than a perfectly controlled Stoic sage. Petrarch, upon discovering these letters, was so distraught at what he had found out about

---

[34] These debates revolved around the influential work of Hans Baron; see C.S. Celenza, *The Lost Italian Renaissance* (Baltimore: Johns Hopkins University Press, 2004), 36–40, for literature.

[35] See Ronald G. Witt, "Introduction," in Salutati, *On the World and Religious Life*, vii–xvii.

Cicero that he took the extraordinary step of chiding in a letter the long-dead Cicero for these worldly propensities. Salutati, enmeshed as he was in the life of an active politician, understood the letters differently. He was in fact happy to be able to round out his picture of Cicero. He also appreciated the fact that the letters offered insights into the "behind the scenes" working of the Roman republic, which he saw as analogous to the Florentine republic he served and loved.[36]

To a correspondent who had facilitated his acquisition of these letters, Salutati wrote regarding Cicero that, after reading these letters, "I saw what sort of man he was in politics, how much he excelled among his friends and indeed among the leading citizens of Rome. And I see how daring he was in war, how strongly he desired glory, and with what techniques he and other Romans cultivated the grandeur of their reputations and made sure their praise was known."[37] Unlike the tortured Petrarch, Salutati is excited about the fact that Cicero and other Romans cultivated worldly glory and were proud of their political achievements.

Salutati goes on, revealing his political sympathies: "I saw, thanks to you, the real basis of the civil wars, and what it was that forced Rome, that very capital of the whole world, to move from a popular model of governance to enslavement to monarchy."[38] For "popular model of governance" Salutati uses the Latin *libertas populica*, literally "liberty of the people" or "popular liberty." What he means is a state that has some basis of participatory governance and that is not subject to another outside state. For Salutati and his contemporaries, this independence marked Florence and was a point of pride. Any opportunity he had to find ancient antecedents was welcome.

But Cicero's letters did more for Salutati than provide information about politics. They also offered him a taste of what sort of man Cicero was in his everyday life, an aspect in many ways just as important to Salutati, who, like his contemporaries, looked to the great men of the past as models for living. He saw Cicero as a human being in the round: "I saw how my Cicero was gentle with his family, how he was disappointed with his son, how he could be hopeless when things were bad, fearful when dangers approached and how, when times were good, he was serene and satisfied."[39] Salutati saw Cicero's interactions with his friends and colleagues and gained so much profit from these letters that, in the final analysis, he could say that he had read

[36] See Witt, *Hercules*, 299–300.
[37] Coluccio Salutati, *Epistolario*, ed. F. Novati, v. 2 (Rome, 1891), 389.
[38] Ibid.
[39] Ibid.

no other work of theory or history "so eagerly and with such delight."[40] It is the human Cicero that Salutati desires to get to know. Occupied daily by the problems and concerns besetting his own republic, Salutati is endlessly fascinated with the ways in which Cicero, an exemplar of Latin eloquence and now ever more human, had found his way in ancient Rome.

The bulk of Salutati's work, his letters most especially, indicates that his service to Florence as chancellor represented more than just a job for him. He came to love his adopted city and was especially eloquent and committed to Florentine *libertas* – "liberty," most literally, but more broadly reflecting a proclivity toward Florence's form of government, a republic, where citizens had the right, and felt the obligation, to participate in government. But what did that "liberty" mean? Was his commitment to republicanism something absolute?

Another way of thinking about these questions is to examine a seemingly puzzling work of Salutati's, called *De tyranno*, or *On the Tyrant*.[41] Salutati's *On the Tyrant* has been difficult for scholars to interpret, since the political message Salutati seems to be sending is at odds with his defense of republicanism. Or at least, that is the way scholars have tended to phrase the problem. Yet it is not so mysterious if considered, again, in context. The problem Salutati is addressing has to do with a key point of dispute among many Florentines: why did Dante, the greatest Tuscan poet and a point of pride for Florence, place Brutus and Cassius in the lowest depths of hell? To understand this question and what lay behind it, it is worth pausing for moment.

First, the ancient world and its legacy were of paramount importance for all Renaissance thinkers, the standard by which they measured themselves and, at least in their aspirations, the revival of which they sought to promote. Yet the problem, as always, was: which antiquity? And whose? In this case, of course, the Brutus in question was the Brutus who, along with Cassius and several others, murdered Julius Caesar in 44 BC. For Salutati and his contemporaries, the question was whether the murder was justified. If Caesar was a tyrant, ruling illegitimately, then the answer was yes. If not, then it was an act of regicide (the killing of a king) and, more than that, an act of betrayal. It was in this latter fashion that Dante had seen Brutus's and Cassius's act, as a betrayal. They are in the bottom of hell, where all is reversed: instead of the warm Mediterranean climate of Italy, it is freezing. And Lucifer, instead of

[40] Ibid.
[41] Coluccio Salutati, *De tyranno*, in Salutati, *Political Writings*, ed. Stefano Ugo Baldassarri, tr. Rolf Bagemihl (Cambridge, MA: Harvard University Press, 2014), 64–143.

being what he once was (God's most beautiful, "light-bearing" angel), emerges as a monster of hideous countenance and proportion: gigantic, winged, ugly, and possessing three heads. In each of his three mouths, Lucifer chews on one of (for Dante at least) history's three greatest traitors: Brutus (described as "writhing, and speechless"), Cassius, and – feeling the most pain, Dante assures us through the character Virgil, his guide through hell – Judas Iscariot, the greatest betrayer of all, who for a few coins had betrayed Jesus Christ.[42] Dante, in other words, puts Brutus and Cassius in bad company.

What about Julius Caesar? On the one hand, for medieval readers, Caesar was one of many exemplary ancient figures, important simply by virtue of being part of the drama of ancient Rome. Bold in war, decisive in politics, Caesar also had a great reputation for clemency. On the other hand, Caesar had also ("against the laws of Rome," as Boccaccio had put it) declared himself dictator for life. Boccaccio made this comment in his commentary to canto 4 of the *Inferno*, where Caesar appears as one of the "virtuous pagans," condemned because they never knew Christ but possessing at least enough virtue that they were not made to suffer hell's most bitter torments.[43] Yet one could also say, as some medieval commentators had done, that Caesar was necessary, the dictator who eventually paved the way for Rome's first emperor, Augustus, under whose reign the birth of Christ – history's most important event – had occurred. It was complicated, and many positions were possible. And Dante, of course, was revered.

Salutati's approach to this topic emerges if we listen to him carefully and set him in the context that made most sense to him: not that of a political scientist developing a "theory" of republicanism but rather a patriotic Florentine who believed that his role as a correspondent and friend was of paramount importance. The truth is that Salutati addressed this subject because he was asked to do so, by a little-known figure named Antonio of Aquila, who was wondering precisely why Dante had made the choices that he had in his poetry.[44] To answer this query, Salutati wrote an extensive treatise. Again, it is revealing that the impetus came from an epistolary query. This was how you philosophized, in other words: not by locking yourself up in a study and theorizing but rather by using a social circumstance such as a letter to stimulate you to develop a position.

[42] Dante, *Inferno*, 34.61–69.

[43] Witt, *Hercules at the Crossroads*, 370, citing Boccaccio, *Il comento alla Divina Commedia*, ed. D. Guerri, Scrittori d'Italia, vols. 84–86 (Bari, 1918).

[44] See Witt, *Hercules*, 367.

After a lot of argumentation in this treatise, Salutati's position is clear: in *On the Tyrant*, he writes: "Can a man raised to power through his own merits, a man who showed such a humane spirit, not to his partisans alone but also to his opponents because they were his fellow citizens – can he rightly be called a tyrant? . . . We may, therefore, conclude with this proposition: that Caesar was not a tyrant, seeing that he held his supremacy in a communal common-wealth lawfully and not by abuse of law."[45] First, then, Salutati maintains that Julius Caesar had popular support for the absolute power that he claimed. Anyone who works in a bureaucracy, especially in a governmental one as did Salutati, can tell you that occasionally strong executive action is needed. Buttressed by the providential nature of the history of Rome at that point (Caesar led to Augustus, under whose ascendancy Christ was born), this position was understandable.

Then there was Dante's reputation to preserve, define, and foster:

> And who can criticize Dante for thrusting into the depths of hell and condemning to extreme punishment those abandoned men who sinned so grievously in treacherously murdering Caesar, the father of his country, while he was administering with such clemency the government which the Senate and people of Rome had conferred upon him in a desperate crisis to put an end to the evils of civil war?[46]

Dante had done the right thing. When Caesar came to the fore Rome was no longer the heroic participatory republic of old, the legend to which Florence always compared itself. Rather, Rome had become a failed state, wracked by civil war, and in need of a strong leader who would lead it out of its morass. Caesar with the consent of the governed was that man, and Brutus and his traitorous allies assassinated him in defiance of all morality. Salutati says: "So we may conclude that our Dante, in this matter as in others, made no mistake either theologically or morally – still less poetically – in condemning Brutus and Cassius as he did. Indeed, not only did he make no mistake, but beyond question he rendered a just judgment."[47]

This last passage shows well where Salutati's loyalties lay at the time: with Dante as a monument of Florentine culture. Note too that Salutati empha-sizes that Dante succeeded "poetically." Poetry was a realm in which all thinkers knew that a certain amount of invention and storytelling was not only permitted but also necessary, and that at times a successful poet might shade the borders of historical truth to arrive at a more permanent, lasting sort

---

[45] Salutati, *De tyranno*, tr. Bagemihl, 115.
[46] Ibid., 139; see Witt, *Hercules*, 383.
[47] Salutati, *De tyranno*, tr. Bagemihl, 141; see Witt, *Hercules*, 384.

of truth: truth of essential representation rather than truth of fact. In this case, Caesar was imagined as a "just ruler," and his killers as exemplars of those who would assassinate such a ruler. Salutati was unconcerned here with other possible interpretations of ancient Roman events, one of which would have been that Caesar was not only seeking to end Rome's civil wars but also that he fomented them, indeed took the memorable step of crossing the Rubicon river in 49 BC, leading a legion under his command into – and against – Roman territory. Ancient Roman history and its place in Florence's present, Dante's place and function in how Florentine culture was to be imagined, and the allegiances of Florence's elite intellectuals: this conversation would continue, and its volume would rise, as Salutati's younger admirers, his circle, began to question the old master.

Before we move to the members of this circle, one more of Salutati's accomplishments needs to be brought to the fore: the introduction of the Greek language into Renaissance humanist culture from the years 1397 to 1400. Decades later, when Italian Renaissance humanists began to write the history of their own movement, almost universally they cited the importance of this extended moment, when Greek came to be taught in a serious and lasting way in the city of Florence, finally allowing intellectuals to add that last, supremely important piece of the puzzle to their images of ancient culture.[48] Salutati played a key role, one that permits us to see just what sorts of cultural dynamics were at work in the Florence of the last decade of the fourteenth century.

Why is Greek important? Tellingly, a Latin citation can help us answer. Here is ancient Rome's greatest Latin lyric poet Horace (65–27 BC), in his classic long poem, the *Ars poetica*, on the rules and habits of good poets and writers: *Vos exemplaria Graeca / nocturna uersate manu, uersate diurna* ("Turn the pages of Greek books day and night").[49] Ancient Roman writers such as Horace, precisely those thinkers whom Renaissance humanists sought to imitate, almost all recognized the shaping effect that Greek literature and philosophy had on their own culture. There was Homer, of course, the original epic poet, who told of the Trojan War and the deeds of heroes and gods in his *Iliad*, and who distilled myth and character study in his *Odyssey*, there focusing on the wily hero Odysseus's quest to return home after that war. There was Plato, the father of philosophy, who established the idea that a higher world existed, one invisible to us on earth but against whose criteria

---

[48] See Patrick Baker, *Italian Renaissance Humanism in the Mirror* (Cambridge: Cambridge University Press, 2015).

[49] Horace, *Ars poetica*, ll. 268–69 in Horace, *Satires, Epistles and Ars Poetica*, ed. and tr. H. Rushton Fairclough (Cambridge, MA: Harvard University Press, 1991), p. 472, my tr.

our souls would one day be measured. And then Aristotle loomed large, having created as he did a kind of architecture of intellectual disciplines, from ethics to metaphysics. The great tragedians Sophocles, Aeschylus, and Euripides had explored questions ranging from eternal fate and fortune to intimate family matters in their great plays.

These were just some prominent Greek writers whom ancient Romans both revered and from whom, in some cases, Romans tried to distance themselves, standing forever in the shadow they sought to outrun. Here is Horace, again, in a letter to the Emperor Augustus, speaking about Rome's relation to Greek culture: *Graecia capta ferum victorem cepit et artes / intulit agresti Latio* – "Greece, the captive, made her savage victor captive, and brought the arts into rustic Latium."[50] Or take Virgil's great epic, the *Aeneid*, which told the tale of the hero Aeneas and his founding of Italy. In a dramatic, haunting scene, Aeneas descends to the underworld, where the dead live on as "shades" – shadows of their former selves who can still talk and think, but who are fated never to emerge. Aeneas meets his father, Anchises, who tells his son:

> Others will hammer out bronzes that breathe in more lifelike and gentler ways, I suspect, create truer expressions of life out of marble, make better speeches, or plot, with the sweep of their compass, the heaven's movements, predict the ascent of the sky's constellations. Well, let them! You, who are Roman, recall how to govern mankind with your power. These will be your special "Arts": the enforcement of peace as habit, mercy for those cast down and relentless war upon proud men.[51]

The Romans recognized that whatever art and culture they had, they had from Greece, even as they distanced themselves from that culture, defining themselves as men of military action, men who would "govern mankind with their power." And yet: Cicero, every humanist's hero, had distilled and "culturally translated" Greek philosophical concepts in a series of works well known to the Renaissance (and to the Middle Ages for that matter). The truth was that, in the same way that educated medieval and Renaissance thinkers were basically bilingual between Latin and their mother tongue, so

[50] Horace, *Ep.*, 2.1, ll 156–57, tr. H.R. Fairclough in Horace, *Satires, Epistles and Ars Poetica*, p. 409; cit. in Alessandro Barchiesi, "Roman Perspectives on the Greeks," in George Boys-Stones, Barbara Graziosi, and Phiroze Vasunia, eds., *The Oxford Handbook of Hellenic Studies* (Oxford: Oxford University Press, 2009), 98–113, at 103, cit. in Christopher S. Celenza, "Hellenism in the Renaissance," in Boys-Stones, Graziosi, and Vasunia, eds., *The Oxford Handbook of Hellenic Studies*, 150–65.
[51] Virgil, *Aeneid*, tr. with notes by Frederick Ahl (Oxford: Oxford University Press, 2007), 6.847–53, cit. Barchiesi, as earlier, 105; cit. Celenza, "Hellenism."

too had educated Romans, Cicero most especially, been schooled bilingually between Greek and Latin.

When all was said and done, no dispassionate observer could deny that to understand the ancient world fully, one needed Greek as well as Latin. It was there, a spectral presence that haunted Latinity and one that Florentine humanists, especially the younger ones in Salutati's circle, believed was needed in Florence. So Salutati, good mentor that he was, arranged for the teaching of Greek in a permanent and lasting way in Florence.

Salutati, however, was not the first humanist to realize the importance of Greek. Writing to a Byzantine correspondent, Petrarch had said: "Without your voice, your Homer is mute to me. Or rather, I am deaf to him. Still, I rejoice even to look at him and often, as I embrace him I say, sighing, 'O Great Man, how ardently would I listen to you!'"[52] Petrarch sent the letter to his Greek friend as a gesture of thanks for a manuscript of Homer's that this friend had sent along. Petrarch tried to learn Greek, studying with a Greek speaker from Calabria named Barlaam (Greek was spoken in certain parts of southern Italy). But Petrarch was never able to achieve fluency: for him, Homer remained "mute" indeed. Boccaccio, too, came to believe that Greek was needed, and he even went so far as to have a chair established at the Florentine university, one held for three years by one of Barlaam's students, named Leonzio Pilato. But Pilato's teaching never took off. Petrarch had met him, and in a letter to Boccaccio, he described Leonzio as morose and difficult. It took the needed environment, the proper historical moment, and the right people to have the teaching of Greek succeed.[53]

As to the people, Salutati pursued a twofold path. First, one member of his circle, Jacopo Angeli da Scarperia, went to Byzantium in 1395 and stayed for about year, studying Greek there. Salutati wrote him, asking that he purchase as many Greek books as he could (funds would be provided), so that they could be brought back to Florence. All genres were important and, Salutati says, they should be copied if possible in "big letters," by which he meant a special type of handwriting called "uncial," in which the letters are all capitals.[54]

Second and more important, Salutati persuaded, with Scarperia's help, a traveling Byzantine diplomat and educator named Manuel Chrysoloras to stay in Florence for three years, from February 1397 to March 1400,

---

[52] Petrarch, *Fam.*, 18.2, v. 3, p. 277, to Nicola Sigero, cit. in Mariarosa Cortesi, "Umanesimo greco," in ed. Guglielmo Cavallo et al., *Lo spazio letterario del medioevo*, vol. 3 (Rome, 1995), 457–507, at 457.

[53] See Cortesi, "Umanesimo greco."

[54] Coluccio Salutati, *Epistolario*, ed. F. Novati, v. 3 (Rome, 1891), 132.

arranging that another professorial chair be set up for the teaching of Greek.[55] This time, it stuck. Chrysoloras's contract specified that he was to teach "Greek literature and grammar" to all citizens of Florence and its territories who desired to learn.[56] Learn they did. Leonardo Bruni, a figure who would become the best-selling humanist of the fifteenth century, put it well: "When you have a chance to see and converse with Homer and Plato and Demosthenes . . . will you deprive yourself of it? For seven hundred years now, no-one in Italy has been able to read Greek, and yet we admit it is from the Greeks that we get all our systems of knowledge."[57] This statement represents enthusiasm, obviously. Yet it also evinces something else, quite important not only in the history of the Italian Renaissance but also in the history of culture more broadly: new generations of intellectuals seek to out-do their predecessors, to contribute something new, and to seek social distinction by that very newness.

Learning Greek, however, represented a matter of importance, and since Florence had no established tradition for teaching Greek, Chrysoloras proved remarkably adaptable and effective.[58] First, he created a basic grammar text-book, called *Questions* (*Erotemata* in Greek) that was modeled on certain basic Latin grammar textbooks that had been in use throughout the Middle Ages. Doing so was no mean feat, since the Byzantine tradition in which Chrysoloras had been educated possessed different ways of thinking about language. Byzantine education tended heavily toward literature and rhetoric. In that respect, the interests of Italian humanists in all things verbal repre-sented a match.

However, the Byzantine and Western systems of learning differed vastly. To give just one representative example, those who taught in the Byzantine tradition divided up Greek nouns into fifty-six types, all of which students had to master. Yet in the Latin language, nouns were divided into only five types. Chrysoloras did not reduce the number that extensively (which would have been impossible), but he did manage to reduce the number from fifty-six to ten. Though there were other attempts contemporary to Chrysoloras to simplify Greek grammar, his *Erotemata* won out, as we can tell from the

---

[55] Salutati's letter to Chrysoloras is in Salutati, *Epistolario*, ed. F. Novati, v. 3 (Rome, 1891), 119–25.

[56] From Chrysoloras's contract as cited by Cortesi, 464.

[57] Leonardo Bruni, *Commentarius rerum suo tempore gestarum*, ed. Carmine Di Pierro, *Rerum italicarum scriptores*, 19.3 (Bologna, 1926) 341–42, tr. G. Griffiths in *The Humanism of Leonardo Bruni*, 23–24, cit. Hankins, *Plato in the Italian Renaissance*, 2 vols. (Leiden, 1989), 1: 30.

[58] See Federica Ciccolella, *Donati graeci: Learning Greek in the Renaissance*, Columbia Studies in the Classical Tradition 32 (Leiden: Brill, 2008).

many manuscript copies of that work that circulated.[59] It was through his work and method that this first generation learned Greek.

These early learners struggled, as do all language learners, with the different facets of learning a foreign language. But the most important aspect was that of translation. This generation of humanists (and not only the ones learning Greek) were aching to learn ever more about the ancient world. Accordingly, Greek to Latin translation emerged as a priority, undertaken by those elite humanists learning Greek and funded by the bankers and merchants and cardinals and prelates who served as the economic engines of culture in the early fifteenth century.

As to the theory of translation, Chrysoloras taught them well, urging his students (once they had mastered the basics) to translate for sense, rather than overly literally, while still respecting the register of the original. Leonardo Bruni, one of Chrysoloras's best students, put it this way when writing about translation: the translator "must possess a sound ear so that his translation does not disturb and destroy the fullness and rhythmical qualities of the original." Bruni argued for a high level of commitment to the enterprise, when he wrote that "the best translator will turn his whole mind, heart, and will to his original author, and in a sense transform him, considering how he may express the shape, attitude, and stance of his speech, and all his lines and colors," while always preserving "the style of the original as well as possible."[60]

One question that preoccupied humanists in this relatively early phase of the humanist movement was how to integrate the manifold perspectives from the ancient world into their own. More specifically, they lived in a society that self-identified, in ways difficult to imagine today, as Christian. And of course much of what they were unearthing about the ancient world had its origins in pagan antiquity. This problem was not new to the early years of the fifteenth century. Giovanni Boccaccio, for example, had argued for the independence of poetry, pagan or not, in his *Genealogy of the Pagan Gods*, suggesting that all poetry came from God, in the final analysis, who imparted to poets a kind of divine madness from which they drew inspiration, the full extent of which they were unaware.[61] Moreover, it was foolish, Boccaccio suggested, to think that poets did not intend a deeper meaning below the surface.[62] And in any case when they introduced many gods into

---

[59] Ibid., 120.

[60] Leonardo Bruni, "On the Correct Way to Translate," in Bruni, *The Humanism*, 217–29, at 220–21. For a critical edition, Italian translation, and ample commentary to this text, see Leonardo Bruni, *Sulla perfetta traduzione*, ed. Paolo Viti (Naples: Liguori, 2004).

[61] Giovanni Boccaccio, *Genealogia deorum gentilium* (Basel, 1532), 14.6–7, pp. 359–61.

[62] Ibid., 14.13, pp. 369–72.

their works, as had Virgil in his epic *Aeneid*, poets did so only in the service of their art.[63] But this new, "post-Chrysoloras" world was different in both quantitative and qualitative ways. It is in fact this very newness that marks the Florentine humanism of the early fifteenth century as one of intellectual history's most exciting periods.

[63] Ibid.

4

FLORENTINE HUMANISM,
TRANSLATION, AND A NEW (OLD)
PHILOSOPHY

IT IS AN APPROPRIATE TIME TO INTRODUCE SOMEONE WHOM WE
have met thus far only in passing: Leonardo Bruni (1370–1444). Bruni
emerged as fifteenth-century Italy's best-selling author: well over three
thousand manuscripts of his works survive and, after the appearance of
printing with moveable type (which reached Italy in the early 1460s, well
after Bruni's death), more than two hundred printed editions containing
Bruni's work were issued through the year 1500.[1] More than this, Bruni was
an active diplomat and statesman, whose career flourished amid one of
Western Europe's most interesting and pivotal periods and whose two
poles – Florence and Rome – represented a key cultural axis and an engine
of the production of Renaissance culture.[2]

As to Rome, the "Eternal City" had been the traditional home of the
papacy, from the days when Christ said to his apostle Peter, "you are Peter,
and on this rock I will build my Church, and the gates of hell will not
overcome it" (Mt. 16:18). Peter, martyred during the reign of Nero in 64
CE, became the symbol of institutional Christianity and Rome the seat of
what became the official religion of Western Europe.[3] A great amount of

---

[1] See James Hankins, *Repertorium Brunianum: A Critical Guide to the Writings of Leonardo Bruni*
(Rome: Edizioni di Storia e Letteratura, 1997), preface; Josef Soudek, "Leonardo Bruni and
His Public: A Statistical and Interpretative Study of His Annotated Latin Version of the
ps.-Aristotelian *Economics*," *Studies in Medieval and Renaissance History* 5 (1968), 49–136; idem,
"A Fifteenth-Century Humanistic Bestseller: The Manuscript Diffusion of Leonardo Bruni's
Annotated Latin Version of the ps.-Aristotelian *Economics*," in E. P. Mahoney, ed., *Philosophy
and Humanism: Renaissance Essays in Honor of Paul Oskar Kristeller* (Leiden: Brill, 1976),
129–43.
[2] On the rich relation between Florence and Rome in the early fifteenth century, see
George Holmes, *The Florentine Enlightenment, 1400–50* (London: Weidenfeld and Nicolson,
1969).
[3] See Eamon Duffy, *Saints and Sinners: A History of the Popes* (New Haven: Yale University
Press, 1997), 1–36.

tradition, in other words, linked Rome and institutional Christianity. So one can imagine the sense of instability – and the resulting creative tensions – when the papacy left Rome in 1308 and then, more to the point, had two, and sometimes three, rival claimants for the papal tiara from 1378 to 1417.[4] Bruni's first major professional experience was in fact to serve as an apostolic secretary to one of those rival popes, Innocent VII, whose court Bruni joined in 1405, having been recommended for the post by Poggio Bracciolini and then endorsed for it by Coluccio Salutati.[5]

Before that moment, Bruni had been the beneficiary of a fine early education in Arezzo, the city of his birth, which in 1384 had submitted to rule by then powerful Florence. Bruni like many other young men came to Florence to study and to seek his fortune. In the 1390s he enrolled at the University of Florence intending to study law. But he soon became enamored of the cultural circle surrounding Salutati, becoming eventually its most important and influential participant. Moreover, he was the most eager member of that first cohort to learn Greek seriously, emerging as one of Chrysoloras's best pupils. By the time of his Rome appointment in 1405, Bruni had put his newly acquired skills to use, translating into Latin what would become one of the most popular Greek texts in the fifteenth century. You might think it was Homer, or a text by Plato or Aristotle. But no. It was instead the "Address to the Youth" of the ancient Greek Church father, Basil of Caesarea (329/30–330 CE).[6]

Basil, a revered Church administrator and theologian, wrote a passionately sincere address to his nephews, laying out why and how they, though Christian, should read the ancient pagan Greek writers. Basil's basic answer was: cautiously but openly. They should emulate bees when approaching pagan literature, "for bees neither approach all flowers equally, nor in truth do they attempt to carry off entire those on which they alight, but taking only so much of them as is suitable for their work, they let the rest go untouched."[7] In any case, "almost all the writers who have some reputation for wisdom have, to a greater or lesser degree, each to the best of his power, discoursed in their works in praise of virtue."[8] A good pilot must steer his own ship with prudence and not "heedlessly give over his ship to the

[4] Ibid., 87–132; Joëlle Rollo-Koster, *Avignon and Its Papacy, 1309–1417* (Lanham, MD: Rowman and Littlefield, 2015).

[5] See Hankins, *Humanism and Platonism*, 1: 1–18. Bruni, *The Humanism*, 21–42.

[6] For the work's fortune, see Luzi Schucan, *Das Nachleben von Basilius Magnus Ad Adolescentes: Ein Beitrag zur Geschichte des christlichen Humanismus* (Geneva: Droz, 1973).

[7] See Basil, *The Letters*, 4 vols., ed. and tr. Roy J. Deferrari (Cambridge, MA: Harvard University Press, 1926–34), 4:378–435, at 391, tr. modified.

[8] Ibid., 4: 399.

winds."[9] Basil's point was that in the by then acknowledged classics, passages might indeed occur that did not harmonize with a Christian viewpoint (he mentions the conduct of Zeus in Homer's work, who though the king of all the gods is depicted performing immoral acts). Yet one needed to approach all ancient literature forming and being formed by Christian principles, open to the many examples of virtue that pagan literature contained and sufficiently self-aware to see the bad examples for what they were: bad examples to be avoided.

Basil touched on topics that resonated especially well for Bruni and his generation. Moreover, when Bruni undertook the translation in 1400–1401, his mentor and father figure Salutati was himself engaged in controversy, as conservative clerics objected to his fostering of the study of the pagan classics.[10] So Bruni's translation had a dual function: helping his mentor and furthering the passion for classical antiquity in which he and his cohort were engaged. Bruni's Latin version was a rousing success, with almost 450 manuscripts and ninety-one printed editions emerging.[11] It is also noteworthy that his translation of Basil's "Address" occurred quite early in Bruni's translating career, the first and, as it happened, most popular of his works in this regard. This and other translations signaled something meaningful about his relationship to the ancient past: Greek was crucial, the final ingredient in the recipe for a mature Florentine humanism, one that, at its best, was not revolutionary but rather served as a source of enrichment, reflection, and debate.

Other translations followed, all seen as directly relevant to contemporary life, as "news," on the one hand but also, on the other, as real sources for the creation of an identity.[12] On the political front, for example, Bruni translated a number of orations by ancient Greece's most famous public speaker, Demosthenes, who argued passionately that the political traditions of Athens must be preserved against the creeping autocracy of King Philip of Macedon.[13] This message resonated deeply for Bruni and, by extension, for the eager Florentine governing elite who consumed Bruni's translations with relish, as proud Florence resisted incursions by autocratic Milan.

Bruni also (and again, quite early, this time in 1405) translated a key dialogue of Plato, entitled *Phaedo*. It is worth pausing with this dialogue, and Bruni's perceptions thereof, since doing so reveals quite a bit about

---

[9] Ibid., 4: 407.
[10] See Witt, *Hercules*, 410–15.
[11] Hankins, *Humanism and Platonism*, 1: 11.
[12] Ibid., 1: 177–92.
[13] Ibid., 191.

philosophy in Bruni's day, his perceptions about its utility, and the way we must foreground social relations if we are to glean an authentic understanding of premodern cultural life.

The *Phaedo* had been known to the West in the Middle Ages (from the twelfth century onward), extraordinarily, since the bulk of Plato's dialogues remained untranslated.[14] But the medieval translation available was too workmanlike in its Latin, remaining far from Plato's high standard of literary art. Accordingly, Salutati, Bruni's mentor, urged him to translate this dialogue, redolent as it was of Platonic theory and so much more.

On one hand, the *Phaedo* possesses arguments that make up the backbone of what is conventionally understood as Platonic philosophy.[15] There are arguments for the theory of the "Forms," the notion that there exist somewhere perfect forms of things that exist imperfectly on earth. In the dialogue the character Socrates says that when we realize that two things are "equal," we simultaneously come to understand the "form" of the Equal itself. In fact, he says, we "remember" that idea, as if we had somehow always known it but had forgotten it, as our souls descended from the heavens into the material bodies in which we find ourselves.[16] Think, for example, of a beautiful piece of music that you love. Once you know it, it is hard to imagine that that very same piece of music had never existed. This is what the theory of forms is like. The forms, moreover, concern important matters of all sorts. When you appreciate someone's physical beauty, this process occurs because you see the eternally beautiful (the form of Beauty) in that person. When you do something good, you are "participating" in the form of the Good. For Plato, it had been greatly important to posit ideas such as the form of the Good. Doing so had allowed him to suggest that there could be an objective, rather than a relativistic, ethics.

The *Phaedo*, too, includes arguments that suggest the human soul is immortal. It survives the body's physical death, Socrates recounts. Human beings are situated as if in a hollow.[17] After people die, those who were most virtuous in life will, after death, be led up to dwell in eternity among the gods. The souls of those who needed further purification would return to earth, to be reborn as bees or wasps if they are highly social. The worst would

---

[14] See Raymond Klibansky, *The Continuity of the Platonic Tradition during the Middle Ages, Together with Plato's Parmenides in the Middle Ages and the Renaissance* (London: The Warburg Institute, 1939), 27.

[15] See for this paragraph Christopher S. Celenza, "The Platonic Revival," in J. Hankins, ed., *The Cambridge Companion to Renaissance Philosophy* (Cambridge: Cambridge University Press, 2007), 72–96, at 72–74.

[16] Plato, *Phaedo*, in Plato, *Opera*, 5 vols. (Oxford: Clarendon, 1995), vol. 1: 73c–77a.

[17] Ibid., 109a–115.

be sent to the river Cocytus that in antiquity was thought to join the river Acheron and lead to the underworld (and which for Dante represented the ninth and lowest circle of hell).

Immortality of the human soul, rewards and punishment after death, and a superior immaterial world that superintends our own earthly world: as attentive readers may have noted, it sounds a lot like Christianity. This family resemblance of Platonism to Christianity was one reason why Saint Augustine (354–430) had proclaimed, as he examined ancient pagan philosophies, that the Platonists were the "closest to us," meaning the closest to Christians.[18] This endorsement, tendered by venerable Augustine and passed along to medieval Christian thinkers, emerged as one very important strand in the DNA of Western Christianity.

Another way to clarify this resemblance is to say that while most of Plato's written work was new to Bruni and his generation, the core messages were familiar. What was new about Plato and Platonism, instead, was far more important. First there was the dialogue form, coupled with a high literary level, apparent to Bruni and others after they had managed to learn Greek fluently. As to the literary level, Plato was a true master of what is called "Attic" Greek, a term that scholars use to designate Ancient Greek prose at its highest, "classic" level. If Cicero had emerged as the exemplar of ancient Latin prose, Plato's writing served as a counterpart for Greek. As to the dialogue form, this too harmonized well with the ideals of Bruni and his cultural cohort. It was not that dialogues did not exist in the Middle Ages, of course. But given their bias toward classicizing Latin, it was hard for members of Bruni's generation to take medieval dialogues seriously. And of course their hero Cicero had written a number of notable dialogues, also models for early fifteenth-century Italian humanists.[19]

Plato's dialogues possess some distinguishing features that mark them as important. The interlocutors in Cicero's dialogues presented long expositions of philosophical positions. By contrast, the interlocutors in Plato's dialogues often could seem more in conversation with each other, trading witticisms, exploring positions from many angles, and, in general, doing what dialogues do at their best: stimulating thought on the part of the reader.

[18] Augustine, *De civitate Dei*, ed. Bernhard Dombert (Leipzig: Teubner, 1909), 8.9.

[19] On dialogues, see David Marsh, *The Quattrocento Dialogue: Classical Tradition and Humanist Innovation* (Cambridge, MA: Harvard University Press, 1980); Christopher S. Celenza and Bridget Pupillo, "La rinascita del dialogo," in S. Luzzatto e G. Pedullà, eds., *Atlante storico della letteratura italiana*, vol. 1, *Dalle origini al Rinascimento*, ed. A. De Vincentiis (Turin: Einaudi, 2010), 341–47; for a later period, see Virginia Cox, *The Renaissance Dialogue: Literary Dialogue in Its Social and Political Contexts, Castiglione to Galileo* (Cambridge: Cambridge University Press, 1992).

A reader might agree with a conclusion reached in a dialogue, or he might not. Either way what was important was that the reader became, after a fashion, another interlocutor, someone who was ready to carry on the conversation that was immortalized and "fixed" on the page. Plato's dialogues also presented an aspirational model of how social life could work among literate elites: whatever the hierarchies that might have existed outside the dialogue, within the dialogue each interlocutor had a right to express his opinion. To a group of thinkers such as Bruni and his fellow humanists, interested as they were in exploring citizenship and social life, this model of behavior was meaningful.

Yet what was newest in Plato's dialogues had to do with how reading them in full offered a new, more expansive vision of what philosophy could be. This newness was important for a generation that, rightly or wrongly, tended to look down on the more academic, specialized sorts of philosophy taught in universities. Turning back to the *Phaedo* can help us understand this element. For alongside all the philosophical "arguments" (those passages, say, where Socrates uses language and logic to persuade his listeners that the form of the Equal exists above and beyond the world in which live day to day), another type of philosophy was embedded in these dialogues. This type of philosophy focused less on precise verbal arguments and more on the development of character, less on setting out syllogisms and logical proofs and more on offering examples of how to live. In the *Phaedo*, for example, readers encounter a setting that could not be more affecting: the action takes place the night before Socrates's death, after he has been convicted by the Athenians of "corrupting the youth." He is imprisoned. We observe him at a moment when he knows that he is going to die and when he has made the final decision to go to his death, rather than take the dishonorable way out by being smuggled out of town, as one of his young friends had offered to do.

Given these dire circumstances, how interesting it must have been to Renaissance readers to see a passage such as this, when the interlocutor Phaedo, who was present with Socrates, tells another interlocutor, Echecrates (who was not), how Socrates comported himself:

> What I wondered at most in him was the pleasant, kind, and admiring way he received the young men's argument, and how sharply he was aware of the effect the discussion had on us, and how well he healed our distress and, as it were, recalled us from our flight and defeat and turned us around to join him in the examination of their argument.[20]

[20] Plato, *Phaedo*, 88e–89a, tr. G.M.A. Grube, in Plato, *The Complete Works of Plato*, ed. John M. Cooper (Indianapolis: Hackett, 1997).

It might sound obvious to say it, but Plato put this passage in the dialogue for a reason: to show that in presenting a model of how to die well – not happy perhaps but tranquil, and most of all concerned with those he loved – Socrates had also offered a model of how to live. This side of philosophy (not the side concerned with verbal arguments but rather the side concerned with how to live among fellow human beings) was indeed something valuable for Bruni and his cohort. This type of philosophizing "counted," in other words. It too represented real philosophy, just as did the argument-oriented styles of philosophy taught in universities.

Soon after the quoted passage, Socrates urged his young friends not to become *misologoi*.[21] That word reflects a combination of the Greek words *misein*, which means "to hate" and *logos*, which at its most basic level means "word," but as understood by Plato, something rather like "inquiring conversation." What Socrates was urging his young followers to do was to avoid becoming "haters of conversation," to engage always in reasoned contact with one another, in short, to keep the conversation going after he was gone. In the same passage, he warns that *misologoi* ("haters of conversation") can become *misanthropoi* – haters of their fellow men.

Bruni himself gave two indications of how he saw the *Phaedo* and the enterprise of its translation, clues that reveal both his character and the cultural matrix in which he was enveloped. The first comes in a letter he wrote to his friend Niccolò Niccoli (1364–1437), himself a formidable figure in the humanism of the early fifteenth century, though not, tellingly, for what he wrote. Rather, Niccoli emerged as a key arbiter of taste, a person whose Latin sensibility was so refined that he seemed one of the best judges of eloquence, and whose sizable personal library made him a cultural resource.[22] He was one of the key members of the Salutati circle and one who was crucially important in the "graphic culture" of this generation of humanists, which is to say the author of a new form of handwriting that became increasingly important over the course of the fifteenth century.[23] Bruni

---

[21] Plato, *Phaedo*, 89d.

[22] On Niccoli, see Martin Davies, "An Emperor without Clothes? Niccolò Niccoli under Attack," *Italia medioevale e umanistica* 30 (1987), 95–148; Giuseppe Zippel, *Storia e cultura del Rinascimento italiano* (Padua: Antenore, 1979); Berthold L. Ullman and Philip A. Stadter, *The Public Library of Renaissance Florence: Niccolò Niccoli, Cosimo de' Medici and the Library of San Marco* (Padua: Antenore, 1972).

[23] See Martin Davies, "Humanism in Script and Print in the Fifteenth Century," in Jill Kraye, ed., *The Cambridge Companion to Renaissance Humanism* (Cambridge: Cambridge University Press, 1996), 47–62; Albinia C. de la Mare, *The Handwriting of Italian Humanists* (Oxford: Oxford University Press, 1973); Berthold L. Ullman, *The Origin and Development of Humanist Script* (Rome: Edizioni di storia e letteratura, 1960).

held Niccoli in the highest esteem. Bruni's letter on translating the *Phaedo* is worth extended quotation, revealing as it does how much community mattered to Bruni and his contemporaries:

> Although I had already, my dear Niccolò, a strong love for your Plato (for such I like to call him for whom you are always contending against the ignorant mob), when I began to translate him, so great was the amount of goodwill I experienced, that it seems to me I have come to love him now for the first time and that before I had merely had affection for him. You can't imagine anything more wisely or eloquently written. This is something I understand now much better than before, since, in translating him, I am compelled to examine intensely from every angle and really chew over everything he said. So I am extremely grateful to Coluccio, my father and teacher, who did me a great service when he requested that I undertake this task. Before, I had merely met Plato. Now, I believe, I know him.[24]

Plato, it is clear from the letter, could be an object of controversy.

Bruni stresses that he now knows more about Plato having translated him, since in translating one needs to examine the author closely. Bruni emphasizes Plato's wisdom and eloquence. And he stresses that it was Salutati, his mentor (so dear to Bruni that he refers to Salutati also as his "father"), who had asked him to translate the *Phaedo*. Later in the letter Bruni says this about Plato, foregrounding the way substance and style interact in Plato's work overall:

> He has the utmost urbanity, the highest method of disputation, and the deepest subtlety; his fruitful and divine sentiments are conveyed with a marvelous pleasantness on the part of the interlocutors, and with extra-ordinary verbal power. In his discourse, there is the greatest facility and much admirable *charis* [grace], as the Greeks say. There is nothing labored, nothing violent; all is said as though by a man who has words and their laws at his command, that best and richest of natures expressing all the sentiments of his mind with the greatest facility and beauty.[25]

Bruni's point, really, is that if you want to teach morals (and even philoso-phical truths) to readers, you need to do it in a way that is appealing, that induces people not only to learn the intellectual architecture of those truths but also to believe them internally. The only way to accomplish this aim? Through eloquence.

Plato, in the original Greek, had this eloquence and then some; and now, for the first time in Western European history, that eloquence was reflected

---

[24] Bruni, *Ep.*, 1.8, p. 15, tr. (modified) in Hankins, *Plato*, 1: 50.
[25] Bruni, *Ep.*, 1.8, p. 16, tr. in Hankins, *Plato*, 1: 50

in Latin. That people should learn from newly discovered ancient texts represented a self-evident truth for Bruni. Soon enough, however, his stance shifted ever so slightly, or rather, the commitments of an emerging public intellectual (such as Bruni was fast becoming) compelled him to reevaluate what sort of author could take hold, even among interested readers. Perhaps Plato for various reasons was too abstruse.

A hint as to why this shift occurred emerges in the second of his two contemporary statements regarding his translation of the *Phaedo*: his dedication of the work to Pope Innocent VII, something that needs to be set in the rich context it deserves. Hindsight allows us to see period 1378–1417 as one of great instability for the institution of the papacy, with two, at times three rival claimants existing at any given time.[26] Innocent VII's papacy was short and stormy, lasting only from 1404 to 1406 and marked by a lack of total acceptance by the Roman citizenry. Still, he was elected by eight cardinals and has gone down in history as the legitimate pope. Bruni won a position as an apostolic secretary at the court of Innocent VII in a way that is quite striking, showing how competitive the search for such positions could be.

We learn of the episode in a letter Bruni sent to Salutati, where he details what occurred. Salutati had recommended Bruni for the position, and Bruni seemed to have it in hand; but then the pope and those surrounding him became concerned at Bruni's relative youth. Another contender was in the wings, Jacopo Angeli da Scarperia (that same Jacopo whom Salutati had asked to seek out Greek manuscripts from Byzantium), who seemed more appropriate in age. The decision was taken to allow them to compete for the position when a dramatic event occurred: a long and complicated letter from a French duke had arrived. Since the pope wanted to respond in a precise fashion, both contenders were asked to draft a response. Even those who had been in support of Jacopo preferred Bruni's version, and Bruni relates, "The Pope himself, having rejected the other contender, congratulated me as he admitted me into that rank and service."[27] Bruni remained in papal service for almost ten years, serving three more popes before returning to Florence.

His time with Innocent (brief as it was given the exiguous length of Innocent's pontificate) proved important for Bruni: the first time in his life that, in a practical sense, his finely honed literary abilities merged with the beginnings of a professional identity. We can see some of this process occurring in the dedication Bruni penned to Innocent upon presenting his Latinized version of the text of Plato's *Phaedo*:

---

[26] See Rollo-Koster, *Avignon and Its Papacy.*
[27] Bruni, *Ep.*, 1.2, p. 4.

Thus I send you, most blessed and holy Father, a precious and truly exquisite thing: Plato's book *On the Immortality of the Soul* [i.e., *Phaedo*]. For when I read him in Greek and saw the many pious and salubrious sayings in this book, it seemed to me a worthy thing to translate, and to dedicate to your holiness, so that you, to Whom heaven has given the care of souls, might know what the best of philosophers believed about the soul ... For it is not the smallest part of religion what happens to the soul after the death of a man.[28]

We see, first, that Bruni offers a title to the work that makes his priority clear, highlighting that the *Phaedo* presents arguments for the immortality of the soul as its first priority. Whereas to his friend Niccoli, Bruni had stressed Plato's eloquence and the high level of his dialogical argumentation, to the pope, Bruni means instead to foreground the way that Plato can be understood within a Christian framework.

Bruni goes on in the dedication to stress that Plato has been considered close to Christian doctrine for so long that some ancient Christian thinkers went so far as to insist that Plato had more than a passing familiarity with ancient Hebrew doctrine. He stresses that this is chronologically impossible, but useful to report in any case.[29] Early on, then, we see that he was balancing the need to be responsible historically (by respecting basic chronology as best he could understand it) with the need to have his work fit into the institutional frameworks within which he was embedded. In this case, he was proposing a dialogue by a pagan thinker to the head of Western Christendom, and he decided to frame the project in as Christian a way as he could.

During the rest of those years at the papal court, Bruni continued translating relatively short Greek texts, both because they represented good practice and because they were of special interest to him. He translated the four "Philippic" orations of the great Greek orator Demosthenes, which argued for the freedom of ancient Athens (like Florence, a republic) over against the tyranny of the Macedonians. And he tried his hand, as did many others, at translating into Latin various of Plutarch's *Lives*, those brilliant short distillations of the lives and careers of illustrious ancient figures, with the lives of Marc Antony and Cato the Younger among them.[30] Bruni never lost his taste for translation and for learning from Greek wisdom, as we shall see.

---

[28] Bruni, *Schriften*, 4, tr. Hankins, *Plato*, 1:50.

[29] Ibid.

[30] See Marianne Pade, *The Reception of Plutarch's Lives in Fifteenth-Century Italy*, 2 vols. (Copenhagen: University of Copenhagen, 2007); and Christopher S. Celenza, "'Parallel lives': Plutarch's *Lives*, Lapo da Castiglionchio the Younger (1405–1438) and the Art of Italian Renaissance Translation," *Illinois Classical Studies* 22 (1997), 121–55.

The period at the papal court also served another important function: it gave Bruni real-world exposure to a complicated and at times dangerous political environment. He saw popes flee Rome under pressure from violent noble Roman families; he saw them return. Through it all, however, he saw that the institution of the papacy, troubled as it was in those years, remained: still the home of the Petrine "rock" on which the Church was built, however precariously perched it might seem at any given time. This experience afforded Bruni a view of institutional culture that remained with him throughout his life, inflecting his vision of Florentine political culture. States need stable institutions to survive, as only those who dedicate significant portions of their lives to serving them really know.

Bruni returned to Florence in 1414, after the last pope that he served, the "anti-Pope" John XXIII (who went down in history as an illegitimate claimant), had to step down from his post at the decision of the Council of Constance, a council that eventually, a few years later, solved the schism with the election of Ottone Colonna as Pope Martin V.[31] The year 1416 saw Bruni earn Florentine citizenship. For this young man who hailed originally from the Tuscan city of Arezzo, Florentine citizenship carried with it prestige, pride, and, most importantly, possibilities. The first of these was a tax break he received for the writing of his monumental work of history, the *History of the Florentine People*, which he worked on from 1415 until his death in 1444.[32] Bruni had already earned a fair amount of money during his time at the papal court. What this tax privilege meant was that he had even more free time to work on his humanistic research. He did so with aplomb, never settling into the life of a retiring scholar but rather continuing to do work that meshed with his evolving view on how humanistic effort could help his adopted city.

It is therefore no surprise that, as his translating work continued, he turned to Aristotle, whom he came to see as more practical in the context of Florence and, importantly, more harmonious with what he and others saw as a primary goal of foregrounding the humanities in public life: teaching virtue to elite citizens.[33] This basic motive can seem difficult to understand

---

[31] See Walter Brandmüller, *Das Konzil von Konstanz, 1414–1418*, 2 vols. (Paderborn: Schöningh, 1991–97); Phillip H. Stump, *The Reforms of the Council of Constance, 1414–1418* (Leiden: Brill, 1994).

[32] See Lauro Martines, *The Social World of the Florentine Humanists, 1390–1460* (Princeton: Princeton University Press, 1963), 168, 171; for the *History*, see Leonardo Bruni, *History of the Florentine People*, 3 vols., ed. and tr. James Hankins (Cambridge, MA: Harvard University Press, 2001–07).

[33] See James Hankins, "Teaching Civil Prudence in Leonardo Bruni's *History of the Florentine People*," in Sabrina Ebbersmeyer and Eckhard Kessler, eds., *Ethik – Wissenschaft oder*

today. We tend to think of the humanities as separate from public life. For fifteenth-century Italian intellectuals, however, this separation was not self-evident. For Bruni, who even in his period of scholarship still had a public profile, it was ever more necessary to bridge the gap. He wanted the new focus on the classical world to arrive at such a point of concentration that it was relevant for him and his contemporaries. Bruni and many other humanists realized that you could not teach political virtue effectively by writing treatises on politics. Instead you needed compelling, readable texts that taught political virtue both by example and by precept.

On the precept side, Aristotle emerged as important. Among many other works of lasting importance, Aristotle, Plato's greatest student, had authored a text Bruni and others found especially compelling: the *Nicomachean Ethics*. For Bruni it was useful precisely because it was so human. At the outset of the work, Aristotle situates ethics, a favorite concern among humanists, under the rubric of politics in general. All inquiries seek the best "end," Aristotle suggests. What he means is that whenever we inquire into how to do something, or how something works, we are guided by what the best final product – the best "end" – will be. However, Aristotle says,

> Even if the end is the same for a single man and for a state, that of the state seems at all events something greater and more complete both to attain and to preserve; for though it is worthwhile to attain the end merely for one man, it is finer and more divine to attain it for a nation or for city-states. These, then, are the ends at which our inquiry, being concerned with politics, aims.[34]

Human conduct and human excellence must be studied in themselves, but they make sense when they are understood within the context of a social community, the state. Already one can see how important such a statement would be for Bruni. He had observed and participated in worldly politics and practical life at the papal court, and he had returned to Florence and become involved with that cultural capital's leading citizens. A vision of politics consequently stood out: each citizen's individual excellence and flourishing were, ultimately, tied to the flourishing of a community.

Lebenskunst? Modelle der Normenbegründung von der Antike bis zur frühen Neuzeit (Berlin, 2007), 143–57; Hankins, "The Virtue Politics of the Italian Humanists," in Patrick Baker, Johannes Helmrath, and Craig Kallendorf, eds., *Beyond Reception: Renaissance Humanism and the Transformation of Classical Antiquity*, forthcoming.

[34] Aristotle, *Ethica Nicomachea*, ed. I. Bywater (Oxford: Clarendon, 1920) 1094b, tr. Ackrill, modified, in *A New Aristotle Reader*, ed. and tr. J.L. Ackrill (Princeton: Princeton University Press, 1989), 1094b.

Aristotle goes on to say that all fields of inquiry should aspire only to that level of certainty that is appropriate for the specific discipline in question. "Precision," Aristotle writes, "is not something one can seek in all discussions any more than in the products of crafts. Now fine and just actions, which political science investigates, exhibit much variety and fluctuation, so that they may be thought to exist only by convention, and not by nature."[35] Aristotle's *Nicomachean Ethics* concerns ethics, of course, so it can be surprising and striking that that he refers to "political science," a term that calls to mind modern university departments. Accordingly, it is helpful to look at the original Greek, *politikê*, which means most literally "politics" and more expansively (but accurately) "that about which we inquire when we talk about socially connected, institutional life." Aristotle saw ethics as part of the world of politics. As such, it was inexact, unlike, say, mathematics. Ethics is a discipline that is inherently historical, in that its precepts will necessarily vary over time. Societal norms change as contexts change. Thus, when it comes to ethics, "we must be content in speaking of such subjects and with such premises to indicate the truth roughly and in outline, and in speaking about things which are only for the most part true."[36] Aristotle goes on to say that one becomes truly proficient in ethics only as one matures and experiences the world. In one sense, ethics can be taught. In another, it must be learned through life experience.

As Bruni began to approach Aristotle seriously, he possessed life experience in spades. It is worth reflecting on the course of his life, not only to the end of his papal service in 1415 but also through the 1420s, as he established himself in Florence. His ten years with the papal court had been marked by dramatic circumstances, studded by outbreaks of violence spurred on by rivalries among the various popes, the Roman people, and even the king of Naples (who believed he had a claim on power in Rome). For a short period, Bruni had even been persuaded to take the job of Florentine chancellor, a position he briefly held from November 1410 to April 1411. Yet he returned to papal service and would remain with the curia, in various guises, until 1415. He had entered papal service at the age of thirty-five and came back to Florence in his mid-forties, by now, too, a married man. Upon arrival, he applied for Florentine citizenship, in addition to that previously mentioned tax exemption from the city, so that he "might more vigorously and freely devote time to his studies," as a contemporary document says.[37]

---

[35] Ibid., tr. Ackrill, modified.
[36] Ibid.
[37] See Emilio Santini, *Leonardo Bruni e i suoi* Historiarum Florentini populi libri XII: *Contributo allo studio della storiografia umanistica fiorentina* (Pisa: Scuola Normale Superiore, 1910), app. 1, docs. 1–4, pp. 132–42.

The petition, both for citizenship and for the tax status, had to move through the different levels of Florence's governing bodies. It did so, giving Bruni an important sign that official Florence, his adopted homeland, was firmly on his side. It was indeed the place for him to settle.

By the 1420s Bruni possessed a broad view of the importance of all kinds of literary, historical, and philosophical study in the formation of citizens. In fact, to use separate terms for these endeavors shortchanges the vision that Bruni, along with other humanists, were propounding. All were linked.

In 1424, for example, Bruni wrote a letter to Battista Malatesta concerning what sort of literature and literary study a woman should undertake.[38] It is true that parts of Bruni's letter reflect traditional views about women (that they are guardians of virtue and should focus on literature that teaches virtues such as modesty and chastity, for instance). Nevertheless, the letter is some-what revolutionary in two ways. First, Bruni argues that women and men alike should study literature. This idea may not seem surprising today, but in his day and age, it was uncommon to have women progress far, especially in the study of ancient, secular literature. Second, he defends the notion that women can and should study potentially scandalous works of ancient poetry, such as Virgil's *Aeneid*, which possessed scenes of gods committing adultery, brutal violence, and other such morally suspect episodes. However, it is the way Bruni makes this latter point that calls out for attention: by citing the many stories in the Bible that themselves present suspect moral conduct.

In the Holy Scriptures, for example, don't we find "Samson's wild lusts, when he put his mighty head in a wench's lap and was shorn of his strength-giving hair? Is this not poetical? And is this not shameful? I pass over in silence the shocking crime of Lot's daughters" – who after the destruction of Sodom and because of the consequent lack of potential husbands had got their father drunk, slept with him, and become pregnant – "and the detestable filthiness of the Sodomites, two circumstances that I, praiser of poets that I be, can hardly bear to relate."[39] In other words, even in the Bible there are tales that on the surface seem immoral: "All of these stories are wicked, obscene, and disgusting, yet do we say that the Bible is not therefore to be read? Surely not. Then neither are the poets to be rejected because of the occasional reference to human pleasures."[40] Nowhere does Bruni say that the Bible is just like any other text, to be discussed and analyzed for the hidden meanings it may contain. Yet the fact that he saw fit to use the Bible as an example, not so

---

[38] In Bruni, *Schriften*, 5–19; tr. in Bruni, *The Humanism*, 240–51.
[39] Bruni, *The Humanism*, 250.
[40] Ibid.

much of holiness or sacred Christian purity but rather as one more text to be discussed, bespeaks a certain secular quality that marked his work and, indeed, that of his generation of humanists.

This pragmatic secularism convinced Bruni that a practical thinker such as Aristotle needed to be in circulation among his fellow Florentines, especially those who, he assumed, were or would be leaders in the Florentine republic. It was not that there was nothing worthwhile in Plato's work, needless to say. But the dialogue format rendered some of Plato's teachings ambiguous, and his literary quality made it difficult for his messages to emerge without extensive interpretation.

On the one hand, Bruni believed that Plato and Aristotle agreed about the most important things. In his "Life of Aristotle," Bruni wrote that, though they did have different followers and different opinions, "it is not to be thought that there was any dissension or disagreement between the philosophers in their general tendency." The philosophers and their followers "seem to have the same doctrine, and to hold the same views about virtue and conduct, good and evil, the nature of the universe, and the immortality of the soul."[41] On the other, Plato's works "are more suitable for men who are already ripe and finished scholars; tender wits will not be able to find sufficient instruction in them."[42] In that same "Life," Bruni reveals the key to his appreciation of Aristotle: Aristotle was "more moderate in his opinions. Thus, he gave support to normal usages and ways of life."[43] Bruni's practical life experience had taught him that you needed texts that fostered the sort of education that could reach the largest group of people. Aristotle was the most important, "because from the way his books are written it is evident that he wished to instruct the young, nourish those of middle ability, and give exercise and polish to the mature."[44]

In addition to his broad reach, Aristotle was to be appreciated because he knew a lot about literature, a preoccupation that Bruni valued. Bruni's reflexive distaste for contemporary philosophers emerges when he writes: "Who indeed of those who in these times would like to be thought philosophers knows the first thing about literature?"[45] Bruni's critique of contemporary, university-based philosophers is on the surface about style, evincing as it does stereotypical critiques of the lack of literary grace in the

---

[41] Text, in Leonardo Bruni, *Opere letterarie e politiche*, ed. Paolo Viti (Turin: UTET, 1996), 504–29; tr. in Bruni, *The Humanism*, 283–92, at 288.

[42] Bruni, *The Humanism*, 289.

[43] Ibid.

[44] Ibid.

[45] Ibid., 291.

ways that scholastic philosophers communicated their ideas. Aristotle, by contrast, "was very careful to acquire knowledge about all the poets as well as a quantity of information respecting literary matters which no one before him had ever worked out."[46] Yet there is more to Bruni's throwaway line. What he is saying is that in matters of importance, a real philosopher needs to move people's hearts as well as their minds, so that persuasion is not something separate from philosophy but rather an integral part thereof. The form and content, though separate and separable conceptually, were interrelated. For Bruni, Aristotle possessed all the qualities needed for an effective philosopher: his work covered diverse areas of human wisdom, it was understandable to many people at several levels of comprehension, and it had the venerable patina of ancient authority.

But there was a problem. Aristotle's works had been available in Latin translations in the West since the thirteenth century. Yet Bruni came to believe that the Latin into which Aristotle's works had been translated was insufficiently elegant to garner the sort of attention and audience that the majesty of Aristotle's argument deserved. This sentiment – that Aristotle's works needed to find expression in an elegance commensurate with their intellectual level – created one of the most interesting, and telling, controversies of the early fifteenth century. For one thing, Bruni did not address extensively in his remarkable "Life of Aristotle" (a work that still impresses with its thoroughness and one that indeed represented a vast improvement over the medieval biographies of Aristotle then in circulation) what we can describe as the "esoteric/exoteric" problem.

Simply put, Aristotle, like many ancient thinkers who also taught, had one class of works that was "esoteric" (the prefix *eso-* in Greek means "within" or "internal") and another that was "exoteric" (*exo-* means "outside" or "public"). The historical Aristotle wrote works of literary art suitable for outside publication (exoteric works), which were in form like Plato's dialogues.[47] These dialogues, however, were not preserved into the Middle Ages. So, when Cicero and others, whom Bruni cites, speak of Aristotle as having been "eloquent," it was the lost exoteric works to which they were referring – works to which Bruni like everybody else had no access.[48]

---

[46] Ibid.

[47] Aristotle says as much, when he refers to "external works": see *Ethica Nicomachea*, 1102a18–28; ibid., 1140a2; and *Ethica Eudemia*, ed. R.R. Walzer (Oxford: Clarendon, 1991), 1217b22.

[48] For two ancient attestations of Aristotle's eloquence that Bruni would have known, see Cicero, *Academica*, 2.38.119, speaking of Aristotle's "flumen orationis aurem" (see Cicero, *De natura deorum. Academica*, ed. and tr. Horace Rackham [Cambridge, MA: Harvard University Press, 1951], p. 620); and Quintilian, *Institutio oratoria*, 10.1.83, "eloquendi

What everyone, Bruni included, did have were the esoteric works, the works that Aristotle used within his school: textbooks, essentially. Works such as the *Nicomachean Ethics* represented something like Aristotle's lecture notes, notes that he or his students later edited and that then, together with Aristotle's other works, were edited, ordered, and made public in antiquity by a later thinker, Andronicus of Rhodes (active in the first century BC).[49] Aristotle's more literary, exoteric works did circulate in antiquity and were known to Cicero among others, but they never made it into the corpus of Aristotelian works that was transmitted over time.[50] Bruni does not address the distinction between the esoteric and exoteric works. But he accepted (because he needed to do so) the idea that Cicero and others had endorsed: that Aristotle had been eloquent. Bruni required this element as part of his conception of Aristotle because Bruni had come to believe in Aristotle's practical utility to his compatriots. That utility could never come to fruition if not presented in an elegant way.

Consequently, when Bruni went about translating Aristotle's *Nicomachean Ethics* from Greek into Latin, he did so by making Aristotle (whose Greek was simple, functional, and precise) sound a lot more like Cicero (whose Latin was ornate, consciously elegant, and even rhythmic). You could argue that Bruni made a mistake in register. Or you could argue that Bruni was not only translating but also culturally transmitting Aristotle to his contemporaries. Or you could say that Bruni was making mistakes, both in particulars and in his general conception of how philosophical texts should be transmitted, studied, and understood.

This latter position is precisely what Alonso Garcia da Cartageña suggested, when he wrote against Bruni's translation. In truth, there was something substantial and important in the critique of this son of a rabbi, Christian convert, learned scholastic thinker, and Church politician who eventually rose to become bishop of the Spanish diocese of Burgos, where he grew up.[51]

---

suavitate" (see Quintilian, *The Orator's Education*, 5 vols., ed. and tr. Donald A. Russell [Cambridge, MA: Harvard University Press, 2001], vol. 4, p. 296).

[49] See David Ross, *Aristotle* (London: Methuen, 1923), 1–19; G.E.R. Lloyd, *Aristotle: the Growth and Structure of His Thought* (Cambridge: Cambridge University Press, 1968), 9–18; Paul Moraux, *Der Aristotelismus bei den Griechen: von Andronikos bis Alexander von Aphrodisias*, 2 vols. (New York: De Gruyter, 1973–84).

[50] See Moraux; and for the Roman side, see Jonathan Barnes, "Roman Aristotle," in Jonathan Barnes and Miriam Griffin, eds., *Philosophia Togata II* (Oxford: Clarendon, 1999), 1–69.

[51] See Alexander Birkenmajer, *Vermischte Untersuchungen zur Geschichte der mittelalterlichen Philosophie* (Münster: Verlag der Aschendorffschen Verlagsbuchandlung, 1922), 129–210.

Before arriving at Alonso's critique, however, we need to step back and open a parenthesis.

To understand this debate and what was at stake, it is best to give a concrete example and to think in broader terms about Aristotle and what he was up to. At the outset of the *Nicomachean Ethics*, Aristotle, as he does in all his major works, discusses the general premises of the field of inquiry, as we have seen. Here are the treatise's first words: "Every art and every investigation, and likewise every practical pursuit or undertaking, seems to aim at some good. Hence it has been well said that the good is that at which all things aim."[52] These two sentences represent a guiding idea integral to Aristotelian philosophy: since all things aim at a certain goal, in any philosophical discipline one must isolate what that particular goal, for that particular discipline, happens to be. Aristotle uses the word *agathon* or, most literally, "good," for what has been described here as a "goal." And what has been translated here as "the good" can be understood as the goal at which all things are aiming. To understand what this means we need to situate "the good" in the context of another key Aristotelian notion, that of causation.

Aristotle, in various places, argues that causation should be understood in a fourfold way, composed of causes that can be described as material, efficient, formal, and final.[53] Take a wooden chair. The chair's "material" cause is the wood, or the material out of which the chair is made. The "efficient" cause is the maker of the chair (the one who "effects" it), the carpenter. The "formal" cause is the "form" of the chair, a concept not to be understood as Plato had understood the forms (as a kind of immaterial, perfect "chair-ness" to which every material chair might be compared and of which every material chair is an imperfect earthly manifestation). Rather the "form" of the chair is something like the chair's plan, that in one sense exists in the carpenter's head and in another should be understood as the shape of the chair as it is physically manifested: matter and form are always linked for Aristotle. Lastly, there is the all-important "final" cause of the chair, the purpose for which it exists: for us to sit on. It is in this last sense that Aristotle meant "the good at which all things aim."

All things have a final cause. One aspect of any inquiry (such as ethics) is to understand what the objects of the inquiry are. Comprehending the objects

---

[52] *Ethica Nicomachea* 1094a, tr. Rackham, in Aristotle, *Nicomachean Ethics*, tr. Horace Rackham (Cambridge, MA: Harvard University Press, 1934), p. 3.

[53] See Aristotle, *Physics*, 2 vols., ed. and tr. P.H. Wicksteed and F.M. Cornford (Cambridge, MA: Harvard University Press), bk. 2, sec. 3, 194b24–195a4 (vol. 1, pp. 128–32); Aristotle, *Metaphysics*, 2 vols., ed. and tr. Hugh Tredennick (Cambridge, MA: Harvard University Press, 1933), bk. 5, sec. 2, 1013a25–1014a (vol. 1, pp. 210–16).

of the inquiry has to do at least in part with understanding their final cause, their purpose. In this case, ethics, the object of inquiry was the human being. In the passage cited, Aristotle was speaking, as he often does, "teleologically" (*telos* in Greek means "end"). Here, at the beginning of the *Nicomachean Ethics*, Aristotle was making a general statement, typical of his style of thinking, before moving to the particulars of the subject matter at hand (here, ethics). The particulars of ethics had to do with human beings, and the good for human beings, in Aristotle's view, is what he calls, in Greek, *eudaimonia*. This word is traditionally translated as "happiness" but is better understood as human "flourishing."

Every person's flourishing will depend on a combination of that person's individual nature (the purpose, in a sense, for which that person was born, his or her "final cause") and the way that person lives his or her life. Living a life is composed of many elements, of course, but for Aristotle the most important concerns the way that a person practices the virtues. Aristotle conceives of the virtues, too, teleologically, in the sense that to exercise a virtue, you needed to practice it. He said that a virtue was a "capacity" or "habit" (*hexis* in Greek), which one had to bring from potentiality to actuality by repeated practice.[54] Simply put, take the virtue of bravery. All of us are born with the capacity to be brave, but you become a brave person only by repeatedly performing brave acts (by bringing your inborn potential capacity for the virtue of bravery into actuality, in Aristotelian terms). Life is like that: you have many parts of your life that need practice to work well. Aristotle's *Nicomachean Ethics* was a work that Bruni admired precisely because it was so real, and so applicable to everyday life.

To return to Bruni and his translation, it is revealing that Bruni translated "the good" as *summum bonum* or the "highest good" in Latin. This expression does not mean the good as Aristotle understood it but rather the highest good. And it is even more telling that Bruni identified *eudaimonia*, human flourishing (which Bruni translated as *felicitas*) as this highest good. Right at the beginning, Bruni disclosed a lack of a basic understanding of Aristotle. For Aristotle the good was general. All things, even trees and rocks, possessed a good toward which they aimed. The highest good, instead, had to do with divinity. Indeed, the highest good for humanity, according to Aristotle in Book Ten of the *Nicomachean Ethics*, was to reach, in so far as each human being could, the divine.[55] Bruni's translation of the good as the highest good thus had the effect of allowing the possibility that even an inanimate object

---

[54] See Aristotle, *Ethica Nicomachea*, 1103a24.
[55] Ibid., 1177b30–1178a1.

might be able to partake of this divine possibility, a notion that would make nonsense out of Aristotle's thinking overall. This mistake, when all was said and done, was only one small error, of course. But it was an important one and, more critically, it signaled a real difference in approach toward Aristotle in general: between how Aristotle had not only been read but also taught and learned in medieval universities and how Bruni and his generation were beginning to understand authoritative works in general.

To understand this difference, we can close this lengthy parenthesis and return to Alfonso Garcia da Cartageña's "Little book against Leonardo" (*Libellus contra Leonardum* as it was known in Latin).[56] Years went by as this controversy played itself out. At the outset, when Bruni translated the *Ethics*, in 1416, he was a mature but still relatively young man in his mid-forties, at the height of his powers and with substantial scholarly and professional experience already behind him. In his widely circulated preface to his translation, Bruni's spared no mercy toward the translator of the medieval version. Though Bruni did not even see fit to name the translator in his preface, it is worth noting that it had been the brilliant Robert Grosseteste, an esteemed Oxford philosopher and theologian, bishop of Lincoln, and respected statesman (1175/9–1253). Bruni wrote that he had misunderstood the Greek, used Greek words in the Latin translations when there were satisfactory Latin ones available, and overall made Aristotle's text "more barbarous than Latin."[57]

Alfonso's critique came almost fifteen years after that moment. By then of course Bruni had become chancellor of Florence, in many respects the most popular humanist writer in Italy, and, finally, a cultural arbiter of values whose opinion was sought after, respected, and often unquestioningly accepted. Alfonso's critique had been quite respectful, foregrounding both the need for Latin translations from the Greek and Bruni's international fame. To his dedicatee, Guzman, Alfonso wrote, "from the times of the early Church and indeed from the era of the ancient Church Councils, we have been almost wholly out of communication with the Greeks, even as Attic sources wither on the vine."[58] It is a matter of great importance, in other words, when anything new emerges from the Greek heritage.

Alfonso wrote that he became acquainted with Bruni's work when, as an ambassador for the king, he was stationed in the westernmost province of

[56] Edited in Alexander Birkenmajer, *Vermischte Untersuchungen zur Geschichte der mittelalterlichen Philosophie*, 129–210; Bruni's "Preface" is at 157–62; Alfonso's *Libellus* is at 162–86.

[57] Bruni, "In libros Ethicorum prooemium," ed. Birkenmajer, 157.

[58] Alfonso, *Libellus*, ed. Birkenmajer, 163. My treatment of this episode is indebted to that of James Hankins, in his "The Ethics Controversy," in Bruni, *The Humanism*, 201–8.

Spain, meaning Salamanca. There he made the acquaintance of several men who had studied law at the famed University of Bologna, with whom he often engaged in learned conversation. One of the men, who had a special taste for humanistic study, mentioned that Bruni was known to be quite learned in both Latin and Greek. Fittingly, Alfonso requested to see some copies of Bruni's work that this interlocutor had in his home, among which were Bruni's translations into Latin of the orations of Aeschines and Demosthenes against and for Ctesiphon, as well as a certain work of Saint Basil (Bruni's translation of Basil's "Address to the youth"). Upon reading these works, Alfonso considered himself in the presence of a "new Cicero," so impressed was he by Bruni's eloquence in rendering the Greek into Latin.[59]

The habit for engaging in learned discussions in the evenings continued over four years, Alfonso goes on, writing to Guzman as follows: "Among other matters, when on one evening the conversation turned to ethics, that brilliant nephew of yours brought a certain new translation of [Aristotle's *Nicomachean*] *Ethics*, which, he proffered, Leonardo had newly committed to paper."[60] Excited as Alfonso was to see the work of Bruni, whom he had come to respect, his enthusiasm soon turned to dismay, as he realized that a work whose precise terminology had wended its way into almost all the branches of learning "had been ridden with loose reins."[61]

"Loose reins." Alfonso's critique reflected not only his own learning but also centuries of tradition, when it came to Aristotle. Perhaps the most important thing to note is something that will seem surprising to modern readers. Though Alfonso was criticizing Bruni's Greek-to-Latin translation, Alfonso himself could not read Greek. How can this be, one might ask? How could you criticize a translation if you cannot read the original language?

Alfonso's reasons as to why his critique was legitimate reveal a great deal about the culture out of which he emerged, even as Bruni's tone-deaf response does the same about evolving humanism. Alfonso says this about Aristotle: "since Aristotle himself did not reason correctly because of his authority, but acquired his authority from reason, whatever is consonant with reason is what Aristotle must be considered to have said."[62] Alfonso believes essentially that the medieval textbook tradition reflected a larger truth of which each individual text and thinker was only a part. He even goes so far as to say that "we ought not to pay attention to what Aristotle says but

---

[59] Alfonso, *Libellus*, ed. Birkenmajer, 164.
[60] Ibid.
[61] Ibid., 164–65.
[62] Ibid., 166.

to what is consonant with moral philosophy, for even Aristotle is not like a prince or potentate handing down philosophy to us; even he can err."[63] Aristotle may, in the texts we possess, seem unclear. But it is not another translation we need, in that case, but rather explanation and commentary: "the text teaches us in brief. The function of the gloss [meaning the commentary] is to explain the meaning of the text."[64] Truth was one, embedded in an authority such as Aristotle, indeed inviolably connected to him as an authority; but it needed commentators, schools, and of course modern interpreters to bring it out into the light of day. Aristotle's own individual text represented only a part – an important one to be sure – of a much larger, polyphonic enterprise.

Bruni's approach, on the other hand, resonates more with modern readers, because he assumes that Aristotle's text represents Aristotle's opinion – the opinion, that is, of the historical Aristotle.[65] To access its meaning correctly, you needed to understand it, first, in the original language (Greek) and then find ways to communicate its main lines into a target language (in this case, Latin). When he first received Alfonso's text criticizing him, Bruni was ungenerous in the extreme, writing to Francesco Pizolpasso, archbishop of Milan (who had sent Bruni Alfonso's criticism): "When I began to read it, I immediately broke out into laughter. For just as Stephen of old was stoned by the Judaizers, that is, by the defenders of the old law, for proclaiming the new truth, so now the defenders of the old version, or rather perversion, come threatening to stone me for publishing a new and true translation."[66] Bruni revealed his attitude a bit more clearly later in the letter: "In truth our whole disagreement has to do with translation; but a translation is correct if it corresponds to the Greek, defective if it does not."[67] Bruni goes on mordantly to express incredulity that Alfonso could even imagine judging whether a translation could be valid or not if he admits he does not read Greek. Bruni's defense of his mistaken *summum bonum* translation relies on one Greek authority, Eustratius, who offers a generic explanation that *t'agathon* ("the good" in Greek) can mean the "highest good" (*summum bonum* in Latin).[68] But Bruni's mistake came not so much in the definition as in the context. It was a mistake he failed to see.

---

[63] Ibid., 204 (this is from a lost letter to Bruni by Alonso as reported by Bruni, in his letter to the archbishop of Milan, Francesco Pizolpasso).

[64] Ibid., 167.

[65] See Hankins, "The Ethics Controversy," 204.

[66] The letter is in Birkenmajer, 193–209; and Bruni, *Ep.*, 7.4, ed. Mehus, v. 2, pp. 81–90; I cite the translation in Hankins, "The Ethics Controversy," 206.

[67] Bruni, *Ep.*, 7.4, ed. Mehus, v. 2, p. 85.

[68] Ibid., p. 87.

The two thinkers, Bruni and Alfonso, later reconciled, so much so that Bruni may have suppressed a subsequent letter to the archbishop of Milan, also critical of Alfonso, from his correspondence, perhaps because of that reconciliation.[69] There was much that separated the two men, and much that united them. As to the latter, both believed in the power of ancient authorities: that one needed them, that they were relevant, and that they were deserving of study. While it is Bruni's attitude toward translation that stands out today, close as it is to what we tend to believe (a good translation can only be judged as such by someone who knows both languages involved), their main difference, really, has to do with the relationship of individuals to institutional, academic culture. For Alfonso, so much academic work had been done on Aristotle, especially on those aspects of Aristotle's thought that were coherent within his extant body of work, that one needed to take that tradition (here, the medieval university tradition) into account: to respect it. For Bruni, that respect was lacking. In truth, had he had a little more of it, he might not have made the error that he did. His mocking letter to Francesco Pizolpasso shows one of his blind spots on that front. It was a blind spot that persisted, in some corners of the humanist movement, throughout its existence.

Still, translation aside, Bruni's position represented the future, in one sense: humanist Latin, by the time of his replies to Alfonso's critiques, was well on its way to being the preferred form of teaching and learning Latin in Italy. So it is worth bringing into relief another debate in which Bruni was involved, this time on the nature of the Latin language itself.

[69] See Francesco Paolo Luiso, *Studi su l'Epistolario di Leonardo Bruni*, ed. Lucia Gualdo Rosa (Rome: Istituto storico per il medioevo, 1980), 138, n. 5; Hankins, "The Ethics Controversy," 372, n. 24.

5

DIALOGUES, INSTITUTIONS, AND
SOCIAL EXCHANGE

THE DEBATE BETWEEN LEONARDO BRUNI AND ALFONSO OF Cartagena revolved around something specific and, in many respects, quite limited: Aristotle's *Nicomachean Ethics*. Yet it signaled much more, including a new view on language, the place of institutions in intellectual life, and finally the way that philosophy should be conceived. As to institutions and philosophy, Alfonso's real concern was not so much for Aristotle's meaning but rather for the institutional apparatus built up around Aristotle and the teaching of his texts. Alfonso does indeed critique Bruni's mistakes, but the anxiety level is high, emotional even, as if he believes he needs to beat back a challenge. Bruni by contrast represents one of the most curious but also lasting and important features of Italian Renaissance humanism: he represents an institutionally enfranchised person striking out against institutional structures. Since the days of Petrarch, humanists had been complaining about the often restrictive, rigid, and intellectually conservative nature of university life. Often they exaggerated, and in most all cases they themselves had spent time at universities and other educational institutions.[1] But what was important was, for want of a better word, the posture – taking the stance of an outsider represents more than just a pose. Instead this stance became part of the genetics of the humanist movement for several generations.

Bruni presents the most prominent bundle of contradictions in this respect. By the 1430s, he was a mature, very wealthy, highly respected stalwart of Florentine political life, well ensconced in the city's most powerful political position, that of chancellor. He had significant institutional backing, in other words. But he was still willing and able, in the debate

---

[1] See David Lines, "Humanism and the Italian Universities," in Christopher S. Celenza and Kenneth Gouwens, *Humanism and Creativity: Essays in Honor of Ronald G. Witt* (Leiden: Brill, 2006), 323–42.

over Aristotle's *Ethics*, to take the stance of the outsider, to maintain that a tradition then almost two hundred years old, buttressed by countless university curricula and by generations of professors, needed revision from the ground up. Retranslation, rethinking, and refashioning would permit philosophy to become something shared outside of the classroom, able to wend its way into the fabric of lived virtue that, Bruni hoped, might take hold among elite Florentines – those who governed, those who participated in political life, those who ruled. In other words, Bruni combined the disruptive side of humanism – that propensity that gazed with a skeptical eye on certain institutional traditions – with a bedrock conservatism concerning the possibilities of politics. Nowhere is this tendency more on view than in the debate over the nature of the ancient Latin language that began in the 1430s.

To understand this debate, its ramifications, and its centrality in any complete understanding of the humanist movement, a look at both traditions and contemporary cultural realities is in order: a look, in other terms, at when Bruni was still young and a self-conscious member of the avant-garde, at what sorts of social contexts shaped his thinking, and then, finally, at the beginnings of this momentous debate. We will thus step backward in time, to the first decade of the fifteenth century.

As to traditions, in Bruni's day as in Petrarch's, for that small, mostly male elite who had the opportunity to be educated beyond an elementary level, bilingualism was the norm: Latin in the classroom, Latin fluency in writing, and the ability to read Latin without problems, on the one hand and on the other, the local vernacular, in Bruni's case Tuscan, a language that by his maturity had already a triumphant history behind it (a history that, as we shall see, Bruni understood and whose societal function he applauded and fostered). Petrarch recognized that the Latin in use did not match that of the ancient Latin he loved so well and did all he could to begin the process of classicizing the Latin prose then in use. Salutati thereafter periodically offered some thoughts, as we have seen, on the history of the Latin language and even went so far in his letter exchange with Giovanni Conversino to equate, notionally, the way one used Latin with a new style of life, one that would match that of the revered ancients in gravity: "Now when you speak like the ancients, why then do you not also live like the ancients?"[2]

But by the time Bruni's generation was in flower, several things had changed, and there is no better work with which to understand this change than Bruni's *Dialogues to Pier Paolo Vergerio*. It represents a first step along the

---

[2] Coluccio Salutati, *Ep.* 2:409.

way to comprehending the language debate and Bruni's position therein. Bruni wrote this short dialogue in the first decade of the fifteenth century. In its reflections on Dante, Petrarch, Boccaccio, and indeed on Salutati himself, it shows most of all a consciousness of generational change.[3]

Bruni's work embraces some of the conventions of the ancient Ciceronian dialogues that he and his cohort respected greatly. These dialogues possessed shared attributes: a beautiful Latin prose, a readable style, and a tendency to break down and explain philosophical concepts in ways understandable to educated, but nonprofessional, readers.

Take Cicero's dialogue *On Friendship*. Cicero, dedicating this dialogue to a friend, first informs his dedicatee that he is assuming a persona, writing his own opinions but doing so in such a way that they will seem to emerge from the mouth of another. After recalling friendly relationships with two older Roman statesmen, Scaevola and Laelius, Cicero writes: "in this book I have written as a most affectionate friend to a friend on the subject of friendship . . . in the present treatise the speaker on friendship will be Laelius, a wise man . . . Please put me out of your mind for a little while and believe that Laelius himself is talking."[4] Cicero makes clear to his dedicatee that this will be a fictionalized conversation but that it will gain in impact by using a real historical person (Laelius) as a spokesman. Cicero was often able (and this dialogue is no exception) to make deep philosophical points come alive for his Latin contemporaries. Take the following passage, which occurs early in the dialogue, which sees Laelius expounding on the soul:

> For I do not agree with those who have recently begun to argue that soul and body perish at the same time, and that all things are destroyed by death. I give greater weight to the old-time view, whether it be that of our forefathers, who paid such reverential rites to the dead, which they surely would not have done if they had believed those rites were a matter of indifference to the dead; or, whether it be the view of those who lived in this land and by their principles and precepts brought culture to Great Greece, which now, I admit, is wholly destroyed, but was then flourishing; or, whether it be the view of him who was adjudged by the oracle of Apollo to be the wisest of men, who, though he would argue on most subjects now on one side and now on the other, yet always consistently maintained that

---

[3] See David Quint, "Humanism and Modernity: A Reconsideration of Bruni's *Dialogues*," *Renaissance Quarterly* 38 (1985), 423–45; Riccardo Fubini, "All'uscita della scolastica medievale: Salutati, Bruni, e i *Dialogi ad Petrum Histrum*," *Archivio storico italiano* 150 (1992), 1065–103; and Ronald G. Witt, *In the Footsteps of the Ancients: The Origins of Humanism from Lovato to Bruni* (Leiden: Brill, 2000), 432–42.

[4] Cicero, *De amicitia*, in Cicero, *De senectute, De amicitia, De divinatione*, tr. William A. Falconer (Cambridge, MA: Harvard University Press, 1923), pp. 108–211, at sec. 1.5–6, p. 113.

human souls were of God; that upon their departure from the body a return to heaven lay open to them, and that in proportion as each soul was virtuous and just would the return be easy and direct.[5]

So much is contained in this brief, casual-sounding conversational point.

When Laelius refers to "those who have recently begun to argue that soul and body perish at the same time, and that all things are destroyed by death," the philosophical group he has in mind is the Epicurean sect, who believed that individual human souls existed only in so far as they were unified to a physical body and that, consequently, when that body died, so too did the soul. When he speaks of the "reverential rites to the dead," Laelius is reinforcing the power of custom in ancient Rome, what was often called the *mos maiorum*, or the "way of our elders," in Latin (in this passage Cicero speaks of the *auctoritas . . . nostrorum maiorum*). Why would our flourishing society have nourished this custom of honoring the dead for so long if, upon dying, all passed into nothingness? When Laelius mentions "the view of those who lived in this land and by their principles and precepts brought culture to Great Greece," he is alluding to the Pythagoreans, who had inhabited southern Italy (what was known as *magna Graecia* or "great Greece"). Their belief had been that souls were reborn. Finally, with his allusion to "the view of him who was adjudged by the oracle of Apollo to be the wisest of men," Laelius signals the view of Socrates. In Plato's *Apology*, the Oracle at Delphi had, famously, designated Socrates the wisest of men because he knew one thing: that he knew nothing. And as we have seen in the *Phaedo* and elsewhere, Socrates argued for the immortality of the human soul.

In this short passage, Cicero manages to set forth a model of learned conversation, where knowledge is assumed, reinforced, and consolidated. It is assumed that one will have heard of the Epicureans and the Pythagoreans, not to mention the rituals of ancestor worship prevalent in Rome. Putting them all together in a seamless and eloquent way fortifies and firms up what one already knows and, in effect, creates an archive both in social memory and in writing. Bruni and his friends loved this sort of thing. It was this precise sort of learning that they sought to imitate and to internalize.

Turning to Bruni's *Dialogues*, we see a similar process occurring, though with different objects and aims.[6] For here, the knowledge "archived" deals with Dante, Petrarch, and Boccaccio. And the larger point that emerges has

---

[5] Ibid., sec. 4.13, p. 121.
[6] Text in Garin, *Pros.*, 44–98; tr. in Bruni, *The Humanism*, 63–84.

to do with generational change. The treatise begins for Bruni, as *On Friendship* had for Cicero, with a dedication, this time to Bruni's friend, Pier Paolo Vergerio (1370–1444/45), who had been born in what is now Slovenia and was then under Venetian dominion. To this distinguished humanist, Church politician, and close contemporary, Bruni writes that he is happy to be in Florence, since there, in addition to its beautiful buildings, "some seeds of the liberal arts and of all human culture, which once seemed completely dead, remained here and grow day by day and very soon, I believe, will bring forth no inconsiderable light."[7] Early then, before 1405, in this and other works (and here, before he was even a citizen of Florence), Bruni contributed to the eventually widespread notion that Florence was a seat of high culture. More than this, his dedication's real purpose is to frame what he is about to relate, which is that "recently, there was a disputation at Coluccio's house."[8]

As Cicero had been wont to do, Bruni makes a transition, at this point, setting the scene and relating the dialogue as it took place:

> Since the feast days for Christ's resurrection were being celebrated and my good friend Niccolò and I had come together, we decided to go visit Coluccio Salutati, easily the leading man of this age in wisdom and eloquence. We had not gone far when we were met by Roberto Rossi, a friend of ours and a man devoted to the liberal arts.[9]

"Niccolò" is Niccolò Niccoli, the literary connoisseur, arbiter of language, critic, and book collector, whose formidable book collection became, after his death, the nucleus of the first great "public" library of the Italian Renaissance, situated in the Dominican complex of San Marco, in Florence.[10] Roberto de' Rossi, another wealthy book collector, had studied Greek with Chrysoloras.

The three friends arrived at Salutati's house, and the old man greeted them kindly and asked them to be seated. But then something strange happened. A silence ensued, long enough that it became awkward. Salutati finally broke the silence, and though he had kind things to say to his young friends, he also gently reproached them, arguing that they neglected to "practice the art of

[7] Bruni, *The Humanism*, 63.
[8] Ibid.
[9] Ibid., 63–64.
[10] On which see Berthold L. Ullman and Philip A. Stadter, *The Public Library of Renaissance Florence: Niccolò Niccoli, Cosimo de' Medici and the Library of San Marco* (Padua: Antenore, 1972); and Christopher S. Celenza and Bridget Pupillo, "Le grandi biblioteche 'pubbliche' del XV secolo," in S. Luzzatto e G. Pedullà, eds., *Atlante storico della letteratura italiana*, vol. 1, *Dalle origini al Rinascimento*, ed. A. De Vincentiis (Turin: Einaudi, 2010), 313–21.

disputation." Nothing is more efficacious than disputation, Salutati says, "where the topic is placed as it were stage center and observed by many eyes."[11] Disputation refreshes the human spirit, sharpens the intellect, "polishes our speech," and "brings it under our ready command. You yourselves can see this in the case of many who read a lot of books and profess themselves men of letters, but cannot speak Latin except with their books because they have refrained from this practice."[12]

What do we learn? First, that gathering together and discussing learned topics in Latin was, if not common, at least not foreign. Second, Salutati's praise of disputation signals a certain public and conversational aspect to the enterprise of gaining wisdom. Reading in private was important, but the sharing of information in public interactions, along with the challenges that inevitably ensued, served as an equally important part of this equation. Third, we learn that, in the case of Renaissance humanism, as in many other cultural movements that proclaim their own newness, traces of past practices remain. In this case, disputation was a feature of the late medieval universities that humanists loved to denigrate for their stodgy inapplicability to everyday life. It was not so much that disputation was new.[13] Instead it was the context where these disputations occurred that represented a change of focus. Held in private homes or other non-university contexts (such as the papal court, as we shall see), these disputations – precisely the kind that Salutati is accusing his young friends of neglecting – represented emblematically the change in perspective for which humanists strove.

As the discussion evolves, Niccoli takes the floor. His main complaint is that serious disputation is impossible, since there has been a precipitous decline in learning and since so much ancient literature has been lost: "so great a loss of books has occurred that no one could talk about the least thing without great impudence."[14] The present is utterly corrupt: "what art, what learning can be found which has not been displaced or completely corrupted?"[15] Philosophy itself has lost its integrity, since self-proclaimed philosophers, joining arrogance and ignorance, claim Aristotle as an ultimate authority and, to boot, are unable to read Aristotle, whom Cicero had termed quite eloquent, in the original. Dialectic, too, has been ruined by "British sophisms" – by which Niccoli means scholastic philosophers. Even

[11] Bruni, *The Humanism*, 64.
[12] Ibid.
[13] On this point, see Alex J. Novikoff, *Medieval Culture of Disputation: Pedagogy, Practice, and Performance* (Philadelphia: University of Pennsylvania Press, 2013).
[14] Bruni, *The Humanism*, 66.
[15] Ibid., 67.

in the realm of grammar and rhetoric, it is hopeless: "to what cause shall we attribute it, Coluccio" – an emboldened Niccoli goes on, speaking directly to the revered old man – "that for so many years now no one has been found who had any distinction in these things?"[16]

Niccoli makes a small, and almost embarrassed exception for Salutati ("you by your presence seem to refute and overthrow my speech"); but Niccoli's tenor reflects his belief that they are living in an era of loss.[17] Presumably this sentiment was one that, if not shared by Bruni and his contemporaries at all times, at least had some currency, enough that Bruni could include an interlocutor, Niccoli, who expressed that opinion. And since the historical Niccoli was known to have been a sharp critic in general, the dialogue evinces a sense of historical verisimilitude. Not only that, but the character Salutati suggests in the dialogue that Bruni was known to agree with Niccoli, saying to Roberto de' Rossi about Bruni that "he would rather be wrong with Niccoli than right with me."[18]

Salutati's larger response is telling, both for the progress of the dialogue and for the state of play in discussions on literature at that moment. Salutati responds in the first instance by saying that one should banish from one's mind what one does not have. Second, he emphasizes the importance of Dante, Petrarch, and Boccaccio, surprised indeed that with such a proud patrimony any Florentine could complain of a lack of humanistic glory. Indeed, Salutati goes on to say that he "does not see why they should not be numbered among the ancients in every aspect of human culture."[19] One can hear echoes of lost conversations here, in which Florentines, proud of their city and anxious about the veneration of all things ancient at the expense of pride in what was modern, sought to valorize their own culture.

Niccoli will have none of it. Praise for this "so-called triumvirate" comes from "the multitude," about whom Niccoli has always been suspicious.[20] Besides, all three had their flaws. Dante's are two in number. First, he made mistakes that no self-respecting scholar would have made. For instance, Dante depicted Marcus Cato (Cato the Younger) as an old man (in *Purgatory*, 1.54), with a white beard, when it was well known to all that he died at the age of forty-eight in the era of the Roman civil wars. Dante placed Brutus, who had slain Julius Caesar, in the lowest level of hell, when Brutus should have been praised as one who fought against tyranny and for the

[16]   Ibid., 69.
[17]   Ibid.
[18]   Ibid., 70.
[19]   Ibid., 72.
[20]   Ibid., 72–73.

Roman republic. Second (and one senses here that Bruni, speaking through Niccoli, believes this is the greater flaw): "granted that Dante had every other endowment, he surely lacked Latinity."[21] Meaning, Dante wrote his masterpiece in the vernacular; those writings we do have in Latin (Niccoli mentions some of Dante's letters) are awkward and inelegant. Niccoli tells old Coluccio: "I shall remove that poet of yours from the number of the lettered and leave him to wool workers, bakers, and the like, for he has spoken in such a way that he seems to have wished to be familiar to this sort of men."[22]

As to Petrarch, he was arrogant and promised far more than he ever delivered. Petrarch discussed endlessly his attempt at a Latin epic, the *Africa*, only to leave it incomplete. And in the rest of his works "he wrote in such a way that in his bucolics there is nothing that smacks of the pastoral or sylvan, and in his orations, nothing that does not greatly desire the art of rhetoric."[23] Since everyone agrees that Dante and Petrarch were better than Boccaccio, there is no need even to go into Boccaccio. But one more thing needs to be emphasized, a flaw that all three possessed: "that they were of a singular arrogance, and did not believe there would be anyone who could judge their works."[24] His final, mordant point, now addressed directly to the shades, as it were, of Florence's three greatest claims to literary fame: "I far prefer one letter of Cicero's and one poem of Virgil's to the whole lot of your works."[25]

Another embarrassed silence, one can imagine, if something like this conversation actually took place. In the flow of the dialogue, Salutati is next. "Smiling in his usual way," he reproaches Niccoli: "How I should wish that you were kinder to your fellow citizens."[26] Bruni set the dialogue dramatically over the course of two days, and the first one ends here, with Salutati repeating his call for his young friends to continue the practice of disputation.

The next day the interlocutors gathered again, this time joined by a young friend of Salutati's, Pietro Sermini. They met at Roberto de' Rossi's gardens, where the discussion continued. When all was said and done, Niccoli was persuaded to speak against his arguments of the previous day, playfully suggesting that the only reason he had denigrated the Three Crowns of Florence was to provoke Salutati into defending them. In the first of what

[21] Ibid., 73.
[22] Ibid., 74.
[23] Ibid.
[24] Ibid., 75.
[25] Ibid.
[26] Ibid.

becomes a series of ambivalent statements, Niccoli, feigning modesty, says to Salutati: "The Florentine poets seemed to call, Coluccio, for your genius, your art of speaking, and your knowledge."[27] This statement means what it says on the surface: that Niccoli considers himself unsuited to praise the Three Crowns and that he believes Salutati would be better suited to do so. But why? Is it because Niccoli believes the Three Crowns and Salutati are so great that he is out of his depth? Or is the reason instead that he sees all of them as part of an earlier generation?

His "defense" of the Three Crowns reveals his answer. Niccoli offers sincere praise for Dante's abundant imagination and copious depiction of all things human and divine, though the praise is tellingly quite vague and without detail.[28] Then when it comes to retracting his statement about Dante's ahistorical depiction of Cato, the defense is simply that Dante engaged in poetic license, representing Cato as old to express his wisdom, traditionally an attribute of old age. The same goes for Dante's placement of Brutus in the lowest circle of hell: it was poetic, with Dante using the figure of Caesar as a legitimate ruler (even though all know he was not, Niccoli says) and Brutus as the representation of a tyrannicide.[29] When it comes to the most serious charge of all, that Dante "lacked Latinity," the defense is only this: "Necessarily he was very well versed in letters and learned and eloquent and fitted for imaginative writings."[30] Niccoli offers no real exposition and no significant argumentation as to why Dante should be considered a preeminent cultural figure.

When it comes to Petrarch, the tenor is similar. Niccoli tells what he heard from Petrarch's friends when he met them in Padua: "they said he had been very handsome, and wise, and the most learned man of his age."[31] Niccoli spends a fair amount of time detailing the praise he has heard from Petrarch's friends: men from another city and another era. As to Florentines, Niccoli says: "Shall we not venture to honor Petrarch for his merits, especially when this man restored humanistic studies, which had been extinguished, and opened the way for us to be able to learn?"[32] Petrarch should be honored as the initiator of serious study of the humanities, but as little else. As to Petrarch's *Africa*, which Niccoli had roundly condemned the previous day, he offers the same sort of wooden defense as he did for Dante: "Who is so

[27] Ibid., 79.
[28] Ibid., 80.
[29] Ibid., 80–81.
[30] Ibid., 81.
[31] Ibid., 82.
[32] Ibid., 82–83.

severe a critic that he would not approve it?"[33] And Niccoli goes on to say that if there is anything in it that is lacking, it is due to Petrarch's inability to complete it before his death. Niccoli's most biting comment comes next: "What they say about preferring one poem of Virgil's and one epistle of Cicero's to all the works of Petrarch" – and of course, on the previous day, Niccoli himself, not an anonymous "they," had enunciated that damning literary comparison – "I often turn around this way: I say that I far prefer an oration of Petrarch's to all the epistles of Virgil, and the poems of Petrarch to all the poems of Cicero."[34] But of course, Virgil wrote no letters that were preserved. And Cicero's poetry – little of which survived – was not considered his finest work (to put it generously).[35] Boccaccio, too, receives a similar amount of vague, faint praise. Poor old Coluccio, when Niccoli asks him to add more praise to the poets under discussion, has only this to say: "I do not see that you have left anything which could be added to their praises."[36] What is a reader to infer?

Something like this conversation may very well have taken place in real life. There is of course no way to know for sure. But the tension presented is real. It has to do with young men, high on their own self-designated membership in the avant-garde, satisfying a respected senior mentor and still preserving their own sense of newness. At this relatively early phase, in other words, Bruni was one of these young men. By the time the debate over the ancient language emerged in earnest, Bruni himself represented the old guard.

If one way of understanding the social world in which Bruni partook is to foreground the way the fifteenth century's many dialogues had their origins in real conversations, another is to see more closely where and how those original conversations took place. Take the milieu surrounding the papal court. Bruni, as we have seen, had himself worked there for many years, and he knew its ins and outs as only an insider would. Proximity matters for intellectuals and for cultural exchange. And the papal court was a place that brought people together from all over Christendom and that unified them using one language: Latin. As a thinker whom we will come to know later, Lorenzo Valla, put it in the 1450s: "For since in the Roman curia it is not allowed to speak anything other than Latin, and since all the Christian nations

---

[33] Ibid., 83.

[34] Ibid.

[35] For a summary of the evidence, see Emma Gee, "Cicero's Poetry," in Catherine Steel, ed., *The Cambridge Companion to Cicero* (Cambridge and New York: Cambridge University Press, 2012), 88–106.

[36] Ibid.

flock there as if to their head, it so happens that all of them give great attention to learning Latin."[37] Latin was the language of social currency in a papal court that included people from the widest reaches of Christianity.

Another thinker, who wrote a somewhat satirical dialogue about the papal court, Lapo da Castiglionchio the Younger, wrote, "There are French, Germans, Hungarians, Scots, and Illyrians [people from the Balkan Peninsula], who are already familiar to us because of the common use of the Latin language and because of long-standing commercial intercourse. Among them there is a difference in manners and lifestyles that is so great anyone could easily see it."[38] The court, in other words, promoted by its very existence and organization a kind of cosmopolitanism, a place both ideal and real where the widely different customs, languages, and ethnicities that made up the fabric of international Christianity could mix and mingle.

So what was the papal court, or *curia romana* as it was known in Latin? Formally, we can think of it as all of the people and institutions that supported the pope, who was himself considered the *vicarius Christi*, or "Vicar of Christ" – Christ's representative on earth.[39] Structurally, in the early fifteenth century, it possessed three branches, one administrative (the "Chancery," or *cancelleria*), one financial (the "Chamber" or *camera*), and one legal (known as the "Tribunal," or *rota*).[40] Though not a part of the papal court, the College of Cardinals also served as an important center of power and patronage. In the 1430s there were twenty-four cardinals, each with his own household, or *familia*, which included a number of employees. Bruni and other fifteenth-century humanists, skilled writers that they were, increasingly sought employment in the papal court and in the households of cardinals. It was in these cultural crossroads that they met, engaged in discussion and debate, and even found time away from their work for (sometimes bawdy) recreation.

Poggio Bracciolini (1380–1459), a close friend of Bruni who spent many years at the papal court and who would later follow in Bruni's footsteps as

---

[37] See Lorenzo Valla, *Orazione per l'inaugurazione dell'anno accademico 1455–1456: Atti di un seminario di filologia umanistica*, ed. Silvia Rizzo (Rome: Roma nel Rinascimento, 1994), 192–201, at sec. 33.

[38] See Lapo da Castiglionchio the Younger, *De curiae commodis*, in Christopher S. Celenza, *Renaissance Humanism and the Papal Curia: Lapo da Castiglionchio the Younger's De curiae commodis* (Ann Arbor: University of Michigan Press, 1999), 103–228, at 173.

[39] Michele Maccarrone, *Vicarius Christi: Storia del titolo papale* (Rome: Facultas Theologica Pontificii Athenaei Lateranensis, 1952).

[40] See Celenza, *Renaissance Humanism and the Papal Court*, 1–80; Elizabeth M. McCahill *Reviving the Eternal City: Rome and the Papal Court 1420–1447* (Cambridge, MA: Harvard University Press, 2013); and Walther von Hoffmann, *Forschungen zur Geschichte der Kurialen Behörden*, 2 vols. (Rome: Loescher, 1914).

chancellor of Florence, put it this way, referring to the time he spent at the court in the days of Pope Matrin V (1417–31): "In the day of Martin V, we used to choose a certain place in the most private part of the court – the *Bugiale*, or 'Theater of Lies.' There the news was reported, and we used to converse about all sorts of things, both for relaxation, which was usually our purpose, and sometimes in a serious way."[41] Poggio tells this anecdote to explain the origins of one of the fifteenth century's most salacious collections of off-color humor, his own Latin collection of tales and jokes called the *Facetiae*, which had wide circulation. But for us, now, what is important is twofold: first, the fact that Poggio highlights the circulation of "news" and, second, the mention of the times when conversations turned to serious matters.

As to news, keep in mind something always difficult to comprehend: this was a world without newspapers, television, and the Internet, from all of which venues we are accustomed to consume news of all sorts. Other contemporaries, beyond Poggio, commented on the fact that news circulated at the papal court. One of these contemporaries, the previously mentioned Lapo, did so in his dialogue about the papal court in 1438. It is a work characterized by admiration for the papal court, satire of many of its tendencies toward luxury and empty formalities, and, above all, the longing of an outsider to be part of the papal court's most desirable in-group for a humanist of that generation.

As he begins, we learn (in Lapo's dedication to Pope Eugenius IV), that he had just lost his patron, a cardinal named Giordano Orsini. Lapo, at odds as to how he would continue to find work and support for his literary endeavors, decides to make a last ditch attempt to gain high-level attention by exposing those at the papal court who, he thought, were not serving it best, even as he would "defend in your eyes" – he tells the pope – "myself and the rest who live chastely and honestly in the curia."[42] The dialogue, by turns funny, bitter, and angry, offers a glimpse into life at the papal court, one that is useful in two respects: first, in showcasing the humanists who were present there and, second, in foregrounding how important the curia seemed as a place where news of all sorts could circulate.

Lapo suggests that "to whichever of the liberal arts you turn your mind and imagination, the Roman curia has in one place quite a number of the most complete, best men."[43] Revealing humanism's consciousness of itself as

[41] Poggio Bracciolini, *Facetiae*, cit. and tr. in Anthony Grafton, *Leon Battista Alberti: Master Builder of the Italian Renaissance* (Cambridge, MA: Harvard University Press, 2002), 51.
[42] Lapo, *De curiae commodis*, 107.
[43] Ibid., 153.

a cultural movement, Lapo continues: "I shall not refer, here, to the professors of holy theology, whose studies have no real kinship to that of ours.
I won't mention the natural philosophers, mathematicians, astronomers, and
musicians, and I shall pass over in silence the interpreters of civil and canon
law."[44] Lapo has, in other words, recognized the prominence of two of the
three "higher" disciplines in the medieval tradition (medicine, theology, and
law), in which one could at a university receive a doctoral degree, as well as
a number of the more mathematical liberal arts. Yet, "although they are like
a great beautification and fortification to the curia, and though the largest
share of the curia is entrusted to their industriousness, still, they do not
contribute anything to this special area of mine – any fruit, that is, the likes
of which I can taste."[45] Lapo wishes to list only those men "whom these
studies, the humanities (*haec studia humanitatis*) – as well as everyday social
intercourse have bound closely to me."[46] We see two things: first, that Lapo
greatly values proximity and friendship and intends in his upcoming description to highlight those whom he has befriended (and perhaps by naming
them to create a social group in which he can claim belonging); and, second,
that his own particular object of fascination is, indeed, the *studia humanitatis*,
the "humanities" of grammar, rhetoric, poetry, history, and moral philosophy. In this highlighting of only those things "he can taste" by a minor
humanist, we see precisely how much an object of fascination the new
culture of humanism had become by the 1430s.

We also see how important the papal court was for bringing leading
humanists together. Lapo has made himself one of the dialogue's two interlocutors, the other being Angelo da Recanate, a close friend in real life.
When Angelo asks Lapo to name the figures he has in mind, Lapo lists several
humanists, a number of whom remain central to our understanding of the
humanist movement even now. In each description, Lapo names the person
in question and then offers a distillation of that humanist's skills and attributes
that make him remarkable.

The first humanist mentioned is a friar of the Camadulese order, who
became that order's general in 1431. About him Lapo writes: "He is a man
endowed with a sanctity of life, a purity, such scruples, such learning, such
humanity, such an excellent abundance and eloquence of speaking ability,
that he can deservedly and most rightfully be judged a kind of phoenix in this
age of ours, a phoenix not born of men but fallen from heaven."[47] Lapo sees

[44] Ibid.
[45] Ibid.
[46] Ibid.
[47] Ibid., 155.

fit first of all to comment on the life of the person under discussion, taking for granted that these attributes (Ambrogio's sanctity, learning, and so on) will be of highest interest to his fellow interlocutor and of course to readers. Though Lapo does not mention Ambrogio's many scholarly accomplishments, it is worth singling out two: his work on the Church fathers and his Greek-to-Latin translation of the *Lives of the Philosophers* by Diogenes Laertius. The first preoccupation signaled an interest among many humanists not only in the secular classical past but also in Christian antiquity.[48] Ambrogio's Greek-to-Latin translations of much related to Greek early Church fathers opened up a world to that other side of antiquity, the Christian side, that would remain a part of learned culture for centuries. And his translations of Diogenes Laertius became a standby for Renaissance thinkers who, as ever, possessed and endless curiosity about the character of ancient philosophers.[49] For Laertius (who was writing in the third century CE), much like Lapo here, discussed first and foremost the "lives" of the ancient philosophers – meaning as much their style of life as their basic biographies – leaving for others analysis of their written texts.[50]

The other brief character sketches that Lapo offers are similar in nature. But it is worth looking at a few in detail, since they portray figures we will meet in more detail and since – more importantly – Lapo's descriptions allow us to reconstruct the ways that humanists "read" other humanists. We can see, in other words, how reputation remained a key form of currency in the social economy that life at the Papal Court represented.

Lapo notes, for example, the rank at which Flavio Biondo (1392–1463 and a key protagonist in the language debate, as we shall see) had arrived, alluding to his status as a papal secretary, noting also that he is "prudent and serious but also . . . learned and well versed in the writing of history. We are indeed in his debt, since he has undertaken to relate and recover the ancients' way of life and describe at length the deeds of our own times in works of history, leaving them behind for posterity."[51] It is noteworthy that Lapo highlights another part of Renaissance humanism, which we can term the "anthropological

---

[48] See Charles M. Stinger, *Humanism and the Church Fathers: Ambrogio Traversari (1386–1439) and Christian Antiquity in the Italian Renaissance* (Albany: State University of New York Press, 1977).

[49] See Marcello Gigante, "Ambrogio Traversari interprete di Diogene Laerzio," in Gian Carlo Garfagnini, ed., *Ambrogio Traversari nel VI centenario della nascita* (Florence: Olschki, 1988), 367–459.

[50] See Christopher S. Celenza, "What Counted as Philosophy in the Italian Renaissance? The History of Philosophy, the History of Science, and Styles of Life," *Critical Inquiry* 39 (2013), 367–401, at 391–92.

[51] Lapo, *De curiae commodis*, 155.

imagination." This strand of thought is a distinctive one that runs through the whole of Renaissance humanism. It is often tied to the humanist propensity – as they read Livy and other works regarding early Roman history – to attempt to understand ancient religion in all its seeming strangeness and difference. Biondo, who discovered Cicero's *Brutus* (a text whose rediscovery spurred the language debate), also wrote works of topography (whereby he attempted to list and explain the buried archaeological features of the city of Rome), and a great historical masterpiece – the first, really, to study in depth the period from the decline and fall of ancient Rome to his own day, thus in effect creating the concept of the Middle Ages.[52] Lapo notes his work with respect, before moving on to others.

One such figure of great interest is Leon Battista Alberti (1404–72), whom Lapo takes care to mention is roughly the same age. Alberti is known these days as perhaps the prototype of that semi-mythical character, the "Renaissance Man." Comfortable and eloquent in both Latin and the vernacular, Alberti wrote witty dialogues and works of serious architectural criticism, and to top it all off, was himself an accomplished and talented architect. Even at this relatively early age, something of Alberti's exceptional side seems to emerge in Lapo's awestruck description: "I so praise his genius that I would compare no one with him."[53] For the word translated here as "genius," Lapo uses the Latin *ingenium*, a word that enfolds the notion of skills, abilities, and most importantly inborn talent. Lapo goes on about Alberti: "For his genius is of this sort: to whichever area of study he puts his mind, he easily and quickly excels the others."[54] Even as the star of Alberti was already in the ascendant, as we can see, Lapo makes sure that his readers know that he, Lapo, is also part of this mix, that he too "belongs" among these luminaries currently at the papal court: "I am, then, on very close terms with these men who are so many, so learned, and so outstanding."[55]

Lapo winds up his survey of prominent curial intellectuals mentioning two who, though not present, nevertheless deserve mention: Francesco Filelfo (1398–81), Lapo's most important teacher, from whom he learned Greek and

---

[52] See Biondo Flavio, *Italy Illuminated*, ed. and tr. J. White (Cambridge, MA: Harvard University Press: 2005); Biondo Flavio, *Historiarum ab inclinatione Romanorum imperii decades* (Venice, 1483); Angelo Mazzocco and Marc Laureys, eds., *A New Sense of the Past: The Scholarship of Biondo Flavio (1392–1463)* (Leuven: Leuven University Press, 2015); Riccardo Fubini, "Biondo Flavio," in *Dizionario biografico degli italiani* 10 (Rome, 1968), 548–51; Denys Hay, *Flavio Biondo and the Italian Middle Ages* (Oxford: Oxford University Press, 1959).

[53] Lapo, *De curiae commodis*, 157.

[54] Ibid.

[55] Ibid.

whom he considered a mentor, and Leonardo Bruni. Both are described as "ornaments of learning and eloquence" and importantly as having "expanded and adorned these studies of ours with their vigilant labors."[56] It is taken for granted that "these studies" are, again, the *studia humanitatis*.

Much had changed in the three decades between Bruni's *Dialogues* and Lapo's *On the Benefits of the Curia*. Marginal Lapo could attempt, as he did, to become part of an "in-group" of humanists, a group whose intellectual, if not professional, standing depended on casting themselves as "outsiders." As Lapo repeatedly refers to "these studies of ours" and so on, he evinces this idea perfectly. Would he have succeeded in joining the innermost circles of the papal court? His untimely death robbed him, and us, of the chance to see. By this time Bruni had become a figure of great cultural capital, so much so that Lapo believed he needed to mention the Florentine chancellor, to associate himself symbolically with Bruni, despite Bruni's absence from the court.

Dialogues such as Bruni's and Lapo's dramatize then current cultural preoccupations, even as they offer insight into how, and in what social spaces, key debates occurred. No debate was more important in this respect than that over the status of the ancient Roman Latin language, for it enfolded concerns about history, self-expression, and the relation of the present to the past.[57] Its first, friendly salvos occurred between that very same Flavio Biondo whom Lapo mentioned and Leonardo Bruni. And the context was that of the papal court, which was resident in Florence at the time and served, as ever, as a center of animated intellectual exchange. It began as a lively conversation, not unlike the sort of "disputation" in which Salutati had urged his young colleagues to engage in Bruni's dialogue of some thirty years earlier. And, as some of these conversations tended to do, it was then memorialized in writing, in this case in a letter, which Biondo Flavio wrote to Bruni:

> Among the learned men of our age there is great discussion and indeed debate at which I have often been present, as to whether the Romans were accustomed to speak in the mother tongue, which is commonly used everywhere in our day by the unpolished and uneducated crowd, or whether, instead, they spoke by making use of "the grammatical art" – what we call "Latin."[58]

---

[56] Ibid., 159.

[57] On which see Tavoni; the literature cited in Celenza, "End Game"; and Maurizio Campanelli, "Languages," in Wyatt, ed., *The Cambridge Companion to the Italian Renaissance*, 139–63.

[58] Biondo, in Tavoni, 198: "Magna est apud doctos aetatis nostrae homines altercatio, et cui saepenumero interfuerim contentio, materno ne et passim apud rudem indoctamque multitudinem aetate nostra vulgato idiomate, an grammaticae artis usu, quod latinum appellamus, instituto loquendi more Romani orare fuerint soliti."

Biondo is precise, and he takes pains to locate a specific conversation that occurred among himself, Bruni, Antonio Loschi, Poggio Bracciolini, Cencio de' Rustici, and Andrea da Firenze (precisely the luminaries Lapo had mentioned in his star-struck account):

> If I remember correctly, Loschi and Cencio seemed to agree with you that the Romans possessed a style of speaking that was ordinary and common to the people, as in later ages. Because of this, even the most learned orators left to posterity what they called "orations." These were compositions that they had delivered in spoken form to the people, which they then, after quite a lot of labor, rendered into "grammatical" Latinity.[59]

Biondo makes several arguments supporting his notion that ancient Latin was a unitary language, spoken in more or less the same way as it was written. We hear in Cicero's *Orator* that there are essentially three registers of Latin discourse, or *oratio*.[60] *Oratio*, Cicero writes, should be neither "metrical [*numerosa*] like a poem, nor completely un-metrical, like the speech of the crowd."[61] *Oratio*, instead, falls between those two registers, somewhat rhythmic but not too much so, so that it does not appear on the surface to have been done on purpose; and it should not seem disconnected so that it appears "common and ordinary" (*pervagatum ac volgare*).[62] This set of propositions, for Biondo, represents the core of the matter.[63] Biondo observes, in other words, Cicero's recognition – an ancient recognition – of the existence of three registers of Latin. For Biondo, this element is one among a number of reasons that allow him to judge that Latin was one language, differently spoken and used according to context and social situation, but not so different as modern vernaculars are from Latin.

Biondo's base texts for his various assertions are Cicero's *Brutus* and *Orator*. Both became increasingly important for humanists after they were rediscovered in 1421 at Lodi.[64] From *Brutus*, Cicero's recounting in dialogue form of

---

[59] Ibid.: "Tecum enim, si recte memini, Luscus et Cintius sentire videbantur, vulgare quoddam et plebeium, ut posteriora habuerunt saecula, Romanis fuisse loquendi genus a litteris remotum, quo doctissimi etiam oratores apud populum illas dicerent orationes, quas postmodum multa lucubratione in grammaticam latinitatem redactas posteris reliquerunt."

[60] Cicero, *Orator*, in Cicero, *Brutus, Orator*, ed. and tr. G.L. Hendrickson and H.M. Hubbell (Cambridge, MA: Harvard University Press, 1962), sec. 195, p. 470.

[61] Ibid.

[62] Ibid., sec. 196, p. 470.

[63] Biondo, in Tavoni, 203: "Hic, Aretine clarissime, hic altum sunt mihi iacenda quaestionis propositae fundamenta."

[64] See Tavoni, 19–24; Martin McLaughlin, "Humanist Criticism of Latin and Vernacular Prose," in Alastair Minnis and Ian Johnson, eds., *The Cambridge History of Literary Criticism*, v. 2 (Cambridge: Cambridge University Press, 2005), 648–55; Timothy Kircher, "Landino,

different ancient orators and their styles, Biondo gathered that some ancients could speak well in public, even though they were not *literati*, meaning educated in literature and language. One example would be an orator named Curio, who according to Cicero in the *Brutus*, though he "knew nothing of literature," was considered by some the "third best speaker of his day" and spoke "not the worst Latin" because of what he had heard in his household growing up.[65] Biondo comments:

> If household usage has such an impact that without learning or literature it could make out of Curio someone who did not speak "the worst Latin," who used "rather elegant words" and who was the third best orator of the City, then it is not possible that the language he heard at home was *not* Latin.[66]

Biondo continues, going over Cicero's account of the two brothers, warriors, and Roman politicians: the Gracchi. Their mother Cornelia provided them with a high level of discourse at home. Addressing Bruni, Biondo writes: "You have heard that it makes a great difference whom one hears at home, with whom one speaks."[67] The example of the Florentines demonstrates this fact, since those who have been raised in the city of Florence are much more eloquent than people raised without. It was the same among the Romans, for Biondo. Those raised in the right way, even women (such as Cornelia and Laelia, the daughter of Cicero's mentor Laelius, among others) could achieve a high level of Latin discourse, even without specific literary training.[68]

There may have been different registers, for Biondo, but in the case of spoken orations we must concede, he argues, "that the words, as they were spoken, were Latin of the sort that we now call 'literate.'"[69] Given this circumstance, and given that there were audiences for both oratory and poetic theater, it must be the case that a broad swath of the population understood the language.

Alberti, and the Invention of the Neo-Vernacular," *Albertiana*, 19 (2016), 29–48, 30; and Remigio Sabbadini, *Le scoperte dei codici latini e greci ne' secoli XIV e XV*, 2 vols. (Florence: Sansoni, 1905–14; reprint edited by Eugenio Garin, Florence: Sansoni, 1967), 1: 99–100.

[65] Cicero, *Brutus*, sec. 210, p. 178.

[66] Biondo, in Tavoni, 205: "Si tantam itaque vim domesticus habebat usus, ut sine doctrina, sine litteris non pessime latine loquentem splendidioribus uti verbis et tertium urbis oratorem faceret Curionem, non latinus esse non potuit sermo ille domesticus."

[67] Ibid., 206: "Magni interesse audivisti, quod quisque domi audiat, quibuscum loquatur."

[68] Ibid., 206–7.

[69] Ibid., 208: "Constet vero primum inter nos necessarium est, sive grandibus, sive abiectis, sive dissipatis, sive coercitis ratione verbis oratum fuerit, verba orationum, dum pronunciarentur, fuisse Latina, qualia nunc dicimus litterata."

The case of theater is revealing, for Biondo, since the plays he has in mind (by ancient playwrights such as Plautus and Terence) were in verse. Again taking his point of departure from Cicero's *Orator*, Biondo reminds Bruni of Cicero's observation concerning the "natural" (meaning not artificial or rehearsed) nature of verse.[70] "In verse," Biondo writes, quoting Cicero, "the whole theater bursts out if one syllable is too short or too long."[71] Even if the audience cannot understand exactly what it is that is bothering them or why, nature itself has implanted in us the ability to judge both the quantities of syllables and the length of vowels.[72] Biondo lays emphasis on this point to buttress his case: the natural knowledge of verse shows that ancient Latin was unitary. People at all levels could understand it, even if what they took away from what they heard would obviously vary according to ability.

Biondo's closing argument, though short, is perhaps his most interesting of all, since it is there where he introduces the idea of a historical rupture. This notion of rupture and the concomitant if sometimes implicit foregrounding of historical change represent the basic undercurrent of the fifteenth-century debate on the Latin language. Even more, the language debate stands at the heart of what the Italian Renaissance was all about. The central question is: are "we moderns" truly different from the ancients we revere? Biondo phrases the issue in this way: "I see that I have one last problem to resolve: why is it, in what era, and because of what causes do I believe that we have exchanged what was among the ancients, as I have tried to show, a universal knowledge of Latin, for our current common language?"[73] Biondo's answer seems almost an afterthought to his other arguments, given its length. He recalls a passage from Cicero's *Brutus*, which given its importance is worth fleshing out more fully than Biondo himself does.

Cicero's interlocutor Pomponius had the floor in the dialogue. Discussing the importance of oratory, he suggested that the "orator's ground . . . and foundation, you see, is a diction that is correct and purely Latin." Those who earned a reputation for this level of Latinity garnered praise not because of "rules and theory but because of good usage [*rationis et scientiae, sed quasi bonae consuetudinis*]."[74] There had been a time, Pomponius went on, when almost

[70]   Cicero, *Orator*, secs. 173 and 183, pp. 452 and 460.
[71]   Biondo, in Tavoni, 210; Cicero, *Orator*, sec. 173, p. 452.
[72]   Biondo, in Tavoni, 210.
[73]   Ibid., 214 (punctuation slightly altered): "Extremam mihi restare video responsionem: qua ratione, quibus temporibus causisque factum credam, ut vulgaritatem hanc nostram cum universae multitudinis latinitate, quam ostendere conatus sum apud priscos fuisse, permutaverimus."
[74]   Cicero, *Brutus*, ed. G.L. Hendrickson (Cambridge, MA and London: Harvard University Press, 1962), p. 222, sec. 258: "Solum quidem, inquit ille, et quasi fundamentum oratoris

every Roman was naturally endowed with a reasonable level of Latinity, unless he had perchance spent much time away from Rome or if there were mitigating circumstances at home. Now, however, this situation no longer obtained. Moreover, in Athens and in Rome there was an influx of impure speakers, so that the time had arrived for a "purging of the language" [*expurgandus est sermo*] and a "set of theoretical arguments [*ratio*] that must be adhered to, almost as a proof that cannot change; nor should one employ that most easily degradable rule: custom."[75] The point is this: reading Cicero here, one could easily infer that even in antiquity, it was imaginable to create a theory of an immutable language subject to rules. It is also noteworthy that the desire for this process of freezing the language was connected to the assumption of a lost, imagined era of purity that could now be revived only with great effort.

This argument struck Biondo so much that it comes near the end of his treatise. Biondo paraphrases Cicero in this fashion: "You see that in the times that had preceded Cicero's era, those who either lived outside of Rome or who had something of the foreign within their homes, in a certain respect departed from the eloquence of Roman speech, so that they were tarnished by that foreignness."[76] If it is true that even in Cicero's day certain foreign traces could be perceived in the use of the Latin language, historical circumstances changed this situation immeasurably:

> But after the City of Rome was taken by Goths and Vandals and began to be inhabited by them, it was not only one or two men who were tarnished, but rather everyone who was polluted and indeed made deeply impure [*penitus sordidati*] by foreign speech. So it gradually happened that, in place of Roman Latinity, we have this common vernacular that has been mixed together with foreign Latinity [*barbarica*, i.e., *latinitate*], that has the character of something inauthentic.[77]

---

vides, locutionem emendatam et Latinam, cuius penes quos laus adhuc fuit, non fuit rationis aut scientiae, sed quasi bonae consuetudinis."

[75] Ibid.: "Confluxerunt enim et Athenas et in hanc urbem multi inquinate loquentes ex diversis locis. Quo magis expurgandus est sermo et adhibenda tamquam obrussa ratio, quae mutari non potest, nec utendum pravissima consuetudinis regula."

[76] Biondo, in Tavoni, 214: "Temporibus vides quae Ciceronis aetatem praecesserant illos qui aut extra Romam vixerant, aut Romae domesticam habuerant aliquam barbariem, a nitore locutionis romanae aliqualiter recessisse, et barbarie illa infuscatos fuisse."

[77] Ibid., 214–15: "Postea vero quam urbs a Gothis et Vandalis capta inhabitarique coepta est, non unus iam aut duo infuscati, sed omnes sermone barbaro inquinati ac penitus sordidati fuerunt; sensimque factum est, ut pro romana latinitate adulterinam hanc barbarica mixtam loquelam habeamus vulgarem."

Biondo soon thereafter signs off on his letter to Bruni, awaiting Bruni's response.

Yet in this last argument something important occurred in the Renaissance Latin language question, something that eventually, in its own subterraneous way, had an impact on the language question overall. Biondo introduced the notion of the historical evolution of language. It is true that he framed the question in terms of "foreignness" (*barbaries*) versus genuine Roman Latinity, so that the notion of a possible restoration of ancient authenticity was still implicitly thinkable. It is also true that this notion was present in medieval sources, most famously in the popular Isidore of Seville.[78] Yet the notion of historical change remained a touchstone of the debate in many fifteenth-century thinkers' discussions.

Bruni's letter of response is shorter than Biondo's query. Its tone reflects Bruni's clarity of mind, even as the letter reveals his views regarding the social functions of language. At the outset Bruni wants to clarify the question at issue, in terms of both its basic premises and its temporal limits. As to the issue itself:

> You think that, for the ancients, there was one and the same language for all, not one language that was a common vernacular and another that was a learned language. I, on the other hand, believe that, just as it is now, the common vernacular was distinct from the learned language.[79]

As to the temporal limits:

> It is also rather important, if you don't mind, that we delineate the question in such a way that it refers to a certain time and place. For when one says "for the ancients," one really is not designating either the time or the place with enough certainty. Let the question then, be the following: whether, in Rome, in the era of the poet Terence and of Cicero, the common people spoke in such a way as those whom we now say speak in a way that is "Latin" [*latine*] and "learned" [*litterate*] or whether there was one language for the crowd and another for those who were learned.[80]

---

[78] Isidore of Seville, *Etymologiae*, 2 vols., ed. W.M. Lindsay (Oxford: Oxford University Press, 1911, reprint 1971), 1: 1.9.1: "Latinas autem linguas quattuor esse quidam dixerunt, id est Priscam, Latinam, Romanam, Mixtam."

[79] Bruni, in Tavoni, 216: "Quaestio nostra in eo consistit, quod tu apud veteres unum eumdemque fuisse sermonem omnium putas, nec alium vulgarem, alium litteratum. Ego autem, ut nunc est, sic etiam tunc distinctam fuisse vulgarem linguam a litterata existimo."

[80] Ibid.: "Pressius quoque, si placet, ita circumscribamus, ut certo tempore locoque diffiniantur. Nam qui apud veteres dicit nec tempus nec locum satis certum designat. Sit igitur quaestio utrum Romae per Terentii poetae et M. Tullii tempora vulgus ita loquebatur ut loquuntur hi quos nunc latine litterateque loqui dicimus, vel alius fuerit vulgi sermo, alius litteratorum."

Bruni's arguments are telling, as he boils Biondo's assertions down to their essential points.

As to oratory, Bruni suggests that when it came to public governmental bodies such as the senate and the courts, the audience was primarily composed of learned men, so that Biondo's arguments do not apply. When it came to the assembly (the *concio*), which included both the learned and the unlearned, even there the orator was mainly addressing not the "bakers and gladiators" but rather "those who were accustomed to governing the republic."[81] The lower orders understood what was going on in the same way that today, Bruni suggests, the unlearned understand the Mass: vaguely.[82]

Bruni makes another point with respect to oratory that touches on the importance of written culture and the way that oral composition does not represent a definitive version of a speech:

> We should not let the fact escape us that the orators themselves wrote their orations down in a manner different from the way they spoke ... It is not that they wrote down something that was completely different but rather that they wrote down what they had said in a way that was more adorned and more elegant. The result was that what they said in the assembly in words that were, perhaps, common and open and thus easy to understand, are read in written form in a way that is more polished [*limatius*] and more compressed [*contractius*].[83]

For Bruni, learned orators in the senate and court were speaking in a fully literate way. Yet even in the assembly, they directed their words to those in the know [*ad scientes*], allowing the unlearned then present in the assembly to understand the discourse as the common people today understand the Latin Mass.[84] Later, when they wrote their speeches down in prose, they polished them up and made sure they were of the highest quality possible.

---

[81] Ibid., 217: "Itaque non ad pistores tantum et lanistas, sed multo magis ad eos qui in reipublicae gubernatione versabantur, et quorum intererat quid populus decerneret, orator loquebatur."

[82] Ibid.: "pistores vero et lanistae et huiusmodi turba sic intelligebant oratoris verba ut nunc intelligunt Missarum solemnia."

[83] Ibid. (punctuation slightly modified): "Nam illud nos latere non debet, oratores ipsos aliter scripsisse orationes suas quam dixerant, quod et apud Graecos et apud Latinos exploratissimum est; non quod diversum scriberent, sed quod ornatius et comptius id ipsum quod dixerant litteris mandabant, ut quaedam in concione dicta verbis forsan vulgates et apertis et ad intelligentiam accomodatis, limatius postea contractiusque scripta legantur."

[84] Ibid.: "In senatu enim et iudiciis ad scientes litteras loquebantur [*sc. oratores*] litterate, in concionibus vero etiam ad scientes."

When it came to the issue of poetry and the audience's natural comprehension of meter in theatrical productions, Bruni could not be clearer: "You think the crowd came together to *understand* the poet's works. I on the other hand think they came to watch the plays."[85] The plays always included great spectacle, with the use of gestures, masks, and music. Even the prefaces to the works of Plautus and Terence clue us in to the extensive use of visual resources, as they describe the play's action and scenery.[86] In the end, "Nothing of the poet's work and no part of their drama was relevant to the speech of the common people. The common people did not seek an understanding of the words but rather the spectacle of the presentations."[87]

Bruni believes, essentially, in a fixed language system, tied to the inevitable divisions of society. On the one hand, there is the elite: its members rule, are learned enough to govern actively in an oratorical culture, and in public situations transmit messages fundamentally only to each other. On the other, there are the masses: they are subject to rule, interested in spectacle, and able to comprehend complex argumentation only within certain limits.

Bruni's key exemplar of this lower community is represented not by "bakers and gladiators," as earlier, but by women:

> I ask you, Flavio, since you are a man who is both learned and well polished when it comes to literature, as well as those who agree with you: can you really get it in your head to believe that nursemaids, little women, and this sort of crowd were born back then in such a way that without the aid of teachers they comprehended things that we understand with so much help from teachers and with so much practice? And that they did so in the same way that those who speak in the way we term "Latin" and "learned" understand such things? And that they understood the poets' comedies without anyone teaching them previously?

Bruni answers his own rhetorical question: "It is utterly absurd to think so."[88]

Part of the reason for the existence of these diverse language communities has to do with the Latin language's complexity, the full extent of which

---

[85] Ibid.: "Tu enim turbam convenisse putas ad carmina poetae intelligenda, ego autem convenisse puto ad ludos scenicos spectandos."

[86] Ibid., 217–18.

[87] Ibid.: "Nichil igitur poetae, nichil eorum fabulae ad sermonem vulgi pertinent. Non enim intellectum verborum, sed spectaculum ludorum vulgus sequebatur."

[88] Ibid., 218–19 (punctuation slightly altered): "Tu ne quaeso, Flavi, cum sis vir doctus ac litteris expolitus, vel alii qui tecum sentiunt, animum inducere potestis ut credatis nutrices et mulierculas et huiusmodi turbam ita tunc nasci ut quae nos tot magistris, tanto usu vix tenemus, illi nullis magistris assequerentur, ut eo modo loquerentur, quemadmodum hi qui latine litterateque loquuntur, intelligerentque poetarum comoedias nullo prius eos docente? Profecto valde absurdum est ita credere."

simply could not, in Bruni's eyes, be grasped by those without formal education, since it was not a natural language. Bruni uses his example of "little women" to clinch his argument. This fact is revealing. It is a truism to state it, but it is no less noteworthy that, like most people in the West before the twentieth century, and like many in the world today, Bruni lived in a society with strong gender separation. Men and women simply did not interact to the extent that they do today, and for Bruni it was unimaginable to conceive of any but the most elite women taking part in the fundamentally public style of education that Latin entailed. The exceptional status of his letter to Battista Montefeltro, examined earlier, only serves as further proof of this notion.

Bruni goes on: vernaculars and Latin are fundamentally different. Unlike the vernacular, Latin is inflected, its verbs decline, and its words have a wide variety of meanings. "Fero [I bring]," Bruni writes, "is a verb and from it" one has the principal parts "tuli [I have brought]" and "latum [having been brought]" and their derivative correlates "sustuli [I have borne]" and "sublatum [having been borne]."[89] Both *abfuit* and *defuit* designate that someone was absent, but the first carries with it a positive connotation, the second a negative one[90]: "I ask you, did the little women, nursemaids, and the illiterate common people really say these things, things that even we who are learned can barely say?"[91]

As to the examples adduced by Biondo via Cicero, to the effect that there were some in ancient Rome who could speak well but who were known not to have any literary training, Bruni argues that those were exceptions.[92] He does concede that having literate people in one's household would have its effects: "I admit it: if relatives and servants are learned [*literati*] and mothers are elegant [*elegantes*] they can aid in the eloquence of their sons."[93] Bruni goes on to commend the ability of contemporary Roman women to speak well, in a way that is purer than Roman men. Still, he is careful to point out that these Roman women of today are speaking a *vernacular*. "It is not that they are inflecting the cases of their nouns, varying their verb forms, or saying word-endings in a literate way, but rather that they pour forth with a speech that is pure, clean, not the least

---

[89] Ibid., 219: "*Fero* verbum est, a quo *tuli, latum, sustuli, sublatum.*"

[90] Ibid.: "*Abfuit* et *defuit* duo sunt, quorum alterum laudem, alterum vituperationem significat."

[91] Ibid.: "Haec ne quaeso mulierculae et nutrices et vulgus illiteratum dicent, quae nos literati vix dicere valemus?"

[92] Ibid., 220.

[93] Ibid.: "Fateor: parentes enim literati, et servi, matres etiam si elegantes sunt, adiuvare eloquentiam filiorum possunt."

foreign-seeming."[94] In the same vein, Bruni goes on: "Even the vernacular has its own excellence, as one sees in Dante and certain others who speak in a pure fashion."[95]

What Bruni will not, indeed cannot, concede is that Latin ever was a vernacular, a common language spoken by all and learned primarily by daily interactions, with schooling existing only for polish. It is a telling fact that the only one of Biondo's arguments that Bruni does not answer is Biondo's last major one: that the language spoken at Rome underwent historical evolution, an evolution that became decisive after the barbarian invasions. In many ways Bruni remained tied to the high and late medieval notion that Latin was a *lingua artificialis*, a language of craft, which possessed, notionally, its own set of invariable rules (wrongly employed and imperfectly discovered as those rules might have been, in Bruni's view, by his medieval predecessors).

Bruni, in this latter respect, was much like his mentor and predecessor as chancellor of Florence, Coluccio Salutati (1331–1406). In the last year of his life, Salutati found himself fending off the implicit and explicit attacks launched by the Dominican Giovanni Dominici (1356–1420). Dominici, in his *Lucula Noctis*, had not so much condemned the study of ancient pagan authors as warned against excesses, arguing that students who devoted too much time to pagan authors might lose sight of true Christianity's essential messages.[96] Salutati, in his unfinished response, stressed that Latin, as *grammatica*, had been an invention of ancient pagan thinkers.[97] Early Christians had profited from this invention (as they had from the invention of Greek), since it allowed them to spread their message among varied constituencies in a uniform way. Latin as such represented the vessel of a foundational culture, which for Salutati was Christian. His main criticism of Dominici was that an ignorance of Latin on the part of the religious makes them unable fully to understand early Christian texts.[98] For Bruni as for Salutati, Latin was also the

---

[94] Ibid., 221: "Non quod casus inflecterent, aut verba variarent ac terminarent literate, sed quod purum et nitidum ac minime barbarum sermonem infunderent."

[95] Bruni, in Tavoni, 221: "Nam et habet vulgaris sermo commendationem suam, ut apud Dantem poetam et alios quosdam emendate loquentes apparet." Cf. Bruni, *Schriften*, 61: "Ciascuna lingua ha la sua perfezione e suo suono, e suo parlare limato e scientifico;" and McLaughlin, *Literary Imitation*, 93.

[96] See Edmund Hunt, ed., *Iohannis Dominici Lucula noctis* (Notre Dame, IN, 1940).

[97] Coluccio Salutati, *Epistolario*, 4 vols. in 5, ed. F. Novati (Rome: Istituto storico italiano, 1891–1911) 4: 216, as cited in Rizzo, *Ricerche*, 21: "An dicere potest aliquis litteras atque grammaticam inventionem non esse Gentilium et, si prohibentur Christianis ista studia, non etiam ipsam grammaticam inhiberi?" See also Rizzo, *Ricerche*, 15–27 for an overview.

[98] Coluccio Salutati, *Epistolario*, 4: 220, as cited in Rizzo, *Ricerche*, 22: "Quo fit ut latine loqui nesciant [*i.e.*, religiosi] et ipsas sacras litteras et dicta doctorum ad intelligentiam non capescant."

foundation of culture. Yet Bruni neither tied Latin's centrality to Christianity nor did he make pronouncements about the invention of Latin. But the main message, regarding Latin's status, is similar: Latin exists (now as it had in the ancient past) as a uniform language of culture, to be employed by the leaders of that culture as an instrument. By this point in his life and career, Bruni had little time for detailed questions such as this. And he represented, in effect, the establishment, convinced as only an insider can be that leadership, cultural and otherwise, remained the province of a relatively small elite.

It is true to say that Bruni was interested in widening the vernacular impact of classicism or, rather, in widening appreciation of the sorts of virtues that he believed the correct appreciation of the classical world could teach. As James Hankins has put it, Bruni's *Lives* of Dante and Petrarch "can be seen as efforts to use traditional vernacular literary genres to spread among the Latinless the civic ideals to whose elaboration and propagation Bruni dedicated the last thirty years of his life."[99] Not only that, but a number of Bruni's own works were translated into the vernacular, and he even composed orations in the vernacular on more than one occasion to help the classicizing ideals he promulgated reach wider audiences.[100] Yet, for Bruni, there was no question that these vernacular efforts were vehicles for the transmission of messages whose full import could only be generated, appreciated, and lent an air of permanence in Latin. Soon, however, the fifteenth-century debate over language took another turn, one that in retrospect seems momentous but in the day-to-day realm in which it emerged belongs to the agonistic rough and tumble of Florentine cultural life.

---

[99] James Hankins, "Humanism in the Vernacular: The Case of Leonardo Bruni," in Christopher S. Celenza and Kenneth Gouwens, eds., *Humanism and Creativity: Essays in Honor of Ronald G. Witt* (Leiden: Brill, 2006), 11–29, at 14.
[100] Ibid.

6

WHO OWNS CULTURE? CLASSICISM, INSTITUTIONS, AND THE VERNACULAR

A ROUND THE SAME TIME AS BRUNI'S EPISTOLARY MUSINGS AND rooted in the same lively conversations that were taking place in and around the papal court, came the intervention into the language debate of Leon Battista Alberti, in the preface to Book Three of his *Della famiglia*, which dates from 1437. Alberti was part of a new generation. Born in 1404, he was emerging in the 1430s as a dazzling new talent, as Lapo's short profile indicated.[1] Alberti, too, represented another "outsider." In his case, it was not a literary affectation.

The illegitimate child of an exiled Florentine aristocrat, Alberti had early training in literature and then university education in law (in Bologna). By the 1430s, when Lapo encountered him at the papal court, then resident in Florence, the citywide ban on the Alberti family had lifted, as we learn from the dedication to the Italian version of Alberti's *On Painting*, where he writes of his wonderment at Florence after returning from exile. This work, *On Painting*, is a masterpiece. A summing up of new Renaissance trends in art making, such as perspective; an intriguing meditation on how painters represent natural phenomena such as color; and, most of all, an affirmation that genius was not dead, that new art, new literature, and new forms of knowledge could exist, and that they could do so in a way independent of antiquity: *On Painting* was all these things and more. Alberti opens the dedication recalling a former belief: "I used to wonder and to grieve that so many outstanding and divine arts and sciences . . . today seem almost completely lost."[2]

---

[1] Most recently, with ample bibliography, see Martin McLaughlin, *Leon Battista Alberti: La vita, l'umanesimo, le opere letterarie* (Florence: Olschki, 2016); and Timothy Kircher, *Living Well in Renaissance Italy: The Virtues of Humanism and the Irony of Leon Battista Alberti* (Tempe: MRTS, 2012).

[2] Leon Battista Alberti, *De pictura* (redazione volgare), ed. Lucia Bertolini (Florence: Polistampa, 2011), proemio.

Then, in that very same dedication, after discussing his exile, he writes:

> I have come to understand that in many men, but most of all in you, my dear
> Filippo [this would be Filippo Brunelleschi, the eventual architect of the
> Dome of Florence's cathedral] and in our very close friend Donato the
> sculptor [Donatello] and in those others, like Nencio [Lorenzo Ghiberti],
> Luca [Luca della Robbia], and Masaccio, there exists a genius for anything
> worthy of praise, a genius for which they should not be ranked behind
> anyone famous in antiquity in these arts. So I have observed that the power
> to attain every sort of praise worthy of its salt lies in our own industry and
> diligence no less than in the gifts bestowed by nature or the time in which we
> live.[3]

Three noteworthy sentiments emerge, all of which can help frame Alberti's
participation in the language debate.

First, Alberti presents his own thinking as an evolution. Having heard
what others have been saying, he has felt small compared to the ancients
whom his age is so keen to rediscover. But then, so the thinking goes, he
simply opened his eyes when he returned to Florence. Doing so, he realized
that his contemporaries had nothing to be ashamed of, even in comparison to
antiquity. Second, there is the foregrounding of Florence and the remarkable
way it has evolved in the years in which the Alberti family has been gone.
True, this is a dedication and thus inclined to favor the recipient,
Brunelleschi, and his home city, Florence. Still, the flourishing of the arts
in Florence could not be denied and seemed remarkable, especially to
Alberti, who had been away a long time. Finally, this dedication served, as
mentioned, to open the Italian edition of this text, in 1436. Scholars have
debated whether Alberti wrote the Italian or Latin version first, with Rocco
Sinisgalli maintaining that Alberti wrote the Tuscan version first, attending
thereafter to the Latin version over a number of years.[4] Absolute priority,
however, is less important than the fact that he considered them both as part
of the same intellectual and cultural universe.

This Latin-Italian bilingualism is important. To understand Alberti, it is
crucial: the need to have an Italian version in circulation highlighted his
belief, which would become ever more persistent with time, that the vernacular could serve as an adequate vehicle of culture, alongside and sometimes
instead of Latin. This bilingualism also signals something deeper. Simply put,

---

[3] Ibid.

[4] See Rocco Sinisgalli, *Il nuovo "De pictura" di Leon Battista Alberti – The New "De pictura" of
Leon Battista Alberti* (Rome: Kappa, 2006); Sinisgalli, "Introduction," in Leon
Battista Alberti, *On Painting: A New Translation and Critical Edition*, tr. Rocco Sinisgalli
(Cambridge: Cambridge University Press, 2011), 3–14.

there emerged an ever-larger market, as it were, for classicism, a market that included highly trained humanists such as Bruni and Alberti but that also included others: merchants, say, who did not have the time and inclination to work through a Latin text but still wanted to read Cicero's orations, or to hear about the exploits of Julius Caesar, or to take life lessons from any number of ancient sources, fashionable as these sources had now become. Thinkers translated a number of Aristotle's texts into the vernacular. The *Ethics* experienced a revival after Bruni's new Latin translation, which itself spurred new Italian translations and a new readership.[5] In the course of the fifteenth century, thinkers used Aristotle, Cicero, and others to justify the preoccupations and predilections of a new, confident mercantile class.

To see both the range – and the limitations – of vernacular classicism, we can take the case (to open a short parenthesis) of Benedetto Cotrugli (1416–69), a merchant from Croatia who settled in Italy and has been credited with the perfection of double-entry bookkeeping. In the middle of the fifteenth century he penned a treatise *On Trade and on the Perfect Merchant* (*Della mercatura e del mercante perfetto*). There he suggested the following:

> Trade, when properly and honestly managed, is not only very fruitful, but also extremely necessary to the government of human communities, and therefore a most noble activity. Cicero said that "merchants are the nerves of the state," by which he meant merchants who were honest, experienced, and learned. For the same reason, Aristotle wanted trade to be one of the main components of the republic.[6]

The text Cotrugli had in mind was Cicero's powerful oration in favor of the Manilian law (*Pro lege manilia*), where Cicero had actually said that tax revenues were the sinews of the state and that those who collected them – the "publicans," who were, in addition to tax collectors, men who engaged in mercantile activity – should be considered the basis of all other societal orders.[7]

---

[5] See Hankins, "Humanism in the Vernacular," 26; David Lines, "Aristotle's Ethics in the Renaissance," in Jon Miller, ed., *The Reception of Aristotle's "Ethics"* (Cambridge: Cambridge University Press, 2012), 171–93; Lines, "Beyond Latin in Renaissance Philosophy: A Plea for New Critical Perspectives," *Intellectual History Review*, 25 (2015), 133–61; Andrea Rizzi and Eva del Soldato, "Latin and Vernacular in Quattrocento Florence and Beyond: An Introduction," *I Tatti Studies in the Italian Renaissance* 16 (2013), 231–42; Brian Maxson, *The Humanist World of Renaissance Florence* (Cambridge: Cambridge University Press, 2013).

[6] Benedetto Cotrugli, *Della mercatura* (Brescia, 1602), 7–8, cit. and tr. Eugenio Refini, "Aristotile in parlare materno," *I Tatti Studies* (2013), 311–41, 317.

[7] Cicero, *Pro lege manilia*, 7.17 (in Cicero, *Pro lege manilia. Pro Caecina. Pro Rabirio Perduellionis* ed. and tr. H. Grose Hodge [Cambridge, MA: Harvard University Press, 1927], p. 28): "Etenim, si vegtigalia nervos esse rei publicae semper duximus, eum certe ordinem, qui exercet illa, firmamentum ceterorum ordinum recte esse dicemus."

As to Aristotle, the text to which Cotrugli pointed was the *Politics*, most obviously, where Aristotle does indeed mention that merchants and trades-men are necessary for the state, though Aristotle also contributes to what was and would be precisely the sort of anti-mercantile prejudice against which Cotrugli and others tried to argue. The truth is that Aristotle thinks that a variety of occupations are necessary to a well-functioning state. But only those people who partake in what he calls *arête*, a word often translated as "virtue," but which we can better understand as "excellence," can govern. Possessing excellence, or true virtue, is a matter of individual development, something tied essentially to self-cultivation and limiting one's own beha-vior. Tradesmen are acquirers of wealth, and to the acquisition of wealth there is no limit.[8] Indeed Aristotle goes so far as to say, "in the most nobly constituted, and the one that possesses men who are just absolutely, and not merely relatively to the principle of the constitution, the citizens must not lead the lives of artisans or tradesmen, for such a life is ignoble and inimical to excellence."[9] This is not to say that he condemns wealth. On the contrary, one thing many fifteenth-century thinkers prized about Aristotle was that he recognized that wealth, if held moderately and exercised prudently, could have a beneficial function in society. Wealth allowed one to exercise the virtue of liberality, to help the poor, to keep the machine of the state well oiled by managing one's own household self-sufficiently.[10]

There will be more to say about the pursuit of virtue and the way the rising use of the vernacular intersected with that enterprise. But to come back to the little-known Benedetto Cotrugli: if his quotations were inexact, the underlying dynamic in both cases was more important. You could find ancient sources that gave value to your chosen style of life – in this case that of a merchant – and you did not have to be a trained scholar to do so. Classicism (loose and sometimes, as here, error prone and unsophisticated) was becoming one important way to advertise and solidify one's own place in the world. Classicism served as what we can call "cultural" capital. And if it had to be addressed in the vernacular, then so be it.

To return to Alberti (and to close that parenthesis), his own participation in the language debate represents another crucial step in legitimizing the vernacular. However, in contrast to the example of Cotrugli, Alberti's intervention shows, more than anything else and despite his surface

[8] Aristotle, *Politics*, ed. and tr. Horace Rackham (Cambridge, MA: Harvard University Press, 1944), 1.3, 1257b, pp. 44–46.
[9] Ibid., 7.9, 1328b35–43, p. 574.
[10] See Hans Baron, *In Search of Florentine Civic Humanism: Essays on the Transition from Medieval to Modern Thought*, 2 vols. (Princeton: Princeton University Press, 1988), 1: 158–257.

intentions, the importance of Latin. To be more precise, it reveals the way any positive evolution in the realm of Tuscan had to be accompanied by a consciousness of the importance of Latin.

At the center of Alberti's theories is recognition of historical change linked to a focus on the utility of discourse to society. He makes no bones about his dissatisfaction with the state of the language question in what is, on balance, one of his most famous and lasting works, *On the Family* (*Libri della famiglia*) – famous now, that is, since the work only circulated in manuscript in the fifteenth century and was not printed until the nineteenth century.[11] The work is a dialogue in the vernacular, structured in four books, which were substantially complete by 1440. Alberti takes pains to outline how a household should be run, a topic that covers everything from education and marriage to finance and children. In the dedication to the third book, Alberti takes on the language question directly and gives arguments as to why he is writing in the vernacular. Unlike Bruni, Alberti addresses the historical argument that Biondo had earlier put forward. Why was it that the Latin language fell into disuse? According to Alberti, "Italy was occupied and possessed more than once by various peoples: Gauls, Goths, Vandals, Lombards, and other similarly barbarous ones who were extremely harsh."[12] Amid invasions and to facilitate communication among different language communities, Latin speakers learned other languages and the newly arrived peoples learned Latin, though the foreigners learned Latin, "I believe, with many barbarisms and corruption in the pronunciation. Because of this mixture our language, which once was quite cultivated and refined, gradually became rough and spoiled."[13]

Alberti's disagreement with Bruni becomes clear as he goes on:

[11] See Leon Battista Alberti, *I libri della famiglia*, eds. Ruggiero Romano and Alberto Tenenti, new ed. Francesco Furlan (Turin: Einaudi, 1994); I cite later from Alberti, "Proemio al III dei *Libri de familia*," in Patota, 3–12.

[12] Alberti, "Proemio," in Patota, 6: "Fu Italia piú volte occupata e posseduta da varie nazioni: Gallici, Goti, Vandali, Longobardi, e altre simili barbare e molto asprissime genti." See Patota, 6, n.18 on the meanings of "nazioni" and "genti" as "peoples."

[13] Alberti, "Proemio," in Patota: 6–7: "Onde per questa mistura di dí in dí insalvatichí e viziossi la nostra prima cultissima ed emendatissima lingua." Alberti does not continue with this argument in the way that Pietro Bembo later did in his *Prose della volgar lingua*, whereby the Italian vernacular was born of the interchange between natives and barbarians; Pietro Bembo, *Prose della volgar lingua*, ed. Carlo Dionisotti (Turin: UTET, 1966), 86: "Del come, non si può errare a dire che, essendo la romana lingua e quelle de' Barbari tra sè lontanissime, essi a poco a poco della nostra ora une ora altre voci, e queste troncamente e imperfettamente pigliando, e noi apprendendo similmente delle loro, se ne formasse in processo di tempo e nascessene una nuova, la quale alcuno odore e dell'una e dell'altra ritenesse, che questa volgare è, che ora usiamo."

Here I cannot agree with those who, wondering at this great loss [of the Latin language], argue that in those days and even before in Italy there was always this one common language, such as we employ today. They go on to say that they cannot believe that in those days women knew things that, today, are difficult and obscure even for very learned men to understand and who thus come to the conclusion that the language in which the learned wrote back then was almost an art and an invention of the schools, that was generally but not thoroughly understood by many.[14]

Alberti offers a markedly different theory here from that expressed by Bruni, especially in so far as he differs from the notion, as he puts it, that even ancient Latin was "almost an art and an invention of the schools [*una quasi arte e invenzione scolastica*]."

If one ponders the significance in Alberti's Tuscan of the word *arte*, the associations that come to mind are revealing. The word had the standard Latinate resonance, that of "craft," easily leading one to think of Latin as a *lingua artificialis*, a notion against which Alberti is arguing here. It is worth noting that the word *arte* also meant "guild" in Alberti's day. Here one observes Alberti's lifelong sense of being an outsider, one who always objected to the tendency of people to gather into groups, a practice that then led them to lead a life that was unexamined, conditioned more by their association with a group than with a tendency to seek individual distinction.[15] His self-expression here is of a piece with his earlier opinion in *On Painting*: everyone is saying that we have and are nothing compared to the brilliant Greco-Roman ancients, but this is untrue. Open your eyes and ears, and you will see and hear that there exist art, language, and philosophy available that are front rank and that can stand on their own as valid. If Bruni's *Dialogues*, back in 1405, represented the concerns and priorities of a new generation trying to get beyond that of Salutati's day, here, in the person of Alberti, we see the struggle of another generation, this one trying to integrate paradigms but then to move beyond them.

---

[14] Alberti, "Proemio," in Patota: 7: "Né a me qui pare da udire coloro, e quali di tanta perdita maravigliandosi, affermano in que' tempi e prima sempre in Italia essere stata questa una qual oggi adoperiamo lingua commune, e dicono non poter credere che in que' tempi le femmine sapessero quante cose oggi sono in quella lingua latina molto a' bene dottissimi difficile e oscure, e per questo concludono la lingua in quale scrissero e dotti essere una quasi arte e invenzione scolastica piú tosto intesa che saputa da molti."

[15] A tendency evident in his autobiography; see Leon Battista Alberti, *Autobiografia e altre opere latine*, eds. Loredana Chines and Andrea Severi (Milan: Rizzoli, 2012), 64–103; and Riccardo Fubini and Anna Menci Gallorini, "L'autobiografia di Leon Battista Alberti: Studio e edizione," *Rinascimento* n.s.12 (1972), 21–78.

So intent was Alberti on defining the terms of this new generation that, with the patronage of Piero de' Medici (the son of Cosimo de' Medici, Florence's greatest patron), he arranged for a competition to be held in 1441 in Florence.[16] The competition, poetic in nature, revolved around the theme of "true friendship." Prospective competitors were asked to submit a poem on the topic. The key factor: the submissions were to be in the vernacular, Italian, rather than Latin. The competition goes by the name of *Certame coronario*, an Italian phrase that means, loosely, "contest for the crown." But both words have Latin resonances. *Certame* in Italian is a direct descendant of the Latin *certamen*, a word that appears in Virgil's seventh eclogue, a poem that details the singing contest between two mythical ancient shepherds, Thyrsis and Corydon. And *coronario* in Italian is related to the Latin *corona*, or "crown," that signifies the "crown," usually of laurel, offered to poets laureate. In other words, the idea was to bring the vernacular into the orbit of classicizing symbols, to recognize the vernacular as a legitimate and serious vehicle of poetic prowess, and to have it all happen publicly, so that the ritual enactment of this competition might confer even more prestige on the enterprise as a whole.

The papal court was then resident in Florence. The cultural prestige of this most ancient Christian institution seemed at the time to merge with Florence's own, increasingly established status as the leading city in the new culture of the Renaissance. It was natural therefore that ten leading members of the papal court should serve as judges for the competition and, moreover, that the site of the contest be Florence's spiritual and religious center, the cathedral, now surmounted by the dome of Alberti's friend and object of admiration, Brunelleschi. How disappointing it must have been that the judges – having heard all the competitors – declined to offer a prize. The reason? No entry was deemed singularly worthy – the judges said that four deserved the crown equally, so that they decided to give it to no one. Underneath the judges' unwillingness to award anyone the crown was the question of language. It was as if something written in the unstable vernacular could never compete with Latin's permanence. Not even when it came to something so all embracing as the topic of friendship; not even when several leading citizens participated (among them Benedetto Accolti, a future chancellor of Florence); not even when a Medici was willing to sponsor the whole event.[17]

[16] See Guglielmo Gorni, "Storia del Certame coronario," *Rinascimento* n.s. 12 (1972), 135–81; and Lucia Bertolini, ed., *De vera amicitia: I testi del primo Certame coronario* (Modena: Franco Cosimo Panini, 1993).

[17] For Accolti's participation, see Gorni, 161; Robert Black, *Benedetto Accolti and the Florentine Renaissance* (Cambridge: Cambridge University Press, 1985), 44–45, 51–52, and 68–69; and Bertolini, 111–39, 295–333.

Alberti wound up responding, when all was said and done, in two ways, one slightly more constructive than the other. As to the first, there is an angry letter to the judges, once thought anonymous but now deemed to be by Alberti himself. He begins sarcastically: "The plebeians and commoners of Florence salute you like men, O most noble apostolic secretaries."[18] In it, he sets out the manner in which the contest had been conceived – and, indeed, accepted – "as something useful for Florence's young people, something worthy of our homeland, and as something, as well, to which everyone has offered their praise."[19] He goes on to suggest that they had, initially, accepted the terms of the competition (so that, in Alberti's implication, they could be seen as reneging on their promise as judges). Since many of the poems had already circulated even beyond Florence and been judged eloquent by learned men, how can the following be the case?

> It is only among you that we hear there are those who ... say that it is unworthy for someone speaking the vernacular to compete with someone learned in Latin [*literatissimo*] and that it is for this reason first of all that these competitions had to be forbidden. Indeed we just can't believe that among some of you most learned men there might be such ineptitude, especially given that we have heard you commonly say things like "we are all born of Jove, and we all buy the same salt."[20]

Alberti begins, at this point, to tighten the screws, rhetorically speaking, expressing a sentiment that was in the air, when he suggests that, after all, "it is a common opinion among all prudent men that virtue, rather than fortune, is that which ennobles us."[21] This opinion had been – indeed, was being – expressed right around 1440 by Poggio Bracciolini, himself one of the querulous secretaries, so that Alberti's letter here offers a sly dig at Poggio, whom we will come to know better in a later context.[22]

---

[18] Alberti, "Protesta," in Patota, 42–52, at 42: "La plebe et i vulgari fiorentini vi saluta come huomini, molto generosissimi segretarii apostolici."

[19] Ibid., 43: "che fosse cosa utile alla nostra gioventù, cosa degna alla patria nostra, cosa ancora lodata presso a tutte le genti?"

[20] Ibid., 46: "Solo tra voi sentiamo essere chi vitupera questa principiata nostra laude, e dice essere cosa indegna che uno vulgare con uno nobilissimo literatissimo contenda, e per questo in prima doversi vietare questi certami. Nollo crediamo che tra alcuni di voi, huomini dottissimi, sia tanto ineptia, sendo in voi questo comune detto che tutti siamo da Giove, e tutti comperiamo il sale tanto l'uno quant' e l'altro."

[21] Ibid.: "essendo comune sentenzia di tutti e prudenti che la virtù, non la fortuna, fia quella che noi nobilita."

[22] See Poggio Bracciolini, *La vera nobilitate*, ed. Davide Canfora (Roma: Salerno, 1999) for the text. Poggio announced his work in a 1440 letter to Francesco Pizolpasso, archbishop of Milan (with whom Bruni had been in contact about his *Ethics* translation); see Poggio, *Lettere*, 2: 359–62.

The angry letter veers into more interesting territory when Alberti brings antiquity into the picture. His charge is that the judges' fetishizing of all things ancient has led them to misconstrue antiquity itself. Alberti says, in a passage worthy of extended quotation:

> If there is anyone who should persist in his critiques, we will ask: was this really always the habit of those ancients whom you put forward, indeed whom you favor in every single word and deed, to such an extent that you like nothing that does not, in some fashion, savor of antiquity? And we will ask whether, in those times, one could find men who were most noble of character and so very learned – and men who had ears that were, shall we say, so very delicate as yours? And we will ask whether, when Plautus appeared on stage covered in flour, with calloused hands, those Latin "princes" turned their noses up at him, whether, indeed, they could even stand the smell of the bakery where that poet toiled to make ends meet?[23]

Alberti's implicit answer is, of course, "yes." His point is that Plautus, who was believed (owing to the ancient biographical tradition) to have worked in a flour mill to support himself, is nonetheless venerated, now, as a key Latin playwright.[24] But in Plautus's own day, he was – to recall the beginning of Alberti's letter here – a "plebeian and commoner." Alberti suggests that there is simply no way, if you look closely at Plautus's life and origins, that he can be seen in his own context as someone who came from an elevated rank of society, someone who would have stood apart by writing in a language different from that which he and his peers spoke day to day, someone who wrote in a secondary language. In other words, Plautus wrote in his own mother tongue.

The most pungent critique follows, as Alberti continues in his imagined dialogue with his elitist, self-satisfied counterparts:

> And we will say: what sort of "humanities" is it, my good man, that teaches you to look down on someone who dedicates himself to virtue, who dedicates himself to things that will help his fellow citizens, to things by

---

[23] Alberti, "Protesta," in Patota, 46–47: "E se pur fusse chi perseverasse vituperandolo, il domanderemo se questo fu usato costume sempre presso agli antichi, quali voi tanto proponete et approvate in ogni fatto et detto, che nulla altro può non dispiacervi se non quanto e' sente dell'antico. E domanderemo se in que' tempi si trovarono huomini generosi, huomini dotti, et vuomini che avessono l'orecchie delicatissime pari a voi. Et domanderemo se, quando Plauto venia in scena tutto polveroso e colle mani callose, que' principi latino lo fastidiavano, se a que' patricii stomacava l'odore del pristino [="pistrino" = mulino] in quale quel poeta se exercitava per pascersi."

[24] On Plautus's biography and the mill, in a text Alberti knew, see Aulus Gellius, *The Attic Nights*, ed. and tr. John C. Rolfe (Cambridge, MA: Harvard University Press, 1947), 3.3.14 (in vol. 1, p. 250); on Alberti and Gellius see McLaughlin, *Leon Battista Alberti*, 137 and 143.

which the rest of us – who are men, just like you, I might add – become more learned, and better fitted out to live well?[25]

So much is contained in this brief and heartfelt exclamation.

First, "humanities." The Italian phrase Alberti uses is *studio d'umanità*, a direct Italianization of the Latin *studia humanitatis*. The *studia humanitatis* had become a recognized marker of the new culture of humanism. It is worth noting that it was in 1438 when we see the first instance of the five subjects of the *studia humanitatis* mentioned together in one place. In that year, Florence's then greatest political figure and patron, Cosimo de' Medici, had asked a certain Tommaso Parentucelli, to give advice on "how to order a library," in other words, how to create a library that would be adequate and in step with the times.[26]

Parentucelli responded with an extensive list that included the mainstays of the medieval tradition: the Bible, patristic works, certain texts of canon law, and a number of scholastic philosophical texts. These traditional texts, in fact, represented the majority of the works he listed. But Parentucelli did add, toward the end of his list, the following statement: "Concerning the humanities and as to what pertains to grammar, rhetoric, poetry, history, and moral philosophy, I believe all this is very well known to you. But if I were about to found a library, though I might not be able to have everything, these especially I would not want to lack." And he went on in his projected inventory to list a number of Latin grammarians, "every single work of Cicero, because all of his works are outstanding," Quintilian, Seneca, Virgil, and a number of other Latin classics (not to mention Latin translations of Plutarch's *Lives*, "because there is quite a lot of history there").[27] Parentucelli became Pope Nicholas V, the first "humanist pope," who fostered Greek-to-Latin translations and laid the groundwork of the Vatican Library. His early suggested library list showed that the power of tradition was still strong when it came to library formation; but it also shows

---

[25] Alberti, "Protesta," in Patota, 47: "E diremo: qual tuo studio d'umanità, o huomo, t'insegna tanto fastidire chi si dia alle virtù, alle cose grate a' suoi cittadini, alle quali cose noi altri, pure vuomini come voi, diventiamo piú dotti e piú atti a ben vivere?"

[26] See Vespasiano da' Bisticci, *Le vite*, 2 vols., ed. Aulo Greco (Florence: Istituto Nazionale di Studi sul Rinascimento, 1970–76), 1:46–47.

[27] The list is in MS Florence, Biblioteca nazionale centrale, Magl. 1.6.30 and is printed in Giovanni Sforza, *La patria, la famiglia, e la giovinezza di Papa Niccolò V: Ricerche storiche*, Atti della Reale Accademia lucchese di scienze, lettere ed arti, 23 (Lucca: Giusti, 1884), 359–81; the cited passage is on p. 380; see also Benjamin J. Kohl, "The Changing Concept of the *Studia Humanitatis* in the Early Renaissance," in *Renaissance Studies* 6 (1992), 185–209; and Cesare Vasoli, "La biblioteca progettata da un Papa: Niccolò V e il 'suo canone'," in *Babel: Littératures plurielles* 6 (2002), 219–39.

that, by the time of Alberti's vernacular adventure, the *studia humanitatis* were understood themselves as foundational and as an anchor of cultural life.

So when Alberti uses the term "humanities" in his letter of protest, it carries weight. He is foregrounding the fact that he understands how deeply Latinate culture had permeated the lives and minds of those who, in his generation, considered themselves the guardians of culture. And he is also suggesting that the judges in this competition need to expand their view of what should be considered acceptable and beneficial. When Alberti asks what sort of "humanities" it is that permits the judges "to look down on someone who dedicates himself to virtue, who dedicates himself to things that will help his fellow citizens," and so on, he is thinking of himself, of course. But Alberti is also asking implicit questions about culture: Whom should culture serve? How? And the rest of his statement shows what he believes: an approach to culture that includes those comfortable in the vernacular must be taken seriously. The energy and devotion that has gone into studying classical culture must now be transferred into the vernacular. Coming from Alberti, whose credentials as a Latinist were impeccable, the critique attracts notice for us today, even if it had little immediate effect.

Alberti's earlier argument, in the *Libri della famiglia*, explicitly points not only to the historical reasons but also to the social functions and utility of language. "Why," he wondered there, in the same dedication to Book Three, "would ancient writers have sought, with so much effort, to be useful to all of their fellow-citizens writing in a language that few understood?"[28] The basic idea is that the learned can make the vernacular "refined and polished [*elimata e polita*]," provided that they devote enough time to the project.[29] This impulse had been seen as far back as Dante's *De vulgari eloquentia*, and it reflects a central tension of the language question overall: the imposition of rules and order on a language will necessarily imply a level of social restriction, in the sense that not everyone will ever be able to access the language in its most "refined and polished" form.

Indeed, one of Alberti's arguments turned one of Bruni's on its head: Bruni had argued that servants could never have properly used a language so complicated as Latin. Alberti, instead, said that even today, "don't we see

---

[28] Alberti, "Proemio," in Patota, 9: "E con che ragione arebbono gli antichi scrittori cerco con sí lunga fatica essere utili a tutti e suoi cittadini scrivendo in lingua da pochi conosciuta?"

[29] Ibid., 10: "E sia quanto dicono quella antica apresso di tutte le genti piena d'autorità, solo perché in essa molti dotti scrissero, simile certo sarà la nostra s'e dotti la vorranno molto con suo studio e vigilie essere elimata e polita." On this point see also Angelo Mazzocco, *Linguistic Theories in Dante and the Humanists: Studies of Language and Intellectual History in Late Medieval and Renaissance Italy* (Leiden: Brill, 1993), 82–105.

how difficult it is for our servants to pronounce words in such a way that they are fully understood" and moreover to use verbal forms and other grammatical particularities of Tuscan correctly?[30] Tuscan too has its own grammatical difficulties and particularities. In other words, Alberti is not calling for a revolution from below. He is aware that any formalized language, Tuscan included, will have those who understand and use it as their different capacities allow. Still, Alberti thinks that the vernacular should have a far larger place than it does in his own contemporary, "high" culture.

Accordingly, he went further and wrote his *Little Grammar*, or *Grammatichetta*, as its Tuscan title runs.[31] This work, the first grammar of the Florentine vernacular, began with a sentiment by now familiar. He wrote as follows:

> I believe that those who argue that the Latin language was not common to all the Latin peoples but belonged only to certain learned men of the schools (of which there are few today) will renounce that error when they see this little work of ours, in which I have gather together the way our language is used in a series of little notes.[32]

Here an important point emerges, one that might at first glance escape notice.

Alberti is suggesting that the written form of a language must coexist and function interdependently with how it is spoken. Since Latin is a secondary language, necessarily fewer will speak it. Yet, he is making the claim that one needs to do the same sort of thing for Tuscan as the ancients had done for Latin. In Alberti's words, in a passage that follows immediately on the one just cited, he writes: "The great minds and scholars of the past did something similar, first among the Greeks and then among the Latins. And they termed these same sorts of instructions – instructions appropriate both to the written and spoken word – *Grammatica*."[33] That word, *grammatica*, was used, we have seen, as a stand-in for "Latin" in the medieval tradition. Alberti gives just a bit

[30] Alberti, "Proemio," in Patota, 8.
[31] Alberti, "Grammatichetta," in Patota, 13–39; see the fundamental edition and study of Cecil Grayson: Leon Battista Alberti, *La prima grammatica della lingua volgare: La grammatichetta vaticana*, Collezione di opere in edited o rare, v. 125, ed. Cecil Grayson (Bologna: Commissione per i testi di lingua, 1964).
[32] Alberti, "Grammatichetta," in Patota, 15: "Que' che affermano la lingua latina non essere stata comune a tutti e' populi latini, ma solo propria di certi docti scolastici, come hoggi la vediamo in pochi, credo deporranno quello errore, vedendo questo nostro opuscholo, in quale io racolsi l'uso della lingua nostra in brevissime annotationi."
[33] Ibid.: "Qual cosa simile fecero gl'ingegni grandi e studiosi presso a' Greci prima, e po' presso de e' Latini; et chiamorno queste simili ammonitioni, apte a scrivere e favellare senza corruptela, suo nome, *Grammatica*."

more thought to the concept, suggesting as he does that rules will make no sense if they cannot be understood and practiced in a living fashion. He ends his brief preface to the *Little Grammar* simply: "As to this art, and what it happens to be with respect to our language, read me and you will understand."[34] That's it. Alberti then moves on to a very short, sober description of the Tuscan language, beginning with the order of the alphabet, a list of the vowels, parts of speech, and so on.

As to technical features of this short text, one element emerges as most salient: the constant presence of the Latin language in the text. Alberti realized that Tuscan and Latin were utterly intertwined and that, for Tuscan to achieve, as it eventually would almost a century later, the kind of status and respect it deserved, its connections to Latin needed to come into relief.

Alberti uses Latin throughout his *Little Grammar* as a touchstone, assuming in fact that his audience, especially those who would refuse to allow Tuscan into the realm of acceptable literary seriousness, would find his references to Latin useful. Take what he says about nouns, simple as it is: "For the most part, things in the Tuscan language have the very same nouns as in Latin. Among its nouns, Tuscan has only 'masculine' and 'feminine'. Latin 'neuter' nouns become masculine [in Tuscan]."[35] This statement represents the simplest of comparisons. In Latin, nouns have three genders: masculine (a word, e.g., such as *hortus*, or "garden" is "masculine" in gender, meaning that if you pair it with an adjective, that adjective has to match in gender), feminine (*mensa*, or "table"), and neuter (*silentium* or "silence"), whereas Tuscan has only two, masculine and feminine, with Latin neuters being subsumed into the Tuscan masculine gender. In the three cases just given (hypothetical and not in Alberti's text) the transformation would be as follows: *hortus* would become *orto* in Tuscan, *mensa* stays the same, and *silentium* becomes *silenzio*. These and other elements like them emerge everywhere in Alberti's *Grammatichetta*. They are quite basic and would have been self-evident to anyone of his audience who had studied Latin in even a rudimentary fashion.

But simple things often seem self-evident in retrospect. The fact is, Alberti was the first to do something like this for the Tuscan language. You would think that something that seems so monumental now would have been recognized as such then. Not so. Alberti served as a lonely voice then, in the early to mid-fifteenth century in Florence, promoting the Florentine

[34] Ibid.: "Questa arte, quale ella sia in lingua nostra, leggietemi e intenderetela."
[35] Ibid., 17.

vernacular among Florence's conservative, Latinate, cultural leaders. The *Grammatichetta* was never printed in the Renaissance or early modern era. It was preserved in a handwritten version in the Medici-sponsored library of San Marco in Florence and was then taken to Rome by Cardinal Giovanni de' Medici, who eventually became Pope Leo X. There, in Rome, a copy was made in 1508 of Alberti's work, the one copy, as it happens, that now serves as the basis for our knowledge of this revolutionary little text. Tellingly, it was bound together with a copy of Dante's *On the Eloquence of the Vernacular*.[36]

Alberti, of course, had other fish to fry in his long and storied life. An active architect, he designed (among other commissions) the upper part of the façade of Santa Maria Novella. One of Florence's two Dominican churches, it was (and is) the home of Masaccio's *Trinity*, one of those paintings of which Alberti was thinking when he wrote admiringly about perspective in his *On Painting*. At the bottom of that painting is an inscription that reads as follows, all in capital letters, all in Tuscan: *IO FU GIA QUEL CHE VOI SIETE, E QUEL CH'I' SON VOI ANCO SARETE*: "I once was what you now are, and what I am you will yet be." The inscription is painted on the representation of a tomb, underneath a haunting skeleton. It is a "memento mori," a reminder of death: a reminder, that is, that death cancels out life and that any achievements one has in life must be measured against death's final triumph. Did Alberti know that his short work on the Tuscan language would have such little circulation? Why was it ignored? Was he an outsider to intellectual life because Florence's elites shut their doors to him, or did he have one of those natures always seeking to distinguish itself from the company it keeps?

These are unanswerable questions, of course. But we can chart where the language debate was going more concretely if we leap forward one generation. For it was then, about thirty years after Alberti's little-heeded grammatical work, that two thinkers would exemplify the trajectories of the language debate.

First, we can begin with the year 1471, which saw the publication in print of a book that, though little known today, was one of early printing's greatest successes. Its full title was *Agostino Dati of Siena's Little Introductory Book on the Precepts of Eloquence*, but it soon became known as the *Little Elegances*, or

---

[36] MS Vatican City, Biblioteca Apostolica Vaticana, Reg. Lat., 1370; see Alberti, *La prima grammatica*, ed. Grayson; Patota; Paolo Brongrani, "Nuovi contribute per la grammatica di L.B. Alberti," in *Studi di filologia italiana* 40 (1982), 65–106; Nadia Cannata Salamone, "Il dibattito sulla lingua e la cultura letteraria e artistica del primo Rinascimento romano. Uno studio del ms Reg. lat. 1370," in *Critica del testo* 8 (2005), 901–51.

Elegantiolae in Latin.[37] The Sienese scholar and educator who authored the book, Agostino Dati, began it by saying that for some time the most learned men have understood that no one unversed in Cicero's work could be expressive and fluent in Latin. "Therefore," Dati writes, "having read over and over the works of Cicero – whom I would term the very father of eloquence – and seen that they were certainly worthy of some brief notes, we shall – if we employ those things – come ever closer to eloquence and leave behind the speech of those who are rather common."[38] What is important here is not the sentiment expressed. Indeed, by 1471, the notion that Cicero should be considered the model of how to write (and occasionally speak) Latin would have been common to many. More noteworthy is the impact of Dati's book. In the incunabular period alone – which is to say from the invention of printing with moveable type up to and including the year 1500 – it went through more than 110 editions.[39]

It was a runaway success, in other words, so much so that one must ask why. Several answers suggest themselves. First, the *Elegantiolae* was short: only about twenty double-sided pages. Second, the nature of the work comes into relief. The *Elegantiolae* is, quite simply, a short, sweet, punchy manual for sounding like Cicero. Dati gets right into a series of ways one can effectively use Ciceronian techniques in one's prose. Number one: variety and alteration (*varietas* and *commutatio*): variety in speech has always given the greatest strength and beauty to the speech of an eloquent man. Dati goes on to give a few suggestions on how to accomplish this goal. Elsewhere he suggests that one might put negatives at the end of a phrase to seem more Ciceronian, for example: "more outstanding than you, I saw no one" – *praestantiorem te vidi neminem.*[40] The book, in short, is a collection of techniques that Dati has acquired by years of teaching and practice. And it filled a need. What we see is that by the 1470s there was no doubt what learned elite members of society needed to do in their education: learn how to express themselves in Latin, the official language of culture and diplomacy and in a Latin, moreover, that was

---

[37] I cite from Agostino Dati, *Elegantiolae* (Venice: Johannes Baptista de Sessa, 1491).

[38] Ibid., a.i(r).

[39] See Robert Black, *Humanism and Education in Medieval and Renaissance Italy: Tradition and Innovation in Latin Schools from the Twelfth to the Fifteenth Century* (Cambridge: Cambridge University Press, 2001), 359–64.

[40] Agostino Dati, *Elegantiolae*, a.i.(v): "Praepositiones perpulchre inter substantiva atque adiectiva nomina inferentur, ut: ferace in agro; ornatissimo in loco; maximas ad res; hanc ob causam; iustis de causis, aliaque huiusmodi complura … Negativa dictio apte in calce orationis ponitur, ut: praestantiorem te vidi neminem. Scipione clariorem in bellicis laudibus invenies neminem. Tua erga me benivolentia et tuo in me animo gratius est nihil. Qui te ardentius amet habes neminem."

fashionably classicizing and historically accurate. Ciceronian Latin by 1471 had arrived at a point of what we can call cultural enfranchisement. It was the language of the establishment. As we shall see in the following chapter, there were reasons why a certain consensus about how to use Latin had emerged. The reasons were tied to history and to the language debate.

Second, and at right around the same time, another side of the language question emerges. We are back in Florence, in fact, at the University of Florence, which had a main branch in Florence's gateway to the sea, Pisa, but another one, dealing with literature, in Florence itself. And it was there, at some point between 1467 and 1470, that a Florentine thinker and educator, Cristoforo Landino, was giving a university course on Petrarch's sonnets, sonnets that had been written in the Tuscan vernacular. That very fact, that a vernacular text could be taught at the university level, was somewhat revolutionary. Dante's *Comedy* had been taught at the University of Florence, on and off, ever since Boccaccio offered lectures on that masterpiece back in the fourteenth century. But the *Comedy* took on that patina – master-piece – early, enfolding as it did poetry, theology, and drama of all sorts.

So when Cristoforo Landino (1424–98) decided to teach Petrarch, it was, in its own small way, a statement that works in the Tuscan language could rise to the level of serious, university study, that even vernacular poetry could be considered to be sufficiently complex, elegant, and full of meaning that it needed an academic apparatus to draw out all its resonances. Landino's lectures were meaningful, in other words. It is worth quoting at length what he says regarding the vernacular in his opening lecture, the one that served to frame the whole course:

> None of you doubt that every language (*sermone*) needs words and ideas (*sentenze*). Words without art (*arte*) will always be improper. They will lack elegance, they will lack composition, they will lack worthiness. And ideas not drawn from the authentic humanities (*veri studi d'umanità*) will always be light and frivolous ... Therefore given that one needs both craft and learning, and since without the Latin language these things cannot be acquired, whoever wants to be a good Tuscan must first be a good Latin.[41]

---

[41] Cristoforo Landino, "Orazione fatta per Cristofano da Pratovecchio quando cominciò a leggere i sonetti di messere Francesco Petrarca in istudio," (1467–70) in R. Cardini, *La critica del Landino* (Florence: Sansoni, 1973), 342–54, at 349–550: "Niuno di voi dubita che ogni sermone ha bisogno di parole e di sentenzie. Le parole sanza arte sempre fieno inette perché mancheranno d'eleganzia, mancheranno di composizione, mancheranno di dignità. Le sentenzie, le quali non saranno tratte da veri studi d'umanità, sempre fieno e frivoli e leggieri ... Se adunque fa di bisogno l'arte, fa di bisogno la dottrina, e queste senza la Latina lingua non s'acquistano, è necessario essere latino chi vuole essere buono toscano."

Every key word in Landino's description has a deep resonance in Latin educational traditions. Take *sermone*, for example, drawn from the Latin *sermo* and translated here as "language." It is a word and concept that enfolds not just "language" in the sense of being able to speak but also "language" as a system of expression and representation. Then there is the notion that "words without art will always be improper." "Art" here means "craft" of course, and craft in this case means both selection and arrangement. The implication is that since learning these things happens to be a key way in which Latin was taught and learned, the same is true for the vernacular. Without this craft, words used in any speech will lack elegance (meaning they will not be sonorous and therefore be unlikely to be persuasive), they will lack composition (i.e., they will seem thrown together as a collection of unrelated parts), and finally they will lack "worthiness." The Italian word employed here is *dignità*, directly related to the Latin *dignitas*, a word that can mean "worth" or "authority" among other things.

What Landino is saying is that language worthy of its salt, Tuscan included, needed craft to be done well. And you learned craft only from Latin, with its rules, techniques of study, and traditions. You also needed the *studia humanitatis*. This is what Landino meant by the "authentic humanities" (*veri studi d'umanita*). It was a sentiment so self-evident by Landino's day that he barely needed to mention it; indeed, it was from the humanities that one drew, in Landino's view, "learning," for which he had used, in Italian, the word *dottrina*, a word, yet again, with a rich Latin resonance (*doctrina*) encompassing "instruction," "erudition," and "demonstrable knowledge," among many other shades of meaning. All things considered, a thinker needs both art and learning, "and since without the Latin language these things cannot be acquired, whoever wants to be a good Tuscan must first be a good Latin."

Landino, in other words, took for granted that Latin and Tuscan were intimately related, and that you needed the tradition and rules that Latin offered to use Tuscan in a way that would, if not guarantee, at least safeguard what you wrote. Alberti, in his own way, had intuited just that a generation earlier, when he had structured his *Grammatichetta* precisely along the lines laid out in the Latin grammatical tradition. Alberti was making a polemical point, of course: insulted at the lack of respect made emblematic in the *Certame coronario*, possessed as ever by the sense that he was an outsider, and committed to his identity as an individual, his motives in writing the *Grammatichetta* were, to say the least, complicated. But the point was there: Tuscan and Latin were linked.

Agostino Dati's *Elegantiolae* showed the reverse side of the same coin. Ciceronian Latin, which generations of intellectuals since Petrarch had studied, documented, and finally perfected as an instrument of creative self-expression, had reached a mainstream level of acceptability. It had entered the schools and had become by the middle of the fifteenth century a necessary accoutrement in an elite education. You could boil it down to a manual. It was necessary. But was it interesting anymore? Where was the avant-garde? If an intellectual wanted to do cutting-edge work, what sort of work did it need to be? The answers to those questions can only emerge if we retrace our steps. For just as a generational conflict concerning the issue of language was playing itself out between Bruni and Alberti, another emerged, equally far-reaching and important, between Poggio Bracciolini and Lorenzo Valla. This time, it had to do as much with philosophy as it did with language. The first step in examining this next phase will be to get to know Poggio more deeply.

7

POGGIO BRACCIOLINI

While I was fleeing the plague, I saw the cathedral of Salisbury, and I sought out the books about which you have written me so many times. What Manuel once saw I don't know. I do know one thing: there are no books by Origen there now, despite the fact that I did not search carelessly; and moreover, there was no one who could say he had ever seen them. We can find quite a number of men who devote themselves to gluttony and lust; very few lovers of literature; and, of course, we can find those barbarians, who are trained more in little debates and sophisms than they are in real learning.[1]

THE YEAR WAS 1420, AND THE WRITER WAS POGGIO BRACCIO-lini (1380–1459), writing his friend, sponsor, and fellow Florentine humanist Niccolò Niccoli, from far away England.

Poggio, like Leonardo Bruni a Tuscan who had come from outside Florence, found a place relatively early in his life at the papal court.[2] He served a succession of popes throughout a long, almost fifty-year career, and like Bruni he became a Florentine citizen and always considered Florence his real home. Poggio belonged to a relatively rare stratum of people in the premodern world: those who traveled extensively. Poggio's service with the papacy during one of its most itinerant periods meant that he saw much of the world. He was at the council of Constance, today on the border between Switzerland and Germany, from 1414 to 1417.[3] There he saw the struggles over the Great Schism end with the election of Ottone Colonna as Pope Martin V. When he was not directly needed, he scoured manuscript libraries for texts known to exist in the Middle Ages but little studied. During

---

[1] Poggio, *Lettere*, 1:20.
[2] On Poggio's life, see the still invaluable Ernst Walser, *Poggius Florentinus: Leben und Werke* (Leipzig: Teubner, 1914).
[3] See on the council Brandmüller, *Das Konzil von Konstanz, 1414–18*; and Stump, *The Reforms of the Council of Constance*.

his time at the council, he found, for example, a full copy of Lucretius's *On the Nature of Things*, a Latin poetic work expressing Epicurean philosophy.[4] Through it all, Poggio's involvement with language and, as we shall see, the language question, was tied intimately to the pragmatic view of the world that he imbibed owing to his travels and to his occupation. Understanding his view of the world through some early letters and then through an analysis of two of his most important works is necessary, before turning, in the next two chapters, to his part in the language debate.

As to the letters, the period in which the epistle cited earlier was composed signaled restlessness, and it saw Poggio accept an invitation from Henry, Cardinal of Beaufort, in England, where he spent five years of his life. The cited letter dates from this period, when Poggio, in service to the cardinal, traveled frequently. We learn from this brief quotation that the plague, though having reached its peak in Europe from 1348 to 1352, nonetheless reemerged on occasion. On his travels fleeing the plague, Poggio went to Salisbury, the site of one of the most striking British Gothic cathedrals, an edifice completed in large part in the thirteenth century. Poggio's concern: manuscripts. Reading between the lines, we see too that Florence's beloved Greek teacher, Manuel Chrysoloras, who had spent the last years of the fourteenth century in Florence teaching Greek to Poggio, Niccoli, and many others, had said back then that Salisbury contained valuable works.

Among them were said to be texts by Origen, an Egyptian Christian writing in Greek, who died in the middle of the third century CE. Respected and admired as a theologian, Origen nevertheless did not achieve sainthood. He had seemed to endorse the heretical position that souls preexisted, difficult to reconcile with the Christian teaching that God created each soul as part of an essential unity with each human body. Origen, too, struggled mightily with the issue of chastity, castrating himself and thus going so far as to take literally the passage in the Gospel of Matthew (19:12): "There be eunuchs which have made themselves eunuchs for the Kingdom of Heaven's sake. He that is able to receive it, let him receive it." So Poggio, with Niccoli's eager encouragement and on the strength of a long ago clue from Chrysoloras, was looking for anything by Origen (fruitlessly, as it turned out in this case). Finally, we also learn that Poggio was not above perpetuating the humanist stereotype that

---

[4] On the impact of which, see Alison Brown, *The Return of Lucretius to Renaissance Florence* (Cambridge, MA: Harvard University Press, 2010); Stephen Greenblatt, *The Swerve: How the World Became Modern* (New York: Norton, 2012); Gerard Passanante, *The Lucretian Renaissance: Philology and the Afterlife of Tradition* (Chicago: University of Chicago Press, 2011); and Ada Palmer, *Reading Lucretius in the Renaissance* (Cambridge, MA: Harvard University Press, 2014).

British academics were logic-chopping "barbarians," rather than "lovers of literature," meaning they were not humanists like him and Niccoli. They were not "like us," he was saying.

The attempt to define a social space by excluding others is common to all cultural movements. There are insiders and there are outsiders, and Poggio, in his little exchange here with Niccoli, was expressing something that was by then so common it verged on self-parody: university-based academics did not "get" humanism. The two men were bonding over their remembrance of their long ago Greek lessons from a respected teacher, they were continuing the mission of finding little-known, possible controversial texts, and they were, finally and for all their bluster, missing each other as friends. Indeed, Poggio's letters to Niccoli from this period are full of explanations as to why he is not yet coming "home," by which he means Florence and, more generally, Italy. In the end, all the explanations boil down to money and the need to secure an income so that he can be free of financial burdens.

Take another letter, for example, in which Poggio writes to Niccoli as follows:

> A certain canonry has been offered to me. It would pay me one hundred florins a year, wherever I might be, or at least eighty. If I get this, I want nothing greater. I would put an end to my desire for acquiring both wealth and rank, and I would be free for literary research, just like I have always wanted. In truth, as I have written you rather often, this was always my intention and was, indeed, the reason I came here: so that I might attain a little something that was enough for me to live a life free for research. If all else fails, I seem already to have achieved that.[5]

These terms and dynamics seem starkly unfamiliar to a modern reader.

The idea of the canonry comes to the fore. Poggio seems to have been offered, though he did not ultimately accept, the canonry of the cathedral of Bordeaux.[6] Poggio would have been entitled to a certain financial income that accrued to that cathedral, in exchange, notionally anyway, for duties he would perform related to oversight of the cathedral. If, say, the cathedral owned land, and on that land produce was grown, and from that produce income would be produced, the farmer would have needed to give a certain portion of that income to the cathedral. And if, for instance, a jurisdictional dispute came up in the territory over which the cathedral held sway, Poggio might have been called upon to help settle the dispute. Even though Poggio

---

[5] Poggio, *Lettere*, 1: 52–53.
[6] See J.A. Twemlow, ed., *Calendar of Entries in the Papal Registers Relating to Great Britain and Ireland. Papal Letters, v.7, AD 1417–1431* (London: Mackie and Co., 1906), p. 295.

never became a priest, he, like many who served in the Church's vast, Europe-wide bureaucracy, took what were called "minor orders," the kind of thing that, today, in the Catholic Church, a lay deacon might possess. What it meant then was that you were "official" from the Church's perspective and that you could be assigned benefices, ongoing gifts in exchange for services that could come with a title – a title such as a canonry, in this case.

Poggio writes to Niccoli, "if I get this, I want nothing greater." Why? Because he would then have time to be "free for literary research," as he has always wanted to do. Should he receive this benefice, he would "put an end" to his desire for "wealth and rank." Poggio means, overtly at least, that he would, essentially, retire from the more active, engaged, public life he has been leading in service to high officials in the Church and, instead, live the quiet but desirable life of a scholar. He says that this is all he ever wanted, really, and that the only reason he left Italy for England was, in the final analysis, to pursue this ambition, to gain enough wealth that he could support his studies.

In some ways, Poggio is expressing the desire of all active people who serve in demanding roles that leave little time for reflection: the hope that, one day, one might have the serenity to pursue one's own interests free of a schedule, free of internal bureaucratic politics, and free of the pressures of a hierarchy. Yet if we step back and look at the passage in context, we realize more is going on here.

In an immediately preceding letter, also directed to Niccoli, Poggio wrote that he was "pleased with what our friend Piero Lamberteschi has offered me, provided that I arrive at something solid. In his last letter to me he confirmed that he was to depart imminently, promising that what he now had in mind he would effect in reality and that, as soon as he got there he would write me again at Florence."[7] Piero Lamberteschi was a wealthy Florentine who like many of his compatriots had a number of business ventures ongoing at any given time.[8] One such enterprise seems to have included a trip to and an extended stay in Hungary. We know that Lamberteschi received the Renaissance equivalent of a visa for this trip in 1423, so something potentially lucrative for Poggio seems to have been a real possibility.[9] Poggio's potential role in this adventure is unknown.

---

[7] Poggio Lettere, 1: 51.

[8] See Gene A. Brucker, Renaissance Florence (Berkeley: University of California Press, 1969), 69–88; Richard Goldthwaite, The Economy of Renaissance Florence (Baltimore: Johns Hopkins University Press, 2009).

[9] Johann Friedrich Böhmer, Regesta Imperii, XI: Die Urkunden Kaiser Sigmunds, 1410–1437, 2 vols. (Innsbruck: Verlag der Wagner'schen Universitäts-Buchhandlung, 1896–1900; repr. Hildesheim: Georg Olms, 1968), v. 1, p. 401, doc. 5667; cit. Phyllis W.G. Gordan, Two Renaissance Book Hunters (New York: Columbia University Press, 1991), 260n4.

The same letter gives a sense of how one went about planning for this sort of career move. Already Poggio was counting on the possibility that his and Niccoli's mutual friend Piero was not blowing smoke; Poggio was planning how to finance his travel: "I will be here" – meaning England – "until I can scrape together a bit of money from my benefice sufficient to fund my travel since otherwise it is not possible."[10] Somehow Poggio had come to believe that this offer, the details of which remain uncertain, was about to materialize.

In a succeeding letter, Poggio's tone changes and he seems to realize, having not heard from Piero, that he should be seriously considering other plans. More than once the name of Piero comes up, its repetition unwittingly foregrounding Poggio's anxiety: "First, of course, I am delighted that you got my letter, the one in which I responded to you and Piero"; "I'll wait until I have a response from Piero"; "make sure to let me know the minute Piero responds."[11] And so on. Poggio becomes more preoccupied with his local situation: "As I wrote you a bit earlier, I cannot come home to you as soon as I should have liked, since a small delay is necessary. As soon as I acquired this benefice, I sought constantly to exchange it for another without a cure, something that, as least up to now I have not found and for which I am exerting every energy."[12] The "cure" refers to the "cure of souls." What it signified, in practice, was the obligation owed for the funds received. In theory, these obligations had to do with pastoral work of some sort – the "care of souls" ("cure" is an Anglicized version of the Latin *cura*, which means "care").

Poggio is seeking, as he makes clear, a benefice "without cure" (i.e., a "sinecure": *sine cura*). In other words, Poggio is looking to trade his current benefice for another that would entail less work and fewer ties to the institution from which it is drawn. As he says in the same letter: "For two months already someone has kept me hung up, promising me as he did that he would give me a certain prebend [a type of benefice specific to English medieval tradition that came from an endowment and had few if any duties attached] in return for this church of mine. Now, however, when I press the matter and want to seal the deal, he has backed away from his promises."[13]

Poggio's letters make a few things clear. Especially at this relatively early stage in his career, he is still looking for income and ever on the alert for new employment possibilities. Writing in 1422, Poggio is in his early forties,

[10]   Poggio, *Lettere*, 1: 51.
[11]   Poggio, *Lettere*, 1: 54–55.
[12]   Ibid., 1: 54.
[13]   Ibid., 1: 54–55.

having served in important administrative roles. Poggio had not come from great wealth, so he is savvy enough to know that he needed to keep open many options. His letters to Niccoli show that their friendship remained a cornerstone of his life, a place to which he could always return when in need of emotional sustenance, news about home, and support in his career. The letters speak about much more than Poggio's career-oriented quests, of course. Often "news" emerges about discoveries of new volumes that have been discovered. From the same letter: "Now concerning the *Orator*, which you say has been found at Lodi ... I believe what those men say: that it is a wonderful acquisition."[14] In this case Poggio is referring to the recent rediscovery of Cicero's *Orator*, a work in which Cicero outlines the "perfect orator" – what sort of man he should be, what sort of training he should have, how his speeches should be structured. It is a companion piece to Cicero's *Brutus*, discovered in Lodi as well, whose impact we have already observed. Together the works added a new set of details to the lived practice of rhetoric in the ancient world, a topic about which Poggio and his contemporaries were endlessly curious.

But at this early stage, it is Poggio's ongoing hunt for financially satisfying career possibilities that comes to the fore. By this point in his life he had held important positions in the service of several popes, roles that for all their prestige did not provide lavish incomes. What they did provide, however, was the opportunity, indeed the necessity, of seeing the world and of doing so in a context shaped by diplomatic work. Writing from England, in this case, Poggio stood at a vantage point seldom shared by his fellow Italian thinkers. His separation from Florence and from Italy allowed him the kind of distance, viewpoints, and dispassionate take on the world that shaped his thinking, even as he continued his employment in different contexts. To understand what this meant for Poggio, a fifteenth-century traveler, we can turn, anachronistic though it may seem, to the work of a nineteenth-century poet, Alfred Lord Tennyson, on Ulysses, the ancient world's most famous voyager:

> For always roaming with a hungry heart
> Much have I seen and known; cities of men
> And manners, climates, councils, and governments,
> Myself not least.[15]

Travel, and lengthy experience living away from home, gave Poggio a kind of cosmopolitanism, an acceptance, if only implicit, that there were different

---

[14] Ibid., 1: 56.
[15] Alfred, Lord Tennyson, "Ulysses," in *Selected Poetry*, ed. Norman Page (London: Routledge, 1995), 69–71, at 70, ll. 12–15.

ways of being in the world, different cultures, and different ways of writing about the world. Two more lines in Tennyson's beautiful poem can help us understand another facet of Poggio's life:

> How dull it is to pause, to make an end,
> To rust unburnish'd, not to shine in use.[16]

Tennyson was of course not thinking of Poggio. But his lines capture something important about Poggio's experience, affect, and style of life: for all his protestations, Poggio was and remained an active man, his stated desire for scholarly leisure notwithstanding.

After serving in England he returned to Italy, to the papal court, going back to Rome in the late 1420s. Poggio went on to become an especially prominent member during its lengthy stay in Florence in the 1430s. During that period, Poggio was one of the original participants in the language debate, though he would not write on the topic until much later, around 1450, as we shall see. He came into his own in the 1430s, serving in important lay positions in the papal court, including that of apostolic secretary.[17] It was during the end of that decade that he wrote some of the works that won him renown and that deserve permanent enfranchisement in the philosophical literature of the fifteenth century. Two especially come to the fore: *On Avarice* and *On True Nobility*.

On Avarice represents one of Poggio's earliest literary works, one about which, even as he wrote it, he expressed misgivings. In the dedicatory preface to his friend Francesco Barbaro, Poggio remarks on the great progress that has been made by Barbaro and others in translating works from Greek into Latin, and he admits that the theme he is proposing is a difficult one for someone like himself, who lacks Greek. Still, he says he wanted to try to writing something "for the common good," a work – at least so he says in the preface – that is intended to argue against avarice.[18] The work helps us learn where Poggio stood, both professionally and financially. And it brings into relief at least one ethos alive when it was written: that of an increasingly wealthy elite confident of its status, somewhat conservative, and able and willing to defend the possession of wealth. The work in question is *De avaritia, On Avarice*, which took the form of a Ciceronian dialogue, one with several interlocutors.

---

[16] Ibid., 70, ll. 22–23.
[17] See W. von Hoffmann, *Forschungen zur Geschichte der kurialen Behörden*, 2 vols. (Rome: von Loescher, 1914), 2:110.
[18] Poggio, *Op.*, 1: 1.

The conversation arose in the environment of the papal court, where, Poggio writes, a number of "papal secretaries were dining together."[19] They discussed a contemporary phenomenon, the roaming preacher Bernardino of Siena, a Franciscan, who had the habit of traveling around Italy and offering long, three-hour sermons urging the rapt local populace in each stopping point to live humbly, to practice the Christian virtues, and to reform their politics to reflect Catholic norms.[20] The interlocutors admit that Bernardino is that rare preacher, one who combines the three characteristics all successful speakers need, who speaks in such a way that "the listeners are instructed, pleased, and moved."[21] Yet, eloquent as he is, even Bernardino has had scant success convincing people to give up their vices and, in any case, Bernardino seems never to have treated the vice of avarice. Or is it a vice? This question becomes the crux of the interlocutors' discussion. Does avariciousness help or harm the public good?

At first, the answer is as clear as day: the avaricious man is nothing less than a monster, whose constant lust for money shapes everything he does: "So he will become a slave to his own private interests, and everything he says, does, and thinks will be directed toward those interests, intent as he will be on himself and his business alone, even as he will be forgetful of the public good."[22] But as the conversation evolves, the direction of the discussion seems to shift, and powerful arguments emerge that make avariciousness seem like not so bad a thing after all. A new interlocutor, Antonio Loschi, takes the floor. He suggests that as far as vices go, avarice, unlike lust, "does not turn one's spirit upside down, disturb the mind, or get in the way of the study of literature and training for the acquisition of wisdom."[23] Many great and admired figures, from rulers to philosophers, have been known to be desirous of money. Almost any profession at all, not to mention trades, have at least at some remove the final purpose of amassing wealth, and with good reason, since "money is quite advantageous, both for common utility and for civil life."[24] Money enables commerce among people, and, moreover, "avarice is a natural thing."[25] And

---

[19] Ibid., 1: 2.

[20] On San Bernardino, see Franco Mormondo, *The Preacher's Demons: Bernardino of Siena and the Social Underworld of Early Renaissance Italy* (Chicago: University of Chicago Press, 1999); and on Poggio's views, see Riccardo Fubini, *Umanesimo e secolarizzazzione da Petrarca a Valla* (Rome: Bulzoni, 1990), 183–219.

[21] Poggio, *Op*, 1.3; this threefold skill set was a commonplace and can be found in Quintilian, *Institutio oratoria*, 3.5.2.

[22] Poggio, *Op.*, 1: 7.

[23] Ibid., 1: 11.

[24] Ibid., 1: 12.

[25] Ibid., 1: 13.

please don't even mention those "hypocrites who . . . under cover of religion get their food without work or sweat and go around preaching poverty to others, not to mention contempt for worldly goods."[26]

This condemnation of the religious (and of precisely the sort of preacher who had earlier been praised) is followed by a statement regarding the way desire for wealth makes civic and cultural achievements possible. It will not be thanks to "those inactive and lazy men, who, owing to our labors live in ease, that we will be able to set our cities up, as we need to do, but rather by the efforts of those who are most fitted out to preserve the human race. Of these men, if no one were to strive for anything beyond his own needs, it will be necessary (and I will skip over the other consequences) for all of us to become farmers."[27] These sentiments (anticlericalism, praise of the active life and of the desire to acquire wealth) are provocative. After all, what's wrong with being a farmer?

But, together, they represent more than just a professional class (in this case that of papal secretaries and administrators) protecting their own interests. Instead, they point to a view of society and of the roles people play, a view that forms part of the long genealogy of secularism. The Christian tradition – of scorn for wealth; focus on the spiritual, inner life of a person; and on treating life in the everyday world as part of a pilgrimage to another, notionally superior realm – is not enough. Desire for money is natural. Moreover, it is not only the case that this natural desire engenders commerce. Without the desire for more than is absolutely necessary for self-preservation, "the practice of the most praiseworthy virtues would be snatched away, namely mercy and charity; and the generous, liberal man would not exist."[28] More than this, "every civic splendor would be taken away, as would civilization and beauty: no one will build churches and colonnades, the arts would cease to exist, and there would be confusion both in our own lives and in affairs in general."[29] Without the "vice" of avarice, you would not, in the final analysis, have civilization at all.

Was this opinion Poggio's own? A better question would be: does it matter? To understand the ramifications of these questions, one must address the fact that, after this clear, vigorous, and rhetorically powerful set of arguments in favor of avarice is made (by the interlocutor Antonio), Poggio gives the floor to another interlocutor. This time it is Andrea, who arrived a bit late to the dinner and was introduced as an expert in theology, so

[26] Ibid.
[27] Ibid.
[28] Ibid.
[29] Ibid.

much so that the interlocutors had fallen silent on his late entrance, claiming they were ashamed to go on with their worldly discussion in Andrea's august presence. But he had encouraged them to go on with their discussion and had listened respectfully as Antonio made the case that the desire for wealth was a natural phenomenon. When it is his turn to speak, he refutes point by point the arguments made. If there were philosophers mentioned who had been avaricious, that should be chalked up to a character flaw, since no philosopher worthy of the name ("philosopher" = "lover of wisdom") could be subject to a vice, such as avarice, that is characterized by a lack of moderation.[30] Though it is true that princes exhibit signs of this vice, it is not to be praised, since they serve as examples for their citizens.[31] And as to the possible civic utility of avarice, this too he characterizes as incorrect: desires should be moderate and an immoderate desire for wealth will pollute society, since an avaricious man will plot against his own country just for the sake of gaining money.[32]

It should be said, first, that Andrea's arguments are good ones. They represent a traditional defense of moderation, representing avarice as an extreme, whereas virtues were thought in the Aristotelian tradition to be means between extremes. Second, Poggio places Andrea's arguments at the end of *On Avarice*, so that one might read them, given that they effectively conclude the dialogue, as the most important arguments and thus as most representative of Poggio's true opinion.[33] Third, Poggio includes, as part of Andrea's stock of anti-avarice arguments, a number of positions taken from early Christian Church fathers. Some of the patristic passages were originally in Greek (like those of John Chrysostom, whose work had been translated into Latin by Ambrogio Traversari), so that, in addition to bearing the authority of ancient Christianity, they also represented "news."[34] All of that said, however, Andrea's arguments are quite traditional.

What is new in *On Avarice* are the arguments that unabashedly proclaim the desire for wealth as positive; beneficial to society; and, in any case, as something that, if you look dispassionately at people's behavior, is just . . . there. It is not a matter of starting abstractly, with a philosophical or religious ideal: traditional Christian charity and humility are good, say; therefore, we

---

[30] Ibid., 1: 20.

[31] Ibid., 1: 20–22.

[32] Ibid., 1: 24–26.

[33] On this point, see Francesco Bausi, "La *mutatio vitae* di Poggio Bracciolini. Ricerche sul *De avaritia*," in *Interpres* 28 (2009), 7–69.

[34] See Charles Stinger, *Humanism and the Church Fathers: Ambrogio Traversari and Christian Antiquity in the Italian Renaissance* (Albany: State University of New York Press, 1977).

should model our behavior on those ideals. Rather, the arguments begin with what people in society actually do, and Antonio the interlocutor – and, of course, Poggio the author – structure them accordingly.

The idea that the acquisition of wealth can be viewed as something natural and as a societal good is an old one; it predates Poggio by two millennia. Aristotle had thought a lot about currency, arguing in his *Nicomachean Ethics* that money is useful as a means of exchange, making concrete something inherently arbitrary – the value we place on things.[35] And in his *Politics*, Aristotle suggested that in a democracy, surplus wealth could and should be aggregated. Some of it could be given to the poor so that they could pursue a trade or other occupations, since if the multitude of citizens is overly poor, "this is the reason for democracy being depraved."[36] Though Aristotle would always maintain that wealth could not be considered the highest good, he saw that it had a natural place in human social life. In that respect, Aristotle's thought mirrored ancient social practices: the wealthy were expected to give generously to their city at large. It was not so much a question of giving to the poor because they were poor. Rather, the obligation to give to the poor had to do with the fact that they were one's fellow citizens. The wealthy, in other words, were also expected to give to their city: to build temples, to sponsor public games, to sponsor beautification projects, and so on.[37]

The Christian tradition was more complicated, since in the Acts of the Apostles the idea of property held in common was forcefully advocated (Acts, 4: 32–35):

> Now the multitude of believers was of one heart and one soul; and not one said that anything he possessed was his own; but they had all things in common . . . and great grace was upon them all. Neither was there anyone among them in want. For those who owned lands or houses would sell them and bring the price of what they had sold, and laid it at the Apostle's; and distribution was made to every man, according as everyone had need.

Christianity's beginnings included arguments about wealth that were oriented toward its redistribution.

Still, early Christian thinkers also recognized the inevitability of the accumulation of wealth in society. Even Christ had said that the poor will always be with us, and further back there had been a similar recognition in

---

[35] Aristotle, *Nicomachean Ethics*, 5.1133b.
[36] Aristotle, *Politics*, 6.5.1320a33.
[37] See Peter Brown, *The Ransom of the Soul: Afterlife and Wealth in Early Western Christianity* (Cambridge, MA: Harvard University Press, 2015).

the Old Testament tradition that charity toward the poor was a necessary social good.[38] But arguments emerged in the early Christian period that wealth was like a tool, one that could be used well or poorly. Take the early Church Father Clement of Alexandria (150–215 CE), who made the case that property and personal wealth should be considered *adiaphora*, a word that in Greek (the language in which Clement wrote) means "things indifferent," things that have no significance on their own. What mattered was how they were used: "If you should use a tool adroitly, then this tool itself becomes adroit ... and such a tool is also wealth. If you should know how to use it properly, then it becomes a means for you to attain true justice. But if you should use it unjustly, wealth itself becomes the handmaid of injustice."[39] What Clement focused on was the character of the person possessing wealth and property. He was urging the wealthy to learn to curb their appetites and make sure to use their wealth to contribute to society. This position evolved into an accepted distinction between "natural law" – the law according to a state of nature – and the "customary law" – the law according to human custom, best summed up by the medieval legal scholar Gratian (active in the twelfth century): "According to the natural law, all things belong to all men in common; only through the 'customary law' or positive law has it come about that this particular thing is called mine and that thing is called yours."[40] In other words, nature had simply established the existence of people and of things. As people organized into communities, to ensure social order, the institution of private property was established.

Thomas Aquinas put it this way: "the ownership of possessions is not contrary to the natural law, but a super-addition thereto, devised by human reason."[41] And Aquinas, like Aristotle, believed that wealth could be used for virtue. Aquinas considered wealth a "good of fortune," and he wrote about wealth in the context of the virtue of *magnanimitas* or "magnanimity," a word that we can translate most literally as "great-souled-ness." The "question" was: "whether goods of fortune lead to magnanimity?" Aquinas offers three "objections" to the idea: first, that virtue stands on its own and does not need "goods of fortune"; second, that magnanimous men often despise goods of fortune as extraneous and unnecessary; and third, that magnanimous men are

---

[38] See Mt. 26:11; and Dt. 15:11.

[39] See Clement, *Quis dives salvetur*, in *Patrologia Graeca*, 9: 631–52, chap. 14, at 617–20; cit. and tr. in Anton Hermann Chroust and Robert J. Affeldt, "The Problem of Private Property According to St. Thomas Aquinas," *Marquette Law Review* 34 (1950–51), 151–82, at 161.

[40] See Gratian, *Decretum* 7.1, cit. and tr., modified, in Chroust and Affeldt, 176.

[41] See Aquinas, *Summa theologica*, 2a2ae, q.66, art.2, ad 1; cit. and tr. in Chroust and Affeldt, 180.

said not to grieve at misfortune, but since everyone "grieves at the loss of what is helpful to him," including goods of fortune such as wealth (no one likes losing money, in other words), goods of fortune cannot lead to magnanimity. Then, in a "contrary" statement (following the logic of the "question" format), Aquinas notes, as he must, what "the Philosopher" – Aristotle – says about the subject: that "good fortune seems to conduce to magnanimity."[42] Thereafter Aquinas offers his solution:

> Magnanimity regards two things: honor as its matter, and the accomplish-ment of something great as its goal. Now goods of fortune lead to both of these things. For since honor is conferred on the virtuous, not only by the wise, but also by the multitude who hold these goods of fortune in the highest esteem, the result is that they show greater honor to those who possess goods of fortune. Likewise, goods of fortune are useful organs or instruments of virtuous deeds: since we can easily accomplish things by means of riches, power, and friends. Hence it is evident that goods of fortune lead to magnanimity.[43]

The short version: wealth can lead to virtue.

Note a few things, however, compared with Poggio's treatment. What would happen if we were to reduce both treatments to "arguments," mean-ing if we were simply to reduce Aquinas's and Poggio's texts to their constituent parts? In that case, we would see both that similar arguments are present in both cases, pro and contra, and that both thinkers take the time to present opposing arguments. Wealth can be useful for charitable works and for exercising virtue, excessive desire for wealth is not useful, and so on.

But it would be a mistake to reduce both texts to arguments. People don't think only in "arguments," and they don't make decisions on purely rational grounds. Rather, people have emotions. Their emotions emerge and solidify owing to many factors, one of the most powerful of which happens to be persuasion. And for most people, intellectuals included, persuasion has to do with style. Accordingly, the first major difference we can note between Aquinas's and Poggio's look at private wealth and its functions regards style. Aquinas pursues the matter in the "question" format, one that fore-grounded clarity, made sure to tell both sides of the story and in so far as possible is neutral rhetorically: it does not seek to inspire emotions, spirited engagement, or even energetic opposition. Poggio on the other hand uses

---

[42] See Aquinas, *Summa theologica*, tr. English Dominican Province, 2nd ed., 2a2ae, q.129, art.8; and Aristotle, *Nicomachean Ethics*, 4.1123b33–1125b1.

[43] See Aquinas, *Summa theologica*, tr. English Dominican Province, 2nd ed., 2a2ae, q.129, art.8, resp.

dialogue with real historical characters who make speeches punctuated by forceful points, moments of humor, and appeals to common human practice, rather than to purely rational argumentation.

More importantly, Poggio accelerates in a quantum fashion an evolution already present in Aquinas, an evolution that brought changing conceptions of wealth into relief. For Aquinas, living as he did amid the high medieval revival of cities, trade, and commerce, it was conceivable to think differently from the Christian tradition that had emphasized the use of wealth as a means of helping the poor and the Church. Indeed, Aquinas explained and agreed with Aristotle that wealth, properly managed and handled with just moderation, could benefit society.

Poggio is in another world entirely, at least when his interlocutor Antonio has the floor. It is as if he is endorsing a return to the ancient pagan tradition of charitable giving, whereby the wealthy were expected to give funds for their city, primarily. It is a vision that is at once more expansive and more restrictive than the Christian vision. It is more expansive in the sense that citizenship comes to seem a primary good, brought into relief as a part of the commonwealth. For the wealthy, one way to exercise citizenship is to contribute wealth to the public good, contributions that can go toward civic enterprises, beautification of public space, and the patronage of artists. Their charitable giving can also go to the poor; but, significantly, it will do so because they are citizens. We see why Poggio's (and the ancient pagan) conception can seem more restrictive than the Christian conception. The Christian conception encompassed a universal Church whose members were all equal in the eyes of God. In theory at least, the poor in one city were no different from the poor in another. Poggio's vision instead, playful as it is, takes one's own city and its particular needs as the starting point. If your city and its citizens are all due the same sorts of protections, laws, and amenities, that set of obligations holds only for your city, not for humanity considered in a universal sense. What we see in Poggio's light, fluffy, and not-so-serious dialogue are the distant, adumbrated, and embryonic beginnings of much later nationalisms.

So: does it matter what Poggio's own opinion was when it came to the desire for wealth? Not really. What matters much more is that the arguments put forward in the dialogue became part of the bloodstream of Western intellectual life. In situations such as these, author's intentions matter far less than the fact that their texts are out of their hands, to be interpreted, reshaped, and appropriated by readers of all sorts in different eras. A similar dynamic obtains with another dialogue by Poggio, this time composed when he was a mature, experienced man of the world.

On True Nobility took on a problem of perennial importance – what distinguishes a person to such a point that he or she can be considered noble – at a time when particular interest in the issue was at its height.[44] There were reasons for this interest. A traditional view would have it that social place served as a marker of nobility: that you should be considered noble if your family had a long, documented history of wealth, titles, military service, and so on. But the Florence in which Poggio was writing in 1440 was remarkable in several ways. By then it was certainly known as a center – arguably *the* Italian center – of culture. Leonardo Bruni, entering his old age, emerged as one of the most respected humanists in Europe. Florence's cathedral, now surmounted by Brunelleschi's stunning, seemingly miraculous dome, served as the spiritual center of an important Church council in 1439, so that the papacy could look upon Florence as a home away from home.[45] The revolutionary art of Donatello was in full swing, his lithe and realistic "David" now ten years old. And most of this was done with the patronage and wealth not of hereditary kings, but of merchants, traders, and bankers: not traditional, titled nobility, in other words.[46] So it was the right time to be thinking about "nobility" broadly conceived – about how citizens in a republic could and should gain prominence – and even more so about what sorts of means they might use to achieve and exercise that status.[47]

The other noteworthy thing about *On True Nobility* is its form: it is a dialogue, and the two main interlocutors are Niccolò Niccoli and Lorenzo de' Medici, an otherwise little known Medici who was the brother of the more famous Cosimo and, along with Niccoli, a great friend of Poggio. Again, Poggio used real, living people as interlocutors to make arguments in the dialogue. It is reasonable to assume that Poggio uses the character Niccoli as a kind of mouthpiece, as we shall see. But it is important to foreground the dialogue as such, as a genre wherein, even if one position expressed has more weight than others, what a reader experiences is polyphony: many voices at once.

---

[44] Poggio, *De nob.*

[45] See Joseph Gill, *The Council of Florence* (Cambridge: Cambridge University Press, 1959); idem, *Personalities of the Council of Florence* (Oxford: Oxford University Press, 1964); and for the problems roiling in the background, see Johannes Helmrath, *Das Basler Konzil, 1431–1449: Forschungsstand und Probleme* (Cologne: Böhlau, 1987).

[46] See, for example, Dale Kent, *Cosimo de' Medici and the Florentine Renaissance: The Patron's Oeuvre* (New Haven: Yale University Press, 2000).

[47] It was a lively fifteenth-century theme. See the collected texts in Albert Rabil, ed., *Knowledge, Goodness, and Power: The Debate over Nobility among Quattrocento Italian Humanists* (Binghamton: MRTS, 1991).

Poggio said at the outset of the dialogue that he decided to write in a deliberately simple way, especially since this was, in his estimation, the first time that the subject would be treated in the way that he planned to do. And the Latin of *On True Nobility* is so good in this respect that one can say that Renaissance humanists, and Poggio in particular by this point, had succeeded in adopting and adapting classical, Ciceronian Latin as a functional language of culture: expressive, fluid, and not filled with jargon.[48] The sharp dialogue proceeds as if it were a real conversation and, like all good writing, conceals the art that lies behind that achievement.

When the character Niccoli takes the stage, the arguments begin to flow. The first set takes the form of a brisk survey of how people in different places conceive of nobility. The character Niccoli is speaking, but the voice is Poggio's: it had to be, since the survey of different customs in different places breathes with the confidence of someone who, like Poggio, has traveled, seen much of the world, and had the habit of summarizing what he needed to say compellingly and concisely.

After clearing away some of the possible meanings of the word "noble," Niccoli moves to Italy's different centers. He minces no words. In Naples, nobility is conceived of as a vehicle for "laziness and indolence" (*desidia atque ignavia*), meaning that, for nobles there, any sort of work at all is regarded as disreputable.[49] Neapolitan nobles spend all their time sitting in the atriums of their homes or riding horses. In Venice, you need to belong to the senatorial class to be considered noble. It is a fixed, limited group, one that only rarely allows access to outsiders. Venetian nobles, however, do consider commerce and mercantile activity worthy endeavors. Roman nobles look down on commerce, seeing pastoral and farming activities as noble pursuits. "We Florentines," Niccoli says, seem to have it right: "Those people are considered nobles who possess an ancient lineage and whose ancestors served the city in governing the republic. Some of these men are dedicated to commerce, while others enjoy their noble status and do nothing except hunt and raise birds."[50] The Genovese are more or less like the Venetians: a closed group of nobles who see commerce as valid; whereas the Lombards (meaning people who live in and around Milan) live from the profits of their lands and also enjoy hunting and birding.[51]

---

[48] See Silvia Rizzo, "I latini dell'umanesimo," in Giorgio Bernardi Perini, ed., *Il latino nell'età dell'umanesimo* (Florence: Olschki, 2004), 51–95.

[49] Poggio, *De nob.*, 42.

[50] Ibid., 46.

[51] Ibid., 44–48.

Poggio, through his mouthpiece Niccoli, has offered a quick sketch of Italy and Italian noble customs in different regions, noting the regionally differing social habits of the aristocracy. Some consider commerce and trade a reasonable part of noble life; others do not and verge more toward hunting. But what is clear is that the customs are different: behavior defines the concept of nobility, and behaviors are conditioned by culture, habit, and locality. There seems to be nothing constant about the idea of nobility as such. The same sense emerges when Niccoli moves on to places outside of Italy, as his survey encompasses the Germans, the French, the English, the Spanish, the Greeks, Egyptians, Syrians, and others. Again, all are so different in what they consider noble that it is difficult to decide on what a common notion of nobility might entail.

To an objection from the interlocutor Lorenzo that one must, in the end, follow custom – the Latin word is *consuetudo*, which also means something like "common usage" – Niccoli replies that, no, one must still look for something deeper, since, even if laws differ from place to place and time to time, they nevertheless stem from the same thing: what he calls in Latin the "fount of fairness and justice."[52] For Niccoli (and, one must presume, for Poggio), there must be some sort of relatively objective means by which one can decide what is and isn't noble.

The crux of the matter surfaces if one zeroes in on an immediately preceding, quite passionate statement made by the interlocutor Niccoli: "How can it happen that a man lounging around and at leisure, never having given himself to an honest endeavor, endowed with no real virtue, wisdom, or learning, relying only on his ancestors and on the age of his family, could in any way be noble?"[53] How indeed. This is the voice, of course, of every outsider who believes his or her talents alone should be the measure of success. It is the sentiment of every person ever told "you don't come from the right family," or "you didn't go to the right school," or "you don't look like us" – in short, "you are not one of us and never will be, no matter your qualifications." And it is the voice, more to the point, of Poggio, a self-made man without private wealth who through education, striving, and energy made himself into what he became: an admired political figure, cultural commentator, and writer.

This last category, writer, is an important lens through which one can look to understand Poggio and what he is up to in this work. One of the

---

[52] Ibid., 58: "Sed tamen omnes eandem originem habent, cum ab equitatis et iustitie fonte descendant."
[53] Ibid.

things that he and other writers of dialogues appreciated was what had been called *argumentatio in utramque partem*, "argument on both sides of the question."[54] Bruni's *Dialogues to Pier Paolo Vergerio*, as we have seen, had the central interlocutor (the redoubtable Niccoli, yet again) argue first against and then for the greatness of Dante, Petrarch, and Boccaccio. We also saw that the second day's argument represented a clever way to maintain the original position: essentially that, because of their extensive and almost exclusive use of the vernacular, the "Three Crowns of Florence" still did not have the sort of cultural cachet that Bruni and his (then) new generation desired. In short, Bruni proffered enough arguments on both sides to satisfy different constituencies, even though his own position could be discerned relatively clearly. The same was true in Poggio's *On Avarice*. And the same mechanism is at work in Poggio's *On True Nobility*.

Lorenzo, the other interlocutor, is given far less to say than Niccoli. But what he does say has a lot going for it from a traditional perspective. Arguing against Niccoli, Lorenzo says he prefers to follow Aristotle's definition of what constitutes nobility: "Now, to return to Aristotle, in the fifth book of his *Politics*, he wrote that nobility consists in virtues united to long-standing wealth; and elsewhere he said that people who seem noble are those who possess virtues and wealth of their ancestors."[55] Wealth, family, reputation: Aristotle's definition was indeed traditional.

But Niccoli will have none of it, arguing that in truth Aristotle was just summing up common opinion and that elsewhere, like in his *Nicomachean Ethics*, Aristotle "seems to believe that that man is noble who, predisposed toward virtue by nature, brings it into actuality by habit and practice."[56] Even Aristotle could be read as supporting the idea that nobility has to do with what you do, rather than what has fallen to you by lot.

The argument continues and, in truth, neither interlocutor persuades the other. Lorenzo persists in thinking that the traditional view of nobility is the right one, linking it at one point to the Greek word *eugeneia*, whose roots (*eu* = "well" and *genos* = "race" or "tribe") indicate "the state of being well born."[57] Niccoli replies that, though that Greek word is indeed translated commonly by the Latin word *nobilitas*, the Latin usage is broader and more connected to everyday activity: "We call men noble on account of deeds done and correct

---

[54] The concept was there in Cicero's *De oratore*, a favorite among humanists (3: 80).
[55] Poggio, *De nob.*, 80, referring to Aristotle, *Politics*, 4.6.1294a21 and 5.1.1301b4.
[56] Poggio, *De nob.*, 82, referring to Aristotle, *EN*, 10.8–9.
[57] Poggio, *De nob.*, 96.

actions that lead to honor and glory for an individual. The Greeks think nobility derives from lineage."[58]

On and on it goes, each interlocutor stating his case as powerfully as he can, each remaining relatively unconvinced of the validity of the other side's opinion. If you were a reader of Poggio's work back then, you could come away from the text with arguments that reinforced your own thinking, predispositions, and prejudices. And a number of contemporaries did respond with treatises and letters of their own both agreeing and disagreeing, weighing in, and becoming part of the conversation.[59] Poggio's work was a "hit," or at least as much of a hit as a work written in the preprint era could be. But for all that one could come away with arguments on both sides of the question, Poggio's own position, voiced by Niccoli in the dialogue, is clear enough. The arguments in favor of nobility as virtue – nobility as measured by action in the world – are longer, more sustained, and more rhetorically vigorous. Poggio did his due diligence in presenting both sides of the question, but for this self-made man, it was action, rather than inheritance, that mattered most.

In many ways, by 1440, Poggio's voice had already become that of the establishment. Far from disenfranchised, he became one of Florence's wealthiest men. He returned to Rome to serve the papal court, continuing in his honored position with Eugenius IV, until that pope's death in 1447. Upon the election of Tommaso Parentucelli as Pope Nicholas V in 1447, the character of the papal court changed a bit. Parentucelli had been the first to mention in one place all five subjects of the *studia humanitatis*. Upon becoming pope, he engaged in an ambitious plan to have the papal court itself become an engine of the humanities, creating and assigning a series of Greek-to-Latin translation projects to prominent thinkers. Poggio, whose ability in Greek was not up to par (as he himself had admitted) when it came to Greek-to-Latin translation, felt pressure from a new generation. This generation was represented most prominently by Lorenzo Valla, and their discussions rose in volume and intensity.

[58]   Ibid.
[59]   See Rabil, ed., *Knowledge, Goodness, and Power.*

8

LORENZO VALLA

So if I am correcting anything, I am *not* correcting Sacred Scripture, but rather its *translation,* and in doing so I am not being insolent toward scripture but rather pious, and I am doing nothing more than translating better than the earlier translator, so that it is my translation – should it be correct – that ought to be called Sacred Scripture, not his.[1]

Who says something like this? The person in question is an intellectual named Lorenzo Valla, Roman in origin but who, because of his difficult, combative, narcissistic personality, spent decades away from home. The context of this statement was, not unusually for Valla, an argument. And the argument happened to be with Poggio, in the year 1450, when Poggio, now by any measure an old, revered, and accomplished man, attacked Valla in writing. The context of Poggio's attack, the ongoing argument between the two intellectuals, and the stakes involved all highlight the crucial point humanism had reached by mid-fifteenth century.

First, Valla himself needs to be introduced. Born in 1406 to a family that had ties to the papal court, Valla was raised during the heady papacy of Martin V (1417–31), when the Great Schism had ended and the papacy was back in Italian hands.[2] Valla's education included contact with some of the age's

---

[1] Lorenzo Valla, *Antidotum Primum: La prima apologia contro Poggio Bracciolini*, ed. Ari Wesseling (Van Gorcum: Assen, 1978), 112: "Itaque, ne multus sim, siquid emendo non Sacram Scripturam emendo, sed illius potius interpretationem, neque in eam contumeliosus sum, sed pius potius, nec aliud facio nisi quod melius quam prior interpres transfero, ut mea tralatio, si vera fuerit, sit appellanda Sancta Scriptura, non illius." Cited in Lucia Cesarini Martinelli, "Note sulla polemica Poggio-Valla e sulla fortuna delle *Elegantiae*," *Interpres* 3 (1980): 29–79, at 63.

[2] John Monfasani has argued for the birthdate of 1406 in his "Disputationes vallianae," in *Penser entre les lignes: Philologie et philosophie au Quattrocento*, ed. F. Mariani Zini (Lille: Presses Universitaires de Septentrion, 2001), 229–50, at 229–31 (now reprinted as essay XII, with

---

luminaries, including Leonardo Bruni, who read and corrected some of Valla's early Latin efforts. Valla also studied Greek with Giovanni Aurispa, a relatively little known humanist who was a member of the earliest generation to go to Constantinople and learn Greek there.

Though settled in Rome for a generation, Valla's family came from the north of Italy, in Piacenza (near Milan). In 1430, Valla headed there to help administer some property his family owned. Within a year, he wrote an early version of a controversial work, entitled *On Pleasure* (*De voluptate*). Later Valla changed the title to *On the True and False Good*.[3] But some key ideas remained the same throughout. The dialogue, structured in three "books," contained as its central element a vigorous defense of the philosophy of Epicureanism in one of its most vulgar versions. Epicureanism, named after its founder Epicurus, represented one of what scholars now term the three "Hellenistic schools" of philosophy, so called because all three flourished in the Hellenistic period, a period immediately succeeding the era of Plato and Aristotle and one marked by the rise of Alexander the Great.[4] The other two schools were Stoicism and Skepticism, and along with Epicureanism, all three had noteworthy roles in the history of ancient philosophy. When it came to moral philosophy, the basis of Epicureanism was the "pleasure principle," meaning in its simplest form that all people have a natural inclination to orient themselves toward pleasure and an equally inborn tendency to flee pain. Therefore, ethics should be structured along those lines.

The more one reads ancient Epicurean sources − and Lucretius's *On the Nature of Things*, another of Poggio's Constance discoveries, represented

---

the same pagination, in John Monfasani, *Greeks and Latins in Renaissance Italy: Studies on Humanism and Philosophy in the Fifteenth Century* (Aldershot: Ashgate, 2004). For recent literature on Valla, see Lodi Nauta, *In Defense of Common Sense: Lorenzo Valla's Humanist Critique of Scholastic Philosophy* (Cambridge, MA: Harvard University Press, 2009); Mariangela Regoliosi, ed., *Pubblicare il Valla* (Florence: Polistampa, 2008); Regoliosi, ed., *Lorenzo Valla e l'umanesimo toscano: Traversari, Bruni, Marsuppini* (Florence: Polistampa, 2009); Regoliosi, ed., *Lorenzo Valla: La riforma della lingua e della logica*, 2 vols. (Florence: Polistampa, 2010); Lorenzo Valla, *Raudensiane note*, ed. Gian Matteo Corrias (Florence: Polistampa, 2007); Lorenzo Valla, *Laurentii Valle Encomion Sancti Thome Aquinatis*, ed. Stefano Cartei (Florence: Polistampa, 2008); Lorenzo Valla, *Ad Alfonsum regem Epistola de duobus Tarquiniis [and] Confutationes in Benedictum Morandum*, ed. Francesco Lo Monaco (Florence: Polistampa, 2009); Lorenzo Valla, *Laurentii Valle Emendationes quorundam locorum ex Alexandro ad Alfonsum primum Aragonum regem*, ed. Clementina Marsico (Florence: Polistampa, 2009); and Salvatore I. Camporeale, *Lorenzo Valla: Umanesimo, riforma, e controriforma; studi e testi* (Roma: Edizioni di Storia e Letteratura, 2002). Still valuable is Girolamo Mancini, *Vita di Lorenzo Valla* (Florence: Sansoni, 1891).

[3] Valla, *De vero*.

[4] See A.A. Long, *Hellenistic Philosophy: Stoics, Epicureans, Sceptics*, 2nd ed. (Berkeley: University of California Press, 1986).

a prime example – the more one realizes that authentic Epicureanism was complicated.[5] "Pleasure" can mean many things, but for ancient Epicureans what it meant at the root level was "satisfying your desires." The more you could reduce your desires, the more pleasure you would experience. Self-control was important, as was the shaping of one's character. But it was a philosophy that could be easily parodied and misunderstood. Ancient practitioners of Epicureanism tended to segregate themselves from society and political life, preferring to gather with small groups of trusted friends. They revered their founder, Epicurus, in ways that seemed extreme. As Lucretius wrote about Epicurus: "He went far beyond the flaming boundaries of the world and in mind and spirit wandered through the unbounded infinite. . . . And so superstition in its turn is trampled underfoot, and his victory makes us equal to the heavens."[6] As a philosophy, Epicureanism gained a bad name in the Christian tradition, as early scripture, without naming Epicureanism specifically, summarized at least one perception of its central tenets as, in Luke's words, "eat, drink, and be merry."[7] The Epicurean notion of divinity – that the divine, though it existed, cared nothing for human affairs – flew in the face of Christian assumptions about a God interested in individuals. Finally, the atomistic materialism of the Epicureans was offensive to Christian sensibilities. All things were made from physical atoms and, when anything dies, human beings included, those atoms dispersed into the void. No individual human soul would survive one's death, in the Epicurean view. This materialism meant no rewards and punishments after death. Life on earth was all we had.

Consequently, Epicureanism presented problems. Valla's dialogue was structured in three parts, or "books," all of which are designed, Valla tells his readers, "to destroy the race [*nationem*] of Stoics,"[8] something he does in part by advocating Epicureanism.[9] What he means is that he wants to argue against what he sees as the dour and unrealistic Stoic idea that virtue should be sought for its own sake – that virtue is its own reward. The perfect Stoic would never show emotions, would participate in society productively without hope of reward, and would live by a code of virtue unmotivated by the pursuit of pleasure. Valla desired to show, instead, that this framework

[5] For the reception of Lucretius in the Renaissance, see Brown, *The Return of Lucretius to Renaissance Florence*; Greenblatt, *The Swerve*; Palmer, *Reading Lucretius in the Renaissance*; Passanante, *The Lucretian Renaissance*.

[6] Lucretius, *De rerum natura*, ed. and tr. W.H.D. Rouse and Martin Ferguson Smith (Cambridge, MA: Harvard University Press, 1992), 1.73–79, p. 8.

[7] See Lk. 12:19–20; Paul 1 Cor. 15:32.

[8] Valla, *De vero*, 51, tr. Lorch.

[9] Valla, *De vero*, 51, tr. Lorch.

was, literally, unnatural – it did not follow nature, which, in our modern terms, has "hard-wired" us to pursue pleasure. Pleasure is a "good." People commonly speak of "goods of our souls, goods of the body, and goods of fortune," and since Stoics believe the last two should not be considered goods at all, Valla believed he must speak against the Stoics.[10]

Throughout Valla makes (or has his interlocutors make) strong arguments in favor of pleasure. At one point, for example, he focuses on female beauty. Valla says, "indeed, what is sweeter, what is more delightful, what is more lovable than a pretty face? ... Now women are graced not only with beautiful faces but also with beautiful hair ... with beautiful breasts, with beautiful thighs, and indeed with beauties of the entire body, whether they be tall, light-complexioned, luscious, or well-proportioned."[11] Nature has created them that way, and women are just as prone to admire and be drawn to male beauty as men are to admire female beauty.

If nature has given us the sense of sight for a reason, it has also given us the sense of taste. Take delicious food, for example. About that, Valla says: "Anyone who dares to defame or forbid such foods seems to me to be praising death rather than life, so that, as far as I am concerned, he should be tortured with the fasting he approves of and even starve to death; in fact, he has my best wishes for such a fate."[12] Valla's interlocutor is highlighting, again, nature, in the broadest sense: there is no one who does not prefer good food. Previously he had highlighted an ascetic tradition of frugality when it comes to food: the notion shared by many that food is something toward which one should remain indifferent, that it exists for nourishment alone, and that one should not fetishize it as something special and worthy of undue attention. The rest of Valla's arguments in the treatise are similar. He repeatedly underscores the natural propensity of human beings to foreground pleasure as a motivating factor in all decisions.

He does make sure, in the dialogue's final book, to affirm official Christian positions, rejecting Epicurean atomism and having an interlocutor make the case that true pleasure was enjoyment of God, something that could only be found through Christian principles. But, just as it was the case with Poggio Bracciolini's opinions, so too with Valla's: his own point of view regarding the dicey stances propounded in his work is less important than the fact that those positions were there, that they saw the light, and that they could then become threads in the texture of different intellectual discussions. And, one

---

[10] Ibid., 91.
[11] Ibid., 98–99, tr. modified.
[12] Ibid., 103.

more thing: in the case of *On Pleasure*, he was doing all this at, more or less, age twenty – or at least he began then.

Thereafter, in 1431 to be specific, Valla was offered a professorship at the University of Pavia.[13] His brief as a professor was to teach rhetoric. But, unable to restrict himself to the disciplinary boundaries to which his contract had committed him, he began attacking his university's law professors, and specifically their use of and (in his view) uncritical interpretation of a famous medieval jurist named Bartolo da Sassoferrato.[14] The only thing that remained to Valla – so great was the animus against him – was to flee.

Valla finally found a long-term home as a courtier, serving as a secretary at the court of Alfonse of Aragon (1396–1458), who reigned over the "kingdom of the two Sicilies," as Naples and Sicily were known at the time.[15] Alfonse, amid almost constant war, was and remained a significant patron of the arts and student of classical literature. He offered support to several humanists, one of whom was Valla, who found a home in Naples and, indeed, wrote almost all of his major works while at Alfonse's court. It is worth taking a look at some of Valla's major works before turning back to his arguments with Poggio.

Taken together, the principal tendencies of Valla's work represent a remarkable unity, one in which three overriding themes come to the fore: a concern for Christianity and a propensity to see himself as a kind of reformer (just what kind of reformer will become clear as we move on); a precise sense of the Latin language – of its proper usage, its functions in society, and the way it can be deployed as an instrument of culture; and, finally, a tendency to write, indeed to think, in an argumentative, dialogical fashion.

The best way to understand this mentality is to return to the quotation that opened the chapter and set it in context. As mentioned it occurred during a protracted written argument that Valla was having with Poggio, one in which, not to put too fine a point on it, Poggio had accused Valla of heresy. What occasioned this accusation was one of Valla's works that, on the surface, might not seem controversial: a series of notes on the Latin version of the New Testament, called the "Vulgate," so called since it had been translated from Greek, the language in which it had been written originally, into Latin, the *lingua vulgata*, or "common language."

---

[13] See Mancini, *Vita*, 65–94.

[14] On whom see Danilo Segoloni, ed., *Bartolo da Sassoferrato: studi e documenti per il VI centenario*, 2 vols. (Milan: Giuffrè: 1962); and Diego Quaglioni, *Politica e diritto nel Trecento italiano: il "De tyranno" di Bartolo da Sassoferrato* (Florence: Olschki, 1983).

[15] Ibid., 95–225.

Valla's notes, called the *Annotations*, were what you could call "philologi-cal" notes, which is to say they were notes that paid very precise – perhaps even picky – attention to the translation, compared to the original Greek.[16] Behind them, however, lay a somewhat revolutionary view regarding the power of language and the responsibility of the critic.

For decades, no love had been lost between Poggio and Valla. They had encountered each other in 1421, when a very young Valla had visited the papal court alongside his uncle, Melchior Scrivani, a papal secretary. When Scrivani died (of a re-outbreak of plague in either 1429 or 1430), Valla had the audacity and ambition to ask to be considered for his uncle's position. But Poggio, along with another curialist, Antonio Loschi, advised the pope (Martin V) against choosing Valla, suggesting that this young and over-confident man would cause dissension in the ranks by attacking the older secretaries (as Valla had indeed already done in writings of his against the Milanese Loschi). The pope took their advice.[17] Denied a job, Valla received a lifelong source of resentment, fueling, if this were even possible, his already competitive nature and contributing to his skepticism toward institutional cultures, that of the Church included.

By 1450, the date of their public argument in writing, Valla was part of the papal court, having been appointed to the office of *scriptor* by Pope Nicholas V and, even more grating to Poggio, becoming one of Nicholas's vaunted Greek-to-Latin translators.[18] The court had been Poggio's professional home for almost fifty years. He was an insider's insider. Now here came this lifelong source of irritation much better poised than he was to serve the cultural interests of the pope. Valla was an expert in Greek, and Poggio wasn't. And that counted for a lot in the pontificate of Nicholas V. Though Valla was not yet at the court's most elite level (he would not be appointed a papal secretary until the papacy of Calixtus III, who served from 1455 to 1458), he was a presence and, Valla being Valla, a presence who had to make himself felt.

The tensions between the two erupted into a series of bitter polemics. Valla had criticized Poggio's self-collected letters for lacking what Valla saw as proper Latin style. Poggio began by writing an "Oration" against Valla, criticizing certain of Valla's works. Among them were the *Annotations* on the New Testament. Whereas in other critiques Poggio took issue with Valla's readings of ancient texts or conclusions about ancient history, in the case of

---

[16] Most recently, see Christopher S. Celenza, "Lorenzo Valla's Radical Philology: The 'Preface' to the *Annotations to the New Testament* in Context," *Journal of Medieval and Early Modern Studies* 42 (2012), 365–94.

[17] See Wesseling, "Introduzione," in Valla, *Antidotum*, 1–53, at 2.

[18] Ibid., 21–25; Mancini, *Vita*, 226–54.

the *Annotations* Poggio framed his critique quite differently, suggesting that Valla had written a book against Saint Jerome and that Valla "hated sacred scripture." To understand this sort of critique, as well as Valla's response, one needs to step back and think about the function of the Latin Bible in the Middle Ages and Renaissance.

First, there is the matter of Saint Jerome. Jerome, who lived from 347 to 420, was considered so authoritative and important in medieval and Renaissance culture that he became known as one of the "four Latin fathers" of the Church. The others were Ambrose (340–397), Augustine (354–430), and Pope Gregory the Great (pope from 590 to 604). All had important parts to play in the ways that early Christianity merged ancient literary culture with evolving Christian norms, accommodated pagan values in the new Christian world, and finally sped along the more general processes of cultural translation that the evolution of Christianity represented. Their work helped Christianity evolve from one of hundreds of ancient Mediterranean religions to what became, by the fifth century, the dominant religion in the West. That final aspect, translation, proved especially important when it came to scripture. In this case the key figure among the Latin fathers was Saint Jerome. Jerome was learned and equally fluent in both Latin and Greek and, when he realized the great weight that Hebrew had in scriptural tradition, made it his business to learn Hebrew as well. When it came to the Old Testament, Jerome realized that the Latin translations then in use were based not on the original Hebrew but on the "Septuagint," a Greek translation (supposedly done by seventy scholars – hence the name) that was widely used. Jerome, accordingly, turned to the original Hebrew texts and based his Latin translation on them.

When it came to the Greek New Testament, Jerome was faced with a difficult task, one that he recounts in a "Preface" to his eventual Latin translation, a preface addressed to Pope Damasus (pope from 366 to 384). The pope had asked Jerome to produce an authoritative Latin version of the New Testament. Jerome addresses the pope as follows: "You urge that I create a new work out of the old, to sit in judgment on copies of the scriptures, dispersed as these are all over the world, and, given that they vary among themselves, to decide which of them agree with the Greek truth."[19] Jerome goes on to say that he fears critique, given that people long accustomed to reading and worshipping with the aid of a certain Latin version will not be inclined to accept a new version. But at least he could take comfort in

---

[19] Jerome, "Praefatio in Evangelio," in Robertus Weber and Roger Gryson, eds., *Biblia sacra iuxta vulgatam versionem* (Stuttgart: Deutsche Bibelgesellschaft, 1994), pp. 1515–16, at 1515.

the fact that he had the backing of the pope himself. What we can take from this statement is that, already in Jerome's day, the Latin-speaking world had Latin translations of scripture to which they were accustomed. Jerome's fears were legitimate. Readers tend in general to be conservative, in the most literal sense: they resist changes in format to texts to which they are habituated, a resistance ever more intense in religious communities.

But Jerome succeeded. He took as many different existing Latin versions that he could find, compared them with one another and with the Greek original of the New Testament, and went on to produce a final Latin version that became the authoritative Latin version used thereafter. As time went by in the Middle Ages, that Latin version itself acquired the aura of something sacred. It was no longer just a text, but rather itself an object of veneration, with everything about it – the order of the words in which it was written, the words themselves – deemed holy. By Valla's day, medieval thinkers had written commentaries, glosses, and interpretations of the Bible, all based on the Latin text.[20] Reference to the original Greek was not deemed necessary. The Latin version had, after all, been commissioned by a pope, presumably under divine inspiration, and carried out by Jerome, considered a saint and deemed one of the most authoritative figures in the Christian tradition. The Vulgate New Testament had itself become something sacred.

So the fact that Valla decided to start looking at the Latin New Testament, comparing it to the Greek, and suggesting different Latin translations at times, was bound to raise hackles. It is tempting for modern scholars, and to an extent true, to believe that Valla was looking at the New Testament "with the eyes of a scholar," as opposed to through a religious lens. This is to say that what he was doing can be understood on one level as treating the Bible like any other text. In so doing, Valla can be seen – again, to an extent correctly – as contributing in a small way to a secularized view of life, one that would not come to final fruition until much later but that has as one of its constituent parts, small as that might seem, the idea that religious texts were just texts to be analyzed, dissected, and studied like any other text. Noting how some contemporaries understood Valla's work, and observing where Valla's work led a century later, one can affirm that this view has a lot to recommend it. On one level, it was precisely this understanding of Valla's work that led Poggio to critique Valla as someone who had written against Jerome.

[20] See Friedrich Stegmüller, ed., *Repertorium Biblicum Medii Aevi*, 11 vols. (Madrid: Consejo Superior de Investigaciones Cientificas, 1950–80), which has lists of almost 24,000 medieval commentaries (up to the year 1500); see also Beryl Smalley, *The Study of the Bible in the Middle Ages*, 3rd ed. (Oxford: Blackwell, 1983).

But there was more to Poggio's anxiety. To grasp it, it is worth looking at what he says in his first "Oration" against Valla, written in 1452.²¹ There are different levels to Poggio's discomfort with Valla. One, surely, is personal, tied to the fact that Valla seems to attack everyone, ancient and modern, extending his vitriol even to pillars of the Christian faith. Valla, Poggio says, has attacked luminaries of the ancient grammatical tradition, such as Priscian, Donatus, and Servius, among others, all of whom wrote foundational texts explaining and expounding Latin grammar.²² And then,

> in dialectic and philosophy Valla asserts that Aristotle and Boethius erred in many places. He proclaims that Cicero, the very teacher of the art of eloquence didn't know how to speak well! He asserts that the ancient jurisconsults did not know the meaning of many words. He condemns everyone but one, Quintilian, whom, like a fanatic, he declares to have been the most learned of all who ever existed, preferring him even to Cicero ... Valla hasn't read that it was not Quintilian but Cicero that blessed Jerome called a golden river of eloquence. And yet Valla condemns Jerome, declaring that Jerome translated many things incorrectly in holy scripture. He goes so far as to profess the belief – such is the stupidity of this man, or rather, this beast – that blessed Augustine held incorrect opinions in his works *On Fate, On the Trinity*, and *On Providence*. Valla takes in everyone, pagan and Christian, people who are outstanding in every branch of learning, and he does so under one and the same cloud of ignorance.²³

In a succeeding passage, Poggio goes on to declare that Valla, unsatisfied with attacking authors from the past, has wielded his pen against luminaries of the present, Leonardo Bruni among them.²⁴

Many noteworthy features emerge from this extended statement, a rant as much as it is a legitimate critique. The first aspect to notice is the *ad personam* nature of the attack. Valla is noteworthy for his "stupidity"; he is a "beast." Modern scholarly readers, accustomed to today's somewhat more detached tone of scholarly argument, may be surprised by the personal animus. But it was, more or less, par for the course then. Many other such invectives, far worse in tone and language, could be cited from the fifteenth century.²⁵ For

²¹ In Poggio, *Op.*, 188–205.
²² Ibid., 189.
²³ Ibid.
²⁴ Ibid.
²⁵ See Charles Nisard, *Les gladiateurs de la république des lettres aux XVe, XVIe, et XVIIe siècles* (Paris: Levy, 1860); David Rutherford, *Early Renaissance Invective and the Controversies of Antionio da Rho* (Tempe: Arizona Center for Medieval and Renaissance Studies, 2005); Ennio Rao, *Curmudgeons in High Dudgeon: 101 Years of Invectives (1352–1453)* (Messina: EDAS, 2007); Johannes Helmrath, "Streitkultur. Die 'Invektive' bei den italienischen

Poggio, Valla is not just wrong in a scholarly sense. He is a bad person, as well, always prone to lashing out without measure.

Second, the list of authorities is noteworthy for its breadth. In Poggio's view, Valla has attacked everyone from stalwarts of the ancient grammatical tradition, to writers on law, to well-known philosophers, to – horrors – Cicero, to Church fathers. All, in Poggio's accounting, are authorities. And, at least here, emphasizing their authoritative status is enough to score a point against Valla. Poggio believes his readers will agree with him that these ancient authors are so worthy of respect and admiration, Cicero especially, that any attacks against them must by that very fact be suspect. They are authorities, building blocks, as it were, in the great enterprise of constructing modern culture by looking back at the past. You might add to what they did, but your responsibility as a modern critic was to read them in such a way that you drew out of them the truths they contained.

The third aspect that emerges is that, in many ways, Poggio was right. Or, more precisely, his contemporaries might have thought he was right. It is worth exploring how, and why, this perspective might be true. To do so one needs to take a deeper look at some of Valla's works, to see how Poggio draws his conclusions, rhetorically slanted as they admittedly are.

To begin, take what Poggio says about Aristotle and Boethius. Poggio's comments point toward one of Valla's works, with the strange-seeming title of the *Re-digging up of all Dialectic* (*Repastinatio totius dialecticae*), more commonly known as the *Dialectical Disputations*.[26] Valla had many goals in that work, but the most prominent one was to effect reform of logic or "dialectic," as the field was known in the Middle Ages. Like all his works, it is "dialogical," meaning that, whatever the outward form, it contains within it a series of viewpoints and arguments, not all of which can be reconciled with one another, and all of which need to be aired for the work to have maximum effect. And, again like all his works, the *Dialectical Disputations* feels angry, as if Valla seems to be challenging his readers to disagree with him.

Valla begins with a well-known story recounting the origin of the word "philosopher," attributed in ancient sources to Pythagoras. Cicero had told the most widely circulated version of the story.[27] Pythagoras, having gone for

Humanisten," in Marc Laureys, ed., *Die Kunst des Streitens. Inszenierung, Formen und Funktionen öffentlichen Streits in historischer Perspektive* (Göttingen, 2010), 259–93.

[26] Lorenzo Valla, *Dialectical Disputations*, 2 vols., ed. and tr. Brian Copenhaver and Lodi Nauta (Cambridge, MA: Harvard University Press, 2012); on it see Nauta, *In Defense of Common Sense*.

[27] Cicero, *Tusc.*, 5.3.8.

various reasons to the Greek city of Corinth, discoursed confidently and learnedly on many different subjects in the presence of the king, Leon. Curious about Pythagoras, Leon asked him what his "art" was – that is, what was the profession to which Pythagoras owed so much wisdom. Here is what Valla says regarding Pythagoras: "When he was asked what he professed to be, he answered that he was not a wise man, as his predecessors had claimed, but a lover of wisdom."[28]

"Lover of wisdom." This indeed is the Greek etymology of the word "philosopher" (*philia* means "love" and *sophia* means "wisdom"). Originally, then, Pythagoras meant to signal the personal trait of humility in describing himself in that fashion. There had indeed been those who might have professed themselves "wise," or *sophoi* in Greek. But the original designation – "philosophy" – was intended to suggest that the search for truth must be undertaken with due humility, that it was an ongoing project, and that no one person or even school of thinkers could ever have found all truth.[29] This, anyway, is what Valla meant to highlight in his use of this anecdote, one that, though repeated by others in the ancient world, has no documentary foundation, since Pythagoras never wrote anything that was preserved. It is a story, in other words, one that Valla uses to highlight the importance of modesty when it comes to the enterprise of philosophy. "How great a praise of modesty" it was when Pythagoras gave that simple answer to the question as to his profession.[30]

No less admirable, Valla goes on, are those succeeding philosophers who got the message, those who "took their name from Pythagoras but were unafraid to disagree with the person who in some ways invented the breed of philosophers ... It was not a man they followed but truth and excellence, which was their immediate aim wherever they found it, without regard to anyone's authority."[31] Think of this statement, and combine it with Poggio's critique as quoted earlier, to the effect that Valla had lashed out at many of literary, religious, and philosophical history's great figures. Again, what we see is the power of generations. Poggio himself, one recalls, had vented about blind allegiance to authority among intellectuals during his stay in Britain, as he had satirized their lack of literary polish. Yet Poggio's critique had occurred back in the 1420s. Valla took up the mantle of reformer with

---

[28] Valla, *Dialectical Disputations*, 1: 3, tr. Copenhaver/Nauta.
[29] See for background on this view Pierre Hadot, *What Is Ancient Philosophy?* (Cambridge, MA: Harvard University Press, 2004).
[30] Valla, *Dialectical Disputations*, 2.
[31] Valla, *Dialectical Disputations*, 1: 3, tr. Copenhaver/Nauta, modified.

vigor, and Poggio, in his *Oration* against Valla, is reduced to saying that Valla in many places did not respect authority enough.

When we look carefully at Valla's critiques of Aristotle and Boethius, or rather, at Poggio's distortion thereof, things become even more textured. What Valla is after, in one respect, is freedom of speech. He says so explicitly when he writes that after Pythagoras and his sterling example, "philosophers have always had the freedom to say straightforwardly what they think, not only against leaders of other groups but also against their own, which is even truer of those not committed to a sect."[32] When Valla uses the word "sect," here, he is subtly sending the message that real philosophers need to preserve the freedom to go where their inquiry takes them. The word "sect" in Latin is *secta* and is related to the Greek *haeresis*. Both derive from verbs that mean most literally "cutting off" and that more broadly mean "to choose." The Greek word *haeresis* is related obviously to "heresy," a word that originally meant "choice" but that came in late antiquity to mean the "wrong choice." Valla thus criticizes thinkers who profess too strong an allegiance to one school of thought; at the same time, he weaves a strand of rhetoric into this evolving tapestry, a strand that would have subliminally suggested religious overtones to a reader. He raises the stakes, in other words.

As to Aristotle, Valla has this to say: "Not to be endured, then, are the modern Peripatetics" – this term meant "Aristotelians" – "who deny me, a man belonging to no sect, the liberty of disagreeing with Aristotle."[33] Valla goes on to give a learned account of how many other schools of thought there were in antiquity, many of whom disagreed with Aristotle. Then he moves to language, ridiculing present-day Aristotelians who believe that they "know" Aristotle; "if in fact," Valla goes on, "knowing is habitually reading him not in his own language but in one that is foreign, not to say inauthentic, not only because most translations of Aristotle's works are bad but also because much that is said well in Greek is not said well in Latin."[34] More to the point, Valla suggests, Aristotle tended to ignore matters of the utmost importance, such as political debate about how to govern provinces, how to lead an army, argue legal cases, practice medicine, and so on. And – not unlike what he said about scripture – "if there are things anywhere in Aristotle that he might have said better, I myself shall do my best to say them better, not to blame the person . . . but to honor the truth."[35] Here and elsewhere, Valla emerges as a thinker who took a somewhat obnoxious

---

[32] Ibid., 3–5, tr. modified.
[33] Ibid., 5, tr. modified.
[34] Ibid., 7.
[35] Ibid., 11.

personal proclivity to seek distinction by disagreeing with everyone around him and turned it into a kind of method, one in which he had such confidence that he believed he could improve upon the ancients.

To return to Poggio's charges regarding Aristotle and Boethius: as to Aristotle, what Valla is proposing in the *Disputations* is quite radical. It is nothing less than to present an alternative to a system of logic (dialectic) that had transcendental categories as its foundation.[36] Since the high Middle Ages in Western Europe, basic instruction in logic had taken the Latin translation of Aristotle's *Organon*, or "Instrument," as its point of departure.[37] The six works in this collection (*Categories, On Interpretation, Prior Analytics, Posterior Analytics, Topics*, and *Sophistical Refutations*) served as an underpinning for education in the liberal arts and became the basis of medieval scholastic logic. One of the key elements of this system was the presupposition that there existed ten transcendental categories superintending all things. With these categories, the thinking went, one could comprehend all of being. For Aristotle, these were: substance, quantity, quality, relation, place, time, position, state, action, and affection.[38] Boethius had provided the standard Latin translation of much of Aristotle's logical work, thus unleashing, in Valla's eyes, terrible, inauthentic terminology into the bloodstream of intellectual life. To these ten categories, Western medieval Latin thinkers added

---

[36] For different perspectives on what Valla was up to, see Paul Richard Blum, *Philosophieren in der Renaissance* (Stuttgart: Kohlhammer, 2004), 44–55; Riccardo Fubini, "Contributo per l'interpretazione della *Dialectica* di Lorenzo Valla," in Graziella F. Vescovini, ed., *Filosofia e scienza classica, arabo-latina medievale e l'età moderna*, (Louvain-la-Neuve: Fédération Internationale des Instituts d'Études Médiévales, 1999) 289–316; Hanna-Barbara Gerl, *Rhetorik als Philosophie: Lorenzo Valla* (Munich: Fink, 1974); Eckhard Kessler, "Die Transformation des aristotelischen Organon durch Lorenzo Valla," in Eckhard Kessler, ed., *Aristotelismus und Renaissance: In memoriam Charles B. Schmitt* (Wiesbaden: Harrasowitz, 1988), 53–74; Jill Kraye, "Lorenzo Valla and Changing Perceptions of Renaissance Humanism," in *Comparative Criticism*, 23 (2001), 37–55; Marco Laffranchi, *Dialettica e filosofia in Lorenzo Valla* (Milan: Vita e Pensiero, 1999); Peter Mack, *Renaissance Argument: Valla and Agricola in the Traditions of Rhetoric and Dialectic* (Leiden: Brill, 1993); John Monfasani, "Was Lorenzo Valla an Ordinary Language Philosopher?" *Journal of the History of Philosophy* 50 (1989), 309–23, repr. with same pagination in John Monfasani, *Language and Learning in Renaissance Italy* (Aldershot: Ashgate, 1994); Nauta, *In Defense of Common Sense*; Alan Perreiah, "Humanist Critiques of Scholastic Dialectic," *Sixteenth-Century Journal* 13 (1982), 3–22.

[37] For the Latin translations of the *Organon*, see Aristotle, *Categoriae vel praedicamenta*, Aristoteles latinus, 1.1–5, ed. Lorenzo Minio-Paluello (Bruges: Desclée de Brouwer, 1961), which included the early Boethian translation, another early medieval composite translation, and the high medieval translation of William of Moerbeke and the *Categoriarum supplementa*, Aristoteles latinus, 1.6–7, ed. Minio-Paluello and Bernard G. Dod (Bruges: Desclée de Brouwer, 1966).

[38] Aristotle, *Cat.*, 4, Latin in Aristotle, *Categoriae vel praedicamenta*, pp. 6–7, 48, 86–87.

six transcendentals (also called *praedicamenta*): *res* ("thing"), *ens* ("being"), *unum* ("one"), *aliquid* ("something"), *verum* ("the true"), and *bonum* ("the good").[39]

The year 1439 saw Valla finish the first version of his attack on this wide-ranging system (he completed a second version in 1448 and a third in 1452). All three redactions of this work showcase Valla's "pruning" of the excesses of contemporary logic as it was taught and learned in contemporary universities ("pruning" is another meaning of the word *repastinatio*, which became part and parcel of the work's extended title). When Valla was criticizing Aristotelians, it was allegiance to this system that he at least partially had in mind.

But he does more than criticize the categories as excessive. Following Quintilian, Valla reduces these metaphysical categories to three: substance, quality, and action. Together, these three categories reflect the mental pattern behind the commonly uttered, everyday sentence: "substance" corresponds to "noun" or "subject," "quality" to "adjective or adverb," and "action" to "verb" or "predicate."[40] Of the six medieval transcendentals, only one remains, *res*, or "thing," which stands, Valla says, as "king" (*rex*) among them.[41] Valla took the predilection of Italian humanists to focus on history and the ordinary, everyday world and transposed it to scholastic logic, focusing on the way our commonplace utterances reflected the knowable meaning of the world. In doing so, he became the first Italian humanist to move beyond exaggerated attacks on scholastic philosophers, instead attempting to challenge them on their own ground.

The complexities of the issue, however, were lost on Poggio, who by the 1450s was a settled member of the establishment. As a person, Valla was annoying, to be sure. But he was also up to something so revolutionary that not only Poggio but also most of his contemporaries missed it. One way to measure the popularity of an author in the Renaissance is to look at how many manuscripts and early printed editions of his or her work existed. The only one of Valla's works to achieve any measure of success in this regard was his *Elegances of the Latin Language*, a brilliant manual of Latin style that became a respected textbook in the late fifteenth and sixteenth centuries. But before turning to that work and surveying a few others, we should return

---

[39] See Jan Aertsen, *Medieval Philosophy as Transcendental Thought: From Phillip the Chancellor (ca. 1225) to Francisco Suárez* (Leiden: Brill, 2012); Jorge Gracia, "The Transcendentals in the Middle Ages: An Introduction," *Topoi* 11 (1992), 113–20.

[40] Valla, *Dialectical Disputations*, 1: 13–17, pp. 200–81.

[41] Ibid., 1: 2, pp. 18–37, esp. 24–27.

to his debate with Poggio over his work on the New Testament, the debate that occasioned the quotation with which this chapter opened.

Placed in context, Valla's response to Poggio is sophisticated. Replying to the charge that he had written his *Annotations to the New Testament* motivated by *invidia* – "hateful jealousy" – Valla, aggressive as always, offers his justification to Poggio. Valla stresses that ancient writers confirm that both the Old and New Testaments had many translators and translations.[42] Valla goes on: "And so what would you say Sacred Scripture is? Surely nothing more than the true translation. But it is this that is uncertain."[43] The words translated here as "true translation," *veram interpretationem*, have capacious meanings. They could equally, and correctly, be rendered as "authentic interpretation."

What is Valla really saying here? One way we can read him (and this is ultimately what is revolutionary about him) is to remark that he is propounding the notion that all texts, even sacred ones, need constantly to be re-translated and reinterpreted. Their meanings are never fixed but will change inevitably according to time and cultural context. Was this Valla's personal intention? Perhaps yes, perhaps no. Valla was so egotistical, resentful of authority, and convinced of his own fundamental rightness that he may indeed have believed that he and only he could provide not only the "true translation" of any text but also that, to boot, once he did it, the questions regarding whatever text it was would be settled. Again, however, discerning an author's own intention is less important than seeing the potential in an author's work, seeing in other words what sort of work an author's writings do in the world. And make no mistake: the Bible was not any other text. Once you start fiddling with the Vulgate New Testament's Latin, how far of a leap is it to believe that, perhaps, the Bible should be read in other languages as well? Valla never advocated doing so of course and indeed never even provided a new Latin translation. But it is no accident that Valla was one of the few Italian humanist authors of whom Martin Luther approved and that more than one scholar has seen in Valla a legitimate precursor of certain attitudes associated with the Protestant Reformation.[44] In other words, once you open the floodgates even a bit, the water starts to flow. Even if it is initially only a trickle, that trickle can serve as a sign and premonition of the flood to come.

When it came to the New Testament, it was precisely to metaphors of water that Valla turned. In his preface explaining his intentions, Valla noted

---

[42] Lorenzo Valla, *Antidotum Primum*, 112.
[43] Ibid.
[44] See Salvatore I. Camporeale, *Christianity, Latinity, and Culture: Two Studies on Lorenzo Valla*, tr. Patrick Baker, ed. Patrick Baker and Christopher S. Celenza (Leiden: Brill, 2014).

that Jerome's own preface to his Vulgate translation suggested that many versions scripture were around. Valla then says: "if within four hundred years those streams were already flowing so wildly, it is almost definite that after a thousand years (for it is indeed so many years from Jerome to now) this stream, which was never cleansed, has taken on some filth and pollution, at least in part."[45] Later in the same preface, Valla likened the New Testament to a magnificent temple whose roof needed repairs, repairs that he himself was carrying out, "because if the temple is not cared for, rain will necessarily enter, and matters divine would be unable to be celebrated therein."[46] Reading Valla on one level (the level on which he is often, but incompletely, read) one might think what he is proposing is simple, as if he is saying, "let's just clean all this up." We know after all that scripture is the center of Christian life, that the Latin version is tremendously important, and that, over time, unskilled scribes and editors have corrupted the text. We need to clean up the stream and fix the roof. The way to do this is to focus on the Greek original, so that we can make sure the Latin is correct. Simple.

Yet Valla was aiming at something more profound. Poggio and others had reason to be concerned. Take what Valla says elsewhere in the same preface:

> Add to this the fact that I am not always examining the Greek words, but rather laying bare any ambiguities occurring in the Latin and illuminating any instances when the regular practice of literal translation may have made things more difficult to understand. I am doing this to alert those who don't know Greek at all or who may have a shaky grasp of Latin about this matter, small though it may be.[47]

Remember that Valla is nowhere coming out and advocating for a new translation. Still, he is saying that the way the New Testament seems to have been translated, in a word-for-word fashion, may have actually obscured its meaning. Jerome himself had once said that he preferred to translate "sense for sense," meaning not necessarily literally, in all cases but one: that of sacred scripture, "where even the order of the words represents a mystery."[48]

---

[45] Valla wrote two versions of this preface, one in the 1430s and the other in 1449; the Latin texts to both are edited by Alessandro Perosa in Lorenzo Valla, *Collatio Novi Testamenti* (Florence: Sansoni, 1970), 3–7 (*Praefatio*) and 7–10 (*Praefatio, forma antiquior*). They are translated in Christopher S. Celenza, "Lorenzo Valla's Radical Philology: The 'Preface' to the *Annotations to the New Testament* in Context," *Journal of Medieval and Early Modern Studies* 42 (2012), 365–94, at 380–83 and 385–87; the cited passage is at 382.

[46] Valla, *Praefatio*, in Celenza, "Lorenzo Valla's Radical Philology," 383.

[47] Ibid., 382.

[48] Jerome, *De optimo genere interpretandi (Epistula 57)*, ed. G.J.M. Bartelink (Leiden: Brill, 1980), 13; par. 5, sent. 2.: "ubi et verborum ordo mysterium est."

Jerome – who if not the Latin Vulgate's translator was at least its final editor, as Valla well knew – had believed that you needed a literal translation when it came to scripture. If the order of the words represented a mystery, then it was up to commentators to unravel the mystery, to explain it to the uninitiated, and to serve as the arbiters of interpretation. Valla, however, sees things differently. He does not wish to rely on commentators. He wants instead, to experience the text directly.

Later, in his debate with Poggio, Valla tries to suggest sympathy with Jerome, to the effect that were Jerome to come back to life, "he would correct what has been corrupted and ruined in certain copies, in just the same way as I am doing in my *Collatio*" – meaning the *Annotations* – "a work that you, Poggio, claim is motivated by hatred."[49] But the truth was that Valla, in his earlier preface to the *Annotations*, was much more explicit regarding his thoughts on Jerome, writing what amounted to a challenge to Jerome's authority. It is worth concluding this chapter with a detailed examination of that challenge.

As mentioned earlier, Jerome had written a preface, directed to Pope Damasus, who had commissioned the project of the Vulgate under Jerome's direction. In it, Jerome expressed anxiety regarding what he was doing. Valla takes the bold step of citing Jerome's preface almost in its entirety and then poking holes in it.

First, here is Jerome, addressing Pope Damasus (and as cited by Valla): "You [Pope Damasus] urge that I create a new work out of the old, to sit in judgment on the copies of the scriptures, dispersed as these are all over the world, and given that they vary among themselves, to decide which of them agree with the Greek truth."[50] Jerome goes on to say that he fears that people used to one version of scripture will be reticent about accepting a new one, even as he can at least reassure himself that he is taking his orders from the pope. And going back to the original Greek is a good idea, since one can "correct those things that were either poorly published by erroneous translators, or wrongly emended by presumptuous ignoramuses, or added or changed by sleepy scribes."[51] All of this sounds reasonable. And, of course, all medieval readers of the Latin Vulgate had read this preface of Saint Jerome. It had become an essential part of the textual tradition of the Vulgate and was indeed by Valla's day an essential part of the packaging of scripture itself.

---

[49] Lorenzo Valla, *Antidotum Primum*, 112.
[50] Valla, *Praefatio*, citing Jerome, in Celenza, "Lorenzo Valla's Radical Philology," 380.
[51] Ibid., 380–81, still citing Jerome.

Valla offers a little humility – mock humility – before he begins his critique:

> Now if such a great and learned man, who on top of that was commanded
> by the Pope, speaks with such care to avoid hatred, what then must I, such
> a little man, do? I, who have been ordered by no one? I, who cannot spread
> out before me so many different exemplars and who thus seem to emend –
> far be it from me – the very emendation of Jerome?[52]

That relatively transparent excuse out of the way, Valla begins his critique.
And he does so in a way that should by now be familiar, employing the
manner and intellectual habits of the dialogue, if not in form, then in content.
In so doing, Valla manages to set himself up in opposition to Jerome.

The specific device Valla uses is that of the "persona." What he says, after
his little bit of false humility just noted, is this:

> Still, if we reckon rightly, what Jerome did then was more hateful than
> what I am doing now, and so one must utilize a sober and careful style of
> speech and not hide the fact that almost everyone will object. Let me
> personify these objectors, as if we were now living in that time, as I take
> on their voice and address Jerome.[53]

The stage is set. Valla will take on the voice of – purely hypothetical –
"objectors" from the distant past. Doing so permits him to launch critiques
directly at long dead Jerome, even as the literary device of the "persona"
allows Valla to distance himself, as if to say only that "some people" might
have objected to what Jerome did, but not, of course, Valla himself.

What are the objections? Here is how the objectors begin: "You say that
Damasus orders you to figure out which exemplars agree with the Greek
truth. Yet you are not doing this. Instead you are creating a new work even as
you condemn all works."[54] From the outset we see that Valla intends to pick
apart what he sees as internal contradictions in Jerome's preface. Here Valla is
simply pointing out that there is very little discussion in Jerome's preface of
the Greek text. Instead of looking at the Greek original and, in a sense,
restoring the original, Jerome, so the objectors suggest, was innovating:
"creating a new work," not something desirable in a world where tradition
was prized. They go on: "In defense of what you are doing, which is twofold,
you bring forward a twofold argument. You condemn all the exemplars as
faulty; you create a new work, since the pope not only commands you to do
but also 'compels' you. So we are asking of you that you clear both of these

---

[52] Ibid., 381.
[53] Ibid.
[54] Ibid.

things up."[55] This statement represents the beginnings of Valla's attempt to find contradictions in Jerome's account. The objectors quote Jerome back at himself, who had said that in looking over all the versions of scripture, "there are almost as many versions as there are codices," meaning that Jerome had suggested that the written version of the scriptures in his day varied so much among themselves that it was necessary to take editorial action. But the objectors say: "Certainly it is possible that there is one out of this diverse collection that is reliable, which it is wrongful to condemn as error-ridden? Still, can anyone who hasn't read all the exemplars that there are in the world really know about all the exemplars?"[56] The objectors are launching the charge that Jerome was careless; that it was impossible that no versions of scripture then in circulation were accurate; and that Jerome certainly hadn't traveled all over Christendom to see all extant versions.

Then Valla's objectors launch a more personal attack, at least an implicit one, against Jerome. If Jerome is indeed suggesting that he is pronouncing on all ancient "exemplars" (manuscript versions of the text of the Bible), then

> that would be to slander the greatest of men, by which I mean not only the pope but also Hilarius, Ambrose, Augustine, and very many others. You seem to mean that none of these men possessed a reliable exemplar, as if to say that they either did not care about doing so or even that they were unaware that they didn't possess a reliable exemplar.[57]

In other words, here are three respected Church fathers other than you, Jerome. How can it be that, in all they wrote and thought about scripture, they were wantonly using unreliable manuscripts? Are you saying that only you, Jerome, came to the realization that there were different and faulty versions of the Bible out there? The implied question was: wouldn't that be tremendously arrogant of you? "So don't condemn others if you don't want to condemn yourself," say the objectors.[58]

Strong language. But there is more, as they move on to the second part of the problem, the idea, that is, that Jerome claims to have been ordered by Pope Damasus to create a new version of scripture. Yet, "how can it happen that he ordered that whatever good exemplars there are should be discovered, as if he thinks there are certain good ones, and that a new work be created from the old, as if he thinks each and every one is bad?"[59] In other

---

[55] Ibid.
[56] Ibid.
[57] Ibid.
[58] Ibid.
[59] Ibid.

words, Jerome, why did you write two things that were mutually exclusive? Valla's objectors are calling Jerome on the carpet, basically saying in no uncertain terms that Jerome's preface, part of scripture since time immemorial, was poorly thought out. It is Valla speaking, of course, and what he is doing more than anything else is clearing the field for himself, suggesting that he too has the right to examine scripture carefully and critically.

So important is scripture, in fact, that Valla believes he has not only the right but also the obligation to bring his talents to the project of interpreting scripture. After all, he knows Greek and, in an earlier version of his preface to the *Annotations*, Valla had said that in Vulgate, "many things are translated in an obscure fashion. This is not the fault of the translator but rather of the rules and demands of translation, at least of that kind of translation that is not sense for sense but word for word, such as this translation, which those who don't know Greek cannot understand. This being the case, they" – and here Valla means contemporary theologians – "pour forth in their expositions many things that are false, unsuitable, and quite inconsistent with the truth."[60] Contemporary theology was bankrupt, and it needed Valla to fix it, to place it on its only true course, that of direct engagement with the original Greek text of the New Testament.

In the longer term, Valla's *Annotations* to the New Testament had legs. The northern European humanist Erasmus discovered them in a manuscript he found in a library outside of Louvain in 1504, when he was on a manuscript "hunt," as he put it. Erasmus had Valla's *Annotations* printed in 1505, and it was then that they entered the bloodstream of religious reform. Erasmus himself used Valla's *Annotations* as the basis for his own set of notes to the New Testament, which encompassed Valla's and added many more.[61] And of course, as mentioned, Valla's attitude toward scripture can indeed be seen as prefiguring the Reformation.[62]

As to Valla, what emerged from his Prefaces to his New Testament work? Well, Jerome was wrong. Valla's contemporary theologians, ignorant as they were, were so wrong that they were practically inventing things. The river

---

[60] Valla, *Praefatio, forma antiquior*, in Celenza, "Lorenzo Valla's Radical Philology," 387.

[61] For Erasmus's letter describing his "hunt," see Erasmus, *Opus epistolarum Des. Erasmi Roterodami*, ed. P.S. Allen (Oxford: Clarendon Press, 1906–58), letter 182, 1–4; for Erasmus's biblical work see Erika Rummel, *Erasmus' Annotations On the New Testament: From Philologist to Theologian* (Toronto: University of Toronto Press, 1986); and H.J. de Jonge, "Novum testamentum a nobis versum," *Journal of Theological Studies* 35 (1984): 394–413.

[62] In addition to Camporeale, as earlier, see Luther on Valla (after Reading Valla's treatise on the *Donation of Constantine*), in Martin Luther, *Martin Luthers Werke. Kritische Gesamtausgabe, part 4, Briefwechsel*, vol. 2, ed. Johannes Ficker (Weimar: H. Böhlaus Nachfolger, 1931), 28.

was dirty; the roof was leaking. Is it any wonder that Poggio hated Valla? Their debate was no isolated phenomenon. Valla crossed verbal swords with many of his contemporaries, and he and Poggio continued to feud. More important than cataloguing insults, however, will be understanding just where and how the two differed. Doing so will entail closing this chapter and opening the next.

To close where we began, we can look once again at that momentous quotation of Valla's as he answered Poggio's charge of violating sacred scripture by suggesting that the translation could be improved: "So if I am correcting anything, I am *not* correcting Sacred Scripture, but rather its *translation*, and in doing so I am not being insolent toward scripture but rather pious, and I am doing nothing more than translating better than the earlier translator, so that it is my translation – should it be correct – that ought to be called Sacred Scripture, not his." Valla's wording cleverly and carefully elides the fact that Jerome had been identified as the translator for a millennium. And we have seen that Valla was certainly willing to criticize Jerome.

What we can draw from this quotation and this debate is the following. Controversies and rival personalities propelled argument. Argument, in turn, propelled discovery, so that, as rivals positioned themselves against one another, they refined their positions. The real difference between Valla and Poggio had to do, unsurprisingly, with their perceptions of the nature of the Latin language. The debate on this fundamental questioned continued. It included Poggio, Valla, and other figures, all of whom had their part to play.

9

THE NATURE OF THE LATIN LANGUAGE:
POGGIO VERSUS VALLA

L ANGUAGE IS THE MOST FUNDAMENTAL MEANS OF HUMAN
expression, of social contact, and of community coherence. Its origin
in vocal communication, derived from person-to-person interaction in
a living, natural fashion, is masked by writing, which inevitably "fixes"
language in a certain form. Certain questions have always accompanied
writers and writing: who gets to write? What form should writing take?
In what "register" should writing occur? Should what is written down have
aspirations to permanence? In other words, should people far in the future be
considered when writing things down? Or is it enough to formalize the way
we speak now, tied as that "vernacular" is to a certain time and place? And
then of course, when we are dealing with the humanities and other academic
areas, there are disciplines: restricted communities of thinkers who often
need equally specialized vocabularies, as shortcuts, to make their work and
communication more efficient. How far should those disciplines go in
communicating with outsiders? What are the boundaries of disciplines,
especially when it comes to the humanities?

These questions occur whenever writing and intellectual communities
coalesce. But they were especially acute in fifteenth-century thinkers'
approaches to the Latin language. In an important sense, these questions
reached their peak in the careers of Poggio Bracciolini and Lorenzo Valla.
Their outlooks differed to such an extent that they stand as exemplars of the
two fundamentally different ways of looking at the Latin language question.
Understanding their views allows us not only to see where this debate was in
mid-century. It also offers hints as to where the debate, and in many ways
Italian Renaissance humanism, was destined to go.

Poggio, who was one of the original group of thinkers present when the
debate began in the 1430s, entered it "officially" only in 1450. In that year, he
wrote a dialogue addressing the question whether there was "one type of

speech for learned men, and another for the common people and the crowd," suggesting that it reflected a discussion he had the year before, in 1449, when he was asked to recall that much earlier conversation at the papal court.[1] Back then, he says, his response had been, essentially, that it all depends on where one grows up. Why is it so difficult to imagine that something now acquired by learning could not then have been mastered by daily usage? We know of many in the environment of the papal court who arrived unlearned and then through the custom of speaking and listening to others could speak Latin in a passable way. If the ancients learned this language along with their mother's milk, it makes perfect sense that they should have been in possession of the language.[2] It should be said that Poggio's examination of this problem does not go far beyond that last point on a theoretical level. Its richness and importance, however, lie in the amount of material he gathers and the way he brings it together. In effect, though he would by no means be the last to address the question, Poggio settles it in all the ways that matter, as we shall see.

Poggio himself is the dialogue's main interlocutor (this is one of those relatively transparent cases where we can assume that the interlocutor's position matches that of the author in real life). He begins the dialogue's main section by recalling his old friend Leonardo Bruni, who, he says, had always encouraged him to write on the topic.[3] Poggio sets out his own arguments first, then toward the end addresses Bruni's points in that long-ago letter that Bruni had written in response to Flavio Biondo. The name of the language, Latin, Poggio begins, comes from the language spoken by the inhabitants of Latium, who were known as the Latini: "Reason itself establishes that this was their only language. Had there been another language different from this one, another name would have been chosen."[4] Without addressing the birth of the vernacular, Poggio mentions the notion that present-day Romans (especially women) preserve some Latin locutions in their speech, and he traces some Latin expressions in the speech of present-day Spaniards.[5] These survivals all show that some isolated remains of a different, ancient tongue survive in the vernaculars of today.

Poggio's next set of arguments draws principally on Quintilian and Cicero. Its aim is to document Latin being spoken and understood in

---

[1] Poggio, *Disceptatio convivialis, III*, ed. in Tavoni, 239–59, at 239.
[2] Ibid.
[3] Ibid., 240.
[4] Ibid.: "Hanc unicam fuisse ipsa ratione constat. Si enim alius ab hoc sermo extitisset, aliud quoque nomen sortitum esset."
[5] Ibid.

a wide variety of circumstances. Poggio uses traditional arguments that had come up earlier in the debate. Cornelia, the mother of the Gracchi brothers, taught them to speak well by her own example; orations being given before broad audiences must have been understood; there is evidence that the audiences of both plays and orations understood what was going on; and there is support for the idea that people without formal learning could still be excellent speakers. Along the way he also gathers evidence from ancient authors such as Aulus Gellius, the historian Livy, the orator Cicero, and the writer Varro, all of whom demonstrated that the ancient Latin language changed *in antiquity*: from Gellius and Livy he finds places where they highlighted the influx of foreign words into Latin (from the Etruscans, Spanish, the Gauls, and so on); from Varro he finds evidence that the ancient Latin language itself changed: what had once been the pronoun *ollum* ("that thing") changed form and became *illum*, for example. And, again, that change occurred in antiquity itself.[6]

Poggio, with his historical sense, comprehended ancient Latin as one long, essentially unitary and organic language that, nonetheless, like all historical phenomena, was constantly changing and reflecting historical circumstances. From Varro, too, he found evidence that common people would occasionally misspeak, declining nouns incorrectly, for example. The fact that their mistakes were noticed as such serves as evidence both that the Latin language was unitary and that the commoners making mistakes were not speaking a wholly different language. Another telling example along these lines comes when Poggio gives the example, drawn from Aulus Gellius, that an ancient Roman figure named Sisenna introduced the verb form *assentio* ("I agree") in place of the traditionally deponent verb *assentior* (same meaning, but morphologically different), and that he was thereafter followed in this usage.[7] Again, this type of example shows that Poggio not only realizes that languages change but also that change was inevitable, a natural property of all things human.

Poggio made short work of Bruni's old letter toward the end of the dialogue. Poggio argued that one can document even private conversations held in Latin, conversations for which a vernacular, had a separate one existed, would have been appropriate.[8] Bruni had highlighted the case of the Mass as something of which the common people had a passive understanding. This example does not work for Poggio. He points out that the

[6] Ibid., 252 (citing Varro, *Ling.*, 7.42).
[7] Ibid., 255 (citing Gell, 2.25, who was himself citing Varro).
[8] Ibid., 257 (citing Flavius Vopiscus, *Aurelian*, 14.1–2).

Mass and the Gospels are repeated ritualistically, the same texts in the same ways, so that it is inevitable that people will have knowledge of them. By contrast, the orations that the common people would have heard in the general assembly in ancient Rome were different each time. And even if ancient authors polished the orations when committing them to writing, they were still originally spoken in Latin.[9] Finally, plays (e.g., those of Terence) were not only sights of spectacle and action, as Bruni had intimated. They were also recited, so that the texts were quite important in understanding their meaning.[10] Soon thereafter Carlo Marsuppini, one of Poggio's interlocutors in the dialogue, convinces the assembled group in the dialogue to go off and have a drink, and the interlocutors disperse.

Poggio's lengthy exposition yields the following message: for him, ancient Latin was a unitary language spoken by all ancient Romans, even if different people spoke Latin with differing levels of ability. He arrived at that position both by common sense and by his knowledge of ancient authors who had provided evidence in their texts that pointed to change even in ancient Latin.

Another way of understanding Poggio's views on the Latin language, its potential, and its use, is to circle back and return to one of his chief motivators: conflict with Valla. Here, his *First Invective* against Valla comes to the fore, the very text to which Valla responded (and wherein he made his extravagant claims about translating scripture).[11] It contained the usual sorts of insults of which Renaissance invectives tend to be full. For example, Poggio writes that "our dear Valla ... has published a book that he titled *On the Elegance of the Latin Language*, though we should rather call it *On the Ignorance of the Latin Language*."[12] Poggio goes on to critique many of Valla's positions in his vaunted *Elegances of the Latin Language* (that is the work to which Poggio refers), calls Valla possibly heretical (for calling Jerome's translations of the Vulgate into question and misunderstanding – in Poggio's view – a word related to the Trinity), and overall amasses a formidable list of critiques, all designed to paint Valla in the worst light possible.[13]

The most telling of Poggio's critiques suggests that Valla's approach to language rejects authority and therefore cannot be trusted. It is worth looking at an extended passage in Poggio's invective. For Poggio, Valla has dared to

[9] Ibid., 258.
[10] Ibid., 259.
[11] See Poggio Bracciolini, "Poggii florentini invectiva in L. Vallam prima," in Poggio, *Op.*, 188–205.
[12] Ibid., 194.
[13] Ibid., 198–200.

recall the philosophy of Aristotle, the eloquence of Cicero, the learning of Varro and other leading lights of the Latin language, not to mention the most learned philosophers Boethius and Albert the Great "without the highest respect and reverence."[14] Poggio goes on:

> This most inelegant of men [meaning Valla] presumes to argue against such men and to snipe at their words and sentiments. You see how great is the blindness, the madness, of this crime. When it comes to Latin words, their proper meaning, force, sense, and construction all are established not so much from reason as from the authority of ancient writers. If you take that away, it is foreordained that both the foundation and sustenance of the Latin language will perish. Usage has always been the master, when it comes to speaking Latin; and usage is found only in the books and writings of ancient authors.[15]

Poggio goes on to accuse Valla of violating this principle and of, in effect, introducing newness into a realm that is based, fundamentally, on past practice and past practice alone.

What stand out, of course, are the phrases "not so much from reason as from the authority of ancient writers" and "usage is found only in the books and writings of ancient authors." With respect to how and why Poggio differs from Valla, both sentiments can be better understood once we discuss Valla's views in more depth. For now, however, it is enough to note that this moment, fueled by anger and polemical energy though it was, represents the capstone of the debate over the status of the Latin language. No one knew it at the time, of course, and others would enter into that debate. Take the phrase "Only in the in the books and writings of ancient authors." Nowhere does Poggio say that Latin is now a "dead" language – indeed, for him as for the rest of his fifteenth-century colleagues, the terminological distinction of a "living" versus a "dead" language was still decades away.[16] But conceiving of a language whose proper usage was present only in books carried with it obvious implications, or rather, one obvious implication: Latin was a dead language. Discovering as they did through research that ancient Latin had

---

[14] Ibid., 203.

[15] Ibid.: "Hic nisi esset insuavissimus, praesumeret redarguere tales viros et eorum verba et sententias carpere. Videte quanta sit huius prodigii caecitas et insania. Latinorum verborum proprietas, vis, significatio, constructio non tantum ratione, quantum veterum scriptorium autoritate constant. Qua sublata latinae linguae fundamentum et sustentaculum pereat necesse est. Latine enim loquendi usus semper fuit magister, qui solum autorum priscorum libris et scriptis continentur."

[16] On this point see R. Faithfull, "The Concept of 'Living Language' in Cinquecento Vernacular Philology," *Modern Language Review* 48 (1953), 278–92.

been a living natural language, humanists came to understand the notion of a dead language.[17]

Poggio was then in his seventies. His younger rival, the polemical Lorenzo Valla, had very different ideas about Latin. Understanding them means understanding how Valla saw himself: as a unique, singular reformer and as – it is no exaggeration to say it – a man of destiny. No one else saw him that way, of course. The history of the manuscript and early printed circulation of Valla's major works shows that his contemporaries, whether put off by his atrocious personality or, more likely, because they didn't understand what he was up to, did not consume Valla's writing in great numbers, the way they did that of Leonardo Bruni, for instance. But it is only by realizing Valla's view of himself as a reformer, exceptional in his abilities and obligations, that we can understand the scope of his view on the Latin language. In the end, Valla saw Christianity, Latinity, and human culture all as intimately linked together. And it is a telling fact that Valla did not really enter into the debate on the status of the ancient Latin language.

One window through which we can peer to observe Valla's views coming into shape happens to be his only work that did have a substantial manuscript and print circulation: the *Elegances of the Latin Language* (*Elegantiae linguae latinae*), that very text Poggio had hoped to impugn.[18] Written like all his major works during his time at the court of Alfonse of Aragon, the *Elegances* remained an object of interest for Valla throughout his life. Later, by the early sixteenth century, the *Elegances* became an admired textbook on Latin stylistics, the place you went if you wanted to make sure you were using Latin correctly, which is to say in a way that was both grammatically sound and sufficiently respectful of proper usage to be up to the best standards of the day. The power of language and Valla's own view on usage represent worthy points at which we can begin.

As to power, Valla expresses himself clearly enough in the Preface to Book One of the *Elegances*. There he begins by sounding a triumphalist note regarding Latin. Even if, compared to the Roman Empire, other ancient empires expanded their power (Valla mentions the Persians, Medes, Assyrians, and Greeks), none "expanded their language to the extent that our people did."[19] The word translated here as "our people" is, in Latin,

---

[17] As noted by Silvia Rizzo, *Ricerche sul latino umanistico*, vol. 1 (Rome: Edizioni di storia e letteratura, 2002).

[18] See D. Marsh, "Grammar, Method, and Polemic in Valla's 'Elegantiae,'" *Rinascimento*, n.s. 19 (1979), 91–116; and M. Regoliosi, *Nel cantiere del Valla: Elaborazione e montaggio delle "Elegantiae"* (Rome: Bulzoni, 1993).

[19] I cite from the critical edition of the *Proemium* to Book One in Regoliosi, *Nel Cantiere*, 120–25; the cited passage is at 125.

simply *nostri*, meaning most literally "our men." But it is worth reflecting on what Valla means here. He is (already, even at this, the earliest stage of his masterpiece) most emphatically not saying that ancient Romans should be considered separately from the present. Instead he is tipping his hand, to the effect that he sees Latin as one, great cultural continuum that, though it has a history of its own, is not and should not be imprisoned only in "the books and writings of the ancients," as Poggio had said.

Culture, Valla suggests, cannot function and indeed could not have survived, without the presence of the Latin language. The divine has given Latin to humankind as a "kind of divine fruit, food not so much for the body as for the spirit."[20] It was only through Latin that the liberal arts survived and thrived. And even as vernaculars – different, common languages – developed over time, Latin served as an "ornament," like a "gem added to gold," or like a *seminarium*, a "seed-bed," in other words a kind of extended field on which many things might grow, battles might be enacted, games might be played.[21]

Over the course of history some might have resented using Latin, but all eventually came around to its usefulness, coming to think of Latin "almost as if it were a god come down to them from heaven."[22] What begins to come into focus is how unique Valla believes Latin to be. He then makes a set of striking statements, so important they should be quoted in full:

> Therefore it is the great sacrament, indeed, the great divinity, of the Latin language that in a holy and religious fashion has been defended among pilgrims, barbarians, and enemies for so many centuries, to such a point that we Romans should not lament but rather rejoice and indeed, with the whole world hearkening, take pride. We have lost Rome, we have lost our kingdom, we have lost power – but this is not our fault but that of the times. And yet we rule over most of the world through this more illustrious power: Italy is ours, as are France, Spain, Germany, Pannonia [meaning the territory that is today partially in Hungary, Austria, and Serbia], Dalmatia [today covering much of Croatia], Illyricum [modern Albania], and many other nations. For wherever the Roman language dominates, it is there that one finds Roman power.[23]

The first thing that comes into relief is Valla's description of Latin as a "sacrament" (*sacramentum* in Latin) and as a "divinity" (*numen*). The word *sacramentum* incorporates the Latin word *sacer*, commonly and correctly

---

[20] Ibid., 120–21.
[21] Ibid., 121.
[22] Ibid., 122.
[23] Ibid.

translated as "sacred." Yet it is interesting to note its basic meaning, which is simply "something set apart," often for the gods but sometimes, too, as something that needed critical and even negative scrutiny, as when Virgil in the *Aeneid* speaks of an "*accursed* hunger for gold" ("auri *sacra* fames") or Catullus writes of a "terrible and *hateful* little book" ("horribilem et *sacrum* libellum").[24] Something "sacred" was something that had a special status, almost as if a boundary were drawn around it. For Valla, Latin is like that: a language, to be sure, but also a medium that drew together a powerful set of symbols, all of which needed careful curation.

The word translated here as "divinity" (*numen*) is even more interesting, for at its root it means simply a "nod," which is to say a "nod" of consent, often from the gods.[25] Gradually it grew to mean divinity itself, and it can signify as much a specific sort of divinity as a divine ambience, or environment. When Valla uses these two words, *sacramentum* and *numen*, to describe Latin, he is not doing so in a casual way. It is instead a measured, calculated means of building the beginning of his case that Latin, special as it is, should be viewed as more than a means of communication. It is, instead, a vehicle of power.

When he uses the word "we," whom does Valla have in mind? He says "we Romans," so on one level, especially given Valla's own family history in Rome, one can see that Valla's "we" has to do with Rome. Of course, Valla's own family was, originally, from Piacenza in the north of Italy; even a moment's reflection reveals that, for Valla, "we Romans" means something much broader and is a concept much more capacious than geography alone might indicate. And yet: "We have lost Rome, we have lost our kingdom, we have lost power – but this is not our fault but that of the times." He means that "Rome" as a stand-in for the center of the Western world's political power is no more. It is striking that Valla says that "it is not our fault but that of the times," reflecting a remoteness from politics that is noteworthy coming from one who for so long sat so close to political power. Valla's politics is, like that of many intellectuals, not a politics of the world but of the mind.

Yet Valla also says: "we rule over most of the world through this more illustrious power: Italy is ours, as are France, Spain, Germany," and so on, as Valla mentions some of the outer reaches of Christendom. He means here that Latin is used in all these places as an official language, despite their different cultures and local vernaculars. Thus, "wherever the Roman

---

[24] Virgil, *Aen.*, 3.57; Catullus, 14.12.
[25] See Lucretius, *De rerum natura*, 2.63; and Virgil, *Aen.*, 1.603.

language dominates, it is there that one finds Roman power" – and for "power" here, the Latin word Valla employs is *imperium*, a word that in antiquity signified the power to command as well as what we think of when we use the word "empire." Again, however, Valla's "empire" seems far from reality, if we restrict ourselves to secular politics.

Of course, we should make no mistake: the preface of any given work is not more important than the work's overall content. Seen in this light, the *Elegances of the Latin Language* is a remarkably practical work, precise and workmanlike in its lists of proper usage. Take Book One, Chapter Eight, "On words that end in –rius or –rium," which is about exactly what it says it is about.[26] It begins as follows: "A *tabularium* [the Latin word means an "archive"] is a place where *tabulae* ["planks," originally, but commonly meaning "tables," as in "tables of writing," or "writings" or "contracts"] are stored. A *sacrarium* is a repository of sacred things, an *aerarium* ["treasury"] is a repository of *aes* ["copper," "bronze," or "brass"], that is, coins and wealth and similar precious things."[27] And so on. The majority of the *Elegances*, with its six books and 475 chapters, is like this: lists that you can use to make sure that you don't use Latin words and expressions incorrectly, dictated by Valla from a posture of omniscience but which, in truth, reflected a stunningly vast learning.

Still, the prefaces do present an architecture of sorts, one that can help us see the outlines of the edifice Valla was (unsystematically, to be sure) trying to build, as well as the one within whose walls he was constrained. The Preface to Book Two is fruitful in this regard.[28] For here, Valla pays tribute to ancient grammarians, most especially to "Donatus, Servius, and Priscian, who stand out to such an extent that all who follow them seem babblers."[29] Then Valla goes on unsurprisingly to heap reprobation on medieval authors. They include Isidore of Seville (560–636), whose *Etymologies* had provided a foundation stone for medieval thinkers, "Papias" (an eleventh-century Italian lexicographer), Eberhard of Bethune (the thirteenth-century author of the *Graecismus*, a Latin poem designed to teach grammar), and others, all of whom had authored books that were stand-by texts in medieval schools.[30]

Overall, the Preface to Book Two shows that Valla believed the ancient works he mentions were indeed great but, implicitly at least at this stage, insufficient. Medieval decadence had created a breach, so that what had been

---

[26] Lorenzo Valla, *Elegantiae linguae latinae* (Venice, 1496), a.iii(v).
[27] Ibid.
[28] Here and for the rest of the Prefaces I cite from Garin, *Prosatori*.
[29] Valla, in Garin, *Prosatori*, 602.
[30] Ibid., 602–04.

incomplete in the ancient tradition remained so in the intervening centuries. The breach was there, and Valla believed he could enter unto it and, with a blast of war, close up any gaps.

Along the way, the Preface to Book Two provides a window into how things worked in Valla's day when it came to the rights of authors (to use anachronistic terminology). After praising Leonardo Bruni and Giovanni Aurispa (the latter one of a pioneering generation of humanists who had traveled to Byzantium to learn Greek and who served as Valla's Greek teacher) for encouraging him to write the *Elegances*, Valla relates an interesting event. Presenting himself as initially unwilling to write the *Elegances* but grateful to Bruni and Aurispa for their encouragement, he then asks: "but what sort of laziness, indeed folly, would I have been guilty of if I had let someone else steal whatever praise I might have deserved?"[31] Not wanting to dignify the plagiarist by naming him (it happened to be a rival named Antonio da Rho), Valla outlines what happened: "Some, having heard the principles I professed either directly or from one of my students – things I have never hidden – decided to insert them into their own work, so as to make them seem like they had discovered these things first."[32] Valla goes on to say that out of friendship he was reading the work of one of these people and, in the offender's presence, no less, he found things that had been stolen from his own work. It had to do with a specific grammatical point, one that had been clumsily rendered and thus made ineffective and unoriginal. Still, Valla was disturbed.

He recounts his conversation with the offender, still unnamed: "I recognize this elegance. I declare that it is my property and that I am able to accuse you of plagiarism."[33] "Property." "Plagiarism." For "property" Valla uses the Latin word *mancipium*, a word with a deeply rooted jurisprudential meaning, denoting a property legally and contractually acquired and provable as such.[34] The expression Valla uses to denote what we call "plagiarism" is, in Latin, the *lex plagiaria*, another term with a deep, ancient legal resonance, whose primary meaning has to do with kidnapping and one that also came to mean stealing a literary work.[35] Then the offender became embarrassed and tried to joke the episode away. Valla remained unmoved, asking what would be left of his own work "if you took all the glory?"[36] Now even quieter, the accused

---

[31] Ibid., 606.
[32] Ibid.
[33] Ibid.
[34] See Cicero, *De oratore*, 1.178, for an example.
[35] Cf. Cicero, *Q.fr.* 1.2.6; Ulpian, *Dig.*48.15.1.
[36] Valla, in Garin, *Prosatori*, 606.

suggested Valla was acting like a bad father who kicked out the children he had raised and educated, whereas he – the accused – was only trying, in a friendly and charitable fashion, to keep the kids at home. It's a big tent, no?

No. Valla concludes by saying that he realized then that he needed to write the book "not only because of the encouragement of great men but also, simply, out of necessity."[37] If not, his insights would circulate as they had been doing in the primarily oral world of education, where no one really owned anything intellectually; then, of course, someone would come along and write them down in a plodding, defective way, and just ruin everything. Just like in the case of the *Annotations*, Valla simply has no choice. He is needed. He must write down his insights, however "unwilling" he may be at the outset to do so.

We can make two observations. First, Valla's "reformer" persona was something he shaped by dialogue and debate, psychologically creating the need for his work by opposing the work and thought of others, whether real or imagined. Second, the fluid world of intellectual property comes into relief.[38] It is noteworthy and, in a sense, a hitherto lost part of the genealogy of copyright law, that Valla takes pains to use legal terminology in the absence of any actual, enforceable laws. You claimed your intellectual property not in a court case but, instead, in the court of public opinion. These prefaces represented ways of communicating these sorts of matters with readers, things that were less technical than the specific, individual points Valla was making in the body of the text but that still served an important function: helping Valla craft his identity in the rough and tumble world of premodern intellectual life.

The same imperatives exist in the Preface to Book Three. There, Valla exemplifies a tendency that would grow stronger after his death and come to final fruition in the life and work of perhaps the finest philologist of the fifteenth century, Angelo Poliziano (1454–94): the search for the most authentic, "superintending" branch of knowledge. Valla begins a process that Poliziano would complete later, in which leading representatives of literary humanism would claim that they, and the sort of work they did, could claim the status of representatives of the "umbrella" discipline *par excellence*, the one without which all the others were like orphans in need of parents. In this case, the matter at hand is the discipline of law, and the clear and present danger, in Valla's eyes, is that those who represent the profession

---

[37] Ibid.
[38] For background see Adrian Johns, *Piracy: The Intellectual Property Wars from Gutenberg to Gates* (Chicago: University of Chicago Press, 2009).

have no literary culture. They are, he writes, in danger of becoming *legulei*, "pettifoggers" who depend more on technicalities to argue cases than what they should aspire to be: *iurisconsulti*, serious lawyers who recognize the wealth that their discipline offers them and society at large.[39]

The case Valla makes is that without a deep understanding of Latin, lawyers will be unable to understand the resonances of the texts they study and will, accordingly, lack the capacity to use the law to full effect. This charge might seem surprising at first: how could Valla, himself formally untrained in law, believe that he could contribute something to what was one of Europe's oldest professional traditions? The answer – as in the case of scripture – had to do with history. Valla had, in his *Annotations on the New Testament*, made a point of noting the way time had passed, first, from the days when the Apostles walked the earth to the time of Jerome, then, from Jerome's day until Valla's own. Here, speaking not of scripture but of law, he makes a similar move. He highlights the fact that though Roman law had a lengthy ancient tradition, it was written down formally and preserved only relatively late.[40] He is speaking of the *Corpus iuris civilis*, the "Body of Civil Law," which was inscribed only under order of Emperor Justinian in years 529–534 CE.[41] It was this body of work on which the (for Valla) modern study of Roman law was based.

But by then, that is, by the sixth century CE, the nature of spoken and written Latin had changed. Just as ancient Romans in the age of Cicero had often mixed Greek together with Latin, in the days of Justinian, after the advent of Goths into the Roman Empire, one found Gothic traits mixed in with Latin. Though he doesn't put it this way, Valla is suggesting that you needed to be a bit of a literary archaeologist to understand the depths of the problem. He even adduces evidence from the realm of material culture: one way we can tell that Gothic speech influenced Latin happens to be "codices written in Gothic script, of which there are a great many."[42] What he means is a bit complicated but worth unraveling.

For Valla and his contemporaries there existed a great divide between what they habitually called *litterae anticae*, "ancient letters," and *litterae Longobardae*, "Lombard letters" or *litterae gothicae*, "gothic letters."[43] "Ancient letters," as it

---

[39] Valla, in Garin, *Prosatori*, 606–12.

[40] Ibid., 608.

[41] See Bruce W. Frier, general editor, *The Codex of Justinian*, 3 vols. (Cambridge: Cambridge University Press, 2016). The *Corpus iuris civilis* was composed of four elements the *Codex*, the *Digest* (or *Pandects*), the *Institutions*, and the *Novellae*.

[42] Ibid., 610.

[43] See Rizzo, *Lessico*, 114.

happened, signified the sort of handwriting employed in the wake of Charlemagne's reforms. It was clear, possessed relatively few abbreviations, and the word spacing was such as to make it legible across different professional communities. "Longobard," or "Gothic" writing, represented many types of handwriting, from the rounded writing of early medieval Irish monasteries; to the stunningly beautiful "Beneventan" script of eleventh-century Monte Cassino; to the spiky, heavily abbreviated forms of writing that scholars today term "Gothic," perfected in thirteenth-century France and often used by university-based scholars.[44] These latter forms all had one thing in common: they were difficult to read, compared to "ancient" letters. What is important to note is that when they used these terms, humanists were making distinctions that lay more in the realm of aesthetics rather than offering historical pronouncement. In this specific case, with his use of "Gothic," Valla may have had any number of scripts in mind. What is important, however, is that he is highlighting a link between texts as bodies of learning and the material form in which they are expressed. He is making a case that links history (the era of Justinian) with physical evidence (manuscripts that can, notionally, be dated and placed owing to their physical form). He does none of these things with the presumptive drive toward exactitude favored by modern scholars, but the tendency is present nonetheless, an early adumbration of disciplinary specializations to come much later.

Valla's Preface to Book Four of the *Elegances* moves in another direction, this time one that will seem familiar: Christianity, with a special focus on Jerome.[45] Valla's point of departure is a statement of Jerome's regarding the study of "pagan" literature, meaning non-Christian literature – meaning everything, more or less, in which humanists took an interest. This debate (whether it was useful or even allowed to read pagan literature) had been a part of Renaissance culture since the days of Salutati, as he and other humanists who saw themselves as dedicated Christians sought to find compatibility between their faith and the eloquent, exemplary ancient literature with which they had grown so entranced and which, indeed, they used as models of style. A millennium earlier of course, Jerome's world was different. He, along with his elite Christian contemporaries, was educated with ancient pagan literature as a basis. Jerome's Latin is redolent of that late pagan world,

---

[44] See Berhnard Bischoff, *Latin Palaeography: Antiquity and the Middle Ages*, tr. Dáibhi ó Cróinin and David Ganz (Cambridge: Cambridge University Press, 1990); and Albert Derolez, *The Palaeography of Gothic Manuscript Books: From the Twelfth to the Early Sixteenth Century* (Cambridge: Cambridge University Press, 2003).

[45] Valla, in Garin, *Prosatori*, 612–22.

when one could scarcely assume that it was possible to be educated in any other way.

Specifically, Jerome, in what became a well-known letter, related to a correspondent a fever dream he had experienced.[46] In the dream he had believed himself dead, sitting in judgment before the Lord. Asked to "state his condition" – meaning who and what he was – Jerome replied: "I am a Christian." To that statement "He who presided said: 'You lie. You are a Ciceronian, not a Christian.'"[47] That line became what we would today call the "sound bite" version of the thrust of Jerome's letter. And indeed, in quoting it and, as we shall see, eventually rebutting its thrust, Valla stays on the level of the sound bite. But the context of the statement is quite important in seeing what Jerome was up to. He was writing, in those dark days, to a woman named Eustochium, who had pledged herself to a life of virginity and communion with Christ. This difficult life choice under any circumstances was made harder in Jerome's view by the climate in Rome, where she was at the time, and whence he was urging her to flee. The city is as much metaphorical as literal, as he likens it to Sodom and writes how difficult it is to preserve one's chastity. Jerome says things to her such as the following: "Be the grasshopper of the night. Wash your bed and water your couch nightly with tears. Keep vigil and be like the sparrow alone upon the housetop."[48] Then, a bit later, Jerome turns to the subject of marriage and, specifically, why it is better to remain unwed: "I praise wed-lock, I praise marriage; but it is because they produce me virgins."[49] As to what Eustochium might say to a worried mother, concerned that her daughter might not marry, Jerome says that the prospective virgin is, in effect, marrying a King – meaning the Lord – rather than making a worldly marriage. The letter goes on and on, extolling the single life dedicated to the Lord over against the married life, and, above all, warning Eustochium against all sorts of distractions that might lead her astray.

One of these potential distractions has to do with the power of literature and speech: "do not seek to be over-eloquent or compose trifling songs in verse."[50] Jerome moves to warn Eustochium against reading pagan literature: "what has Horace to do with the Psalter, Virgil with the Gospels and Cicero

[46] Jerome, *Ep.* 22, in Jerome, *Select Letters of St. Jerome*, ed. and tr. F.A. Wright (Cambridge, MA: Harvard University Press, 1991), 52–157.
[47] Jerom, *Ep.* 22, p. 127, tr. modified.
[48] Ibid., p. 89, tr. modified.
[49] Ibid., p. 95.
[50] Ibid., 125.

with Paul?"[51] She should stick to scripture. It is then that Jerome relates his own struggle, telling how, while in Jerusalem and despite wanting to give up the secular classics he could not bring himself "to forgo the library that with great care and labor" he had collected when in Rome.[52] He would stick to scripture for a bit but then return to reading Cicero and Plautus. And thereafter, he felt ashamed when, on returning to scripture, its language sounded "harsh and barbarous."[53] Jerome's anecdote about becoming ill follows; he went into a fever-induced fugue state and was accused by God of being a Ciceronian rather than a Christian, and, he relates, he was physically beaten because of his ill-considered reading habits.[54] The episode moved him to such an extent that, he writes, he promised the Lord never to read secular books again, and he assures Eustochium that from that moment on he "read the books of god with greater zeal than I had ever given before to the books of men."[55] When he woke up from the dream, he had black-and-blue bruises as evidence that it was far more than just an average dream. He goes on to warn her against excessive love of money and luxurious clothes, and before a final, prayer-filled exhortation suggests that "love finds nothing hard: no task is difficult if you wish to do it"; in other words, focus yourself on your love of Christ and you will be able to persist in the vows you have taken.[56]

Jerome's letter was at once the fervid statement of a true believer, an exhortation to a woman (for whom, he would have assumed with the prejudices of his era, there was no need for an expert command of Latin), and an exemplary performance, designed by its very structure and deliberate emotional resonance to convince Eustochium to keep going down the difficult but rewarding path she has chosen. It should be noted, regarding Jerome's comments on reading, that he has of course already done a lot of intensive reading, in the typically slow, heavy-on-the-memorization style of his day, and he has done so in a world where far more secular classics were available than in Valla's era.

So perhaps, especially given what we know about Valla, it is unsurprising that he seems a bit angry with Jerome, as if, just as in the case of scripture, Valla feels the great saint's spectral presence and resents it, as if it were a shadow darkening all his efforts – his necessary efforts – to shine light on the culture of his day. He begins his Preface to Book Four of the *Elegances* as follows:

---

[51] Ibid.
[52] Ibid.
[53] Ibid.
[54] Ibid., 127–29.
[55] Ibid., 129.
[56] Ibid., 153.

I am well aware that there are some – especially those who consider themselves of the more pious and religious sort – who dare to condemn my project and my work, as something unworthy of a Christian man, since I urge people to read secular books, the sorts of books that caused Jerome, in his telling to be beaten at god's tribunal and to be accused of being a Ciceronian rather than a Christian. He then promised never again to read secular books. This charge is not applicable to this work so much as it is to me and other literary men, blamed as we are both for our study of literature and for our learning thereof.[57]

The word translated here as "charge" is *crimen* in Latin, a word that can indeed also mean what it looks like in English: "crime." The fact that a blameworthy attribute appears so close to Jerome and that Valla seeks to differentiate himself from Jerome reveals, again, Valla's anxiety regarding Jerome.

Valla goes on to say that he wants to respond to the accusation of those who would criticize his devotion to literature, because, he says, "they are for the most part to blame when it comes to the downfall, the shipwreck, really, of Latin culture."[58] Implicitly, then, we see that Valla is accounting for history, the passage of time, and the epoch in which he lives with all of its current problems. His own times are not like Jerome's. It is not enough to follow unreflectively Jerome's move away from secular literature, a millennium ago as it was. Instead it is time to build a case as to why all fields can benefit from an increased attention to classical literature. In this respect, no field is more worthy of cultivation, more central, than Christianity itself, which can only benefit from an increased attention to classical literature. After ridiculing the idea that one could plausibly give up classical literature ("What books would these be, pray tell? All rhetorical writers, all historians, all poets, all philosophers, all legal writers, as well as the others?"), Valla offers a classic dichotomous critique.[59] How can you say, he asks his nameless critics, that one can forbid only works of eloquence? "Do you think that in these ancient books there is contained only eloquence, rather than also the memory of times gone by and the history of nations, without which no one is not a boy?"[60] "Boy" versus man – grown-ups know how to handle their classical literature.

As Valla moves on he offers an interesting comparison between what he calls "philosophy" and "eloquence." So as not to misunderstand what he is up to

[57] Valla, in Garin, *Prosatori*, 612.
[58] Ibid.
[59] Ibid.
[60] Ibid., 614.

here, an extended look at what he says is necessary: "I don't want here to make a comparison between philosophy and eloquence, something many already have done, showing as they have that philosophy is scarcely consistent with the Christian religion and that all heresies have flowed from the fountain of philosophy, whereas rhetoric possesses nothing that is not praiseworthy."[61] Rhetoric allows you to engage in discovery, to arrange arguments correctly, to offer, as it were, the bones and sinews of an oration, to give it ornament, which is to say to give it flesh and coloration; finally rhetoric allows you to fix things in memory, to engage in appropriate pronunciation, which is to say, to give an oration spirit and to bring it to life.[62]

This "comparison" represents a classic case of what rhetoricians call a "passing over," or *praeteritio*, in Latin. When Valla says he doesn't want to make a comparison between philosophy and rhetoric ("eloquence" as he uses the term), that is if course precisely what he is doing.

What Valla means here should not be taken on a superficial level. One theme that runs throughout the Italian long fifteenth century's intellectual history is the search for the most authentic kind of philosophy considered in that word's most elemental meaning: "love of wisdom." When Valla is criticizing philosophy here, he is not doing so to suggest that one should not engage in philosophy. He is saying rather that those who have claimed the name "philosopher" for themselves have been going about their business in the wrong way. He means that the discipline as currently practiced in its institutional setting has, in essence, gone astray. It has stopped trying to affect people's emotions to make them better people. It is precisely this that rhetoric, or as Valla calls it interchangeably, eloquence can do: move people and meet them, as it were, where they are making decisions. In focusing so intently on language (not in a picky way but rather on how the arrangement of an oration helps create its meaning), rhetoric represents philosophy in its most authentic sense.[63]

Given the power of eloquence, it is wholly appropriate that eloquence be added to the other arts (such as painting, sculpture, epigraphy, and music) that commonly occur in religious contexts and that indeed help give glory to God. Far from something that a Christian should shun, eloquence instead is something one should study and assiduously cultivate.[64] There is no other way to do this than to study ancient, non-Christian exemplars of eloquence.

---

[61] Ibid., 616.

[62] Ibid.

[63] See Nancy Struever, *Theory as Practice: Ethical Inquiry in the Renaissance* (Chicago: University of Chicago Press, 1992).

[64] Valla, in Garin, *Prosatori*, 616–18.

Again, today is not Jerome's era. Jerome assumed for himself a classical education, one that he had simply absorbed. This sort of mastery is not possible today without study. Besides, Valla goes on, Jerome was himself quite the rhetorician, one who, especially in his debates with others, indeed used the arts of eloquence to his advantage: "Who is more eloquent than Jerome? Who is a greater orator?"[65] So did all the other great Church fathers, all of whom "embedded the precious gems of the divine Word in the gold and silver of eloquence without trading in one branch of learning for another."[66] Done well, in other words, the employment of eloquence helps Christianity thrive. Its most heroic – which is to say its early – exemplars, the Church fathers, knew this to be so. They were like "bees that flew around in far-flung fields and then made the sweetest honey as well as wax, all with a wondrous craftsmanship."[67] Today's theologians instead are like ants that steal from their neighbor and tuck away a little piece of grain in their hideaway. Valla concludes by saying he would prefer to be a servant of the queen bee rather than the king of the ants. "And," he goes on, "I am certain that young people of good conscience will agree, despite their hopeless elders."[68]

Were the youth going astray? Were they, under the influence of self-proclaimed university-based "philosophers," losing their way, spending time on useless mental exercises, and veering ever closer to irreligious mind-sets? These questions animated Valla to some extent, and they grew in intensity during the fifteenth century, representing a preoccupation among some reform-minded thinkers, most especially the Florentine Platonist Marsilio Ficino, whom we shall meet in more detail later. But for Valla, far more important than any one consistent program, whether religious, philosophical, or ideological, was being independent in all those realms, and doing so in a combative way.

These tendencies emerge in the Prefaces to Books Five and Six. In the Preface to Book Five, Valla makes it clear that he has taken an enforced break from the *Elegances*, for three years. Given his fear that others will steal his work, he feels even more pressure to complete it. Valla says that, among prudent men at least, "no one has dared to consider everything together" regarding grammar, as he has.[69] It is thus high time that he lay out the plan

---

[65] Ibid., 618.
[66] Ibid., 620.
[67] Ibid., 622.
[68] Ibid.
[69] Ibid., 624.

for the rest of the books. Book Five will be on verbs, and Book Six, he says, will be *de notis auctorum*: "on the errors of the authors." Ancient authors, that is. The word used for "errors" is *notis*, whose basic form is *nota* – a word that can have many resonances. But Valla's meaning is clear. These are things that he will have marked out for notice in ancient authors, things that in his view do not meet his own standards for proper Latin usage. Here it is important to pause, to realize just what a radical move that is – how Valla's quest to be original and different was, in many ways, so outside the mainstream that he was bound to have difficulty being accepted in the culture of his day.

The Preface to Book Six, in fact, allows Valla to give one side of why what he is doing is appropriate. He says, in effect, that ancient authors themselves criticized predecessors, and that what he is doing is akin to purifying gold. True, once you purified the gold, you might have less in terms of weight and mass, but what you did have was all the purer. And the Latin word Valla uses for "purify" is *expurgare*, which in Latin as in its English cognates has a strong resonance: "purging," "cleansing," and so on. Valla sees himself as the cleansing agent, one that is so powerful and all-embracing that he believes he can correct the usage of ancient authors: authors who were, unlike him or of course anyone in his day, native speakers of Latin.

As in so much else, Valla, in the final analysis, was an outlier in the long fifteenth-century's extended language debate. Valla, tellingly, did not really address the question whether ancient Latin had been a natural or artificial language. But in his many sallies against Poggio, Valla hinted that he believed ancient Latin had been something for which one needed schooling to perfect. Here is how Valla represented his own position, in dialogue form:

LORENZO: So then, you avow that little children spoke "grammatically."
POGGIO: I believe it and avow it.
L: And why then did they send children to a grammar teacher?
P: So they might learn the theories and causes [*rationes et causas*] of the language they knew.
L: There you go again. I wish I spoke properly grammatically without knowing something about the causes and theories of grammar! But I have to admit that in this matter you are far ahead of me, since you've never cared too much about the teachings of this art. What are you saying? Either grammar is an art and thus something that was handed down by the learned and not by nursemaids; or what everyone

says *is* an art is not an art, as you alone, more than anyone else, seem to know.[70]

Valla suggests that Poggio is arguing contrary positions. Valla's view is that Poggio, on the one hand, admits that *grammatica* (i.e., Latin as a school subject) is a craft (an *ars*), which implies that it is a skill with underlying principles and techniques that can, and that need to be, taught and learned. On the other hand, Poggio seems to be saying that there was a time when this was not so, that (as Valla has the character Poggio phrase it) "grammar was not, then, a skill [*artificium*] as it is now, but rather usage and custom."[71] What we can see is that Valla, in truth, is not preoccupied with the everyday language of the common people in antiquity. Instead, he sees the Latin language as an instrument of culture, something that exists both inside and, ideally, outside of time.

Valla's positions on the place of historical analysis and Latinity reflect this larger view, even as they exemplify his radically reforming side. As to Valla the reformer, he believed that the custom, or *consuetudo* in Latin, of the ancients should be respected. His source base, however, was in practice restricted, as he excluded a number of ancient authors from the ranks of those whose Latin was sufficiently pure. When he found clearly documented cases of ancient usage, if he did not believe that that usage reflected the idealized clarity that a proper Latin should have, he was unafraid to suggest changes in practice. Valla thought that even the ancients could make mistakes.

One example can serve to prove the point.[72] Valla insisted in the *Elegantiae* on differentiating between the subjective and objective genitive (for Valla "active" and "passive") when it came to personal pronouns. Valla writes:

> Every genitive ... is understood in either an active or a passive way. You can also add in a possessive way, which I understand as being very close to

---

[70] Valla, *Apologus II*, in Tavoni, 260–73, at 270–71: "Laur.: Ergo grammatice locutos fuisse confiteris infantes. Po.: Sentio et confiteor. Laur.: Cur igitur ad preceptorem grammatices mittebantur? Po.: Ut discerent lingue, quam norant, rationes et causas. Lau.: Eodem revolveris. Utinam ego recte grammatice loquerer, nec aliquid causarum ac rationum grammatice nossem! Quanquam in hac tu re longe antecellis, qui nunquam de huius artis preceptis magnopere curasti. Quid ais? Aut ars grammatica est, et ab eruditis, non autem a nutricibus, tradebatur; aut ars non est, quam omnes fatentur esse artem, ut tu unus plus omnibus sapere videare, et ceteros tanquam tardissimo ingenio damnare, qui artem fecerint id quod usu et sua sponte percipi poterat."

[71] Ibid., 270: "Po.: Tu vero pro mea causa loqueris, qui non artificium olim fuisse grammaticam, ut nunc est, sed usum et consuetudinem volo, eoque pueris quoque et infantibus scitu facilem."

[72] Brilliantly examined by Lucia Cesarini Martinelli, in "Note sulla polemica Poggio-Valla e sulla fortuna delle *Elegantiae*," *Interpres* 3 (1980), 29–79.

the active way. Examples of the active way include: "providentia dei" [God's providence], "bonitas dei" [God's goodness]. Examples of the passive way include "timor dei" [the fear of God], "cultus dei" [the worship of God]."[73]

Despite Valla's seeming certainly here, the truth is that the ancients had not been clear on this distinction, and ambiguities throughout the classical period are clearly observable.[74] But Valla suggests that the genitive forms of the possessive pronoun, for example, the forms *mei, tui,* and *sui,* should always possess, as one scholar has phrased it, "the objective function, whereas the possessives, *meus, tuus,* and *suus,* preserve the subjective function. *Amor meus* will refer to my love for someone else, *amor mei* the love of someone else toward me."[75] Valla has some limited evidence for this claim, as he suggests that the archaic forms *mis, tis,* and *sis* (analogous to *meus, tuus,* and *suus*) always reflected the subjective function of the genitive. But in truth there is not that much evidence of how those archaic forms were used. Moreover, though Valla's way does represent the majority tendency in Cicero's work, exceptions can be found even there.[76]

The ancients, in short, had no hard and fast rule that regulated this phenomenon. Valla feels free to invent one; the rule he invents is appealing to him precisely because it respects the idealized inner logic that Latin, as the preeminent language of culture, must possess – a logic that he, as a reformer, needs to supply. Valla is different from Poggio precisely because Valla does not think that "only the books and writings of ancient authors," as Poggio had put it, served as the authoritative foundation upon which one might build the edifice of proper Latinity. Instead, human reason and the practice of language – which never ends – must also play a role. Latin was inside of time, in the sense that the proper ancient historically and chronologically identifiable sources could be documented and understood in context. That historical understanding served as a foundation for human reason. Yet Latin was also outside of time, in the sense that its evolution represented the evolution of culture. As such, proper Latin's empire could never end, since if it did, true culture would end with it. It deserved the zeal of a reformer to keep it

---

[73] *Elegantiae,* 2.1, cited in Cesarini Martinelli, 71–72: "Genitivus omnis, ut taceam si qui sint alii modi, aut active aut passive accipitur; adde etiam possessiva, quod pene pro activa accipio. Active, ut 'providentia dei', 'bonitas dei'. Passive, ut 'timor dei', 'cultus dei'. Ibi deus providet et benigne agit, non ipsi providetur et benigne fit; hic timetur et colitur, non timet et colit'."

[74] See Cesarini Martinelli, 72–73.

[75] Ibid., 72.

[76] Ibid., 73–74.

pristine, reflective of ancient norms (even if those norms were not always overtly articulated or even scrupulously adhered to by the ancients), and adequate to the times.

No one else in the fifteenth century approached Latin in this way, with this sense of reforming, ideological fervor and this faith, impractical as it may seem in retrospect, that reform of language could lead to a reform in other realms of culture. As to the language debate, Poggio's position, buttressed as it was by so much evidence, became the norm: in the ancient world, Latin had been a living, natural language. We who use Latin today need to respect ancient, classical usage, so that it can serve its proper function as a language of scholarship and diplomacy. Standards are needed, and the criterion of judgment for these standards can be found only in ancient authors. They are the arbiters. We are not. Valla's views concerning this rich intersection of learning and culture are so different from what became the standard position, and his calls for reform so noteworthy, that we must delve further into his thought to understand him in all his exceptional fullness.

10

VALLA, LATIN, CHRISTIANITY, CULTURE

Latin needed reform. Christianity needed reform. Everything needed reform, in Valla's eyes. Five works combine to tell us much of we need to know: a letter from 1440; an oration a treatise Valla wrote against one of the Church's beliefs regarding its property and rights; a speech of "praise" for a respected medieval philosopher that, as it unfolds, offers as much criticism as it does praise; and, finally, a dialogue that discusses one of the most dramatic – and current and still insoluble – questions in the history of philosophy: to what extent do human beings act freely in the world and to what extent are their actions circumscribed by larger forces?

The 1440 letter, to a friend from Valencia, Joan Serra, is a good place to begin. Serra had written Valla previously, to tell Valla that he kept encountering people who all said the same thing: that Valla had a bad habit of attacking authoritative figures. Valla's return letter serves as an extended reply and justification for his gladiatorial style. First, Valla says this: "I have hardened myself to the scurrilous and abusive chatter of fools."[1] What Valla cares about is praise from the educated, and he assumes that those who slander him behind his back are not only ignorant but also cowardly: "Let whoever calls himself a grammarian avenge the insult to grammarians. Let the dialectician avenge dialectic, and the philosopher philosophy. Let the legal scholar vindicate the interpreter of civil law. Surely there must be one man among such a crowd brave enough to write against me rather than simply barking with the rest of the pack."[2] Those afraid to write against him spend their time "snarling like a dog rather than fighting like a man."[3]

---

[1] See Lorenzo Valla, *Correspondence*, ed. and tr. Brendan Cook (Cambridge, MA: Harvard University Press, 2014), 77.
[2] Ibid., 79.
[3] Ibid.

Speaking of his *Elegances of the Latin Language*, Valla writes that he nowhere criticizes Virgil, Ovid, Lucan, Cicero, Caesar, Livy, and a whole host of other ancient authors. But, as to ancient grammarians, "if I add something to what Priscian and the other grammarians say, does this amount to a crime?"[4] Valla presents that instance not as warring against the ancients but rather as defending them. Though he admits he corrects Priscian and some others on occasion, he says: "unless I am mistaken, it is rather ground for praise that I am seen to have honored earlier generations and instructed later ones."[5] What he means is that, where he has here and there corrected ancient grammarians such as Priscian, it is because in his view they were incomplete, not having accounted for the usage present in those earlier authors (Virgil, Ovid, Cicero, and so on).

Yet again Valla presents it as necessary. After all the terrible medieval grammarians, medieval jurists, and medieval philosophers (and he lists a host of them), Valla had no choice but to intervene: "I would rather be illiterate than their peer, so far am I from thinking any of them learned. Were the ancients alive, I believe they would say the same."[6]

Valla goes on: "When therefore, in view of the general corruption and deformation of Latin, I realized that there was a need for me to write about the refinements of the language, how could I have failed to reproach those who took the leading part in its perversion?"[7] When all is said and done, Valla knows where he stands: "I have done more for the Latin language with the six books I have mentioned" – he means the *Elegances* – "than anyone who has written on grammar, rhetoric, logic, civil and canon law or the meaning of words these past six hundred years."[8]

Valla goes on to say that in the past writers have always criticized their predecessors when needed. Then he goes just that little extra step, one that shows where he is coming from, one that reveals what sort of personality we are dealing with here: "What other reason could there otherwise be for writing, if not to castigate the errors, omissions or excesses of others?"[9] Valla then goes through different disciplines, detailing ways in which practitioners criticize their predecessors. Philosophy as a discipline is divided into warring schools of thought. Oratory is full of practitioners who, though they borrow from one another, are never fully satisfied with the definitions of others; even

---

[4] Ibid., 81–83.
[5] Ibid., 83.
[6] Ibid., 83–85.
[7] Ibid., 85.
[8] Ibid.
[9] Ibid., 87.

modest Quintilian criticizes his predecessors.[10] Historians and poets also disagree among themselves. And even – and here, again, we see Valla pushing things perhaps just a bit further than he should have done – Christian authorities can be seen to have presented critiques, not only of predecessors but even of one another. If the Apostle Paul criticized pagan philosophy as well as other religions, "Doesn't Luke in the Acts of the Apostles, object from the outset to almost everyone who had tried to describe the same events?"[11]

A quick parenthesis as to Luke: the author of the Acts of the Apostles was also the author of the gospel according to Luke, and there, at the beginning of the gospel (*not* at the beginning of Acts) Luke does have four prefatory verses (to Theodorus, the addressee of the gospel) suggesting that he is providing an account of birth, life, and death of Christ *ex ordine*, "in an orderly fashion," or "in the order that things happened."[12] But those are prefatory verses to the gospel, not Acts (though it is true that others beside Valla had assumed that Luke was talking about both the gospel and Acts). And in any case, Luke's words are gentle, not polemical, as he presents himself as another voice to add to the already many accounts of the beginnings of the Jesus movement.

Back to Valla. Don't get Valla started on Jerome, "whose example is by itself enough to comfort me, if I may compare small things to great."[13] It is worth looking in detail at Valla's treatment of Jerome in this letter, where Valla goes on as follows:

> Others, however, will find in him a demonstration of how to correct their predecessors. They must consider how, following in the footsteps of so many great men and inaugurating what was essentially a new religion, Jerome was at last accepted and praised after constant and nearly universal attacks. Indeed, Augustine was foremost among his persecutors ... [Jerome] gave the impression that God had somehow neglected to instruct earlier generations in the truth, holier though they doubtless were, whereas I merely discuss secular literature, neither devised nor endorsed by God.[14]

Valla presents Jerome as courageous, someone who was willing to take the heat in the public arena for what he believed to be right, eventually winning the prize of public recognition for his labors. Valla is doing the same, in his own view, and only, he insists, in the realm of secular literature, not in the area of scripture. Well, one asks, what about the *Annotations*? In their absence

[10] Ibid., 87–89.
[11] Ibid., 91.
[12] Lk. 1:1–5.
[13] Valla, *Correspondence*, 91.
[14] Ibid., 91.

from this account in Valla's letter, the *Annotations* loom as powerfully present, even as Jerome emerges as one of Valla's exemplary presences, both a hero to be imitated (in his courage and resolve) and a fellow critic to be emulated, in the truest sense of the word "emulation" and as Valla would have understood the Latin concept (*aemulatio*): a rivalrous imitation, one in which one seeks not only to equal but also to surpass the model.[15]

Rhetorically, Valla's letter to Serra practically bursts with valuable information. First, the letter manifests the most straightforward exposition of Valla's combative nature – his clearest justification for the way he conducts his life. Finishing up a section on Saint Augustine and the way in which that Church father disagreed with many others, Valla writes: "He condemned in some degree every single writer of our faith that he took up, with the exception of the prophets, apostles, and evangelists. This may be called the defining quality of all the greatest men: the more learned a man is, the more he is employed (and should be) in castigating error in others, for trained eyes detect more than untrained ones."[16] Read one way, this proclamation can seem like a classic definition of how scholarship is supposed to work. We build on the work of our predecessors; we correct errors based on new evidence; and gradually, haltingly, we approach the truth, even if we may never reach it in an ultimate sense. Yet, Valla really doesn't talk much about "building," which implies collaboration. Instead his focus, both in technique but also in tone, seems to focus on destruction.

In one respect, and again if we read him as generously as possible, Valla can also be read as making a generational statement. A truly wise man, he goes on, "must never shrink from his duty . . . for fear of inviting resentment. He must desire neither to wound nor shame – who indeed wants to fight the dead? – but to instruct the young and, whenever possible, to restore the others to their senses."[17] Here again, Valla presents himself as, in effect, one of the only productive voices of his generation, willing, since it is necessary, to disagree with authors of the past, for a dual purpose. The first is to instruct the younger generation, in danger as they are of being led astray by a corrupt educational system and a cultural clique more concerned with not rocking the boat than with making any real scholarly progress. Second, Valla also says that the wise

---

[15] See Quintilian, *Institutio oratoria*, ed. and tr. Donald A. Russell (Cambridge, MA: Harvard University Press, 2002), 10.5.5: "Neque ego paraphrasin esse interpretationem tantum volo, sed circa eosdem sensus certamen atque aemulationem." See McLaughlin, *Literary Imitation*, esp. 243; and G.W. Pigman III, "Versions of Imitation in the Renaissance," *Renaissance Quarterly* 33 (1980), 1–32.

[16] Valla, *Correspondence*, 93.

[17] Ibid.

man needs, in so far as possible "to restore the others to their senses." The verb translated as "restore to their senses" is *reformare* and was used in one of Valla's favorite biblical texts, Paul's *Letter to the Romans*, to mean mental transformation: "And be not conformed to this world; but be reformed in the newness of your mind, that you may prove what is the good, and acceptable, and perfect, will of God."[18] Valla sees himself in serious, one could even say portentous, terms, juxtaposing himself with early Christian legends and subtly evoking biblical language. It was all part of one package, with Christianity, Latinity, and culture playing a role.

Nowhere is the link between Latin and Christianity more prominent than in Valla's *Oratio in principio sui studii*, or "Oration in the beginning of his study," what was then termed a *praelectio*.[19] This custom is not often practiced today, but then, in universities, a professor would give a public introductory lecture to the course he was to teach.[20] Delivered in October 1455, just as Valla began a term at the university of Rome as a professor of rhetoric, the "Oration" begins with Valla recognizing how common these opening orations are and wanting to offer "something rather new." This he does by asking what it is to which all the branches of learning owe so much. His answer? The Apostolic See, the place where among so many different cultures coming together, one thing was central: the Latin language.

Valla offers a sketch of Latin's development in antiquity. Many great ancient Roman writers were not born Roman citizens, but they became so through their use of Latin. Artisans benefit from competition with others. In the same fashion, competition among writers raised the quality of Latin. Moreover, just as coins facilitated commerce and engendered travel, so too did Latin, once it was properly fostered, do the same for intellectual life. Valla writes: "before the invention of coins almost no one knew about any of the good things produced by other peoples and indeed could neither travel very far nor stay for too long away from home; with the invention of coins commerce began to flourish, travel became more frequent, and indeed there began to exist an abundance of goods."[21] Latin, Valla goes on, "not only brought liberal arts to the provinces, it also allowed the talents of those

---

[18] Romans 12:2.
[19] Lorenzo Valla, *Orazione per l'inaugurazione dell'anno accademico 1455–1456: Atti di un seminario di filologia umanistica*, ed. Silvia Rizzo (Rome: Roma nel Rinascimento, 1994), 192–201, for the text of the oration.
[20] On the custom, see Maurizio Campanelli, "L'*Oratio* e il 'genere' delle orazioni inaugurali dell'anno accademico," in Valla, *Orazione*, pp. 25–61.
[21] Valla, *Orazione*, sec. 20.

from the provinces to have access to the arts."[22] Cicero, Virgil, Seneca, Livy, Priscian, and a number of others are cited as examples of people who gained great esteem in Rome, though they were not born there.[23] Their use of Latin, he suggests, was an essential element in gaining citizenship.

Valla's use of artisanal and commercial metaphors should be brought into relief. This strategy allows him to jar his listeners and readers a bit, changing the habitual focus on literature as separate from political culture and suggesting, instead, that language as such is ever present, something as common as tradecraft or economic exchange. Through practice and guidance one can improve it, just as artisans do in their various trades. And without language as currency, relations between nations would be impossible.

The empire, as it grew, was united by power and language, hand in hand. But after its fall, the many disciplines that relied on Latin suffered too. It was only the Apostolic See that prevented a complete collapse. Why? "Without a doubt, it was the Christian religion that stood out as origin and cause." The reason? "Since both the Old and the New Testament existed written in that very Latin language that God made sacred on the cross, together with Greek and Hebrew," and since Christians preserved Latin, even as they rejected Roman power, this one precious instrument was allowed at least to survive.[24] The evolution of Christianity, in other words, elevated Latin to an even higher level of sacredness.

As Christianity grew, so too did the papal court, where "it is not allowed to speak anything other than Latin."[25] And so, "given that our religion is eternal, so too will Latin literature be eternal."[26] Popes who help Latin thrive, Valla concludes, also help Christianity thrive.[27] When Valla wrote this oration, the humanist pope, Nicholas V, had been dead for more than

---

[22] Ibid., sec. 20: "sic propagata lingua Latina non solum he artes ad provincias sunt profecte, set etiam provincialium ad istas ingenia accessere."

[23] Ibid., sec. 21.

[24] Ibid., sec. 30: "Cuius rei sine dubio caput et causa extitit religio christiana. Cum enim utrunque testamentum extaret scriptum latinis litteris, quas duas in cruce una cum grecis et hebraicis consecravit, cumque tot hominum clarissimorum ingenia in illis exponendis consumpta essent, nimirum hi qui christiani censebantur nomina, quanquam imperium romanum repudiassent, tamen nefas putaverunt repudiare linguam romanam, ne suam religionem profanarent."

[25] Ibid., sec. 33: "Nam cum in curia romana non nisi latine loqui fas sit et ad eam tamquam ad caput cunte christiane nationes privatim publiceque concurrant, fit ut singule operam dent lingue latine discende, et ob id libris omnibus latine scriptis et ut quisque maxime aliquo in genere doctrine excellit, ita cupidissime ad hanc se curiam conferat et velit in hac tamquam in clarissima luce versari."

[26] Ibid., sec. 36: "quia religio nostra eterna, etiam latina litteratura eterna fore."

[27] Ibid., secs. 38–40.

half a year. Nicholas had tirelessly supported Valla and many other humanists in his massive Greek-to-Latin translation project, and Valla was likely feeling his absence and trying to sway the new pope, Calixtus III, to continue to support learning. Still, this oration's extraordinary distillation of Valla's view that Christianity, Latinity, and culture were intimately linked remains potent.

The same message, in a slightly different key, is present in two other works by Valla, each in its own way a keystone of his thought: his treatise on the *Donation of Constantine* and his *Encomium of Saint Thomas*.[28] If Valla is known today, it is certainly because of his *Declamation on the falsely believed and lying Donation of Constantine* (*De falso credita et ementita Constantini donatione declamation*).[29] For it was in this treatise, so the story goes, that Valla used his knowledge of the Latin language to unmask the "Donation of Constantine" as a forgery. The "Donation" may be unfamiliar to modern readers, but it was well known as a point of controversy in the Middle Ages.[30] According to the traditional version, in the second decade of the fourth century, Constantine, the first Christian emperor, was cured of leprosy miraculously, with the intervention and prayer of the then pope, Sylvester, as a primary cause. So grateful was Constantine that he decided to give a series of privileges along with territorial control of much of Western Europe to the pope. Thereafter, Constantine removed himself to Byzantium, locating the capital of the "Roman" Empire there and eventually renaming the city after himself (Constantinople). And there was a document to "prove" that this gift had taken place.

Valla's achievement, according to traditional accounts (which are correct as far as they go) was to show that some of the language used in the *Constitutum Constantini* (as the document was known) derived from a later

---

[28] See Lorenzo Valla, *On the Donation of Constantine*, ed. and tr. Glenn Bowersock (Cambridge, MA: Harvard University Press, 2007); there the Latin edition is based on Lorenzo Valla, *De falso credita et ementita Constantini donatione*, ed. Wolfram Setz, in the *Monumenta Germaniae historica*, 10 (Weimar: Böhlau, 1976); Valla, *Laurentii Valle Encomion Sancti Thome Aquinatis*, ed. Stefano Cartei (Firenze: Polistampa, 2008); and for an English translation of the *Encomium*, Valla, "Encomium of St. Thomas," tr. Patrick Baker, in Salvatore I. Camporeale, *Christianity, Latinity, and Culture: Two Studies on Lorenzo Valla*, tr. Patrick Baker, ed. Patrick Baker and Christopher S. Celenza (Leiden: Brill, 2014), 297–315.

[29] See Wolfram Setz, *Lorenzo Vallas Schrift gegen die Konstantinische Schenkung De falsa credita et ementita Constantini donatione: Zur Interpretation und Wirkungsgeschichte*. Bibliothek des Deutschen Historischen Instituts in Rom, 44 (Tübingen: Niemeyer, 1975); and Camporeale, *Christianity, Latinity, and Culture*.

[30] See Johannes Fried, *Donation of Constantine and Constitutum Constantini: The Misinterpretation of a Fiction and its Original Meaning* (Berlin and New York: de Gruyter, 2007).

period than that of the document itself, meaning that it could not have been written when it was purported to have been written and was, instead, a later forgery. If Valla appears in textbooks of Western history, it is this unmasking for which he is centrally featured, with his use of language seen as a predecessor of "scientific" philology, which is to say the use of technical linguistic and historical evidence to date and place documents from the past. Yet, there is so much more to be said about this work that it is worthwhile stepping back and examining its constituent parts.

The first of these parts is the document of Donation itself. The "Donation of Constantine" refers to the notional gift of the Emperor Constantine, as mentioned. The consensus of modern scholarship is that the document in which this gift was formalized (the *Constitutum*) was produced in the environment of the papal court in the eighth century, almost five centuries after Constantine's supposed gift.[31] It is often indicated, therefore, as a forgery," which at the most literal level it surely is, and Valla is seen as the first to identify it as such in a definitive way. Yet to understand Valla's approach in its entirety, it is productive to reflect on what a forgery might mean, not only in the premodern world but also in the preprint world. Suppose that consensus emerged, in the eighth-century curial environment whose members went on to produce the document, that Constantine had indeed ceded the rights to the western territories to the pope. How central would a document be in "proving" that this Donation had indeed taken place, in a world in which catastrophic loss of documentation was not uncommon?

Medieval archives often possessed mechanisms for ensuring authentication.[32] Yet given (what now seems like) the instability of the world of medieval documentary culture, arguments about proof were likely to include, and to hinge upon, more than simply documentation.[33] Indeed, this is precisely what occurred during the medieval centuries in which the legitimacy of the Donation (rather than the authenticity of the document) constituted matter for intense debate. To offer two from among a number of possible (and similar) examples, the historian and bishop Otto of Freising (1114–58) did not discuss the Donation with reference to the *Constitutum*.

---

[31] Johannes Fried, as earlier, has made the important step of separating, conceptually, the "Donation" from the document, showing that each had, in a sense, a separate existence in different intellectual and cultural communities throughout the Middle Ages. This and the succeeding paragraph follow his emphasis; see Alfred Hiatt, *The Making of Medieval Forgeries: False Documents in Fifteenth-Century England* (Cambridge: Cambridge University Press, 2004), 136–42, whose approach to the Donation has also informed what follows.

[32] Bischoff, *Latin Palaeography*, 34–37.

[33] See, e.g., Michael Clanchy, *From Memory to Written Record*, 3rd ed. (Oxford: Wiley-Blackwell, 2013), 295–329.

Instead he wondered in his *Chronicle* how there could have been emperors subsequent to Constantine who disposed of the very same land Constantine was supposed to have alienated.[34] Even Gratian, the foremost of the early legal scholars at the University of Bologna (where the study of law was reborn in the Middle Ages) did not include the *Constitutum* in his *Concordance of Discordant Canons*.[35] Though his immediate successors added a version of the document, arguments for most of the Middle Ages turned on other factors: whether the pope or emperor was the supreme leader of Christendom, whether the Donation was legally possible (did the emperor have the right to alienate the property under discussion?), whether the pope, with his ecclesiastical responsibilities, could legitimately have accepted such a gift, and so on. Different versions of the document circulated, needless to say, along with different summaries its content.

So it is unsurprising that much of Valla's argumentation, too, turns on factors other than just the text of the *Constitutum*. He, like everyone in his era, took part in a culture shaped by manuscripts, and no one was more aware than Valla just how precarious these could be. The force of his argumentation is compelling, all of it rooted in Valla's acute sense of history.

If the claim sounds implausible that a powerful secular ruler, expert in military affairs, would simply hand over large swaths of property for which he and his predecessors had paid hefty prices in blood and treasure, that is because it is implausible. It is an implausibility that Valla brings into stark relief with a variety of techniques. Valla begins by addressing unnamed princes directly: "Would any one of you, had he been in Constantine's place, have thought he should act to bestow upon another person, by gracious liberality, the city of Rome? ... I cannot be persuaded to believe that any sane person would do this."[36] Princes go to great effort to acquire dominion: "But if dominion is apt to be sought by so great an effort, how much greater must be the effort to keep it!" It is simply implausible to think you would just give hard-earned dominion away.

When Valla wanted to make critical points in his Preface to his *Annotations*, he used the rhetorical device of personification. Here, in his treatise on the Donation, he does the same. He takes on, for instance, the persona of Constantine's sons, who ask their father how he could do something like alienating property that they, by right, should have inherited: "Father, do you really deprive, disinherit, and cast off your sons, you who loved your

---

[34] Fried, 13.
[35] Ibid., 19.
[36] Valla, *On the Donation*, p. 11.

sons very much until now?"[37] Valla impersonates the Roman Senate: "Caesar, if you are unmindful of your own family ... nevertheless the Senate and People of Rome cannot be unmindful of its right and reputation ... Shall we accept an Empire of those whose religion we scorn?"[38] And Valla ventriloquizes Pope Sylvester: "I am a priest ... I could not be induced by any argument to agree with you unless I wished to be untrue to myself, forget my station, and almost deny my Lord Jesus."[39] Plausibility: the first major section of Valla's treatise, the part intended to grab readers' attention, to make sure they would keep reading, has to do simply with common sense. Rulers don't give land away if they are not compelled to do so by surrender.

There are significant arguments about the text itself, through which Valla shows himself a connoisseur of the traditions, history, and instability of different forms of writing. If, he asks, such a monumental Donation indeed took place, why are there no other testimonies, such as would normally have been expressed in the various traditional forms of public writing (inscriptions, bronze tablets, and so on)? He writes: "But this Donation of Constantine, so splendid and unexampled, can be proven by no document at all, whether on gold or on silver or on bronze or on marble or, finally, in books, but only, if we believe that man [here Valla refers to person who added the *Constitutum* to Gratian's *Decretum*] on paper or parchment."[40]

Valla is also justly celebrated for the etymological arguments, such as when he highlights the absurdity of the document containing the term "Constantinople" when "Byzantium" had not yet acquired that name, or when he shows that words are used that would have made no sense in the document's supposed chronological context (such as the use of the term "satrap," for which there is no other contemporary evidence, or the use of the word "ecclesia" for "church" – referring to the building – when *templum* would have been more appropriate in that case).[41]

The criticisms that Valla makes add up to more than an "unmasking" of a forged document. Taken together they amount to a strong critique of the Church as it situated itself in Valla's day, which is to say as the custodian of universal Christendom and simultaneously as a regional political power: "The Pope himself makes war on peaceful nations and sows discord among states and rulers ... Christ lies dying of starvation and exposure among so

[37] Ibid., 21.
[38] Ibid., 23.
[39] Ibid., 31–33.
[40] Ibid., 63.
[41] Ibid., 75, 67, 79, respectively.

many thousands of poor."[42] It is true that when Valla wrote this text he was in the employ of Alfonse of Aragon, who was at odds with the then pope, Eugenius IV. But the incisiveness, range, and sheer amount of Valla's criticisms belie the notion that this text was little more than the product of a paid rhetorician. There is a vision behind the text about Christianity, Latinity, and culture, a vision also manifested in Valla's *Encomium of Saint Thomas*.

Valla delivered the *Encomium*, an oration, on March 7, 1457, the feast day of St. Thomas Aquinas, at the seat of the Dominican order in Rome, Santa Maria sopra Minerva.[43] As it turned out, this was his last work, and it stands as a small masterpiece of restrained refection: restrained for Valla, that is. For here too, Valla launches a critique, but it is a subtler critique than those to which his readers are accustomed. He had been asked, after all, to speak at a commemorative occasion honoring Thomas Aquinas, and in so far as it was possible for him to do, given his guiding assumptions concerning philosophy and theology, he took the obligation seriously. As is often the case, his critique emerges not against the *auctoritas*, in this case Aquinas, but rather against those who make uncritical use of the authority. Valla followed the same procedure, for example, when dealing with Aristotle in the Preface of his *Repastinatio totius dialecticae*, where it is not Aristotle himself but his uncritical followers who bear the brunt of critique.[44]

In Aquinas's case, over time he became the Middle Ages' greatest scholastic philosopher, one whose interpretations of Aristotle have come to seem emblematic of an entire mind-set. His question-oriented style, as we have seen, manifested numerous advantages when it came to laying out the pro and con of an argument, provided great mental training, and embodied one of medieval theology's most lasting and important genres of writing. Aquinas's reputation was, in the fifteenth century, not as high as it is today in that emblematic sense.[45] But it was getting there, and he was in any case the Dominican Order's leading philosopher, occupying, in terms of his reputation within the Order, the highest possible rung.

Valla's entire *Encomium*, in fact, represents an attempt to put Aquinas in his proper place, in the most literal sense of that expression. What rung should

---

[42] Ibid., 155–57.
[43] In addition to Camporeale, *Christianity*, for context see the important work of John W. O'Malley, "Some Renaissance Panegyrics of Aquinas," *Renaissance Quarterly* 27 (1974), 174–92; O'Malley, "The Feast of Thomas Aquinas in Renaissance Rome: A Neglected Document and Its Import," *Rivista di storia della Chiesa in Italia* 35 (1981), 1–27.
[44] See Lorenzo Valla, *Dialectical Disputations*, ed. and tr. Copenhaver and Nauta, 2–13.
[45] See Paul Oskar Kristeller, *Le Thomisme et la pensée italienne de la Renaissance* (Paris: Vrin, 1967); Kristeller, *Medieval Aspects of Renaissance Learning*, ed. and tr. Edward P. Mahoney (Durham, NC: Duke University Press, 1974), 29–91.

Aquinas occupy, and why? Valla notes the difference, for example, between "martyrs," who died because of their faith, and "confessors" (*confessores*), who "lived a chaste and spotless life accompanied by divine signs and miracles."[46] Aquinas is a "confessor" and as such possessed innumerable virtues, but he was not a martyr, Valla reminds his audience, and he should not be accorded that sort of veneration (unlike other Dominicans, such as Peter Martyr). Aquinas's birth was prophesied, as was that of the Dominican Order's founder, Dominic. Valla thenceforth begins what one might term a relational strategy, evaluating Aquinas against others to whom he has been compared. In this case, Dominic is a founder, and Thomas is a continuator, not to be regarded as on the same level as the founder, one assumes, but important nonetheless: "Dominic founded the house of the Preachers; Thomas covered its floor with marble. Dominic built its walls; Thomas decorated them with the finest paintings."[47] The impression is that there can be only one founder, but that there could have been more who contributed to ornamenting the original foundation. As it happened, Aquinas was the most prominent of those later contributors, but he still should not be confused with the founder.

Similarly, Valla has in mind the larger history of Christian thinkers, a history in which the early Church fathers loom large. Valla expresses surprise at how Aquinas has been regarded: "It has not escaped me that certain people who held an oration here, on the same subject as today's, not only made Thomas second to none of the doctors of the Church, but also placed him above them all."[48] What is more, "The reason they gave for being able to put him above everyone is, they say, that he used logic, metaphysics, and all philosophy to prove theology, things which the earlier doctors are supposed barely to have tasted with the tips of their tongues."[49] Recognizing how risky it seems even to appear to criticize Aquinas on his feast day, in Rome's central Dominican Church, Valla says that he still cannot disguise what he thinks. Furthermore, since he did not rise to speak of his own accord but was instead asked to do so by the Dominicans themselves, he feels he must speak his mind.

Valla has already adumbrated his two principal concerns: the need to protect the exemplary, authoritative status of the ancient Church fathers and the concomitant desire to put the focus where he believes it belongs when treating of theology: not on dialectic and metaphysics but rather on the

---

[46] The quotation is from Valla, *Encomium of Saint Thomas* (tr. Baker), sec. 2.
[47] Ibid., sec. 9.
[48] Ibid., sec. 13.
[49] Ibid.

message of the early Church and of its earliest and greatest thinkers. These two themes dominate the remainder of the *Encomium*. Valla admires the copiousness of Aquinas's writings in sincere terms of praise but he also marvels, he says, at something else Aquinas is supposed to have said: "that he never read a book that he did not fully understand."[50] What is the audience to think? That Valla offers sincere praise? Or that he is instead subtly mocking Aquinas for vaunting an omni-comprehensive intelligence no human being could achieve? Or could audience members believe either of the two opinions, depending on their predilections, receptivity to possible irony, or even on Valla's delivery, something about which we cannot know anything definitively?

Valla goes on immediately to touch on one of the two themes mentioned: "But those things which they call metaphysics and modes of signifying and the like, which modern theologians regard with wonder like a recently discovered ninth sphere or like the epicycles of the planets, I regard with no great wonder at all."[51] Valla indicts what he sees as an overemphasis on metaphysics and dialectic at the expense of more important concerns. This move leads him to the other concern, the Church fathers: "I will not make this case with my own arguments (although I could) but by citing the ancient theologians – Cyprian, Lactantius, Hilary, Ambrose, Jerome, Augustine – who were so far from treating such matters in their works that they did not even mention them."[52] The fathers do not devote themselves to detailed discussions of metaphysics and logic for two reasons. First, they do not "seem to lead to the knowledge of divine truths."[53] Second, both of these areas operate with crucial terminology that has roots in Greek philosophical discussion and, ultimately, in the Greek language. Even if latterly coined Latin words exist to reflect certain Greek concepts (concepts around which

---

[50] Ibid., sec. 15.

[51] Ibid., 16. "Modes of signifying" = *modi significandi*. Valla is referring to philosophers of the thirteenth and fourteenth centuries who studied the specialized ways that different words acquired meaning in propositions and sentences. Martin of Dacia and Boethius of Dacia are most commonly named when studying this tendency, though they profited from the earlier work of twelfth-century "speculative grammarians" such as William of Conches (the term "speculative grammarians" is often used to refer to both groups). See Costantino Marmo, *Semiotica e linguaggio nella scolastica: Parigi, Bologna, Erfurt, 1270–1330* (Rome: Istituto Storico Italiano per il Medioevo, 1994); Jan Pinborg, "Speculative Grammar," in Norman Kretzmann, Anthony Kenny, and Jan Pinborg, eds., *The Cambridge History of Later Medieval Philosophy* (Cambridge: Cambridge University Press, 1982), 254–69; Pinborg, *Die Entwicklung der Sprachtheorie im Mittelalter* (Münster: Aschendorff, 1967); and Irène Rosier, *La grammaire spéculative des Modistes* (Paris: PUF, 1983).

[52] Valla, *Encomium of Saint Thomas*, sec. 16.

[53] Ibid., sec. 18.

much discussion in metaphysics and dialectic revolve, such as the ten categories of Aristotle), they are not organic to the Latin language and thus not
organic to the kind of thinking and writing about religion that the Church
fathers prized. The Latin fathers "dreaded words which the great Latin
authors . . . never used."[54] Once again one observes that solid Latin, meaningful Christianity, and human culture are linked for Valla, a presupposition
he takes with him into his evaluation of the fathers and their exemplary value.

The fathers mentioned are so important that Valla uses them to end his
oration. He argues that to understand Aquinas, if he is indeed to be considered as having the kind of status that a father should have, he must be
paired with a Greek father, the way one might pair the older Latin fathers
with Greek counterparts. And after suggesting that Aquinas should be
considered above a series of medieval theologians (St. Bernard, Peter
Lombard, Gratian, and Albert the Great, among others), this is precisely
what Valla does. Ambrose is paired with Basil, Jerome with Gregory
Nazianzen, Augustine with John Chrysostom, Gregory with (for us pseudo)
Dionysius the Areopagite, and Aquinas with John Damascene. Though Valla
does not expatiate on these pairings beyond a few words each, there is
a rationale to them. Ambrose considered himself a "rival" to Basil; Jerome
claimed to have been a "pupil and disciple" of Nazianzen; Augustine "often
followed" and "emulated" John Chrysostom; and Gregory the Great (pope
490–504) is the first to have mentioned Dionysius the Areopagite (Valla
mentions that Gregory "is the first of the Latins . . . to mention" Dionysius
and notes that Dionysius was unknown to the Greeks as well).[55] As to
Aquinas and John Damascene, Valla writes that their pairing is justified,
because "John wrote many logical and well-nigh metaphysical works."[56]

All things considered, one observes a restrained and balanced Valla. Yet
Valla adds what could be read as another note of ambiguity. Sacred writers
"always make music in the sight of God," and each pair has its part to play in
the musical group Valla outlines: "The first pair is Basil and Ambrose, playing
the lyre; the second, Nazianzen and Jerome, playing the cithara; the third,
Chrysostom and Augustine, playing the psaltery; the fourth, Dionysius and
Gregory, playing the flute." The fifth? "John Damascene and Thomas,

[54] Ibid., sec. 19.
[55] For Valla's part in the story of the interpretation of ps.-Dionysius the Areopagite, see
John Monfasani, "Pseudo-Dionysius the Areopagite in mid-Quattrocento Rome," in
J. Hankins, J. Monfasani, and F. Purnell Jr., eds., *Supplementum Festivum: Studies in Honor
of Paul Oskar Kristeller* (Binghamton: MRTS, 1987), 189–219, reprinted with the same
pagination as essay IX in J. Monfasani, *Language and Learning in Renaissance Italy*
(Aldershot: Ashgate, 1994).
[56] Valla, *Encomium of Saint Thomas*, sec. 23.

playing the cymbals," which are, Valla says, an "instrument that emits happy, cheerful, and pleasing music."[57] What sort of praise is this? "Happy," "cheerful," and "pleasing" are positive attributes, but do they imply the requisite gravity, holiness, and depth due on the occasion of Thomas's feast day? Valla does not address these questions and closes his oration piously.

When Valla wrote and delivered this oration, unbeknownst to him he had very little time left to live. It is difficult to know whether this seemingly always dissatisfied and cranky scholar was content with his lot as he neared the end of his life. He had managed to achieve a lifelong dream: a high-level position at the papal court, one that had eluded him most of his life and had become a source of difficulty owing to his conflict with Poggio and other curialists. Nicholas V, the humanist pope, had employed Valla as one of the team of Greek-to-Latin translators so important during that pontificate; during Nicholas's reign Valla occupied the position of *scriptor*, a relatively high-level writer of official papal documents.[58] Then, when Alfonse Borgia became Pope Callixtus III (significantly, he was a Spanish churchman and ally of the house of Aragon, Valla's longtime employer in Naples), Valla became a papal secretary, reaching the highest rung of the papal court.[59] And all this despite his scabrous personality, frequently radical attacks on certain central Christian practices, and his penchant for stirring up trouble in any workplace he entered.

One wonders about the fact that Valla, at least today, can be read as being at odds with the very institution with which he affiliated himself so strongly. A few factors emerge that can help explain this seeming inconsistency.

First, for Valla as for most Renaissance thinkers, the writings whose contents we study today – in Valla's case his *Dialectical Disputations*, the *Elegances*, his work on the *Donation*, the *Encomium*, and so on – all represent something like "side projects." This is not to say that they were unimportant to their authors, just that they were written in one's free time. Valla was almost continuously employed, from his early days of controversy at the University of Pavia, to his longest stint at the court of Alfonse of Aragon in Naples, and finally to his time at the papal court, under the pontificates of Nicholas V and Calixtus III. In all of those contexts, Valla had things to do to earn his bread: to give lessons, to write letters, to defend the interests of his patron, and so on. It is stunning and, whatever one thinks about Valla as a person, admirable that amid all these responsibilities, Valla was able to

[57] Ibid., sec. 24.
[58] Mancini, *Vita*, 237.
[59] See A. von Hoffman, *Forschungen zur Geschichte der kurialen Behörden vom Schisma bis zur Reformation*, 2 vols. (Rome: von Loescher, 1914), 2: 114.

develop a consistent, critical viewpoint and produce a body of work still worth reading today. His messages – that the precise deployment of language is of utmost importance to thinking critically; that institutions sometimes forget their roots; that people, especially in academic contexts, sometimes venerate authority unquestioningly – emerge clearly enough. But the works in which he developed those messages did not gain him any significant income. So if it seems puzzling on the surface that he was able to rise so high in a Church that he criticized fairly openly, this is why: the authorities did not care all that much. His works were circulating in hand-written copies, squabbling among underlings was not that uncommon, and in any case people were constantly debating this or that point of politics or theology.

Second, and related specifically to Valla, he remained an outlier in the fifteenth century in many respects. Most of his work did not circulate heavily in manuscript and even in the new world of printing (a world that we will examine soon). The only work with indubitable "market share," as it were, was the *Elegances*. And even there, what draws our gaze versus what did so in the Renaissance seem at odds. Valla's comments in the Prefaces about language, power, and empire attract attention today, since they show us one of the most brilliant, if quirkiest, Renaissance intellectuals wrestling with, and explaining, his era's fascination with the Latin language. It is almost unimaginable today that a dead language could have such purchase on intellectuals. Yet it did, and Valla's sentiments present an extreme version as to why: if you could somehow zero in on the right elite language, then power, culture, and politics would follow in train.

While such a notion might seem improbable on the face of it, it is surely true at anything but the most superficial of levels. All you need to do is look at the way the early twenty-first-century media revolution has cannibalized political discourse in so many ways, and it becomes ever clearer that control of the medium means the ability to control the message in a significant if not absolute way. Valla's views on language represent a "strong" version of his contemporaries' concern with the problem of what sort of language was suitable for public use. Most who wrestled with the question of what sort of language did the ancient Romans speak had no such high-minded, broad views. What mattered to contemporaries (aside from the occasional debater) was the text itself, rather than the more ideologically inclined Prefaces. For all his bluster, Valla was good at what he did, able to back up many if not all of his claims to superiority by an exhaustive knowledge of Latin and literary history, so much so that his work in that respect did indeed make it into classrooms. You could ignore the ideological statements in the Prefaces and still get quite a lot out of the *Elegances*: stylistically sophisticated, accurate, and comprehensive recommendations on how to use the Latin language well.

One final work deserves our attention. Though the dialogue *On Free Will* was not Valla's last work, it is appropriate to focus on it now, since it looked toward the future, toward the sixteenth century, really, and toward the way Christianity would evolve during the Protestant Reformation.[60] The dialogue is also noteworthy because it alerts us to the various ways Renaissance thinkers talked about, and engaged in, philosophy.

On this latter front, Valla's own letter of dedication seems clear – on the surface. Writing to his dedicatee, a Spanish bishop, Valla begins as follows: "I would prefer, O Garsia, most learned and best of Bishops, that other Christians and, indeed, those who are called theologians, would not depend so much on philosophy or devote so much energy to it, making it almost an equal and sister (I do not say patron) of theology."[61] Valla is recalling one of his most powerful models, Saint Paul, who in his letter to the Colossians had written: "Beware lest any man cheat you by philosophy and vain deceit, according to the tradition of men, according to the elements of the world, and not according to Christ."[62] Paul was speaking, of course, of pagan philosophers and what they professed. But he was also describing a way of thinking about the world that suggested that all things worth pondering could be approached through human reason alone, which depends radically on sense perception, rather than with the aid of faith. And he was speaking, as well, of empty rhetoric. The message was this: do not think that, just because you cannot see God, God does not exist. And: do not let slick talkers convince you otherwise. "Philosophy" comes to signify this emptiness. So Valla, it should be remembered, is using the term in that Pauline fashion. He is not arguing against philosophy pure and simple, understood as, simply, the love of and pursuit of wisdom. For Valla, wisdom could only be pursued through Christian channels.

Just what those Christian channels were, however, was the issue at stake for fifteenth-century Italian thinkers. As we shall see, Valla will not be the last person to wrestle with this problem. But he is one of the most interesting and, in this dialogue, perhaps the most subversive. "Free will," or *liberum arbitrium* in Latin, is what is at issue in the dialogue. Valla has two interlocutors, himself and a friend of his, Antonio, with whom, Valla writes, he had a bit of

---

[60] Valla, *De libero arbitrio*, in Garin, *Prosatori*, 524–65; "Dialogue on Free Will," tr. Charles E. Trinkaus Jr., in Ernst Cassirer, Paul Oskar Kristeller, and John Herman Randall Jr., *The Renaissance Philosophy of Man* (Chicago: University of Chicago Press, 1948), 155–82.

[61] Valla, *De libero*, 524; tr. Trinkaus, 155.

[62] Paul, Col. 2:8.

a friendly argument concerning whether or not human beings truly have free will. Valla also tells his dedicatee that part of what he wants to do is to show that Boethius had argued incorrectly about the question.[63] The problem of free will has most profoundly to do with God: how one conceives of Him, what sort of relationship one presumes that human beings have with God, and what sort of action one assumes God takes in the world of day-to-day human affairs.

A few things were nonnegotiable: God is omniscient, meaning he knows all things. He is omnipotent, meaning that he has unlimited power: there is nothing He cannot do. God is one, despite the plural nature of the Holy Trinity of Father, Son, and Holy Spirit, who though able to be conceptualized as separate beings, all resolve into God's eternal Oneness. And, finally, God is "good," meaning exactly what it sounds like. God does not do evil things. As to human free will, it represented the core of a certain type of ethics, inherited from Plato and adopted by Christianity, whereby a world was presumed to exist, immaterial and eternal, beyond our own. In that supra-mundane world, one would reap the rewards of what one had done on earth. One who lived a good life – one who performed good acts in life, in other words – would be rewarded with heaven. Those who did not would go to hell. And for those who had committed sins not sufficiently severe to earn damnation, there was a purgatory, where one would be cleansed of sin before entering paradise.[64] This divine social economy depended in one version on human free will: your own choices about what you did served as the basis for how you would or would not be rewarded in the afterlife.

Yet there had been, since the days of Saint Augustine, a sneaking suspicion that it would be limiting the omnipotence of God, if human beings, small and powerless as they were compared to an eternal, omniscient being, could "earn" their salvation through their own actions. Augustine tried to maintain what later scholars would term a "compatibilist" position: that you could have both human free will and God's omniscient omnipotence, side by side.[65] But it was a difficult thing to do, especially so as Augustine resonated so deeply with the idea that salvation had to do with God's grace, freely given on His part. The individual Christian needed to submit to God's will, in the

---

[63] Valla, *De libero*, 526; tr. Trinkaus, 156–57.

[64] See Jacques LeGoff, *The Birth of Purgatory* (Chicago: University of Chicago Press, 1984), for the eleventh-century origins of purgatory as a place.

[65] See Augustine, *De civ. Dei*, 5.10; and *De libero arbitrio libri tres*, ed. William M. Green, Corpus scriptorum ecclesiasticorum latinorum, vol. 74, sect. 6, part 3 (Vienna: Hoelder-Pichler-Tempsky, 1956), esp. Book Three, at pp. 89–154.

full knowledge that one could never know one was saved.[66] Later, in the Middle Ages, Peter Lombard, Thomas Aquinas, and other theologians, interested in protecting human free will, refined an idea that had been floating around in the atmosphere of Christian theology, something that they called "cooperating grace," pairing it with what was called "prevenient" or "operating" grace. What this meant was that God would freely give you His grace if you were saved but that through your freely chosen actions you could "work together," or *cooperari* in Latin, with Him to help the process along. As Peter Lombard put it in the twelfth century, "operating grace is that which comes before good will; for by it man's will is freed and prepared that it might be good and that it might effectively will the good; but cooperating grace follows a will that is already good by offering help."[67]

If that sounds fuzzy, it is because it is. The truth is that this is a philosophical question of long standing, a kind of "if / then" problem that does not allow for a satisfying logical solution. If God truly knows all things, this means that there is nothing across time that He does not know and observe. He sees the past, present, and future as if it were an eternal present, all there for Him at all times. (This conclusion, regarding God's trans-temporal knowledge, was precisely the point at which Boethius, in the early sixth century, had arrived, in his *Consolation of Philosophy*.[68]) If you do something now, God will have foreseen that that is exactly what you were going to do, precisely when you were going to do it, and exactly in the way that you did it. "Omniscient" – "all knowing" – means exactly what it sounds like. If you have the ability or capacity to do something that God cannot foresee, that means that God is not omniscient. He is not God, by the definition that we have been using.

Then there is omnipotence – being all-powerful – and its relationship to goodness. Every day we are surrounded by events that by any normal definition are far from good. Fatal accidents, crimes, murders, innocent people who are loved by their families and neighbors brought low by accidents, crimes, and sundry other seemingly random events. How can a God who is both good and all-powerful allow these things to occur? Again, does the very fact that these tragic events occur somehow show that if there is a God, He cannot be described as "good," at least in the everyday language that we use to describe goodness? Also, wars, floods, and other analogous catastrophes: how can it be that this "God" allows all this to exist?

---

[66] See Augustine, *Conf.*, 8.12 for his conversion and realization of the necessity of grace.
[67] See Peter Lombard, *Sent.*, 2.dist.26.1.2; cf. Aquinas, *ST*, 1a2ae, q. 111, esp. art. 2 and 3; and q.113, esp. art.3.
[68] Boethius, *Cons.*, 5.3.

What kind of "power" does He have, if a litany of evil can be visited on human beings daily?

True, you could point to our smallness: you could say that we, finite as we are, know so little that we must simply accept that these terrible tragedies form part of a larger plan whose broad outlines only God in His infinite wisdom truly comprehends. Yes, you could say that. But does it console a mother who has lost a young child to a disease whose cure is unknown? Does it help the citizens of a town destroyed by an earthquake or flood?

Questions analogous to these have preoccupied Western thinkers since antiquity, and they became ever more acute with the gradual rise of Christianity. For Christians conceived of their God as omniscient, omnipotent, and good, on the one hand. On the other, the Christian God is also a personal God; He is conceptualized as being personally interested in individual human beings. For Valla, the question boils down to this (as his interlocutor Antonio puts it): "whether God's foreknowledge stands in the way of free will."[69] Antonio's dilemma is as follows: "If God foresees the future, it cannot happen otherwise than he foresaw," with the result that "for God either to praise this one for justice or accuse that one of injustice and to reward the one and punish the other, to speak freely, seems to be the opposite of justice, since the actions of men follow by necessity the foreknowledge of God."[70] If you do something evil and God knew this was going to happen, you were in effect destined to do it. How can you really be blamed? How is punishment after death just? What, then, is the nature of the divine social economy?

In Valla's *On Free Will*, two crucial moments occur on the way to addressing the main question of whether, given God's foreknowledge, one can conceive of human free will in a nontrivial fashion. The first has to do with separating God's foreknowledge from the motivations behind human action. Valla has his interlocutor Lorenzo (himself, in fictionalized dialogical form) present a hypothetical situation. Let us go back to Roman antiquity and take the case of Sextus Tarquinius, a figure of universal hatred and opprobrium. Sextus, one of the sons of Rome's last king (Tarquin the Proud), raped the pure Lucretia, that very Lucretia who thereafter took her own life, rather than live with the dishonor of her status, sullied as she believed herself to have been.[71]

---

[69] Valla, *De libero*, 532; tr. Trinkaus, 161.
[70] Valla, *De libero*, 532–34; tr. Trinkaus, 162.
[71] Livy, *Ab urbe condita*, 1.57–58.

Let us say, "Lorenzo" goes on, that Sextus early on went to Apollo, the oracle, who could predict the future, and asked what his fate would be. In that case, "we may pretend that the oracle replied, as was customary, in verse as follows: 'an exile and a pauper you will fall, / Killed by an angry city.'"[72] Sextus, upon hearing his fate, might then have replied angrily to the oracle, requesting that the oracle predict a better fate of what would lie ahead. To this (again all hypothetical) statement the oracle would have responded: *Ego nosco fata, non statuo; ego denunciare fortunam possum, non mutare* – "I know the fates, I do not decide them; I am able to announce Fortune, not change her."[73] The oracle says, in effect, I am not to blame. Well then, whom might Sextus accuse? "Accuse Jupiter, if you will, accuse the fates, accuse fortune whence the course of events descends."[74] More confusion from hypothetical Sextus: why is Jupiter so unjust? The oracle: "that is the way things are, Sextus. Jupiter, as he created the wolf fierce, the hare timid, the lion brave . . . so he fashioned some men hard of heart, others soft, and further, he gave a capacity for reform to one and made another incorrigible."[75] That is all.

Then emerges the most startling passage of this first, important section: "For this was the point of my fable, that, although the wisdom of God cannot be separated from His power and will, I may by this device of Apollo and Jupiter separate them. What cannot be achieved with one God can be achieved with two."[76] Valla, in other words, is proposing a solution to a profound problem in the realm of the Christian religion by using the device of "two gods."

Now, exaggeration would be unwise: it is after all only a literary device, first of all. Second, the work in which it appears happens to be a dialogue, a literary genre in which a certain amount of play is encouraged. Valla himself writes the dialogue in a humorous spirit, with puns and short set pieces as the rule. On the other hand, a Christian proposing a solution to a theological problem that involves two gods – two pagan gods, one might add – does make one's ears perk up. As we have seen in other cases, what matters is the fact of the text being out there, rather than Valla's intentions. How might one have read that text back then?

In any case, the "solution" is obviously not a solution, as the interlocutors soon come to realize, a moment that opens up the second great major point of the dialogue and makes it seem a kind of foreshadowing of debates to

---

[72] Valla, *De libero*, 546; tr. Trinkaus, 170.
[73] Ibid.
[74] Ibid.
[75] Valla, *De libero*, 550; tr. Trinkaus, 173.
[76] Ibid.

occur later, and more openly, in the sixteenth century. True, the interlocutors realize, one can conceptually separate God's foreknowledge from human free will. But that is not a satisfying solution at all, since, even if an individual human being might believe he or she is acting freely, God still knows, exactly, what those actions will turn out to be. Preserving God's omnipotence, in other words, means, in a strict logical sense, destroying human free will. There really is no way out of the conundrum.

As this realization dawns on the interlocutors, Valla offers a very lengthy citation from Paul's Letter to the Romans, one in which Paul had, quite starkly, defended God's omnipotence and limited human free will. Valla also hearkens back to a number of Old Testament citations, citations in which God's absolute majesty and ultimate unknowability are affirmed. Here is part of Valla's citation of Paul, where Paul is speaking of God:

> Therefore he hath mercy on whom He will; and whom he will, he hardeneth. Thou wilt say therefore to me: Why doth He then find fault? For who resisteth His will? O man, who art thou that repliest against God? Shall the thing formed say to him that formed it: Why hast thou made me thus? Or hath not the potter power over the clay, of the same lump, to make one vessel unto honor, and another unto dishonor?"[77]

This Pauline citation represents a stark viewpoint: God possesses absolute power and, given His status as infinite, there is simply no way human beings can know if anything they might do can affect God's opinion.

Our realm is finite, and it is not for us to question what God does, including allowing what seems to us to be evil to exist. As Valla says: "Indeed, a very worthy cause is adduced as to why He hardens one and has mercy on another: that he is most wise and good; and it is impious to feel otherwise as if to say that He, who is absolutely good, can do what is not good."[78] That is all one needs to know.

As in the case of most of his other works save the *Elegances*, Valla's *On Free Will* did not command much attention in his lifetime. But Valla in this instance can serve for us as a harbinger of what would come later: of a world in which the volume of discussion rose precipitously and one where much of what he said in *On Free Will* and elsewhere served as inspiration, fodder for debate, and controversy. To understand Valla's impact, we need to take a leap forward in time.

In the early sixteenth century, in northern Europe, two brilliant thinkers, the Netherlandish humanist Erasmus of Rotterdam (1466–1536) and the

---

[77] Rom. 9:18–21; cited at Valla, *De libero*, 554; tr. Trinkaus, 176.
[78] Valla, *De libero*, 554; tr. Trinkaus, 176–77, modified.

German reformer Martin Luther (1483–1546) engaged in a debate over free will.[79] Both were deeply religious. Erasmus took religious orders and became a Catholic priest by the age of 25. Luther was a Catholic, Augustinian friar, and a trained theologian, who, relatively early in life, had a spiritual crisis. Though Luther did not know Valla's work at the time, the crisis was related to precisely the issues Valla raised in *On Free Will*. Luther later in life reported the details of this episode: caught in a storm and fearing for his safety, he prayed to Saint Anne and promised to become a monk if his life were spared. It was, and he did, joining the Augustinian order. But he was wracked by continual crises of conscience, ever tormented by the sins he perceived he was constantly committing in his heart. Under guidance from his supervisor, Johann von Staupitz, Luther was able to move from constant introspection on his own sins to thinking about Christ as savior and redeemer. And then when Staupitz was made dean of theology at the University of Wittenberg, he called Luther there, where Luther in short order became a priest, earned two bachelor's degrees and then a doctorate in theology. He was asked to stay on as a distinguished member of the faculty.

Yet despite Luther's success, that haunting voice remained within him, one that told him God was so great that there was nothing we could do to satisfy Him. At the same time Luther grew impatient with traditional Catholicism. A visit to Rome left him unimpressed, as he saw too much luxury and not enough evangelism. The Catholic practice of selling indulgences also grated on him. This practice is difficult to explain to modern readers, but it had a long history in the Church.[80] Late ancient theologians had theorized the existence of a "treasury of merit," a heavenly bank wherein all the good works done by Christ and the saints reposed, offering a kind of infinite credit of goodness. In the early Christian world, those who were alienated from the Church (having been designated as "lapsed" by their bishop for this or that sin) could regain entry into the church after a period of penance. By praying to Christ and the saints one could have access to the stored-up good works in the treasury, earn some remittance from penance, and reenter the communion of the faithful ever more expeditiously.

[79] Biographical details in what follows rely on Johann Huizinga, *Erasmus and the Age of Reformation* (Princeton: Princeton University Press, 1984); Erika Rummel, *Desiderius Erasmus* (London: Continuum, 2004); James D. Tracy, *Erasmus of the Low Countries* (Berkeley: University of California Press, 1996); Martin Brecht, *Martin Luther*, 3 vols. (Stuttgart: Calwer, 1981–87); Volker Leppin, *Martin Luther*, 2nd ed. (Darmstadt: Primus, 2010); Heiko Oberman, *Luther: Man Between God and the Devil*, tr. Eileen Walliser-Schwarzbart (New Haven: Yale University Press, 1989).

[80] See Henry Charles Lea, *A History of Auricular Confession and Indulgences in the Latin Church*, 3 vols. (Philadelphia: Lea Bros., 1896).

As the centuries wore on, however, and as the Church of necessity grew into a political as well as spiritual entity (given its sociopolitical evolution in the Middle Ages), people saw more direct ways to access the treasury of merit. Indulgences represented that way. An indulgence consisted of the Church offering a remission from penance for a sin that has been forgiven. During the Middle Ages one could earn an indulgence by going on a pilgrimage to a holy site, say, or doing a series of meritorious good works (e.g., of charity). They also began to be conceived as something one could do to help the dead, already in purgatory, lessen their time there and enter heaven more quickly. Eventually, however, financial contributions to the Church also began to "count" as a good work.

So by Luther's day, some indulgences were simply sold by the Church as a means of generating revenue. Given Luther's own sensitivities, the visit of a Dominican friar to Germany sent him over the edge. The Dominican, named Tetzel, had been sent to Germany by the papacy to help rebuild the Basilica of Saint Peter, and Tetzel – at least according to Luther's later account – seemed particularly mercenary about the job he was sent to do. His anger over this episode fueled what became known as the "95 theses," a set of theological questions set forth very much in the way a late medieval theologian would do: the tone is one of earnest concern rather than overt anger.[81] But they are firm in their emphasis, and especially so when they came to the power of the pope and the practice of indulgences. The pope, Luther wrote in thesis 5, "possesses neither the will nor the power to remit any penalties, except for those imposed either at his own discretion or by canon law." Luther went on to specify that the notion that anyone on earth, the pope included, could forgive anybody anything after death was fallacious (thesis 13): "Those who die are released, by death, from all penalties, they are already dead as far as canon law is concerned, and thus have a right to be released from all penalties." Throughout the 95 theses, too, Luther gestures toward what "true Christians" believe.

Without knowing it and, likely, without intending to do so, with his 95 theses, Luther kicked off what would become known as the Protestant Reformation, with the 1517 episode serving as a symbolic first salvo in a process that, in truth, had been brewing for some time.[82] One of the places where it had been developing was in the mind of Lorenzo Valla, who in his

---

[81] Latin text in Martin Luther, *Werke: Kritische Gesamtausgabe*, 58 vols. (Weimar: Böhlau, 1883–1948), 1: 233–38.

[82] See Euan Cameron, *The European Reformation*, 2nd ed. (Oxford: Oxford University Press, 2012); Carlos M.N. Eire, *Reformations: The Early Modern World, 1450–1650* (New Haven: Yale University Press, 2016).

treatise on the Donation of Constantine, his *Annotations on the New Testament*, and his *On Free Will* foreshadowed much of what Luther and his later followers would hold dear.

To be clear, Valla never came out and openly advocated breaking off from the Catholic Church, changing the language of scripture, or changing Catholic dogma regarding free will. But then again, neither did Luther at the beginning of his reform efforts. It was only upon meeting growing resistance from the Church that he decided a break was inevitable. Luther knew, and liked, Valla's work on the Donation, especially after it was print-published by a fellow German reformer, Ulrich von Hutten.[83] The treatise's message – that the papacy that had lost touch with its early Christian roots – struck home with Luther. As to the *Annotations*, in them Valla had unwittingly brought into question the sacred status of the Latin Vulgate: the Catholic Church's official translation of the New Testament. Valla never advocated replacing the translation; but how far a step is it, really, to think that one might express the New Testament's truths more effectively in a native language, rather than Latin? Luther did precisely this, and his own German translation of the New Testament is as admired in German-speaking lands as the King James translation of the Bible is in English-speaking ones.[84]

But free will was a different issue altogether, the central philosophical difference that would come to separate Luther's growing reform movement from Roman Catholicism. In the years 1517–20, Luther wrote a series of works that outlined a different way of thinking about Christianity, personal salvation, and the structure of the Church, all of which Valla had prefigured.[85] Luther came to a series of conclusions that can be summarized with three Latin phrases: *sola gratia* ("by grace alone"), *sola fide* ("by faith alone"), and *sola scriptura* ("by scripture alone"). The true Christian can be saved only by the freely given grace of God. "Good works" simply did not count toward salvation, for all the reasons we have seen in Valla: God was too great and we were too small, a differential so vast that meaningful comparison was impossible. One believed and knew these things (and indeed one needed to live) by faith alone. One must surrender to the fact of one's smallness,

---

[83] See Brecht, *Martin Luther*, 1: 346; David M. Whitford, "The Papal Antichrist: Martin Luther and the Underappreciated Influence of Lorenzo Valla," *Renaissance Quarterly* 61 (2008), 26–52.

[84] See Hanz Volz, *Martin Luthers deutsche Bibel: Entstehung und Geschichte der Lutherbibel*, ed. Henning Wendland (Hamburg: Wittig, 1978).

[85] The most important of these were *An den christlichen Adel deutscher Nation*, in Luther, *Werke: Kritische Gesamtausgabe*, 6: 404–69; *De captivitate babylonica ecclesiae praeludium*, in Luther, *Werke: Kritische Gesamtausgabe*, 6:497–573; and *Von der Freiheit eines Christenmenschen*, in Luther, *Werke: Kritische Gesamtausgabe*, 7:1–38 (42–73, Latin version).

believe unwaveringly that God is good and that whatever He throws one's way, bad as it might immediately seem, is part of a larger plan that is, ultimately, good. Finally, Christianity's doctrines must be understood and gleaned from scripture alone. In practice this meant that most if not all medieval theology was irrelevant. If Valla had objected on stylistic as well as theological grounds to some of what he found in medieval theology, for Luther instead it was all about theology. Scripture gave you all you need to know. Not only that, but each Christian had the responsibility to read and understand scripture for himself. One did not need a mediating class of people, priests, to interpret a text, the Bible, written in a language you could not understand, Latin. For Luther, Christianity consisted of the priesthood of all believers, and scripture could and should be translated in such a way that it reached them all where they stood. What sort of Pandora's box had Valla opened with his philological notes?

What all of this meant, in practice, according to Luther, was that human free will was a nonissue, nonexistent in a philosophical sense since everything one did was, ultimately, foreordained because able to be seen in advance by God. Therefore "good works" could not earn one salvation or even help along the way. Realizing only belatedly how far from Roman Catholic theology Luther was straying, Pope Leo X issued a bull, *Exsurge Domine*, in 1520. Luther responded with a series of "Assertions," one of which categorically denied the existence of free will, after which Pope Leo issued *Decet romanum pontificem*, in which Luther was excommunicated.

It was with the claim regarding free will that Erasmus found fault. A youth of modest means from Rotterdam in the Netherlands, Erasmus found a home in the Church, after impoverishment struck upon the death of his mother in 1492. He became an excellent Latinist and, because of his talents, was able to travel widely, studying and teaching at different centers of learning. Erasmus developed a specific type of Christian piety, one that focused on personal spiritual training and the need through education to spread what he called the "philosophy of Christ," something that could not be done, he came to believe, through scholastic argumentation but had rather to be entrusted to eloquence.

Erasmus had been an early adopter of some of Valla's work. He was one of the first northern Europeans to recognize how important a text Valla's *Elegances* was, writing in his *On the Method of Study* (*De ratione studii*) – and addressing himself to students – that, when it comes to Latin grammar, "you should diligently pore over Lorenzo Valla, who wrote most elegantly about the Elegances of Latin speech."[86] As important, Erasmus discovered Valla's

---

[86] Erasmus, *De ratione studii*, 3.

Annotations to the New Testament in manuscript as he was on what he described as a "hunt" for manuscripts in 1504 in the library of an abbey outside of Louvain. Erasmus was so impressed that he had Valla's *Annotations* print-published, writing in his Preface to the work that Valla was brave to persist despite criticism, even though his critics "called it presumption in a grammarian . . . to let loose his impertinent pen on Holy Scripture itself."[87] Erasmus defended the idea that one needed both Greek and Latin to understand scripture and suggested that only scholarship that relied on those languages could reveal scripture's true meaning.

In many ways, angry, interior Luther and jovial, social Erasmus actually agreed on many things. Both were committed to close interpretation of scripture, for example, not believing the Latin text as such to be sacred. Both, too, shared a passion for a Christianity that was simple rather than scholastic, communicative rather than rebarbative. And Erasmus even went so far as to publish his own *Annotations* on the New Testament, adopting almost all of Valla's points, adding many of his own, and even going a step further: adding his own Latin translation of the New Testament.[88] Whatever his intentions, offering a "new" translation of a text some thought sacred was a potentially revolutionary act.

But Erasmus never went so far as to advocate translating the Bible into the vernacular, as did Luther. Instead, their real break came over the question of free will. Erasmus, peace loving as he was, had been reluctant to enter into the debate initially. The truth was that he admired Luther early on and had even been critical of some of what he believed to be the Catholic Church's excesses. But by the early 1520s it was becoming clear that what had seemed a theological dispute (common enough) was evolving into something much weightier. So Erasmus, persuaded by friends and goaded by Luther, in 1524 wrote a treatise defending the idea of free will. It is telling that Erasmus, this otherwise admirer of Valla, distanced himself from Valla in this instance. After mentioning the many writers throughout Christian antiquity and the Middle Ages who have defended free will, Erasmus says that no one has completely denied free will save the ancient heretic Manicheus and the medieval heretic John Wycliffe. And then: "Lorenzo Valla's authority, who almost seems to agree with them, has little weight among theologians."[89] Later in the work,

[87] Cit. and tr. (modified), in Rummel, *Desiderius Erasmus*, 75.
[88] Erasmus, *Novum instrumentum omne, diligenter ab Erasmo Roterodamo recognitum et emendatum* (Basel: Froben, 1516).
[89] See Erasmus, *On Free Will*, in Erasmus, *Controversies: De libero arbitrio / Hyperaspites* 1, ed. and tr. Charles Trinkaus, *Collected Works of Erasmus*, 76 (Toronto: University of Toronto Press, 1997), sec. 2.

Erasmus gives his own arguments, which are indeed traditional: why would we have been given the exemplary lives of the saints to ponder, full of good works as they are, if good works were useless? "Why does one so often hear of reward, if there is no merit at all? How would obedience of those following God's commandments be praised, and disobedience de damned? Why does Holy Scripture so frequently mention judgment, if merit cannot be weighed at all?"[90] And, of course, it is impossible to understand God as being just if He essentially foreordains the damnation of some. Toward the end, as throughout, Erasmus urges moderation.

Luther, in his reply, begins by stating how impressed he is both by Erasmus's eloquence and by his gentle moderation. Yet, Luther being Luther, he then proceeds to a point-by-point refutation of Erasmus, always bringing things back to the necessity of faith on the part of the Christian and the infinity and immensity of God. Toward the end of his treatise, Luther avers that he is glad he does not possess free will. The reason? "If I lived and worked to all eternity, my conscience would never reach comfortable certainty as to how much it must do to satisfy God."[91] You simply could not know you were saved. This is why you needed to submit, to entrust yourself to God, and to persist in life despite not knowing your final fate. A popular perception at the time was that Erasmus's skepticism toward the Church helped lay the groundwork for the acceptance by many northern Europeans of Luther's ideas, however much Erasmus may have come to regret his role in the end. While the problems, questions, and debates behind the Protestant Reformation came to a head in the era of Erasmus and Luther, there can be no doubt that Valla had a role to play – a spectral one, perhaps, but important none the less.

The European cultural landscape had changed a great deal by then, as Erasmus and Luther crossed rhetorical swords against a backdrop of rapid religious change. So, just as we have gone forward in time to see one trajectory on which Valla's thought played itself out, it is appropriate now to circle back and to see what sorts of material, cultural, and political conditions were in play in the 1450s, a crucial time in a number of respects.

[90] Ibid., sec. 53.
[91] Martin Luther, *De servo arbitrio*, in Martin Luther, *Werke. Kritische Gesamtausgabe*, 58 vols. (Weimar: Böhlau, 1883–1948), vol. 18, pp. 551–787, at 783.

11

A CHANGING ENVIRONMENT

V ALLA DIED IN 1457. THAT DECADE, THE 1450S, SERVES AS a kind of fulcrum, one on which the Italian Renaissance delicately balanced amid transitions in the culture of reading and writing, libraries and the storage of information, and a growing if still inchoate sense that Europe as such both existed and, simultaneously, was under threat. To understand where Renaissance culture was going, we need to delve into those three aspects, beginning with printing with moveable type.

It was in the mid-1450s in Germany (in Mainz) that three technologies came together to issue forth with the first book printed with moveable type, the so-called 42-line Bible (so named because of the number of lines on each page).[1] The first of these was block printing, known to Chinese culture for centuries, whereby a block would be carved in reverse, then pressed in ink, and the image stamped on a page. The second was paper, again a Chinese invention. Costing about one-sixth the price of parchment (treated animal skins), paper appeared in Italy in the thirteenth century, making its way to France and Germany in the fourteenth. Old rags were shredded in a mill and mixed with water; the resulting mixture was poured over specially prepared matrices; the paper was pressed, hung to dry, and then cut and sized. The third element was the press, long known in Europe, used for grapes to make wine and, in the south of Europe, for olives to make oil. Three names appear in the sources, Johann Gutenberg, Johann Fust, and Peter Schöffer.

---

[1] What follows relies on Lucien Febvre and Henri-Jean Martin, *The Coming of the Book: The Impact of Printing, 1450–1800*, 3rd ed. (New York: Verso, 2010); Anthony Grafton and Eugene F. Rice Jr., *The Foundations of Early Modern Europe, 1460–1559* (New York: Norton, 1994), 1–10; Adrian Johns, "The Coming of Print to Europe," in Leslie Howsam, ed., *The Cambridge Companion to the History of the Book* (Cambridge: Cambridge University Press, 2014), 107–24; Andrew Pettegree, *The Book in the Renaissance* (New Haven: Yale University Press, 2010).

Gutenberg's is the most famous, but one can imagine a collaboration whereby, at some point, someone had the idea to take the blocks from block printing and use that basic idea with individual letters; take the concept of the matrix, used to hold macerated rags (in the papermaking process), and repurpose the matrix to hold engraved letters in reverse; and take the press, and use that idea to press a page of those letters – placed in reverse on a matrix – and press them down onto paper.[2] The 42-line Bible was printing's first great triumph.

Looking backward, it is tempting, and justified to an extent, to stress the revolutionary character of printing with moveable type.[3] But retrospection is always a bit deceiving. People rarely realize they are living through revolutions; and readers, especially, tend to be a conservative lot (in the literal sense), preferring continuity to change. Printed books were made to look like manuscripts. They remained un-paginated, often left details such as the title and author to the end of the book, and at times were even printed on parchment (treated animal skins). And indeed, it can be difficult to tell the difference between a manuscript and an early printed book, especially in the first five decades or so of printing. But people soon realized that the new art of printing had immense potential. By 1465 printing spread beyond Mainz in Germany and indeed moved south to Italy, when two German printers, named Sweynheym and Pannartz, went to a provincial town east of Rome, Subiaco, the site of a Benedictine monastery where, as it happened, there were several monks of German origin. Two years later, Sweynheym and Pannartz moved to Rome, where in the next seven years they would produce editions of "at least forty-eight more books," as one scholar has tallied the number.[4]

One early enthusiast was Leon Battista Alberti, writing in around the year 1466. He recounted that he had been in Rome and that

> It happened that we greatly approved of the German inventor who in these
> times has made it possible, by certain pressings down of characters, to have
> more than two hundred volumes written out in a hundred days from an

---

[2] See Grafton and Rice, 1–10.
[3] See Elizabeth Eisenstein, *The Printing Press as an Agent of Change* (Cambridge: Cambridge University Press, 1980); Anthony T. Grafton, "The Importance of Being Printed," *Journal of Interdisciplinary History* 11 (1980), 265–86; Adrian Johns, *The Nature of the Book: Print and Knowledge in the Making* (Chicago: University of Chicago, 1998); "Forum" in the *American Historical Review*, 107 (2002): Anthony Grafton, "How Revolutionary Was the Print Revolution?" pp. 84–87; Elizabeth Eisenstein, "An Unacknowledged Revolution Revisited," pp. 87–105; Adrian Johns, "How to Acknowledge a Revolution," pp. 106–28.
[4] Brian Richardson, *Printing, Writers, and Readers in Renaissance Italy* (Cambridge: Cambridge University Press, 1999), 4.

original, with the labor of no more than three men; for with only one downward pressure a large sheet is written out.[5]

One leading scholar of print culture in Italy, Brian Richardson, has pointed out how new all this must have seemed by recalling an example: that of Vespasiano da Bisticci. Vespasiano by profession was what was called a *stationarius* – "stationer," most literally, but meaning something more like "book-producing entrepreneur." A famous tale circulated, to the effect that, at Cosimo de' Medici's request, in a period of 22 months and with the aid of 45 scribes, Vespasiano produced 200 books, an achievement that was considered almost a miracle. Now, as anyone could see (and as someone such as Alberti marveled), with the new "art of writing artificially," as it was called, that production process could be accelerated immeasurably. Printing arrived in Venice in 1469 and, as Richardson notes, "by the end of the century, printing had taken place in nearly eighty towns or cities in Italy, many more than in Germany or France."[6] Printing, though invented elsewhere, was nourished in Italy, feeding on the energy of the Renaissance and on the growing desire of ever-larger cohorts of readers to have access to a great variety of texts, from the Bible to Cicero.

Bibliographers have a term to describe any early printed book from the origin of printing until the year 1501: *incunabulum* (sometimes rendered in English as "incunable"), a word that designates "in swaddling clothes" or "in the cradle," in Latin.[7] It is estimated that around six million books in approximately forty thousand editions saw the light during the incunabular period, more books than were produced in total since Greco-Roman antiquity. At first it all seemed like an accelerated way of producing manuscripts. But by the end of the fifteenth century, one could not help but notice how printing was proceeding, so much so that in 1501, Pope Alexander VI produced a papal bull, in which one could read the following:

> The art of printing is very useful in so far as it furthers the circulation of useful and tested books. But it can be very harmful if it is permitted to widen the influence of pernicious works. It will therefore be necessary to maintain full control over the printers so that they may be prevented from bringing into print writings which are antagonistic to the Catholic faith or which are likely to cause trouble to believers.[8]

---

[5] Cit. and tr. in Richardson, *Printing, Writers, and Readers in Renaissance Italy*, 3.

[6] Ibid., 4.

[7] The word came into use in the seventeenth century; see Jacqueline Glomski, "*Incunabula Typographiae*: Seventeenth-Century Views on Early Printing," *Library* 2 (2001), 336–48.

[8] Alexander VI, Bull "Inter multiplices," cit. and tr. Grafton and Rice, 10.

Pope Alexander had a point. Scarcely two decades later, Martin Luther's Reformation spread much faster than it might have done, had printing been unavailable. "Broadsheets," single-leaf publications (like a poster) circulated widely with Luther's messages, as did short pamphlets.[9] Each was relatively easy and fast to produce.

As printing transformed the way people read and wrote, a longer-range transformation was occurring in how information was stored. The fifteenth century in Italy saw the emergence of a certain variety of "public" library, as a place, an idea, and an aspiration, that has a notable position in the cultural history of the Renaissance. The Italian Renaissance library as a *place* represents the best of Renaissance architecture: classicizing yet functional, fifteenth-century Italian libraries served as tastemakers throughout early modern Europe in the centuries to come. As an *idea*, the notion that a monumental place for gathering cultural riches should be linked to the prestige of a state formed part of the political backbone of early modern Europe. And as an *aspiration*, the notion of a "public" library – one that should exist, as many Renaissance men wrote, "for the common good" – supplied the distant intellectual beginnings of our modern open-access libraries.

To understand this transformation, we need to reach back to Petrarch. When he used the phrase "the ornament of a public library" (*bibliothecae decus publicae*), to what was he referring?[10] In his storied life, he had gone from patron to patron, city to city, to find a home for his intellectual labors. Along the way he had amassed a substantial collection of books, perhaps more than two hundred volumes; at one point in his life he had evinced a hope to leave his books to the republic of Venice, where he had spent several happy years. The plan did not ultimately come to fruition, but the fact that he designated his prospective bequest as "public library" found echoes in the years to come.[11]

The very next intellectual generation saw Renaissance humanism, finally, become firmly located in a place, Florence, as we have seen, with the figure

[9] See Heinz Dannenbauer, *Luther als religiöser Volksschriftsteller, 1517–1520* (Tübingen: Mohr, 1930); Mark Edwards, *Printing, Propaganda, and Martin Luther* (Berkeley: University of California Press, 1994); Britt-Marie Schuster, *Die Verständlichkeit von frühreformatorischen Flugschriften: eine Studie zu kommunikationswirksamen Faktoren der Textgestaltung* (Hildesheim: Olms, 2001).

[10] Petrarch, *Epistolae variae*, in Petrarch, *Epistolae de rebus familiaribus et Variae*, 3 vols., ed. G. Fracasetti (Florence: Le Monnier, 1859–63), vol. 3, Ep. 43, p. 413.

[11] Nereo Vianello, "I libri di Petrarca e la prima idea di una pubblica biblioteca a Venezia," in *Miscellanea marciana di studi bessarionei (a coronamento del V Centenario della donazione nicena)* (Padua: Antenore, 1976), pp. 435–51.

of Coluccio Salutati looming large. He too had gathered an exceedingly large collection of books, more than eight hundred volumes, which he was happy to put at the disposal of those eager members of his circle who flocked to the "Athens on the Arno." Salutati, too, called for a public library, this time in his treatise *On Fate*. There he wrote that there should "be founded public libraries into which a copy of all books would be collected; let the most learned men be placed in charge of the libraries, who would revise the books with most diligent collation, and who would know how to remove all discord of their [textual] differences with the judgment of correct definition."[12] Salutati saw the public library as an important center, both for gathering written material and for ensuring its integrity. During the next two generations, from the 1420s to the 1470s, real plans were made and real action was taken to create these public libraries.

Most striking of all is the common language behind the plans, the common culture. Princes of the Church, civic leaders, private scholars: all were, more or less, united in their desire to leave books "for the common good." In the Tuscan city of Pistoia, in a 1423 will, Sozomeno da Pistoia wishes to leave his books to the *opera*, or building commission, of the church of San Iacopo. The provision: that they be kept "in a certain place that is common, one well-adapted to allow all who wish to study the books to be able to study them." The inheritors of the books cannot give them away, since he "wants the books in perpetuity to remain in common use of those who wish to study them . . . They should also be bound and ordered together in that same such place."[13]

Then there was the *éminence grise* of Florentine humanism, Niccolò Niccoli. In his 1430 will he left his books to Santa Maria degli Angeli, the seat of the Camaldolese order in Florence. He desired to leave all his books, "both sacred and profane, both Greek and Latin, and the 'barbarian' ones [i.e., in other languages] which he had from everywhere with great enterprise, diligence, and energy gathered from the time of his youth, not

---

[12] Coluccio Salutati, *De fato et fortuna*, ed. Concetta Bianca, (Florence, Olschki, 1985), 49: "ut sicut hactenus aliquando factum fuit, constituantur bibliothecae publicae, in quas omnium librorum copia congeratur praeponanturque viri peritissimi bibliothecis, qui libros diligentissima collatione revideant et omnem varietatum discordiam recte diffinitionis iudicio noverint removere."

[13] Cit. Luciano Gargan, "Gli umanisti e la biblioteca pubblica," in Guglielmo Cavallo, ed., *Le biblioteche nel mondo antico e medievale* (Rome: Laterza, 1988), 163–86, at 172: "in quodam loco communi et acto ad studendum in eis [libris] omnibus studere volentibus in illis." "cum vellet ipsos in perpetuum stare ad communem usum volentium in ipsis studere in loco acto et deputato per dictos operarios in civitate Pistorii et in ipso tali loco omnes ligati simul et ordinati."

shunning toil and sparing no expense." And he made sure to say that the books were to be left "both for the monks that were then in the service of God, and for the use of all the scholarly citizens."[14] Though his books were to be preserved in an ecclesiastical library, Niccoli still saw them as benefits for the public good. A commission was appointed after his death, one over which Cosimo de' Medici eventually assumed control; the books eventually formed the nucleus of the library of San Marco in Florence, one of its two Dominican houses and, by the end of the fifteenth century, a center of learned discussion.

The examples multiply. Cardinal Giordano Orsini, a major patron of humanism, in 1434 wishes to unite a favorite Roman Church, San Biagio, to the Basilica of St. Peter. He will give his collection of well over three hundred books to the little church to form a library. Why? So that the "number of learned and knowledgeable men increase both in the said church of St. Peter and in the City of Rome."[15]

Amid all this innovation there was retrospection as well, for the very same people who left their books with such largesse also often specified how they wanted the libraries to look and to work: like medieval mendicant libraries. Those repositories of knowledge of Dominicans and Franciscans, with the benches arranged, church-like, in two rows and with important books chained to the benches, served as the basis for the Italian Renaissance public library.[16] The first such library opened its doors in Florence in 1444. Though Niccolò Niccoli had donated his books to Santa Maria degli Angeli, after he passed away they wound up in the hands of his executor, the great Florentine patron Cosimo de' Medici. Cosimo nurtured a close tie to the convent of San Marco, just then being taken over by the Dominicans. And it was there that the architect Michelozzo designed the beautiful library of San Marco, comparable in its simple elegance to Brunelleschi's Hospital of the Innocents, and equally to become part of the fabric of Florentine culture. True, there were "Renaissance" innovations in the structure, most notably the use of

---

[14] Ed. Berthold Louis Ullman and Phillip Stadter, *The Public Library of Renaissance Florence: Niccolò Niccoli, Cosimo de' Medici and the Library of San Marco* (Padua, Antenore, 1972), 293: "Ad hec omnes libros suos tam sacros quam gentiles, tam grecos quam latinos aut barbaros, quos undique magna industria diligentia studio ab adulescentia nullum laborem subterfugiendo nullis impensis parcendo coegit, sanctissimo cenobio Sancte Marie de Angelis ... legavit, cum monachis ibidem Deo servientibus, tum etiam omnibus civibus studiosis usui futuros."

[15] Orsini, "Testament," ed. in Christopher S. Celenza, "The Will of Cardinal Giordano Orsini (ob. 1438)," *Traditio* 51 (1996), 257–86, at 277–78.

[16] Cf. Armando Petrucci, *Writers and Readers in Medieval Italy: Studies in the History of Written Culture* (New Haven: Yale University Press, 1995), 203–20.

classicizing columns within. Still, there were to be chains on the books. And as to the disposition of the books – in special cabinets called *armaria*, set together in rows, with the principal collection in a defined center – this style of arrangement came directly from the respected medieval tradition. The culture of the book, written culture, is inherently conservative, changing slowly and even in moments of change recalling older traditions.

Orsini said it best. He wanted to create a "library with glass windows and iron bars, and enough benches and tables for sitting down and for storing the books," as well as the chains that are necessary to hold them, just as is usually done in other libraries."[17] He suggests that there should be two beneficed custodians to keep watch over the books night and day, "as happens in the libraries situated in the mendicants' places in Florence and Bologna, better if possible." They should not just be bookmen; instead, they should be "priests of good reputation and honest conversation who should also care for the souls of the parishioners of San Biagio."[18] To be noted is that Orsini made concrete plans, that he specified (as had Niccoli) that his books were to be used by people outside of the realm of clerical life, and that he looked backward to the medieval mendicant tradition as a model. His library was never realized, as it happens: one of the many instances when a testament cannot guarantee a real-life outcome.

But San Marco did come to fruition as a library. The achievement of San Marco served, in the next decades, as a theme on which numerous local variations would be played. The basic constituents, however, were in place by this point. The idea of the public library, to have books be available "for the common good" or "for the common use of the learned," reflected a key tenet of Italian humanism: that established, corporate institutions (such as small, specialist university communities) did not satisfy the cultural needs of the time, and that something new was necessary. The physical manifestation of the public library put that tenet into practice, even as it reflected continuity with past practices. Inevitably, too, the library as a monument would play a role in the power politics of the Italian states of the fifteenth century, serving as a key marker of state prestige.[19]

---

[17] Orsini, "Testament," 278: "una libraria cum fenestris ferratis et vitratis et cum scannis et tabulis necessariis tam ad sedendum quam ad ponendos libros et fiant cathene necessarie ferree et cum astis ferreis, sicut fieri solitum est in aliis librariis, ubi dicti libri ponantur."

[18] Ibid., 278: "Volo etiam quod dicti libri ponantur in dicto loco et deputentur per capitulum continuo unus vel duo beneficiati qui habeant et teneantur dictos libros custodire die noctuque, sicut fiet in librariis sitis in locis mendicantium Florentie et Bononie, et melius, si potest ... et quod dicti duo beneficiati sint presbiteri et bone fame et conversationis honeste, qui etiam habeant curam animarum parochianorum dicte ecclesie Sancti Blasii."

[19] See Petrucci, *Writers and Readers*, 142–43.

The history of libraries, like the history of intellectual life, was woven together with that third element, political change. It is worth pausing to understand these vicissitudes before continuing the story of how libraries evolved. The 1450s saw alterations in the political life of Renaissance Italy, not least of which was the 1454 Peace of Lodi.[20] This balance-of-power–style treaty, brokered by Cosimo de' Medici and the Milanese mercenary leader Francesco Sforza, created forty years of relative (if often tense) peace on the Italian peninsula and brought to the forefront five leading states: Milan, Venice, Florence, papal Rome, and the Kingdom of Naples. These states, as well as their many satellites and allies, competed in the give-and-take game of Renaissance statesmanship, each seeking to outdo the other in power, prestige, and wealth.

Culturally, too, changes were afoot. The Ottoman Turks had been threatening Western Europe since they founded their empire in 1299, gradually moving westward.[21] Today we remember Manuel Chrysoloras as the brilliant Greek teacher whom Salutati persuaded to stay in Florence for three years, educating luminaries such as Bruni. But one of the reasons that Chrysoloras was in Italy then, in in the 1390s, was to try to drum up allies against the Turks. Thereafter the Turks grew so strong that, by the middle of the fifteenth century, they mounted an attack on Constantinople, still held by the Greeks. Constantinople fell to the Turks in 1453, an event that generated an impulse toward unity and consolidation on the part of the Italian states.[22]

A minor humanist, Angelo Decembrio, wrote a dialogue concerning libraries and other cultural matters, called *On Literary Polish*. When he arrived at the function and importance of Greek literature, he had this to say:

> Indeed, after Constantinople was devastated by the barbarous infidels and
> its ruler, a great man, was slaughtered, and the ruler's brother had fled with
> those of his people who were left, it is scarcely believable how many of our

---

[20] See Felice Fossati, "Francesco Sforza e la pace di Lodi," *Archivio Veneto*, 5th series, 60–61 (1957), 15–34; Vincent Ilardi, *Studies in Italian Renaissance Diplomatic History* (Aldershot: Ashgate, 1986); Ilardi, "Lodi, Peace of," in Paul F. Grendler, ed., *Encyclopedia of the Renaissance*, 6 vols. (New York: Scribner's, 1999), 3: 442–43; Randall Lesaffer, "Peace Treaties from Lodi to Westphalia," in Randall Lesaffer, ed., *Peace Treaties and International Law in European History: From the Late Middle Ages to World War One* (Cambridge: Cambridge University Press, 2004), 9–44; Garrett Mattingly, *Renaissance Diplomacy* (Boston: Houghton Mifflin, 1955; Baltimore: Penguin, 1964), 71–86; Giovanni Pillinini, *Il sistema degli stati italiani, 1454–94* (Venice: Universitaria editrice, 1970); Giovanni Soranzo, *La lega italica (1454–55)* (Milan: Vita e pensiero, 1924).

[21] See Colin Imber, *The Ottoman Empire*, 2nd ed. (New York: Palgrave Macmillan, 2009).

[22] See Steven Runciman, *The Fall of Constantinople* (Cambridge: Cambridge University Press, 1965); for relevant contemporary reactions, see Agostino Pertusi, ed., *La Caduta di Costantinopoli*, 2 vols. (Milan: Mondadori, 1997).

own have almost gone Greek! It is as if they'd been educated in Attica or Achaia. They have acquired this ability by carefully studying Greek books.[23]

If Decembrio highlighted the increased interchange, suggesting that after 1453 an increased impulse to study Greek could be seen, more typical was the sentiment of an anonymous annotator of a Greek manuscript (today held in the British Library): "Indeed there has been nothing worse than this that has ever happened or ever will happen."[24] Most revealingly, a Church politician and diplomat, Enea Silvio Piccolomini, suggested immediately after the event that it was as if the Church had lost one of its two eyes.[25] He also criticized the sitting pope, Nicholas V, for what seemed an inadequately forceful reaction, calling for a crusade and suggesting that there must be held a "general convention" whose goal would be to come to a "consensus of the nations" against the Turks to mobilize a crusade.[26]

A few years later, in 1458, Piccolomini became Pope Pius II, reigning until 1464, when he died in the port city of Ancona of a fever, just as he saw the crusading forces he mobilized gather there arrive in full.[27] He and others called for crusades against the Turks, who continued to threaten Europe, taking and holding for almost a year the southern Italian city of Otranto, publicly beheading hundreds of men who refused to convert to Islam.[28] Eventually the Ottomans were driven out of Italy. But the threat of other religious traditions, coupled with the sense that a thousand-year Christian tradition was under assault, led not only to a sense of political unity. It also led to renewed efforts to gather information and to have it centrally available. Public libraries in this period became state libraries: monumental locations of beauty and grandeur that also served a political function – helping control the storage of information. Power politics, religious anxiety, and the evolving dynamics of the new communicative medium that printing with moveable type represented: the libraries built in the second half of the fifteenth century emerged against this background.

---

[23] Angelo Decembrio, *De politia litteraria*, ed. Norbert Witten (Munich: Saur, 2002), 1.8.9.

[24] Annotation on Greek manuscript, MS London, British Library, Add. 34060 f.1v, in A. Pertusi, ed., *Testi inediti e poco noti sulla caduta di Costantinopoli*, ed. A. Carile. Il Mondo medievale: sezione di storia bizantina e slava 4. (Bologna: Pàtron Editore 1983), #22, p. 214.

[25] Piccolomini, in Pertusi, *La Caduta*, 2:56: "Ex duobus oculis alterum amisisti."

[26] Ibid., 58–60.

[27] See Emily O'Brien, *The 'Commentaries' of Pope Pius II (1458–1464) and the Crisis of the Fifteenth-Century Papacy* (Toronto: University of Toronto Press, 2015).

[28] See Margaret Meserve, *Empires of Islam in Renaissance Historical Thought* (Cambridge, MA: Cambridge University Press, 2008); Hankins, *Humanism and Platonism*, 1: 293–424.

The Vatican Library is the most prominent of all.[29] For the first time in its history, the papacy in the 1450s took on the classicizing, humanist coloration it would retain throughout the next century. Tommasso Parentucelli had been part of the background of the creation of the library of San Marco, having written for Cosimo de' Medici a "canon," or list of books necessary in the founding of a good library.[30] When Parentucelli became Pope Nicholas V in 1447, the stage was set for the papal court to encourage more humanist interaction. To the *curia Romana*, Nicholas brought skilled classicists such as Lorenzo Valla, as we have seen, who began translating the ancient Greek historian Thucydides into elegant humanist Latin. And it was under Nicholas's tenure as pope that plans were made to found the Vatican Library. In a 1451 letter accompanying an envoy of his looking for rare books throughout Europe, Nicholas wrote: "for some time now we have judged and now we give our attention with all enthusiasm to this project: that – for the common convenience of all learned men – we might have a library of all books, both Latin and Greek, a library appropriate to the worth of the Pope and the Apostolic See."[31] It is not surprising that Sixtus IV used similar language in the 1475 Bull (entitled *Ad decorem*), which is traditionally understood as founding the Vatican Library, or that both men's conceptions formed part of an emerging consensus.[32]

---

[29] See Franco Bonatti and Antonio Manfredi, eds., *Niccolò V nel sesto centenario della nascita*, Studi e Testi, 397 (Vatican City: Biblioteca apostolica vaticana, 2000); Leonard Boyle, "Sixtus IV and the Vatican Library," in Clifford M. Brown, John Osborne, and W. Chandler Kirwin, eds., *Rome: Tradition, Innovation, and Renewal* (Victoria, BC: University of Victoria, 1991), 65–73; Boyle, "The Vatican Library," in Grafton, ed., *Rome Reborn*, xi–xx; Boyle, "Niccolò V fondatore della Biblioteca Vaticana," in Bonatti and Manfredi, eds., 3–8; Christopher S. Celenza and Bridget Pupillo, "Le grandi biblioteche 'pubbliche' del XV secolo," in S. Luzzatto and G. Pedullà, eds., *Atlante storico della letteratura italiana*, vol. 1, *Dalle origini al Rinascimento*, ed. A. De Vincentiis (Turin: Einaudi, 2010), 1: 313–21; Carmela Vircillo Franklin, "'Pro communi doctorum virorum comodo': The Vatican Library and its Service to Scholarship," *Proceedings of the American Philosophical Society* 146 (2002), 363–84; Anthony Grafton, ed., *Rome Reborn: The Vatican Library and Renaissance Culture* (New Haven: Yale University Press, 1993); Eugene Müntz and Paul Fabre, *La Bibliothèque du Vatican au XVe siècle, d'après des documents inédits*, Bibliothèque des écoles françaises d'Athènes et de Rome, 48 (Paris: Thorin, 1887).

[30] Vespasiano da Bisticci, *Le vite*, 1: 46–7: "Et per questo Cosimo de' Medici avendo a ordinare la libreria di Sancto Marco, iscrisse a maestro Tomaso, gli piacessi fargli una nota come aveva a stare una libreria."

[31] Cit. in Müntz and Fabre, 47–48: "Jamdiu decrevimus atque id omni studio operam damus ut pro communi doctorum virorum comodo habeamus librorum omnium tum latinorum tum grecorum bibliothecam condecentem pontificis et sedis apostolice dignitati."

[32] 1475 Sixtus IV Bull *Ad decorum*, cit. Boyle, "Sixtus IV and the Vatican Library," 73 n.17: "Ad decorem militantis ecclesie, fidei catholice augmentum, eruditorum … commodum et honorem."

And then there were what we can term "signorial" libraries. The libraries of the signories – those characteristic fifteenth-century Italian despotisms ruled by strongmen, or *signori* – tell different stories, adding contours to the map of the Italian Renaissance library. That of Urbino was the creation of the *condottiero* leader Federigo da Montefeltro, whose familiar, craggy-nosed portrait in profile by Piero della Francesca remains a touchstone image of the Italian Renaissance.[33] About Federigo and his library, the Florentine bookshop-owner and biographer Vespasiano da Bisticci wrote that "he alone had the spirit to do what no one had been able to do for over a thousand years, or more: to have created a library, the worthiest that has been created from that time to now."[34] The Urbino library's development shows the creation of an ideal Renaissance library. The fact that many of its books eventually (centuries later) wound up in the Vatican Library reminds one that, to understand the importance of Italian Renaissance libraries, we need to see them as more than collections of books, but rather as part of an integral cultural moment, an idea put into practice over time.

Another signorial library was that of Ferrara, which resulted from the patronage of the Este family, who ruled the city in the fifteenth century.[35] Ferrara's case is noteworthy because we possess a unique contemporary source for the way libraries were talked about at a Renaissance court: Decembrio's *On Literary Polish*. Eavesdropping on the interlocutors allows us to enter a world at once familiar and foreign. The interlocutors, most noteworthy among them Prince Leonello D'Este (the dramatic date of the dialogue is the 1440s, during his reign), discuss matters we would expect: for example, with what books should a good library be stocked, how to detect forgeries, what is the place of vernacular rather than Latin literature, and so on. At one point, Prince Leonello discusses how to care for books:

> Some people, actually, keep the books in small chests or cabinets, and they only take them out and put them back individually when the books need to be read. In effect, they keep them on reserve in a "private" or "secret" library, rather than in one that is public and often frequented. The dust itself, when it is more condensed, will stick to these books, even when they

---

[33] See Marcello Simonetta, *Federico da Montefeltro and His Library* (Vatican City: Biblioteca apostolica vaticana, 2007).

[34] Vespasiano, *Le vite*, 1: 386: "et a lui solo è bastato l'animo di fare quello che non è ignuno che l'abbia condotto da anni mille o più in qua, d'avere fatta fare una libraria, la più degna che sia mai stata fatta da quello tempo in qua."

[35] See Giulio Bertoni, *La Biblioteca Estense e la cultura ferrarese ai tempi del duca Ercole I (1471–1505)* (Turin: Loescher, 1903); Domenico Fava, *La Biblioteca Estense nel suo sviluppo storico* (Modena: G.T. Vincenzi e Nipoti di D. Cavalotti, 1925).

are covered up while traveling – all the more so when the room's floors are cleaned. To combat this inconvenience, one should sprinkle the floor beforehand with water. Also, you should rather attentively make sure that the individual books, before the library is opened, are suspended on their shelves, chained, for example, as happens in the libraries of the monks.[36]

Again, we see the ongoing dialogue between past and present, retrospection and innovation, private and public that fifteenth-century Italian library culture represents.

We also hear the interlocutors making recommendations that surprise us. One should keep the right herbs in the library to induce users to study; make sure that chirping birds and little dogs are out of the way, in cages, because they make noise; and perhaps also have a picture of Saint Jerome studying, because that too will make people more studious.[37] Ferrara's imagined library brings into relief both the familiarities and the differences of Renaissance culture.

Then there was Venice. The republic of Venice benefited from the largesse of the cleric Basilios Bessarion (1403–72), an émigré from the Byzantine world who converted to Roman Catholicism, became a cardinal of the Roman Church, and was highly esteemed for his classical learning.[38] His private library, well known to papal scholars in Rome, was unsurprisingly strong in Greek works (a special aim of his collecting practice, he tells us in a 1468 document): "and though I have always leaned with my whole heart toward this matter, now, with even more intense zeal and owing to the slaughter of Greece and the woeful capture of Byzantium, I have practically exhausted all my powers, energy, care, ability, and industry in acquiring Greek books."[39] Yet here, too, we see the mix of retrospection and innovation that library culture could represent: retrospection, in that Bessarion had very little interest in collecting works of his fellow humanists; innovation, in that the very size and scope of his gift was noteworthy.[40]

San Marco in Venice, the ultimate destination of Bessarion's library, perhaps more than any other Italian Renaissance library, presents us with

[36] Angelo Decembrio, *De politia*, 1.3.
[37] Ibid., 1.5.
[38] See John Monfasani, *Bessarion Scholasticus: A Study of Cardinal Bessarion's Latin Library* (Turnhout: Brepols, 2011); Lotte Labowsky, *Bessarion's Library and the Biblioteca Marciana: Six Early Inventories* (Rome: Edizioni di storia e letteratura, 1979).
[39] Ed. in Labowsky, 147: "quamvis autem huic rei toto animo semper incubuerim, ardentiori tamen studio post Graeciae excidium et deflaendam Byzantii captivitatem in perquirendis graecis libris omnes meas vires, omnem curam, omnem operam, facultatem industriamque consumpsi."
[40] See Monfasani, *Bessarion Scholasticus*, 1–26 and *passim*.

the idea of the public library in its purest form. Bessarion had initially committed his private library to the monastery of San Giorgio, situated on an island in Venice's territory. He was eventually persuaded that prospective readers might be impeded by the location of San Giorgio, "considering that the monastery itself is on an island unreachable except by ship."[41] Accordingly, in 1468, with the permission of Pope Paul II, Bessarion revoked his original bequest, "so that (we are told in the legal instrument recording the transaction) all wishing to study or read or even to go to the library might have easier access, and so that scholars might more easily profit from the books."[42] Here too, the monument reflecting the wish did not actually come to fruition until almost a century later, when the brilliant architect Jacopo Sansovino designed the library of San Marco, which still stands today.[43]

Like much else in Italian Renaissance culture, an idea born in the fifteenth century led to a later concrete practice. This is the way culture works: ideas arise; they become part of a genealogy only recognizable in retrospect; and then later practices erase, or elide, those original ideas. It was in the wills and testaments of fifteenth-century Renaissance men that a recognizably coherent idea for libraries that benefited the public good emerged. It was an idea that came to only partial fruition in the fifteenth century, an era when Italian states were wrestling with threats from abroad, struggling to see if they might overcome their centuries-long petty enmities, and seeing if they could present some sort of unity in the face of outside threats. That latter objective they failed to achieve, spectacularly so, as events in the fifteenth century's last decade would prove decisively. For our purposes, it is enough to know that Italy's leading intellectuals in the second half of the fifteenth century were working against a differently complected background when it came to the world of reading, writing, and the storage of information. To begin to understand what was occurring in a more finely grained way, we can turn, again, to Florence.

[41] Ed. in Labowsky, 150: "ad illud ex civitate predicta nisi navigio iri non potest."
[42] Ibid.
[43] See Marino Zorzi, *La libreria di San Marco: Libri, lettori, societa nella Venezia dei Dogi* (Milan: Mondadori, 1987).

FLORENCE: MARSILIO FICINO, I

O NE THING WAS CLEAR IN FLORENCE IN THE 1450S: THE MEDICI family was in charge. Recent historiography has complicated that picture, stressing that Medici power was never as universal as later, laudatory accounts might lead one to believe. To a substantial extent, this is true. Not a decade went by when there were not conspiracies, dissatisfaction, and coalitions of other families who wanted a piece of the pie. Later, Machiavelli, with his signature astuteness, would obliquely reveal many of the flaws in Medici leadership in his magisterial *Florentine Histories*. In his view, the Medici allowed too much to depend on one person at a time, and on one family; they did not build institutions that could outlast them and help Florence flourish and grow; they did not nourish a "public" culture, often employing a culture of doing favors for friends to build political support. Again, all true, or at least arguably so. But one can also exaggerate revisionism.[1]

From the 1450s on, everywhere you looked, you would have seen evidence of Medici wealth and power. You could have started in the Medici family's own neighborhood, known as San Lorenzo, after the church of San Lorenzo. In 1442, the neighborhood council met and heard from Cosimo de' Medici, who (a document recording the meeting tells us)

---

[1] For Machiavelli, see his *Istorie fiorentine*, in Niccolò Machiavelli, *Opere*, 3 vols., ed. Corrado Vivanti (Turin: Einaudi-Galimard, 1997–2005), 3:304–732, esp. books 3–8, at 3: 423–732. For recent historiography on Florence, see Riccardo Fubini, *Quattrocento fiorentino: politica, diplomazia, cultura* (Pisa: Pacini, 1996); Fubini, *Politica e pensiero politico nell'Italia del Rinascimento: dallo stato territoriale al Machiavelli* (Florence: Edifir, 2009); Fubini, *Italia quattrocentesca: politica e diplomazia nell'età di Lorenzo il Magnifico* (Milan: FrancoAngeli, 1994); John Najemy, *A History of Florence, 1200–1575* (London: Blackwell, 2008); Nicolai Rubenstein, *The Government of Florence under the Medici (1434–1494)*, 2nd ed. (Oxford: Clarendon, 1998), esp. 278–374.

asked permission to build the main chapel . . . Provided that the choir and the nave of the church . . . were assigned to him and his sons, together with all the structures so far erected, he would pledge himself to complete that section of the building within six years, out of the fortunes that God had granted him, at his own expense and with his own coats of arms and devices.[2]

Also, the document goes on, no other coats of arms could be placed in the choir and nave of the church, that is, in the main, most visible public spaces that there were.

The meaning of all this? San Lorenzo was to be known as a Medici church. There were many reasons for doing this, and of course patronage of this sort was not new in the Renaissance. But that coat of arms, six red balls against, usually, a gold background, is everywhere in Florence. Cosimo engaged the services of Brunelleschi, the same architect who had done the cupola of the Duomo, to design the new nave. Brunelleschi would die before seeing his plans fulfilled. But his ideas merged with those of others, the Medici included, to produce the nave as one sees it today, part of a tradition of high artistic involvement at that Church. This tradition culminated later, in the 1520s, with Michelangelo's new sacristy, which included his tombs of Giuliano di Lorenzo de' Medici, adorned with allegories of "night" and "day," and that of Lorenzo di Piero de' Medici, flanked by "dusk" and "dawn." Again, circumstances conspired to prevent Michelangelo from seeing his design fully completed. But later – after the Medici were ousted and then spectacularly re-installed with ducal titles backed by the Spanish – the prominent artist and biographer Vasari was hired to install Michelangelo's statues, which remain some of the most important and lasting monuments of high Renaissance sculpture.

It was different in Cosimo's day. Florence was a republic, meaning it was accustomed to corporate self-governance: no royalty allowed. This was why, whenever Cosimo undertook to engage in some major project, he "let it appear that the matter had been set in motion by someone other than himself" so as to escape envy, as Vespasiano da Bisticci, the "stationer" we met in the last chapter, noted in his biography of Cosimo.[3] But changes were afoot in Italy in the middle of the fifteenth century, with the number of hereditary lordships rising and making their presence felt in their own city-states, often with monumental architectural projects (such as libraries, as we have seen).

[2] Cit. and tr. in Dale Kent, *Cosimo de' Medici and the Florentine Renaissance: The Patron's Oeuvre* (New Haven: Yale University Press, 2000), 183–84.
[3] Vespasiano, *Le vite*, 2: 392, cit. and tr. in Kent, *The Patron's Oeuvre*, 185.

If Cosimo masked his own status as "first among equals" within the Florentine citizenry by strategic misdirection (as Vespasiano suggested), he and his family nevertheless cultivated many of the same social habits and gestures as did other, openly hereditary aristocrats throughout Italy, patronage included.

Cosimo died in 1464, one of Europe's wealthiest men. Before he died, in addition to artistic patronage, he also offered support to a number of intellectuals. One of the most interesting of these was Marsilio Ficino (1433–99), the son of a Medici family physician. Ficino proved, with Cosimo's initial support, to be one of most dedicated scholars of Greek philosophy, a religious reformer who saw himself as playing a prophetic role, and finally one of the most noteworthy intellectuals of the second half of the fifteenth century. And yet, as we shall see, one of Ficino's main stumbling blocks to wider appreciation had to do with language and genre.[4]

The story of Ficino's involvement with Cosimo de' Medici has become legendary. And like a lot of legends, there have been exaggeration, burnishing of stories, and the creation of myth in the service of a larger narrative. But there is also a core of truth behind the lore.

Ficino himself is the one who created the legend, later in life, when he was an already well-established presence in Florence. In 1492, he brought out, with a local publisher, an edition of the work of Plotinus in translation.[5] Plotinus (204/5–70), a late ancient philosopher living in Rome but writing in Greek, had caught Ficino's scholarly attention in the 1480s. By that point Ficino had become the leading Platonic philosopher in the West, having

---

[4] For literature on Ficino, which is vast, see Christopher S. Celenza, "Marsilio Ficino," in the *Stanford Encyclopedia of Philosophy*: http://plato.stanford.edu/entries/ficino/. Touchstones are Michael J.B. Allen, *Synoptic Art: Marsilio Ficino on the History of Platonic Interpretation* (Florence: Olschki, 1998); Amos Edelheit, *Ficino, Pico, and Savonarola: The Evolution of Humanist Theology 1461/2–1498* (Leiden and Boston: Brill, 2008); Arthur Field, *The Origins of the Platonic Academy of Florence* (Princeton: Princeton University Press, 1988); Sebastiano Gentile, "Il ritorno di Platone, dei platonici e del 'corpus' ermetico. Filosofia, teologia e astrologia nell'opera di Marsilio Ficino," in C. Vasoli, ed., *Le filosofie del Rinascimento* (Milan: Mondadori, 2002), 193–228; Hankins, *Plato*, esp. 1: 267–366; Hankins, *Humanism and Platonism*, vol. 2, esp. pp. 187–470; Paul Oskar Kristeller, *Il pensiero filosofico di Marsilio Ficino* (Florence: Le Lettere, 1988); Kristeller, *The Philosophy of Marsilio Ficino* (New York: Columbia University Press, 1943); Kristeller, *Supplementum*; Raymond Marcel, *Marsile Ficin, 1433–1499* (Paris: Belles Lettres, 1958); Cesare Vasoli, *Quasi sit Deus: Studi su Marsilio Ficino* (Lecce: Conte, 1999).

[5] Florence: Miscomini, 1492; I have consulted the copy in the Garrett Library of Johns Hopkins University; see Frederick R. Goff, *Incunabula in American Libraries* (New York: Bibliographical Society of America, 1972), P-815. The Preface was widely reprinted; see Henri Saffrey, "Florence, 1492: The Reappearance of Plotinus," *Renaissance Quarterly* 49 (1996), 488–508.

translated all of Plato's dialogues from Greek into Latin and also offered commentaries to many of them as well. His passion for Plotinus grew as he began to realize how much Plotinus was indebted to Plato. Moreover, Ficino was fascinated by the manner in which Plotinus, living half a millennium later than Plato, also synthesized a number of other philosophical elements that had intervened in the years between when Plato died and Plotinus lived (Aristotle, the Stoics, Skeptics, and Epicureans among them). And of course in that time Christianity had arisen as well. Ficino, an ordained Catholic priest since 1473, was particularly interested in putting all the elements together into a kind of grand unified theory of philosophy and religion. Plotinus himself had been anti-Christian. But the more Ficino read him, the more he became convinced that Plotinus simply needed to be interpreted wisely and well to become part of what Ficino saw as one unified tradition of religious wisdom. This "ancient theology," or *prisca theologia* as he put it, went back to the era of Moses, continued through Plato, Christ, Plotinus, and many others, and would be capped off by none other than Ficino himself.

But it was important that this tradition be presented and understood correctly, and here is where mythmaking and legend enter into the picture. In his Preface to the Plotinus translation, Ficino makes a remarkable effort to give his overall project, culminating in the Plotinus edition, a venerable pedigree, reaching back to Cosimo's leadership and Florence's central cultural and religious role.

Ficino begins by alluding to the year 1439: "Great Cosimo, the father of his country by senatorial decree, at the time when a council was being negotiated among the Greeks and Latins in Florence under Eugenius IV, frequently heard a Greek philosopher by the name of Gemistos Plethon disputing like another Plato on the Platonic theology."[6] It is true, of course, that a council had been called to unify the Western, Roman Catholic branch of the Church with the Eastern, Orthodox side.[7] The council had begun in Ferrara, but after an outbreak of plague there it moved to Florence, where Cosimo provided much financial support. It is also true that a number of Byzantine theologians had arrived with the Greek delegation, including the fascinating Gemistos Plethon (1355–1452/4).[8] Cosimo had been designated

[6] Tr. in Saffrey, "Florence, 1492," 492.
[7] See Gill, *The Council of Florence;* and Paolo Viti, ed., *Firenze e il Concilio del 1439,* 2 vols. (Florence: Olscki, 1994).
[8] See Wilhelm Blum, *Georgios Gemistos Plethon: Politik, Philosophie und Rhetorik in spätbyzantinischen Reich (1355–1452)* (Stuttgart: Hiersemann, 1988); Vojtech Hladky, *The Philosophy of Gemistos Plethon: Platonism in Late Byzantium, between Hellenism and Orthodoxy* (Aldershot: Ashgate,

the title *pater patriae* after his death by the Florentine government, as well. So Ficino starts his Preface by asserting things everyone knows and upon which all would agree. His next move is interesting, as he suggests what Cosimo thought when he heard Plethon: "From Plethon's fervid lips Cosimo was straightaway so inspirited, so ensouled, that from that time forth he conceived deep in his mind a kind of Academy, to give birth to it at the first opportune moment."[9] Here is where one needs to step back a bit and offer context.

Plethon, like other Byzantine intellectuals, had never lost contact with ancient Greece's fundamental philosophical and religious texts. Deep study of those texts, meditation on the religious tradition in which he was situated, and his own unique personality had all led him to believe that a radical restructuring of religion was necessary, with an expansion of what we might call worship possibilities as the primary motivation. Put simply, Pletho wanted to expand Christianity into what amounted to a polytheistic religion. Now, Christianity both Eastern and Western had always been a bit less monotheistic than it seemed on the surface. There was the concept of the Trinity, first of all: one god with three unique natures, to each of which one could legitimately offer worship and prayer. Then, from antiquity onward, the saints were worshiped.[10] In the early Christian period, as more saints mounted up, the holidays to celebrate them were often timed to coincide with traditional pagan Roman holidays, even as many Roman temples and monuments were repurposed as Christian churches. Christianity, unsurprisingly, absorbed, transformed, and adopted as its own traditional pagan Roman customs.

But there was always this matter of Christianity's official monotheism. Despite all the diverse strands that made up Christianity's multicolored tapestry, it was still one tapestry. And this is why what Ficino says in his Preface – that Cosimo became so enraptured by Plethon that he decided to found a "kind of Academy" – is, if not impossible, at least unlikely. Or rather, it is likely only if we expand our vision and try to understand what the word "Academy" meant for Ficino.[11]

2014); Francois Masai, *Pléthon et le platonisme de Mistra* (Paris: Les belles lettres, 1956); Brigitte Tambrun, *Pléthon: Le retour de Platon* (Paris: Vrin, 2006); C.M. Woodhouse, *George Gemistos Plethon: The Last of the Hellenes* (Oxford: Oxford University Press, 1986).

[9] Tr. in Saffrey, "Florence, 1492," 492.

[10] See Peter Brown, *The Cult of the Saints: Its Rise and Function in Latin Christianity*, 2nd ed. (Chicago: University of Chicago Press, 2015).

[11] See Hankins, *Humanism and Platonism*, 2: 187–395.

There is no better way to accomplish this end than by following along in his Preface and observing, first, how Ficino continues to emphasize the paternal metaphor: while Cosimo, struck with Plethon's messages, "was intending in some sense to give birth to the great thing he had conceived, he destined me, the son of his favorite doctor Ficino" – this is Dietifeci Ficino, Ficino's father – "while still a boy, to undertake the labor, guiding me from that day forth to this very thing. Moreover he labored that I should not only have all the books of Plato in Greek, but also the books of Plotinus."[12] Already we can see that Ficino is: thinking in terms of family, with a strong father, Cosimo, at the top, whose vision would direct the progress of intellectual life; claiming for himself a special status, as the chosen one – in this case chosen by Cosimo to reveal to the world the great truths contained within the Platonic tradition, and signaling the importance of books. At a very basic level, Ficino is stating that Cosimo provided the books that one would need to carry out this important intellectual work. Some of this is indeed true. Cosimo did use his wealth, as we have seen, to build libraries, and Medici wealth was indeed behind the purchase of some singularly important Greek books, Platonic texts among them. What Ficino elides here is all the rest of Cosimo's patronage. But of course Ficino's purpose is to present his translation of Plotinus to the world.

Then we arrive at the first more or less documentable statement:

> After this, in the year 1463, in the thirtieth year of my life, Cosimo commissioned me to translate first Thrice-Great Hermes, and thereafter Plato. Hermes I finished in a few months while Cosimo was still alive; Plato I had also begun at that time. Although Cosimo was also eager for Plotinus, he said nothing to me about translating it, lest he should appear to be weighing me down with too great a burden all at once.[13]

Ficino, looking back from a distance of three decades, wants to attribute the project of translating all of what he believed to be "Platonic" wisdom to Cosimo, long dead, of course. "Hermes thrice-great" (*Hermes trismegistos* in Greek, since he was thought to be the greatest priest, king, and philosopher) represented a keystone for Ficino. One in a long line of ancient sages, Hermes was thought to have been Egyptian, a rough contemporary of Moses, and one element in an international, interreligious polyphony of wisdom, whose many voices combined to make up the one unitary, ultimately Christian wisdom Ficino was eager to uncover, represent, and promote. "Hermes" had acquired this reputation in late antiquity (about which

---

[12] Tr. in Saffrey, "Florence, 1492," 492–93, modified.
[13] Tr. in Saffrey, "Florence, 1492," 493, modified.

we will say more shortly). In fact, the texts that are now attributed to this mythical sage (known as the *Hermetic Corpus*) were authored, in Greek, in late antiquity and were given their patina of foreign, "Egyptian" wisdom then.[14] For now, it is enough to know that Ficino thoroughly believed in their worth and authenticity and that he wanted to include them in the battery of texts that "Cosimo" promoted, way back when.

Next in the Preface Ficino continues to extend the family metaphor, to suggest that much if not all of his project must be attributed to Cosimo's instincts, and to introduce a new member in the family: "Such was Cosimo's kindness to his household, such was his discretion towards all, that I myself could hardly divine that he wished me to undertake Plotinus. However, as long as he was alive, Cosimo kept his desire to himself. But from heaven he expressed or rather inspired it."[15] The way Cosimo's soul did this from beyond the grave was to inspire Pico della Mirandola to come to Florence. Ficino goes on:

> Pico, born in the very same year I was starting on Plato, and coming to Florence the same day – almost the same hour – I was publishing him, after greeting me asked me immediately about Plato. To him I said, our Plato has today emerged onto our thresholds. Then he heartily congratulated me on this, and straightway ... and neither I nor he knows whence the words came – he led, or rather impelled, me to translate Plotinus.[16]

The picture we have is of a lively community, given its initial impetus by Cosimo, fostered by Ficino's tireless labor, and moved forward by the presence of a young genius, Pico. One more thing needs to be mentioned: Ficino's Preface to Plotinus was addressed to Lorenzo "the Magnificent" de' Medici, grandson of Cosimo, who became one of late-fifteenth-century Italy's most renowned leaders.

There will be more to say about Pico, Lorenzo, and others in due time, but it is worth emphasizing that Ficino's picture of a golden age is what remained and became memorialized about the Florence of his era. The elements (in the memorialized version) included the primacy of Plato and what was perceived to be Platonic wisdom in Florence's intellectual and cultural life (so much so that older traditions of writing about the Renaissance called it an "age of Plato" as compared to the notional "age of Aristotle" that the Middle Ages seemingly represented); Ficino having founded a formal "Platonic Academy" to spread

---

[14] See Brian P. Copenhaver, ed. and tr., *Hermetica: The Greek Corpus Hermeticum and the Latin Asclepius in a New English Translation* (Cambridge: Cambridge University Press, 1992).

[15] Tr. in Saffrey, "Florence, 1492," 493.

[16] Ibid.

the word; the linking of politics and culture, to the effect that Lorenzo de' Medici was believed to have bought in completely to Ficino's Platonic vision; and a harmony of the arts, whereby Botticelli's greatest works were considered Platonically inspired. And while there are as always some small grains of truth in those ideas, all require qualification so substantial as to make them imperfect explanatory notions.

It is best to start with Ficino's early years, the 1450s to be precise, when we can at least make some surmises about his education and when he begins to have something of a presence in Florence, to judge from some early letters. As to his education, he had a solid but traditional Latinate education, with a focus on scholastic philosophy and less emphasis than one might imagine on the new Latin of Italian humanism. Finally, he learned enough Greek by the late 1450s to begin to translate Greek works.[17]

The 1450s also saw Ficino begin a custom he would maintain his entire life: writing philosophical letters to friends. In 1458, for example, he wrote a letter, in Latin, entitled "On the four sects of the philosophers."[18] In it, Ficino gave short, summary accounts of four "sects" or "schools" of philosophers: Platonists, Aristotelians, Stoics, and Epicureans. For the most part, at this relatively early stage in his career, Ficino draws on Latin sources, primarily. Accordingly, he presents nothing all that surprising in his account. Ficino delineates the major differences in opinion found among the four schools. He says for example that there are significant differences between Plato and Aristotle. They agree on God as the first cause, but Aristotle in contrast to Plato "thinks that the world has existed and will exist perpetually."[19] Another difference emerges:

> Aristotle thinks that man's soul is a certain simple, rational, and incorporeal nature, which perfects and moves the body to which it is joined. But whether soul is immortal or resistant to death, he did not sufficiently say. And so, some Peripatetics think that Aristotle meant that a soul of this sort was eternal and divine. But others, and not a smaller number perhaps, interpret their teacher in this way: they argue that Aristotle thought the soul would die with the body.[20]

A number of features of this short passage deserve comment.

First is the fact that it occurs in a letter. It is not all that remarkable that a Renaissance intellectual would place a serious discussion of a philosophical

[17] Hankins, *Plato*, 1: 269–78; Field, *The Origins*, 129–74.
[18] Marsilio Ficino, "De quattuor sectis philosophorum," in Kristeller, *Supplementum*, 2: 7–11.
[19] Ibid., 2: 8.
[20] Ibid.

matter in a letter. But it is worth highlighting nonetheless in Ficino's case, since his letter writing served as a serious vehicle of his overall philosophical enterprise. In fact, one might even say that Ficino's letter writing was his most successful way of doing philosophy. He created, over the course of his life, a Europe-wide network of correspondents. With each one, and in each individual letter, Ficino practiced what we might call "applied philosophy." His most deeply held assumption was that philosophy was useless if it was not practiced and shared among people. Even here, in this early, unremarkable letter on the "sects" of the philosophers, Ficino is responding to a request from a correspondent to elucidate the differences among ancient philosophical schools. The request created the opportunity to think about the topic, and the thinking is expressed in writing, so that one moved from an informal, conversational mode to a written, more formal one.

Second are the results of that process, which is to say Ficino's position on the thorny issue of what Aristotle thought about the human soul and its possible survival after death. The humanists we have thus far encountered – from Petrarch in his maturity, to Bruni, and even through Valla, did not agonize over issues such as this one. Petrarch's own tormented religiosity left no room for doubt: a card-carrying Christian, he believed the human soul was immortal and that it would reap rewards and punishments in the afterlife based on its owner's conduct during his or her life. Bruni was, for all intents and purposes, secular in his intellectual outlook.[21] If pressed, he certainly would have affirmed Church doctrine. But he and most of his cohort, Poggio included, just did not think these were subjects on which one needed to spend too much intellectual capital. After you died, you'd find out, was the unarticulated sentiment. Intellectuals in this world should focus on problems of this world. And Valla – well, Valla would have been happy to charge Aristotelians with disbelieving in the immortality of the human soul, if it happened to help him in whatever argument in which he was contemporaneously engaged.

But Ficino was different. We are still in the 1450s, of course. Ficino was relatively young, and we have the benefit of looking with hindsight over the course of his life. We know what he will say later in life. And one theme to which he comes back, over and over and in different contexts and genres, is the peril of irreligiosity for human society. What this meant precisely was far different in the fifteenth century from what it might mean today. But there can be no doubt that for intellectuals, the massive amount of sometimes religiously destabilizing textual discoveries in the long fifteenth century had

---

[21] See Witt, *In the Footsteps*, 393–442.

an effect. Only later in life would Ficino need to wrestle explicitly with what all this meant for him. But even here, in this short letter, two aspects stand out, as clues leading us down the trail of what is to come.

The first is the position on Aristotle and the soul. Aristotle's most powerful statement about this problem came in a text known as *On the Soul*, or *De anima*, as the work was known in its Latin translation.[22] He was inscrutably unclear on what he meant. Aristotle believed that all human knowledge depended radically on the senses, meaning that everything you know, you know because your senses at some point were in contact with the outside world. In *On the Soul*, Aristotle talks about the "affections" of the soul, emotions such as anger, fear, and so on, about all of which "there seems to be no case in which the soul can act or be acted upon without involving the body."[23] If you are afraid, your fear emerges because your imagination (which Aristotle conceived as almost corporeal, or bodily) transmits impressions to your mind of some sort of unwanted physical consequence resulting from that of which you are afraid. Thinking all by itself, Aristotle concedes, seems to be an exception, yet even here, "if this too proves to be a form of imagination or to be impossible without imagination, it too requires a body as a condition of existence."[24]

Another way to put this is to say that Aristotle saw everything in "hylomorphic" terms, which is to say that every existing thing represented a unity of matter (the Greek word is *hyle*) and form (*morphe*). Human beings were no exception. You might be able to think about the human soul and the human body separately (you can separate them conceptually), but neither had a real existence without the other. A consequence of this approach is that the soul – the individual human soul – as such cannot exist without the body. When the body dies, the soul ... well, what does happen to the soul? Did it too die, since it lacked its material partner, the body, on which it might further rely? Or was it somehow transformed, living on in some respect? These were the fundamentally challenging questions for any Christian when dealing with Aristotle.

They were made even more problematic given some of Aristotle's other statements, which themselves reached back to his own complicated relationship with his mentor and teacher, Plato. Plato had been a great supporter of the idea that the individual human soul was immortal. In dialogues including

---

[22] Aristotle, *De anima*, ed. David Ross (Oxford: Clarendon, 1961); English tr. in Aristotle, *On the Soul*, in Aristotle, *Complete Works of Aristotle: The Revised Oxford Translation*, ed. Jonathan Barnes, 2 vols. (Princeton: Princeton University Press, 1984), 641–92.

[23] Aristotle, *De an.*, 1.1.403a5–7; Aristotle, *Complete Works*, 641.

[24] Aristotle, *De an.*, 1.1.403a7–10; Aristotle, *Complete Works*, 641.

Phaedo, Phaedrus, The Republic, and a number of others, Plato propounded the idea that the human soul represented the essence of each individual. The body was made of matter and matter was corruptible and non-eternal, whereas the soul was something divine and immortal. For Plato, it preexisted in an immaterial realm, that of the Forms, where other immaterial, ideal exemplars resided. At a certain point, when the time was right and the gods agreed, an individual immaterial soul would descend into the realm of material things, to be united to a human body.[25] That soul-body dyad existed on earth, lived a life as a person, and based on what that person did in that life would receive rewards or punishments in the afterlife. That soul could also be reincarnated into a lesser form of life in subsequent reincorporations, coming back, Plato suggested in one dialogue, as donkeys, wolves, bees, or ants (among other creatures).[26] Only those who lived a perfect, contemplative life would after death reside permanently in the placid, immaterial realm of the Forms, subject to no physical pain, eternally contemplating, and free of care.

On the one hand, as early Christianity evolved, thinkers adopted much of this Platonic framework. Augustine had said the Platonists had come "the closest to us," meaning the closest to Christian ideas, in his influential and much read *City of God*.[27] Immortality of the soul, rewards and punishments after death, and an immaterial realm that superintended the material world: all these harmonized with Christian beliefs and, in truth, stood behind and before them as a point of origin. On the other hand, from a Christian perspective, when it came to the soul, one aspect especially of Plato's theories was suspect: reincarnation. The Christian view held that God created each individual as an individual and, importantly, that each individual was unique. This is why, when Aristotle's texts became the basis for high medieval university education, some of what he had to say regarding hylomorphism made sense, especially when it came to people: simply put, each person was an individual made of matter and form, unique, unlike any other individual person, and thus, in a way, a perfect example of how God could indeed create unique individuals and care for them as such.

But then there was that touchy matter of the soul. You could say that each individual was a unity of matter and form, body and soul, but then what happened after death? Without the promise of some sort of individual survival of earthly, bodily death, how could there be rewards or punishments

---

[25] See Plato, *Republic*, 10.614–10.621 (the myth of Er).

[26] Plato, *Phaedo*, 81e–82b.

[27] Augustine, *City of God*, 8.9.

after death? In his *On the Soul*, Aristotle had argued that the "mind," or *nous*, was a "faculty" of the "soul," or *psyche*, meaning that the mind and what it did, thinking, was a part of the soul, a part that depended on and was enveloped in the soul and its functioning. And the soul was fundamentally natural and physical, dependent as we have seen on sensation and impressions derived from the natural world through the senses.

Yet, in one puzzling section of *On the Soul*, Aristotle departed from this fundamentally physical (and typically premodern) notion, positing a part of "mind," or *nous*, that was in Greek *poetikos*, most literally "poetic" but which can best be translated as "active" or even "able to create." He described it as follows: the *nous poetikos* is "distinct, unaffected, and unmixed, being in its essence actuality."[28] Soon thereafter Aristotle described it as "immortal and eternal."[29] So on the surface this definition seems almost perfectly apt for a Christian perspective: there was a certain part of the soul that, though immaterial, was set apart and eternal. But there was one problem: Aristotle did not specify that the *nous poetikos* was proper to individual human beings. He left it open: he did not say those two key qualities, immortality and being eternal, were *not* proper to the individual human soul. But you could also interpret his statements as pertaining to a kind of universal, general mind, as if the eternal, immortal, totally "separate" mind could be thought to exist in the universe at large.

When medieval thinkers discussed this problem, they proposed different solutions. One of the most influential was that of Averroes (1126–98), an Islamic scholar living in then Muslim southern Spain. Profiting from the Islamic world's unparalleled study of Aristotle in the Middle Ages (it was this world that preserved, studied, and commented on Aristotle's texts well before the Western twelfth-century revival of Aristotelian studies), Averroes and other Islamic scholars took Aristotle to have been "the greatest philosopher who ever lived," almost divine, in truth, and worthy of extensive research and explication.[30]

---

[28] Aristotle, *De anima*, 3.5, 430a17–18; tr. D.W. Hamlyn, in J.L. Ackrill, ed., *A New Aristotle Reader* (Princeton: Princeton University Press, 1987), 196, modified.

[29] Aristotle, *De anima*, 3.5, 430a23; tr. Hamlyn, 196.

[30] For a sketch of the "unity of the intellect" theory, see Martin Pine, *Pietro Pomponazzi: Radical Philosopher of the Italian Renaissance* (Padua: Antenore, 1986), 78–86; the problem is framed nicely in John Marenbon, *Later Medieval Philosophy (1150–1350): An Introduction* (London: Routledge, 1987), 66–82; see also Jamal Al-Alawi, "The Philosophy of Ibn Rushd: The Evolution of the Problem of the Intellect in the Works of Ibn Rushd," in S.K. Jayyusi, ed., *The Legacy of Muslim Spain*, 2 vols. (Leiden: Brill, 1994), 2: 804–29; and Herbert Davidson, *Alfarabi, Avicenna, and Ibn Rushd, on Intellect: Their Cosmologies, Theories of the Active Intellect and Theories of Human Intellect* (Oxford and New York: Oxford University Press, 1992).

Averroes's work especially was well known in the West, so much so that even Dante in his *Inferno*, 4, had included Averroes among the "virtuous pagans," among whom were non-Christian thinkers who had made signal contributions to philosophy and who stood as exemplars of an ethical life. Dante designated Averroes as the thinker "who wrote the great commentary," something certainly true, for Averroes had written extensive commentaries on most of Aristotle's works, commentaries that were translated into Latin along with Aristotle's works in the twelfth-century revival of learning. When it came to Aristotle's *On the Soul*, Averroes solved the problem of Aristotle's ambiguities on the issue of personal immortality by suggesting that, after individuals died, their souls were in effect subsumed into the universal active intellect. Meaning: each individual participated after death in the universal intellect, losing his or her individuality in the process. Personal immortality went by the wayside in the search to explain Aristotle's position. Something of the individual's soul remained, but only as a trace, not as something that possessed its own formal individuality.

Averroes's solution to the dilemma present in Aristotle's *On the Soul* represented one way, a powerful and coherent one at that, to interpret Aristotle's work. But it was a difficult, indeed heretical one for Christians to accept. So in the Middle Ages, when thinkers took on this problem, they tended to do one of two things: either they rejected it entirely, saying that it was the wrong interpretation of Aristotle and that anyone who understood Aristotle correctly would realize that the great thinker really was referring to individuals, to human souls, when he talked about that one "immortal and eternal" part; or they fell back on what used to be known as the "theory of the double truth": the truth of philosophy, which is to say that human reason, unaided by faith, taught us that the individual soul did indeed perish as such after death. But the truth according to faith, which we must as good Christians simply believe, taught us instead that individual immortality remained, and that it was precisely that individual identity that would, in the end, be subject to rewards and punishments in the afterlife and, even more important, would be resurrected at the end of time and when God's providence so decreed. Without preserving individual immortality, resurrection was off the table, and the whole social economy of the divine would be evacuated.

It should be noted, parenthetically, that the notion that one could endorse "two truths," one from philosophy, one from faith, seems absurd on the surface and one that no self-respecting thinker schooled in Aristotelian logic could ever endorse in a full-throated fashion. It was derived fundamentally from an accusation hurled against thirteenth-century scholastic philosophers (members of the arts faculty of the University of Paris) by Bishop Stephen Tempier, who issued formal condemnations in 1270 and 1277. The latter set was especially robust, containing 219 positions said to be held by some; in the Bishop's letter of introduction he states clearly his concern regarding the possibility that there were some thinkers who claimed that there could exist two truths.[31] Scholars have scoured the writings of medieval thinkers and have found no one who openly said such a thing in a bald-faced manner.[32] But there were thinkers who came close, and who said that any branch of knowledge functioned according to its own principles and that the results drawn therefrom might not agree completely with truth in an absolute sense; it was only the divine will, at some level impenetrable and unknowable, in which absolute truth resided.[33] There were those who took the traditional notion that scripture hid many levels underneath its surface meaning far enough into other, non-scriptural realms, that one could imagine concern, especially from those outside of the classroom.

By Ficino's day (to close the parenthesis) no real synthesis or solution had arrived to the problem of individual immortality of the soul. So (to return to his short summary of the schools of philosophers), it is worth recalling what Ficino says: "Aristotle thinks that man's soul is a certain simple, rational, and incorporeal nature, which perfects and moves the body to which it is joined."[34] Fair enough. This statement serves as a fine summary of Aristotle's basic definition for the human soul: it is the form of the body but separate from the body, and it serves as a principle of motion. Then things begin to grow complicated, as Ficino continues: "But whether soul is immortal or resistant to death, he did not sufficiently say."[35] Also true, as we have seen. Even at this relatively early age Ficino is a sober enough reader

---

[31] See David Piché, ed., *La condemnation parisienne de 1277. Texte latin, traduction, introduction et commentaire* (Paris: Vrin, 1999), p. 74: "Dicunt enim ea esse vera secundum philosophiam, sed non secundum fidem catholicam, quasi sint duae contrariae veritates."

[32] See Jan A. Aertsen, Kent Emery Jr., and Andreas Speer, eds., *Nach der Verurteilung von 1277. Philosophie und Theologie an der Universität von Paris im letzten Viertel des 13. Jahrhunderts* (Berlin: de Gruyter, 2001); Luca Bianchi, *Censure et liberté intellectuelle à l'université de Paris (XIIIe–XIVe siècles)* (Paris: Les Belles Lettres, 1999); Richard C. Dales, "The Origin of the Doctrine of Double Truth," *Viator* 15 (1984), 169–79; Alain de Libera, *Penser au Moyen Age* (Paris: Editions du Seuil, 1991); John F. Wippel, "The Condemnation of 1270 and 1277 at Paris," *The Journal of Medieval and Renaissance Studies* 7 (1977), 169–201.

[33] See for one example Boethius of Dacia (one of the arts faculty members Bishop Tempier had in mind), in his *De aeternitate mundi*, in Boethius of Dacia, *Opera*, vol. 6: *De aeternitate mundi, De summon bono, De somniis*, in Corpus Philosophorum Danicorum Medii Aevi, 6.2 (Copenhagen: Bagge, 1976), p. 54.

[34] Marsilio Ficino, "De quattuor sectis philosophorum," in Kristeller, *Supplementum*, 2:8.

[35] Ibid.

of texts to recognize the ambiguity at the heart of Aristotle's vision of the soul. Ficino goes on: "And so, some Peripatetics think that Aristotle meant that a soul of this sort was eternal and divine. But others, and not a smaller number perhaps, interpret their teacher in this way: they argue that Aristotle thought the soul would die with the body."[36]

We can see that Ficino summarizes the basic medieval bifurcation in interpretations of Aristotle, as outlined earlier. Even more noteworthy is the fact that Ficino subtly deflects the import of the implicit question as to what Aristotle himself meant. In one sentence Ficino moves from Aristotle, the authority, to the Peripatetics, which is to say those who counted themselves interpreters of Aristotle. This move might not seem to be that momentous. And on the face of it, it is not. We have a young Ficino doing his duty and answering a friend's question about the differences among philosophers. But this strategy of protecting the authority is something in which Ficino, as it turned out, engaged for his entire career. Aristotle in this small statement remains sacrosanct; when it came to individual immortality, "he did not sufficiently say." His interpreters, on the other hand, are the ones who profess a diversity of opinion. It is precisely with the interpreters, rather than the authority, that one could disagree. This strategy serves the function, then, of protecting Aristotle and clearing the way for Ficino to advance a correct interpretation. Here in this early letter, he does no such thing, of course. But later, as his career advanced, this approach to texts and interpretation – signaled early on in this 1458 epistolary treatise, a seedling, as it were – grew and became Ficino's intellectual signature.

One other small matter in this little treatise deserves attention: his summary of Epicureanism. For Ficino at this stage in his career, much of his knowledge of Epicurean philosophy would have come from its most famous ancient Latin exponent, Lucretius, the first-century BCE philosopher-poet about whom almost nothing is known save his *On the Nature of Things*, a lengthy poem of more than seven thousand lines in six books. In it, Lucretius summarized in beautiful Latin hexameters much of ancient Epicurean philosophy. The poem was known in a reduced form during the Middle Ages; but after it was rediscovered by Poggio during the Council of Constance, it aroused interest, as did other controversial ancient texts during the long fifteenth century, texts whose basic outlines might have been known earlier but only came into clear view when they could be read as a whole.[37]

---

[36] Ibid.
[37] See Chapter 7, n.4.

In the case of Lucretius, two elements especially come to the fore when considering the impact this text had on Renaissance thinkers: atomism and his conception of the divine. Atomism held that all things were composed of particles so small they could not be broken down into smaller particles. Whether a rock, or tree, or – and here is the controversy – a human being, when anything ceased to exist, it dispersed into these particles, which whirled without pattern in the void of space until they recombined into something else. There was no question of an immortal soul, rewards and punishments, and so on. If Aristotle at least possessed some ambiguity on this question, the case of Epicureanism was clear. When you died, you ceased to exist. When it came to God – or "the divine" – Epicureanism and Lucretius were also limpid: God existed but took no notice of human affairs. As Ficino put it in this short treatise, Lucretius's god is "is eternal, wisest, and most blessed; it does nothing, has no duty, and cares for nothing."[38] Of the four schools of philosophy that Ficino portrayed in this short treatise, he spent the most time, comparatively, on Epicureanism, fascinated by and perhaps fearful of how interesting this alien but coherent philosophy seemed to be. Later in life, he hinted that in his youth he went through a Lucretian period.[39] We see a trace of that period here, perhaps. But, just as Ficino's early thoughts on Aristotle manifest what would become a lifelong inclination to protect authoritative figures and stake out an interpretive place for himself, his interest in Epicureanism can serve as a window onto another important Ficinian trajectory: his tendency to explore realms of religion that fell far outside what now seem to be the boundaries of Christian religious orthodoxy. To understand how these two themes played themselves out in his life and work, we need to return to his early years.

As Ficino was coming into maturity and finishing his early education, he began translating Greek. Despite the mythmaking in which he engaged in the previously noted Preface to Plotinus, Ficino's representation of his translating practice was right on the money. Early in the 1460s he began translating certain dialogues of Plato, interrupting that work to translate the Hermetic Corpus. Other early Greek-to-Latin translations included a number of recondite later Platonists (the ramifications of which we shall examine later).[40]

Ficino also, with the spirited energy of relative youth, began consolidating resources. One important step on this road consisted in his acceptance of

---

[38] Marsilio Ficino, "De quattuor sectis philosophorum," in Kristeller, *Supplementum*, 2:9.
[39] See Hankins, *Plato*, 1: 279–80 and 2: 454–59; Marcel, *Marsile Ficin*, 221–27.
[40] See Sebastiano Gentile, "Sulle prime traduzioni dal Greco di Marsilio Ficino," *Rinascimento*, 2nd series 30 (1990), 57–104.

substantive patronage from Cosimo in the early 1460s. A 1463 archival document preserves the record of a gift by Cosimo to Ficino of a small property a few miles north of Florence, in a village called Careggi. The property came with a house; Ficino could both reside there when he wished and, importantly, earn income from the farming done on the property.[41] We have a letter from a year earlier, in 1462, in which Ficino wrote to Cosimo: "spiritedly do I devote myself to the Academy you arranged for us on the estate in Careggi, as if I worship rightly at a shrine of contemplation."[42] We also know, from another archival document, that in 1462 Cosimo gave Ficino a house in Florence, allowing Ficino income from the rent.[43]

Land, income, Cosimo, philosophy: the picture we have from these early years is of a Ficino assiduously cultivating Cosimo and beginning the process of publicizing (through letters intended to be public) and memorializing these relationships. Ficino's mention, in his later Preface to Plotinus, of an "Academy," along with other such clues, led a much earlier generation of scholars to believe that Ficino inaugurated a formal Platonic "school," with regular meetings. While this development seems not to have occurred in the formal fashion once supposed, what is clear is that Ficino for a time served as one important hub of Florentine intellectual life, a hub understood broadly as Platonic.

To express his vision of philosophy and religion – the two were inextricably linked in Ficino's mind – Ficino went in many directions, so many in fact, that later ages look back on him as inconsistent. In context, it all made sense. First, there were his letters. Over the course of his life, he collected his letters in twelve books, dedicated to admired friends or patrons.[44]

He thought a lot about friendship and about how friendship stimulated philosophy, the pursuit of wisdom. In one letter, to a German correspondent, Ficino catalogued his friends. Among them, he included patrons, in the first

---

[41] Florence, Archivio di Stato, Notarile antecosmiano A 376, 10r–11r; see Sebastiano Gentile, S. Niccoli, and Paolo Viti, *Marsilio Ficino e il ritorno di Platone: Mostra di manoscritti, stampe, a documenti* (Florence: Le Lettere, 1984), 175–76.

[42] Ficino in Kristeller, *Supplementum*, 2: 87–88; Gentile, Niccoli, Viti, 176.

[43] Florence, Archivio di Stato, Notarile antecosmiano A 376, 36r–36v; Gentile, Niccoli, Viti, 176. These gifts were noted by contemporaries; see Vespasiano, *Le vite*, 2: 204.

[44] Ficino's letters are in Marsilio Ficino, *Op.*, 607–964; critical editions of the first two books: Marsilio Ficino, *Lettere*, ed. Sebastiano Gentile, 2 vols. to date (Florence: Olschki, 1990–2010); English translations in Marsilio Ficino, *Letters*, tr. by the Language Department of the School of Economic Science, 10 vols. to date (London: Shepheard-Walwyn, 1975–2015); the early modern Tuscan translation of them by Felice Figliucci is available in Ficino, *Le divine lettere del gran Marsilio Ficino*, 2 vols. (Rome: Edizioni di Storia e Letteratura, 2001).

rank. These were people, such as the Medici, who sustained him and without whom his work would be impossible to pursue. Second, Ficino listed "familiar friends – fellow conversationalists, so to speak."[45] The word he uses for "fellow conversationalist" is *confabulatores*, which can also mean something in the neighborhood of "fellow storytellers." The use of the word indicates that Ficino did not believe philosophy was only about dry argumentation; rather, it needed to be shared, cultivated, and worked out in a context of give and take among different thinkers. About his "fellow conversationalists," he says that they are "almost pupils [*discipuli*], still, they aren't really pupils, since I wouldn't want to imply that I had taught or am teaching any of them, but rather, in a Socratic fashion, I ask them all questions and encourage them, and I persistently call forth the fertile geniuses of my friends to bring about birth." Ficino uses a metaphor developed in Plato's dialogue on knowledge, *Theaetetus*, where Socrates presents himself not as an omniscient teacher but rather as a philosophical "midwife," whose function is to bring about the birth of ideas through gentle questioning. Third, Ficino mentions his *auditores* or "students." These include a number of people who would go on to become important thinkers and carriers of the torch. Among the people listed, we find some of Florence's most prominent citizens, from various members of the Medici family, to Cristoforo Landino, Benedetto Accolti, and Giorgio Antonio Vespucci (a relative of the famous explorer), and Niccolò Valori, Carlo Marsuppini, and Bindaccio dei Ricasoli, among a number of others.[46]

One way, then, that Ficino understood his Academy (to use that term in the broadest sense imaginable) was simply as a network of friends both in Florence and far away. They were linked, not in a formal, regular fashion, but rather by the bonds of Platonic love, which was for Ficino a force that both bound the universe together and drove natural processes. In his view love had its most important effects on the human soul, which he saw as something semi-material.[47] This notion can be puzzling to moderns, since we are more accustomed to thinking of the "mind" as something immaterial but that still needs to function in a material world to which it is unconnected. Instead, in Ficino's day, the soul and matter were thought to be linked. One of the key

---

[45] Ficino, *Op.*, 936–37: "consuetudine familiares (ut ita loquor) confabulators."

[46] Ibid., 936–37.

[47] For an overview, see Katherine Park and Eckhard Kessler, "The Concept of Psychology," Katherine Park, "The Organic Soul," and Eckhard Kessler, "The Intellective Soul," in Charles B. Schmitt and Quentin Skinner, eds., *The Cambridge History of Renaissance Philosophy* (Cambridge: Cambridge University Press, 1988), at 455–63, 464–84, and 485–534, respectively.

elements in this linkage was termed "spirit," which Ficino defined in this fashion: "Spirit is defined by doctors as a vapor of blood – pure, subtle, hot, and clear. After being generated by the heat of the heart out of the more subtle blood, it flies to the brain, and there the soul uses it continually for the exercise of the exterior senses."[48] In another place Ficino writes: "since spirit is closely akin to the soul, the soul has no difficulty in entering into this spirit and first permeating the whole of it, and then with spirit as a mean it totally permeates the whole body."[49] So is the soul for Ficino material? Immaterial? It is in truth a distinction he is not really making. But what is clear is that just as soul and spirit collaborate in human affairs, so too do they do so in matters of the universe: "what doubt will occur to anyone that love is inborn in all things toward all things?"[50]

That last question occurs in a dialogue Ficino wrote called *On Love*, one place where we can see a perfect meshing of his scholarly and philosophical interests.[51] He completed a first version in 1469, right when he was riding high on Medici patronage and after he had completed the first round of his translations of Plato. The dialogue is based on Plato's classic dialogue on love, the *Symposium*. In it, Plato has a series of interlocutors, Socrates of course among them, who participate in a "symposium," an all-male dinner and drinking party, which by tradition was followed by animated discussion on some topic of mutual interest.

The topic suggested was love, and the means for the discussion was that each participant was to make "the finest speech he can in praise of love."[52] There are in total seven speeches in the dialogue, with each interlocutor making a special case for love. For one, love binds fellow warriors together in honor, so that in fighting an enemy they are also fighting for one another.[53] Another suggests love links humanity and the gods.[54] Another (the character Aristophanes) offers a myth: once all people had dual bodies, bodies whose faces and limbs faced in opposite directions.[55] Some were all male, some were

---

[48] Marsilio Ficino, *De triplici vita*, ed. and tr. Carol Kaske and John R. Clark (Tempe: MRTS, 1998), 1.2, 11–15.

[49] Ficino, *Platonic Theology*, 7.6.1 (vol. 2, pp. 234–35), tr. modified.

[50] Ficino, *Commentaire / Commentarium*, 3.1, p. 53.

[51] See Ficino, *Commentaire / Commentarium*; for an English translation, see Marsilio Ficino, *Commentary on Plato's Symposium on Love*, tr. Sears Jayne (Dallas: Spring, 1985); and Paul Richard Blum, "Einleitung," in Ficino, *Über die Liebe oder Platons Gastmahl*, ed. Paul Richard Blum (Hamburg: Meiner, 1994), XI–XLVII.

[52] Plato, *Symposium*, 177d; English tr. in Plato, *The Symposium*, tr. Christopher Gill (London: Penguin, 1999), p. 9.

[53] Plato, *Symposium*, 178d–179b.

[54] Ibid., 186a–188e.

[55] Ibid., 189a–193d.

all female, and some were androgynous. When they all had the idea to scale Olympus and make war on the gods, Zeus broke them all in half, so that thereafter they would wander the earth looking for their "other half," the main reason, Aristophanes says, why people in love say that they feel "complete."

Another intervention, this one of Socrates, suggests that one should begin with what is natural (human love spurred on by physical attraction) but then move upward. Socrates offers wisdom he says he heard from a woman of Mantinea (a Greek city), named Diotima. You fall in love with one person, physically beautiful to you, but then you realize that this person partakes of something larger, beauty itself, something that is divine and eternal. The lover will then realize that beauty is everywhere, if only he has the mental resources to seek it out: in human practices and laws, when they are well arranged, and in knowledge of the truth. Continuing to contemplate all this, the lover with the properly disposed mind will see that beauty – the eternal kind – appears "as in itself and by itself, always single in form. All other beautiful things share its character, but do so in such a way that, when other things come to be or to cease, it is not increased or decreased in any way nor does it undergo any change."[56] Love, in this respect, served as a kind of motive force for human beings. Naturally implanted in us (for all are inclined to seek out beauty) this propensity was something to be cultivated and trained so that we could rise up from our human, every-day, material concerns and experience the divine.

Ficino admired this notion, and he used it as a basis for his own *On Love*, an odd but influential text that sat between the genres of commentary and original work in a noteworthy fashion. On the one hand, it was unexceptional to write commentaries to admired works, and Ficino did many of these. You took a work such as, say, Plato's *Phaedrus* (another text Ficino loved), excerpted a number of key passages, and explained them. The goal was to explicate the meaning of the author: you, the commentator, had something to say, but the balance of the work looked toward the author's views, even if – as in Ficino's case – you used that occasion to express your own philosophical viewpoint. On the other hand, there were original works, where you were yourself considered the author. Ficino's *On Love* represents a kind of hybrid, an homage-like rewriting of Plato's *Symposium*, one that, he hoped, would take into account Plato's theories on love and culturally translate them for Ficino's own era and community. As one slightly later contemporary, a professor of Aristotelian studies named Agostino Nifo

---

[56] Plato, *Symposium*, 211b; tr. Gill, p. 49.

(1473–1546) put it in 1529: "Now Ficino, amplifying what Plato handed down about Love, in part by allegorizing, in part by adding, made a not unlearned compilation of much regarding love."[57]

In form, Ficino's *On Love* represents an account of an evening that nine philosophical friends spent together, friends who included Ficino's father, some of his teachers, and two of his students.[58] After their dinner, two had to depart, leaving seven to continue the conversation. When all was said and done, five of the guests gave speeches, all of which can be seen as contributing to Ficino's vision of love and its place in the universe, a vision best summed up in the exhortation of one of the speakers to the group: "As to you, my dear friends, I urge and beg you to embrace love – certainly something divine – with all your strength."[59]

As the dialogue proceeds, what becomes clear is that love, for Ficino, represents a central element of the universe, one that must be understood within his overall view of the cosmos. This view reached back to Plato, first of all. Both in his *Symposium* and in his dialogue *Phaedrus*, Plato hinted at something that later Platonic thinkers would make explicit: our natural, inborn desire for beauty is there for a reason, implanted in us by the divine to be trained in the proper way. That reason had to do with the need to return to the divine. For Plato, our souls at one point existed unencumbered by materiality or, put more simply, they existed without a physical body. Plato suggested that there was some capacity of choice involved, as disembodied souls could choose the sort of person they wanted to become in their next life.[60] Still, return to an embodied state was a step down on the scale of being; it was that natural desire for beauty that enabled us to rise up out of our physicality. It is this sort of love that represents a good kind of madness: "that which someone shows when he sees the beauty we have down here and is reminded of true beauty," as Plato said in the *Phaedrus*.[61] The more one trained that tendency to use the desire for beauty to remind oneself that an

---

[57] Agostino Nifo, *De amore*, in Agostino Nifo, *Libri duo, De pulchro primus, De amore secundus* (Leiden, 1549), 90–277, at 91. The treatise was finished in 1529 and originally published in 1531; see Jill Kraye, "Ficino in the Firing Line," in Michael J.B. Allen and Valery Rees, eds., *Marsilio Ficino: His Theology, His Philosophy, His Legacy* (Leiden: Brill, 2001), 377–97, esp. 382–85; Pierre Laurens, "Introduction," in Ficino, *Commentaire / Commentarium*, IX–LXIX, at LXV–LXVI.

[58] See Laurens, "Les interlocuteurs du *De amore*," in Ficino, *Commentaire / Commentarium*, XCI-XCII.

[59] Ficino, *Commentaire / Commentarium*, 2.8, p. 43.

[60] See Plato, *Republic*, 10.614–10.621.

[61] Plato, *Phaedrus*, 249d; English tr. in Plato, *Phaedrus*, tr. Alexander Nehamas and Paul Woodruff (Indianapolis: Hackett, 1995), p. 37.

eternal, divine, incorruptible beauty existed outside the realm of our world, the closer one could come to union with the divine. This process occurred through the various cycles of reincarnation, with Plato suggesting that a very select few might one day reside permanently among the gods, in a world free of the pain, corruptibility, and decay that any enmattered state entailed.

For Christians, reincarnation of this sort was plainly heretical: God created each person as an individual, body and soul. But there remained in Christianity a very potent legacy of Platonism, to the effect that part of our job as human beings was to discipline ourselves through prayer and medita-tion, so that we might return to God. For Ficino, this idea of return to the divine became a central factor in his thought. It was only later, when he approached the work of Plotinus in a serious way, that he worked his ideas out in full. But in the era of his *On Love*, in the late 1460s, Ficino was relying as much on inherited medieval traditions as on recondite, little known later Platonists such as Plotinus. Take, for example, what Dante Alighieri had said in his *Convivio*, or *Banquet*, a much earlier, vernacular rather than Latin, symposium-inspired piece of work, one in which Dante mixes poetry that he has written with prose explanations, a kind of self-commentary that had far-reaching effects. On "love," in that work, Dante suggested that "love is nothing other than the spiritual unification of the soul with what it loves" and that the human soul, depending on God as it does, "naturally desires and wants to be unified with God."[62] What Dante meant, well over 150 years before Ficino was writing his *On Love*, was that everything that exists has a natural desire implanted in it, a tendency that moves it along and that attracts it to certain things.

That entire set of sentiments would have been perfectly familiar to Ficino; whether or not he was drawing in some direct way on Dante, it is worth pointing out how similar Ficino's thinking was to Dante's regarding love.[63] It is also worth pointing out that Ficino decided to translate into the Tuscan vernacular Dante's treatise on government, *On Monarchy*, which Dante had written in Latin and in which he had argued for an early version of the separation of Church and state.[64] In Ficino's Preface to that translation, he said that Dante was "celestial, when it came to his homeland, Florentine,

---

[62] Dante, *Convivio*, 3.2., in Dante, *Tutte le opere*, ed. Luigi Blasucci (Florence: Sansoni, 1965), p. 142.

[63] On Ficino and Dante, see Jean Festugières, "Dante et Marsile Ficin," *Bulletin du Jubilé* 5 (1922), 535–43; Kristeller, *Studies*, 41.

[64] See Dante Alighieri, *Monarchia*, Cola di Rienzo *Commentario*, Marsilio Ficino, *Volgarizzamento*, with introduction by Francesco Furlan (Milan: Mondadori, 2004), 3–162 for the text; on Ficino's translation see Prue Shaw, "La versione ficiniana della 'Monarchia'," *Studi danteschi* 51 (1978), 289–408.

when it came to where he was from, by profession a poetic philosopher," and one who, even if he was not a Greek reader, still "adorned his books with many Platonic sentiments."[65] And it is, finally, even more noteworthy – to return to Ficino and his *De amore* – that he decided to make it available in both Latin and the vernacular. What we see is that Ficino was drawing on inherited traditions at this phase of life, even as he was reworking Plato, whose *Symposium* had not been known to the West; that Ficino believed that these messages were too important for society overall to be restricted to a Latin-reading elite; and that, finally, Ficino's thinking from the beginning of his public prominence was oriented outward toward the city and its participants, a sincere and almost touchingly naïve belief that Plato's ideas on love, interpreted rightly, could help the society in which he lived find its way.

[65] Marsilio Ficino, "Proemium," in Kristeller, *Supplementum*, 2: 184–85, at 184.

13

FICINO, II

ONE OF THE MAIN REASONS FICINO FEARED FOR THE FUTURE OF his city and culture had to do with a dangerous tendency he perceived toward irreligion. The years 1469–74 saw him author two works, one large, the other small, one Latin, the other in both Latin and the vernacular. The first of these was the *Platonic Theology*, the second his *On the Christian Religion*. These two texts, Ficino's translations, and finally his letters serve to flesh out the nature of his overall cultural project, one that was intended to heal a society he feared was ill.

Ficino's principal concern, as he wrote in the Preface to his *Platonic Theology* (dedicated to the then young Lorenzo "the Magnificent" de' Medici) was that people tended to separate philosophy from religion.[1] For Ficino they were united, inextricably linked, to such an extent that it seemed folly to separate them. Plato, interpreted rightly, was the key, for "whatever subject he deals with, he quickly brings it round, in a spirit of utmost piety, to the contemplation and worship of God."[2] It can appear startling that Ficino could seem to endorse Plato, the thinker who had written openly and admiringly about homosexual love between men and much younger boys, who was a pagan polytheist, and who had advocated reincarnation. For those earlier thinkers in the Middle Ages who appreciated Plato, it was because they understood from Augustine that Plato and the Platonists had "come the closest" to Christianity, as Augustine had written in the *City of God*.[3] They

---

[1] Marsilio Ficino, "Proem," in Ficino, *Platonic Theology*, 1: 8–13.

[2] Ibid., 1: 9.

[3] Augustine, *City of God*, 8.9. See Eugenio Garin, *Studi sul Platonismo medievale* (Florence: Le Monnier, 1958); Stephen Gersh, *Middle Platonism and Neoplatonism: The Latin Tradition* (Notre Dame: University of Notre Dame Press, 1986); Tullio Gregory, *Platonismo medievale: studi e ricerche* (Rome: Istituto storico italiano per il medioevo, 1958); Hankins, *Humanism and Platonism*, 2: 7–26; Raymond Klibansky, *The Continuity of the Platonic Tradition During the Middle Ages* (London: The Warburg Institute, 1939; repr. with supplement,

knew doctrines attributed to Plato, such as the immortality of the soul and the notion that there was a world that stood above and superintended our own and was the home of immaterial purity.

But they did not have to wrestle, as did Ficino, with Plato's actual works, for the most part. Of all of Plato's more than thirty surviving works, medieval thinkers had very few available in Latin, and the ones they did have were relatively uncontroversial. In the early fifteenth century, as we have seen, Bruni and his cohort appreciated Plato for his dialogues and for the effect they had on him and his contemporaries, as they provided models of how learned conversations including different viewpoints might be conducted among notional social equals. Still, Bruni with his eminent practicality soon turned to Aristotle as his preferred philosopher, thinking him more suitable for a larger proportion of the citizenry, realizing that Plato was more dangerous to the multitude and thus more suitable for mature, educated men.

Ficino, however, was much more interested in integrating what he believed important about Plato with Christianity. He was an excellent translator and scholar, and he left nothing out. When he came to scandalous passages, Ficino explained them by means of allegory.[4] Most importantly, Ficino believed that to further his vision of a new, deeper type of Christianity, one that would be informed by the ancient theological tradition that included Plato, he needed to reach many segments of society. It was this very impulse that drove the composition of his *Platonic Theology*.

Though it is considered Ficino's most important independent philosophical work, the *Platonic Theology*, it must be said, has not made it onto any canonical lists of classic works of philosophy. Part of this neglect has to do with the general disregard that Italy's long fifteenth century has suffered in the intellectual realm. But the truth is that Ficino's *Platonic Theology* is in many ways a difficult or even, one dares to say, an off-putting work. On the one hand, there are passages, especially in the Preface, that are lyrical in the way they evince Ficino's deeply felt motivations. He writes, for example,

> Anyone who reads very carefully the works of Plato that I translated in their entirety into Latin some time ago will discover among many other matters two of utmost importance: the worship of God with piety and

Munich: Kraus, 1981); Klibansky, *Plato's Parmenides in the Middle Ages and the Renaissance: A Chapter in the History of Platonic Studies* (Toronto: University of Toronto Libraries, 2011); Klibansky, ed., *Plato Latinus* (London: The Warburg Institute, 1940); John Marenbon, *Aristotelian Logic, Platonism and the Context of Early Medieval Philosophy in the West* (Aldershot: Ashgate, 2000), esp. studies XII and XV.

[4] See Hankins, *Plato*, 304–59.

understanding, and the divinity of souls. On these depend our whole perception of the world, the way we lead our lives, and all our happiness.[5]

Ficino is signaling to his prospective patron, Lorenzo de' Medici, that he, Ficino, is diligent ("in their entirety"). Ficino with the utmost sincerity is foregrounding religious ritual and the nature of humanity. As to ritual, Ficino says that God must be worshiped with "piety and understanding." He is convinced that there are hidden depths in traditions not traditionally considered Christian, Platonism among them, that must be brought to society's attention, so that the profundity, centrality, and necessity of Christianity can shine as brightly as they deserve to do. As to the nature of humanity, Ficino is adamant that all need to be convinced, not just as a matter of course but also as a matter of importance, that the nature of humanity includes at its very center the human soul, a soul that is immortal and divine.

On the other hand, the way Ficino makes his case regarding these two propositions can seem haphazard and unsystematic. One reason for this seeming haphazardness lies in the unique cultural situation in which Ficino found himself, one in which the fruits of Renaissance discoveries were being digested and assimilated. Before outlining his approach, it will be worthwhile to digress and consider just what those discoveries entailed, by focusing on Ficino's engagement with Neoplatonism. That appellation has tended to be used to describe a late ancient philosophical movement that had as its first great representative the philosopher Plotinus.

Plotinus, a devoted teacher with a large following, had been persuaded late in life to write down some of his teachings. These are known as the *Enneads*, a set of fifty-four chapters (six sets of nine), all of which both summarized and expounded on many of Plato's ideas and thoughts.[6] Living when he did in the third century CE, Plotinus had a long tradition of philosophical and religious thought behind him. His work, in effect, represents a kind of gathering together of many of Plato's key ideas, even as Plotinus supplemented them with guiding notions from other philosophical traditions, Aristotelian thought included.

[5] Ficino, "Proem," in Ficino, *Platonic Theology*, 1: 9–11.
[6] Plotinus, *Enneads*, 7 vols., ed. and tr. A.H. Armstrong (Cambridge, MA: Harvard University Press, 1966–88); see Werner Beierwaltes, *Das wahre Selbst: Studien zu Plotins Begriff des Geistes und des Einen* (Frankfurt am Main: Klostermann, 2001); Lloyd P. Gerson, *Plotinus* (London: Routledge, 1994); Gerson, ed., *The Cambridge Companion to Plotinus* (Cambridge: Cambridge University Press, 1996); Pierre Hadot, *Plotinus, or, the Simplicity of Vision*, tr. Michael Chase (Chicago: University of Chicago Press, 1993); Dominic J. O'Meara, *Plotinus: An Introduction to the Enneads* (Oxford: Oxford University Press, 1993); John Rist, *Plotinus: The Road to Reality* (Cambridge: Cambridge University Press, 1967).

Perhaps most important is Plotinus's position on the structure of being, or what we can call his ontology. He believed the universe of being (not necessarily coextensive with the physical universe we observe) had at the top a great, unified, generative principle, which he called the One.[7] The One resided above what we traditionally consider being, so high on the scale that it is difficult to conceptualize. It had one main enterprise, which was to think. That process of thinking led it to "overflow" into other, lower levels of being. The next down the scale was termed "Mind," after which one found "Soul," which was itself followed by a fourth realm of being which, finally, included nature – the things we see and hear and physically experience through our senses and, of course, the realm of being in which we as human beings find ourselves.[8]

Plotinus had inherited from Plato and Platonism the basic notion that the immaterial was better than the material: matter, as we see around us every day, is corruptible. Things are born, they grow, but then they age, die, and pass away. It was only in the realm of the immaterial that seemingly perfect, eternal, and immortal things were thought to exist. The purest manifestation of this perfection was the One, for Plotinus. Individual human beings, once their formerly perfect, immaterial souls had passed downward, all the way into matter – into a body, now in part participated in the corruptible, material, mortal world. But only in part: for their souls contained sparks of the divine, seeds that, if properly cultivated, would grow and permit them to reascend that hierarchy and, eventually, to reach union with the One.[9] That union would be ecstatic, beyond all imaginable human experience and, because it was so difficult to accomplish, reserved to the very few: to the true philosophers who, turning within themselves by meditating, found that divine spark and did the difficult work of personal, spiritual exercise that enabled the great return to the One.[10]

Now if some of this sounds like Christianity, that is because it is like Christianity, notwithstanding the fact that Plotinus did not identify as a Christian and indeed was hostile to the new religion.[11] "The One" – in its supremacy, unitary nature, and power – resembles, if not completely, the Christian God, itself inherited from the God of the Hebrew Bible, who

[7] Plotinus, *Enneads*, 6.9.
[8] Ibid., 5.1 and 5.2.
[9] Ibid., 4.3, 4.4, 4.7; 3.8.
[10] Ibid., 6.9.10.
[11] See Werner Beierwaltes, *Platonismus im Christentum* (Frankfurt am Main: Klostermann, 1998); John Rist, "Plotinus and Christian Philosophy," in Gerson, ed., *The Cambridge Companion to Plotinus*, 386–413.

proclaimed himself coextensive with being: "I am Who Am."[12] The notion that our existence on earth was possibly deceptive, since it relied on our human imperfection, had been epitomized for Christianity by Saint Paul, who had written, "For now we see through a glass darkly; but then face to face: now I know in part; but then shall I know even as I am also known."[13] That Pauline sentiment also embedded within it the idea that those who lived rightly would someday see "face to face," meaning that the souls of the saved would be "face to face" with all powerful, all knowing God – not, in the end, all that unlike what Plotinus two centuries after Paul described as ecstatic union with the One.

There were differences of course. One major one was that the Christian God was a personal god, interested both in humanity at large (having sent his Son to earth to die as atonement for human sinfulness) and in human beings as individuals. The One of Plotinus was not nearly so definable. We human beings were in a sense "descended" from the One; and yet, far down the scale of being as we were, we were not "created in His image and likeness," as Genesis had memorably described God's act of creation.[14] The One was in a real sense the author of all that flowed downward from it, but, by definition, it could not be fully conceived by the human mind.

Another difference lay in what we might call translatability. Monotheism had become by Plotinus's day rather common among intellectuals scattered across the Mediterranean.[15] This monotheism was first and foremost philosophical, which is to say that many intellectuals by the third century CE believed that there was some one supreme being of some sort who ruled all things.[16] If you were Egyptian, you might call it Amoun Ra. If you were Roman, you might call it Jupiter, if Greek, Zeus, and so on. But the Judeo-Christian God insisted on formal and nominal supremacy and exclusivity. "You shall have no other Gods before me," as the commandment (stated in both Exodus and Deutronomy) held and as Paul would reiterate, as

[12] Ex. 3:14.
[13] I Cor. 13:12.
[14] Gen. 1:27.
[15] See Polymnia Athanassiadi and Michael Frede, eds., *Pagan Monotheism in Late Antiquity* (Oxford: Oxford University Press, 1999), esp. the editors' introduction, 1–20; Polymnia Athanassiadi, *Mutations of Hellenism in Late Antiquity* (Farnham, Surrey: Ashgate, 2015).
[16] See for the following paragraph Jan Assman, "Translating Gods: Religion as a Factor of Cultural (Un)Translatability," in Sanford Budick and Wolfgang Iser, eds., *The Translatability of Cultures: Figurations of the Space Between* (Stanford, CA.: Stanford University Press, 1996), 25–37; and Assman, *Of God and Gods: Egypt, Israel, and the Rise of Monotheism* (Madison: University of Wisconsin Press, 2008).

Christianity absorbed and then separated itself from Judaism: "For even if there are so-called Gods ... for us there is but one God."[17] For many Christians, the relative malleability of the pagan supreme being served as an irritant. Correspondingly, Christian rigidity engendered pagan enmity.

But the similarities were there and, in a sense, all the more powerful precisely because of the differences. If the One did not take a personal interest in us human beings, the One as the author of nature had at least planted seeds in us, seeds that we might cultivate through personal, spiritual training (what was called *askesis* in Greek) as a means of returning to our divine nature. Moreover, the soul was believed immortal and, importantly, the one supreme being (both the One and the Christian God) were understood as good, supremely so, which meant in practice that the universe as such was good, if only we could learn to accommodate ourselves to its variability and challenges.

Ficino looked back on Plotinus with admiration, seeking to integrate Plotinus into his own thinking. But it couldn't happen until Plotinus could be made to seem more human, and for that process too we need to look back to late antiquity. Plotinus himself had a brilliant student named Porphyry (234–305), who also served as Plotinus's biographer and editor. In his biography of Plotinus, Porphyry painted the picture of a great-souled, natural teacher, one who cared so little about writing that he needed to be persuaded to write down his teachings.[18] Plotinus in Porphyry's telling was relentlessly inward focused, as well, living the philosophy he preached: only through self-discipline could one really master oneself, find those divine seeds, and eventually reach ecstatic union with the One. This union was so difficult that Plotinus himself only achieved it four times, Porphyry said, in the time they were together.[19] Unwittingly, Porphyry was signaling the problem with Plotinus, a problem that straddled Platonic philosophy and Christianity as they evolved side by side: what was to be done about ordinary people, who could never be expected to master the kind of ascetic self-discipline that Plotinus suggested was necessary to reach the divine? Concomitantly, what was the place of the true philosopher in society? If even the great Plotinus was only able to reach the divine so rarely, what hope was there for the rest of us? Not much, it would seem.

Into this mix, on the Platonic side, came another philosopher, Iamblichus (c. 240–325), who began as a student of Porphyry, only – in the event – to

---

[17] Ex. 20:3; Dt. 5:7; 1 Cor. 8:5–6.
[18] Porphyry, "Life of Plotinus," in Plotinus, *Enneads*, vol. 1, 2–87; secs. 3–5 on writing.
[19] Ibid., sec. 23.

become his antagonist.[20] What divided them happened to be the questions just mentioned. Plotinus like all his contemporaries had believed that there existed what he and others called "sympathies" in the universe.[21] These were, in effect, linkages between things earthly and divine, properties that, though hidden on the surface, existed as part of the deep fabric of being. You might find a plant, for instance, believed by convention to have a relationship to the sun, itself a heavenly body invested with a lot of power. Take the lotus, which, when the sun sets, folds its petals but then opens them on the sun's rising, or other plants that seem to follow the course of the sun, or rocks that had a natural relationship to some celestial body, and so on.[22] The world, nature, was full of physical existence of all different sorts, and those manifestations of existence were all connected, the heavenly to the earthly. Think, today, of any sort of plant that has a naturally occurring medicinal property (eucalyptus, say, for sore throats). Whereas our tendency is to offer a natural explanation for that medicinal property, for premodern people, the propensity was to assume that the property was natural but that the natural status of the property formed part of a divine social economy. As with medicine, so too with access to the divine. The world was thought to be full of physical things that, if approached properly, with the right rituals, could be used to access the divine. And here is where the differences between Plotinus's approach and that of an emerging consensus about rituals, both pagan and Christian, emerged.

For Plotinus, reaching the divine was an interior process, one that a true philosopher needed to discipline himself correctly to achieve – on his own power, with his own mind at his service. To get where we need to go – to arrive at and become like the divine – Plotinus says, "We cannot get there on foot; for our feet only carry us everywhere in this world, from one country to another. You must not get ready a carriage, either, or a boat. Let all these things go, and do not look. Shut your eyes, and change to and wake another

---

[20] For some of the arguments that follow, see Christopher S. Celenza, "Late Antiquity and Florentine Platonism: The 'Post-Plotinian' Ficino," in M.J.B. Allen and V.R. Rees, eds., *Marsilio Ficino: His Theology, His Philosophy, His Legacy* (Leiden, Boston, Cologne: Brill, 2002), 71–97; on Iamblichus, see Henry J. Blumenthal and E. Gillian Clark, eds., *The Divine Iamblichus: Philosopher and Man of the Gods* (Bristol: Bristol Classical Press, 1993); John Dillon, "Iamblichus of Chalcis (circa 240–325 AD)," *Aufstieg und Niedergang der römischen Welt*, 36.2 (1988), 862–909; and Gregory Shaw, *Theurgy and the Soul: The Neoplatonism of Iamblichus* (University Park: Pennsylvania State University Press, 1995).

[21] See, for example, Plotinus, *Enneads*, 4.3.11.

[22] See for one example, another later Platonist, Proclus, in his *De arte sacrificali* in *Catalogue des manuscrits Alchimiques grecs*, 8 vols., ed. Bidez et al. (Brussels: Lamertin, 1924–32), 6: 139–51, at 149.

way of seeing, which everyone has but few use."[23] Relying on anything in nature as a kind of automatic way of channeling divine power was suspect in Plotinus's eyes. Porphyry, Plotinus's student and biographer, vacillated on this point.

But Iamblichus turned in the opposite direction. He believed instead in something that he called *theourgia* in Greek, commonly rendered in English as "theurgy." The roots of the Greek word reveal his thinking: *theion* means "divine" and *ergon* means "work." So theurgy could signify "doing divine work" or even "working the divine." In practice, what this indicated was that rituals grew increasingly important in defining and shaping how one accessed the divine. How could lowly, mortal humans, embedded in matter as they were, think they might influence the immortal, perfect gods? Through theurgy. Iamblichus says:

> Of the works of theurgy performed on any given occasion, some have a cause that is secret and superior to all rational explanation, others are like symbols [a word that can also mean something like "passwords"], conse-crated from all eternity to the higher beings, others preserve some other image, even as nature in its generative role imprints (upon things) visible shapes from invisible reason-principles.[24]

The gods have embedded these and other properties in the universe, so that accessing them through the right sorts of rituals means one is participating in a divine plan. Theurgy signified, in Iamblichus's formulation, the operation of "ineffable acts correctly performed, acts which are beyond all under-standing, and by the power of the unutterable symbols which are intelligible only to the gods."[25] You perform a ritual – sing a sacred song, say, accom-panied by the right symbols, or offer an animal sacrifice, or recite prayers that possess magical words ... and the effect is automatic. If the ritual is done correctly, if the right materials are used, and if the right circumstances are observed, then the efficacy of the whole process does not depend on your mind or mental state but rather on the ritual. Iamblichus goes on: "For in fact the actual tokens of themselves perform their proper function even without our conscious thought, and the ineffable power of the gods, towards whom these things draw us up, of itself recognizes its own images, but not by being

---

[23] Plotinus, *Enneads*, 1.6.8.
[24] Iamblichus, *De mysteriis*, ed. Edouard des Places (Paris: Les Belles Lettres, 1966), 2.11; passage cit. and tr. in John Dillon, "Iamblichus' Defence of Theurgy: Some Reflections," *The International Journal of the Platonic Tradition* 1 (2007), 30–41, at 34. See also the fundamental study of Shaw, as earlier.
[25] Iamblichus, *De mysteriis*, 2.11; tr. Dillon, "Iamblichus' Defence," 37.

summoned up by our intellectual activity."[26] The gods will answer those sorts of prayers, since they have created a chain of causation in the universe that sits, waiting to be activated.

The first thing to note: this position regarding ritual is very much not in the spirit of Plotinus's views. Plotinus conceded that these hidden sympathies existed, but he believed the philosopher's only job was to turn within to ascend. Second: Iamblichus's view (in contrast to that of Plotinus) is pluralistic (if we think of philosophy not as a rarefied practice to be shared fully only by a necessarily small elite). Many people can benefit from the practices and rituals involved, rituals that were seen as legitimate expressions of religion, or rather, of philosophy, keeping in mind that philosophy was considered the pursuit of a style of life. This large number of possible beneficiaries included philosophers (indeed, Iamblichus and those who followed him believed that philosophers too needed to practice these rituals), but it also encompassed a wider variety of people. Accordingly, the third matter worthy of observation is how similar some of these impulses were to certain tendencies in Christianity. In Iamblichus's day, Christianity had accrued large numbers of followers. But, still, it was one among a number of religious outlets available in the ancient Mediterranean world.[27] By the end of the fourth century, however, Christianity had evolved into a much stronger religion. And pagans and Christians, opposed to each other though they were, were arguing over the same things.

In the case of ritual, the Christian approach emerged in the doctrine of sacraments. By the era of Saint Augustine (354–430), a belief about them was solidified in Christianity, to which a name would be given much later: sacraments were held to function *ex opere operato* – "from the work having been worked," meaning that sacraments would work properly if the rituals surrounding them were done correctly. The question in Augustine's day had been the following: if, for example, a corrupt priest administered the sacrament of the Eucharist, would the sacrament function correctly, turning (as was believed) the bread and wine into the body and blood of Christ and allowing the recipient access to divinity? Or would the priest's vitiated character instead somehow invalidate the sacrament, thereby denying the participant all the benefits the sacrament was believed to confer?

Augustine answered these questions decisively, arguing definitively and influentially that the character of the priest had nothing to do with the

---

[26] Ibid., tr. Dillon, "Iamblichus' Defence," 38.

[27] See Ramsey MacMullen, *Paganism in the Roman Empire* (New Haven: Yale University Press, 1981).

efficacy of the sacrament.[28] Sacraments are visible signs of the conferral and possession of God's grace; they represented ways of automatically accessing divinity. Behind Augustine stood all the debates among Platonists.

It is tempting when writing history to succumb to what we might call a fallacy of origins – the scholar's search becomes a search for origins: who said it first? Who did it first? Far more important is to see the texture of conversations. This case is no exception. It is not that the Platonists did all this first and then Augustine adopted their doctrines, or conversely that Platonists were reacting only to Christian ideas. Rather, it was a common conversation, held among proponents who had different views about religion, but who (as often occurs in the case of such vitriolic debates) were quarreling over the same problems. Was religion/philosophy reserved for only a few? Or was it something that could and should be shared by all? Could our human actions in the world cooperate somehow with the divine? Or was the divine so far from us that our earthly actions could not even be imagined as attracting the notice of the divine?

These questions and others like them have never had definitive answers. They have been asked continually throughout the history of philosophy and the history of religion, the Christian religion included. Which is why, when Ficino began discovering and translating these late ancient Greek pagan texts, the possibilities took on an explosive patina, as if one were on the edge of theological acceptability, an edge whose outer limits one could discern only once they were crossed.

Some of the earliest Greek-to-Latin translations on which Ficino worked in the 1460s happened, in fact, to be works of later Platonists, Iamblichus especially, works that are still preserved in Ficino's early versions in two manuscripts in the Vatican Library.[29] What Ficino discovered there was something unlike anything else he had previously encountered. Plotinus, Porphyry, and Iamblichus (especially the latter two) had reserved a special place in their thinking for Pythagoras.[30] This mysterious ancient thinker had preceded Plato and Socrates, had thought that number was the prime

---

[28] Augustine, *Traité anti-Donatistes*, 5 vols. (Bruges: DeBrouwer, 1963–65), esp. 2, *De baptismo libri VIII*, ed. G. Bavard, at VI.4–5 (pp. 412–14). The connections between the pagan and Christian views were noted by Gregory Shaw, "Theurgy: Rituals of Unification in the Neoplatonism of Iamblichus," *Traditio*, 41 (1985), 1–28.

[29] See Gentile, "Sulle prime traduzioni." The manuscripts are MSS Vatican City, Biblioteca Apostolica Vaticana, Vat. Lat. 5953 and 4530.

[30] See Mark J. Edwards, "Two Images of Pythagoras: Iamblichus and Porphyry," in Blumenthal and Clark, *The Divine Iamblichus*, 159–72; Dominic J. O'Meara, *Pythagoras Revived: Mathematics and Philosophy in Late Antiquity* (Oxford: Oxford University Press, 1989).

principle ruling the universe, and had established a religious identity along-side the more overtly rationalistic positions often associated with him – the mathematical Pythagorean theorem (wherein the square of a triangle's hypo-tenuse equals the sum of the squares of the other two sides) being especially noteworthy.[31] But Pythagoras had, by design, written nothing.

As the centuries after his death wore on, Pythagoras became an especially appealing blank slate onto which one could inscribe one's own passions, predilections, and theories. Of all the three great late ancient Platonists, it was Iamblichus who made the most of Pythagoras. He wrote a ten-volume set of works concerning Pythagoras and Pythagoreanism, of which four survived into Ficino's day.[32] By 1463, Ficino translated or paraphrased these works.[33] It is worth noting that this moment occurred when he was not yet thirty, when he still had the lion's share of Plato's dialogues in front of him, and when he was far from working on Plotinus. It is reasonable to assume both that these works of Iamblichus had special interest for Ficino and that they remained with him, coloring and inflecting his view of what Plato, Plotinus, and others had meant in their thinking.

Most important was the twofold notion regarding Pythagoras to which Iamblichus adhered and gave expression: that Pythagoras was both divine and sent down by the gods to help save humanity. As Iamblichus put it: "through some unutterable, almost inconceivable likeness to the gods, his hearing and mind were intent upon the celestial harmonies of the cosmos."[34] Pythagoras established standards of behavior, he educated his followers well, and he believed that friends should hold all things in common: the latter a sentiment that Ficino would have seen in Plato's *Republic* and, importantly, in the *Acts of the Apostles*.[35]

The result of all this early exposure to later Platonism was manifold. Ficino would have seen, first, that Iamblichus, a known anti-Christian, had embraced – even theorized – doctrines such as theurgy, which had powerful affinities to known Christian practices (in this case, sacraments). Moreover,

---

[31] On Ficino and Pythagoras, see Christopher S. Celenza, "Pythagoras in the Renaissance: The Case of Marsilio Ficino," *Renaissance Quarterly* 52 (1999), 667–711.

[32] The four works are Iamblichus, *Protrepticus*, ed. Ermenegildo Pistelli (Stuttgart: Teubner, 1888); *De communi mathematica scientia*, ed. Nicola Festa (Stuttgart: Teubner, 1891); *In Nicomachi Arithmeticam introductionem*, ed. Ermenegildo Pistelli (Stuttgart: Teubner, 1894); *De vita pythagorica*, ed. L. Deubner (Leipzig: Teubner, 1937); there is an English translation of the last work in Iamblichus, *On the Pythagorean Life*, tr. with notes and an introduction by Gillian Clark (Liverpool: Liverpool University Press, 1989).

[33] See Gentile, "Sulle prime traduzioni."

[34] Iamblichus, *De vita pythagorica*, sec. 15; tr. Clark, p. 27.

[35] Plato, *Republic*, 5.462b–d; Acts, 4:2.

for Ficino, ideas regarding salvific figures suddenly came to seem not just the
property of Christianity as it was known and understood in Ficino's day but
rather as part of an age-old tradition, which many thinkers, in many contexts,
had served to represent for humankind. Christ, of course, had been sent by
God to save humanity. But so (as an earlier tradition seemed to indicate) had
Pythagoras. The *Acts of the Apostles* indicated that, ideally, Christians should
hold all things in common. But that very notion had an ancient pedigree,
stemming from Pythagoras and the ideal community he had created and that
was manifested in Plato's work as well. Recall that Ficino was an ordained
priest of the Roman Catholic Church. What do you do, in that case, when
you find out from hitherto lost texts that beliefs you held sacred and proper to
your religion alone also inhered in the thinking of non-, or even anti-
Christians, some of whom had walked the earth well before the providential
birth of Christ?

Ficino's answers were manifold, but all of them shared one central
assumption: Christianity enfolded within itself the truth. The more interesting problem for us, looking back at a remarkable, but in many ways alien,
culture was this: what was the nature of Christianity? This question, perhaps
the guiding one of his life and career, motivated Ficino to write a work
On the Christian Religion, a text that he considered so important that (like his
On Love) he issued it in both Latin and vernacular versions. Written in
1474–75, the work came at a noteworthy moment in his career. He had
become a fully ordained priest in 1473, and he had finished writing his
Platonic Theology (in 1474) without yet having it published in print. *On the
Christian Religion* represented the first time Ficino had one of his works
printed. He brought out the vernacular version first, presenting it to
a friend, Bernardo del Nero, following it soon thereafter with a Latin version
that he dedicated to Lorenzo de' Medici.[36] In the Preface to Del Nero,
Ficino says, "since religion is a gift and a virtue belonging to all in common, it
seemed to me to be a good idea to compose this book not only in the Latin
language, but also in Tuscan, so that the book, treating of universal virtue as it
does, would be common to all."[37]

Early in the work, Ficino makes a powerful case that religion and humanity are linked and that religiosity is part of human nature: "man, the most
complete of all living creatures, stands out and differentiates himself from
inferior beings in this way most of all: the property thanks to which he joins

---

[36] See Cesare Vasoli, "Il *De christiana religione* di Marsilio Ficino," in *Bruniana et Campanelliana*,
13 (2007), 403–28; Kristeller, *Supplementum*, 1: LVIII–LX; the Preface to the vernacular
version is edited in Kristeller, *Supplementum*, 1: 10–12.

[37] Ficino, "Preface," in Kristeller, *Supplementum*, 1:11.

himself to even more perfect beings, which is to say to divine beings."[38] Animals do not share this propensity to worship and to try to reach the divine. Moreover, "if religion were vain, man would be the most incomplete of all animals and, for this, deranged and wretched in the highest degree."[39] Human beings worship, they incline toward God, they even at times deny themselves things (in the enterprise of fasting, say); all of this would represent only folly were religion something untrue, unnecessary, or ineffective.[40]

The naturalness of religion represents one of Ficino's main emphases in *On the Christian Religion*, one that he believed to his core and that he carried with him throughout his life. Another firm conviction is the importance of attending to the youth. Children are born naturally respectful of religion, Ficino says. But then, when they mature and reach the age of reason, their education can sometimes turn them from religion. They reach a point when they begin to study "the causes of things with great diligence" and they then "begin to want not to affirm anything at all, if it is not something for which they have been studying the key causes." The result: "Soon, for the most part, they turn away from religion, if they do not place their trust in the laws and in the prudence of their elders."[41] This sense that the future of society rested on the still undeveloped shoulders of the young never left Ficino, indeed only intensified over time. He came to believe that everything he did, in effect, served to teach different constituencies of society; and none was more important than the young, so easily led astray as they might be by an education that was not structured correctly.

Yet a third element also emerged in Ficino's *On the Christian Religion*: the notion that every monotheistic religion has something good that inheres in it:

> Divine providence does not allow that, in any span of time, any region of the world be completely without religion, though he does permit – in different places and eras – different worship rituals [*modi d'adoratione / ritus adorationis*] to exist. Perhaps it is the case that such a variety – regulated as it is by God, generates a kind of wondrous beauty in the universe.[42]

---

[38] I cite from Marsilio Ficino, *Libro di Marsilio Ficino della Cristiana Religione* (Florence: Niccolò di Lorenzo, undated but before March 25, 1475; Hain-Copinger, 7071), un-paginated, chap. 1 and from Marsilio Ficino, *De christiana religione*, in Marsilio Ficino, *Op.*, pp. 1–77, at p. 2. There are some small differences between the vernacular and Latin versions, noted in Kristeller, *Supplementum*, 1: 7–8.

[39] Ficino, *Libro*, chap. 1; *Op.*, p. 2.

[40] Ibid.

[41] Ficino, *Libro*, chap. 3; *Op.*, p. 3.

[42] Ficino, *Libro*, chap. 4; *Op.*, p. 4.

It is important to God that he be worshiped and honored, whereas the way it occurs is less so: content, not form, matters.

What this conviction meant in practice was that Ficino presented throughout his life a curious mixture of tolerance and provincialism: tolerance, in the sense that he was more than willing to entertain the notions that non-Christian religious practices, including Judaism and Islam, shared in that core of truth (as did the wilder reaches of later Platonism, as we have seen); provincialism, in that he was convinced that in the final analysis it was Christianity that would encompass and represent all of those truths, provided it were understood and shaped correctly and under the right sort of guidance: guidance that he was more than ready to provide.

It was in his most extensive work of philosophical synthesis, the *Platonic Theology*, that all these tendencies came to fruition. It was here that Ficino gathered arguments expressing a Christian Platonism at the highest and most technical levels; it was here that he planted "seeds," as he put it, for all different segments of society to induce them to the correct beliefs regarding religion; and it was here, finally, that he argued for what, on balance, he considered the most important belief of all: that the human soul was immortal.[43]

Ficino worked on his *Platonic Theology* – with its telling subtitle *On the Immortality of the Soul* – from 1469 to 1474, when it was substantively complete. He did not print-publish the work until 1482.[44] He dedicated it to Lorenzo de' Medici, who, Ficino hoped, would continue to support his work as Cosimo had earlier done. Ficino's goal was not to persuade anyone who resolutely denied Christianity (an almost unimaginably small minority in any case). Instead his hope was to solidify the faith of those whom he called the *ingeniosi*, or *acuta ingenia* – the "acute wits" – precisely the kind of people who had been educated in the ways outlined earlier, or those indeed who, partaking of the Renaissance's new culture of openness to hitherto unknown but possibly dangerous texts, might have been wavering in their faith. They needed "bait," Ficino says, to "lure" them to religion, and that bait had to be philosophical.[45]

---

[43] On the *Platonic Theology*, see Kristeller, *Il pensiero*; Ardis Collins, *The Secular Is Sacred: Platonism and Thomism in Ficino's Platonic Theology* (The Hague: Nijhoff, 1974); on seeds, see Hiroshi Hirai, "Concepts of Seeds and Nature in the Work of Marsilio Ficino," in Allen and Rees, *Marsilio Ficino*, 257–84.

[44] Marsilio Ficino, *Theologia platonica de immortalitate animae* (Florence: Antonio Miscomini, 1482), Hain-Copinger 7075; see Kristeller, *Supplementum*, 1: LX.

[45] See Michael J.B. Allen, *Synoptic Art: Marsilio Ficino on the History of Platonic Interpretation* (Florence: Olschki, 1998), esp. 1–49; Ficino uses the wording *acuta ingenia* in his Preface to his translation of Plotinus: "Non est profecto putandum acuta et quodammodo philosophica

Accordingly, in the *Platonic Theology*, Ficino tries to attract different types of possible contemporary readers. For those Renaissance enthusiasts who loved and admired classical literature, Ficino presented many quotations from classical authors. Ficino himself had solid grounding in Aristotelian thought, as did many others. Thus, throughout the *Platonic Theology* he employs Aristotelian concepts, many of which had been woven into the enterprise of doing philosophy, given the attention to Aristotle in medieval university culture. Ficino also offered countless quotations of and references to scripture. Here the imagined reader was reactionary, someone who perhaps saw and disapproved of all the new enthusiasm for classical authors, someone Ficino wanted to reassure and convince that this new vision of Christianity was, indeed, still Christianity. Ficino, in short, wanted to appeal to everyone.

All these goals were noble ones, and the ambition of the enterprise, broad as it was, cannot help but inspire admiration. But it would be difficult to say that Ficino's *Platonic Theology* was a success, or at least completely so. Part of the reason for dissatisfaction has to do with genre. Ficino deals, for example, with scholastic philosophical concepts. But his allusive play in the text forgoes the clarity and precision that undergirded scholastic thinking, with its embrace of the "question" and "commentary" genre. He also deals with Platonic works. But by sacrificing Plato's dialogue format, Ficino loses the literary and emotional appeal those works possess. Finally, though he included fashionably humanistic classical allusions, his Latin was not written in the elevated, smooth, classicizing idiom most humanists had come to prize in his day. Though he tried to reach different constituencies, he addressed none of them in such a way that it would draw their attention completely.

Let us take as an example a section in Book Eighteen of the *Platonic Theology*, its last book, and one in which Ficino is attempting to resolve sticky questions regarding the immortality of the soul.[46] Ficino begins the book familiarly enough, in his tolerant mode, where he argues that Judaism, Christianity, and Islam all share some fundamental assumptions about creation writ large.[47] One of these assumptions had to do with the nature of the link between body and soul and what, precisely, happened to the body after, or beyond, physical death. The Catholic doctrine was (and is, for that matter)

---

hominum ingenia unquam alia quadam esca praeterquam philosophica ad perfectam religionem allici posse paulatim atque perduci. Acuta enim ingenia plerunque soli se rationi committunt, cumque a religioso quodam philosopho hanc accipiunt religionem subito commune libenter admittunt."

[46] Ficino, *Platonic Theology*, 18, v. 6, pp. 64–219.
[47] Ibid., 18.1, v. 6, pp. 64–65.

that, at the end of time and when God so decrees, human souls will be resurrected and in that process will be joined to real, physical bodies – not metaphorically or figuratively, but as a matter of literal truth.[48]

About this process Ficino says: "The three laws" – he means Judaism, Christianity, and Islam – "confirm this resurrection in the first place by invoking divine authority. For they say that God had often foretold through the prophets and apostles that he would raise many men in various ages from the dead; and that holy men, moreover, even those deprived of life, had continued to perform miracles, and continue to do so every day."[49] The first implication, then, is that bodily death does not mean annihilation. Something in the physical remains can, in certain cases, remain potent enough to effect wonders in the world, things that seem to be outside the normal course of nature but that, because of God's providence and power, flows through the otherwise lifeless bodies. Death, in this respect, is not death.

From the distant past, Ficino moves to the present: "Certainly in our own age, in the year 1477 in December and January, certain relics of the apostle Peter discovered in the town of Volterra made twelve miracles known, and they were prodigious miracles and made known to the people at large."[50] The recent occurrence of the example, along with the geographic specification, serves to testify for the miracles' authenticity. The fact that it was known to a significant number of people does the same. Ficino continues: "These and similar facts are the best witnesses of the resurrection, so much so that in his *Metaphysics* Avicenna asserts that one must believe divine authority when it proclaims the resurrection."[51] Here a modern reader backs up a bit. Who is Avicenna? Why is he relevant? Avicenna (c. 980–1037), an Islamic medieval philosopher, was known for his loosely Platonic interpretations of certain standard (sometimes paradoxically Aristotelian) texts, as well as for his medical writings.[52] Ficino is signaling his broad reading here, as well as his belief that thinkers from different, even non-Christian, traditions can have something useful to say.

---

[48] For the history of the concept of resurrection, see Fernando Vidal, "Brains, Bodies, Selves, and Science: Anthropologies of Identity and the Resurrection of the Body," *Critical Inquiry* 28 (2002), 930–74; Caroline Walker Bynum, *The Resurrection of the Body in Western Christianity, 200–1336* (New York: Columbia University Press, 1995).

[49] Ficino, *Platonic Theology*, 18.9, v. 6, pp. 169–71.

[50] Ibid., 171.

[51] Ibid.

[52] See Louis Gardet, *La pensée religieuse d'Avicenne* (Paris: Vrin, 1951); Lenn Goodman, *Avicenna* (London: Routledge, 1992); and Dimitri Gutas, *Avicenna and the Aristotelian Tradition* (Leiden: Brill, 1988).

Then he goes on to present four instances of what he calls a *ratio*, a Latin word that in this context means "proof."[53] The first of these will suffice to understand both Ficino's tone as well as the sense of confusion of genre that the *Platonic Theology* presents. It is worth quoting in full:

> First proof. Since one natural composite is made from the soul and the human body, and the soul is affected by a natural instinct for the body, obviously the soul is bound to the body not only because of the universal order but also because of the order of its very own nature. Hence it comes about that it is contrary to the order of the universe and of its own nature alike that the soul remain apart from the body. But after the body's death souls do remain everlastingly; and since that which is contrary to nature cannot be everlasting, the result is that at some point souls are going to receive their bodies back.[54]

Ficino wants, first, to foreground the power of nature and the natural order; he is saying that the human soul is in its most natural state when it is bound to the body. This sentiment shows Ficino fully in line with classic, Aristotelian teaching on the nature of hylomorphic unity: the idea that a thing is really only a thing if its form and matter are united. The soul is the form of the human being, whereas the body is the matter. Therefore, it is "contrary to the order of the universe and of its own nature alike that the soul remain apart from the body." Ficino however is aware of death – the death of a person's earthly physical body, after which, he says, souls "remain everlastingly." But he has already said that souls possess a natural instinct for the body. Since this instinct, this joining, is a part of nature and since "that which is contrary to nature cannot be everlasting," then at some point souls and bodies must be rejoined; hence, we have the first "proof" for resurrection.

This argument, as well as the other three immediately following, depends for its effectiveness on logical premises arranged in such a way that they seem incontrovertible: logic used in the service of faith. In truth, his argument would have been more effective if it had been written in *quaestio*-format, the standard language of medieval philosophy, whereby a proposition is set out, arguments pro and contra are enumerated, and, finally, a solution is offered. Needless to say, however one might argue for the notion of human bodily resurrection, belief, finally, depends on faith in the notion that, at some as yet undetermined point, human, earthly time will come to an end. God will have decided that the world as it is has existed long enough. He will offer a *recreatio*, a "new" or "second" creation, one in which, after eons of motion, all things

---

[53] Ficino, *Platonic Theology*, 18.9, v. 6, pp. 171–73.
[54] Ibid., p. 171.

will be at rest.[55] In the final analysis, "it is God's measureless power that is the efficient cause of the resurrection. So it is most appropriate that the infinity of life that raises the dead be the same infinity that preserves the dead free from death for eternity."[56] Life on earth as we know it now is different from what it will be like then: "At present on earth and disjoined from the God, the soul unites, sustains, and lifts the body contrary to the nature of its elements; but later, conjoined with supercelestial God, the soul is able to raise it with itself to the sublime region of the aether."[57] "Aether." Ficino accepted the Ptolemaic notion that above the terrestrial universe (that region that is available to us through our senses) there existed a fifth element, or "quintessence," beyond the four familiar ones of earth, air, water, and fire.[58] The universe was believed to be arranged in concentric spheres. Those spheres on the innermost level housed the terrestrial world (everything, essentially, below the moon). The outer levels housed the visible celestial bodies (the planets, some stars) that moved through the universe surrounded by "aether," an element with no density. Ficino says that it is there, eventually, where the resurrected will reside. They will become closer to and more like God. Ficino thus offers a Christian transformation of the Platonic notion of becoming "similar to God" (homoiôsis theô): that process by which you become like a god, the whole goal of the philosophy of Plotinus, which Ficino is seeking to reorient here and to adapt to Christian theological imperatives.[59] And yet, given all that Ficino mixes into his discussion, there remains a lack of clarity and precision that makes that last point possess less impact than it ought to do.

If it were more persuasively and consistently written, Ficino's *Platonic Theology* could be considered his most important work. As it stands, however, his translations and commentaries, on the one hand, and his letters, on the other, take pride of place in having had the greatest influence on his own and succeeding generations.

Ficino's greatest contribution to translation was his *Complete Works of Plato*, which he had completed in draft form by 1469.[60] Since antiquity

---

[55] Ibid., 174–75.
[56] Ibid., 177.
[57] Ibid., 179.
[58] See Michael J. Crowe, *Theories of the World from Antiquity to the Copernican Revolution* (New York: Dover, 1990); Owen Gingrich, *The Eye of Heaven: Ptolemy, Copernicus, Kepler* (New York: American Institute of Physics, 1993).
[59] See Plato, *Theatetus*, 176a, for *homoiôsis theô*. Damascius, active in the sixth century CE, used the term *theôsis*, in his *De principiis*, ed. C.A. Ruelle (Paris, 1889), 100; for a more recent edition, see Damascius, *Traité des premiers principes*, ed. and tr. Leendert G. Westerink and Joseph Combés, 3 vols. (Paris: Belles Lettres, 1986).
[60] See Hankins, *Plato*, I: 300–18; Kristeller, *Supplementum*, I: CXLVII–CLVII.

Plato's work had been organized into nine sets of four (sets called "tetra-logies"), the result of an influential edition produced in the early first century CE, well over three centuries after Plato's death.[61] In those intervening years, works crept in to what was considered the body of Plato's work, some of which scholars today consider inauthentic. For Ficino, however, there was no question that the thirty-six texts in the traditional set (thirty-five dialogues plus the letters attributed to Plato) were authentic. Ficino did not follow the ordering of the Platonic texts as presented in the tetralogies as he approached his translating enterprise; his edition, when published, employed his own order, rather than the traditional one.[62]

Translating Plato and presenting Plato's work to his contemporaries represented a key element of Ficino's overall program. It can seem puzzling that he waited as long as he did to have them print-published. The date he chose was 1484, a date that scholarship has revealed as astrologically impor-tant in Ficino's eyes.[63] This fact reminds us, if we ever need reminding, that Ficino lived in a premodern world. Indeed, in his "Life of Plato," which originated as a letter to a friend and then wound up in his *Complete Works of Plato*, Ficino takes pains at the outset to delineate the position of the planets when Plato was born.[64]

But through it all is Ficino's conviction that Plato somehow represented a point of evolution far beyond that of everyday humanity. Even Plato's style was divine: "His style, I say, is similar more to a divine oracle than to human eloquence, now thundering deeply, now flowing with the sweetness of nectar, but always enfolding the hidden things of Heaven."[65] Overall, Ficino here and elsewhere indicates the need for the modern interpreter to bring out of any project the core of truth that exists within it.

In this case, the project is Plato, and the interpreter is Ficino himself. What is the core of truth? In the case of Plato, we can return from his translating enterprise to his *Platonic Theology*: there, Ficino wrote that it was his intention "to paint a portrait of Plato as close as possible to the Christian truth."[66] The interpreter has a mission that is highly active in its basic parameters and

---

[61] See Diogenes Laertius, 3: 56–61, in Diogenes Laertius, *Lives of Eminent Philosophers*, 2 vols., ed. and tr. R.D. Hicks (Cambridge, MA: Harvard University Press, 2000–05), pp. 326–31.

[62] Ficino's principal Greek manuscript did follow the ordering of the traditional Thrasyllan tetralogies: MS Florence, Biblioteca laurenziana, Plut. 85.9; for Ficino's ordering see Kristeller, *Supplementum*, 1: CLI-CLII.

[63] Hankins, *Plato*, 1: 302–4.

[64] Ficino, *Op.*, 769; *Letters*, 3:33.

[65] Ficino, *Op.*, 1129; cit. and tr. in Hankins, *Plato*, 1: 316.

[66] Ficino, *Platonic Theology*, Preface, v. 1, pp. 10–11.

intentions: that mission is not to find the intention of the author under study. It is, rather, to bring the truth out of the author under study, a truth that the author may not even have understood himself to be revealing. In the case of Ficino's translations of Plato, it is interesting to note that, unlike earlier translators in the fifteenth century (e.g., Leonardo Bruni), Ficino did not expurgate Platonic passages that seemed inappropriate.[67] As mentioned, passages throughout Plato contain open talk of homosexual conduct between men and boys.

Plato's *Phaedrus* is just such a dialogue, and it is worth examining it and Ficino's response to it, to see both the advantages and the limitations of Ficino's approach. In the *Phaedrus*, Socrates and Phaedrus, the interlocutors, discuss the nature of love, the power of oratory, and even toward the end the nature of writing. Throughout the dialogue gentle teasing occurs between the two, with the implications that Phaedrus has a crush on Lysias (an orator whose speech on how to persuade a reluctant boy to engage in sexual relations serves as the jumping off point for the dialogue's discussions on love) and that Socrates has a crush on another young man. When Ficino explains these and other passages elsewhere in his commentaries on Plato, he uses allegory, rather than literal interpretation, or he focuses on other parts of the dialogue, or he draws out what seems to him to be the dialogue's central message.

The structure of Plato's *Phaedrus* is as follows: the two interlocutors meet and talk. Phaedrus tells Socrates that Lysias has authored a wonderfully captivating speech on "love." The speech, which Phaedrus reveals he has in his possession, makes the case that a boy should yield (should grant sexual favors, in other words) to a prospective older partner who wanted only sex, who was not so besotted with the boy that the boy would be stifled and suffocated.[68] Socrates then critiques the speech and says he could do better.[69] So he delivers a speech on the same theme (the boy should yield to the older man not in love) using a structure and ordering of language that he, Socrates, believes better reaches its objective: persuasion.[70]

But then Socrates has a pang of conscience.[71] So he feels compelled to deliver another speech, one that will honor love as the divinity that love is, rather than presenting love as only a base tendency to satisfy one's physical

---

[67] Hankins, *Plato*, 1: 312–14.

[68] Plato, *Phaedrus*, in Plato, *Euthyphro, Apology, Crito, Phaedo, Phaedrus*, ed. and tr. Harold N. Fowler (Cambridge, MA: Harvard University Press, 2014), 227c–234e.

[69] Ibid., 235c.

[70] Ibid., 237a–241d.

[71] Ibid., 242c.

desires.[72] Socrates makes the case that physical love and the propensity to seek out, touch, and possess physical beauty is something implanted in us by the gods. To realize this gift's true potential, we must realize that the physical beauty represents, really, a symbol of that eternal, nonphysical, divine beauty, beauty that is permanent and unchanging. The real "lover," then, will indeed have physical relations with the boy. But he will then care for the boy, help educate him, help him succeed, and help him become a man.

Every person's soul, Socrates says, can be likened to a chariot in the sky, one in which the driver of the chariot is struggling with two horses, the tendencies of each verging in opposite directions. One horse wants always to rise higher; the other, unruly, aims ever downward. The responsibility of the driver is to keep them in balance and to direct them in such a way that all reach their proper objective. The human soul is the same: it possesses countervailing tendencies, both good and bad, and the well-trained and well-disposed person (the charioteer) must regulate those tendencies in all matters, love included. The interlocutors go on to discuss rhetoric – the art of persuasion – as well as, finally, writing, an art that can, in the way it "fixes" live speech and dialogical interaction, also deaden animated inquiry.[73]

Like his ancient models, Ficino believed each Platonic dialogue had what in antiquity was termed a *skopos*, an "aim" or "main purpose" – a reason why it was written that represented the main point the dialogue was supposed to make.[74] So when it comes to Plato's *Phaedrus*, Ficino distinguished between that dialogue and Plato's *Symposium*, noting that he had already commented on it (in his *On Love*, as we have seen). Ficino writes: "The *Symposium* principally treats of love and of beauty as a consequence; but the *Phaedrus* talks about love for beauty's sake."[75] Ficino then almost completely bypasses the overt references to homosexual sex: "take note of the modesty of Socratic love; for Socrates begins with his head veiled since he is about to say something less than honorable."[76] With this statement Ficino refers to Socrates's first speech, the one for which he feels immediate regret and that leads to the second speech on the true nature of love.

Ficino goes on to write:

Socrates defines base love as a certain passion or lust that rebels against the reason; it overwhelms opinion which is trying to do what is right and

[72] Ibid., 244a–257a.
[73] Ibid., 258c–279c.
[74] See Michael J.B. Allen, "Introduction," in Marsilio Ficino, *Commentaries on Plato*, ed. and tr. Michael J.B. Allen (Cambridge, MA.: Harvard University Press, 2008), at xvi–xvii.
[75] Ficino, *Commentaries on Plato*, ed. and tr. Allen, 39.
[76] Ibid., 41.

enraptures it instead with the pleasure of shape. In pursuing the definition, Socrates assigns us two leaders: one is our inborn desire for pleasure, the other is a sort of legitimate opinion that we gradually acquire through learning and that directs us towards what is honorable.[77]

It is in this fashion that Ficino begins to explain Plato's myth of the charioteer, with its two horses as stand-ins for different parts of our consciousness, one drawn toward beauty but corruptible, the other with the potential to guide us heavenward, but needing training.[78]

This example is one from among thousands that we could cite of Ficino using allegory and exposition to explain Plato, something Ficino does confidently, without feeling that he needed to omit any of the more salacious or scandalous parts of Plato, instead seeing them as interpretive challenges. Still, in this commentary, as in other commentaries and, indeed, as in his *Platonic Theology*, for every clear passage such as the ones just cited, Ficino verges far more often toward abstract and dense explanations, ones that weave together later Platonic texts, biblical passages, and a deep familiarity with medieval philosophical tradition. Again, what we see is a hybrid genre, one that did not fit into standard ways of approaching texts, a kind of dead end.

It is for these reasons that his letters represent, on balance, the best way to see what sort of impact Ficino had on his contemporaries. His correspondence was vast and multi-faceted, and while this is not the place for a full accounting of Ficino's letters, a brief glimpse will be useful, both to see how they were part of Ficino's social economy and as a springboard to an examination of what that social economy looked like.

Sometimes Ficino's correspondence was intended to keep his friends in the know, as in for example a 1477 letter where Ficino updates Bernardo Bembo, a Venetian diplomat and friend, on the course of his work: "I am composing a book on the providence of God and the freedom of human will, in which I refute, to the best of my ability, those pronouncements of the astrologers which remove providence and freedom."[79] Here we see Ficino letting his friend know that he was dealing with one of the thorniest problems in his day and one in which we see, yet again, the porous boundaries between premodern and modern, superstition and science.

---

[77] Ibid.

[78] On this theme, see the classic studies of Michael J.B. Allen, *Marsilio Ficino and the Phaedran Charioteer: Introduction, Texts, Translations* (Berkeley: University of California Press, 1981); and Allen, *The Platonism of Marsilio Ficino: A Study of His Phaedrus Commentary, Its Sources and Genesis* (Berkeley: University of California Press, 1984).

[79] Ficino, *Op.* 771; *Letters*, 3: 48.

Everyone assumed, as we have seen, that the heavens had influence on earthly matters, an assumption that was certainly not wrong, if we consider the way the position of the moon impacts the tides through its gravitational pull. But the problem in Ficino's day, and indeed throughout the Middle Ages before him, was one of extent: just how much influence did the heavenly bodies – stars, planets, comets, and so on – have on human life? Was the web of universal forces that was assumed to exist so powerful, so all embracing, that it essentially controlled human action? For Ficino, as indeed for many before him, the danger was that if that latter proposition were true, then human free will would be extinguished. In that fashion the entire divine social economy of rewards and punishments after death would cease to make sense. Here, in this letter, all we get is a glimpse of Ficino's opinion (decidedly in favor of human free will) and a window, as well, into how premodern "publication" tended to work. You informed your friends about your work in progress; whetted their appetites for it; and thus hoped that, when and if your work emerged in a finished state, they would help circulate and diffuse it to their own network of friends and intellectual interlocutors. In this case, we know that Ficino did in fact write this work, but that he never had it print-published, nor did he circulate it widely.[80] But the letter lets us see that he was concerned about this problem and that he devoted significant amounts of time to it.

Most of Ficino's letters offer us, more than half a millennium later, insight into his personality. He was possessed of a gentle sense of humor, was an inveterate networker, and was always on track to spread his message. The conclusion of the letter in which he offered a biography of Plato sums much of this up. Citing a second-century CE Platonist, Ficino says: "With Apuleius of Madaura, let us freely proclaim: 'We, the family of Plato, know nothing except what is bright, joyful, celestial, and supreme.'"[81] That same letter, earlier on, offers an interesting hint about Ficino's – and Florence's – intellectual milieu, as the 1470s ended:

> There are some common rhymesters who without meriting it, usurp for themselves the name of poet. Roused as much by the difference in conduct as by the malice of envy, they mock shamelessly any man of excellence. And to these men a certain supreme license is allowed against good men rather than bad, especially in our time.[82]

[80]   Kristeller, *Supplementum*, 2: 11–76.
[81]   Ficino, *Op.* 770; *Letters*, 3: 48.
[82]   Ficino, *Op.* 770; *Letters*, 3: 47.

Who was this "rhymester," this unnamed poet who, when Ficino was revising this final version of this letter, seems to have gotten under his skin?

As we shall see, Ficino was and remained a leading intellectual in Laurentian Florence, that period, later glamorized, in which Lorenzo "the Magnificent" de' Medici (1449–92) served as Florence's leading citizen. Still, by the late 1470s, other voices were emerging, all of whom vied for a share of that most important currency in Renaissance cultural life: reputation.

I4

THE VOICES OF CULTURE IN LATE
FIFTEENTH-CENTURY FLORENCE

What heaven wants is not a miracle.
Many a portent at that moment came:
At once up in the sky the sun grew dim . . .

On the next morning King Marsilius,
greatly perturbed and in great agitation,
for all the sages of Toledo sent . . .

To Saragossa all those sages came
To give that matter their respected views –
Astrologers, magicians, necromancers,
Interpreters, diviners – all of them
(and they were many) valiant and well known.[1]

These lines are from a lengthy poetic epic of twenty-eight chapters, written
in Tuscan by Luigi Pulci (1432–84), precisely the troublesome "rhymester"
to whom Ficino was referring.[2] Pulci's *Morgante* was what we might call an
"anti-epic," a poem that mirrored some of the traditions of epic poetry,
mingled them together with the characters and plot devices of medieval
romances, and added enough vulgar burlesque – much of it drawn from the
bawdy oral poetry declaimed on the streets of Florence in the fifteenth
century – that it represents something truly unique.

---

[1] Luigi Pulci, *Morgante*, 2 vols., ed. Giuliano Dego (Milan: Rizzoli), cant. 25: 73, 81, and 82; tr.
in Luigi Pulci, *Morgante: The Epic Adventures of Orlando and His Giant Friend Morgante*, tr.
Joseph Tusiani, introduction and notes by Edoardo A. Lèbano (Bloomington: University of
Indiana Press, 1998), pp. 590–92.

[2] On it see Constance Jordan, *Pulci's* Morgante: *Poetry and History in Fifteenth-Century Florence*
(Washington, DC: The Folger Shakespeare Library, 1986). See also James Coleman and
Andrea Moudarres, eds., *Luigi Pulci in Renaissance Florence and Beyond: New Perspectives on his
Poetry and Influence* (Turnhout: Brepols, 2017).

In the 1470s in Florence, Pulci was a rival of Ficino's, so much so that Ficino referred to Pulci not only obliquely, in the letter that became the biography of Plato, but also, as we shall see, directly in other letters, even going so far as to confront Lorenzo de' Medici about Pulci, a confrontation that led to Pulci's removal from Florence. On the surface the two men, Ficino and Pulci, represent two of several cultural tendencies in the air then: the one austere, inclined toward scholarly study, veering toward Platonic wisdom, and private; the other, decidedly vernacular, earthy, funny, and very public. There is some truth in that general distinction. But beneath the surface, there emerge more similarities than one might otherwise imagine.

First, we might as well reveal what an attentive reader will already have suspected, regarding the passages cited earlier. Pulci is satirizing Ficino. The action and logic of the *Morgante* is set in the world of Charlemagne (742–814), the medieval emperor who, with an aggressively Christian program of reform, unified and indeed gave shape to Europe in some ways as we know it today. His exploits became the subject of poetry in the Middle Ages, most famously the *Chanson de Roland*, or *Song of Roland*, the first major French vernacular epic. The action is set in the southwest, in Spain, where Christians led by one of Charlemagne's trusted men, Roland, were fighting Muslims. The tale grew and was retold in different languages and contexts in the Middle Ages; in Italian, "Roland" became "Orlando," and it was partially on this series of myths and poems that Pulci drew. In his telling, the character who had been the Muslim ruler Masilla becomes "Marsilio," and in the earlier quotation and elsewhere, the kind of foreignness and shadiness that some associated with Ficino came through. For example, "King Marsilio" is associated with "astrologers, magicians, necromancers" – practitioners of arts and practices from which Ficino sought to dissociate himself but which, especially as he gradually moved to interpret the more recondite parts of the later Platonic tradition, stuck to his reputation, fairly or not.

Before he wrote the *Morgante*, in fact, Pulci had Ficino in his sights, having written a series of sonnets against Ficino. Pulci said things such as the following:

> Those who make such a big argument
> about the soul, where it enters and where it exits
> or, how the pit sits in the peach
> have studied up there a big old melon.
> They cite Aristotle and Plato,

> and they hope that the soul rests in peace
> among sounds and songs; and they dance around so much
> that it muddles up your head.[3]

Elsewhere:

> Marsilio, this philosophy of yours / no one really feels."[4]

And:

> You animal, who fled here from the Maremma [an area in southwestern
> Tuscany, with a reputation as rustic].[5]

The analogy today would be a Twitter feud among celebrities. But it would
be an imperfect analogy to say the least. Twitter exists in a realm without
space, and in a temporal zone that has a very short time window: amid the
vast amounts of information that come our way daily, one day's controversy
is often forgotten when the next day's arrives.

In the Florence of the 1470s, however, things were different. A feud such
as this one had substantive implications for the way culture would proceed.
You could find yourself without patronage – without, that is, financial
support for your work – if you did not defend your place in the cultural
landscape. Ficino, who did not have the gift for competitive vernacular
rhyming of which Pulci was availing himself, wrote letters in Latin.

One, for example, was to Luigi Pulci's brother Bernardo. Ficino begins
the letter as follows: "I know that your brother is a tremendous shame to you,
since he is considered an unstable liar by everyone."[6] Ficino goes on to urge
Bernardo to continue in his own considerable virtue and not to worry that
his brother's vices might obscure his own good character.

Ficino wrote also to another person who had connections to Pulci through
marriage, Bernardo Rucellai, a leading citizen, a member of one of
Florence's most prominent families, and someone who had recently married
one of Lorenzo the Magnificent's sisters. In this letter, Ficino characterizes
Pulci as a barking dog, one who "barks because of his nature and habit."[7]
Ficino writes, regarding the abuse heaped on him by Pulci, "I would rather

[3] Luigi Pulci, *Libro dei sonetti*, excerpted in Carlo Muscetta and Daniele Ponchiroli, eds., *Poesia del Quattrocento e del cinquecento* (Turin: Einaudi, 1959), 177. See also Salvatore Nigro, *Pulce e la cultura medicea* (Rome: Laterza, 1978), 65–66.
[4] Cit. in Arnaldo della Torre, *Storia dell'Accademia platonica di Firenze* (Florence: Carnesecchi, 1902), 822.
[5] Ibid.
[6] Ficino, *Op.*, 661; Della Torre, *Accademia*, 823.
[7] Ficino, *Op.*, 661; *Letters*, 1: 169.

be censured by the words of an unjust man than by the facts themselves."[8] He says, "every man who disparages others, necessarily disparages himself first."[9] And he goes on for a time in the same vein, taking the high road and suggesting that Pulci has taken, and will likely continue to take, the low road: reputation management, in other words.

But then two interesting statements occur, ones that let us look deeper into this moment and into some of Ficino's real fears about his society. First, Ficino writes to Bernardo as follows:

> Now you are striving in vain to correct that lost soul, the giant Pulci, for the madman neither hears nor listens to reason. That wicked man will never spare good men, for he has never respected God. How can a madman, who hates God, love men, who are the images of God? No one attacks divine matters more aggressively nor more foolishly than the little man you ask me to correct.[10]

We learn first of all that Rucellai had written to Ficino, in the hopes that Ficino might have been able to talk some sense into Pulci. We gather, also, that Ficino speaks of Pulci as if Pulci were irreligious and known to be so.

Second, Ficino writes, a bit later in the letter: "I need not accuse our present generation of anything, Bernardo, except that it has produced this small but evil portent," meaning Pulci.[11] This statement is part of Ficino's managing his reputation, as outlined earlier; however, it also fits with Ficino's larger views about the state of religion in his day and the possibly dangerous tendencies afoot, tendencies manifested in none other than Pulci.

Around the same time, the mid-1470s, and just before his conflict with Ficino began, Pulci had engaged in another polemic. This time it was against a Florentine priest named Matteo Franco (1448–94), who has been variously described by his contemporaries as well as by later scholarship either as perhaps a bit too worldly, more in love with the trappings and luxury of his status than with the saving of souls, or as someone who simply ran afoul of the easy-to-provoke Pulci, who was always on the lookout for another argument.[12]

Either way, what is important from our vantage point is to bring into relief what Pulci was saying in a series of sonnets connected to his arguments with

---

[8] Ibid.

[9] Ibid.

[10] Ficino, *Op.*, 661; *Letters*, 1: 170.

[11] Ibid.

[12] See Stefano Carrai, *Le muse dei Pulci: Studi su Luca e Luigi Pulci* (Naples: Guida, 1985), 78–84; Edoardo A. Lèbano, "Introduction," in Pulci, *Morgante: The Epic Adventures*, xi–xxxiii, at xvi–xvii; Guglielmo Volpi, "Un cortigiano di Lorenzo il Magnifico ed alcune sue lettere," *Giornale storico della letteratura italiana* 17 (1891), 229–76.

292 INTELLECTUAL WORLD OF THE ITALIAN RENAISSANCE

Franco. In one, he doubts the miracles in the Bible, taking aim, just to take two examples, at the story of Peter walking on water until he was sunk by his doubts (Mt. 14.29) and at the miracle of Lazarus being raised from the dead (Lk. 7: 12–17): the latter a point in the sonnet at which Pulci refers to the Bible as "barking" ("dunque la Bibbia abbaja").[13] In another, Pulci ridiculed pilgrims, those devoted late medieval Christians who believed that traveling to a holy site would allow some of the benefits of that holiness to rub off on them. Things had reached such a pitch, and Pulci's evident irreligiousness had been so bandied about, that in 1473 Pulci was persuaded by Lorenzo de' Medici's sister (who was also Rucellai's wife) to reassess his mores and to affirm his Christian faith.[14] It was then that his polemic with Matteo Franco, the priest, broke out.

Franco accused Pulci of practicing forbidden magical arts, or at least of having been present at a household where these were known to occur.[15] Elsewhere Franco accuses Pulci of being someone who "with tongue and pen makes war on God."[16] In another poem, Franco berates Pulci for having a "lance that is not the right size," of having a "disgraceful life," and of being a "little Muhammed."[17] And so on. Their poetic war went like this, each of them hurling rhyming, allusive, punning insults at the other. Pulci gave as good as he got, suggesting that Franco was not a priest of integrity, and that he was too interested in love and not enough in saving souls.

Pulci's sonnets and his epic were meant to be recited and heard. They were oral as much as written, as were Matteo Franco's works against Pulci. Franco's and Pulci's exchanges formed part of an interesting and, in truth, still understudied facet of Renaissance Italy: the performative side, whereby what was written was also somehow not complete until and unless it became public in some fashion.

In this respect Ficino's letters – recondite, more measured, and of course Latinate though they were – formed part of the very same world. Why else would you collect your letters? More importantly, and more relevant to the situation at hand, why would you take the time to write letters responding, in various guises and to various addressees, to someone such as Pulci? Why would you care?

[13] See *Sonetti di Matteo Franco e di Luigi Pulci*, ed. Filippo de Rossi (Lucca, 1759), sonnet CXLVI, pp. 146–47, at 147.
[14] Lèbano, "Introduction," xvii.
[15] *Sonetti di Matteo Franco e di Luigi Pulci*, 15.
[16] Ibid., 39: "E con lingua, e con penna a Dio fa guera [sic]."
[17] Ibid., 43 ("la lancia tua non è a misura"), 45 ("vita scelerata"), 46 ("Maumetezzo").

The reasons for this sort of behavior clue us in to the environment in which people such as, not only Pulci and Franco (provocateurs and poets of the street) but also Ficino (in some ways more high minded but no less "public" in orientation) carried out their day-to-day lives. No scholar who today writes grant applications for funding can find this competitive world altogether unfamiliar. Still, the differences between then and now are stark enough that they are worth bringing into relief, especially if we want to approach the polyphonic cultural world that late fifteenth-century Florence represented. The public, local aspect represents a factor of paramount importance. Living divided, online lives as we tend to do today, it is well-nigh impossible to imagine oneself back in the environment of Pulci, Franco, and Ficino. But we need to try, for it is the only way to understand their work in a well-rounded fashion.

Let us return to Ficino's letters in the context of his conflict with Pulci. Ficino was in contact with a prominent Florentine, Bernardo Rucellai, who was a relative by marriage of Pulci, as we have seen. Ficino also made sure to reach out to the Medici family with letters both to Lorenzo the Magnificent and to his beloved brother Giuliano, for whom, as we shall see, a tragic fate lay in store imminently. To Lorenzo, for instance, Ficino wrote regarding Pulci: "So let that little imp bite your Christian priests with impunity, as he was long ago allowed to bite Christ."[18] Later in the letter, Ficino says that, while philosophy can keep his and others' minds clear from the trifling slights of people such as Pulci, nevertheless that very same philosophy now impels Ficino to tell Lorenzo this one thing: "that I should indicate to you the very way to discharge your duty . . . that is, with the slightest tilt of the head show that you are displeased at what above all displeases God."[19] Ficino makes Lorenzo into an arbiter, one so powerful that with a nod of his head he can regulate the small universe of competing intellectuals and cultural figures who swirl around him. And then to Lorenzo's brother, Giuliano, Ficino says:

> I am not surprised that that dog continually snarls at me, for it is his custom to snarl at good men and men of learning, as it is his custom to snarl at the soul and at God . . . Let him snarl in the company of the great and the humble, so long as it is publicly [palam] understood that his snarling gives no pleasure to the Medici.[20]

[18] Ficino, *Op.*, 725; *Letters*, 2: 12.
[19] Ibid.
[20] Ficino, *Op.*, 725; *Letters*, 2: 13.

Reputation, culture, and patronage all stood together in a delicate, precarious equilibrium, one for which agonistic, public polemic was needed to keep it in balance.

Pulci too directed sonnets and letters to Lorenzo. These were not scabrous productions directed against Lorenzo but rather writings designed to shore up Lorenzo's support. They tended to contain the same sorts of puns, jokes, and vulgar witticisms as the rest of his sonnets; vulgarities, however, that were aimed at others and that, presumably, were intended to provoke laughter in Lorenzo, something they surely did.[21]

Pulci's cultivation of Lorenzo de' Medici was no exception. In fact, if you were to think of late fifteenth-century Florence, especially in the 1470s and 1480s, as a wheel, Lorenzo would be the hub; connected to this hub you would see many spokes. One of these would have been, not so much Pulci alone, but rather everything he represented: day-to-day, vernacular humor, a bawdy poetry that was as important for its orality (the ways it would have been performed, sung, and heard in public contexts) as for the written versions we now possess, which we are condemned to study in isolation from their real, original, authentic context.

Lorenzo himself was a vernacular poet, taking his part in that literary side of Florentine culture, and leaving behind one of the Renaissance's most emblematic poetic songs, the "Song of Bacchus," one that he composed to be sung in a choral setting in the environment of Carnival, that Pre-Lenten time when all traditional customs were topsy-turvy, a celebration in preparation for the forty days of denial to follow. He captures the mood well:

> Quant' è bella giovinezza
> Che si fugge tuttavia
> Chi vuol essere lieto, sia
> Di doman non c'è certezza

> How beautiful is youth,
> Though it flies away
> Let whoever wants to be happy, be so,
> Tomorrow holds nothing certain.[22]

Laced throughout the poetic song were mythological references, especially to the power of Bacchus (god of wine), together with his mythological bride, Ariadne, who "because time flies and is a trickster, are always happy

---

[21] See Jordan, *Pulci's* Morgante, 27–42.

[22] Lorenzo de' Medici, "Canzona di Bacco," in Muscetta Ponchiroli, *Poesia del Quattrocento e del cinquecento*, 194–96, at 194.

together." Satyrs, nymphs, and other mythological personae make appearances. The poem, like other Laurentian verses, is rich with the heady aroma of ancient mythology. Finally, the poem signals something else: complete comfort with Tuscan as a language of high literature.

Elsewhere Lorenzo addressed the use of the vernacular in an explicit fashion, arguing for the use of Tuscan in the Preface to his Commentary on his sonnets, the *Comento de' miei sonetti* (which remained unfinished at his death in 1492).[23] He writes that for any language to be regarded as truly praiseworthy, it needed first of all to be "copious, abundant, and able to express well what the mind has understood and expressed in a conceptual form."[24] It also needs a certain "sweetness and harmony," and it has to have a history of having had "things written [in the language] that are nuanced, and serious, and necessary to human life."[25] Finally, it requires another attribute: that things have come to such a pass "that what was naturally proper to one city or province alone becomes universal and almost common to all," as had been the case of Latin during the Roman Empire.[26] If Tuscan does not quite have the last attribute, Lorenzo argues, it nonetheless does possess the first three, as the work of Dante, Petrarch, and Boccaccio, "our Florentine poets," shows.[27] So, "no one can blame me if I have written in that language into which I was born and raised, especially given that once, Hebrew, Greek, and Latin were all, in their day, natural mother tongues."[28]

The tone of Lorenzo's Preface breathes confidence, showing that appreciation for the Florentine vernacular had reached a new maturity in his era. It would take another generation to be theorized definitively, as we shall see. But in Lorenzo's era, there was no doubt that ancient Latin had once been a native language and hence was no longer a living language; that Tuscan was a language that could and should be used for literature of high cultural import; and that the proper way to go about realizing Tuscan's full potential was by understanding the attributes of Latin that had made it a success – lessons to which Poggio and Alberti, each in his own way, had contributed decisively.

There were many ingredients in the culture of Lorenzo's Florence, other spokes, as it were. One was the University of Florence. If you travel to

---

[23] Lorenzo de' Medici, *Comento de' miei sonetti*, in Lorenzo de' Medici, *Opere*, ed. Tiziano Zanato (Turin: Einaudi, 1992), 565–773, at 565–88. See also Tiziano Zanato, *Saggio sul Comento di Lorenzo de' Medici* (Florence: Olschki, 1979), 11–44.

[24] Lorenzo de' Medici, *Comento*, 578.

[25] Ibid., 578–79.

[26] Ibid., 580.

[27] Ibid., 581.

[28] Ibid., 584–85.

European cities famous for their universities in the Middle Ages (Bologna, Naples, Paris, and Oxford come to mind), you will find in each a rich legacy of the university, a "university district." If you go to Florence, you find the *via dello Studio*, or "university way": a small, unimpressive street that, in its diminutiveness, indicates the place the university traditionally held in Florence. This relatively meager presence of a university helps explain why Florence had been receptive to Renaissance humanism back in the days of Coluccio Salutati: without an imposing, inherently conservative intellectual tradition (such as universities often represent), Florence's intellectual and cultural elite was readier to embrace new cultural possibilities than it might otherwise have been.

The best way to understand how varied the intellectual interests were is to listen to what one thinker, Cristoforo Landino, who taught for many years at the University of Florence and authored many interesting if still little-studied works, had to say about Lorenzo and his cultural patronage: "So large a troop was there of the best and most learned minds, and so many and varied were the opinions on each subject, disputed with such subtlety, that within those magnificent precincts you would have thought that not only the Academy, the Lyceum, and the Porch had migrated there from Athens, but every school of Paris."[29] What Landino meant by "Academy" was Platonism. The Lyceum referred to Aristotelianism, and the "Porch" to Stoicism. And then there was the phrase "every school of Paris," by which Landino meant that a wide variety of scholastic theology was cultivated in the environment of Florence.

Lorenzo's patronage was of key importance for these developments. His interests were far broader than any one school of philosophy or style of thought. Or rather, his interests ran more along the lines of what one would expect from a culturally inclined politician and patron of culture: to have everything around him occur at the highest level, with the most variety, and with the best talent available.[30] In this respect, Lorenzo's work with the University of Florence might stand as his most noteworthy accomplishment. He reformed the university, so that it wound up with a relatively small outpost in Florence, and a larger one in Pisa, a subject city and Florence's gateway to the sea (thus bringing Florence in line with other Italian cities, such as Venice, whose university resided in one of its subject cities, Padua).[31]

---

[29] Cristoforo Landino, *De vera nobilitate*, ed. Maria Teresa Liaci (Florence: Olschki, 1970), 26; cit. and tr. in Hankins, *Humanism and Platonism*, 2: 285.

[30] See Hankins, *Humanism and Platonism*, 2: 273–316; Francis William Kent, *Lorenzo de' Medici and the Art of Magnificence* (Baltimore: Johns Hopkins University Press, 2004).

[31] See Jonathan Davies, *Florence and Its University During the Early Renaissance* (Leiden: Brill, 1998) for the period up to 1473; and Armando Verde, *Lo studio fiorentino, 1473–1503*, 5 vols. (Florence: Olschki, 1973–94).

It was only with his tireless aid, financial support, and even administrative involvement that the university went from what many saw as a second- or third-tier university to a leading institution.

Lorenzo accomplished this end through the thinkers and scholars he hired to teach, about whom the reigning assumption was that they needed to be prominent and important. As one of Lorenzo's relatives wrote to him in 1473, it was necessary for a university "to have famous and outstanding men, because they bring along with themselves numerous students, even as they bring honor and reputation to universities."[32] Students in sufficient numbers would bring revenue, so that one would have bottom-line capital; and the reputations of these scholars would add that other form of capital: cultural capital, which itself accrued from their reputations, to be transferred to that of the university that was rich enough in resources to hire them, and thus to the city with which that university was affiliated. Lorenzo helped recruit some of the best scholastic philosophers, men whose principal interest lay in teaching and studying the works of Aristotle.

Lorenzo also fostered the career of Cristoforo Landino, who took it upon himself to teach and to promote the emerging vernacular classics, Dante's *Comedy* and Petrarch's collection of love poetry, the *Canzoniere*. Indeed, Landino's work at the university and the written texts it produced represented one reason – the key reason, arguably – that Lorenzo himself was able, later, practically to take for granted the preeminence of Tuscan, along with its suitability as a high language.[33]

First, Landino decided to teach Petrarch's poetry at the university even before the 1473 reforms, thus bringing Petrarch's vernacular work officially into the orbit of the university world.[34] We have seen what Landino said in his opening oration to that course. But it is worth highlighting once more that he linked the development of the vernacular to the Latin *studia humanitatis*: any good language needed *arte* (or "craft"), and *dottrina* ("learning"), he had said; both come from studying the *veri studi d'umanità* (the "authentic humanities"). These were expressed in Latin; so, "whoever wants to be a good Tuscan must be a good Latin first."[35] Landino's work helped contribute to a set of assumptions: content and form were linked. You needed, if

---

[32] Letter of Filippo de' Medici to Lorenzo of February 16, 1473, published in Armando Verde, "Domenico di Fiandra: intransigente tomista non gradito nello studio fiorentino," *Memorie dominicane* 7 (1976), 304–21, at 313; and Hankins *Humanism and Platonism*, 2: 286–87 n.29.

[33] The work of Simon Gilson has been crucial here; see his *Dante and Renaissance Florence* (Cambridge: Cambridge University Press, 2005).

[34] Ibid., 135–38.

[35] Cardini, *La critica del Landino*, 349–50.

you were to be thoroughly educated, to understand matters drawn from antiquity both because they provided good lessons for life and because of the way in which they were expressed: in Latin. Note too that he is saying all this at the beginning of a course on vernacular, that is, Tuscan, poetry, thus making a durable and important link. Tuscan, if it were to become a literary language with the requisite amount of permanence and durability, needed to be informed by the debates, theories, and research that by then had gone into Latin. Humanist training in Latin, by this point, was understood as a necessity.

Landino, however, did more than teach Petrarch's vernacular poetry. He also taught Dante's *Comedy* and, in a burst of energy, wrote a Commentary to that great work in 1480–81, a time when, as we shall see, Florence was in need of a patriotic cultural politics.[36] Landino's Preface to his Commentary reveals both his intentions and, in its linking of the vernacular and classical Latin, the effects Landino's work had. Two aspects prove especially note-worthy. First, Landino brings Dante into the orbit of the classics:

> Now, given that I have recently interpreted and commented in Latin on the allegorical meaning of Virgil's *Aeneid*, I deemed that it would be neither disadvantageous nor unwelcome to my fellow citizens, were I – with whatsoever learning and diligence I could muster – to examine, in a similar fashion, the hidden and secret, but altogether most divine mean-ings of the *Comedy* of the Florentine poet Dante Alighieri. And since I wrote about the Latin poet in the Latin language, just so would I interpret the Tuscan in Tuscan.[37]

In case the Florentine aspect was not clear, after having enumerated some other commentators on Dante, Landino went on: "This alone do I affirm: that I have liberated our fellow citizen from the barbarism of many foreign tongues by means of which he had been corrupted by commentators."[38] Landino meant by that (somewhat overwrought but nevertheless indicative) statement that there had been by his day commentaries on Dante in other, non-Tuscan vernacular dialects. Now it was time to bring the enterprise of

---

[36] Cristoforo Landino, *Comento sopra la Comedia*, 4 vols., ed. Paolo Procaccioli (Rome: Salerno, 2001); see the excellent discussion in Gilson, 163–238.

[37] Landino, *Comento*, 1: 219–20: "Ora perché havevo novellamente interpretato, et alle latine lettere mandato l'allegorico senso della virgiliana *Eneide*, giudicai non dovere essere inutile a' miei cittadini, né ingiocondo, se con quanto potessi maggiore studio et industria, similmente investigassi gl'arcani et occulti, ma al tutto divinissimi sensi della *Comedia* del fiorentino poeta Danthe Alighieri; et chome el latino poeta in latina lingua haveveo expresso, chosí et toscano in toscana interpretassi."

[38] Ibid., 1: 221: "Questo solo affermo, havere liberato el nostro cittadino dalla barbarie di molti externi idiomi, ne' quali da' comentatori era stato corropto."

interpreting Dante where it belonged (Florence), and to signal that Dante was part of an elite group of writers, one who could be mentioned together with Latin classics such as Virgil.

Second, we can note that Landino's enterprise was symbolically blessed by none other than Marsilio Ficino, who enthusiastically allowed Landino to include a letter of endorsement to the whole enterprise in that very same Preface. Ficino's tone is rhapsodic, as if a divine mystery were being revealed to a grateful elect: "Florence, grieving for so long but finally happy, is full of joy in the highest degree because her poet, Dante, has been revived now after two centuries, restored to his own homeland, and finally crowned."[39] Addressing Dante himself, Ficino says: "As you enter these city walls, the blissful Graces take your hand; the lovely Nymphs bestow kisses on your brow."[40] As if to ratify precisely the merging of classicizing and vernacular trajectories that was occurring, Landino presented, first, the Latin version of Ficino's letter, followed by a Tuscan translation.

Florence, culture, classicism, and the vernacular: what all this meant for Florence, its university, and its cultural life emerges most clearly in the life and career of Angelo Poliziano (1454–94). Poliziano was born Angelo Ambrogini in the Tuscan territory known as Montepulciano (or in Latin *Mons politianus*). He had a difficult childhood, with his father having been murdered in a clan rivalry. Because of his early promise as a student, he made it to Florence, where he drew the attention of Lorenzo de' Medici, who took young Poliziano into the Medici household. Lorenzo nourished Poliziano's talent for ancient languages.[41]

One of the first literary and scholarly tasks that Poliziano undertook, while still a teenager, was a verse translation of parts of Homer's *Iliad*, the great foundational epic on war, something he looked back on much later in life with great nostalgia.[42] The timing, around the year 1472, could not have

[39] Ficino, "Letter on Dante," ed. in Landino, *Comento*, 1:268–70, citation at 268 (Latin version) and 269 (Tuscan); I translate form the Tuscan. The letter is also included as the final letter in Book Six of Ficino's *letters*, in *Op.*, 1: 840. On the letter, see Sebastiano Gentile, "Intorno a *Proemio XIII*," in Landino, *Comento*, 1: 114–18.

[40] Ficino, "Letter on Dante," in Landino, *Comento*, 1:268 (Latin version) and 270 (Tuscan).

[41] For his early years, see Ida Maïer, *Ange Politien: La formation d'un poète humaniste (1469–1480)* (Geneva: Droz, 1966).

[42] See Angelo Poliziano, *Miscellanea*, in Poliziano, *Op.* [speaking about his early studies], K ii(v)–K iii(r): "Etenim ego, tenera adhuc aetate, sub duobus excellentissimis hominibus Marsilio Ficino Florentino, cuius longe felicior quam Thracensis Orphei cithara veram (ni fallor) Eurydicen, hoc est amplissimi iudicii Platonicam sapientiam revocavit ab inferis, et Argyropylo Byzantio Peripateticorum sui temporis longe clarissimo, dabam quidem philosophiae utrique operam, sed non admodum assiduam, videlicet ad Homeri poetae blandimenta natura et aetate proclivior, quem tum latine quoque miro ut adolescens ardore,

been more appropriate, since it was then that Lorenzo ordered a war against the subject city of Volterra, which had audaciously blocked Florence's desired involvement in an alum mine on Volterran territory.[43] The Florentine war had a dual aim: to protect and foster Florence's interests in its subject territories and to remind everyone at home in Florence that Lorenzo, though young, had the stomach for war. Even at an early age, Poliziano had experienced almost unimaginable violence with the death of his father. Now, entering Lorenzo's household, translating the poetry of war was one of his first accomplishments.

The year 1478 saw an event of great violence in Florence. Known as the conspiracy of the Pazzi, it represented an attempt by a rival family to murder Lorenzo and his brother Giuliano.[44] Poliziano, as it happens, gives us something close to an eyewitness account, in his *Commentary on the Conspiracy of the Pazzi*.[45] Why would a family in Florence, a proud "republic," decide that the only way to satisfy its political goals would be to kill the leading representatives of another family? In republics, where self-governance and freedom from tyrannical authority reign supreme, this sort of thing is just not done. The answer lies in considering just what sort of republic Florence was and in how its politics worked – both official, "on the books" politics as well as its symbolic politics. The young Poliziano's *Commentary* tells us a lot about the symbolic politics especially, to which we will return momentarily. But it is worth commenting on the official politics as well, to understand why eruptions such as the Pazzi conspiracy were not only possible but also inevitable.

Florence's status as a republic emerged, especially in the early fifteenth century, as one of its points of pride.[46] Thinkers such as Bruni and others

miro studio versibus interpretabar. Postea vero rebus aliis negotiisque prementibus, sic ego nonnunquam de philosophia, quasi de Nilo canes, bibi fugique, donec reversus est in hanc urbem maxime Laurenti Medicis cum benivolentia, tum virtutis et ingenii similitudine allectus princeps hic nobilissimus Ioannes Picus Mirandula."

43 As noted by Francesco Bausi, in his "Introduzione," in Angelo Poliziano, *Due poemetti latini*, ed. Francesco Bausi (Rome: Salerno, 2003), XI–LVI, at XII–XIII.

44 See Lauro Martines, *April Blood: Florence and the Conspiracy Against the Medici* (Oxford: Oxford University Press, 2003); Marcello Simonetta, *The Montefeltro Conspiracy: A Renaissance Mystery Decoded* (New York: Doubleday, 2008).

45 Angelo Poliziano, *Della congiura dei Pazzi: Coniurationis commentarium*, ed. Alessandro Perosa (Padua: Antenore, 1958); Poliziano, *Coniurationis commentarium / Commentario della congiura dei Pazzi*, ed. Leandro Perini (Florence: Firenze University Press, 2012); English tr. by Elizabeth B. Welles, in Benjamin Kohl and Ronald G. Witt, eds., *The Earthly Republic* (Philadelphia: University of Pennsylvania Press, 1978), 305–22.

46 For recent literature on civic humanism, see Nicholas S. Baker and Brian Maxson, eds., *After Civic Humanism: Learning and Politics in Renaissance Italy, 1300–1600* (Toronto: Center for Reformation and Renaissance Studies, 2015); James Hankins, ed., *Renaissance Civic*

repeatedly looked toward *Florentina libertas* – "Florentine liberty" – as one of the defining characteristics of their collective political lives. By it they meant, first and most importantly, freedom from outside control. Florence was not, and never intended to become, a client state of some other larger power. It may be difficult to understand this notion today, given that the international political community tends to recognize "sovereignty" as a norm: the notion is that each nation-state has its own borders and within those borders has a right to develop a politics according to its own wishes and desires. This norm did not exist in a robust fashion in fifteenth-century Italy, whose fiercely independent, though in truth small, city-states were compelled often to ally with outside powers. Sometimes these powers included northern European states such as France or the predominantly German-Austrian Holy Roman Empire. Quite often these alliances included other states on the Italian peninsula. There were even occasions, especially toward the end of the fifteenth century, of Italian states allying with the Ottoman Turks, Muslims who in other circumstances were stigmatized as "infidels" but who, when the right moment occurred, were seen as useful partners against other rival Italian cities.[47] The point is that these foreign policy arrangements were always precarious.

This precariousness was mirrored within Italian city-states, Florence included. Here, within the city walls, the tensions that emerged had to do with family and kinship ties, as each district of the city had its important families, each with its own, often interlocking, webs of influence. Wealth mattered, but the primary coin of the realm, to which wealth contributed conspicuously, was reputation. Within Florence, if one were wealthy, one had to manage one's reputation carefully. Cosimo de' Medici, Lorenzo's grandfather, seemed to have been born with the perfect knack for politics in republican Florence.[48] When he died in 1464, the city government referred to him henceforth with the honorific *pater patriae*: "father of the homeland." But he earned that title not by having held any special political office during his life. Instead he had always maintained that he was a citizen like any other. But he found clever ways to put his finger on the scale when it came to local politics. Florence governed itself by

Humanism: Reappraisals and Reflections (Cambridge: Cambridge University Press, 2000). On Florence's structure as a republic, see Nicolai Rubenstein, *The Government of Florence under the Medici (1434–1494)*, 2nd ed. (Oxford: Clarendon, 1998).

[47] See Anthony D'Elia, *A Sudden Terror: The Plot to Murder the Pope in Renaissance Rome* (Cambridge, MA: Harvard University Press, 2009).

[48] See Frances Ames-Lewis, *Cosimo 'il Vecchio' de' Medici, 1389–1464* (Oxford: Oxford University Press, 1992); Dale Kent, *The Patron's Oeuvre*; Kent, *The Rise of the Medici: Faction in Florence 1426–1434* (Oxford: Oxford University Press, 1978).

a system of nine elected officials, called "priors," who were chosen from the different professional guilds in the city.[49] You had to be at least thirty years old, a guild member, and free of debt. Your name was then eligible to be put with others in a bag. The names chosen – by lot – would serve. The nine men would move as a group into Florence's main government building, called the Palazzo della Signoria, and there they would live and govern the city for a two-month term. Thereafter a new group of nine would be elected. But there was a special official, called a "scrutineer," whose responsibilities included monitoring the eligibility of those men whose names would go into the bags. In practice, that meant one could fill the bags with candidates who were likely to be "friendly." And it was on this process that Medici control of the government rested.

Cosimo, however, was a master at seeming like a regular citizen, or rather, at behaving just as a regular citizen believed he might act if he were rich. He dressed well but not lavishly; he offered patronage to Church-related enterprises; he opened his home (large and well built but not preciously opulent) to visiting dignitaries. To those many citizens who liked him and his family – a large number that included many who were linked to the Medici by marriage, through business and trade, and with other forms of patronage – the Medici were beloved.

But there were others in fifteenth-century Florence: other families, other bankers, other merchants – other people, in short, who wanted a piece of the pie. As long as Cosimo was Florence's "leading citizen," those tensions were kept sufficiently at bay that Medici leadership was strong. But as Lorenzo took over that role in 1469 (upon the death of his father, Cosimo's son Piero de' Medici), things seemed less certain. For one thing, Lorenzo was not even twenty years old: a youngster in the eyes of some of Florence's old hands and thus, seemingly, easy prey. For another, political "styles" (for want of a better word) across the Italian peninsula were changing as well. Military leaders had always had a role in Italy, as *condottieri* – military experts whom the city could hire to fight its wars – often decided that they could do just as good a job at ruling as they had done shoring up the aims of those by whom they had been employed, since after all, the *condottieri* had the military power and thus an effective monopoly of force. One also saw the rise of hereditary dynasties in a number of Italian cities. Along with this tendency toward consolidated rule came social cues: knightly festivals, lavish social differentiation in the form of different dress from normal citizens, and importantly titles to accompany nobility.

---

[49] See Rubenstein, *The Government of Florence under the Medici.*

The fear in Florence, by the time Lorenzo came of age, was that the Medici might be tending in just that direction. Where Cosimo had been careful to act the part of an ordinary citizen, Lorenzo by contrast started cultivating some of those social habits that seemed in their opulence to presage a move toward tyranny. Not that Lorenzo was claiming any titles for himself – yet. But all the other cues were there. In 1475, for example, he staged a lavish tournament, whose themes were drawn from classical mythology, in which his brother Giuliano was a key participant. Poliziano was there, and to celebrate the event he wrote a set of poems in Tuscan that later acquired the title *Stanze per la giostra*: "Stanzas for the Joust."[50]

The joust was a tournament-like event with a rich history in the Middle Ages: formal in nature, it pitted knights against each other, who would, on horseback, and bearing a weapon, ride directly at one another and see who could knock whom off his horse. There were occasional injuries, perhaps the most spectacular having occurred later, in sixteenth-century France, when in 1559 King Henry II was killed when a splinter that broke off from his opponent's lance pierced his eye.[51] Usually, however, jousts were ritualized celebrations (Henry's was held to celebrate his daughter's wedding); for the most part these were not dangerous events. They were, however, powerfully connected to the idea of nobility and courts, stressing two things: martial prowess (however formalized and staged this might have been) and idealized courtly love, whereby the competing knights were striving for the love of a (usually unattainable) woman, whose purity and beauty fired them to reach the heights of glory.

Nobility, courts, and courtly customs: Florence prided itself precisely on not having nobility and on the notion that all citizens were equal under law. So the very fact that the Medici staged this event itself was cause for concern. Lorenzo's brother, Giuliano, took center stage, and in Poliziano's telling is described as the joust's winner. It didn't help matters among the disaffected that Lorenzo himself had staged, paid for, and himself "won" a similar tournament in 1469.

Poliziano (and it should be remembered that when he wrote his *Stanze* he was only in his early twenties) showed with his composition an early and abiding interest in different registers of language. He wrote not only in Tuscan (rather than Latin) but also in *ottava rima*, a metrical form beloved

---

[50] Angelo Poliziano, *Stanze*, in Angelo Poliziano, *Stanze, Fabula di Orfeo*, ed. Stefano Carrai (Milan: Mursia, 1988), 35–135; English translation in Angelo Poliziano, *The Stanze of Angelo Poliziano*, tr. David Quint (University Park: Pennsylvania State University Press, 1993).

[51] See Frederic J. Baumgartner, *Henry II, King of France, 1547–1559* (Durham, NC: Duke University Press, 1998).

by Boccaccio, back in the fourteenth century, used for longer, "epic"-worthy themes. Poliziano wrote deliberately echoing the sentiments used in classical forms, beginning in this fashion:

> My daring mind urges me to celebrate the glorious pageants and the proud games of the city that bridles and gives rein to the magnanimous Tuscans, the cruel realms of the goddess who adorns the third heaven, and the rewards merited by honorable pursuits; in order that fortune, death, or time may not despoil great names and eminent deeds.[52]

The Tuscans, which is to say the Florentines, are elevated, high and mighty enough to take their place alongside other peoples whose deeds poets sang. Then of course there is the "goddess who adorns the third heaven" – Venus, goddess of love – whose cruel realms will serve as another pole around which Poliziano's poetic composition will revolve. And then, finally, "the rewards merited by honorable pursuits" – what he means here is glory: worldly glory, the kind of glory that you win when you do something beloved and appreciated by your fellow citizens. The goal of this sort of poetic commemoration is that "fortune, death, or time may not despoil great names and eminent deeds." The goal is to be remembered here on earth.

Is this all too much? Did this twenty-year-old poet have such lofty goals in mind? This poetic account, after all, remained unfinished for reasons we will later come to understand. But there is something to the sentiments underlying Poliziano's initial stanza that call to mind one of the strange and noteworthy features of the epoch he inhabited, which was, all in one: medieval ("pageants"), "Renaissance" (Venus and the ancient gods), and modern (worldly deeds and civic glory are worth celebrating and preserving for their own sake). We see that here, in "Renaissance" Florence, at its high point, arguably, there is no cultural supersession, no essential moment when the Middle Ages yield to the Renaissance. Instead, threads of different traditions, practices, and ideologies felicitously intertwine in young Poliziano's *Stanze*.

Immediately after the passage quoted he then addresses love directly (as a god, as was traditional): "O fair god: you who inspire through the eyes unto the heart sweet desire full of bitter thought, you nourish souls with a sweet venom, feeding yourself on tears and sighs, you ennoble whatever you regard ... Love, ... now lend your hand to my intellect."[53] Love, then, will be Poliziano's guide and inspiration. Soon thereafter, he addresses

---

[52] Poliziano, *Stanze*, 1.1; tr. Quint, 3.
[53] Ibid., 1.2; tr. Quint, 3.

Lorenzo directly, to come to one of the main points of the *Stanze*: "let us sing of your glorious brother, who delights his renowned family with a new trophy, a second branch."[54] The "second branch" here refers to the laurel, which was both the emblem for poetic as well as military triumph. In this case, Poliziano means that Giuliano won the joust, even as Lorenzo in 1469 had won a joust as well. The family's glory accrues through repeated triumph. Then there emerges the subject of the poem: "in the lovely time of his green ages, the first flower yet blossoming on his cheeks, fair Julio [meaning Giuliano de' Medici], as yet inexperienced in the bittersweet cares which Love provides, lived content in peace and liberty."[55] Throughout, the story of Giuliano's triumph emerges in Poliziano's gentle verse, and along the way there are matters drawn from mythology that illuminate Florentine culture in the round.

One such occasion occurs during an *ekphrasis* – an extended description – of an intricately carved door, on which images are engraved that narrate the birth of Venus, goddess of love. Poliziano draws from a myth in the ancient Greek author Hesiod, whose *Theogony* told the tales of the origins of the ancient Gods: another Greek text, like Homer, on which the young Poliziano was cutting his teeth as a translator. Its contents remind us that the birth of any god is accompanied by violence:

> In the stormy Aegean the genital member is seen to be received in the lap of Tethys [Tethys is a goddess of the sea] to drift across the waves, wrapped in white foam, beneath the various turnings of the planets; and within, born with lovely and happy gestures, a young woman of non-human countenance, is carried on a conch shell, wafted to shore by playful zephyrs; and it seems that heaven rejoices in her birth.[56]

The myth involved the god Kronos, a Titan and the father of Zeus (thus one of the original gods who ruled in a mythical golden age), who in a violent act of succession killed and castrated his father Uranus, god of the sky).[57] Uranus's severed members fell to the ocean and their fertile power was realized in the birth of Venus. Then, later, Zeus would overthrow Kronos, beginning the regime of the gods in an act of aggression and a paradigm of struggle. The violence (its presence, its nearness to a politics of the gods) would have been self-evident to Poliziano, and as we shall see, he had more

---

[54] Ibid., 1.6; tr. Quint, 5.
[55] Ibid., 1.8; tr. Quint, 5.
[56] Ibid., 1.99; tr. Quint, 51.
[57] Hesiod, *Theogony*, in Hesiod, *Theogony. Works and Days. Testimonia*, ed. and tr. Glenn Most (Cambridge, MA: Harvard University Press, 2007), ll. 167–206.

occasion to view violence close to home. But in the case of this *ekphrasis*, one cannot help bring to mind one of the Western world's most famous paintings, Botticelli's *Birth of Venus*, begun about a decade after Polizano began this poem. Almost all its elements are described in and, likely, come from Poliziano's *Stanze*, so that we see clearly how the vernacular became an important vector for the sorts of classicizing pursuits that scholars of Poliziano's level pursued.[58]

The *Stanze* also represented a chance for Poliziano to celebrate the Medici and to integrate himself into the cultural landscape. As the second book begins, Poliziano offers celebratory verses in honor of the Medici, after reintroducing "Julio, the younger brother of our laurel" (by "laurel" Poliziano means Lorenzo, whose Latin name, "Laurentius," served as a convenient way to symbolize both military and poetic success, since the laurel was itself a symbol for both in antiquity).[59]

Poliziano proceeds, offering a succession-oriented brief history of the Medici in the fifteenth century: "who is not aware of the ancient glory and renowned honor of the Medici family, and of great Cosimo, the splendor of Italy, whose city calls herself his daughter? And how much esteem has Piero" – son of Cosimo, father of Lorenzo and Giuliano – "added to his father's worth, with what miraculous means has he removed evil hands and cruel discord from the body of the state?"[60] Poliziano stresses the patrilineal power of the Medici men, with emphasis on how much they have done to secure that most difficult to attain status: peace and concord. And then: "From Piero and the noble Lucrezia" – this was Lucrezia Tornabuoni – "Julio was born and, before him, Laurel": – Lorenzo – "Laurel, who still burns for a beautiful Lucrezia."[61] This latter Lucrezia was the idealized love object for Lorenzo (Laurel) when he competed in the prior tournament of 1469. Now, Giuliano (Julio) takes up the mantle of courtly love and the quest for honor: Julio, of whom the god Cupid says (addressing his own mother, the goddess of love Venus): "I will not show any pity to him until he carries off a new triumph for us: for I have shot an arrow into his heart from the eyes of the fair Simonetta."[62] Simonetta, a legendary beauty in Florence then, becomes Giuliano's idealized love object. Tragically, she will die, in fact,

---

[58] For the case of Botticelli's "Spring," see Charles Dempsey, *The Portrayal of Love: Botticelli's Primavera and Humanist Culture at the Time of Lorenzo the Magnificent* (Princeton: Princeton University Press, 1992).

[59] Poliziano, *Stanze*, 2.2; tr. Quint, 69.

[60] Poliziano, *Stanze*, 2.3; tr. Quint, 69.

[61] Poliziano, *Stanze*, 2.4; tr. Quint, 69.

[62] Poliziano, *Stanze*, 2.10; tr. Quint, 73.

a year after the tournament. But for the moment, she exists in the theater of Poliziano's mind, a perfect beauty after whom Julio longs and by whom he will be inspired.

The gods continue to observe and to voice their opinion, predictions, and commands in the *Stanze*, as Venus speaks in response to Cupid, taking an interest still in the Florentines and their earthly affairs and, now, in Julio most of all:

> But first Julio should arm himself, so that he may fill the world with our fame; and one is now singing the arms of strong Achilles and with his style is renewing ancient times, ever singing the examples of love: whence we shall see our glory, my fair son, rise in flight above the stars.[63]

Giuliano, in the view of the gods, appears as the new branch on the strong Medici tree, now that Lorenzo himself has emerged as a leader. And then there is the one who "is now singing strong Achilles." Here, Poliziano is referring to himself and to his translation of parts of the *Iliad*. He inserts himself onto the front lines of Florentine culture yet also defines, however cryptically and with a kind of malleable shorthand, what that culture is to be, when Venus says that he, Poliziano, *rinnuova in suo stil gli antichi tempi*, most literally, "renews in his style ancient times."

Those three concepts – renewal, style, and ancient times – what do they mean for Poliziano? After all, linking them had been an (arguably the) imperative of the Renaissance since the days of Petrarch. What makes Poliziano distinctive? To propose answers to these questions we need to return to and flesh out Florentine history and culture in the late 1470s and 1480s.

First, there is the matter of the Medici. Poliziano's *Stanze* remained unfinished, ending relatively shortly after the passages reported earlier. One reason is that the beautiful Simonetta, Florence's new muse and Giuliano's idealized love object, herself died young, in 1476. About her, Lorenzo said, in his *Commentary* to his own sonnets: "It seemed impossible to believe that so many men loved her without jealousy and that so many women praised her without envy."[64] If the death of the tournament's muse was one factor contributing to Poliziano leaving the *Stanze* unfinished, another, certainly, was a death of much greater moment, one for which he provides us the closest we have to an eyewitness account.

---

[63] Poliziano, *Stanze*, 2.15; tr. Quint, 75.
[64] Lorenzo de' Medici, *Comento*, "Argumento," to the first sonnet, 589–93, at 592–93; cit. and tr. Quint, x.

This event occurred in the year 1478. By now, Lorenzo was clearly Florence's leading citizen, and the Medici continued in their dominance of city affairs, however tenuous that dominance would come to seem. In his *Stanze* Poliziano had said, about Florence under Lorenzo's leadership, that it "rests tranquilly, happy in peace" (*Fiorenza lieta in pace si riposa*).[65] From one perspective this sentiment was certainly true. Lorenzo had assumed the role of leading citizen of Florence after the death of his father, Piero, in 1469, and Florence's position in the uneasy balance of power in Italy remained strong. He and his allies in the early 1470s solidified their political positions by having pro-Medici scrutineers appointed to vet potential priors.[66] Accordingly, within the city, as always, there were those other families who believed themselves just as entitled to the respect and prestige that the Medici commanded.

One of these was the rival Pazzi family, who like the Medici were bankers and who persuaded the then pope, Sixtus IV (Francesco della Rovere) to withdraw his formidable account from the Medici bank in Rome and commit it to that of the Pazzi.[67] Also in play, for the pope and the Medici, was a city of strategic importance, Imola, which sat on the western border of the Romagna region and was as such a gateway to trade, being relatively close to the Adriatic. The Romagna region was traditionally part of the papal states, and the pope wanted to install a loyal ally, named Francesco Salviati, as his archbishop there. But on the other side of Imola, as it happened, was Tuscany, itself under Florentine control. Imola, small though it was, loomed large in the power politics of the Italian city-states, so large in fact, in this case, that Lorenzo schemed to avoid Salviati's installation, citing a rule that any archiepiscopal appointments in Tuscan territory had to be cleared with Florence.[68] All the ingredients were in place for an explosive situation.

Matters reached such a pitch, in fact, that the conspirators – for at a certain point this is precisely what that group of people became, having added a few members by early 1478 – wound up hiring a professional solider, a mercenary named Montesecco, to organize the attack. The pope addressed some of them this way (Montesecco later said, in a confession): "Now I don't want anyone to die in any way, because it is not within the realm of our respon-sibilities to consent to anyone's death. True, Lorenzo is a lout and behaves badly toward us. But still I would not want his death at all. But a change of

[65] Poliziano, *Stanze*, 1.4.
[66] Martines, *April Blood*, 88–110; André Rochon, *La jeunesse de Laurent de Medicis (1449–1478)* (Paris: Les Belles Lettres, 1963); Rubenstein, *The Government*.
[67] Martines, *April Blood*, 98–99.
[68] Ibid., 152.

state: yes."[69] Meaning: do what you need to do have a change of government occur. The rest of the conspirators understood well what the pope meant and proceeded in their plan. When two different ideas (assassinations planned at lavish banquets) fell through, they settled on an idea that seems shocking even now: to carry the assassination out in a church, and not just in any church, but in Santa Maria del Fiore, Florence's famous Duomo. Even the paid assassin, Montesecco, thought this idea was crazy and backed out. But the conspirators persisted nevertheless, and the event – which is to say the assassination attempt on Lorenzo and Giuliano – took place on April 26, 1478.

When all was said and done, Poliziano was part of an effort to explain what had happened, and his *Commentary on the Pazzi Conspiracy* represents his account of the whole tawdry episode. We can let Poliziano take it from here as he narrates what happened at the Mass:

> As soon as the communion of the priest was over and the signal had been given, Bernardo Bandini, Francesco Pazzi, and the other conspirators surrounded Giuliano in a circle. First Bandini struck the young man, forcing his sword through his chest. Giuliano, dying, fled a few steps; they followed. Gasping for breath the youth fell to the ground. Francesco stabbed him again and again with his dagger. Thus this upright young man was murdered."[70]

This, then, was the first result of this awful conspiracy: that young Giuliano, whom Poliziano had been portraying in his *Stanze* as the virile flower of Florentine youth, was no more. The conspirators also, as we learn in the *Commentary*, made an attempt on Lorenzo's life, wounding him in the neck, but Lorenzo "turned upon his murderers with his unsheathed sword, watching carefully and guarding himself."[71]

Lorenzo was spirited out of the nave of the church and into its sacristy. Poliziano says: "Then I, who had withdrawn to the same place with some others, shut the bronze doors."[72] This moment is important, because Poliziano is establishing his own eyewitness status with his readers: he was there and his account will thus have more inherent value. Soon thereafter, Poliziano persists in this eyewitnessing. He tells us that Lorenzo's friends escorted him out of the Church and to the Medici palace by a circuitous route, so that Lorenzo might not have to see the body of his slaughtered

---

[69] See the "Confessione" of Montesecco in Gino Capponi, *Storia della reppublica di Firenze*, 2 vols. (Florence: Barbéra, 1876), 509–20, at 514; see also the analysis of Martines, in *April Blood*, 150–73.

[70] Angelo Poliziano, *Coniurationis Commentarium*, ed. Perini, 16; tr. Welles, 312.

[71] Ibid.

[72] Ibid., 18; tr. Welles, 313.

brother. Then, Poliziano relates: "I went straight to the house by the shortest route and came upon Giuliano's body wretchedly lying there, fouled with the blood of many wounds."[73] But Poliziano, supported by his friends, was led inside the Medici palace. There then follows one of those telling passages that can be read in many ways:

> The whole house was full of armed men and full of cries in favor of the Medici, which resounded off the roof in a great din. It was something to see: boys, old men, young men, priests, and laymen seizing arms to defend the Medici house as though it were the public safety.[74]

The passage means precisely what Poliziano surely intended: that Florence's many Medici allies rallied around the Medici in an hour of need. Poliziano also tells us unwittingly that the Medici palace had become far more in the minds of Florentines than a private home; it had begun to be identified with the city-state itself: one reason among many that their enemies objected to their growing power.

The conspiracy was ultimately unsuccessful, as a small band of conspirators tried and failed to take over Florence's actual governmental center, the Palazzo della Signoria. A strengthened Lorenzo made sure that the conspiracy was understood in the way he wanted it to be understood: as a vile, treacherous act, whose consequences could leave no doubt as to who was supreme in Florence. Poliziano's *Commentary* was part of this campaign, a way of explaining for all time the conspiracy's elements and consequences. He did so in Latin, echoing Sallust, whose *Conspiracy of Catiline* served as Poliziano's model, at least in part. And explain the consequences Poliziano did, with vigor.

If the conspiracy itself (in a Church, in public, intended to be carried out with bloody hand-to-hand combat) may seem startling to modern eyes, the retribution was even more outré. Once Medici supporters had retaken definitive control of the Palazzo Vecchio, the scene unfolded in this way:

> They hung Jacopo di Poggi [one of the conspirators] from the windows; they led the captive cardinal [this was Raffaele Riario, another in the extended web of conspirators] to the palazzo with a large guard and had much difficulty in protecting him from attack by the people. Most of those who followed him were killed by the crowd, all torn apart, their bodies mangled cruelly; in front of Lorenzo's doors someone bought, now a head fixed on a spear, now a shoulder.[75]

---

[73] Ibid., 18; tr. Welles, 314.
[74] Ibid.
[75] Ibid., 20; tr. Welles, 315–16.

"Justice," such as it was, emerged from the reactions and behaviors of a crowd that had been whipped into a frenzy and that, like the lynch mobs of the Reconstruction era in U.S. history, carried out their actions in a way that was visceral, bloody, and atavistic: the worst of humanity emerging even in the best of times, whether during the cultural flowering of the Renaissance or in the booming and industrializing United States of the late eighteenth and early nineteenth centuries.

Lynching, when we hear of it our modern context, is shocking, and justifiably so. It runs against everything we tend to assume as our natural rights to protect and acquire life, liberty, and property, rights that emerged as principles during the eighteenth-century Enlightenment and have been pursued as ideals in Western societies since then, with slavery and its terrible consequences being one of the most egregious failures of those ideals. In late fifteenth-century Florence, however, we should remember that those ideals barely existed. Poliziano's predecessors in the humanist movement had indeed articulated ideas such as the rights to property and notions of equality before the law.[76] But these ideas were not considered "rights" the way we think of that term today, with its implications of universality. They were for Florentine citizens only. And even then, we see that street justice, as here, in the case of the Pazzi conspiracy's consequences, could take precedence over any high-minded ideals.[77] This is not to devalue the contributions of civic humanists such as Bruni, whose thinking on this issue served as a very important, and still insufficiently recognized, part of the long intellectual genealogy of Western theories of human rights. It is to say, more simply, that Poliziano's world was still much closer to a "face-to-face" premodern society than we sometimes recognize. Poliziano's account of this conspiracy continues in this vein. There is more public violence, more retribution, more from Lorenzo that served, like his war against Volterra, to show that the Medici were not to be trifled with.

The conspiracy, and Poliziano's accounting thereof, serves as a kind of punctuation mark to the era of Lorenzo and the now dead Giuliano's fair youth. In Poliziano's other major work of vernacular poetry, *Orfeo*, he tells the story of the myth of Orpheus and Eurydice. That myth had its own tragic overtones: Eurydice, Orpheus's wife, was being chased by a satyr and, as she attempted to flee the sex-crazed half-man, half-goat, she fell into a nest of vipers, was bitten by one, and died.[78] Orpheus (whose musical abilities were

[76] See William Connell, "The Republican Idea," in Hankins, ed., *Renaissance Civic Humanism*, 14–29.

[77] See Lauro Martines, *Strong Words: Writing and Social Strain in the Italian Renaissance* (Baltimore: Johns Hopkins University Press, 2001).

[78] See Angelo Poliziano, *Fabula di Orfeo*, in Poliziano, *Stanze. Fabula di Orfeo*, 139–64.

outstanding) sang songs so sad that all the gods and nymphs pitied him. Advised to go down into the underworld to seek his wife, he did, and the gods of the underworld allowed him to take Eurydice back with him. She would live on one condition, that he not look back after her. Almost by accident, however, he did look back, and in so doing lost Eurydice forever.

At one point in Poliziano's *Orfeo*, when Orpheus is making his impassioned speech to Pluto, supreme god of the underworld, the character Orpheus speaks as follows, addressing the god: "In the end, everything returns to you; every mortal thing returns to you. Whatever lies under the moon as it circles, naturally arrives in your domain ... each mortal life falls back to you again, whatever lies under the circling moon must finally arrive in your domain, but everyone must take these roads at last."[79] This sentiment seems a far cry from Lorenzo's "whoever wants to be happy, let him." And yet the final line of that couplet of Lorenzo – "for tomorrow promises nothing certain" – portended, unwittingly to be sure, a series of almost unimaginable changes in the last two decades of the fifteenth century. Poliziano matured greatly in the 1480s, and his work, life, and thought were all spurred on by the emergence of a new and important member of the Florentine intellectual community, Pico della Mirandola.

---

[79] Poliziano, *Fabula di Orfeo*, ll. 205–8; see also Julia Cotton Hill, "Death and Politian," *Durham University Journal* 46 (1953–54), 96–105.

15

"WE BARELY HAVE TIME TO BREATHE." POLIZIANO, PICO, FICINO, AND THE BEGINNING OF THE END OF THE FLORENTINE RENAISSANCE

"I, AND OUR OWN POLIZIANO, HAVE OFTEN READ WHATEVER letters we had from you, whether they were directed to us or to others. What arrives always contends to such an extent with what there was previously, and new pleasures pop up so abundantly as we read, that because of our constant shouts of approbation we barely have time to breathe."[1] This statement appears in a letter written in the mid to late 1480s, from Giovanni Pico della Mirandola to a Venetian intellectual, Ermolao Barbaro, with whom Pico and Poliziano had a close correspondence. It shows in its enthusiasm that the three thinkers saw their enterprise as collective. And their letter exchanges, in their own way, also led to the composition of one of Poliziano's most interesting works, called *Lamia*, itself a kind of capstone to Italian Renaissance reflection on the nature of philosophy. To understand all this, it is important, first, to introduce Pico della Mirandola.

Giovanni Pico, Count of Mirandola (1463–94), more commonly known as Pico, was the scion of a noble family who ruled the small independent town of Mirandola, near Modena in northern Italy.[2] A true prodigy if ever there was

---

[1] Garin, *Pros.*, 806: "Legimus saepe ego et noster Politianus quascumque habemus tuas aut ad alios, aut ad nos epistolas; ita semper prioribus certant sequentia et novae fertiliter inter legendum efflorescunt veneres, ut perpetua quadam acclamatione interspirandi locum non habeamus."

[2] See Eugenio Garin, *Giovanni Pico della Mirandola: Vita e dottrina* (Florence: Le Monnier, 1937), still the best biography. See also Pier Cesare Bori, "The Historical and Biographical Background of the *Oration*," in Pico della Mirandola, *Oration on the Dignity of Man: A New Translation and Commentary*, eds. Francesco Borghesi, Michael Papio, and Massimo Riva (Cambridge: Cambridge University Press, 2012), 10–36; William G. Craven, *Giovanni Pico della Mirandola, Symbol of his Age* (Geneva: Droz, 1981); M.V. Dougherty, *Pico della Mirandola: New Essays* (Cambridge: Cambridge University Press, 2008); Gian Carlo Garfagnini, ed., *Convegno internazionale di studi*, 2 vols. (Florence: Olschki, 1997); Engelbert Monnerjahn, *Giovanni Pico della Mirandola: Ein Beitrag zur philosophischen Theologie des italienischen Humanismus* (Wiesbaden: Franz Steiner, 1960); Louis Valcke and Roland Galibois, *Le*

one, he had extensive experience with both Greek and Latin by the time he was ten years old. At thirteen, he went to Italy's leading law school, the University of Bologna. As so many humanists before him had done, when parental shackles were loosened (in this case because of the death of his mother), he left law school to pursue his studies of humanistic subjects freely, something that, with his private wealth, he was well positioned to do. His passion for philosophy took him to the University of Ferrara. And his desire to expand the range of his studies took him to Florence for a short stay in the 1470s, where he met Poliziano, among other members of Florence's intelligentsia.

Thereafter Pico studied at the University of Padua, a hotbed of scholastic philosophy, and he also began to widen his range from the customary Latin and Greek sources to those in other languages, including Hebrew and Arabic, which he studied in Padua with a Jewish convert and influential intellectual, Elia del Medigo. Pico's travels in pursuit of the most advanced philosophical knowledge continued; he wound up, for a time, at the University of Paris, whose reputation as Europe's center for theological study was undiminished. Now in his early twenties, Pico seems to have conceived an audacious plan: to draw up a series of 900 propositions covering all realms of human knowledge, propositions that he hoped eventually to debate and to defend in public.[3] With this plan in mind, he went to Florence for a more extended stay in the year 1484.

There, when Pico arrived, one of those magical moments in cultural history occurred, when just the right people at just the right time found themselves in proximity and, in large part, in sympathy with one another. There was Poliziano, about ten years older than Pico, who like the young count had been a prodigy. Their different backgrounds notwithstanding, they had had an immediate meeting of the minds when they met briefly in the 1470s, both devoted as they were not only to the ancient world but also to some of its more recondite corners: for Pico, the wilder reaches of different philosophical traditions; for Poliziano, Latin and Greek literature that others might have considered of secondary importance but that he, instead, saw as possessing an intrinsic value appropriate to his own cultural moment.

Then, there was Ficino. By now, in 1484, Ficino was an older, quite venerated figure. He had made it through the turbulent years of the Pazzi conspiracy and, though he would never have the same close relationship with Lorenzo the Magnificent as he had enjoyed with Lorenzo's grandfather,

périple intellectuel de Jean Pic de la Mirandole (Québec: Les Presses de l'Université Laval, 1994); Paolo Viti, ed., *Pico, Poliziano, e l'umanesimo di fine Quattrocento* (Florence: Olschki, 1994).

[3] See Stephen A. Farmer, *Syncretism in the West: Pico's 900 Theses (1486): The Evolution of Traditional Religious and Philosophical Systems* (Tempe: MRTS, 1998).

Cosimo, Ficino still flourished under the umbrella of Medici patronage, broad as this had become under Lorenzo's intellectually omnivorous support. Ficino was a leading figure, even if, by the 1480s, other voices were beginning to emerge. Ficino later commemorated his meeting with Pico as an almost divine occurrence, supported and favored by an astrological conjunction that seemed propitious.[4] It is hard for us today to imagine how central the "stars" and their relative positioning could seem to some intellectuals then; but to Ficino – and Pico, for that matter – it was of no little importance. It was in fact in that very year, 1484, that Ficino had decided to print-publish his *Complete Works of Plato*. The work had been finished years earlier, but he waited to have it printed until then, precisely owing to this astrological conjunction.[5] So when Pico arrived in the same year, the occurrence seemed to have been favored by the heavens.

The years from 1484 to 1486 stand out for the excitement and close collaboration that existed among the triad of Ficino, Pico, and Poliziano. The balance of friendship and intellectual engagement would shift a bit in the coming years. Ficino, always maintaining his lively personality in his letters and sustaining his friendly tone, began to be engaged in the 1480s in the more esoteric reaches of Platonism. As it happened, Pico too was looking at the same sorts of texts, going beyond Ficino's capacities (as a young energetic upstart was wont to do) by looking into texts in Hebrew and Arabic, two languages Ficino could not read.

Then, as the year 1486 came about, one of the strangest series of events in Pico's life occurred, events that remind us powerfully of the premodern world in which he and his compatriots lived. Just as Poliziano cannot really be understood without the background of clan violence against which he lived, so too must Pico be set against his lived reality, replete with unarticulated assumptions that are difficult to imagine today.

Pico was about to set out for Rome, where he planned to lay the groundwork for his planned, massive debate.[6] On the way, however, he stopped in the Tuscan city of Arezzo, a city steeped in tradition, the place whence the luminary Bruni had hailed. Pico was not there, however, to celebrate humanist genealogy. Instead, with about twenty armed men at his side, he kidnapped a beautiful woman: a widow named Margherita, who had been remarried to none other than a member of the Medici clan (Giuliano di Mariotto de' Medici, from another branch of the illustrious Florentine

[4] In his Preface to his translation of Plotinus, f. a.ii (r).
[5] Hankins, *Plato*, 1: 302–3.
[6] The account that follows is heavily indebted to Bori, "The Historical and Biographical Background."

family). We possess a robust record of what went on, and it is worth delving
in, to see how this formidable intellectual, Pico, also engaged in behavior so
shocking that he was lucky to escape alive.

We hear first from an envoy to Florence, Aldobrandino Guidoni, who was
in Tuscany on behalf of his employers, the noble family of the Este, lords of
Ferrara and Mantua. Guidoni says that Pico

> enjoyed in this city [Florence] great distinction ... It truly seemed that his
> erudition and knowledge were beyond belief ... The poor Count [poor,
> obviously, not meant literally here but referring rather to the grim tide of
> events to follow] made it known in those days that he intended to travel to
> Rome; and it seemed that he had loaded all of his things and sent them to
> Perugia. Then he followed afterward with all of his servants, and there were
> twenty people on horseback and on foot; and he had two crossbowmen on
> horseback; and they went to Arezzo, where his most beautiful beloved had
> gone.[7]

We learn, first of all, that when you were a person of Pico's status, you
traveled with an armed retinue. Fair enough. But you normally did not do
things like this (what follows is testimony from Giuliano, the husband,
writing from Arezzo to Lorenzo the Magnificent in Florence):

> Yesterday morning, as my lady Margherita was going with her servant to
> the old Duomo outside Arezzo for a stroll, she was taken against her will by
> the Count of Mirandola's men, was put on a horse and was carried off with
> some of his servants in the company of the aforementioned Count who, for
> this purpose, had lodged the previous evening in Arezzo with about twenty
> horses and crossbowmen ready to cause harm. They led her away, galloping
> as fast as they could.[8]

It was not unusual for Lorenzo to receive letters containing requests, or that
informed him of news he needed to know, and so on. But this one must have
seemed unusual. It provoked a minor diplomatic incident, as the city government of Arezzo wrote to the city government of Florence that Margherita
had been taken away in an act of betrayal. But there were other voices, too,
that suggested instead that Margherita was hopelessly enamored of Pico and
would have followed him anywhere. Pico's own sister wrote to another
relative suggesting just that.

---

[7] Tr. Bori, in "The Historical and Biographical Background," 11; the documents are collected
in Marcello Del Piazzo, "Nuovi documenti sull'incidente Aretino del Pico della Mirandola,"
Rassegna degli Archivi di Stato 23 (1963), 271–90.
[8] Tr. Bori, in "The Historical and Biographical Background," 12.

In any case, the people of Arezzo were not pleased at what was perceived as a brazen act of kidnapping. The *podestà* of the city (in effect, the police captain) rang a central bell and summoned up to two hundred men to track Pico and his kidnapping party down, which they did. Eighteen of Pico's men were killed and, as one contemporary wrote, "the magnificent *signore* himself [Pico] was seriously wounded; and if he hadn't had a good horse beneath him, he would have found himself in the company of those eighteen."[9] We think of intellectuals as retiring creatures. But, like his friend Lorenzo the Magnificent, who with deft swordsmanship defended himself from his attackers during the Pazzi conspiracy, Pico was an aristocrat. And to be raised as an aristocrat in Renaissance Italy meant to be raised with arms as well as books.

Pico was taken prisoner, and his fate seemed forbidding. But then, with some back-channel intervention from Lorenzo, who wrote to the Aretines expressing regret and sympathy for the "injustice done to Giuliano" (the aggrieved husband), Pico was released after paying a substantial fine. The same Ferrarese envoy, Guidoni, wrote to his employer, Ercole I D'Este, that Pico was no longer held in the esteem in which he once was: "The whole of this city is saddened, for this Count Giovanni had the reputation of being the most learned man that there had been in this city in a long time. He was deemed a saint; now he has lost his good name and reputation."[10] "A saint": *uno sancto*, in the Italian dialect in which Guidoni wrote. In one sense this remark is a throwaway indication on Guidoni's part: he is saying that the Aretines had considered Pico as a person of superior wisdom and goodness. Yet, the otherwise little known envoy's comment does tell us something about Pico's character and about how he saw himself. He was, as was Ficino, convinced that momentous changes were on the way, changes he himself might help bring about through study and research.

Eventually Pico made it back to Florence, and his friendship with Ficino grew more intense and, eventually, somewhat rivalrous. One of Pico's first letters to Ficino gives us a sense of the tenor of his thinking: "This, my dear Marsilio, is my passion, these are the flames with which I burn, and for me there is not only the promise but the gift of joy, which is not fleeting and vain but stable: the true image of the future glory that will be revealed in us."[11] Like so many thinkers of his day, Pico felt the presence, powerfully, of instability, and was willing, hoping, to do something about it. For some,

[9] Ibid., 13.
[10] Ibid., 14.
[11] Pico, Letter to Ficino, in Pico, *Op.*, 1: 367–68; Tr. Bori, in "The Historical and Biographical Background," 17.

such as the slightly later Machiavelli, it was political reform that was necessary, shorn for the most part of anything having to do with speculative
philosophy and religion.[12] But, for Pico, only transformation through intellectual breakthroughs seemed possible. The passage just cited echoes Saint
Paul's letter to the Romans, where Paul speaks of a future glory yet to come,
one that in its magnitude would tower over the paltry present.[13] Pico, too,
was suffused with this sense that there was a great change coming and, more
importantly, that he had a role to play, a role to be inaugurated by his great,
planned debate in Rome.

Pico was chastened, somewhat, by his embarrassing kidnapping episode,
suggesting in a letter to a contemporary that he had learned his lesson: "He
who has shipwrecked only once can cry out to Neptune. If he falls again and
strikes the same rock, no one will offer a hand or have pity on him."[14] Still, he
stood firm on the notion that love (divine, not carnal by now) was
a motivating factor in all he did, arguing in other works that celestial love
is the most powerful and, interestingly, that love between men (rather than
between a man and a woman) represented the purest and most powerful
expression of this type of higher love.

Pico wrote, for example, a work in Tuscan, entitled *Comment on a Poem of
Girolamo Benivieni* (Benivieni was a Florentine contemporary and friend who
had written a "Poem on Celestial and Divine Love," to which Pico wrote his
Comment).[15] Pico in his *Comment* singles out "heavenly love," which, he
writes

> involves no danger of coitus, but rather is directed entirely toward the
> spiritual beauty of the soul, or the intellect. This spiritual beauty is much
> more complete in men than in women, as is true of any other attribute. This
> is why most men who have been affected by heavenly love have loved some
> young man of virtuous character (the more beautiful his body, the more
> attractive his virtue) rather than become effeminate and pursue a flock of
> harlots, who not only do not lead a man to any degree of spiritual perfection
> but, like Circe, completely transform him into a beast.[16]

Was Pico thinking of his recent misadventure in Arezzo? Was he renouncing
female companionship? Was he declaring a new sexual identity? None of

[12] See Christopher S. Celenza, *Machiavelli: A Portrait* (Cambridge, MA: Harvard University Press, 2015), for Machiavelli and instability.
[13] Rom., 8: 18–19, as noted by Bori, in "The Historical and Biographical Background," 17 n.25.
[14] Pico, *Op.*, 1: 378–79; tr. Bori, in "The Historical and Biographical Background," 21.
[15] Pico della Mirandola, *Commento alla canzone di amore*, in Pico, ed. Garin, 443–581.
[16] Ibid., 537–38; tr. Bori, 26, modified.

these questions permits a definitive answer. What we can say is that he was preparing himself mentally for his great debate, focusing his intellect, and attempting to reach a new phase of maturity.

As to the debate, he was aware of the objections others might have, both to the scope of the project and to the apparent audacity he was displaying in putting himself forward at such an early age. In December 1486 Pico went so far as to have his nine hundred theses printed in Rome in preparation for the debate, adding that he would personally pay the travel expenses of any scholars wanting to attend who could not afford the trip on their own.

The plan was remarkable, if one compares it to the medieval tradition out of which it emerged. "Disputations" were a regular and important part of life in medieval universities. One variety of these disputations included debate on what were termed "quodlibetal questions" (*quaestiones quodlibetales*). The term derived from the Latin word *quodlibet*, meaning "whatever you please," and these events, which could last up to two days, would have a maximum of between twenty and twenty-five questions to be debated. Another variety of debates were known as *quaestiones disputatae*, "disputed questions," where the topics for debate were rather more settled in advance than in this case of quodlibetal debates. Pico's intentions have been read in both ways.[17] Either way, given the setting and taking Pico's age into account, it was clear that Pico's plan was far from normal, in keeping perhaps with his sense of his own extraordinariness.

Pico divided his theses into different categories, and it will be helpful to take a look at a few to understand the tenor of what he was trying to do.[18] Take, for example, a set of his "conclusions" (this was the term he used for his theses) "according to Porphyry," the later Platonist and student and biographer of Plotinus:

> By the father in Plato we should understand the cause which from itself produces every effect; by the maker that which receives matter from the other.
> The demiurge of the world is the supra-mundane soul.
> The exemplar is nothing but the intellect of that demiurgal soul.[19]

---

[17] See Farmer, 6, who argues for the quodlibetal position; and M.V. Dougherty, "Three Precursors to Pico della Mirandola's Roman Disputation and the Question of Human Nature," in Dougherty, *Pico della Mirandola: New Essays*, 114–51, who argues for the notion that Pico's proposed debate stood in a tradition of medieval *quaestiones disputatae*.

[18] The 900 theses are edited and translated in Farmer, *Syncretism*, 209–553.

[19] Pico, "900 Theses," 22.1–22.3, in Farmer, *Syncretism*, 306–7.

Thus far we see a set of statements that, though strikingly unfamiliar to modern ears, are not that controversial.

Pico is simply interpreting ideas about the cosmos, drawn from Porphyry (indirectly, to be precise, since Pico takes his statements from a later Platonist, Proclus, who had been recapitulating Porphyry's arguments).[20] They have to do at root with Plato's creation myth as represented in his dialogue *Timaeus*, on which all later Platonists had opinions. The "father" in this case is what later Platonists, reading Plato and explicating him, would have called the "One," meaning the supreme entity out of whom the universe flows. The "demiurge" is the being who creates the world; Pico identifies this being with the "supra-mundane soul," meaning a variety of soul that exists above and beyond our world. And the "exemplar" occupies another part of that later Platonic system of hierarchies. Abstruse, yes; unusual, no: it is part of the way one interpreted Platonic philosophy, making links among the original texts of Plato and the way later interpreters understood them.

But then one runs into these statements, immediately following:

> Every soul participating in the volcanic intellect is seminated on the moon.
>
> From the preceding conclusion I deduce that all Germans are large in body and white in color.
>
> From the same conclusion I deduce that all Germans of the apostolic seat should be the most reverent.
>
> Just as Apollo is the solar intellect, so Aesculapius is the lunar intellect.
>
> From the preceding conclusion I deduce that the moon in ascending gives health at birth.[21]

Now, you could go ahead and try to figure out the exact series of astrological meanings inherent in these statements. For the truth is that these sorts of astrological notions were not only taken seriously in Pico's day; they were used as a way to guide one's life – whether you were a leader trying to find just the right day to begin a battle or, closer to home, Ficino, trying to see when precisely would be the best time to publish your masterpiece (he chose the astrologically propitious year of 1484, as we have seen, to publish his *Complete Works of Plato*). In truth, there are better ways to spend our time; a more profitable way to think about this variety of thesis is that it reminds us, again, of the premodern world in which Pico lived.

There were, however, other theses in which Pico presented opinions that seemed suspect to the Church, so much so that the then pope, Innocent VIII,

---

[20] They are drawn from Proclus's commentary on Plato's *Timaeus*; see Farmer, 307, n. to 22.1–3.

[21] Pico, "900 Theses," 22.4–22.8, in Farmer, *Syncretism*, 306–7.

having heard of the scope of Pico's planned disputation, had it canceled and, indeed, condemned Pico's work, and specifically all the theses that promoted "certain arts, disguising themselves as natural philosophy harmful to the Catholic faith and humankind, sharply damned by the canons and doctrines of Catholic learned men." The pope said that excommunication would be in store for anyone who thought "to read, to copy, to print, or to have read, copied or printed; or to hear others reading it in whatever fashion."[22] Pico touched a nerve, and it is worth asking how and why the sorts of things about which he was writing concerned the Roman curia to the extent that they did.

For one thing, it was Pico's rhetoric that seemed out of bounds, even if, to him, it might have seemed appropriate. Take what he says on the first page of the printed edition of his theses:

> The following nine hundred dialectical, moral, physical, mathematical, metaphysical, theological, magical, and cabalistic opinions, including his own and those of the wise Chaldeans, Arabs, Hebrews, Greeks, Egyptians, and Latins, will be disputed publicly by Giovanni Pico of Mirandola, the Count of Concord.[23]

First, Pico is claiming to cover all the traditional areas of philosophy ("dialectical" through "metaphysical"). Then he moves to theology, then to magic and the Hebrew art of Cabala; and not only this, Pico is claiming also to cover the world, as it were: the Chaldeans (which designates people from an area of southeast Babylon but whose name also encompassed a series of mystical texts thought to be very old, on par with Moses in age), Arabs, Hebrews, and Egyptians, as well as Greek and Latin sources. His first claim, then, is that he is covering a body of knowledge that no one else could have hoped to master, in a variety of languages that was similarly broad.

Pico goes on to distinguish himself yet again: "In reciting these opinions, he has not imitated the splendor of the Roman language, but the style of speaking of the most celebrated Parisian disputers, since this is used by almost all philosophers of our time."[24] What Pico is saying is this: I know well how to write Latin in the style favored by humanists of our day (Ciceronian and classicizing), but for the purposes of this event I will adapt myself and my style to the conventions of scholastic philosophy, conventions that include scholastic Latin. Both in his language and his self-proclaimed breadth of knowledge, Pico is presenting himself as exceptional. It was in part this very claim that seems to have bothered the authorities. The same papal bull of Innocent

[22] Cit. and tr. Farmer, *Syncretism*, 16.
[23] Pico, "900 Theses," First Preface, in Farmer, *Syncretism*, 211.
[24] Ibid.

VIII, cited earlier, also condemned Pico's tendency in the 900 theses to renovate "the errors of the pagan philosophers" and to foster positively the "deceits of the Jews."[25]

As to the "pagans," the problem is that Pico speaks of things such as "gods," for example, as if this concept were unproblematic in a Christian world, where, even if one routinely prayed to saints as intermediaries, the basic idea was that there was only one God. This propensity comes to light in a series of "conclusions according to Proclus," a fifth-century CE later Platonist, who had synthesized a number of his Platonic predecessors' arguments. Take this conclusion: "Between the extreme paternal gods, Saturn and Jove, Rhea necessarily mediates through the property of fertile life."[26] Proclus, in his own *Platonic Theology* (a text much beloved by Ficino, Pico, and others) had set forth a series of seven "orders," represented by the names of the planetary gods, which stood in a hierarchical relation to one another. Saturn, Jove, and Rhea stood in an intimate relation to on another, making up the first three of these.[27]

Now it is not the case that Pico is advocating the worship of these "gods," nor is he coming out and criticizing any existing Christian frameworks in a practical sense. But there is something about how he phrases this statement that could indeed be troublesome: it sounds a lot like the trinity, for one thing, with the number three foregrounded; it implies, in its direct, seemingly factual statement, that these "gods" existed; and so on. True, the idea was to set this proposition and the other 899 out for debate. But what if someone were wavering in his faith? What if that notional person was wavering precisely because he was reading all these newly discovered later Platonic texts, like that of Proclus, texts that, though they were written by anti-Christians in late antiquity, seemed nonetheless to propound theories and doctrines that did indeed bear at least a family resemblance to Christian dogmas (as in this case the Proclan theory resembled the trinity)? One can see how fears might emerge, especially since the newly arrived printing press had offered possibilities for dissemination that dwarfed anything available in the manuscript era.

Or take these two conclusions "according to the ancient doctrine of Mercury Trismegistus the Egyptian" (otherwise known as "Hermes Trismegistus," the thinker believed to be an ancient Egyptian source of wisdom, also roughly contemporaneous with Moses):

---

[25] Cit. and tr. Farmer, *Syncretism*, 15.
[26] Pico, "900 Theses," 24.12, in Farmer, *Syncretism*, 318–19.
[27] See Proclus, *Theologia platonica*, 6 vols. ed. and tr. Henri D. Saffrey and Leendert Westerink (Paris: Les Belles Lettres, 1968–97); 5.3, pp. 16–17; cf. Farmer, 319, n. to 24.12.

Nothing in the world is devoid of life.

Nothing in the universe can suffer death or destruction.

Corollary: Life is everywhere, providence is everywhere, immortality is everywhere.[28]

These propositions too could seem quite dangerous. It is not that Pico is advocating "pantheism," the notion that the universe, including its physical, sensible manifestation (what we see, hear, and touch), is to be identified with God and vice versa. But it is close enough to make one start to wonder: to wonder, perhaps, if one might doubt the long Judeo-Christian tradition that maintained that all-powerful God stood apart from the created world and indeed was its Creator; to wonder, indeed, if the physical universe was all there was; to wonder if human agency might be divinely powerful, provided one engaged in the right rituals and activated the right parts of nature (Godly as "nature" might in this version of things seem to be). Again, it was not that Pico, here at least, was advocating this sort of thing. But a curious reader, a reader wavering in his faith, might be set off in the wrong direction.

Then there were the "deceits of the Jews," as the pope's Bull would have it. Here the point of contention revolved around the fact that Pico had become an enthusiastic believer in the Cabala, a Hebrew word that means "tradition" or "handing down" and that designated a series of interpretive practices, all of which centered on the notion that everything about scripture and the tradition of scripture – down to the very letters of the words – was holy.[29] As in later Platonism, members of this tradition adhered to the idea that God (for Platonists, the One), all-powerful and almost unknowable, had created levels to the universe. In Cabalistic tradition there were ten "numerations," known in Hebrew as the ten "sefirot."

Here is what Pico has to say on this front: "there are no letters in the whole Law which in their forms, conjunctions, separations, crookedness, straightness, defect, excess, smallness, largeness, crowning, closure, openness, and

[28] Pico, "900 Theses," 27.5–27.6, in Farmer, *Syncretism*, 340–41.
[29] See Giulio Busi, "Who does not Wonder at this Chameleon? The Kabbalistic Library of Giovanni Pico della Mirandola," in Giulio Busi, ed., *Hebrew to Latin, Latin to Hebrew: The Mirroring of Two Cultures in the Age of Humanism* (Turin: Aragno, 2006), 167–96; Busi, "Toward a New Evaluation of Pico's Kabbalistic Sources," *Rinascimento* 48 (2009), 165–83; Brian P. Copenhaver, "Maimonides, Abulafia and Pico: A Secret Aristotle for the Renaissance," *Rinascimento* 47 (2007), 23–51; Copenhaver, "The Secret of Pico's Oration: Cabala and Renaissance Philosophy," *Midwest Studies in Philosophy* 26 (2002), 56–81; Fabrizio Lelli, ed., *Pico e la cabbalà* (Mirandola: Centro internazionale di cultura, 2014); Moshe Idel, *La Cabbalà in Italia* (Florence: Giuntina, 2007); Chaim Wirszubski, *Pico della Mirandola's Encounter with Jewish Mysticism* (Cambridge, MA: Harvard University Press, 1989).

order, do not reveal the secrets of the ten numerations."[30] On one level, what Pico is saying is that when one interpreted texts – here the Law (Hebrew scripture) – every element was important. But there were cabalists who went further, arguing, as Pico is reflecting here, that even the shapes of the letters might have, imbued within them, a power that could, with the right sort of interpretation, be released and indeed have phenomenological effects on the world. Every Christian would have been familiar, to an extent, with a similar operation when, at every Mass, the central sacrament of the Eucharist was performed: the priest's words channeled divine power and made the bread turn into the body of Christ, which congregants then consumed, unifying themselves to divinity in the most intimate way possible. But, again, Pico seems here to be going just a bit too far, bringing in a tradition, Judaism, thought to have been superseded by Christianity and discussing and endorsing a part of that tradition that lay at the outer reaches of respectability.[31]

True, Pico and others might say that in his broad embrace of non-Christian religious ideas, he was only researching and hoping to find the true nature of Christianity, which in this view is much more capacious than tradition allowed.[32] But it all just seemed too extravagant for the Church. Pico's proposed debate was shut down, and in March 1487, a committee of clerics was drawn together under orders from the pope.[33] Pico, offended by this development, then published a justification of his work, on which the committee did not look kindly.[34] By the summer Pico was compelled to sign a statement formally submitting to the Church's authority in this matter, even as, initially unbeknownst to him, a warrant for his arrest had been issued. Pico fled Rome when he heard about the warrant. Captured near Lyon, he was taken to Paris by agents of the pope, where, however, the French King Charles VII (a friend of Lorenzo de' Medici) protected Pico,

---

[30] Pico, "900 Theses," 28.33, in Farmer, *Syncretism*, 358–59.

[31] Supersessionism goes back to Paul, Gal. 3:28: "There is neither Jew nor Gentile, neither slave nor free, nor is there male and female, for you are all one in Christ Jesus." See also Heb. 10.

[32] For Christian cabalism, see Joseph Dan, ed., *The Christian Kabbalah: Jewish Mystical Books and Their Christian Interpreters* (Cambridge, MA: Houghton Library of the Harvard College Library, 1998).

[33] See Alberto Biondi, "La doppia inchiesta sulle *Conclusiones* e le traversie romane di Pico nel 1487," in Garfagnini, ed., *Giovanni Pico della Mirandola: Convegno*, 197–212; Paul Richard Blum, "Pico, Theology, and the Church," in Dougherty, ed., *Pico della Mirandola: New Essays*, 37–60; Francesco Borghesi, "Chronology," in Pico, *Oration*, 37–51; Garin, *La vita*, 31–36.

[34] On Pico's "Apologia," see Amos Edelheit, *Ficino, Pico, and Savonarola: The Evolution of Humanist Theology 1461/2–1498* (Leiden: Brill, 2008), 286–348.

confining him to a royal castle to secure his safety.[35] He was permitted to return to Florence under royal protection, where the tenor of his work changed definitively, as we shall see.

Most interestingly, however, a work that went unprinted during Pico's lifetime is the work for which he has become most famous, which today is known as the *Oration on the Dignity of Man*, though Pico had only given it the title *Oration*. In its original version it had been intended as the formal oration Pico would deliver to open the debate. There has been quite a bit of scholarship surrounding this work, and it has generated diverse interpretations since its appearance.[36] Clearing the scholarship away for moment, it is important to say something that should be obvious but is too often obscured: Pico's *Oration* is a stunning, fascinating work, one that well deserves the reputation it has acquired.

The *Oration* begins with a rapturous statement about the nature of humanity, one that signals Pico's direction and orientation:

> Most esteemed fathers, I have read in the ancient texts of the Arabians that when Abdallah the Saracen was questioned as to what on this world's stage, so to speak, seemed to him most worthy of wonder, he replied that there is nothing to be seen more wonderful than man.[37]

It is a measure of what Pico was up to and of the sorts of strategies he employed that scholars even today are not sure to whom he is referring here, with his reference to "Abdallah the Saracen." Different candidates have been proposed, all of whom can be located in the long medieval Islamic tradition.[38] More significant, however, is the effect that a statement such as this was intended to have on Pico's audience during the debate that never occurred. It is as if Pico were saying, Here we are, in Rome, the seat of international Christendom, and to show you – many of whom are distinguished clerics – how much I know and how willing I am to strain the boundaries of orthodoxy, I will begin with a reference to a thinker of whom you probably have never heard and whose writings you necessarily will not have read.

[35] See Léon Dorez and Louis Thuasne, *Pic de la Mirandole en France (1485–1488)* (Paris: Leroux, 1897).
[36] See Francesco Borghesi, "Interpretations," in Pico della Mirandola, *Oration on the Dignity of Man: A New Translation and Commentary*, 52–65; M.V. Dougherty, "Introduction," in Dougherty, ed., *Pico della Mirandola: New Essays*, 1–12, at 1–6.
[37] Pico della Mirandola, *Oration*, ed. and tr. in Pico della Mirandola, *Oration on the Dignity of Man: A New Translation and Commentary*, 108–277.
[38] See Pico, *Oration*, 109, n.3, for the different candidates.

Pico then goes on to make a classic rhetorical move stressing his own newness.[39] He says that he went through all the classic opinions on why "man" (standing in, obviously, for humanity as a whole) is so unique and worthy of wonder. Some had said, "man is the intermediary between creatures, a companion of higher beings, a king of things beneath him."[40] Others had said man was located midway between nature and the divine and "only slightly inferior, as David affirms, to angels."[41] All of these reasons are indeed impressive, Pico affirms. But (and here is where Pico wants to set himself off from tradition and make himself seem singular and unique) those reasons "are not the main grounds on which man may rightfully claim for himself the privilege of the highest admiration."[42] Pico fell to pondering, and wondering, and, finally, he came to see precisely what it was that made man not only unique but also inhabiting a "condition to be envied not only by beasts but even by the stars and the intelligences dwelling beyond this world."[43]

It was this: God created everything in the heavens and in the earth, all the stars and celestial spheres, all the oceans, mountains, animals, and earthly things. But, at the end, God (to whom Pico refers as the *artifex* in Latin, which means "craftsman" but that also possesses resonances of "builder," "architect," and "planner" and that also refers to the Platonic "demiurge" of the *Timaeus*) was unsatisfied. Why? Because He "still longed for there to be someone to ponder the meaning of such a magnificent achievement, to love its beauty and to marvel at its vastness."[44] But then, God was further stymied:

> There was nothing among his archetypes [these were in the nature of "templates" and were an important part of the Platonic tradition] from which He could mold a new progeny, nor was there anything in His storehouses that He might bestow on His new son as an inheritance, nor was there among the seats of the world any place for this contemplation of the universe. Every place was by then filled; all things had already been assigned to the highest, the middle, and the lowest orders.[45]

---

[39] On this posture in the history of philosophy, see Stephen Menn, "The *Discourse on the Method* and the Tradition of Intellectual Autobiography," in Jon Miller and Brad Inwood, eds., *Hellenistic and Early Modern Philosophy* (Cambridge: Cambridge University Press, 2003), 141–91.

[40] Pico, *Oration*, 111.

[41] Ibid.

[42] Ibid.

[43] Ibid., 113.

[44] Ibid.

[45] Ibid., 115.

Already we see where Pico is going: man is unique, fitting into no fixed scheme.

Finally, God decided that man should possess one distinguishing characteristic: he should "share in common whatever belonged to every other being."[46] This characteristic would be what distinguished humanity: human beings, in so far as they are human, are distinct from yet somehow united to all things. As Pico puts it, regarding God:

> He therefore took man, this creature of indeterminate image, set him in the middle of the world, and said to him: "We have given you, Adam, no fixed seat or form of your own, no talent peculiar to you alone. This we have done so that whatever seat, whatever form, whatever talent you may judge desirable, these same may you have and possess according to your desire and judgment."[47]

This statement is extraordinary enough on its own: human beings are plastic, they can mold themselves, and they can freely follow their interests. What comes next is even more important, as God continues to speak: "Once defined, the nature of all other beings is constrained within the laws We have prescribed for them. But you, constrained by no limits, may determine your nature for yourself, according to your own free will, in whose hands we have placed you."[48] Thus God has given a profound freedom to mankind and, it should be said, a kind of loneliness and even danger accompanying that freedom: "It will be in your power to degenerate into the lower forms of life, which are brutish. Alternatively, you shall have the power, in accordance with the judgment of your soul, to be reborn into the higher orders, those that are divine."[49]

On one hand, then, we hear things that are familiar: a focus on the human soul as that part of a person that can be trained through spiritual exercise, so that, instead of inclining toward base, earthly lusts and desires, one develops the strength to look upward toward the divine. On the other hand, we should not undervalue the loneliness that is there in Pico's vision, implicit as it may be. The explicit tone of the *Oration* breathes full-throated optimism. Man's freedom is owed to a good and generous God, and isolating and understanding that freedom serve as a way to praise God, since He gave it to mankind. As Pico says: "O supreme liberality of God the Father, and

---

[46] Ibid.
[47] Ibid., 117.
[48] Ibid.
[49] Ibid.

supreme and wonderful happiness of man who is permitted to obtain what he desires and to be what he wills."[50]

But remember: Pico wrote the *Oration* to be delivered at the start of a debate that never occurred; moreover, he did so at a time in his life (only in his early twenties) when he was at a manic phase of activity both intellectual and otherwise (as his abortive kidnapping attempt testifies). It is as if Pico sees himself as a stand-in for human capacity, multiform and unlimited as it is; and it is also as if Pico, in his life and at that moment, saw himself, most of all, as the one who could lead humanity into that new age where all could realize this God-given potential, if only they had the right framework in which to do so. Pico says, regarding man: "If he – being dissatisfied with the lot assigned to any other creature – gathers himself into the center of his own unity, thus becoming a single spirit with God in the solitary darkness of the Father, he, who had been placed above all things, will become superior to all things."[51] The process of bringing one's superior status to fruition is difficult. One needs to unify oneself with God in that "solitary darkness" before arriving at this superior status.

Much of the rest of the *Oration* refers to names, phenomena, and traditions that will seem unfamiliar. Angelology, Hebrew mysticism, and many recondite aspects of the Platonic tradition emerge. But there is a moment when Pico offers a practical nugget to his listeners, clothed though it is in unfamiliar language. After a section on the Cherubim (angels who were thought to stand just below the Seraphim, who were the highest-ranking angels), Pico writes as follows:

> So too, emulating the cherubic life on Earth, curbing the drive of the emotions through moral science, dispersing the darkness of reason through dialectic (as if washing away the squalor of ignorance and vice), may we purge our souls, lest our emotions run amok or our reason imprudently run off course at any time. Then may we imbue our purified and well-prepared soul with the light of natural philosophy so that afterward we may perfect it with the knowledge of things divine."[52]

Put in simple terms, Pico offers a sequence of philosophical disciplines. First is "moral science," meaning ethics or moral philosophy. A person's character, its basic training, comes first. Then "dialectic," or logic, follows, to be used by young people of good character to clear away ignorance and to "purge" themselves of damaging emotional swings. Thereafter comes

---

[50] Ibid.
[51] Ibid., 121.
[52] Ibid., 143.

"natural philosophy," a discipline that allows one to see how nature works, so that, subsequently, one can arrive at what is most important: theology, where one will find the only proper framework for understanding where and how the natural phenomena one has studied and observed really fit.

Pico was not advocating practical education reform, of course, and his sequence of fields was not especially original, reflecting as it did both ancient and medieval traditions. But, buried in the ecstatic and esoteric language of the *Oration* though it is, this order of disciplines is noteworthy since Ficino had similar concerns, with the central question being: how should we educate our young people? Pico's arrangement, with moral philosophy coming first, reflects a general anxiety that Ficino too experienced: the creeping sensation that something was terribly wrong with contemporary society. Ground up reform, which would include imbuing young people with the right moral character – before they went on to other educational experiences – represented a clear priority.

Before we return to Ficino, however, Pico's career following the abortive debate comes into relief. It is a poignant story and one that possesses no little mystery as well. With his debate canceled by the higher echelons of Church leadership, Pico returned to Florence an altered, and chastened, man. There was no abatement in his work ethic, as the years 1488 until his death in 1494 were highly productive ones.[53] His orientation, however, changed in a marked fashion, as he became more contemplative, more internally spiritual, and more connected to his friend and soul mate Angelo Poliziano.

During this period Pico wrote some significant works, perhaps the most momentous of which was *De ente et uno*, or *On Being and the One*.[54] The issue involved, whether "one" is superior to "being," seems, today, far less vital than one might imagine. For Pico and his cohort, it was an important concern, reflecting views about the nature of God and, secondarily, about the structure of the universe. At root, Pico's *De ente et uno* represents a drive toward harmony between seemingly discordant philosophical positions, specifically those of Plato and Aristotle, respectively.

For Plato, and more importantly for the way Ficino and other Platonists interpreted Plato, One – unity, in other words – stood above being.[55] In a practical sense what this meant was that God, having created the

[53] See Francesco Borghesi, "A Life in Works," in Dougherty, ed., *Pico della Mirandola: New Essays*, 202–19, at 216–19.
[54] See Pico della Mirandola, *De ente et uno*, ed. Raphael Ebgi and Franco Bacchelli (Milan: Bompiani, 2010); and Stéphane Toussaint, *L'esprit du Quattrocento: Pic de la Mirandole: Le* De ente et uno *et* Réponses à Antonio Cittadini (Paris: Honoré Champion, 1995).
[55] See Chapter 13; and Plato, *Parmenides*, 137c–147a; *Sophist*, 238d–240a.

phenomenological universe, placed what Ficino and many others (Pico included for that matter) termed "seeds" in both the earth and in people, seeds that with the right sort of cultivation could be developed and that would, when developed, allow closer contact between the human and the divine. Inside you, for example, there is a seed of the divine; but without meditating on that seed, "finding" it, as it were, you might never cultivate it enough to bring it to fruition. You might stay, for example, in the realm of physical, bodily lust and other desires, never lifting yourself toward the divine by the right sort of training. But what was clear was that God, as the Christian version of the One, was above all recognizable being. These seeds and other mechanisms could, if properly cultivated, help your soul become like God, but it was as if by analogy.

On the Aristotelian side, "one" and "being" were considered coextensive. In a Christian context (one that had been articulated best by Thomas Aquinas in the thirteenth century) what this meant was that though there was of course room to see God as at the top of any naturally established hierarchy, God was linked in a direct way to being – to what existed on earth – rather than seen in some fundamental way as separate from being. God is a superior – indeed, the superior being – but is conceived of as within the realm of being. It was this latter position that Pico advocated in *De ente et uno*, arguing that it is not the case that all being, in which God is included, is knowable by us, since we, and our corresponding imaginations, are finite. It is also not the case that God is beyond, or outside the realm of, being as such.

Pico left his *De ente et uno* unfinished. It was part of a plan to write a much larger work that would have set forth the inherent concord that Pico believed existed among all philosophies and that could be found if only one searched hard enough and in the right fashion. Pico dedicated what he had written of *De ente et uno* to Poliziano, as it happens, and that dedication can serve as a way in, not only to Pico's thinking concerning concord but also to the nature of the Florentine intellectual community in the late 1480s and early 1490s. It is important enough to warrant quoting extensively. Pico begins thus, writing to Poliziano:

> You were telling me recently about a conversation you had had with Lorenzo de' Medici on "being" and "unity," and how his stance, based on the arguments of the Platonists went against Aristotle (whose *Ethics* you will be teaching this year). I admire Lorenzo above all (whose intelligence is so deep and versatile that it seems adapted to all things) because, despite being continually occupied in public affairs, he is always discussing or

thinking about matters relating to learning, as if he had nothing else about which to concern himself.[56]

The first thing we learn, then, is that, yet again, a Renaissance thinker is developing his ideas in the context of a conversation; and it is all the more noteworthy that, at whatever remove, Lorenzo de' Medici formed part of the conversational circle, busy with affairs of state though he might have been.

Pico goes on to say this:

> Now since those who believe that Aristotle disagrees with Plato disagree also with me, since I conceive of their philosophy as in agreement, you were asking both how one might defend Aristotle in this matter and how he agrees with his teacher, Plato. Back then I said what came to mind, confirming what you said to Lorenzo during the discussion rather than adding anything new. But that wasn't enough for you.[57]

Pico goes on to say that Poliziano wanted more, along the lines of Pico's projected project, on the concord of Plato and Aristotle.

As it happens, though his dreams about his work were unique and ultimately not to be realized, the sentiment he is expressing regarding concord was common, much more so than scholars have tended to indicate.[58] Among the many echoes of antiquity that we can hear in the Renaissance is that of a vision of philosophy that stressed concord, rather than division. If our tendency today is to classify, divide, and categorize thinkers from the past, often implicitly setting them against one another as if they were in competition, that impulse, though it existed in the Renaissance and indeed across the history of Western philosophy, was not always and everywhere as strong or as self-evident as it is today. For Pico, and Ficino for that matter, a certain corner of late ancient philosophical thinking, one that had precisely to do with concord, emerged as foundational.

The easiest way to understand this mentality is to dive in. Take the example of a thinker who today is little known but who in his day was an important representative of Platonic philosophy: Olympiodorus, an Alexandrian Platonic thinker active in the sixth century CE, who wrote a commentary on Plato's famous dialogue on rhetoric, entitled *Gorgias*. Olympiodorus commented on the relationship between Aristotle and Plato in this way: "concerning Aristotle we must point out that in the first place he

---

[56] Pico della Mirandola, *De ente et uno*, "Proem," p. 202.
[57] Ibid.
[58] On this theme in the Renaissance see Frederick Purnell, "The Theme of Philosophic Concord and the Sources of Ficino's Platonism," in Garfagnini, ed., *Marsilio Ficino e il ritorno di Platone*, 2: 397–415.

in no way disagrees with Plato, except in appearance. In the second place, even if he does disagree, that is because he benefited from Plato."[59] Another late ancient thinker, Simplicius (a rough contemporary of Olympiodorus), also writing a commentary, said that Plato and Aristotle may indeed have disagreed as to the *onoma* (the Greek word means "name"), but that they were in agreement when it came to the *pragma* (the central matter, or the underlying message).[60] These two examples are, relatively speaking, drops in a bucket. The assumptions that underlay them were as follows. Philosophy is the search for wisdom, and wisdom entails matching one's thinking to the truth. There can only be one truth when it comes to deeply rooted, fundamentally important, and momentous matters. So when we are presented with cases, such as that of Plato and Aristotle, where there is obvious disagreement in what they are saying (in their words), it is up to us to find the deeper truth that may indeed lie hidden but that underlies what they are saying.

There was no denying, of course, that ancient philosophers had been divided into schools of followers, which in Greek had been termed *diadochoi* and in Latin *successores*.[61] For the most part, when modern scholars focus on the history of philosophy, they zero in on the philosophers' different verbal arguments: how the arguments are structured; how they offer internal coherence within a larger "system"; and, when comparing philosophers, how their arguments differ.[62] But in the late ancient tradition of which Olympiodorus was a part, it was more important to draw out the hidden truth that might underlie differences, rather than focus on the differences alone. The more you could do this, the better a philosopher you were deemed to be and, importantly, the more "followers" you yourself might garner. It all partook of the part oral, part written world that was such an

---

[59] Olympiodorus, *Commentary on Plato's Gorgias*, tr. Robin Jackson, Kimon Lycos, and Harold Tarrant (Brill: Leiden, 1998), 41.9, p. 267. Cit. in Lloyd P. Gerson, "What Is Platonism?" *Journal of the History of Philosophy* 43 (2005), 253–76, at 259 n.24; see also Gerson, *Aristotle and Other Platonists* (Ithaca: Cornell University Press, 2005), for the late ancient tendency toward concord.

[60] Simplicius, *Commentary on Aristotle's Physics*, 1249.12–13, as cited and translated in Gerson, "What Is Platonism?" 259 n.25.

[61] As in Diogenes Laertius, *Lives of the Philosophers*.

[62] See Leo Catana, "The Concept 'System of Philosophy': The Case of Jacob Brucker's Historiography of Philosophy," *History and Theory* 44 (2005): 72–90; Catana, *The Historiographical Concept 'System of Philosophy': Its Origin, Nature, Influence and Legitimacy* (Leiden: Brill, 2008); Christopher S. Celenza, "What Counted as Philosophy in the Italian Renaissance? The History of Philosophy, the History of Science, and Styles of Life," *Critical Inquiry* 39 (2013), 367–401.

unarticulated staple of premodern intellectual life that we often miss its importance, focused on written documentation as we tend to be.

Both Pico and Ficino fit perfectly into that tradition. Pico, for example, as he was writing all his work, deemed the local reception and discussion of his work and thought far more important than memorializing it in print forever. He had his 900 "Conclusions" published in print; but that was so that he might spread the news far and wide that they were to be debated and discussed orally, not because it necessarily represented his final view on the subject. He did not have printed any of his letters or most of his other work, which awaited a later generation (his nephew, specifically) to be gathered up, edited, and printed. He cared more about the conversation on the ground, whether epistolary or oral, with his friends and friendly rivals. We have seen, for example, that his dedication of *De ente et uno* to Poliziano took as its point of departure a conversation. And, importantly, it feels conversational, as if he is simply continuing in writing a discussion that had earlier been interrupted.

Take, for example, the letter exchange with Ermolao Barbaro, with which this chapter began. Through it we can see both how authorship can be deemed collective, in a sense, and how important community was in Pico's world. He begins a letter from the late 1480s to Barbaro in this fashion: "I, and our own Poliziano, have often read whatever letters we had from you, whether they were directed to us or to others. What arrives always contends to such an extent with what there was previously, and new pleasures pop up so abundantly as we read, that because of our constant shouts of approbation we barely have time to breathe."[63] This letter exchange has become rather well known among scholars of the Renaissance, the main reason being the discussion between Pico and Barbaro concerning the nature of philosophy and its relationship to rhetoric.[64] But the communal sensibility calls out for comment first of all. One must imagine the letter arriving, Pico receiving it and immediately reading it together with Poliziano, as they used their respected friend's thoughts as a stimulus to their own. The exchange led, as we shall see, to the composition of one of Poliziano's most important works.

Barbaro had written Pico complaining of university-based philosophers, arguing that they were not sufficiently cultured and that they lacked sophistication in Latin: a standard humanist complaint. More surprising, however, was Pico's response, contained in the very letter from which the earlier quotation is drawn. For in it, Pico defended medieval philosophers and, to boot, wrote in

---

[63] Garin, *Pros.*, 806.
[64] See Francesco Bausi, *Nec rhetor neque philosophus: Fonti, lingua e stile nelle prime opere latine di Giovanni Pico della Mirandola (1484–87)* (Florence: Olschki, 1996).

the persona of a scholastic philosopher arguing that rhetoric and oratory should be placed below philosophy. Pico writes that it is more praiseworthy "to have the Muses in our hearts and not on our lips," and he goes so far as to suggest that language, all things considered, is arbitrary: Arabs, Egyptians, and so on all might say the same things, but they would not be doing it in Latin.[65] Besides, take Lucretius: he wrote beautiful Latin but said scandalous things.

Yet, at the end of the letter, Pico playfully says that he has only denigrated eloquence (meaning rhetoric) at the expense of philosophy, so that he could then hear Barbaro praise eloquence. Again we observe conversation propelling further research and reflection. Pico ends his letter by complimenting Barbaro, saying that Barbaro is "most eloquent among philosophers and, among the eloquent, most philosophical."[66]

Barbaro's response is commensurate to Pico's letter, both in the eloquence in which it is expressed and in the sophistication of the points he makes. Referring right away to the substantive quality of Pico's letter, Barbaro says that he was expecting a letter from Pico and received instead a "volume." Barbaro notes the fact that Pico had written his letter in beautiful and elegant Latin, though he had been at the same time defending those who were not that proficient in Latin elegance. Barbaro avers that in doing so, Pico showed unwittingly that those who do not possess Latinate eloquence cannot defend themselves. They are, Barbaro says, "like slaves, like women, like animals."[67] What seemed funny then seems today terrible, of course. But beyond the prejudices of his era, we can see that Barbaro is trying, already in his letter, to outline a position whereby one could balance the need for verbal elegance with philosophical precision.

Then follows an interesting passage, one that might escape a reader's attention but that deserves to be highlighted. Barbaro relates an anecdote about the University of Padua regarding what one of the philosophers there had said about Pico: "One of their number in the University of Padua (I am making nothing up, Pico, and will relate the whole silly but true story), an audacious and insolent little man, one of that sort who hold the humanities in joking contempt, said: 'Whoever this Pico is, a grammarian, I believe, has stepped into shoes too big for his feet.'"[68] The first thing we learn, then, is that this is the way "news" was transmitted. Barbaro, with his ear to the ground and close to one of Italy's leading places for university-based, scholastic philosophy, has heard gossip from a philosopher there about Pico, and he lets Pico know what was said.

[65] Garin, *Pros.*, 814 and 818.
[66] Ibid., 822.
[67] Ibid., 844.
[68] Ibid., 846.

What follows, however, deserves to be quoted extensively. Barbaro relates more of what this unnamed philosopher says about Pico, reporting it as a quotation:

"But I hear that he [Pico] makes use of examples, histories, fables, and the testimony of poets. And so I myself am aware of nothing that he writes for us. If everything he says is true, well then, to what wretched state have we been reduced? Has it really come to this, that it is necessary to bind our authority with stories and fables? Really, where is it then that one treats of hypotheses, of inductions, and of enthymemes? And why not? I am a philosopher, and I want philosophical demonstration! The rest I leave to orators. You will claim that not everything can be learned by means of demonstrations, and that at times there is a place for probable arguments. But in that case the matter is like a game of dice. Some probable things work in our favor, others not so much."[69]

So much is contained in this short passage, one that, we should remind ourselves, is Barbaro's indirect report (touched up for emphasis, to be sure) of comments a university-based philosopher made about the sort of project in which Pico was engaged. Everything this unknown philosopher says – every technique mentioned, every strategy to which he alludes – did indeed represent what Pico and a whole cohort, lost to standard histories of philosophy, considered philosophically legitimate.

Take the first major accusation, that Pico in his work "makes use of examples, histories, fables, and the testimony of poets." "Examples." The word Barbaro's philosopher uses is *exempla*. While this term and its associations are relatively unfamiliar today, the use of "examples" represented a core way of thinking about the course of one's life and how to improve it, from the ancient world to well beyond the Renaissance. Scholars today group these practices and ideas under the word "exemplarity."[70] At its core, it is simple: you look both to history and to present-day examples of conduct, to see what sort of behavior you should cultivate and what sorts of behavior you should avoid. The use of the discipline of history (the second accusation of Barbaro's philosopher) was seen as valuable in this respect as well. As Livy had put it long before the Renaissance: "It is this especially in the study of history that is healthy and profitable: that you observe instances of every kind of conduct, a record clearly displayed from which you may

---

[69] Ibid., 848.

[70] See Matthew Roller, "The Exemplary Past in Roman Historiography and Culture," in Andrew Feldherr, ed., *The Cambridge Companion to the Roman Historians* (Cambridge: Cambridge University Press, 2009), 214–30; Roller, "Exemplarity in Roman Culture: The Cases of Horatius Cocles and Cloelia," *Classical Philology* 99 (2004), 1–56.

select for yourself and your country what to imitate and from which you may avoid that which is shameful through and through."[71] It was a sentiment with which many in the Renaissance would have agreed completely.

Examples, history: the question was, were they part of philosophy? For Barbaro's Paduan colleague, the answer was, quite decisively, "no." For Pico, however, and many others like him, the answer was much more complicated. In one restrictive and technical sense you could say that "philosophy" was exclusively the field cultivated by professors in universities who taught Aristotle. But for most thinkers it was a broader endeavor, something by means of which you could live a better life.[72] For that enterprise, "examples" and "histories" (not to mention "fables" and the "testimony of poets") served as perfectly legitimate building blocks. The complaint of Barbaro's philosopher is, in truth, the complaint of every institutionally based thinker who wants to wall off his field and include within the walls only those who think exactly like him. Pico didn't fit the mold.

The Paduan philosopher goes on: Pico writes nothing "for us." Stories and fables have no place. "Where is it then that one treats of hypotheses, of inductions, and of enthymemes?" These were, of course, all staples of the tradition of studying logic that was still quite alive in university-based courses on philosophy. But the philosopher will have none of it: "I am a philosopher, and I want philosophical demonstration!" He wants "demonstration," or *apodeixis*, the purest and best form of making philosophical arguments, one that had its fullest ancient expression in Aristotle's *Posterior Analytics* and that had been the subject of commentary and debate throughout the Middle Ages. The most basic way to understand demonstration is to say that it is a syllogism in which principles that are understood and whose meaning is evident produces certain knowledge: "All men are mortal. Socrates is a man. Therefore" – we can demonstrate that – "Socrates is mortal." But this basic theme had many variations and led to much debate about how, say, one could prove the existence of God in a demonstrable way. This sort of logic represented a core tool for reasoning in philosophical faculties, and it had great value in Pico's day as well.[73] But as often happens, those within the walls of a discipline made more of their own field than they should have

---

[71] Livy, *Ab Urbe Condita*, 1.10.

[72] On this theme, see Celenza, "What Counted."

[73] See Owen Bennett, *The Nature of Demonstrative Proof According to the Principles of Aristotle and St. Thomas Aquinas* (Washington, DC: Catholic University of American Press, 1943); Eileen F. Serene, "Demonstrative Science," in Norman Kretzmann, Anthony Kenny, and Jan Pinborg, eds., *The Cambridge History of Later Medieval Philosophy* (Cambridge: Cambridge University Press, 1982), 496–517.

done, seeing it as the be all and end all of, in this case, philosophy broadly conceived.

The philosopher's last objection is telling: "You will claim that not everything can be learned by means of demonstrations, and that at times there is a place for probable arguments. But in that case the matter is like a game of dice." "Precisely," Pico and many others might have said. Proof by means of syllogisms represents one, and the best, way of achieving certainty when it comes to logical argumentation. But philosophy was, is, and always will be much deeper and broader than purely verbal argumentation. This realization regarding the breadth of philosophy is not only modern.[74] It reaches back to Greco-Roman antiquity and has popped up here and there in the history of Western thought whenever institutionally enfranchised forms of learning have clashed with thinkers who wish to challenge those institutionally buttressed forms of thought.

Much of what was most important about Italian Renaissance humanism had precisely to do with this realization. Most humanists did not express it this way, of course, but one significant underlying tension of the period from Petrarch to Pico and beyond had to do with institutions and with intellectual enfranchisement: who belonged? What was the most authentic intellectual discipline? How should thinkers situate themselves with regard to both past and future? These central questions and more emerge in one of the long fifteenth century's most interesting and underappreciated philosophical works (one that, as it happens, was engendered by Pico's correspondence with Barbaro), to which we now turn.

---

[74] See Pierre P. Hadot, *Philosophy as a Way of Life*, ed. Arnold I. Davidson, tr. M. Chase (Oxford and New York: Blackwell, 1995); Hadot, *What Is Ancient Philosophy?* (Cambridge, MA: Harvard University Press, 2002).

16

ANGELO POLIZIANO'S *LAMIA* IN
CONTEXT

I N THE FEVERED ENVIRONMENT OF THE LATE 1480S IN FLORENCE,
Pico and Angelo Poliziano (1454–94) became intimate friends and intellectual colleagues. Their relationship evolved into the closest friendship each
would come to possess in life. Pico, as we have seen, spoke of himself and
Poliziano almost as a unit in the correspondence with Ermolao Barbaro,
suggesting that when one of Barbaro's letters arrived, Pico and Poliziano
were so enthused that they "barely had time to breathe." That correspondence also included an element that might seem to have passed by in an
instant but that had momentous consequences: the moment when Barbaro
informed Pico that a Paduan colleague had said that Pico was just some
"grammarian" who had stepped into shoes too big for himself. The word
employed there, in Latin, was *grammaticus*. As it happens it is, in a sense,
around that word that all of the intellectual energy and ferment in Poliziano's
Lamia swirls.

To understand how and why Poliziano wrote the *Lamia*, it is necessary to
pick up on his career after the 1478 Pazzi conspiracy, of which he had
written such a memorable account. Once that event had come and gone,
Lorenzo the Magnificent hired Poliziano to tutor his children.[1] Soon,
however, Poliziano ran afoul of Lorenzo's wife, the Roman Clarice
Orsini, whom some considered snobbish. Poliziano took his leave from
Florence briefly, spending some time in Mantua, then ruled by Ercole
I d'Este and graced by the presence of the painter Mantegna. But
Poliziano soon patched up his relationship with the Medici and returned
to Florence. He began teaching ancient literature at the University of
Florence in 1480, focusing his energies on poetry first and foremost but,
as he always seemed to do, moving beyond and among the boundaries of

---

[1] See Maier, *Ange Politien*, 351–57.

various disciplines.[2] As early as 1480, in fact, Poliziano engaged in a series of philosophical conversations about Aristotelian logic with a little known Dominican named Francesco di Tommaso at Florence's church of Santa Maria Novella, which di Tommaso memorialized in a little known dialogue.[3] We also know that, when he was even younger, Poliziano had studied for a time with Marsilio Ficino. When Poliziano wrote a funeral elegy for a recently deceased humanist, Bartolomeo Fonzio, almost thirty lines were dedicated to Ficino, whom Poliziano described as having refuted the heretical Epicurean Lucretius, so much in vogue then. For the still young Poliziano, Ficino appeared as a "new Orpheus, measuring out Apollonian poetry."[4] Later in his life Poliziano downplayed his early attractions to the study of philosophy, claiming that at that early age he had been most interested in Homer. But overall, the picture we receive is of a young man with a startlingly omnivorous intellect, one that was never satisfied with any one institutionally bounded discipline.

When Poliziano began his teaching career at the University of Florence, it almost seems as if he was predestined to do things in unorthodox ways. At the very outset of his teaching career in Florence, Poliziano chose to lecture on Quintilian, an author from the first century CE who had written a manual of rhetorical education, and Statius, also from the first century CE, who had written a poetic text titled *Silvae*, or "Woods," but which also meant "matter" of all sorts. Quintilian was a prose author and Statius a poet, so one can see a kind of balance in Poliziano's chosen authors. But, late Latin authors as they were, they were not, perhaps, the first authors one might have had in mind – not "blockbusters," as Cicero and Virgil might have been.[5] Poliziano defended his choices in the oration he gave to open the course, among other things citing a line of Tacitus: "We should not say that what is different is automatically worse."[6] What he meant was that one needed to cultivate the habit of reading widely and not being imprisoned in one era or style. This need to seek distinction through difference remained characteristic of him throughout his teaching career.

[2] See Lucia Cesarini Martinelli, "Poliziano professore allo studio fiorentino," in *La Toscana al tempo di Lorenzo il Magnifico*, multi-authored, 3 vols. (Pisa: Pacini, 1996), 2: 463–81.

[3] See Jonathan Hunt, *Politian and Scholastic Logic: An Unknown Dialogue by a Dominican Friar* (Leiden: Brill, 1995).

[4] See Poliziano, *Ad Bartholomeum Fontium,* in *Due poemetti latini*, ed. F. Bausi (Rome: Salerno, 2003), pp. 2–45, at v. 183.

[5] See Cesarini Martinelli, "Poliziano professore."

[6] Tacitus, *Dialogus de oratoribus*, 2.18, in Poliziano, "Oratio super Fabio Quintiliano et Statii Sylvis," in Garin, *Pros.*, 870–85, at 878; cit. and tr. in Fantazzi, "Introduction," in Poliziano, *Silvae*, vii–xx, at ix.

Take the way he wrote and delivered his opening orations to the university year. This custom is all but unheard of today, but in Poliziano's era (and as we have seen in the case of Lorenzo Valla), it was customary for a professor to compose and deliver an opening oration to the course he was to teach, called a *praelectio* in Latin. Normally, the contents of any given *praelectio* are unsurprising: you would give a general lecture about the subject at hand, explain its importance, and focus a bit on the specific material's importance.[7] You would not, if you were teaching poetry, compose a *praelectio* in meter, imitating the style of the poet or poets to be covered and replicating in your *praelectio* the kind of poetry that the course would treat. But that is exactly what Poliziano did, during the first phase of his teaching career.

He composed a poetic *praelectio* as a way of introducing his university courses on Virgil in 1482. Entitled *Manto* (the name refers to an ancient prophetess), Poliziano adapted and extended traditional approaches in an innovative fashion.[8] He told the story of where Virgil was born, in what circumstances, and what sort of works Virgil had written, all of which were commonplaces of the premodern biographical tradition. But he did so in meter, and he wove into his poetic descriptions quotations from and allusions to minor poets.

Poliziano made Virgil's life and work almost mythic, in his own way. At one point in *Manto*, Poliziano addresses Virgil directly:

> At your birth, Maro [Maro was part of Virgil's extended Latin name] Calliope left the heights of Parnassus, hastening to join her sister Muses, and she took you into her tender arms and cradling you, she caressed you and kissed you three times; three times she chanted prophecies and three times she wreathed your temples with laurel. Then the other Muses competed with each other to offer tiny gifts at your cradle.[9]

"Calliope." She was the Muse of epic poetry. Inspired by her impression of the fateful young Virgil, the other Muses too blessed the still young poet with their gifts. Virgil is portrayed therein as truly set apart, and as one who had instilled in him the ability to tell the tale of Rome in the form of epic.

The other poetic *praelectiones* share this kind of distinctiveness. Poliziano's title for them, *Silvae*, is a telling word, evoking the work of Statius. Poliziano

---

[7] See the examples in Karl Müllner, ed., *Reden und Briefen italienischer Humanisten* (Munich: Fink, 1970), 3–197; cf. also Cardini, *La critica del Landino*, 287–382, who publishes different preliminary orations of Cristoforo Landino; and Campanelli, "L'*oratio* e il 'genere' delle orazioni inaugurali dell'anno accademico."

[8] Poliziani, "Manto," in *Silvae*, 2–29.

[9] Ibid., 9, tr. Fantazzi, slightly modified.

understood the word to mean what he termed, in Latin, *indigesta materia*, literally "undigested matter."[10] What it pointed to, really, was a whole approach to poetry and indeed to culture that linked together interpretation with creativity. Statius himself, in his preface to the first book of the *Silvae*, expressed a humorous anxiety in his dedication of the work to his friend Lucius Arruntius Stella: "Much and long have I hesitated, my excellent Stella, distinguished as you are in our chosen area of pursuits, whether I should assemble these little pieces, which streamed from my pen in the heat of the moment, a sort of pleasurable haste, emerging from my bosom one by one, and send them out myself."[11] Statius says that all the works contained therein were composed in great haste. But he hints that it was worth bringing the poems together anyway, even though they might lack a formal unity. Poliziano, in the preface to his *Manto*, dedicated to Lorenzo the Magnificent, writes as follows:

> You compel me, Lorenzo, to publish an unpolished, uncorrected poem; even to have recited it once in public would have seemed too shameless. Surely it would have been enough that such an imperfect creature, which might be numbered among those insects called ephemera, should have lived for but a day.[12]

Of course, these sentiments are commonplaces: an author behaves with humility, perhaps exaggerated, toward a patron or a friend; in making that humility part of the writing project in question (by including it in the Preface), he also sets the tone for readers.

However, Poliziano's sense of his own distinctiveness and the affinities he senses between himself (and his moment) and the world of Statius calls out for comment. Statius, as well as Quintilian, wrote in what scholars have traditionally termed Latin's Silver Age.[13] The Golden Age belonged to earlier writers who already by the first century CE were becoming classics. Cicero

---

[10] See Poliziano, *Commento inedito alle Selve di Stazio*, ed. Lucia Cesarini Martinelli (Florence: Sansoni, 1978), Preface; Fantazzi, "Introduction," xi.
[11] Statius, *Silvae*, ed. and tr. D.R. Shackleton Bailey, with corrections by Christopher A. Parrott (Cambridge, MA: Harvard University Press, 2015), pp. 26–27.
[12] Poliziano, "Manto," in *Silvae*, 3, tr. Fantazzi.
[13] See for the classic example, J. Wight Duff, *A Literary History of Rome in the Silver Age* (London: Unwin, 1927); Richard Jenkyns, "Silver Latin Poetry and the Latin Novel," in John Boardman, Jasper Griffin, and Oswyn Murray, *The Oxford History of the Classical World* (Oxford: Oxford University Press, 1986), 677–97; Gordon W. Williams, *Change and Decline: Roman Literature in the Early Empire* (Berkeley: University of California Press, 1978); for a more current perspective, see Gian Biagio Conte, *Latin Literature: A History*, tr. Joseph B. Sodolow, rev. by Don Fowler and Glenn Most (Baltimore: Johns Hopkins University Press, 1999), 401–591, on the "Early Empire."

and Virgil stood out on this front: Cicero, the defender of the Roman republic and cultural translator of Greek philosophical ideas for a Roman milieu; Virgil, patronized by Augustus, telling the tale in exquisite meter of Rome's origins and its predestined greatness. Silver Age authors, instead, perhaps because of the increasingly capricious rule of unstable emperors such as Caligula and Nero, wrote poetry less "epic" in both the technical and commonsense meaning of that term. The result was that the Silver Age stood out as an environment ripe for satire, with Juvenal serving as the exemplar of the species. And Seneca's Stoicism, emphasizing the transitory nature of the world and the limited place human beings have for action, stands as much as an exemplar of the age as does his own suicide.

"Silver Age" is a term that scholars have, in recent years, "problematized," to use a clunky academic term of art, examining as they have the literary richness of that environment and the many splendid works that emerged. But looked at from a distance, what appears is a change in mood, as it were, a more limited vision of what literature and philosophy might be able to accomplish. Was there a connection with the new styles of politics that emerged, as the Roman republic faded into the distance and people became accustomed to the realities of empire? A simple, one-to-one correspondence would be impossible to prove, of course. But the change is there.

Accordingly, when we notice Poliziano's affinities for Silver Age authors, it would seem reasonable to take changing political circumstances into account. An earlier generation of scholars suggested, for example, that as Medici power increased, the more action-oriented, overtly political "civic" humanism of Bruni's generation ceded to Ficino's contemplative Platonism.[14] Under this interpretation, the Medici fulfilled their expected obligations when it came to the patronage of intellectuals but did so in such a way that pesky advocates of Florence's republican, civic traditions were sidelined, if not silenced. In retrospect that interpretation seems exaggerated, since the Medici supported so many types of intellectual endeavors. But intellectuals, in general, do tend to follow the operations and contours of political power. In the case of Ficino, there might be some (but just some) explanatory power in linking his somewhat unworldly style to a new, more absolutist local Florentine politics.

But in the case of Poliziano, things look different, and that difference, in turn, shines light on Ficino as well. Poliziano's politics, such as it was, was

[14] This line of thinking was associated with Eugenio Garin; see his *Rinascite e rivoluzioni: movimenti culturali dal XIV al XVIII secolo* (Rome: Laterza, 2007), esp. chap. 3, 89–129; *La cultura filosofica del Rinascimento italiano* (Florence: Sansoni, 1961), 102–8; and the examination of the problem in Field, *The Origins*, 3–51.

linked intimately to the Medici. His *Stanze* celebrated in unapologetic terms the personae of the two young Medici citizens destined to take the lead in Florence's governance (though of course Giuliano's life was cut short in the Pazzi conspiracy). Poliziano's *Commentary* on the Pazzi conspiracy formed part, we have seen, of a Medici effort to win the propaganda battle as the conspiracy's dust settled. Poliziano's politics is relatively straightforward: support the regime.

Yet, the form of his work and the subterraneous anxieties we can see therein reflect something deeper and indeed have a connection (tenuous but still there) with some of the same factors active in the "Silver Age" of Latin literature. Put simply, the problem has to do with canons. Looming over figures of the Silver Age was the sense that there had, at times for more than a century, been in existence authors whose work was already considered "classic," which is to say it had the consensus of the learned that it was not only essential but also necessary for authentic learning. Virgil, for example, became part of elite education early on, so that people growing up in, say, the mid to late first century CE, would have had large parts of the *Aeneid* memorized, with passages always at hand and always coming to mind whenever an apt situation presented itself.[15] When major authors occupy that sort of broad realm in your own intellectual space, it can be difficult to imagine that you can do something truly new, that you can add something.

Poliziano and those of his generation found themselves up against a problem that had a family resemblance to that of the Silver Age. But it was a problem that, though similar, had a different complexion. Poliziano came to maturity at the tail end of a great wave of rediscovery. For centuries after him, a key part of elite education would yet again be based on certain classic ancient authors, and the writing one learned would be modeled on Cicero's prose. If you were to "rewind" to one century before Poliziano's maturity, you would have found yourself in a world in which certain texts of Cicero were unknown, Lucretius was known only through incomplete copies, and most of Plato was not known directly. But by Poliziano's day, almost all the classical Greco-Roman literature and philosophy that we now possess and that, again, would be taken for granted as the basis of elite education, had been rediscovered. In his day, the question changed: it was no longer, "what else can we find?" Rather, the question became, "what do we do now?"

---

[15] See Stanley Bonner, *Education in Ancient Rome: From the Elder Cato to the Younger Pliny* (London: Routledge, 2012), esp. 212–26.

We see in Poliziano's case a certain set of approaches that would not have been unfamiliar in the Silver Age and in the earliest phases of late antiquity. Nowhere is this tendency more manifest than in Poliziano's *Miscellanea*, or *Miscellanies*. To understand the *Miscellanies*, we need to understand one of the authors who lay behind Poliziano's approach, Aulus Gellius, the second-century CE author whose *Attic Nights* preserved notes from conversations he had during long winter nights in Attica, so he tells readers in the Preface.[16] Divided into twenty books (of which Book Eight is lacking except for its index), this text recorded notable short questions and answers on topics relating to literature, history, philosophy, geography, and a host of other subjects. The *Attic Nights* is thus a miscellany, with no apparent order to its contents. Yet there are moments of intellectual virtuosity within it, all the more powerful precisely because of their lack of overall intellectual arrangement. This type of learned genre of writing has different functions across diverse cultural environments. One of the most prominent is the manner in which this genre allows its practitioners to reflect on a sense of "classicism" already achieved, even as they use this apparently artless form to define their own intellectual identities, shaped as those are by the classics that loomed before them: giants on whose shoulders they could only hope to stand.[17]

Gellius had been known to Augustine, to twelfth-century scholars, and to Petrarch.[18] Yet in the fifteenth century Gellius's Preface was rediscovered, and it was a fortuitous time: the 1420s and 1430s, when the making of excerpt notebooks came to be seen as an important vehicle by which scholars could control and have at their disposal a quantity of information that was increasing exponentially.[19] Gellius's Preface, in which he described his method, told thinkers of the early fifteenth century something they were ready to hear:

> But in the arrangement of my material I have adopted the same haphazard order that I had previously followed in collecting it. For whenever I had taken in hand any Greek or Latin book, or had heard anything worth

---

[16] On Aulus Gellius, see Leofranc Holford-Strevens, *Aulus Gellius: An Antonine Scholar and His Achievement* (Oxford: Oxford University Press, 2003) and Leofranc Holford-Strevens and Amiel Vardi, eds., *The Worlds of Aulus Gellius* (Oxford: Oxford University Press, 2004); the text and translation used here is Aulus Gellius, *The* Attic Nights *of Aulus Gellius*, 3 vols. ed. and tr. John C. Rolfe (Cambridge, MA: Harvard University Press, 1927–28).

[17] See Anthony Grafton, "Conflict and Harmony in the *Collegium Gellianum*," in *The Worlds of Aulus Gellius*, 318–42; and on "classicism" see James I. Porter, "What Is 'Classical' about Classical Antiquity?" in James I. Porter, ed., *The Classical Traditions of Greece and Rome* (Princeton: Princeton University Press, 2006), 1–65.

[18] See Grafton, "Conflict and Harmony," 320–22; the following section is heavily indebted to Grafton.

[19] Grafton, "Conflict and Harmony," 324.

remembering, I used to jot down whatever took my fancy, of any and every kind, without any definite plan or order; and such notes I would lay away as an aid to my memory, like a kind of literary storehouse, so that when the need arose of a word or a subject which I chanced for the moment to have forgotten, and the books from which I had taken it were not at hand, I could readily find and produce it.[20]

Gellius suggests that a man of good literary taste ought to be conversant with different branches of learning, presenting in the *Attic Nights* a "kind of foretaste of the liberal arts; and never to have heard of these, or come in contact with them, is at least unbecoming, if not positively harmful, for a man with even an ordinary education."[21]

This short Preface can be seen as a manifesto for a style of life that humanists were at once celebrating and creating: one where the reading of venerated ancient material never ends, questions about that material arise, and resolution of those questions in the context of civil conversation became an ideal often aimed at, if, perhaps, less often achieved. By Poliziano's day, these questions were even more alive. Poliziano found himself in a position to be addressing certain questions in that style. In his *Miscellanies*, he did so in a virtuosic manner. He completed one "century," or set of one hundred, of these notes during his lifetime, and he left behind an incomplete second century, which was only published in the twentieth century.[22]

Poliziano consciously claims Gellius as an inspiration among the Latins (and Aelianus among the Greeks); in the very first note Poliziano uses a small-seeming matter in Cicero's *Tusculan Disputations* to open up a much broader discussion.[23] Cicero's *Tusculan Disputations*, a much beloved, five-book dialogue, was intended to explain the way certain Stoic ideas could help one lead a fulfilling life amid all of life's misfortunes: how to deal with the fear of death, how to bear pain and the inevitable ups and downs of life, how to control our emotions, and so on. It was a broad-ranging, beautifully written piece of work, a classic Ciceronian text in which he took some often very complicated and technical philosophical concepts drawn from Greek traditions, distilled them to their essence, and culturally translated them for his

---

[20] Aulus Gellius, *The Attic Nights*, pref.

[21] Ibid.

[22] The first *Centuria* is still best read in Poliziano's un-paginated *Opera Omnia* (Venice: Aldus Manutius, 1498); for the second century, see Angelo Poliziano, *Miscellaneorum centuria secunda*, eds. Vittore Branca and Manlio Pastore Stocchi (Florence: Olschki, 1978).

[23] The note is *Misc.* 1, in Poliziano, *Opera Omnia*, B ii(v)–B v(v). It is treated in Eugenio Garin, "*Endelecheia* e *Entelecheia* nelle discussioni umanistiche," *Atene e roma* 5 (1937), 177–87; Jill Kraye, "Cicero, Stoicism, and Textual Criticism: Poliziano on *katorthoma*," *Rinascimento* second series, 23 (1983), 79–110, at 83–84.

Roman readers, presenting philosophy in an idiom and register that that was appropriate.

The first book presents conversations about the soul. At a certain point Cicero, defining various positions on the soul, says that for Aristotle the soul could be described using the Greek term *endelecheia*, a term that means "a source of constant motion."[24] This discussion attracted Poliziano's attention in his *Miscellanies*, since it enfolded different ideas about how the human soul worked and was constituted. The passage had also garnered notice in Florence. In fact, Poliziano opens the discussion by referring to a revered Byzantine thinker who had taught at the University of Florence and with whom Poliziano himself had studied, John Argyropoulos.[25]

Poliziano writes that Argyropoulos used to say that Cicero had got this term, *endelecheia*, wrong, not understanding that the Aristotelian term should be *entelecheia* (with a "t" instead of a "d"). *Entelecheia* (with a "t") encompasses within it the meaning of the Greek word *telos*, which means "end" or "goal." *Entelecheia* thus denotes the traditional Aristotelian position; it is in fact the word that Aristotle himself uses to describe the soul as a point of completion, the "form" of the person in so far as the form in this case represents the actualization of the hylomorphic entity (the union of matter or *hyle* in Greek, and *morphe*, or "form") that the person represents. Cicero's word, instead, suggests that the soul is, as it was for Plato, a principle of motion. The fact that Argyropoulos, Poliziano's old teacher, had been in the habit of saying (so Poliziano reports) that Cicero had been ignorant, not only of Greek but also of philosophy, impels Poliziano to find a way of buttressing Cicero's reputation. Poliziano wanted to discuss just what the meaning of the "soul" really was. And it all hung on one letter.

Poliziano uses this textual difficulty to open a discussion that is as wide ranging as it is precisely informative. He begins casually enough, indeed almost playfully, casting his short text as a "defense of Cicero" and more broadly as a defense of the Latins against the Greeks. Still, he goes further than fifteenth-century cliché. Poliziano adduces a series of ancient authorities who praised Cicero's wide-ranging philosophical knowledge and his abilities in Greek. He even retells an anecdote from Plutarch's *Life of Cicero*, to the effect that a Greek contemporary of Cicero, Apollonius Molon, after hearing Cicero speak in Greek, expressed wonder at Cicero's abilities and lamented that what the Greeks thought of as their own unique purchase on eloquence

[24] Cicero, *Tusculan Disputations*, ed. and tr. J.E. King (Cambridge, MA: Harvard University Press, 1945), 1.10.22, p. 28.
[25] For Argyropoulos's teaching see Arthur Field, *The Origins of the Platonic Academy of Florence* (Princeton: Princeton University Press, 1988), 107–26; Hankins, *Plato*, 1: 350.

had now passed to the Romans.[26] Throughout his text, Poliziano goes beyond shoring up Cicero's abilities, once again seeking distinction for himself and his work by bringing to bear texts little known to his contemporaries, especially those who fancied themselves philosophers.

In this case (and as he does elsewhere in his work, as we shall see), Poliziano takes account of the work of a series of thinkers who are still little known, but whom Poliziano had just begun fully to understand. These were the late ancient commentators on Aristotle, thinkers with names such as Alexander of Aphrodisias, Porphyry (in his commentary on Aristotle's *Categories*), Themistius (in his paraphrase of the second book of Aristotle's *De anima*), and Simplicius. These thinkers among others are all mentioned in Poliziano's discussion.[27] All flourished in late antiquity, devoting their energies to commenting on Aristotle's texts from different perspectives. Here affinities emerge between Poliziano's interests and the long, ancient post-classical period, encompassing the Silver Age as well as late antiquity.

Poliziano's argument is twofold. One trajectory is a standard one for Renaissance thinkers: manuscript transmission, when everything was copied by hand, is inherently unreliable. The difference of one letter, a "d" versus a "t," would be unsurprising. Given that Cicero was closer in time to Aristotle than the late ancient commentators, it is likely that he had it right, even if later readings were different. Cicero may have had access to the now lost exoteric Aristotelian works, in which the conception of soul as continuous motion, as in Plato's *Phaedrus*, might have been more prominent.[28]

The other strand of Poliziano's argument is far more interesting, reflecting as it does a theory that, as we have seen, has late ancient roots and that was shared by Pico and Ficino, each in his own way: the notion of a fundamental concord between Plato and Aristotle.[29] For Poliziano, the difference in terminology reflects the fact that different terms, even different fundamental conceptions, do not have to reflect foundational differences between philosophers. Like his friend Pico della Mirandola, from whom he says here that he draws inspiration, Poliziano, like many late ancient commentators, believed both that Plato and Aristotle agreed on certain fundamental issues and that the enterprise of philosophy was so large that a division of labor was necessary. If the soul could indeed be seen as the body's final actuality (*entelecheia*),

---

[26] Poliziano, *Misc.* 1, in *Opera Omnia*, B iv(r).

[27] Ibid.

[28] Ibid., B iv(v)–B v(r); Poliziano means the definition of soul expounded in Plato, *Phaedrus* 245c.

[29] See Lloyd P. Gerson, "What Is Platonism?" *Journal of the History of Philosophy* 43 (2005), 253–76; and Gerson, *Aristotle and Other Platonists* (Ithaca: Cornell University Press, 2005).

there was also room to concede that it could be seen as an "animating force" or principle of motion (*endelecheia*). Philosophy was large enough to have room for different though ultimately compatible views on important subjects, even if individuals might not always possess intellects capacious enough to encompass these ideas.

Poliziano, Pico, and a broad conception of philosophy: together these three permit us to recall that Pico had been called a mere "grammarian" by a scholastic philosopher at the University of Padua. It is time to return to the ramifications of that accusation and to how Poliziano dealt with them. And to do that, Poliziano's teaching career at the University of Florence comes yet again into relief.

Having spent the first half of the 1480s teaching literature at the university, Poliziano, toward the end of that decade, began to gravitate to an author who might seem surprising for a literary humanist and philologist: Aristotle. During that decade, too, Poliziano gained prestige. The university was run by a group called the "Ufficiali dello Studio" (literally the "officers of the university"), which in practice was something akin to a modern board of trustees.[30] Among other obligations fulfilled, the Ufficali directly issued yearly contracts to their professors. As the 1480s progressed, the language of Poliziano's contracts indicates both that he was to have almost complete freedom to teach whatever he wanted and that his bottom-line prestige rose as well, as he became the highest paid of Florence's professors of literature.[31]

As to Aristotle, there were several reasons for Poliziano's attraction to the ancient Greek thinker. First, he had had an early interest in philosophy as a very young man, as we have seen. Second, Poliziano was attracted to Greek, to the idea of teaching Greek authors, and especially to the idea of teaching a Greek author who had, over the past two centuries, become canonical in universities, but canonical in a particular way: in Latin translation, rather than in the original Greek. Poliziano's sensibilities ran ever more toward the notion of going directly to the source, in the language of the source, if possible. Third, as we have seen in the case of his *Miscellanies*, he also took an interest in the late ancient commentators on Aristotle, most of whom were almost completely unknown to late medieval thinkers.

It was a fact that Aristotle had become canonical in Latin translation in late medieval universities. It was also true that an entire interpretive tradition had

---

[30] See Jonathan Davies, *Florence and Its University During the Renaissance* (Leiden: Brill, 1998); and Armando Verde, *Lo studio fiorentino, 1473–1503: Ricerche e documenti*, 5 vols. to date (Florence: Olschki, 1973–94).
[31] See Christopher S. Celenza, "Poliziano's *Lamia* in Context," in Celenza, *Poliziano's Lamia*, 1–46, at 4–10.

emerged, with many major scholastic philosophers having written dense commentaries on Aristotelian works. What this meant was that there were, especially by Poliziano's day, university-based thinkers who were quite protective of their disciplinary "turf," as it were, seeing Aristotle as "belonging" to them and to the field of philosophy as they understood it. Then, too, there was Poliziano's friendship with Pico and the fact that Pico had been called a "grammarian" as a term of opprobrium. So in the *Lamia*, Poliziano makes bold to suggest a definition of what it is precisely that grammarians can accomplish. In doing so, Poliziano winds up suggesting, in effect, that the grammarian is, in the final analysis, the more authentic philosopher, or lover of wisdom. How he gets there is a marvel to behold.

The *Lamia*, first and foremost, was another *praelectio* – not in verse this time, but distinctive and, again, unusual. The course Poliziano was to teach in 1492 was on Aristotle's *Prior Analytics*, one of his six foundational works on logic and language that had been a staple of medieval and Renaissance learning. The *Prior Analytics* focused on deductive reasoning and the various forms that syllogisms could take, so it was an important, if difficult, part of how reasoning was taught and learned. Toward the very end of the *Lamia*, in fact, Poliziano himself suggests that the two books of the *Prior Analytics* are "rather thorny," even as he suggests that he is uniquely prepared to teach them.[32]

But it is how he begins the *Lamia* that sets the tone for the treatise: "Let's tell stories for a while, if you please, but let's make them relevant, as Horace says. For stories, even those that are considered the kinds of things that foolish old women discuss, are not only the first beginnings of philosophy. Stories are also – and just as often – philosophy's instrument."[33] Remember that the text to which, eventually, Poliziano will be addressing himself is Aristotle's *Prior Analytics*, a dense work on logic. Poliziano, instead of opening with some statement about the work in question or even identifying it, begins by stressing the power of *fabellae*, the word translated here as "stories." Poliziano, in beginning the *Lamia* in this fashion, sends messages. The first is an appeal to authenticity and primacy ("first beginnings of philosophy"). There is also a tweak at the outset toward Aristotelians. For when he uses the word "instrument," or *instrumentum* in Latin, Poliziano is employing the word by which Aristotle's six foundational works on logic (of which the *Prior Analytics* were part) were known: *organon*, in Greek, or *instrumentum* in Latin. From the beginning, then, he is linking a very distinctive notion – narrative,

[32] Poliziano, *Lamia*, in Celenza, *Poliziano's Lamia*, 191–253, at sec. 71
[33] Ibid., sec. 1.

fable, story – to a type of philosophy that had traditionally been expressed quite differently in terms of written genre.

Then of course there is the creature itself, *Lamia*: a vampiric, soul-sucking (usually female) monster, whom ancient sources had named and who was alive, too, in the vernacular culture of the Italian late Middle Ages and Renaissance.[34] Poliziano's first excursion into the realm of fable is, accordingly, a doozy. He tells the story of the *Lamia*, a tale he says he has heard since he was a boy, when his grandmother would scare him by telling him of these creatures who "devoured crying boys."[35] As a boy, this was the monster Poliziano dreaded most, he says, as he expands into a more scholarly, but no less story-oriented, account of what the *Lamia* represented. Poliziano cites Plutarch (c. 50–c. 120CE), who had suggested that the *Lamia* had "removable eyes." He specifies: "That is, she has eyes that she takes out and replaces when she pleases . . . Now then, every time she goes out of the house, she attaches her eyes and goes wandering around . . . through all the public places, and she looks around at each and every thing . . . you'll have covered up nothing so well that it escapes her." But then: "when she comes back home, right at the doorway she pops those eyes out of her head and puts them back in a little compartment. And so she is always blind at home, always sighted in public."[36] This then is the nature of this particular monster: it can see only when out and about, only to lose that ability when home and alone. Why then would Poliziano want to begin a university course on Aristotle's *Prior Analytics* with an explanation of this monstrous figure? Because Florence is full of Lamias: "I ask you, Florentine countrymen, haven't you ever seen Lamias like this, who know nothing about themselves and their own business but are always observing others and their affairs?"[37]

Poliziano then relates an encounter he had with a bunch of Lamias:

> When I was walking around, by chance one day a number of these Lamias saw me. They surrounded me, and, as if they were evaluating me, they looked me over, just like buyers are accustomed to do. Soon, with their heads bowed crookedly, they hissed together, "It's Poliziano, the very one, that trifler who was so quick to call himself a philosopher." Having said that, they flew away like wasps who left behind a stinger.[38]

---

[34] See Celenza, "Poliziano's *Lamia* in Context," 20.
[35] Poliziano, *Lamia*, sec. 2.
[36] Ibid., secs. 3–4.
[37] Ibid., sec. 5.
[38] Ibid., sec. 6.

Gossip, insults, and an attempt at public humiliation: these, then, were the elements that led to the *Lamia*'s composition in an immediate sense.

Poliziano then turns quickly to the question of names and naming:

> Now as to the fact that they said I was "so quick to call myself a philosopher," I really don't know what it was about the whole thing that bothered them: whether I was a philosopher – which I most certainly am not – or that I wanted to *seem* to be a philosopher, notwithstanding the fact that I am far from being one.[39]

What was it about that word, "philosopher," that got those gossipy Florentine academics so up in arms?

The question obviously needed investigation, and it is precisely this that Poliziano proposed to do:

> So why don't we see, first of all, just what this animal is that men call a "philosopher." Then, I hope, you will easily understand that I am not a philosopher. And yet, I'm not saying this because I believe *you* believe it, but so that no one ever might happen to believe it. Not that I'm ashamed of the name "philosopher" (if only I could live up to it in reality!); it's more that it keeps me happy if I stay away from titles that belong to other people ... First, then, we'll deal with the question, "what is a philosopher" and whether being a philosopher is a vile or bad thing. After we have shown that it isn't, then we'll go on to say a little something about ourselves and about this particular profession of ours.[40]

Poliziano thus spells out what the oration will look like; and he gets down to business right away, beginning, in a decidedly unsystematic way, to set forth a kind of alternative history of philosophy by examining the figure of Pythagoras. But he does so laden with humor and ridicule.

The first step is to report a little known, but recently revived, facet of the Pythagorean tradition: the so-called sayings of Pythagoras. Pythagoras, like Socrates after him, was thought not to have written anything. But he developed a kind of cult following, a "school," that gathered around him and preserved, according to some, his oral teachings, passing them down generation by generation until later thinkers interested in the tradition wrote them down.[41]

---

[39] Ibid.

[40] Ibid., sec. 7.

[41] See Walter Burkert, *Lore and Science in Ancient Pythagoreanism*, tr. Edwin L. Minar (Cambridge, MA: Harvard University Press, 1972); on this tradition in the Renaissance, see Christopher S. Celenza, *Piety and Pythagoras in Renaissance Florence: The Symbolum Nesianum* (Leiden: Brill, 2001); Florence Vuilleimier Laurens, *La raison des figures symboliques à la Renaissance et à l'âge classique* (Geneva: Droz, 2000).

The problem is that the sayings as we have them are quite mysterious, so that not all of them have meanings that are readily apparent on the surface. Taken completely out of any context, they can seem somewhat ridiculous.

So Poliziano goes forward accordingly, referring to Pythagoras without naming him (and recalling the fact that later members of the Pythagorean school would themselves refuse to name Pythagoras, referring to him only as "he himself"): "I've certainly heard that there once was a certain man from Samos, a teacher of the youth . . . But as soon as he took one of those students under his wing, in a flash he took away his power of speech!"[42] Here Poliziano alludes to the tradition regarding Pythagoras that within his school there were two categories of students: the "listeners" (or *akousmatikoi* in Greek) and the "learned" (*mathematikoi*).[43] Some ancient sources, which Poliziano well knew, suggested that you had to spend five years in the first category (where you were allowed only to listen, not to speak) until you graduated to the second. Right away, then, we see Poliziano using the *Lamia* as an occasion to mock what can sometimes seem like the excesses and myopic viewpoints of professors.

Then he gets to Pythagoras's sayings ("Now if you hear the precepts of 'He Himself' you are going to dissolve with laughter, I just know it") and, with the rhythm of a stand-up comedian, Poliziano says: "But I'm going to tell you anyway."[44] Poliziano goes on to recount the Pythagorean sayings:

> "Do not," he used to say, "puncture fire with a sword." "Don't jump over the scale." "Don't eat your brain." "Don't eat your heart." "Don't sit upon the sixth."[45] "Transport mallow, but don't eat it." "Don't speak against the sun." "Refuse the royal road, travel instead on the wide roads." "When you get out of bed, fold up the bedspreads, and wipe out the mark of your body." "Don't wear a ring." "Erase, also, the mark of the pot in the ashes." "Don't let swallows into your house." "Don't urinate into the sun." "Don't look into the mirror by lamplight." "Step first with your right foot, wash the left one first." "Don't defile the cutting of your nails and hair, but do spit in them."[46]

One can imagine the reactions of the audience as they were told these precepts just like that, with no explanation.

The point behind these sayings had always been a bit vague, in truth. In Pythagoras's day, they would have made most sense as rituals: behaviors

---

[42] Poliziano, *Lamia*, sec. 8.

[43] See Burkert, *Lore and Science in Ancient Pythagoreanism*.

[44] Poliziano, *Lamia*, secs. 8–9.

[45] That is, the sixth part of an ancient measure.

[46] Poliziano, *Lamia*, sec. 9.

and practices that you would have followed if you considered yourself a member of the "school" of Pythagoras.[47] Later, as time went by and lists of the precepts continued to be transmitted, there developed a minor interpretive tradition surrounding them, seeking to understand what, if any, secret meanings they carried.[48] Tellingly, in Poliziano's own day, one of the thinkers who took a crack at understanding them was Marsilio Ficino.[49] So we can see in Poliziano's comic mockery of Pythagoras some similar jibing directed at Ficino; by that point, too, Poliziano's close friend Pico had departed from his earlier close alliance with Ficino. In Poliziano's teasing references to Pythagoras, we have a sense that, by the early 1490s, the earlier tripartite alliance of Ficino, Poliziano, and Pico (which Ficino had done so much to memorialize) was no longer what it once was; and we can notice yet again Renaissance thinkers seeking to define a place for their own, emerging, new generation, as we have seen in the case of Bruni (in relation to Salutati) and Alberti (in relation to Bruni and Poggio).

After this listing of the Pythagorean sayings, Poliziano goes on to highlight two tales that had circulated in antiquity regarding Pythagoras's relationship to animals.[50] Both tales have to do with Pythagoras and his perceived wonder-working charm. In these cases, Pythagoras employed his power to modify the natural behavior of animals. Both, significantly, occur in a Greek text by the later Platonist Iamblichus that was much beloved by Ficino and indeed was one of the first Greek works to which Ficino turned after his very early translations of Plato. One was a tale regarding a bear, which was "terrifying in its savagery and was a bitter plague on bulls and men." Pythagoras petted the bear and gave it bread and apples to eat and somehow made the bear swear that it would not harm any other animals thereafter. The other was a tale about how Pythagoras interacted with a bull, a story that Poliziano, again, relates with the timing of a club comic ("Don't you want to hear about the bull?"), which is worth relating more or less in full:

> He saw the bull of Taranto once by chance in a pasture as it was munching away, stripping off the greens from a bean field. He called the herdsman

---

[47] See Burkert, *Lore and Science in Ancient Pythagoreanism*.

[48] See Celenza, *Piety*, for some late ancient and medieval approaches.

[49] See Ficino's annotations to Iamblichus in MS Vatican City, Vat. Lat. 4530, f.43v–48r and his "Commentariolus" to the Pythagorean sayings in MS Vatican City, Vat. Lat. 5953, f. 316v–318v, as edited by Kristeller, *Supplementum*, 2: 98–103; cf. Christopher S. Celenza, "Pythagoras in the Renaissance: The Case of Marsilio Ficino," *Renaissance Quarterly* 52 (1999), 667–711, at 691–93; and Celenza, *Piety and Pythagoras*, 21–26.

[50] The stories and the citations that follow are in Poliziano, *Lamia*, secs. 11–12. The tales are in Iamblichus, *De vita Pyth.*, 13.60–1 and Porphyry, *Vita Pyth.*, 23–4.

over to tell him to inform the bull not to eat that stuff. The herdsman said, "But I don't speak bull. If you do, you'll do a better job of it." Without delay, He Himself went right up to the bull and talked to him for a minute, right in his ear. He ordered the bull not to eat any bean-like food, not only now but forever. And so that bull of Taranto grew old in the temple of Juno. He was thought to be holy, and he customarily fed on human food that the happy crowd gave him.

Note that in both cases professor Pythagoras, with his different inducements, persuaded the animals to refrain completely from conduct that was natural to them: in the case of the bear, eating animals; in the case of the bull, grazing in a nearby bean field.

As if to firm up the only implied link between Pythagoras's conduct and typical professorial modes of dealing with students, in the next line Poliziano refers to Pythagoras as a "professor, a salesman really, of such a revolting kind of 'wisdom.'"[51] Poliziano then tells the traditional story about Pythagoras having invented the word "philosopher." Whereas most other Renaissance descriptions used this account in such a way that it pointed toward Pythagoras's modesty (as we have seen in the case of Valla), Poliziano tells more of the story, and his tone changes somewhat, from one of mockery to one of reverence for the mission of philosophy.

The story went that an ancient tyrant of the Greek city of Phlius asked Pythagoras what he did for a living after he had discoursed wisely on a number of subjects. Pythagoras said that he had no particular profession but that he was, rather, a *philosophos*, a "lover of wisdom." The king still didn't understand and asked Pythagoras for further explanation. So Pythagoras replied that (as Poliziano tells the story) "human life was like one of those festivals that was held, known throughout all of Greece, with the greatest fanfare and games."[52] At these festivals, all sorts of people were represented. Some came to sell merchandise, others engaged in contests of athletic prowess, and "There too the tightrope-walker does risky tricks, the tumbler jumps around, the con-man works his magic, the poison-mixer blows in and out, the little holy-man hallucinates, the student of virtue trifles, and the poet lies."[53] People of a higher station also came to the fairs, so that they could "see places and contemplate unknown men, techniques, and talents, as well as the noblest artisans' works" and there were still others, who came for other reasons: out of a desire for money or luxury, or in the

---

[51] Poliziano, *Lamia*, sec. 13.
[52] Ibid.
[53] Ibid., sec. 14.

hope of winning the kind of public esteem that would lead to rule, or even for physical pleasure.[54]

Yet, there is one more type of person, the best type indeed: "those who excel and who are the most honorable sorts possible are those eager to look at the most beautiful things, who gaze upon this heaven and on the sun and the moon and the choruses of stars."[55] The grouping of celestial bodies here referenced "possesses beauty because of its participation in that which is the first intelligible thing, what He Himself understood as the nature of numbers and reasons."[56] As Poliziano relates serious matters (Pythagoras was said to have believed that number represented the central principle of all existence and that the world was structured rationally), he also has a bit of an occasion for more mockery, again referring to Pythagoras as "He Himself." But then he finishes his excursus on Pythagoras in a serious fashion, alluding to the central nature that runs through all things (again, for Pythagoras, number) and saying that "it is a specific type of knowledge of these things that is called 'sophia' – the word that, translated into Latin, is 'sapientia', or 'wisdom'. And the man studious of this 'sophia' has now been called, by himself, a 'philosopher.'" We have, as it were, the origin story of the word "philosopher." Tied to Pythagoras as it is (and drawn for the most part from Cicero's *Tusculan Disputations*), it occasions some of Poliziano's humorous jibing.[57] But the tone is, in truth, rather reverential, as if to say that the pursuit of true wisdom is indeed a serious matter.

The question then becomes: in what does wisdom consist? Here again, Poliziano's approach contains surprises, as he follows a winding road. Poliziano says that once, in earliest antiquity, even those who practiced "mechanical crafts" – trades, in other words – could be considered wise. But then there emerged another thinker, a towering presence much as Pythagoras had been and who, again like Pythagoras, goes unnamed. He is "a certain Athenian old man, who was, as they say, tall-shouldered."[58] We learn from the rest of Poliziano's description that this tall-shouldered gentleman is Plato and we learn, too, that Plato redefined what it meant to be wise and to pursue wisdom and, in short, to be a philosopher. The mechanical arts, first of all, were out. Reading the *Lamia*, it is not apparent on the surface what Poliziano thought about this Platonic demotion of tradesmen.

---

[54] Ibid., secs. 14–15.
[55] Ibid., sec. 16.
[56] Ibid.
[57] Cicero, *Tusculan Disputations*, 5.3.8–9, pp. 430–32.
[58] *Lamia*, sec. 17.

Plato had held that to possess authentic knowledge of a given subject, one needed both to be able to practice that subject successfully and to give an "account" of it, which is to say a set of reasons, all linked together, of why that subject existed. If you only knew how to do something (being a blacksmith, say), you had what Plato termed a "knack," or *empeiria* in Greek – a skill, to be sure, but not true knowledge of the sort that could lead to wisdom.[59] Poliziano recognizes this Platonic predilection implicitly; if he disapproves, one notices it only in his tone, a kind of wistfulness about a lost era in antiquity, when there was a broader scope for what could be considered wise and thus implicitly a similar amplification of whom one could consider a philosopher.

Poliziano accounts for other positions that Plato held: that it was necessary to know dialectic ("that art by which the true was distinguished from the false"), that empty rhetoric was to be shunned, and that the philosopher needed eventually to come to an understanding of what subtends the world apparent to us – to wit, that "there is a nature that always exists and is not in flux under the influence of corruption and generation."[60] Plato had said that true philosophers needed to be well born, Poliziano recounts, and that philosophy is best pursued by more than one person, just as in a hunt, the quarry is more easily pursued by a group of hunters rather than just by one. On this model, philosophy's "quarry" is the "hunt for the truth."[61] True philosophers should spurn the love of money, should avoid gossip, and should not care at all about other people's affairs: "Such was the image of a true and legitimate philosopher that that old Athenian man outlined for us."[62]

What is clear from this description is that the philosopher – the authentic, true philosopher as hinted here – must be very rare in real life. Poliziano says as much, averring that philosophers of this sort "are almost as rare as white ravens" and then admits that he is about as far as one could be from the idealized figure just represented.[63] Thus far, then, we can infer two things: first, that it must be the case that those Lamias – which is to say those teachers of Aristotle who, Poliziano suggested, had judged him unworthy to teach philosophy – are not living up to image of the idealized philosopher whom

---

[59] See Plato, *Gorgias*, 461b–465c.
[60] Poliziano, *Lamia*, secs. 20–21.
[61] Ibid., sec. 23.
[62] Ibid., sec. 28.
[63] Ibid. For the "white raven" image see Juvenal, *Satires*, 7.202, in Susanna Morton Braund, ed. and tr., *Juvenal and Persius* (Cambridge, MA: Harvard University Press, 2004), p. 314; and Ari Wesseling, "Commentary," in Angelo Poliziano, *Lamia: Praelectio in priora Aristotelis analytica*, ed. Ari Wesseling (Leiden: Brill, 1986), 21–115, at 62.

Poliziano had sketched through the mouth of the unnamed Plato. Second, however, the implied absolute perfection of the philosopher (he doesn't care about money, he is interested in no one's business but his own) represents an impossibility in practical terms.

In this latter respect Poliziano evinces a Stoic viewpoint, one that he could have picked up from any number of sources, including one that he had translated from Greek into Latin, the *Encheiridion*, or "Handbook" by the ancient Stoic philosopher Epictetus. There Epictetus had sketched a similarly idealized figure, the "wise man" (or *sophos* in Greek), a person whose behavior, perfect as it was, could serve in truth only as a source of imitation and aspiration, rather than as a template for how to behave in the real world. Poliziano had defended Epictetus early on, in a 1479 letter to a contemporary.[64] So right away we understand that Poliziano is positing an ideal.

What remains to be seen is whether being a philosopher along those lines is a good or bad thing. The first tack he takes is to list various eminent leaders who had little taste for philosophers: Socrates was made to suffer the penalty of hemlock, and the Roman emperor Domitian kicked philosophers out of the city.[65] But, of course these antagonists to philosophy (the Athenian *demos* and Domitian, respectively) were full of vice, and unlearned. More surprising, Poliziano suggests, is that good and learned people have campaigned against philosophy. For example, the little known Dio of Prusa (born in the provinces of the empire, in what is now Turkey and, again and tellingly, a figure from the first century CE, chronologically on the same plane as Poliziano's beloved Silver Age authors) wrote scathing orations against philosophy. The figure Hortensius came out against philosophy; despite this fact, the great Cicero dedicated a dialogue to this otherwise little known thinker, a dialogue that, though lost to us, was a favorite of Augustine. Why did the ancient comic writer Aristophanes satirize philosophers so, as he did most memorably in his *Clouds*, where Socrates comes in for some heavy ribbing?[66] Still, Poliziano goes on, these and other examples might be chalked up to jealousy or to the fact that sometimes, perhaps too much philosophy is just too much, like in the case of sweet-tasting things, where they can be seen as good in moderation but negative when consumed excessively.[67] Poliziano is deliberately teetering on a kind of

---

[64] See his letter to Bartolomeo Scala in Garin, *Pros.*, 912–25. For Poliziano's translation, see Maïer, *Ange Politien*, 374–80.

[65] Poliziano, *Lamia*, secs. 29–30.

[66] Ibid., secs. 31–32.

[67] Ibid., sec. 33.

precipice and asking his listeners to do so as well, as he oscillates between a veneration for philosophy's highest aspirations and a frank recognition of its limits as traditionally understood.

Lest one think, however, that Poliziano is penning an anti-philosophical screed, he then says this (to anyone who might think that philosophy is unnecessary or unprofitable):

> But not needing to philosophize also means not needing to live according to the virtue of the soul. Just as we live by means of the soul, so also do we live well thanks to the soul's virtue, in the same way that, just as we see by means of our eyes, so too do we see well by means of the virtue of the eyes. Therefore, whoever doesn't want to live well, let him not philosophize, and whoever wants to live in a base fashion, let him, then, not follow philosophy.[68]

The soul represents the instrument of our lives: it is that essential part of a person, what is left when we peel away our physical needs, our little everyday envies, and our fallible senses. If the soul is the instrument of our lives, then philosophy can be seen as the instrument of the soul.

There follows sincere praise of philosophy and what it can do. No one can truly be happy without philosophy, because philosophy well practiced represents the best way to control one's own life. The soul has three parts, reason, anger, and desire, "with the first one being divine and the latter two brutish, will we, I ask, really be mild in the way we train desire, almost allowing desire itself (that many-headed beast) and beyond that anger (that raging lion) to grow?"[69] The division of the soul into three parts reaches back to Plato's *Republic*.[70] "Reason" (the faculty of discrimination, where thought occurs without the pressure of emotions), "anger," which we can also call "spirit" (that vital part of the soul that is fired up when soldiers go into battle, say, or when one is engaged in a debate), and "desire" (not subject to reason, this part of the soul wants only to be satisfied, and as soon as possible, as in the case of lust): these separate parts are all, of course, unified in one person. Poliziano's point (he is by no means original here) is that the right sort of philosophy can help moderate these three innate human predispositions, keeping them in the right relation with one another and correcting for the natural tendency every person will have to err in any given area. Philosophy, real philosophy, is care of the soul, as Poliziano had mentioned earlier:

---

[68] Ibid., sec. 34.

[69] Ibid., sec. 38.

[70] Plato, *Republic*, 4.435–439. Poliziano's wording loosely echoes that of Cicero, describing Plato's theory of the soul in *Tusc.*, 1.10.20; see Wesseling, "Commentary," 71.

"In the same way that medicine cures the body, so too does philosophy cure the soul."[71]

Philosophy possesses countless other benefits. For one thing, if we look at life as lived among people in society – civil life – there are many noble arts, from trades to governance. Here, again, we see the nod toward another view, less complimentary perhaps toward philosophy; once more we are at the edge of the precipice, as it were, as Poliziano describes the arts that function in civil life and their relation to philosophy:

> Is it not among these arts, inasmuch as they are nobler, that the good itself is principally to be found? But that art which alone judges the straight and narrow, which employs reason itself and surveys the entire good – well, that art can either employ or command all on account of its very nature. All things considered, there is no art, other than philosophy, that is like that. Why then would anyone be ashamed to be a philosopher?[72]

This type of statement represents one of the traditional ways in which practitioners of a certain variety of philosophy have made the claim that philosophy should be seen as a "regulative" discipline: philosophy judges the true and the false and as such its practitioners sit above others arts (such as politics, say), whose participants have other, vested interests and are not pure partisans of truth and truth alone.

However, is this conception realistic? More importantly, does it matter or, rather, does it matter as much as its proponents tend to imagine that it does? Plenty of intellectual enjoyment and peace can be had in philosophy, Poliziano says. Why else would so many thinkers have pined away for *otium*, "leisure," understood here as "free time for purely intellectual pursuits," the most desirable of which is often deemed philosophy?[73]

But then Poliziano turns somber. As he makes the transition from writing about how philosophy can be seen as an advantageous pleasure to why philosophy is necessary, yet again we begin to sense that authentic philosophy is rare, practiced by few, and in any case part of a social economy that includes as much pain as pleasure and more than its share of woe. The reason is that we are, in a word, nothing, and we deal, in the main, with only surface matters. Take a beautiful person. On the outside, the symmetry and harmony of his or her features please the eyes. But if we could see within him or her, "things would appear that are foul and disgusting, deformed even."[74] And

---

[71] Poliziano, *Lamia*, sec. 37.
[72] Ibid., sec. 39.
[73] Ibid., sec. 41.
[74] Ibid., sec. 47.

don't get Poliziano started about sex: "Do I even have to mention those obscene pleasures, which always have regret as their companion?" Overall, the real question to ask is: "Please, what among all our affairs is solid and lasting?"[75]

The answer, Poliziano intimates, is very little. It is our own nature that makes us sometimes think otherwise. It is a passage so striking that it merits extended quotation:

> It is our weakness and the shortness of our lives that sometimes make us think anything remains or endures. It is for this reason that some of the ancients were of the opinion that our souls, put into our bodies as if into a prison, were suffering penalties for great crimes – an opinion which, even if not entirely true, cannot also seem absurd, on the face of it. For since our soul is joined and indissolubly connected to our body, extended and unfolded through every bodily member and every channel of the senses, it seems in my view to be afflicted with a punishment no different from that with which Mezentius, that character in Vergil, punished his wretched citizens. For this is how our poet tells the tale: "He used to join dead bodies to the living, matching hands to hands and mouths to mouths – what savage torture – and, as they overflowed with blood and gore, he killed them in that way, in a wretched embrace and with a slow death."[76]

The soul as the essence of the person being trapped in the prison of the corruptible body with its fallible senses: this conception was not new. But in its somber and melancholic elegance, the passage, buttressed as it is by a well-chosen quotation from Virgil, represents one of the most existentially stark depictions of the human condition, and in one of the most concentrated ways, across which one is likely to come.

In an ideal sense the only thing that matters is the soul: "There is, therefore, nothing in human affairs worth study or care beyond that which Horace delightfully calls that 'tiny bit of divine breath' which causes human life in this whirlwind of things to be governed safely none the less."[77] Then, finally, rapturously and (though it goes by too quickly to be noticed), just a little scandalously: "For God is our soul, God indeed, whether it was Euripides or Hermotimus or Anaxagoras who dared say it first."[78] The soul was traditionally seen, indeed, as divine. And it is true that a long pre-Christian line of thinking emphasizes the divinity of the human soul. But the fact that Poliziano in this last sentiment elides two different frames of reference is notable.

[75] Ibid.
[76] Ibid., sec. 48; see Virgil, *Aen.*, 8.485–89.
[77] Ibid., sec. 49.
[78] Ibid.

Placed early as the word is in the sentence (in Poliziano's Latin as in the English translation), "God" would have called forth in the minds of his listeners their God, the god closest to them, the Christian God. Poliziano then, like a composer shifting keys for emphasis, goes back to the pagan Greeks, to the playwright Euripides and to the pre-Socratic philosophers Hermotimus and Anaxagoras, all three of whom had made statements connecting the human soul to the divine. There is nothing expressly heretical about any of this, of course. It is simply striking that Poliziano believes himself operating in a world (in delicate contrast to his friend Pico and friendly rival Ficino) in which there is no need to justify this sort of thing, no reason even to begin to separate, conceptually, a pagan and Christian outlook or to make the case that there really was some underlying but ultimately Christian harmony. Poliziano just doesn't seem to care that much, a stance and a pose that are in utter harmony with his bleak view of human existence, his consciousness of human limitation, and his understanding, born of many years of studying antiquity, of loss: for every time Poliziano discovered a text, or filled in a fragment, or proposed a new reading, he did so against a background of loss, realizing that for every new discovery, hundreds if not thousands of texts from the past were gone forever.[79]

The back and forth, dialogical tendency of the *Lamia* is thus unsurprising and indeed continues, as Poliziano presses on with his extended consideration of what the philosopher is like and how he lives his life. To his imagined audience, Poliziano says: "But, you say, there is no financial reward available for philosophers."[80] True enough, he replies, but then, neither is there a reward for us when we go to the theater, which we do because it is enjoyable. Why should there be a reward for philosophers? In truth, "philosophy doesn't *do* anything. It only frees one for contemplation."[81] It is like sight, Poliziano says, which, though it does not actively perform any tasks, does show one the way.

Then there is the kind of person the philosopher tends to be:

Now, the philosopher is an unsophisticated man. He's not really action-oriented. He doesn't even know the specific road one uses to go to the forum, or where the senate holds its sessions, or where the people gather, or

---

[79] On this theme, see Francesco Caruso, *Philology as Thanatology: A Study on Angelo Poliziano's Intellectual Biography*, unpublished PhD dissertation, Johns Hopkins University, 2013. Anna De Pace has rightly pointed out (as Caruso notes) that some of Poliziano's rather bleak outlook is conditioned by skepticism; see Anna de Pace, *La scepsi, il sapere, e l'anima: Dissonanze nella cerchia laurenziana* (Milan: LED, 2002).

[80] Poliziano, *Lamia*, sec. 50.

[81] Ibid., sec. 51.

where legal disputes are settled. He doesn't know the city's laws, decrees, and edicts. He doesn't even dream of the political platforms of candidates, or of assemblies, banquets, or carousing.[82]

Poliziano is sketching a "type": that of the absent-minded, deliberately unworldly, head-in-the-clouds intellectual. This figure is familiar enough. Still, placed against the extended background of the civic culture of Florence, nominally still a republic, wherein all citizens were at least in theory eligible to take part in government, Poliziano's description has an extra added valence. It would be a stretch to say that this statement represents some kind of veiled republicanism, as if in sketching the absent-minded figure Poliziano is also criticizing the life of the mind versus the life of action. But it would not be straining the bounds of plausibility to suggest that this description might have rung some of those sorts of bells in the minds of some of his listeners.

There is more along these lines. The philosopher doesn't know any of his neighbors, he is inept in public, "And so if you bring this man into court, or before a praetor, or, again, into a public assembly, and you command him to speak about those things that are under discussion and that are before his eyes and in his hands, he is at a loss."[83] The philosopher, in short, is not fitted out by nature or inclination for public, civil life.

But maybe this unworldliness is not such a bad thing. The philosopher does not pry into the business of others, and he is unintimidated by people of high rank. Indeed, "Sometimes he is so ignorant of things that he is unaware that he doesn't know them!"[84] The philosopher floats so high above the earth that he notices only things of great moment, while the smaller, day-to-day realities of necessity escape his notice. And when it comes to the philosopher being unimpressed by ancestry, about this matter, too, he is basically correct, since:

> After all, the philosopher knows that in the lineage or family tree of anyone there are almost innumerable slaves, barbarians, and beggars, and that there is no king not born from slaves and no slave who does not have kings as ancestors. The long stretch of time has intermingled all those things that are far apart.[85]

Poliziano, the self-made scholar, a man who depended his whole life on his own genius when it came to securing patronage, professorships, and esteem

[82] Ibid., sec. 52.
[83] Ibid., sec. 53.
[84] Ibid., sec. 56.
[85] Ibid., sec. 57.

for his work, seems especially animated by this latter concern. This lengthy description of the "type" that the philosopher represents (idealized, formalized, and humorous as it is) ends, and Poliziano is set to move to the *Lamia*'s most interesting and important section, his definition and defense of what sort of profession he himself practices, why it is important, and why it represents a more authentic form of the pursuit of wisdom.

Before getting there, however, Poliziano offers a strange interlude, one that should not have been strange at all, really, but (because of one detail) again serves to highlight the different levels on which the *Lamia* operates. Poliziano decides to tell his audience the myth of the cave. If that myth rings familiar, it is because it comes from Plato's celebrated *Republic*, Book Seven, and has served as one of the most important representations of how and why we are sometimes so focused on the immediate world surrounding us that we, as it were, lose the forest for the trees.[86]

The myth runs as follows. Imagine a cave with people inside it. At one end of the cave is an opening, through which light can enter; at the other there is a wall. The people inside the cave are facing the wall and are bound in that position by chains, so that any images they see from outside are, in effect, shadows on the wall. If one of those people somehow manages to free himself and go outside into the real world, he will see light, and nature, and all the real things of the earth with a clarity and precision that he never could have imagined previously. If he then returns to the cave, he will at first have trouble seeing in the dark and will find it difficult to accustom himself to this once familiar world. Then, when his sight readjusts, those compatriots of his, chained as they are, will refuse to believe all he tells about the outside world – the real world – and they will ridicule this truth teller, as if he is making everything up. He will see all the customs of the cave dwellers as somehow invalid, and he won't want thenceforth to participate in them.

Poliziano ends his retelling of this myth in the following way:

> Now, I would interpret the sense of this image if I weren't speaking among you, Florentine men, who are endowed with such great intelligence and eloquence. I will suggest this much: those who were bound in the darkness were none other than the crowd and the uneducated, whereas that free man, liberated from his chains and in the daylight, is the very philosopher about whom we have been speaking for a time. I wish I were he! For I don't fear the envy and possible slander that might come with the name, or at least not so much that I wouldn't want to be a philosopher, were it allowed.[87]

---

[86] Plato, *Republic*, 514a–517c.
[87] Poliziano, *Lamia*, sec. 67.

Two things are noteworthy here. The first is obvious and unsurprising: Poliziano yet again evinces sincere praise for the idealized philosopher. The second, however, throws a slightly different light on the matter. The reason is that Poliziano, though retelling what was even then a relatively well-known myth drawn from Plato, had commenced his account by saying this: "Now I'd like to bring before you the most elegant image of that Platonist, Iamblichus, whom the consensus of ancient Greece is accustomed to call 'most divine.'"[88] Poliziano, for some reason, chose to relate this famous myth not from its original, and well-known, source in Plato's *Republic* but rather by recourse to the version (for all intents and purposes identical to Plato's) in Iamblichus's *Protrepticus*, the late ancient Platonist's hortatory summary of Platonic philosophy.[89] It is as if Poliziano is determined to read the myth through a little known, ancient but not "classical" source.

In a certain fashion, Poliziano's choice has something to do with Ficino, who was known to be a fan of Iamblichus and especially of the fact that Iamblichus was seen (as Poliziano's comment indicates) as important for religion. Also, speaking in this indirect fashion allows Poliziano to report a Platonic myth without naming Plato. This move on Poliziano's part also, finally, helps effect a transition to the oration's next major section, when he allows the Lamias back on stage.

Here is Poliziano, allowing his part real, part imagined enemies the chance to speak:

> Here is what they say: "Poliziano, you labor in vain when you argue and declaim to your listeners that you are no philosopher. You have nothing to worry about. No one is so stupid that he believes this about you! When we were saying that you were 'so quick to call yourself a philosopher' (a word that really burns you up, as we see), even we didn't believe that you were in fact a philosopher. We are not so perversely ignorant that we would accuse you of philosophy. No, this is what got us angry: it is that you behave somewhat presumptuously (not to use a stronger word), since for three years now you've been calling yourself a philosopher, even though you had never before paid any attention to philosophy. This is the reason we also called you a 'trifler,' since for a time you have been teaching things you don't know and never learned."[90]

What becomes clear is that his critics are using the term "philosopher" as, predominantly, a professional designation, even as they arrogate to

[88] Ibid., sec. 57.
[89] Iamblichus, *Protrepticus*, chap. 15.
[90] Poliziano, *Lamia*, sec. 68.

themselves, subtly and without saying so in so many words, the honorific sense of the word, that sense that implies the "love of wisdom."

Poliziano moves on to his response:

> So now I really hear and understand what you are saying, what you mean, good Lamias. But if you can make the time, just listen to me for a second. I confess I am an interpreter of Aristotle. How good I am at it is inconsequential to say but, yes, I do confess that I am an interpreter of Aristotle, not a philosopher. I mean, if I were the interpreter of a king, I wouldn't, for that reason, consider myself a king.[91]

This statement represents the real beginning of Poliziano's constructive argument explaining just what it is that he believes he does, in a professional sense.

He will lead up to mentioning his own profession as that of the *grammaticus*, which we can (here, in this context) best translate as "philologist." Recall that the term *grammaticus* was used, in a derisive sense, to describe Pico, Poliziano's dear friend, in a letter exchange between Pico and his friend Barbaro. Barbaro had reported that a self-identified philosopher at the University of Padua described Pico in this fashion, as a *grammaticus* who had stepped into shoes too big for himself when he attempted to enter the world of philosophy. The same sort of things, one intuits, are being said about Poliziano too: the questions regarding names, disciplines, and professional identities all reaching a fever pitch until, finally, Poliziano attempts to settle things here, in the *Lamia*.

Poliziano's first step is to find ancient precedents for what he does: "Now, let us take, from among our own, Donatus and Servius, for example, or, from among the Greeks, Aristarchus and Zenodotus: they do not repeatedly call themselves poets just because they interpret poets."[92] Poliziano foregrounds ancient philologists who interpreted and commented on poetry. Both Donatus and Servius wrote commentaries on (along with introductory biographies of) Virgil, and in so doing they had not only elucidated scholarly problems, they also helped establish Virgil as a canonical author.[93] Zenodotus and Aristarchus (Poliziano inverts their chronological priority) did similar things for Homer.[94]

---

[91] Ibid., sec. 69.
[92] Ibid.
[93] See Sabine MacCormack, *The Shadows of Poetry: Virgil in the Mind of Augustine* (Berkeley: University of California Press, 1998), 3.
[94] See L.G. Reynolds and N.G. Wilson, *Scribes and Scholars: A Guide to the Transmission of Greek and Latin Literature*, 4th ed. (Oxford: Oxford University Press, 2013).

Poliziano goes on to name other members of the ancient philological tradition, none of whom are explicitly identified, he takes pains to point out, as practitioners of the disciplines on which they comment. Poliziano says it best: "Indeed, the functions of philologists are such that they examine and explain in detail every category of writers – poets, historians, orators, philosophers, medical doctors, and jurisconsults. Our age, knowing little about antiquity, has fenced the philologist in, within an exceedingly small circle."[95]

Earlier, Poliziano had sketched the ideal philosopher: unworldly, supremely unconcerned with the business of others and, importantly, almost completely without appreciable effect on the world around him. Amid Poliziano's sincere admiration for that idealized figure, it was difficult not to sense just a bit of discomfort, as if to say, yes, in theory, the perfectly inward, contemplative life might be best – but only in theory. And besides, why are those who self-identify as philosophers so far from that ideal?

Here, instead, we see Poliziano doing two things: he is setting out a new, more practical ideal of what philosophy ought to represent, disregarding the contemporary uses of the word itself and getting back to its original meaning; second, he is playing a game, an elevated version of university politics, making a claim that what he does for a living actually represents the highest and most important academic discipline: it is not philosophy but rather philology that should be considered regulative.

Think of the range of disciplines: "poets, historians, orators, philosophers, medical doctors, and jurisconsults." Each of those fields could legitimately be considered the province of one or another specialty. But for Poliziano, instead, the *grammaticus* stands above them all, because only he can read the full range of sources without being enclosed within the walls of any one discipline, whose boundaries are, after all, artificial and to a certain extent arbitrary, more the result of institutional affinities than of authentic connections: "Our age, knowing little about antiquity, has fenced the philologist in, within an exceedingly small circle. But among the ancients, once, this class of men had so much authority that philologists alone were the censors and critics of all writers." Poliziano recalls implicitly the heroic days of the ancient Alexandrian philologists, those critics such as Aristarchus, who edited the text of Homer for posterity.

The issue of naming arises, yet again: "For 'grammatikos' (philologist) in Greek means nothing other than 'litteratus' in Latin."[96] Poliziano takes offense at the fact that someone who teaches grammar to children is today

---

[95] Poliziano, *Lamia*, sec. 71.
[96] Ibid., sec. 72.

termed a *grammaticus;* among the ancient Greeks, the proper term for this occupation was *grammatista,* even as today, in Latin, it should be *literator.* What Poliziano is doing is twofold: he is distinguishing what name should count for what occupation, and he is reclaiming for himself and what he represents the name of *grammaticus,* "philologist," as it has been translated here. All in all, Poliziano believes that the true meaning of philology, one that the ancients understood and that the modern age does not, has been lost.

Having staked out the general terms, Poliziano now makes it more personal: "But let's save philologists for another time. I come back to myself."[97] His intention in what follows is to settle the naming question and to outline what he has done. As to "philosopher," Poliziano says he only comments on philosophers, just as he comments on legal and medical texts. No one in those latter two fields ever confuses him with a lawyer or a doctor, so why should there be this confusion in the case of philosophy? But then the Lamias come back on stage, with another accusation. Fine, they say, you are not a philosopher: "How could you be a philosopher when you have had no teachers and have never even cracked open any books of this sort?"[98]

Pedigree is what is at issue here, and the self-made (and proud of it) Poliziano will have none of it. It is not pedigree (with whom you have studied or where you are from) that matters, but what you do and, in a scholar's case, what you read, what you comment on, and what you write. On the reading front, Poliziano alludes to without naming directly his familiarity with late ancient Greek commentaries: "I also won't cite my bookshelves, filled to the rooftops as they are with ancient commentaries, especially those of the Greeks, who usually seem to me to be the most outstanding of all learned men."[99] He is saying to his accusers, subtly but unmistakably: I read Greek and you don't. I am familiar with some newly discovered commentaries on Aristotle that are in Greek and are things with the likes of which you are utterly unfamiliar.

Poliziano emphasizes what he believes (correctly) to be his superior command of sources in their original languages. He also alludes to the fact that there was a long tradition of interpretation of Aristotle that had, for the most part, been utterly lost. He was in a position to recuperate parts of this tradition and did so, as he brought these texts into his work.

We can also observe that, for Poliziano, as for many in his cohort, something deceptive exists in the way reading, writing, and publicly commenting

---

[97] Ibid., sec. 73.
[98] Ibid.
[99] Ibid., sec. 75.

were linked. Immediately following the just quoted section, Poliziano takes pains to outline what he has done recently:

> Quite some time ago I lectured publicly on Aristotle's *Ethics*, and recently I lectured on Porphyry's *Isagoge*, the *Categories* of Aristotle himself along with the *Six Principles* of Gilbert of Poitiers, Aristotle's little book called *On Interpretation*, then (out of the usual order) the *Sophistical Refutations*, which is a work untouched by the others and almost inexplicable.[100]

Poliziano is managing his reputation. In addition to what he may or may not have published in written form (for some of the courses he mentions we have corresponding *praelectiones*), it is also important to him that he taught the works under consideration. Publicly lecturing, as well as what we more traditionally consider publication in written form, "counted" in his view. He claims, too, that the road he has taken is original, relatively speaking, a road that others have not traveled.

This unique trajectory is what has made him ready, now, to lecture on the *Posterior Analytics* (in case one had forgotten the real purpose of the *Lamia*, which was to introduce his course on that Aristotelian work): "Because of all this, those two volumes of logical works called the *Prior Analytics* are calling me now ... I go at them all the more willingly, eagerly, and spiritedly, because they are almost passed over in all schools by the philosophers of our age, not because they are of little use, but because they are acutely difficult."[101] Poliziano, to an extent, exaggerates his originality, since we know of others who taught Aristotle's logical works in his context.[102] But he is surely right that it would have been rare to see them taught in the light of the late ancient Greek commentary tradition. And so, he says, he is quite willing to forgo the title "philosopher": "Who then would legitimately blame me if I should take on this job of interpreting these most difficult things but leave the title 'philosopher' to others? Really, call me 'philologist,' or if you like it better call me 'dilettante,' or if not this, call me nothing at all."[103]

Poliziano, in short, has turned things around: those who have, in his context, traditionally claimed the title of "philosopher" have left behind the true search for wisdom and indeed were unaware of the qualities that an ideal philosopher should possess. That very set of ideal qualities, as Poliziano has outlined it, is just that, an ideal, impossible perhaps to arrive at in this life but still worth keeping in mind as an exemplar.

---

[100] Ibid., sec. 78. See Celenza, "Poliziano's *Lamia* in Context," 42–43.
[101] Ibid., secs. 78–79.
[102] See Wessling, "Commentary," 110–11.
[103] Poliziano, *Lamia*, sec. 79.

Yet, that very impossibility left the matter of philosophy (to be understood as the love of wisdom) uncertain. In what did it consist? For Poliziano, in his context, it had to do with philology in precisely the way he understands it: as a kind of intellectual omnivorousness, one in which the practitioner reads widely; is unafraid to take on projects that fall outside of this or that disciplinary tradition; and who is, if only implicitly, wary of institutions; wary of the ways, that is, that they can induce one to ignore matters that lie outside of specific disciplinary traditions, concerned as institutions often are with social reproduction and with the replication of existing curricula.

Regarding this latter point, Poliziano obviously does not express himself in those terms. Yet there are things Poliziano does not say explicitly but that we can reasonably infer. He concludes the *Lamia*, a text that began by praising the capacity of stories and fables, with one more tale. It has to do with birds, resembles the earlier Pythagorean animal-taming fables in aiming its not-so-subtle satire at university-based intellectuals, and is worth hearing in full:

> Once, almost all the birds approached a night-owl and asked her if, instead of nesting henceforth in holes in houses she might not rather nest in the branches of trees, among leaves, for merry-making is sweeter there. To follow up, they showed her a newborn oak, small and delicate. In it, they claimed, the owl could settle down with gentility at some point and build her very own nest for herself. But she said she wouldn't do it. Instead she advised them not to trust the little tree, because there would come a time when it would generate sap, the plague of the birds. Yet, they pooh-poohed that lonely owl's advice, since they are lightweights, and a flighty sort. And then the oak tree grew, its branches spread outward, and then it was leafy. There you have it: all those birds, gathered together, flew around in the branches, sporting, playing, and singing. Meanwhile that oak had generated sap, and men were taking notice. Then suddenly all of those little wretches were equally entrapped, and their late regret – that they had spurned that healthy advice – came to them in vain. And this, they say, is why all birds, whenever they see a night owl, greet her upon meeting her, serve as an escort, pursue, besiege, and fly around her. Indeed, mindful of that advice, now they admire her as wise, and they surround her in a dense throng, for the express purpose of learning something from her at some point. Yet, I think they do so in vain. In fact, I think they do so sometimes to their greatest detriment, because those ancient night owls were really wise. Today, there are many night owls who, to be sure, possess the plumage, the eyes, and the perch. But they don't possess wisdom.[104]

---

[104] Ibid., sec. 81.

It is difficult to imagine that Poliziano did not have university culture in mind, with his image of the oak. Once it was new, appealing, a place where you might set up shop and be happy with your own little nest. The ancient owl was wise enough to avoid the tree, realizing it would "generate sap." Still, the rest of the birds didn't listen and, before they knew it, they found themselves entrapped. But then there is a slight transposition in the fable, a shifting of perspective: we realize that, today, many owls (professors) possess the plumage and the perch (professorial chairs), around whom the rest of the birds (students, acolytes) flutter, habituated as they have been by tradition to do so, but, perhaps, having forgotten why.

It is as if, with this short fable, Poliziano has recapitulated the history of the medieval university. Listening to him, we can imagine ourselves back in the days of the great medieval masters, such as Abelard, who had groups of students following him around precisely because what he offered then was new, and interesting, and different. The classroom and the curriculum were, respectively, where he was and what he designed. But then, as later successors took his place, they set up shop in a fixed location, where, to be sure, there were more students, where traditions began and were reinforced by repeated practice, where schools of thought developed and set curricula emerged and, in short, all the rituals and practices associated with university life came into being. It might have been at Paris (that was, indeed, the trajectory that followed Abelard). But Poliziano's little story could stand for any number of late medieval universities, which, in the two hundred fifty or so years since they emerged as institutional realities had, by Poliziano's day, multiplied (from 1300–1500, the number of European universities went from eighteen to sixty).[105] You start out new and interesting and you become old and boring.

This was of course Poliziano's story, as it was for many other humanists. The pose of the outsider had been a part of the movement since its beginnings, as far back as Petrarch. The paradox was that most humanists had quite a lot to do with late medieval universities. Almost all had at least studied at universities and a number of them, including Poliziano, taught at universities as well. On one hand, then, the pose of the outsider was useful, a stance one could take to seek distinction and point toward one's own uniqueness. In that respect, designing one's image as an outsider can be regarded as much as

---

[105] See Jacques Verger, "Patterns," in H. De Ridder-Symoens, *A History of the University in Europe*, 2 vols. to date (Cambridge: Cambridge University Press, 1992–96), 1: 35–67, at 55–65, for the numbers; and on the formation of universities, Marsha Colish, *Medieval Foundations of the Western Intellectual Tradition* (New Haven: Yale University Press, 1997), 265–73.

a social as an intellectual mechanism. Those who fostered this self-image certainly had a point: it is inevitable that educational institutions will at times develop programs and traditions that are not as vital as they were when they first emerged. It is the nature of the beast.

On the other hand, those who hold to this outsider pose miss a lot, whether they are humanists from the past or contemporary critics of higher education's relative conservatism and its propensity to let bureaucracy get in the way of innovation. They miss the way that students are trained in subjects useful to them; they miss the positive side of tradition, whereby many of the subjects taught and studied need to be cultivated with a long-term view in mind; and they miss the usefulness of universities to society. Most attendees of universities, in the Renaissance as now, do not go on to be specialized scholars or avant-garde intellectuals. Their educations give them skills, background, and social capital, all of which allow them to function in society.

Still, even in the Renaissance, the level at which Poliziano was operating was rare, and in most ways, he was right to say that his scholarship, in its scope, was far ahead of his contemporaries. In Poliziano's case, however, his intellectual omnivorousness set him apart in several ways. It allowed him to point the way toward the sort of scholarly work that often appeals today, simply because, read in a certain way, he seems like us. Setting authors in their historical context, using a wide variety of sources to interpret an author such as Aristotle, and digging down into how texts were transmitted when thinking about the meaning of specific words: these strategies resemble modern scholarship in many respects. His search for individual distinction endears him to our era, when being "original" and having an "identity" seem so important.

Looked at in another light, Poliziano's originality shared some of the same limitations that one saw in Alberti and in Valla. Alberti, pushing as he did for a formalization of the Florentine vernacular for which contemporaries just weren't ready, remained a voice in the wilderness on that front: prophetic, perhaps, when it came to the language question, but also lonely. Valla, too, presaged debates and concerns that would emerge much more forcefully in the sixteenth century, in his case having to do with the nature of the Christian religion and its institutional expression. Yet Valla too remained in many ways unintegrated: an institutional man who had trouble being part of institutions. As to Poliziano, like Valla he avoided taking a direct position in the debate over what sort of language the ancient Romans spoke. But his contribution, such as it was, serves to mark a certain sort of an ending to that debate, to which we now turn.

ENDINGS AND NEW BEGINNINGS: THE LANGUAGE DEBATE

POLIZIANO'S LAMIA REPRESENTED A KIND OF CULMINATION IN his own work, both by chance and by intention. Written and delivered in 1492, it was a summing up of what he believed important when it came to the mission of philosophy considered in its broadest sense. He died two years later, on September 24, 1494, only forty years old; hence, the element of chance. His dearest friend, Pico, would die a scant two months after that.[1] In a sense their joint project died with them both. The *Lamia* also, intentionally, represented a forceful presentation of Poliziano's approach to real philosophy, an approach wherein the essence of philosophy was twofold: to have the exemplary ideal of the unworldly philosopher always in front of oneself, but then, second, to lead one's life in such a way that one was unafraid to ask why, to read widely, and to work beyond and around traditional academic disciplines. Poliziano's *Miscellanea* make much more sense in light of the *Lamia*: each chapter of that work, both the published first "century" (or one hundred short chapters) and the unpublished second century represent Poliziano's continual quest to dive deep into historical, philological, and philosophical problems, and then to go wherever that search might lead. They are more than philological notes. They represent, instead, a way of life.

But that search for originality had another side to it, as well, one that was quite meaningful and that, in context, serves to punctuate the language debate and to foreground the two directions in which things traveled thereafter. Poggio Bracciolini's much earlier statement, right around 1450, that proper Latin usage was found "only in the books and writings of the ancients," implied, de facto, that Latin was a dead language and that to use it correctly, one needed to use ancient writers as models. The next question

---

[1] See Garin, *Giovanni Pico*, 47.

was: what sort of models should one use? How should one express oneself in Latin, still the language of education, the Church and to a certain extent diplomacy? These questions came to a head in an epistolary debate between Poliziano and Paolo Cortesi (1465–1510) that occurred sometime between 1485 and 1491.[2]

Among scholars of Renaissance Latin, this debate has become well known, and with good reason. It enfolds several interesting factors: style, the inter-active, personal way in which people came up with intellectual positions and the manner in which intellectuals sought approval from one another. Cortesi, in his early twenties, had sent Poliziano, who was a decade older, a book in which he had collected his own letters, which he hoped to publish. In doing so, Cortesi partook of the familiar humanist custom of sending one's work to a respected colleague to obtain his judgment.[3] It is difficult to forget how Poliziano opened his letter to Cortesi, in which he confessed that Cortesi's letters were not pleasing to him, redolent as they seemed of too excessive an imitation of Cicero: "I am sending back the letters that, in your earnestness, you gathered together. If I may speak freely, I am ashamed to have spent my good time so poorly."[4] Cortesi's shortfall?

> As I have understood you, you are unaccustomed to approve any style of writing that does not portray Cicero's features ... Those who engage in composition solely by imitating seem like parrots who say things they don't understand. Men like this, what they write lacks strength and life, energy, emotion, and innate character; they lie down, they sleep, they snore. There is nothing there that is true, nothing solid, nothing effective. Someone might say: you don't express yourself like Cicero. What then? I am not Cicero. Still, I represent myself, I believe.[5]

[2] For the debate, see Peter Godman, *From Poliziano to Machiavelli: Florentine Humanism in the High Renaissance* (Princeton: Princeton University Press, 1998), 45–51; McLaughlin, *Literary Imitation*, 202–6; Silvia Rizzo, "Il Latino di Poliziano," in Vincenzo Fera and Mario Martelli, eds., *Agnolo Poliziano: Poeta, scrittore, filologo* (Florence: Le Lettere, 1998), 83–125, at 102–4; Roberto Ricciardi, "Cortesi, Paolo," in *Dizionario biografico degli italiani*, 29 (1983), 766–70. Texts in Garin, 902–11. The debate probably occurred sometime between 1485 and 1491; see McLaughlin, *Literary Imitation*, 202; Rizzo, 102–3 n.45; Ricciardi, "Cortesi, Paolo," 767.
[3] For this custom, see Anthony Grafton, *Leon Battista Alberti: Master Builder of the Italian Renaissance* (New York: Hill and Wang, 2000), 53–58.
[4] Garin, *Pros.*, 902: "Remitto epistolas diligentia tua collectas, in quibus legendis, ut libere dicam, pudet bonas horas male collocasse."
[5] Ibid.: "Non enim probare soles, ut accepi, nisi qui lineamenta Ciceronis effingat. ... Mihi certe quicumque tentum componunt ex imitatione, similes esse vel psittaco vel picae videntur, proferentibus quae nec intelligunt. Carent enim quae scribunt isti viribus et vita; carent actu, carent affectu, carent indole; iacent, dormiunt, stertunt. Nihil ibi verum, nihil solidum, nihil efficax. Non exprimis, inquit aliquis, Ciceronem. Quid tum? Non enim sum Cicero; me tamen, ut opinor, exprimo."

Cortesi replied, beginning his own letter no less memorably: "Nothing has ever happened that was so far beyond my imagining than your returning my book of letters."[6]

What followed, in Cortesi's letter, represented the simplest, most realistic, and ultimately the most cogent defense of a flexible Ciceronianism seen in the Renaissance.[7] In Italy, this set of ideas signified an ending, of sorts, as well as a beginning. In many respects the debate over the Latin language ended with Cortesi. His position, which we shall examine later, proved dominant in the long run. What began was the wide-scale adoption of classicizing standards in an Italian prose whose essential features were just then beginning to be the objects of sustained study.

Returning to Poliziano and Cortesi, it is useful to highlight the social and cultural environments out of which each emerged. Poliziano, as we have seen, rose to prominence by individual skill and talent, gaining a professorship at the Florentine university in 1480. He came from relatively humble circumstances, and for him, the search for academic and social distinction always remained tied to his work. Poliziano developed a philologically omnivorous mind-set that, in its voracious intake of information, was tied intimately to his need to seek distinction by individual achievement.

Paolo Cortesi was markedly different. He came from a family with close ties to the papal court. His father, Antonio (d. 1474), had served in various curial offices from the court of Martin V (r. 1417–31) to that of Sixtus IV (r. 1471–84).[8] Paolo Cortesi himself became, early in his life and career, a member of the court, being named a *scriptor* in 1481.[9] As such he observed, professionally, a very different use of the Latin language. Since the 1450s and the pontificate of Nicholas V (r. 1447–55), the papal court had increasingly turned to humanist norms in its use of Latin. Yet members of the court also had to be practical men. They were habituated not only to scholarly achievement and elegant Latinity; they also needed, because of the demands of their duties, to develop a language that was both classicizing in its norms and sufficiently standardized to make communication suitable among the papal court's many diverse, international constituencies.[10] The result? What to

[6] Cortesi, in Garin, 904: "Nihil unquam mihi tam praeter opinionem meam accidit, quam redditus a te liber epistolarum nostrarum."
[7] For literature on Ciceronianism, see John Monfasani, "The Ciceronian Controversy," in *The Cambridge History of Literary Criticism*, vol. 3, The Renaissance, ed. Glyn P. Norton (Cambridge: Cambridge University Press, 1999), 395–401.
[8] See Gianni Ballistreri, "Cortesi, Antonio," in *Dizionario biografico degli italiani*, 29 (1983), 754–56.
[9] Cf. Ricciardi, "Cortesi, Paolo."
[10] Cf. John D'Amico, *Renaissance Humanism in Papal Rome: Humanists and Churchmen on the Eve of the Reformation* (Baltimore: Johns Hopkins University Press, 1983): chap. 5; D'Amico,

Poliziano might have seemed a matter of careful research and reading that then expressed itself in an individual yet classically based style, could easily have seemed to members of the papal court too eclectic and impractical.

Cortesi conveyed this need to communicate clearly and in a classicizing fashion most famously in his response to Poliziano. By the end of the fifteenth century, most humanists believed that ancient Latin had been, more or less, a natural language, one learned from birth, even if there were obviously differing levels of polish. Cortesi took these insights to their logical conclusion. He argued that those who use Latin today (as one must, given its centrality as an international language of culture and diplomacy) are like strangers in a strange land, who need a guide. The way Cortesi arrives at that point reveals much about the social circumstances in which humanist debate took place, even as the argument itself is a landmark in the history of the Latin language question in the Renaissance. Cortesi's real response, within this letter, begins when he says that he never claimed to say that he only approved those who imitate Cicero. "But," Cortesi goes on, "since you are summoning me to this disputation, it might not be a waste of time to make my opinion clear, not to mention to defend my side, even as I recognize that your words were characteristic of one who wants to persuade, not to harm."[11]

The word *disputatio*, as used here, has as we have seen a rich significance that points backward, to the history and practice of medieval university life, even as it foregrounds something unique about the culture of humanism in the long fifteenth century. Humanists from this period, at their best, cultivated a style of thinking and writing that was, at its roots, public and hence dialogical. When transferred to the epistolary realm, this mentality implied that a letter, especially one as challenging as Poliziano's, demanded a response, a response that, ideally, was to be tendered within a culture of public civility and polish in which protagonists could disagree strongly and remain on good terms, as we know Poliziano and Cortesi in fact did.

Arguments to support different positions mattered, and here Cortesi's point becomes clear as he weaves together metaphors of birth, growth, and loss. It can be assumed, Cortesi writes, given the state of the "research on eloquence" (*studia eloquentiae*), that men of our day have "almost lost their inborn voice" (*et quasi nativam quandam vocem deesse*). Given this dire

---

"The Progress of Renaissance Latin Prose: The Case of Apuleianism," *Renaissance Quarterly*, 37 (1984) 351–92.

[11] Cortesi, in Garin, *Pros.*, 906: "Sed quoniam me in hanc disputationem vocas, non erit fortasse alienum tempus purgandi iudicii nostri et tuendi mei, cum plane cognoscam verba tua esse suasoris, non lacessentis."

situation, Cortesi has grown accustomed to arguing that, "in our day nothing can be said beautifully and in a variegated manner," if the people who have lost their voice "do not propose for themselves someone to imitate, since pilgrims without a guide travel unskillfully in a strange land, and year-old infants cannot walk around unless they are in a carriage or are borne about by a nurse."[12] Good Latin is a specific kind of aid: nourishment. It is the sign of a sick stomach that its owner prefers poor food while shunning food that is healthy and of the best quality. Cortesi goes on: "Even now, I would dare to state the following, and to state it often: No one after Cicero garnered such praise for writing, except those reared and raised by him, almost as if it were done by the nourishment of milk."[13] Cortesi does not propose to imitate Cicero as an ape would a man, but rather as a son would a father:

> For the ape, like a laughable imitator, portrays only the body's deformities and imperfections, whereas the son offers anew the face, the gait, the posture, the style of motion, the appearance, the voice, and finally the shape of the body, even as he possesses in the context of this similitude something of his own, that is inborn and different, to such a point that when they are compared one with the other they appear dissimilar.[14]

The physical metaphors continue in Cortesi's presentation. One can gather, from the flow of his argument, that he believes it is necessary to see Cicero as a classic who was, in a sense, out of human proportion. Cicero's richness (*copiam*) was so evident and clear (*dilucidam*) that someone regarding Cicero's work believes Cicero to be imitable, even as the aspirant will always fall short of the ideal in the end.[15] Cicero himself had argued for the exemplary

[12] Cortesi, in Garin, *Pros.*, 906: "Et primum de iudicio libenter fatebor, cum viderem eloquentiae studia tamdiu deserta iacuisse, et sublatum usum forensem, et quasi nativam quandam vocem deesse hominibus nostris, me saepe palam affirmasse nihil his temporibus ornate varieque dici posse, nisi ab iis qui aliquem sibi praeponerent ad imitandum, cum et peregrini expertes sermonis alienas regiones male possint sine duce peragrare, et anniculi infantes non nisi in curriculo aut nutrice praeeunte inambulent."
[13] Ibid.: "Ausim nunc etiam affirmare idem quod saepe: neminem post Marcum Tullium in scribendo laudem consecutum praeter unum aut alterum, qui non sit ab eo eductus et tamquam lactis nutrimento educatus."
[14] The metaphor of filial imitation is present in Seneca, *Ep. Mor.*, 84.8: "Etiam si cuius in te comparebit similitudo quem admiratio tibi altius fixerit, similem esse te volo quomodo filium, non quomodo imaginem: imago res mortua est." On differing degrees of imitation, see Pigman, "Versions of Imitation in the Renaissance"; on apes and imitation, see Kenneth Gouwens, "Erasmus, 'Apes of Cicero,' and Conceptual Blending," *Journal of the History of Ideas* 71:4 (October 2010), 523–45.
[15] Cortesi, in Garin, *Pros.*, 906: "Dicam idem iterum: habere hoc dilucidam illam divini hominis in dicendo copiam, ut existimanti se imitabilem praebeat, experienti spem imitationis eripiat."

function of the perfect orator in his own *Orator*: "Consequently in delineating the perfect orator I shall be portraying such a one as perhaps has never existed."[16] For Cortesi, Cicero himself had achieved the same level of exemplarity. The problem, in Cortesi's view, is that his own contemporaries are not sufficiently aware of this fact. Men are naturally drawn to eloquence, Cortesi writes, but they never frame this aspiration within the parameters of their own ability; rather, they simply desire it. When attempting to imitate Cicero's fluency of expression, his *facilitas*, then, they neglect his power and his sting, his *nervos et aculeos*. They wind up "very far from Cicero." It is useless to attempt to combine highlights from too many sorts of works. If one does so, what will emerge is something "strange, whose disharmonious limbs do not hold together."[17] Many great writers of the ancient past have Ciceronian tendencies, from Livy to Lactantius, and all retain their individuality despite this fact. Again, Cicero seems almost outside the order of nature: "one must think very seriously about the problem of imitation, esteeming Cicero to be a wondrous man (*hominem mirabilem*)," since "from him so many different minds have flowed, as if from a kind of perennial fount."[18]

The best authors, and Cicero is the best of the best, "leave behind seeds" in the spirits of those who read them, and those seeds, later, grow on their own.[19] Those unwise thinkers who look to garner praise for their work without wanting to imitate anyone produce the worst sort of writing: "at times they appear base and uncultivated [*sordidi et inculti*], at other times sumptuous and prosperous [*splendidi et florentes*]." In this entire style of writing, it is as if "a number of seeds that are absolutely inimical to one another were scattered about in one and the same field."[20] The project of literature, then, is one of constant, fertile retrospection and advance. True progress is only possible by

---

[16] Cicero, *Orator*, in Cicero, *Brutus. Orator*, ed. and tr. G.L. Hendrickson and H.M. Hubbell (Cambridge, MA: Harvard University Press, 1930), pp. 306–509, at p. 311, sec. 7: "Atque ego in summo oratore fingendo talem informabo qualis fortasse nemo fuit."

[17] Cortesi, in Garin, *Pros.*, 908: "Itaque dum abundantiam sermonis et, ut ipsi aiunt, facilitatem imitantur, nervos et aculeos deserunt, et tum a Cicerone absunt longissime. . . . Fit enim nescio quid monstruosum, cum membra cohaerentia male dissipantur."

[18] Ibid.: "Ex quo intelligitur, maxime et cum iudicio ponderandam esse imitationem, et eum ipsum hominem mirabilem fuisse, ex quo tam diversa ingenia tamquam ex perenni quodam fonte defluxerint."

[19] Ibid., 910: "Relinquunt enim in animis semina, quae in posterum per seipsa coalescunt."

[20] Ibid.: "Qui autem neminem imitari et sine cuiusquam similitudine laudem consequi videri volunt, nihil, mihi crede, roboris aut virium in scribendo prae se ferunt, et illi ipsi, qui se niti dicunt ingenii sui praesidiis et viribus, facere non possunt quin ex aliorum scriptis eruant sensus et inferciant suis, ex quo nascitur maxime vitiosum scribendi genus, cum modo sordidi et inculti, modo splendidi et florentes appareant, et sic in toto genere tamquam in unum agrum plura inter se inimicissima sparsa semina."

re-elaborating a past tradition that, in its organic coherence, provides a model that in its variegated richness resembles nothing so much as a treasury.

This treasury, used correctly, provides learning as well as, inseparably, pleasure, and an inadequate prose, dissonant as it is, can bring no pleasure: "What pleasure can be obtained by words whose meaning is too varied, oblique words, phrases that are broken up, a rough arrangement, an unfortunate metaphor that is too daring in its intention, or rhythms that have been intentionally interrupted?"[21] Moreover, the practice of imitating no one leads one to wander around aimlessly, whereas following a dependable guide leads one to stay on the straight way:

> Now I believe there is as much of a difference between the man who imitates no one and the man who follows a dependable leader as there is between someone who roams around randomly and someone who travels on the straight way. The first, wandering in out of the way places, wallows in difficulties, whereas the other man without fault or trouble moves with intention from the course he has proposed to the place he needs to go.[22]

It is worth exploring this notion of pleasure, combined as it is with the need for the author of spoken and written prose to be on the "straight way."

Here as elsewhere, Cortesi seems to be recapitulating certain features of this language debate that by the late fifteenth century comprised the question's genetic structure. There are echoes in this section of passages familiar to most humanists, in Cicero's *Orator*, where Cicero discussed the proper method of oratorical speech (and more generally, *oratio*, signifying also written prose), which, he wrote, should not be "in meter, as if it were a poem [*numerosa ut poema*]," or completely "outside the realm of meter, like everyday speech [*or*, like the speech of the common people] [*extra numerum, ut sermo vulgi est*]."[23] Cicero continued: "The one style seems too rhythmical, so that it appears to have been done on purpose, the other seems too disconnected, so that it appears common and ordinary; the result is that you would take no pleasure in the one style and hate the other."[24]

---

[21] Ibid.: "Quid enim voluptatis afferre possunt ambiguae vocabulorum significationes, verba transversa, abruptae sententiae, structura salebrosa, audax translatio nec felix, ac intercisi de industria numeri?"

[22] Ibid.: "Ego autem tantum interesse puto inter eum qui neminem imitatur et qui certum ducem consectatur, quantum inter eum qui temere vagetur et qui recta proficiscatur. Ille devius inter spinas volutatur, hic autem ex proposito itinere ad constitutum locum sine lapsu et molestia contendit."

[23] Cicero, *Orator*, sec. 195.

[24] Ibid.: "alterum nimis est vinctum, ut de industria factum appareat, alterum nimis dissolutum, ut pervagatum ac vulgare videatur; ut ab altero non delectere, alterum oderis" Cf. Cicero,

To return to Cortesi's statement, the Ciceronian echoes are contained in the language of pleasure (*quid enim voluptatis* and Cicero, *delectere*) as well as in the looser similarity between the words *vagetur* (Cortesi) and *pervagatum* (Cicero). Cicero's usage, in the latter case, of the word *pervagatum*, combined as it was with *vulgare*, referred to his idea that a prose completely free of rhythmic considerations would be "common," meaning like everyday speech. Yet the roots of the words are similar, as are the fundamental points at issue: the language of prose mirrors the character of the speaker. Practice in writing, which is necessary to develop a prose that is effective on its listeners and readers, implies self-control and work, which themselves imply a style of life that would lead the practitioner to stay on the straight way and not wander about aimlessly.[25]

Finally, Cortesi points out, "There is no one, my dear Poliziano, who has garnered praise for eloquence without having practiced some variety of imitation. Among the Greeks not only the orators Demosthenes, Hyperides, Lycurgus, Aeschines, and Deinarchus, but also the philosophers, those masters of virtue, meant to be imitators of someone."[26] Cortesi's implication is that culture is really impossible without this process of intellectually fertile retrospection, and he is right on target with respect to philosophy as well. He and many others until the late eighteenth century saw philosophy in the mold of *diadochoi* or "successors," whereby each individual school of philosophy had an acknowledged head. Later members of the school would elaborate what were believed to be that initial philosopher's key ideas in the only way deemed appropriate and possible: creative exegesis and imitation.[27]

De oratore., 3.49.184–90 and Quintilian, 11.2.47 and 9.4.19, for this meaning of "vinctum"; and Quintilian, 2.11.7 and 8.6.62 for this meaning of "dissolutum."

[25] For "practice," cf. Cicero, *De oratore*, 3.190: "Hanc igitur, Crassus inquit, ad legem cum exercitatione tum stylo, qui et alia et hoc maxime ornat ac limat, formanda nobis oratio est." The possibilities inherent in the *studia humanitatis*, especially rhetorically oriented moral philosophy, to allow one to lead a directed life, that is, one that was not "aimless," represented a topos in fifteenth-century humanist thought; it is expressed in Leonardo Bruni's *Isagogicon*, which I cite from the translation in G. Griffiths, J. Hankins, and D. Thomson, *The Humanism of Leonardo Bruni*, 267–82, at 267: "As it is, we generally make the mistake of living without a defined purpose, as though we were wandering about in the dark like blind men on whatever by-way chance should offer us, instead of traveling safely and confidently along the beaten track."

[26] Cortesi, in Garin, *Pros.*, 910: "Praeterea, Politiane, sic habe neminem eloquentiae laudem consecutum, qui non sit in aliquo imitationis generis versatus. Apud Graecos non modo oratores Demosthenes, Hyperides, Lycurgus, Aeschines et Deinarchus, sed etiam illi philosophi, virtutum magistri, alicuius imitatores esse voluerunt."

[27] On this point, see Celenza, "What Counted as Philosophy," and Hadot, *Philosophy as a Way of Life*, 71–77.

The association of pleasing Latinity with philosophy was something on which Cortesi continued to reflect as the years went by. To open a brief but meaningful parenthesis, Cortesi took this linkage up later, in 1504, in his commentary on the *Four Books of Sentences* of Peter Lombard.[28] Peter Lombard's *Sentences* gathered excerpts from scripture, the Church fathers, and other sources.[29] The collection was designed to cover theological matters both with respect to the *res* (the things themselves) – God, for example – and the *signa* (signs), such as sacraments. The *Sentences* formed part of the core of medieval theological speculation since the late twelfth century and were endorsed by the fourth Lateran Council under Innocent III in 1215. Most major high and late medieval scholastic thinkers tried their hand at a commentary.[30]

Cortesi took the opportunity of writing on the *Sentences* to attempt to bring eloquence to a task that, increasingly, had become a vehicle for ever more specialized speculation. His comments in his Preface are revealing, given what they disclose about his attitudes toward true philosophy.[31] Dedicating his treatise to the newly elected Pope Julius II, Cortesi writes: "For some time now, great Pope, there has been the greatest controversy among men, as to whether philosophers should employ grace of Latin speaking style in their studies."[32] Cortesi suggests that different solutions have been proposed. Some philosophers believe that it is their province to invent words at will, that they should have as much freedom as did the ancients, not wanting to be too constricted in their choices.[33] "However, some" Cortesi goes on,

---

[28] Cf. Ann Moss, *Renaissance Truth and the Latin Language Turn* (Oxford: Oxford University Press, 2003), 64–68.

[29] See Peter Lombard, *Sententiae in IV libris distinctae*, 2 vols., ed. Victorin Doucet (Grottaferrata: Collegium S. Bonaventurae ad Claras Aquas, 1971–81); Marsha Colish, *Peter Lombard*, 2 vols. (Leiden: Brill, 1994).

[30] Cf. Friedrich Stegmüller, *Repertorium commentariorum in Sententias Petri Lombardi*, 2 vols. (Würzburg: Schöning, 1947); Victorin Doucet, *Supplément au Répertoire de M. Frédéric Stegmüller* (Florence: Collegium S. Bonaventurae ad Claras Aquas, 1954).

[31] Cf. Giovanni Farris, *Eloquenza e teologia nel 'Proemium in librum primum sententiarum' di Paolo Cortese*, Quaderni di civiltà letteraria (Savona: Sabatelli, 1972), who offers an edition of the *prooemium*, drawn from Paolo Cortesi, *In quattuor libris sententiarum* (Basel, 1540), from which I cite.

[32] Cortesi, "Proemium," ed. Farris, 22: "Diu Pont. Max. summa est hominum contentione certatum, Philosophorum ne esset studiis latini sermonis adhibendus nitor . . . ."

[33] Ibid.: "Sunt enim multi philosophi qui cum facultatem verborum faciendorum voluntariam esse opinentur nihiloque minus eis in pariendo licere quam priscis illis licitum fuerit arbitrentur; negant quicquam esse causae cur verborum pariendorum licentiam priscorum angustiis praefiniri velint."

think that philosophy is like a kind of marble edifice, and they believe that there is no justification for covering it up with superficially flattering stucco, even as they think it is not right to besmear the radiance of a very beautiful face with make-up [cf. Cicero, *Orator*, sec. 78]. To some, who are even harsher in judgment, a philosophy that is rather obscure and stern seems pleasing, one that is neither welcoming to those who approach it nor ready to give up its riches with largess to the crowd.[34]

Given that philosophy is something of great moment, Cortesi writes, it is against these sorts of thinkers that the will take up arms.[35]

These later reflections of Cortesi indicate something important (to close the parenthesis): the diversity of opinion between Poliziano and Cortesi with respect to the proper style of Latin prose should not be overdrawn and turned into something that might seem to reflect a different underlying message. In many respects, Poliziano is in exact agreement about the core principles: creativity meant not so much a break with the past as an individual expression of what was useful and best about that past. He and Cortesi agreed on the need for true philosophers to engage in this process of creatively using the past; and they both insisted that since the search for wisdom is important for humankind, its messages needed to be communicated in a way that is clear and relevant to contemporary society. Poliziano argued for just these ideas in his *Lamia*, though there, too, he expressed a worry that was probably at the root of his real objection to Cortesi in this earlier letter exchange.[36] It was not so much imitation that worried Poliziano as intellectual sterility. Poliziano's primary concern was the tendency of intellectuals to cease reflection once caught up in a tradition that by repeated practice became too rigid in its fundamental assumptions. These institutionally reproduced traditions often prove unresponsive to history, that is, to the need for intellectuals to adapt to changing circumstances. The two thinkers agreed on that much.

Their debate, however, is noteworthy for two reasons: first, in the long run it was Cortesi's position that won out, finding expression de facto in the way Latin prose was taught and used institutionally thereafter: a moderate Ciceronianism was the Latin style taught and used in schools, universities,

[34] Ibid.: "Nonnulli autem cum philosophiam quasi marmoream quandam aedem constituant, nullo modo ei tectorium induci debere censent, nec fas esse putent pulcherrimi vultus candori illiniri fucum. Quibusdam etiam severioribus, philosophiam squallidiorem et horridiorem esse placet, quae nec aspectu invitet adeuntes, nec opes vulgo largiendo effundat."

[35] Ibid.: "In quo quidem cum permagna res agatur utilitatis hominum, causa est contra eos arma capiendi."

[36] See Chapter 16.

and academies.[37] This style was moderate in the sense that its practitioners made allowances for necessary neologisms and therefore did not consider the Ciceronian lexicon the only possible one among ancient authors used as models. Still, the basic periodic structure and word order of the Ciceronian sentence remained the school model, and hence the model for elite Latinity, in the old world and the new, until relatively modern times.[38]

Second, Poliziano's conception of creativity, expressed here so curtly and in fact without a lot of sustained thought as to the specific matter at hand, itself lived on, the result of about five intellectual generations of humanist striving. This conception entailed that thinkers must constantly be engaged in a process of Socratic self-examination, always on the lookout that the traditions and ideas they had inherited did not become fixed ideas, repeated only because a respected master had taught them. In the world of Italian humanism, however, this mentality found expression, in the generation after Poliziano, in the vernacular rather than in Latin.

The divergence between Poliziano and Cortesi is emblematic of the two trajectories that the new Latin of the Renaissance would take thereafter. On one hand, you needed a Latin that was both fashionably classicizing (and thus in line with new Renaissance norms and expectations) and reproducible. Latin had many public uses. If you were at the papal court, for instance, one of Europe's most international places, you might have to give a funeral oration, or a welcome speech to a visiting delegation. Events such as these (and many other analogous ones) were not the place for eclecticism. Latin had a ceremonial function and, to be in step with the times, it needed to sound classical. Cicero was the right model, as Agostino Dati had realized as early as 1471.

On the other hand, Latin, and more specifically style in Latin, represented an instrument of self-fashioning. In this respect, Poliziano (and others like him) might indeed prefer to write in an eclectic fashion, using classical models but combining them, or using different ancient authors' styles according to the occasion at hand, as Poliziano had done when he relied on the style of the ancient writer Sallust, back in 1478, to describe the Pazzi conspiracy against the Medici.

Writing in an eclectic but still recognizably classicizing fashion could in this respect serve a number of functions: that of self-fashioning, to be sure, so

---

[37] On this point, see Monfasani, "The Ciceronian Controversy."
[38] On the fortunes of Latinity, see Jürgen Leonhardt, *Latin: Story of a World Language*, tr. Kenneth Kronenberg (Cambridge, MA: Harvard University Press, 2013); Francoise Wacquet, *Latin: Or, the Empire of a Sign*, tr. John Howe (London and New York: Verso, 2001).

that individual distinction might be achieved by control of Latinity's different registers (recall when Poliziano wrote to Cortesi: "I am not Cicero: I express myself"). Using Latin eclectically could also serve as a means of both inclusion and exclusion. If, for instance, you used a word or phrase that was attested only once or twice in antiquity, or by a little-read but interesting author, those who recognized your citation immediately became part of an in-group, even as those who didn't were by that very fact excluded.[39] Take, for one example, the beginning of Poliziano's *Lamia*, where Poliziano suggested that stories and fables were the "beginnings" of philosophy and philosophy's "instrument." There Poliziano echoed the words of the Silver Age author Apuleius (124–170 CE) and specifically a relatively rare work of his, the *Florida*.[40] That little, barely noticeable gesture advertised to Poliziano's listeners and readers that he considered this minor work of Apuleius part of the vast treasury of ancient Latinity upon which one might draw. You might have noticed it if you were a contemporary reader or listener, or you might not. Either way, for Poliziano, it was another brick, however small, in the never-ending edifice he was constructing.

Latin as a consistent, teachable, and useful instrument of public culture versus Latin as a means of creative self-expression: this was the polarity that emerged as Poliziano and Cortesi finished their debate. Like the Poggio moment earlier in the fifteenth century ("only in books"), this parting of the ways seems much easier to recognize in hindsight. It is not that debates over Cicero and his status as a model ended with the exchange of Poliziano and Cortesi.[41] Indeed, plenty of people straddled both worlds or took their writing in Latin to almost ridiculous extremes.

The great northern European humanist Erasmus (1466–1536) – a fan of Lorenzo Valla, as we have seen – wrote a satirical dialogue called *The Ciceronian* in which he ridiculed those (and he had in mind Italians especially) who relied only on Cicero as a model of Latinity. One of his interlocutors claims to have removed all books not written by Cicero from his sight, and he says other things: "I have a picture of him [Cicero], nicely painted, not only in my private chapel and in my study, but on all the doors too; and I carry his portrait about with me, carved on gems, so that all the time he's present to my thoughts. I never see anything in my dreams but Cicero."[42] The interlocutor in question

---

[39] See D'Amico, "The Progress of Renaissance Latin Prose: The Case of Apuleianism."

[40] Apuleius, *Florida*, 15.24.

[41] See JoAnn DellaNeva, ed., *Ciceronian Controversies*, tr. Brian Duvick (Cambridge, MA: Harvard University Press, 2007).

[42] Erasmus, *Ciceronianus*, tr. Betty I. Knott, in *Collected Works of Erasmus* (Toronto: University of Toronto Press, 1974), v. 27, pp. 337–448, at 346.

claims to have memorized all of Cicero; to have gathered together and subdivided all the places in Cicero's work where he uses meter in his prose; and, most importantly, studiously to avoid any word, phrase, or verbal form not employed by Cicero. When he does not find the verb form *amamus* (which means "we love") in Cicero, he implies he avoids using that form, apparently undisturbed by the silliness of not being able to say "we love" in his own Latin.[43] Numerous other occasions abound when the interlocutor's slavish imitation leads him into taking positions that, when aired in the way they are aired in *The Ciceronian*, seem absurd. The dialogue is funny (somewhat, in the slightly stilted way that these things tend to be), but of course, it misses the point in many ways. It tends to appeal today because of the way individualism has been and continues to be fetishized, so that the slavish imitator becomes a figure all too easy to ridicule. But the truth was that most everyone believed that you needed models to write – and to live – well.

Living well was the province of philosophy: not the narrow sort of thing taught in classrooms as academic philosophy, but the broader field of intellectual endeavor that investigates (as Poliziano did so brilliantly in his *Lamia*) the sorts of things you need to do to live a fulfilling and productive life.

As to writing, this search for models came to represent the core of how the "language question" was resolved in Italy. This phrase (*questione della lingua* in Italian) has traditionally designated a series of debates reaching back to Dante's *On the Eloquence of the Vernacular*, debates that eventually culminated in the widely accepted choice among Italian intellectuals to accept Tuscan as the basis for literary Italian.[44] The figure credited with crystallizing this position is Pietro Bembo (1470–1547), a Venetian – surprisingly, perhaps, given Italy's intense regionalism.[45] But Pietro had the benefit of being part of a distinguished diplomatic family, whose peregrinations exposed him to a wide variety of cultural settings. His father, Bernardo Bembo (1433–1519) served Venice in many ways, not least as an ambassador. Young Pietro had the good fortune to accompany his father on many diplomatic voyages, including a lengthy stint in Florence, where Pietro developed an abiding love for the Tuscan language, believing, eventually, that it would have a capacity to move the emotions equal to that of ancient

[43] Ibid., 348.
[44] See Robert A. Hall, *The Italian Questione della lingua: An Interpretive Essay* (Chapel Hill: University of North Carolina Press, 1942); Bruno Migliorini, *Storia della lingua italiana* (Milan: Bompiani, 1998), 281–388; Maurizio Vitale, *La questione della lingua* (Palermo: Palumbo, 1964).
[45] On him see Carlo Dionisotti, *Scritti sul Bembo*, ed. Claudio Vela (Turin: Einaudi, 2002), esp. 143–67; Carol Kidwell, *Pietro Bembo: Lover, Linguist, Cardinal* (Montreal: McGill-Queen's University Press, 2004).

Greek and Latin; if, that is, it were correctly employed. But the Tuscan that Bembo came to endorse was not the Tuscan spoken in the late fifteenth and early sixteenth centuries. Rather, he believed the language had reached a high point in the work of Petrarch and Boccaccio.

Why would a theorist of language deliberately choose a variety of dialect that had been cultivated a century and a half before his current moment? There are, in Bembo's case, three answers: the culture out of which he emerged, the example of Latin and Greek, and the cultural imperatives of a new era. As to the culture he came from, it was principally that of diplomacy. Much like Paolo Cortesi, who was raised within a family with close ties to the papal court, Pietro Bembo's experience at his ambassador father's side taught him one thing most of all, with respect to language: if you wanted to communicate clearly, you could not afford to speak or write in a way that would be restrictive in terms of time and place. If the language you chose were fully understood only in a certain region, or if it were dotted with dialect expressions that emerged only in the time in which you lived, you would of necessity limit yourself to particular audiences. Bembo's choice to focus on Petrarchan and Boccaccian Tuscan was undergirded by a twofold assumption: first, a certain amount of uniformity was necessary; second, this uniform language needed in some form still to be spoken in a native way and not contained "only in books," as Poggio had written regarding Latin.

The exemplary functions of Latin and Greek, however, were never far from Bembo's mind. He was a truly outstanding Latinist, one whose Latin competency emerged as one among a number of reasons why he was chosen to be a papal secretary as the pontificate of the Medici pope, Leo X, began in 1513.[46] By Bembo's day, he and the rest of his cohort had absorbed the fifteenth-century debate over the Latin language, coming to realize that ancient Latin had been a living, natural language, now dead but in some senses all the more admirable because of the permanence and rule-bound aspect that had allowed it to survive so many centuries. Like others, Bembo was eager to transpose the permanence and cultural prestige that Latin by tradition possessed into a new linguistic realm that could harness the energy of a living language.

In line with the best thinking of his day, when it came to Latin, Bembo believed that Cicero was the model to follow in prose (as was Virgil in epic poetry), as he wrote in a letter concerning imitation to Pico della Mirandola's nephew Gianfrancesco Pico in 1512.[47] As to Greek, Bembo spent two years

---

[46] See Dionisotti, *Scritti*, 155.

[47] See Giorgio Santangelo, ed., *De imitatione: Le epistole "De imitatione" di Giovanfrancesco Pico della Mirandola e di Pietro Bembo* (Florence: Olschki, 1954); and the letters in JoAnn DellaNeva, ed., *Ciceronian Controversies*, 16–125.

studying the language with one of the Byzantine world's most distinguished scholars and philologists, Janus Lascaris (1434–1501), whose Greek *Grammar* became one of the great successes of the printing house of Aldus Manutius and served as an introductory Greek textbook for countless Westerners.[48] In fact, it was Bembo himself who brought Lascaris's grammar to the attention of the soon-to-be legendary printer Aldus.[49]

A refugee from the 1453 sack of Constantinople, Lascaris was one of many learned Greeks who made their way west and taught their native language to eager students.[50] Lascaris settled in the Sicilian city of Messina, which is where Bembo went to work with him. It is a curious and remarkable fact that Bembo went to Messina in 1492, right after he had met with none other than Poliziano and Pico, who had come to Venice to search for and collate manuscripts. Moving to Messina and studying with the man who "wrote the book," as it were, Bembo not only learned Greek to a very high degree, he also absorbed the notion that poetry, Greek poetry especially, moved people's emotions. That affective energy, too, came to seem crucial to Bembo, as he thought about language. If poetry were to flourish in Italy, real poetry that could "blend the useful with the sweet," as Horace had suggested in classical antiquity, it had to be written in a language that could move people.[51] Bembo saw in all his travels that, though Petrarch's fourteenth-century poetry was written in Tuscan, it was still known up and down the Italian peninsula and that it moved people indeed.

Then there were the conditions, desires, and imperatives of a new era. Printing with moveable type had found its way to Italy in the 1460s. At the outset, printers made books deliberately to look like manuscripts – handwritten books – since readers did not want surprises and since printers wanted to make sure they sold their products. The "art of writing artificially," as it was known early on, seemed an accelerated way to produce the sorts of books that had gone before: evolution, rather than revolution.[52] But by the late

---

[48] See Paul Botley, *Learning Greek in Western Europe, 1396–1529: Grammars, Lexica, and Classroom Texts* (Philadelphia: American Philosophical Society, 2010).

[49] See Daniel S. Houston, *The Aldine Lascaris: A Greek Textbook in the Italian Renaissance*, unpublished PhD dissertation, Johns Hopkins University, 2015.

[50] See Massimo Ceresa, "Lascaris, Giano," in *Dizionario biografico degli italiani*, 63 (2004), 785–91; for larger context, see John Monfasani, *Byzantine Scholars in Renaissance Italy: Cardinal Bessarion and other Emigrés* (Aldershot: Ashgate, 1995); Monfasani, *Greeks and Latins in Renaissance Italy* (Aldershot: Ashgate, 2004).

[51] See Horace, *Ars Poetica*, in Horace, *Satires, Epistles, and Ars poetica*, ed. and tr. H. Rushton Fairclough (Cambridge, MA: Harvard University Press, 1991), ll. 343–44: "omne tulit punctum qui miscuit utile dulci, lectorem delectando pariterque monendo."

[52] See Chapter 11.

fifteenth century printing became an acknowledged cultural force, as the first, halting steps in the new industry yielded to the emerging reality of mass book production, larger audiences, and new modes of reaching people (on this latter front, pamphlets, especially, being relatively inexpensive to produce, became one of the key ways in which the messages of the Protestant Reformation spread, from 1517 onward).

The last decade of the fifteenth century saw the emergence in Venice of the printing house of Aldus Manutius, who became for a time the leading printer in Europe.[53] Aldus had studied as a youth with the eminent humanist teacher Guarino da Verona and had been close friends with Pico della Mirandola, before being selected, with Pico's help, to serve as the tutor to Alberto and Leonello, members of the royal house of Carpi. Prince Alberto later gave Aldus enough financing to begin his new life as a printer, a profession he carried out with brio. Settling in Venice, Aldus, among other accomplishments, printed the first complete set of Aristotle's works in Greek (all the more impressive given that fonts had to be created expressly for that purpose) and established a series of Greek and Latin "classics" published in small format.[54] He transformed printing, in short, making this art the gold standard for book production.

Bembo was a close collaborator with the Aldine printing press, overseeing the production in 1501 of a printed edition of Petrarch's verse.[55] The union of the new technology of printing with the vernacular, and the fact that Petrarch's Italian poetry was presented in the same series of books in which Aldus was publishing classics such as Virgil, was quite meaningful. Bembo like others realized that allowing for diffusion as printing did, it had power; for that reason alone, the language question was all the more important.

Bembo tried his hand early at a work in Tuscan prose, called the *Asolani*, so named after the town, Asolo (near Venice), in which the conversation he fancifully recreated in dialogue form occurred.[56] The subject was love, and

[53] See Martin Davies, *Aldus Manutius: Printer and Publisher of Renaissance Venice* (Tempe: MRTS, 1999); Carlo Dionisotti, *Aldo Manuzio: umanista e editore* (Milan: Polifilo, 1995); Martin Lowry, *The World of Aldus Manutius* (Ithaca: Cornell University Press, 1979).

[54] See Ralph Hexter, "Aldus, Greek, and the Shape of the Classical Corpus," in David S. Zeidberg, ed., *Aldus Manutius and Renaissance Culture* (Florence: Olschki, 1998), 143–60; Giovanni Orlandi, ed. and tr., *Aldo Manuzio editore: dediche, prefazioni, note ai testi* (Milan: Polifilo, 1975); Richardson, *Printing, Writers, and Readers in Renaissance Italy*, 126–28.

[55] See Cecil Clough, "Pietro Bembo's Edition of Petrarch and His Association with the Aldine Press," in David Zeidberg, ed., *Aldus Manutius and Renaissance Culture* (Florence: Olschki, 1998), 47–81.

[56] Pietro Bembo, *Gli Asolani*, in Pietro Bembo, *Prose e rime*, ed. Carlo Dionisotti (Turin: UTEP, 1966), 311–504.

Bembo showed himself to have been influenced by Ficino's theories on love, Platonizing as these were, whereby love is viewed as something that, practiced correctly, elevated both the lover and the beloved. Structured in three books, the *Asolani*'s interlocutors set forth arguments both against and for love, with the Ficinian Platonizing arguments at the end. The dialogue is important for many reasons, but with respect to the language question, its principal significance is that Bembo was writing it in the last years of the fifteenth century and had it print-published in 1505: early for a work with serious (if also courtly and diverting) pretensions to appear in the vernacular. It was a way of "test driving," as it were, the theories regarding language that Bembo was beginning to develop even then.

Moreover, it was part of a new, larger reality: printing with moveable type was one sign that members of the new culture, like Bembo, must not only imitate and take what was best from ancient Greco-Roman culture. They also had to surpass that culture and do something new, finding means of self-expression that were appropriate to the current moment. As Bembo wrote in his "Letter on Imitation" to Gianfrancesco Pico:

> So this, Pico, can be our rule in everything of this kind: first, that we set before ourselves for imitation the best of all models; then, that we imitate that person with the aim of equaling him; and finally, that all our efforts have in view outstripping the man we have equaled.[57]

Language, of course, was paramount, as was the material form – the book – in which it appeared.

Scattered notes here and there in Bembo's correspondence confirm his early work (as early as 1500) on what must be considered his masterpiece, the *Prose della Volgar Lingua*.[58] But the work did not appear in full and in print until 1525. Again, Bembo used the beloved dialogue form, structuring his work in three "books." Bembo, by then a cardinal, dedicated the work to then Cardinal Giulio de' Medici (who would soon become Pope Clement VII). Bembo had four interlocutors, all of them historical personages; throughout the *Prose*, antiquity is the model to which the interlocutors repeatedly return.

In Book One, early on, for example, the interlocutor Carlo Bembo (the author's brother in real life) suggests that modern Italians should be like ancient Romans. To the ancient Romans, he argues, the Latin language was

[57] Bembo to Pico, in DellaNeva, *Ciceronian Controversies*, 81 (tr. Duvick).
[58] Petro Bembo, *Prose della volgar lingua*, in Bembo, *Prose e rime*, 71–309. For the correspondence see Pietro Bembo, *Lettere*, 4 vols., ed. Ernesto Travi (Bologna: Commissione per i testi di lingua, 1987); and Kidwell, *Pietro Bembo*, 223.

much closer, since "they were all born into Latin and imbibed it along with the milk of their nursemaids," whereas "they learned Greek normally much later in life, when they were already grown, and they used Greek rarely and, indeed, many of them happened neither to use nor even ever to have learned Greek."[59] For Italians today the situation is similar, but the two languages in question are Latin and Italian, with present-day Italians having the same relationship to Latin as the ancient Romans did to Greek: "The same thing happens to us when it comes to Latin, which we (and not all of us but rather few of us) learn not from our nursemaids and in our cradles but rather from teachers in schools. Once it is learned, it's not that we use it all the time; rather, we use it rarely and sometimes not at all."[60]

Antiquity is the frame of reference, of course, and the argument can proceed with that framework in mind. Another interlocutor sums things up more succinctly:

> Since the Romans had two languages, one that belonged to them and that was natural (and this was Latin), the other foreign (and that one was Greek), so too do we possess two ways of speaking: one that belongs to us and is natural and domestic, which is the vernacular, and the other foreign and not natural, which is Latin.[61]

Embedded in these early arguments are a few key concerns guiding Bembo's thinking.

First is the stark, no-nonsense recognition that there are languages you learn at home, naturally, and languages you learn in school. For modern-day Italians, Latin falls into the latter category. Second, and somewhat at variance with the first, an underlying and unresolved open question exists regarding unity, plurality, and registers. Will or should there be only one literary language? If so, would it need to be refined to such a point that one would need schools and other institutions to teach and to preserve it?

These very questions continue to preoccupy the interlocutors. One can admit, for instance, that the vernacular is natural, whereas Latin is not. But: what was the vernacular? "Italy," recall, was not one, large, relatively unified nation, such as, say, France or England, with a central metropolis such as Paris or London, whose linguistic tastes and aspirations could serve, ideally at least, as models for the larger whole that those countries represented. No, Italy was composed still of small city-states that were often at war, settling sometimes into uneasy alliances with one another but never coming close to

---

[59] Bembo, *Prose*, 1.3, p. 80.
[60] Ibid.
[61] Ibid.

representing anything like the emerging national unities that newer, sovereign states such as France and England embodied. Each of Italy's city-states possessed its own dialect, dialects that really were different, with dissimilar words for the same things and pronunciations so radically diverse that it was possible for people from different city-states, uneducated people especially, not to understand each other. It was not a matter of slightly different accents.

Accordingly, when one of the interlocutors (Giuliano de' Medici) maintains that the literary language of Italy should be the Florentine vernacular currently in use ("since writing, just like clothing and armaments, needs to draw near and adapt itself to the usage of the times"), the argument is dispatched rather quickly.[62] The real reason has to do, yet again, with the importance of models and the inherent differences between written and everyday language.

The interlocutor Carlo Bembo, responding to this argument, asserts that written culture has always been different from the everyday language used in the streets. If that had not been so, "Virgil would have been praised less than any number of everyday speakers in town squares."[63] Here is the truth, Carlo suggests: "Written language, my dear Giuliano, must not draw near to the language of the people." If it does, it will be at the cost of seriousness and greatness. Carlo continues: "The reason this occurs is that writers most definitely should not care only for the pleasure of those people who are alive while they are writing but rather – and in truth much more – for those people who will live after they write."[64] This future-oriented aspiration is why, Carlo avers, writers hope for fame for their work that will last forever, rather than for a short time. And (to return yet again to the respected examples of antiquity), precisely this "eternalizing" of a language is what Virgil and Cicero did for Latin and Homer and Demosthenes did for Greek.[65]

Two bards, two orators; poetry and prose: these are the principal concerns. Thus Carlo begins to zero in on what the *Prose*'s main contribution to the history of the Italian language will be, as he focuses his (and the reader's) attention on Petrarch and Boccaccio: "Do you believe that, if Petrarch had composed his poems in the language of the everyday people of his time, those poems would have been as elegant, as beautiful, as precious and noble, as they are? If that is in fact what you believe, your belief is quite wrong."[66]

[62] Ibid., 1.17, pp. 115–17.
[63] Ibid., 1.18, p. 118.
[64] Ibid.
[65] Ibid., 118–19.
[66] Ibid., 119.

The same distance between written and everyday speech obtains for Boccaccio, though Carlo admits that in some of Boccaccio's stories he approached the language of the people for rhetorical reasons.

Models are needed, in the final analysis, because literature of any sort exists ultimately for elite readers. Even Virgil, when he wrote about shepherds and farmers (as he did in his *Georgics*) did so in such a way that almost no farmer could fully understand him. Indeed, Virgil wrote in such a way that almost no one from a city could well and completely understand him unless that notional reader had been educated and become familiar with literature.[67] Whatever the subject matter, whatever the language, levels of comprehension will vary. Models are thus essential, but in a manner that might seem contradictory. As the dialogue progresses, the interlocutor Carlo (still the mouthpiece of the author Pietro Bembo) makes a noteworthy point. Just as in antiquity Cicero and Virgil had to consider earlier writers who came before them (Carlo mentions the early Latin writer Ennius), so too did Petrarch and Boccaccio have to reckon with Dante, as well as other early vernacular Italian writers.

Historically, authors who have not modeled their works on the best that has come before them have been judged poorly: Bembo says that the late Latin writers Seneca, Suetonius, Lucan, and Claudian all would have "written in a more praiseworthy fashion in both prose and verse ... if they had written in the style of those ancients – and I mean Virgil and Cicero – instead of in their own style."[68] What we have here is a majority opinion, confidently enunciated: if an elite scholar such as Poliziano had maintained that Silver Age authors were very much worth studying, Bembo here is instead stating the obvious. Authors such as Seneca, Suetonius, Lucan, and Claudian are valuable, but their work pales in comparison to that of Cicero and Virgil, since the style of those two classics in prose and verse represented a point of perfection.

The point – and the tension – is this: just as Cicero had (in his *Orator*) declared that "in delineating the perfect orator I shall be portraying such a one as perhaps has never existed," and just as Cortesi had seen Cicero as a model who was in some respects timeless, so too does Bembo share the same basic, possibly antagonistic assumptions regarding models and history.

On one hand, humanism (if it had taught the previous five generations of thinkers anything) had alerted all intellectuals to the reality of history and context. Valla's view of Aristotle was new and interesting and important

[67] Ibid., 120.
[68] Ibid., 1.19, p. 122.

because he saw Aristotle not as an authority, singular and immutable, out of time, but rather as one of a number of great ancient figures, whose work could be understood as important, yes, but as inhabiting one specific moment in history. The implication behind that view, one that other humanists shared implicitly or explicitly, was that there was room "for us," as it were, meaning that, though we understand that we need to study the ancients, we also need to work in the world we have now and not be imprisoned by ancient exemplarity. Or as Alberti had put it in his *On Painting*: all you had to do was look around you to see that our best contemporary artists were doing work that could rival the ancients in greatness, work that was all the more meaningful because it was happening now, today, in our lifetimes and in our world. It is no surprise that Alberti, in his *Grammatichetta*, had made an early, angry, cogent argument for the integrity of the Florentine vernacular.

On the other hand, it is also unsurprising that Alberti's exuberance had scant success in his era. There was always another assumption hovering above a lot of what humanists did, one that attended their work inside and outside of institutions. It is this: you need institutions to have culture. To have institutions you need to have traditions; to have traditions, you need to have models. The most forceful exponents of this supposition had long, sustained, insider-style exposure to enduring late medieval and Renaissance institutions. Take Poggio Bracciolini, for example, who had said that one learns proper usage "only from the books and writings of the ancients." For all his raillery and salty bonhomie, Poggio was an institutional man at root, whose long service at the papal court had convinced him beyond convincing that institutions were inevitable parts of society.

The same goes for Paolo Cortesi, who stemmed from one of the most influential curial families in Rome and who was an esteemed member of the papal court. Cortesi, we recall, had considered Cicero a "wondrous man . . . from whom so many different minds have flowed, as if from a kind of perennial fount." In so many ways, precisely this sort of idealization represented the contrary of what has often been viewed as essential to Italian humanism: the contextualization of figures in their own time (as in Valla's view of Aristotle). Cortesi was sophisticated enough to know what, five generations earlier, had shocked Petrarch: that Cicero had been a flesh-and-blood politician, whose foibles and flaws existed side by side with his elegant writing. But Cortesi was also both clear-eyed about the reality in which he existed and, of course, an heir to the fifteenth century's language debate. Latin was "alive" in so many ways (as a language of education, religion, and diplomacy) that calling it "dead" makes little sense. But he knew as did everyone else that it was not "living" as were native languages, imbibed in the home, from parents and nursemaids, as any vernacular was bound to be. And Cicero was "wondrous" in precisely the way Cortesi claimed: as an influencer, whose prose both set the gold standard for writing in Latin and had become so well known and studied by the late fifteenth century that there had evolved speedy ways to teach and learn the art of sounding like him in one's own writing (as Agostino Dati's *Elegantiolae* showed).

Cortesi, engaged humanist intellectual though he was, also had responsibilities in the world of politics and diplomacy. He saw that a relatively standard but still classicizing Latin was needed, a language that was international and translatable across Europe's evolving order of large, competing bureaucracies. His conflict with Poliziano could not be more emblematic of the fate of the language question going forward. Eclectic, individualized Latin was for scholars trying to prove a point. Ciceronian Latin was for the rest of cultured society.

The very same assumptions (regarding models, Cicero's status, and the existence of an elite) run through Bembo's *Prose*. Cortesi had said, regarding the "best authors" in general and Cicero more specifically, that they "leave behind seeds" in the spirits of those who come after them; he had also said that it was important not to have too many seeds in the same field. When Bembo, in his *Prose*, discusses the modeling capacities of Petrarch and Boccaccio, the same notions are present. Both of those great authors had dealt with and reconciled themselves to worthy writers who had come before them (as Cicero and Virgil had done with Ennius and other early authors) but then had emerged as points of perfection, completing as they did an evolutionary process they might not even have known was occurring. In the same way that otherwise respectable but, inevitably, second-tier authors such as Seneca and Lucan would have done well to stick more to the models provided by Cicero and Virgil, so too should "we" ("we" who have the benefit of so much history behind us) realize that Boccaccio's prose and Petrarch's poetry provide the same sort of perfected models worthy of imitation. In the end, one can see, both in poetry and prose, that "the great growth of the Tuscan language arrived at its final point with Petrarch and Boccaccio; and that, from that point onward, no one has been observed who has even reached that point, let alone gone beyond it."[69]

This last quotation occurs at the beginning of the second book (of three) of the *Prose*, and it emerges at a point when the interlocutors have, essentially, settled the principal question at hand, which was: what sort of language should one use for serious literary works? The answer: Tuscan, derived from

[69] Bembo, *Prose*, 2.2, p. 131.

the fourteenth century. It is worth noting that the first book, in which the main thesis is presented, argued over, and defended, was substantially complete by 1512 (though Bembo did not publish the whole in print until 1525). What this meant was that Bembo's main arguments and theories were largely formed by that relatively early point. It is a particular merit of Bembo's genius that he was somehow able, in the final two books, to discuss matters that were quite technical, such as meter and rhetoric in Book Two and then proper Tuscan grammar as a whole in Book Three (the largest of the *Prose*), in dialogue form.

Even more significant is that Bembo's ideas dominated. He can, in his own way, be called the father of modern Italian. It didn't happen overnight, of course: long-term phenomena almost never do. Moreover, Bembo's desire to unify the Italian language was by no means unique to him. It was a dream that reached back to Dante and his *On the Eloquence of the Vernacular*. But Bembo inhabited a moment when ever more people evinced a similar desire. Take the Neapolitan Benedetto di Falco, who in his 1535 *Rimario* (a guide for poets to rhyming words) wrote:

> If only it pleased the heavens ... that some Roman court [here meaning a powerful state or regime], such as is today the Venetian court, with the advice of the learned were to reform the Italian language, so that there were one language common to all and so that, in general, it could be used without blame, just as, once, there was one Latin language used throughout the world.[70]

For di Falco, Neapolitan though he was, it was Tuscan that should have that exalted role, since so much foundational literature had by then been written in that variety of Italian (though like others of his era di Falco sought to expand the group of writers one might imitate).[71]

There were plenty of other theories as to how one might create a literary language. In his foundational work *The Courtier*, Baldassare Castiglione's interlocutors accept the received wisdom, which had been so neatly articulated by Bembo (and it is no accident that Bembo himself appears as one of *The Courtier's* interlocutors): that, for the ancients, Latin was as natural as the vernacular is today. They agree, too, that Tuscan, and especially fourteenth-century Tuscan, represented the best of the vernaculars. But they also made the case that it would be imprudent to model current language on a version of the language that was almost two centuries old. If someone were sent to

---

[70] Benedetto di Falco, *Rimario* (Naples, 1535), I.3.r–v.
[71] See Hermann Haller, *The Other Italy: The Literary Canon in Dialect* (Toronto: University of Toronto Press, 1999).

Florence today (one interlocutor suggests), and he had to speak of some serious diplomatic matter in front of the Florentine Senate, or even for that matter if he were jesting with Florentine friends, he would avoid using "those old Tuscan words. Were he to use them, beyond making a fool of himself, he would give no little annoyance to whoever was listening."[72]

In the end, though as in all dialogues multiple opinions are represented, Castiglione's view is stated by the same interlocutor, who maintains that, since writing and speaking are linked, someone wanting to write and speak well should use words and expressions that "are customary in Tuscany and in other places in Italy and that have a certain charm when pronounced."[73] This position, which others shared, reflects a preference for what is often referred to as the *lingua cortigiana*, or "language of the court." The idea was that one would, by one's cosmopolitanism, grace, and education, distill, as it were, the best usage of the day and produce a language suitable for current use in Italy's courts that would also be appreciated as literature in the years and decades to come.

If that sounds vague and impossible, it is because it was. And so, after all the debates and accounting for local provincialisms, it is accurate to say that by the end of the sixteenth century, Bembo's ideas regarding Latin not only were widely accepted; they were also reinforced by new, professional bodies that evolved in the sixteenth century to regulate language.

Just as, in the fifteenth century, various Italian states had come to see libraries as part of the state itself (as possessions that were, loosely though inevitably, "public" and as part of the "common good"), so too in the sixteenth century did ever more realms of culture fall under that same umbrella of an idea. A good, flourishing state needed military strength, a workable political order, international relations commensurate with its size and influence, and a cultural apparatus that seemed worthy and that "belonged" to the state.

While it would be impossible to cover in substance all the developments that were occurring in the sixteenth century and that put pressure on states to develop in all these areas, culture included, we can point to at least three. The "Italian wars," which began in 1494 and ended with the Peace of Cateau-Cambrésis in 1559, left behind a new order. Major Italian states now fell under the protection of larger European powers: Milan and Naples went to the Spanish, and Florence too eventually came under the dominion of the Spanish, retaining at times strained ties to the French.

---

[72] Baldassarre Castiglione, *Il libro del cortegiano*, ed. Ettore Bonora (Milan: Mursia, 1972), 1.29, p. 66.
[73] Ibid., p. 67.

Second, the Protestant Reformation, begun in 1517 and signaling the beginning of the end of the old dream of a united "Christendom," presented challenges large and small all over Europe.[74] More realignments occurred, with several northern powers following Luther's version of Christianity, or John Calvin's, or other new models that emerged. In the Catholic south, finally, the Catholic Reformation, traditionally known as the Counter-Reformation, gained momentum and culminated in the Council of Trent, begun in 1545.[75] When it ended, after numerous sessions, in 1563, the Church affirmed its commitment to a Catholic theology that leaned heavily on the interpretations of the great thirteenth-century scholastic thinker Thomas Aquinas; established a new critical text of the Latin Vulgate Bible (thus opposing the wish of Luther and other Protestant reformers to have scripture translated into vernaculars); and endorsed the Index of Prohibited Books, which forbade certain books from being published or studied publicly.

What these changes all fostered was, to put it broadly but accurately, the search for order. Language was one of those realms in which order was sought, increasingly on an international stage. In 1539, for example, Francis I (1494–1547), the first Valois king of France and great patron of Italian artists (Leonardo da Vinci among them), signed into law an ordinance (the "Ordonnance de Villers-Cotterêts"), whose 192 articles had far-reaching effects on many aspects of French life.[76]

Amidst articles having to do with everything from matters pertaining to the Church to judicial questions, two articles (110 and 111) stood out from the others. Together, they proclaimed that all official decrees and proclamations emanating from the French royal house, lower courts, and other entities, as well as any official contracts, must be issued in French, since there were too many misunderstandings based on "l'intelligence des mots latins" – "the understanding of Latin words."[77] These articles represented

---

[74] See Euan Cameron, *The European Reformation*, 2nd ed. (Oxford: Oxford University Press, 2012); Carlos M.N. Eire, *Reformations: The Early Modern World, 1450–1650* (New Haven: Yale University Press, 2016).

[75] See John W. O'Malley, *Trent: What Happened at the Council* (Cambridge, MA: Harvard University Press, 2013); O'Malley, *Trent and All That: Renaming Catholicism in the Early Modern Era* (Cambridge, MA: Harvard University Press, 2002).

[76] See Gilles Boulard, "L' Ordonnance de Villers-Cotterêts: le temps de la claret et la stratégie du temps (1539–1992)," *Revue Historique* 301 (1999), 45–100; Piero Fiorelli, "Pour l'interprétation de l'ordonnance de Villers-Cotterêts," *Le Français moderne* 18 (1950), 277–88.

[77] "Ordonnance de Villers-Cotterêts," in *Recueil general des anciennes lois françaises*, 29 vols. (Paris: Belin-Le-Priers, 1821–33), vol. 12, part 2.

a major change, one that had far-reaching effects in France and helped solidify Parisian French as the French national language, even as they gave cohesion to an evolving but unmistakable sense of French national identity.

Roughly a century later, in 1635 to be precise, Cardinal Richelieu, King Louis XIII's chief minister, recognized and, effectively, founded the French Academy. Its chief purpose, as one of its founding articles states, was "to work with all the effort and diligence possible to give precise rules for our language and to render it pure, eloquent, and capable of treating the arts and sciences."[78] Toward that end the Academy was to compose a dictionary, a grammar, and manuals of rhetoric and poetics, and it was also to work on standardizing French orthography.

One of the models the French had in mind was an academy founded in Florence in 1583, called the *Accademia della Crusca* (*cruscate* was a word that connoted informal, playful literary and philosophical discourses).[79] It grew, as these things often did, out of the informal discussions of a group of acquaintances that had been taking place in the 1570s.[80] This group was joined in 1582 by a momentous figure, Lionardo Salviati, who became its leader.[81] In taking a name that had embedded within it a bit of play, it sought to distinguish itself from other, seemingly stodgy institutions. Salviati emphasized the root meaning of the word *crusca*, "bran," so that the Academy's name also came to connote sifting, as in sifting the wheat of proper linguistic usage from the chaff of impoverished, inelegant, everyday speech.

Salviati died in 1589, but not without leaving behind him a substantial legacy: with procedures and frameworks in place, the Academy concentrated all its attention thereafter on the preparation of a dictionary, which became the *Vocabolario degli accademici della crusca*, printed in 1612 and recognized immediately as a groundbreaking work. The editors' Preface makes clear where they stood. After outlining how the Tuscan language has flourished

---

[78] *Statuts et règlements de l'Académie Françoise*, at www.academie-francaise.fr/sites/academie-franc aise.fr/files/statuts_af_0.pdf, accessed August 17, 2016, article 24, p. 19.

[79] See the Accademia's website: www.accademiadellacrusca.it/it/laccademia/storia; Severina Parodi, *Quattro secoli di Crusca: 1583–1983* (Florence: Accademia della Crusca, 1983); *La Crusca nella tradizione letteraria e linguistica italiana: Atti del Congresso internazionale per il IV centenario dell'Accademia della Crusca* (Florence: Accademia della Crusca, 1985)

[80] See David S. Chambers and Francois Quiviger, eds., *Italian Academies of the Sixteenth Century* (London: Warburg Institute, 1995); Marianne Pade, ed., *On Renaissance Academies* (Rome: Quasar, 2011).

[81] See Peter M. Brown, *Lionardo Salviati: A Critical Biography* (Oxford: Oxford University Press, 1974); Lionardo Salviati, *Regole della Toscana favella*, ed. Anna Antonini Renieri (Florence: Accademia della Crusca, 1991).

and is indeed recognized as a model, they discuss the authors they held in esteem as authorities:

> In compiling the present *Vocabolario* (keeping in mind the judgment of the most Illustrious Cardinal Bembo, of the Deputies in their corrected edition of Boccaccio in 1573, and finally of the knight Lionardo Salviati), we have deemed it necessary to recur to the authority of those writers who lived when this language [Florentine Tuscan] flourished in the highest degree, which was from the time of Dante, or a little before him, up until a few years after the death of Boccaccio. We could say that this period, altogether one entire century, runs from the year of our Lord 1300 to 1400, more or less. The reason is – as Salviati brilliantly argued – that those writers who worked before 1300 can be considered in much of their language excessively ancient, whereas those writers from 1400 onward corrupted no little part of the purity of speech possessed by that wonderful century.[82]

So much is contained in this paragraph.

First is the victory of Bembo. The Venetian's theories and predilections regarding the Tuscan language became, within a century of the 1525 publication of his *Prose*, common opinion about how the language should be used and who counted canonically as a true authority. Boccaccio was one of those authors of course, and the mention of the 1573 work of a group of editors appointed by the city of Florence (the "Deputies") clues us in to this fact: Boccaccio's work was coming to seem a cornerstone of "official" Florentine culture, so much so that it (like libraries in the fifteenth century) became part of the state's cultural apparatus, an inheritance just as worthy of preservation as a fine building or work of art.

Then there are the seeds of much later criticism of the Italian fifteenth century, as the editors suggest that writers after the year 1400 "corrupted" the purity of what Dante, Petrarch, and Boccaccio had achieved. The early twentieth-century Italian critic and philosopher Benedetto Croce much later called the fifteenth century in Italy a *secolo senza poesia* – a "century without poetry." Doing so, he rode the waves of earlier, nineteenth-century criticism of the fifteenth century as one of classicizing, Latinate pedantry that, in its turn to the ancient world, ignored the contemporary environment.[83] The Academicians in their Introduction seem to prefigure that sense that,

---

[82] *Vocabolario degli accademici della Crusca* (Venice: G. Alberti, 1612), "A' lettori"; I have consulted the second impression (Venice: Iacopo Sarzino, 1623), *.3v; also available online at http://vocabolario.sns.it/html/_s_index2.html.

[83] See Christopher S. Celenza, *The Lost Italian Renaissance: Humanists, Historians, and Latin's Legacy* (Baltimore: Johns Hopkins University Press, 2004); Rocco Rubini, *The Other Renaissance: Italian Humanism between Hegel and Heidegger* (Chicago: University of Chicago Press, 2014); for Croce, see Benedetto Croce, "Il secolo senza poesia," *La critica* 30 (1932), 161–84.

along with the fifteenth century's accomplishments, a kind of decadence existed there as well.

But of course, in so many ways, the Academicians who put the *Vocabolario* together and who composed its Introduction were the heirs of the fifteenth century. Most of all, they inherited the notion that the five-generation humanist discussions over the Latin language had revealed: that languages had histories; they evolved; they were born; and, if not preserved, they could die. That biological metaphor (birth, growth, decline) had been part of discussions on language since Cicero. But the consciousness regarding doing something about it came to its high point when Cortesi (who was the representative of a consensus) made the case that part of preserving a language meant canonizing, and part of canonizing a language meant having models. For Latin it would be Cicero (something with which Bembo agreed, as we have seen). For Italian, Bembo had suggested Boccaccio as a model for prose, Petrarch for poetry.

The authors of the *Vocabolario*'s Introduction go a bit further. They state that to ensure that the language manifested in their enterprise was pure, of the authors they chose, "if not all, at least most, were either Florentine writers or writers who had adopted in their works the words and idioms of that state."[84] They signal repeatedly that they tried to be as thorough as possible. Then they begin to name names, in a lengthy but important sentence:

> In gathering together the writers' words, from some of the most famous, who are also understood by all as such, owing to their works having been published, writers who could be considered as in the front rank – Dante, Boccaccio, Petrarch, Giovanni Villani [a fourteenth-century historian of Florence], and others like them – we have without distinction taken all their words and, for the most part, used selections from their works as examples in the entry.[85]

A dictionary, one might say, is born: fourteenth-century Florentine authors will serve as the foundation, the entries in the dictionary will have citations from respected texts to show how the words were used in context, and the final product will be something worthy of this already great linguistic tradition.

The *Accademia della Crusca*, as mentioned, was one of the bodies on which the French Academy later modeled itself. These academies became exemplary of a new phenomenon: the attempt to codify and regulate language in an organized fashion; harnessing the technology of print; and linking the enterprise to the prestige, power, and cultural cohesiveness of a given region. The French

---

[84] *Vocabolario degli accademici della Crusca*, ★.3v.
[85] Ibid.

400 INTELLECTUAL WORLD OF THE ITALIAN RENAISSANCE

example signaled something important: that a large, diversely populated nation could come together, with a unified language as one of its instruments.

The *Crusca*, by contrast, signifies something more complicated. It is the oldest academy for language in the Western world: the exemplar. Yet, despite its continuous existence and notwithstanding the many luminaries who took part in the activities of the *Crusca* over many decades and centuries, it wound up in some respects substituting one variety of bilingualism for another. If in the fifteenth century Latin (and a classicizing Latin at that) was viewed as the literary language of durability, permanence, and seriousness, by the era of Bembo and beyond it was Tuscan that assumed that mantle. But that variety of Tuscan was still the property of the educated. Well into the early twentieth century, before radio and eventually television made it possible to hear spoken language in a relatively standard format, most Italians were proficient in their local dialect alone, and illiteracy rates remained high.[86] Bembo's assumption, we recall, was that, though Petrarch wrote in a "native" language, he nevertheless did not write "his poems in the language of the everyday people of his time." Bembo exemplifies in this respect a kind of elitism with which literature has always had to reconcile itself. Finally, with respect to Italy, it was not in the cards, at least in the Renaissance, to unify the peninsula around the language of only one city-state, Florence, given Italy's deeply embedded regionalism.

Nevertheless, Bembo's approach and the way it played itself out did codify the Italian language. If it didn't open the doors to everyone, it did at least widen the playing field significantly. The sixteenth century, to give one example, saw a noteworthy rise in women authors, who may indeed still have been excluded from the sorts of public culture toward which users of Latin could gravitate – politics, Church diplomacy, and (for the most part) university life – but who represented eager participants in the new and revived culture of Renaissance Italian literature.[87] The worlds opened up by Italian (mostly male, Latinate) humanists were diffused, adopted, and appropriated across various cultural communities, by diverse protagonists, in different fields.

---

[86] See Giulio Lepschy, *Mother Tongues and Other Reflections on the Italian Language* (Toronto: University of Toronto Press, 2002); Tullio De Mauro, *Storia linguistica dell'Italia unita* (Rome: Laterza, 2005), 118–26.

[87] See Virginia Cox, *Women's Writing in Italy, 1400–1650* (Baltimore: Johns Hopkins University Press, 2008); Cox, *The Prodigious Muse: Women's Writing in Counter-Reformation Italy* (Baltimore: Johns Hopkins University Press, 2011); Cox, *Lyric Poetry by Women of the Italian Renaissance* (Baltimore: Johns Hopkins University Press, 2013); Diana Robin, *Publishing Women: Salons, the Presses, and the Counter-Reformation in Sixteenth-Century Italy* (Chicago: University of Chicago Press, 2007).

EPILOGUE

Perhaps he believes philosophy is a book, a man's fantasy, like the *Iliad* and *Orlando furioso*, books of the sort that it is of lesser importance whether what is written in them is true. Mr. Sarsi, the matter at hand is not like this. Philosophy is written in this enormous book that is ever open before our eyes (I mean the universe). But it cannot be understood if, first, one does not learn to understand the language and to know the characters in which it is written. It is written in mathematical language, and the characters are triangles, circles, and other geometrical figures. Without means such as these it is impossible, in human terms, to understand a word; without these, one just wanders around a dark labyrinth in vain.[1]

When Galileo wrote these words, in 1623, he was responding to a Jesuit, Orazio Grassi (who had used the pseudonym Sarsi). Grassi had earlier published works in which he had employed some of Galileo's work without attribution and argued against Galileo's theories regarding comets. Galileo's bracing, funny, and lively *Saggiatore* ("The Assayer"), from which this quotation is drawn, pleased the pope when it was read to him, represented Galileo's own position with brio, and has become a classic in the literature of the scientific revolution.[2]

What draws a reader's attention today is twofold and immediately apparent: first, the framing of the universe as a "book" and, second, natural science as an effort to read the book and to uncover the truths that it contains. For us, what jumps out most of all is the fact that Galileo wrote the *Saggiatore* in Italian, and more specifically in Tuscan. One can suggest a host of reasons as to why: the need to communicate to targeted readers who were more

---

[1] Galileo Galilei, *Il saggiatore*, ed. Ottavio Besomi and Mario Helbing (Rome: Antenore, 2005), 6.34–36, p. 119.

[2] For the circumstances of its composition, textual history, and reception, see Ottavio Besomi and Mario Helbing, "Introduzione," in Galileo, *Il saggiatore*, 11–68.

comfortable reading and hearing the vernacular, the concurrent imperative to make sure his patronage connections remained firm, the ability to distinguish himself from those in the papal court accustomed to the use of Latin, and so on.

Whatever the reason, it is worthy of note that Galileo chose not to write in Latin. He had written learned texts in Latin before, of course: his *Starry Messenger* (*Sidereus nuncius*), announcing what he had seen through a telescope, appeared in Latin in 1610. Unsurprisingly, it was subject to quick and international diffusion, having been written in Latin, the international language of scholarship. But then, in 1613, when he wanted to have his opinions on sunspots reach a local but important audience, he wrote his *Istoria e dimostrazioni intorno alle macchie solari* (*History and Proofs Regarding Sunspots*) in Tuscan.

What all this means is that Galileo had Tuscan at his disposal, a language that by his day had become canonical, with the *Accademia della Crusca*'s *Dictionary* as the first formal expression of that status. Behind that moment – before, in other words, Tuscan became canonical – lies a story, with its beginnings in the fourteenth century and its real ending in 1525. The story has to do with Italian intellectuals and their reflections on the ancient Latin language: whether the language ancient Romans spoke was natural, learned in the home, and, in short, a "mother tongue," or whether the ancients had a separate vernacular and needed to learn Latin in schools (as did those Italian intellectuals who engaged in this generation-by-generation debate). Only when that debate regarding Latin had played itself out, when the history behind it had been excavated by Italian scholars and the major positions sketched, could thinkers then turn to "canonizing" the Florentine vernacular. However fragmentarily, this is one story that has run through this book.

Galileo's usage of the word "philosophy" is also worthy of attention. In the quotation he uses it to mean "natural philosophy," that branch of philosophy that dealt with how the physical universe worked and how one might offer explanations thereof that (ideally) corresponded to observable data. For Galileo, the need to have explanations that allowed for observable data was important. It has become so much a part of modern theories of what science does that it has tended at times to obscure the back story of "philosophy": as a set of disciplines, as a field in continuous evolution, and as a field of contestation. In this latter respect, it is worth foregrounding that philosophy's parameters were not, for the most part, bounded by what we today consider different schools of philosophy. Rather, in the period that this book brings into relief, the main polarity had to do with institutions (often universities) and views of authority. Did you see yourself as part of an institution?

Or as an outsider? Did you believe that your job as an intellectual was to build on authorities? Or to use them only as a springboard and then to surpass them, discarding them when needed?

A quotation from Galileo, immediately preceding the one with which this Epilogue began, offers a way in: "I seem to notice in Sarsi the firm belief that in philosophizing it is necessary to lean on the opinions of some famous author. It is as if our mind must remain entirely barren and fruitless when not married together with that of another."[3] This statement, too, has a lot of appeal today: Galileo as the bold thinker who, freeing himself from hidebound strictures inducing the veneration of authority, allows observation, experiment, and inductive reasoning to form the basis of his science and his worldview. This view has a lot to recommend it in the case of Galileo. Behind him, however, lies an even more complicated story than in the case of language. Galileo's anti-authority and anti-institutional attitude (he taught at the University of Padua for a time, a hotbed of Aristotelian thinking) was nurtured in an environment of patronage. Part of the way that patronage manifested itself was in what we might call anti-institutional institutions.

In Galileo's case, he was the beneficiary of membership in an academy, founded in 1603, called the *Accademia dei lincei*, the "Academy of the Lynx-eyed" (the lynx was thought to have sharp vision).[4] Like other Renaissance and early modern academies, its purpose was to foster the sort of work that was not happening in other institutions. In this case, the founder, Federico Cesi, was an ardent enthusiast of botanical research; but the *Lincei* embraced Galileo and his work, inducting him as a member in 1611 and serving as the sponsor of his *Saggiatore*. In leaving one set of institutions behind (he had taught at the University of Pisa in addition to Padua), Galileo joined another. First, there were courts: he tried without success to find patronage at Mantua but then succeeded in 1610 in Florence, becoming chief mathematician to the Medici. Then, retaining Florentine ties, he joined the Roman *Accademia dei Lincei*, set up to address problems in a new way, untethered to traditional institutional methods and decidedly social and personality based.

This tension – between existing institutions that have their own rhythms, repeated schedules, and dominant personalities versus the need to find new social spaces for creating and preserving knowledge – also had a deep background in the Italian long fifteenth century, as we have seen. At its core, it had to do not with disciplines as we define them today, but with the most

[3] Galileo, *Il saggiatore*, 6.34, p. 119.
[4] See David Freedberg, *The Eye of the Lynx: Galileo, His Friends, and the Beginnings of Modern Natural History* (Chicago: University of Chicago Press, 2002).

404 INTELLECTUAL WORLD OF THE ITALIAN RENAISSANCE

basic assumptions concerning philosophy in its most elemental meaning: the love of wisdom. Should that pursuit, seeking wisdom, take place inside existing institutions? Or was their inherent conservatism so restrictive (wittingly or not) that one needed distance? Was publication of one's thoughts in formal treatises the best or only means of searching for wisdom? Or – especially relevant in a pre- and early print world – was the social element just as important? In other words, did the people with whom you interacted, in conversation or in its written cousin, letter writing, constitute your primary audience? If one concern that ran through Italian Renaissance intellectual life had to do with language, the other (and they were linked) had to do with precisely these problems regarding philosophy.

It is no accident that Galileo's other great vernacular work, the *Dialogue on the Two Chief World Systems*, was in fact a dialogue, that it enfolded within it some of the same ambiguities about philosophy, and that it allowed Galileo to make the case for a perspective that was unpalatable to some. In this instance, it was the Copernican view of the universe rather than the Ptolemaic, with the sun, rather than the earth, as the body around which other celestial bodies revolved. Behind it, however, were works such as Bruni's *Dialogues*, which gently but clearly allowed the concerns of a new generation to emerge; Valla's many-faceted, always dialogical work, specimens of which, even if they were not all formally dialogues, invited debate, proposed unpopular opinions, and solicited by their very presence response and continued conversation; or, finally, Poliziano's brilliant *Lamia*, which stood in opposition to the very same types of institutional politics against which Galileo himself marshaled resources (excessive adherence to authority, to seemingly unchanging curricula, to professors unwilling to think the world anew). Galileo, as he looked out into the vast, physical world, was heir to the mental habits of the Italian thinkers who had gone before him. They had, from Petrarch to Poliziano and beyond, scrutinized, dissected, and interpreted material that was in books and on the page. Those habits persisted, changed, and transmuted in an almost infinite variety of expressions, of which Galileo's work was one. How many more early-modern figures might we understand just a little better, with a bit more depth, if the Italian long fifteenth century and its sometimes hidden contributions to intellectual life were understood in their fullness?

BIBLIOGRAPHY

MANUSCRIPTS

MS Florence, Biblioteca Laurenziana, Plut. 85.9
MS Florence, Biblioteca Nazionale Centrale, Magl. 1.6.30
MS Florence, Biblioteca Riccardiana, Ricc. 991
MS Vatican City, Biblioteca Apostolica Vaticana, Reg. Lat. 1370
MS Vatican City, Biblioteca Apostolica Vaticana, Vat. Lat. 3196
MS Vatican City, Biblioteca Apostolica Vaticana, Vat. Lat. 4530
MS Vatican City, Biblioteca Apostolica Vaticana, Vat. Lat. 5953
MS London, British Library, Add. 34060

SOURCES CITED

Accademia della Crusca, ed., *La Crusca nella tradizione letteraria e linguistica italiana: Atti del Congresso internazionale per il IV centenario dell'Accademia della Crusca* (Florence: Accademia della Crusca, 1985)

    ed., *Vocabolario degli accademici della Crusca*, 2nd impression (Venice: Iacopo Sarzino, 1623)

    ed., *Vocabolario degli accademici della Crusca* (Venice: G. Alberti, 1612)

Aertsen, Jan, *Medieval Philosophy as Transcendental Thought: From Phillip the Chancellor (ca. 1225) to Francisco Suárez* (Leiden: Brill, 2012)

    Kent Emery Jr., and Andreas Speer, eds., *Nach der Verurteilung von 1277. Philosophie und Theologie an der Universität von Paris im letzten Viertel des 13. Jahrhunderts* (Berlin: de Gruyter, 2001)

Al-Alawi, Jamal, "The Philosophy of Ibn Rushd: The Evolution of the Problem of the Intellect in the works of Ibn Rushd," in S.K. Jayyusi, ed., *The Legacy of Muslim Spain*, 2 vols. (Leiden: Brill, 1994), 2: 804–29

Alberti, Leon Battista, *De pictura* (redazione volgare), ed. Lucia Bertolini (Florence: Polistampa, 2011)

    On Painting: A New Translation and Critical Edition, tr. Rocco Sinisgalli (Cambridge: Cambridge University Press, 2011)

    Grammatichetta e altri scritti sul volgare, ed. Giuseppe Patota (Rome: Salerno Editrice, 1996)

I libri della famiglia, eds. Ruggiero Romano and Alberto Tenenti, new ed. Francesco Furlan (Turin: Einaudi, 1994)

La prima grammatica della lingua volgare: La grammatichetta vaticana, Collezione di opere inedited o rare, v. 125, ed. Cecil Grayson (Bologna: Commissione per i testi di lingua, 1964)

Alighieri, Dante, *Autobiografia e altre opere latine*, eds. Loredana Chines and Andrea Severi (Milan: Rizzoli, 2012)

Monarchia, with Cola di Rienzo, *Commentario*, Marsilio Ficino, *Volgarizzamento*, with introduction by Francesco Furlan (Milan: Mondadori, 2004)

De vulgari eloquenti, ed. and tr. Steven Botterill (Cambridge: Cambridge University Press, 1996)

Convivio, ed. Franca Brambilla Agena, 2 vols. (Florence: Le Lettere, 1995)

Monarchia, ed. and tr. Prue Shaw (Cambridge: Cambridge University Press, 1995)

Inferno, tr. Mark Musa (New York: Penguin, 1984)

Opere minori, eds. Domenico de Robertis, Gianfranco Contini, and Pier Vincenzo Mengaldo, 2 vols. (Milan: Ricciardi, 1979)

The Divine Comedy, Italian text and translation, with a commentary by Charles S. Singleton, 3 vols. (Princeton: Princeton University Press, 1970–75)

Tutte le opere, ed. Luigi Blasucci (Florence: Sansoni, 1965)

Allen, Michael J.B., *Synoptic Art: Marsilio Ficino on the History of Platonic Interpretation* (Florence: Olschki, 1998)

The Platonism of Marsilio Ficino: A Study of His Phaedrus Commentary, Its Sources and Genesis (Berkeley: University of California Press, 1984)

Marsilio Ficino and the Phaedran Charioteer: Introduction, Texts, Translations (Berkeley: University of California Press, 1981)

and V.R. Rees, eds., *Marsilio Ficino: His Theology, His Philosophy, His Legacy* (Leiden, Boston, Cologne: Brill, 2002)

Ames-Lewis, Frances, *Cosimo 'il Vecchio' de' Medici, 1389–1464* (Oxford: Oxford University Press, 1992)

Aquinas, Thomas, *The Summa Theologica of St. Thomas Aquinas*, 2nd ed., 22 vols. (London: Burns, Oates, and Washbourne, 1913–42)

Aristotle, *Ethica Eudemia*, ed. R.R. Walzer (Oxford: Clarendon, 1991)

A New Aristotle Reader, ed. and tr. J.L. Ackrill (Princeton: Princeton University Press, 1989)

Complete Works of Aristotle: The Revised Oxford Translation, ed. Jonathan Barnes, 2 vols. (Princeton: Princeton University Press, 1984)

Categoriarum supplementa, Aristoteles latinus, 1.6–7, ed. Lorenzo Minio-Paluello and Bernard G. Dod (Bruges: Desclée de Brouwer, 1966)

Categoriae vel praedicamenta, Aristoteles latinus, 1.1–5, ed. Lorenzo Minio-Paluello (Bruges: Desclée de Brouwer, 1961)

De anima, ed. David Ross (Oxford: Clarendon, 1961)

Nicomachean Ethics, tr. Horace Rackham (Cambridge, MA: Harvard University Press, 1934)

Metaphysics, 2 vols., ed. and tr. Hugh Tredennick (Cambridge, MA: Harvard University Press, 1933)

Metaphysics, ed. W.D. Ross (Oxford: Clarendon, 1924)

Ethica Nicomachea, ed. I. Bywater (Oxford: Clarendon, 1920)

Ascoli, Albert Russell and Unn Falkeid, eds. *The Cambridge Companion to Petrarch* (Cambridge: Cambridge University Press, 2015)

Assman, Jan, *Of God and Gods: Egypt, Israel, and the Rise of Monotheism* (Madison: University of Wisconsin Press, 2008)

"Translating Gods: Religion as a Factor of Cultural (Un)Translatability," in Sanford Budick and Wolfgang Iser, eds., *The Translatability of Cultures: Figurations of the Space Between* (Stanford, CA: Stanford University Press, 1996), 25–37

Athanassiadi, Polymnia, *Mutations of Hellenism in Late Antiquity* (Farnham, Surrey: Ashgate, 2015)

and Michael Frede, eds., *Pagan Monotheism in Late Antiquity* (Oxford: Oxford University Press, 1999)

Augustine (St., of Hippo), *Traité anti-Donatistes*, 5 vols. (Bruges: DeBrouwer, 1963–65)

De libero arbitrio libri tres, ed. William M. Green, *Corpus scriptorum ecclesiasticorum latinorum*, vol. 74, sect. 6, part 3 (Vienna: Hoelder-Pichler-Tempsky, 1956)

De civitate Dei, ed. Bernhard Dombert (Leipzig: Teubner, 1909)

Baker, Nicholas S. and Brian Maxson, eds., *After Civic Humanism: Learning and Politics in Renaissance Italy, 1300–1600* (Toronto: Center for Reformation and Renaissance Studies, 2015)

Baker, Patrick, *Italian Renaissance Humanism in the Mirror* (Cambridge: Cambridge University Press, 2015)

Ballistreri, Gianni, "Cortesi, Antonio," *Dizionario biografico degli italiani*, 29 (1983), 754–56

Barchiesi, Alessandro, "Roman Perspectives on the Greeks," in George Boys-Stones, Barbara Graziosi, and Phiroze Vasunia, eds., *The Oxford Handbook of Hellenic Studies* (Oxford: Oxford University Press, 2009), 98–113

Barnes, Jonathan, "Roman Aristotle," in Jonathan Barnes and Miriam Griffin, eds., *Philosophia Togata II* (Oxford: Clarendon, 1999), 1–69

Baron, Hans, *In Search of Florentine Civic Humanism: Essays on the Transition from Medieval to Modern Thought*, 2 vols. (Princeton: Princeton University Press, 1988)

Basil (St., of Caesarea), *The Letters*, 4 vols., ed. and tr. Roy J. Deferrari (Cambridge, MA: Harvard University Press, 1926–34)

Baudoux, Bernardus, "Philosophia 'Ancilla Theologiae,'" *Antonianum* 12 (1937), 292–326

Baumgartner, Frederic J., *Henry II, King of France, 1547–1559* (Durham, NC: Duke University Press, 1998)

Bausi, Francesco, "La *mutatio vitae* di Poggio Bracciolini. Ricerche sul *De avaritia*," *Interpres* 28 (2009), 7–69

Nec rhetor neque philosophus: Fonti, lingua e stile nelle prime opere latine di Giovanni Pico della Mirandola (1484–87) (Florence: Olschki, 1996)

"Introduzione," in Poliziano, *Due poemetti latini*, XI–LVI

Beierwaltes, Werner, *Das wahre Selbst: Studien zu Plotins Begriff des Geistes und des Einen* (Frankfurt am Main: Klostermann, 2001)

Platonismus im Christentum (Frankfurt am Main: Klostermann, 1998)

Bembo, Pietro, *Prose e rime*, ed. Carlo Dionisotti (Turin: UTET, 1966)

Lettere, 4 vols., ed. Ernesto Travi (Bologna: Commissione per i testi di lingua, 1987)

Bennett, Owen, *The Nature of Demonstrative Proof According to the Principles of Aristotle and St. Thomas Aquinas* (Washington, DC: Catholic University of American Press, 1943)

Bertolini, Lucia, ed., *De vera amicitia: I testi del primo Certame coronario* (Modena: Franco Cosimo Panini, 1993)

Bertoni, Giulio, *La Biblioteca Estense e la cultura ferrarese ai tempi del duca Ercole I (1471–1505)* (Turin: Loescher, 1903)

Besomi, Ottavio and Mario Helbing, "Introduzione," in Galileo, *Il saggiatore*, 11–68

Bianchi, Luca, *Censure et liberté intellectuelle à l'université de Paris (XIIIe–XIVe siècles)* (Paris: Les Belles Lettres, 1999)

Biondi, Alberto, "La doppia inchiesta sulle Conclusiones e le traversie romane di Pico nel 1487," in Garfagnini, ed., *Giovanni Pico della Mirandola: Convegno*, 197–212

Birkenmajer, Alexander, *Vermischte Untersuchungen zur Geschichte der mittelalterlichen Philosophie* (Münster: Verlag der Aschendorffschen Verlagsbuchhandlung, 1922)

Bischoff, Bernhard, *Latin Palaeography: Antiquity and the Middle Ages*, tr. Dáibhí ó Cróinin and David Ganz (Cambridge: Cambridge University Press, 1990)

Bisticci, Vespasiano da', *Le vite*, 2 vols., ed. Aulo Greco (Florence: Istituto Nazionale di Studi sul Rinascimento, 1970–76)

Black, Robert, *Humanism and Education in Medieval and Renaissance Italy: Tradition and Innovation in Latin Schools from the Twelfth to the Fifteenth Century* (Cambridge: Cambridge University Press, 2001)

  Benedetto Accolti and the Florentine Renaissance (Cambridge: Cambridge University Press, 1985)

Blum, Paul Richard, *Philosophieren in der Renaissance* (Stuttgart: Kohlhammer, 2004)

  "Einleitung," in Ficino, *Über die Liebe oder Platons Gastmahl*, XI–XLVII

  "Pico, Theology, and the Church," in Dougherty, ed., *Pico della Mirandola: New Essays*, 37–60

Blum, Wilhelm, *Georgios Gemistos Plethon: Politik, Philosophie und Rhetorik in spätbyzantinischen Reich (1355–1452)* (Stuttgart: Hiersemann, 1988)

Blumenthal, Henry J. and E. Gillian Clark, eds., *The Divine Iamblichus: Philosopher and Man of the Gods* (Bristol: Bristol Classical Press, 1993)

Boccaccio, Giovanni, *Decameron*, tr. Wayne Rebhorn (New York: Norton, 2013)

  Boccaccio's Expositions on Dante's Comedy, tr. with introductions and notes by Michael Papio (Toronto: University of Toronto Press, 2009)

  Esposizioni sopra la Comedia di Dante, ed. Giorgio Padoan (Milan: Mondadori, 1965)

  Il comento alla Divina Commedia, ed. D. Guerri and Scrittori d'Italia, vols. 84–86 (Bari, 1918)

  Genealogia deorum gentilium (Basel, 1532)

Boethius of Dacia, *De aeternitate mundi, De summon bono, De somniis*, in Corpus Philosophorum Danicorum Medii Aevi, 6 (Copenhagen: Bagge, 1976)

Böhmer, Johann Friedrich, *Regesta Imperii, XI: Die Urkunden Kaiser Sigmunds*, 1410–1437, 2 vols. (Innsbruck: Verlag der Wagner'schen Universitäts-Buchhandlung, 1896–1900; repr. Hildesheim: Georg Olms, 1968)

Bonatti, Franco and Antonio Manfredi, eds., *Niccolò V nel sesto centenario della nascita*, Studi e Testi, 397 (Vatican City: Biblioteca apostolica vaticana, 2000)

Bonner, Stanley, *Education in Ancient Rome: From the Elder Cato to the Younger Pliny* (London: Routledge, 2012)

Borghesi, Francesco, "Chronology," in Pico della Mirandola, *Oration on the Dignity of Man*, 37–51

  "Interpretations," in Pico della Mirandola, *Oration on the Dignity of Man*, 52–65

  "A Life in Works," in Dougherty, ed., *Pico della Mirandola: New Essays*, 202–19

Bori, Pier Cesare, "The Historical and Biographical Background of the Oration," in Pico della Mirandola, *Oration on the Dignity of Man*, 10–36

Botley, Paul, *Learning Greek in Western Europe, 1396–1529: Grammars, Lexica, and Classroom Texts* (Philadelphia: American Philosophical Society, 2010)

Boulard, Gilles, "L' Ordonnance de Villers-Cotterêts: le temps de la claret et la stratégie du temps (1539–1992)," *Revue Historique* 301 (1999), 45–100

Boyle, Leonard, "Sixtus IV and the Vatican Library," in Clifford M. Brown, John Osborne, and W. Chandler Kirwin, eds., *Rome: Tradition, Innovation, and Renewal* (Victoria, BC: University of Victoria, 1991), 65–73

"The Vatican Library," in Grafton, ed., *Rome Reborn*, xi–xx

"Niccolò V fondatore della Biblioteca Vaticana," in Bonatti and Manfredi, eds., *Niccolò V nel sesto centenario*, 3–8

Bracciolini, Poggio, *La vera nobilitate*, ed. Davide Canfora (Roma: Salerno, 1999)

Dialogus contra avaritiam (De avaritia) (Livorno: Belforte, 1994)

Lettere, 3 vols., ed. Helene Harth (Florence: Olschki, 1984–87)

Opera Omnia, 4 vols., ed. Riccardo Fubini (Turin: Bottega d'Erasmo, 1964–69)

Brandmüller, Walter, *Das Konzil von Konstanz, 1414–1418*, 2 vols. (Paderborn: Schöningh, 1991–97)

Brecht, Martin, *Martin Luther*, 3 vols. (Stuttgart: Calwer, 1981–87)

Brongrani, Paolo, "Nuovi contribute per la grammatica di L.B. Alberti," *Studi di filologia italiana* 40 (1982), 65–106

Brown, Alison, *The Return of Lucretius to Renaissance Florence* (Cambridge, MA: Harvard University Press, 2010)

Brown, Peter, *The Ransom of the Soul: Afterlife and Wealth in Early Western Christianity* (Cambridge, MA: Harvard University Press, 2015)

The Cult of the Saints: Its Rise and Function in Latin Christianity, 2nd ed. (Chicago: University of Chicago Press, 2015)

Brown, Peter M., *Lionardo Salviati: A Critical Biography* (Oxford: Oxford University Press, 1974)

Brucker, Gene, *Giovanni and Lusanna: Love and Marriage in Renaissance Florence* (Berkeley: University of California Press, 1986)

Renaissance Florence (Berkeley: University of California Press, 1969)

Bruni, Leonardo, *Epistolarum libri VIII*, ed. Lorenzo Mehus, 2 vols. (Florence, 1741; repr. with intro. by James Hankins, Rome: Edizioni di Storia e letteratura, 2007)

Sulla perfetta traduzione, ed. Paolo Viti (Naples: Liguori, 2004)

History of the Florentine People, 3 vols., ed. and tr. James Hankins (Cambridge, MA: Harvard University Press, 2001–07)

Opere letterarie e politiche, ed. Paolo Viti (Turin: UTET, 1996)

The Humanism of Leonardo Bruni: Selected Texts, ed. and tr. Gordon Griffiths, James Hankins, and David Thompson (Binghamton, NY: MRTS, 1987)

Humanistisch-philosophische Schriften mit einer Chronologie seiner Werke und Briefe, ed. Hans Baron, Quellen zur Geistesgeschichte des Mittelalters und der Renaissance, 1 (Leipzig: Teubner, 1928; reprint, Wiesbaden: Sändig, 1969)

Commentarius rerum suo tempore gestarum, ed. Carmine Di Pierro, *Rerum italicarum scriptores*, 19.3 (Bologna, 1926)

Burkert, Walter, *Lore and Science in Ancient Pythagoreanism*, tr. Edwin L. Minar (Cambridge, MA: Harvard University Press, 1972)

Busi, Giulio, "Who does not Wonder at this Chameleon? The Kabbalistic Library of
    Giovanni Pico della Mirandola," in Busi, ed., *Hebrew to Latin, Latin to Hebrew*, 167–96
    "Toward a New Evaluation of Pico's Kabbalistic Sources," *Rinascimento* 48 (2009),
    165–83
    ed., *Hebrew to Latin, Latin to Hebrew: The Mirroring of Two Cultures in the Age of Humanism*
    (Turin: Aragno, 2006)
Bynum, Caroline Walker, *The Resurrection of the Body in Western Christianity, 200–1336*
    (New York: Columbia University Press, 1995)
Cameron, Euan, *The European Reformation*, 2nd ed. (Oxford: Oxford University Press,
    2012)
Campanelli, Maurizio, "L'Oratio e il 'genere' delle orazioni inaugurali dell'anno accade-
    mico," in Valla, *Orazione*, pp. 25–61
    "Languages," in Wyatt, ed., *The Cambridge Companion to the Italian Renaissance*, 139–63.
Camporeale, Salvatore I., *Lorenzo Valla: Umanesimo, riforma, e controriforma; studi e testi*
    (Roma: Edizioni di Storia e Letteratura, 2002)
    Christianity, Latinity, and Culture: Two Studies on Lorenzo Valla, tr. Patrick Baker, ed.
    Patrick Baker and Christopher S. Celenza (Leiden: Brill, 2014)
Cannata Salamone, Nadia, "Il dibattito sulla lingua e la cultura letteraria e artistica del
    primo Rinascimento romano. Uno studio del ms Reg. lat. 1370," *Critica del testo* 8
    (2005), 901–51
Capponi, Gino, *Storia della reppublica di Firenze*, 2 vols. (Florence: Barbéra, 1876)
Cardini, Roberto, *La critica del Landino* (Florence: Sansoni, 1973)
Carrai, Stefano, *Le muse dei Pulci: Studi su Luca e Luigi Pulci* (Naples: Guida, 1985)
Caruso, Francesco, *Philology as Thanatology: A Study on Angelo Poliziano's Intellectual
    Biography*, unpublished PhD dissertation, Johns Hopkins University, 2013
Casamassima, Emanuele, "L'autografo della seconda lettera del Petrarca a Urbino V
    (*Senile* IX 1)," *Quaderni petrarcheschi* 3 (1985–86), 103–34
Castiglionchio, Lapo da, the Younger, *De curiae commodis*, Celenza, *Renaissance Humanism
    and the Papal Curia: Lapo da Castiglionchio the Younger's De curiae commodis*, 103–228
Castiglione, Baldassarre, *Il libro del cortegiano*, ed. Ettore Bonora (Milan: Mursia, 1972)
Catana, Leo, *The Historiographical Concept "System of Philosophy": Its Origin, Nature,
    Influence and Legitimacy* (Leiden: Brill, 2008)
    "The Concept 'System of Philosophy': The Case of Jacob Brucker's Historiography of
    Philosophy," *History and Theory* 44 (2005), 72–90
Cavallo, Guglielmo, ed., *Le biblioteche nel mondo antico e medievale* (Rome: Laterza, 1988)
Celenza, Christopher S., *Petrarch: Everywhere a Wanderer* (London: Reaktion, 2017)
    "What Did It Mean to Live in the Long Fifteenth Century?" in Rivka Feldhay and F.
    Jamil Ragep, *Before Copernicus: The Cultures and Contexts of Scientific Learning in the
    Fifteenth Century* (Montreal: McGill-Queen's University Press, 2017)
    Machiavelli: A Portrait (Cambridge, MA: Harvard University Press, 2015)
    "Coluccio Salutati's View of the History of the Latin Language," in N. van Deusen,
    ed., *Cicero Refused to Die: Ciceronian Influence Through the Centuries* (Leiden: Brill,
    2013), 5–20
    "What Counted as Philosophy in the Italian Renaissance? The History of Philosophy,
    the History of Science, and Styles of Life," *Critical Inquiry* 39 (2013), 367–401
    "Lorenzo Valla's Radical Philology: The "Preface" to the *Annotations to the New
    Testament* in Context," *Journal of Medieval and Early Modern Studies* 42 (2012), 365–94

ed., *Angelo Poliziano's* Lamia *in Context: Text, Translation, and Introductory Studies* (Leiden: Brill, 2010)

The Lost Italian Renaissance (Baltimore: Johns Hopkins University Press, 2004)

Piety and Pythagoras in Renaissance Florence: The Symbolum Nesianum (Leiden: Brill, 2001)

"Pythagoras in the Renaissance: The Case of Marsilio Ficino," *Renaissance Quarterly* 52 (1999), 667–711

Renaissance Humanism and the Papal Curia: Lapo da Castiglionchio the Younger's De curiae commodis (Ann Arbor: University of Michigan Press, 1999)

"Parallel lives': Plutarch's *Lives*, Lapo da Castiglionchio the Younger (1405–1438) and the Art of Italian Renaissance Translation," *Illinois Classical Studies* 22 (1997), 121–155

"The Will of Cardinal Giordano Orsini (ob. 1438)," *Traditio* 51 (1996), 257–286

"Marsilio Ficino," in the *Stanford Encyclopedia of Philosophy*: http://plato.stanford.edu/entries/ficino/

"The Platonic Revival," in Hankins, ed., *The Cambridge Companion to Renaissance Philosophy*, 72–96

"Late Antiquity and Florentine Platonism: The 'Post-Plotinian' Ficino," in Allen and Rees, eds., *Marsilio Ficino: His Theology, His Philosophy, His Legacy*, 71–97

"Hellenism in the Renaissance," in Boys-Stones, Graziosi, and Vasunia, eds., *The Oxford Handbook of Hellenic Studies*, 150–65

and Kenneth Gouwens, eds, *Humanism and Creativity: Essays in Honor of Ronald G. Witt* (Leiden: Brill, 2006)

and Bridget Pupillo, "Le grandi biblioteche 'pubbliche' del XV secolo," in S. Luzzatto and G. Pedullà, eds., *Atlante storico della letteratura italiana*, vol. 1, *Dalle origini al Rinascimento*, ed. A. De Vincentiis (Turin: Einaudi, 2010), 313–21

and Bridget Pupillo, "La rinascita del dialogo," in S. Luzzatto and G. Pedullà, eds., *Atlante storico della letteratura italiana*, vol. 1, *Dalle origini al Rinascimento*, ed. A. De Vincentiis (Turin: Einaudi, 2010), 341–47

Ceresa, Massimo, "Lascaris, Giano," *Dizionario biografico degli italiani*, 63 (2004), 785–91

Cesarini Martinelli, Lucia, "Poliziano professore allo studio fiorentino," *La Toscana al tempo di Lorenzo il Magnifico*, multi-authored, 3 vols. (Pisa: Pacini, 1996), 2: 463–81

"Note sulla polemica Poggio-Valla e sulla fortuna delle *Elegantiae*," *Interpres* 3 (1980): 29–79

Chambers, David S. and Francois Quiviger, eds., *Italian Academies of the Sixteenth Century* (London: Warburg Institute, 1995)

Chroust, Anton Hermann and Robert J. Affeldt, "The Problem of Private Property According to St. Thomas Aquinas," *Marquette Law Review* 34 (1950–51), 151–82

Ciccolella, Federica, *Donati Graeci: Learning Greek in the Renaissance* (Leiden: Brill, 2009)

Cicero, *Letters to Atticus*, 4 vols., ed. and tr. D.R. Shackleton Bailey (Cambridge, MA: Harvard University Press, 2014)

Letters to Quintus and Brutus, ed. and tr. D.R. Shakleton Bailey (Cambridge, MA: Harvard University Press, 2002)

Cicero's Letters to Atticus, with translation and commentary by D.R. Shackleton Bailey, 7 vols. (Cambridge: Cambridge University Press, 1965–70)

Brutus, Orator, ed. and tr. G.L. Hendrickson and H.M. Hubbell (Cambridge, MA: Harvard University Press, 1962)

De natura deorum. Academica, ed. and tr. Horace Rackham (Cambridge, MA: Harvard University Press, 1951)

De oratore, ed. and tr. E.W. Sutton and H. Rackham (Cambridge, MA: Harvard University Press, 1948)

Tusculan Disputations, ed. and tr. J.E. King (Cambridge, MA: Harvard University Press, 1945)

Pro lege manilia. Pro Caecina. Pro Rabirio Perduellionis ed. and tr. H. Grose Hodge (Cambridge, MA: Harvard University Press, 1927)

De senectute, De amicitia, De divinatione, tr. William A. Falconer (Cambridge, MA: Harvard University Press, 1923)

Clanchy, Michael, *From Memory to Written Record*, 3rd ed. (Oxford: Wiley-Blackwell, 2013)

Abelard: A Medieval Life (Oxford: Blackwell, 1999)

Clough, Cecil, "Pietro Bembo's Edition of Petrarch and His Association with the Aldine Press," in Zeidberg, ed., Aldus Manutius and Renaissance Culture, 47–81

Colish, Marsha, *Medieval Foundations of the Western Intellectual Tradition* (New Haven: Yale University Press, 1997)

Peter Lombard, 2 vols. (Leiden: Brill, 1994)

Coleman, James and Andrea Moudarres, eds., *Luigi Pulci in Renaissance Florence and Beyond: New Perspectives on His Poetry and Influence* (Turnhout: Brepols, 2017)

Collins, Ardis, *The Secular Is Sacred: Platonism and Thomism in Ficino's Platonic Theology* (The Hague: Nijhoff, 1974)

Connell, Wiliam, "The Republican Idea," in Hankins, ed., *Renaissance Civic Humanism*, 14–29

Conte, Gian Biagio, *Latin Literature: A History*, tr. Joseph B. Sodolow, rev. by Don Fowler and Glenn Most (Baltimore: Johns Hopkins University Press, 1999)

Copenhaver, Brian P., "Toward a New Evaluation of Pico's Kabbalistic Sources," *Rinascimento* 48 (2009), 165–83

"Maimonides, Abulafia and Pico: A Secret Aristotle for the Renaissance," *Rinascimento* 47 (2007), 23–51

"The Secret of Pico's Oration: Cabala and Renaissance Philosophy," *Midwest Studies in Philosophy* 26 (2002), 56–81

ed. and tr., *Hermetica: The Greek Corpus Hermeticum and the Latin Asclepius in a New English Translation* (Cambridge: Cambridge University Press, 1992)

Cortesi, Mariarosa, "Umanesimo greco," in Guglielmo Cavallo, ed., *Lo spazio letterario del medioevo*, vol. 3 (Rome, 1995), 457–507

Cortesi, Paolo, *In quattuor libris sententiarum* (Basel, 1540)

Cotrugli, Benedetto, *Della mercatura* (Brescia, 1602)

Cox, Virginia, *Lyric Poetry by Women of the Italian Renaissance* (Baltimore: Johns Hopkins University Press, 2013)

The Prodigious Muse: Women's Writing in Counter-Reformation Italy (Baltimore: Johns Hopkins University Press, 2011)

Women's Writing in Italy, 1400–1650 (Baltimore: Johns Hopkins University Press, 2008)

The Renaissance Dialogue: Literary Dialogue in Its Social and Political Contexts, Castiglione to Galileo (Cambridge: Cambridge University Press, 1992)

Craven, William G., *Giovanni Pico della Mirandola, Symbol of His Age* (Geneva: Droz, 1981)

Croce, Benedetto, "Il secolo senza poesia," *La critica* 30 (1932), 161–84

Crowe, Michael J., *Theories of the World from Antiquity to the Copernican Revolution* (New York: Dover, 1990)

Dales, Richard C., "The Origin of the Doctrine of Double Truth," *Viator* 15 (1984), 169–79

Damascius, *Traité des premiers principes*, ed. and tr. Leendert G. Westerink and Joseph Combés, 3 vols. (Paris: Belles Lettres, 1986)
 De principiis, ed. C.A. Ruelle (Paris, 1889)

D'Amico, John, "The Progress of Renaissance Latin Prose: The Case of Apuleianism," *Renaissance Quarterly*, 37 (1984) 351–92
 Renaissance Humanism in Papal Rome: Humanists and Churchmen on the Eve of the Reformation (Baltimore: Johns Hopkins University Press, 1983)

Dan, Joseph, ed., *The Christian Kabbalah: Jewish Mystical Books and Their Christian Interpreters* (Cambridge, MA: Houghton Library of the Harvard College Library, 1998)

Dannenbauer, Heinz, *Luther als religiöser Volksschriftsteller, 1517–1520* (Tübingen: Mohr, 1930)

Dati, Agostino, *Elegantiolae* (Venice: Johannes Baptista de Sessa, 1491)

Davidson, Herbert, *Alfarabi, Avicenna, and Ibn Rushd, on Intellect: Their Cosmologies, Theories of the Active Intellect and Theories of Human Intellect* (Oxford and New York: Oxford University Press, 1992)

Davies, Jonathan, *Florence and Its University During the Early Renaissance* (Leiden: Brill, 1998)

Davies, Martin, *Aldus Manutius: Printer and Publisher of Renaissance Venice* (Tempe: MRTS, 1999)
 "An Emperor without Clothes? Niccolò Niccoli under Attack," *Italia medioevale e umanistica* 30 (1987), 95–148

Decembrio, Angelo, *De politia litteraria*, ed. Norbert Witten (Munich: Saur, 2002)

de la Mare, Albinia C., *The Handwriting of Italian Humanists* (Oxford: Oxford University Press, 1973)

D'Elia, Anthony, *A Sudden Terror: The Plot to Murder the Pope in Renaissance Rome* (Cambridge, MA: Harvard University Press, 2009)

DellaNeva, JoAnn, ed., *Ciceronian Controversies*, tr. Brian Duvick (Cambridge, MA: Harvard University Press, 2007)

De Pace, Anna, *La scepsi, il sapere, e l'anima: Dissonanze nella cerchia laurenziana* (Milan: LED, 2002)

Del Piazzo, Marcello, "Nuovi documenti sull'incidente Aretino del Pico della Mirandola," *Rassegna degli Archivi di Stato* 23 (1963), 271–90

Dempsey, Charles, *The Portrayal of Love: Botticelli's Primavera and Humanist Culture at the Time of Lorenzo the Magnificent* (Princeton: Princeton University Press, 1992)

Derolez, Albert, *The Palaeography of Gothic Manuscript Books: From the Twelfth to the Early Sixteenth Century* (Cambridge: Cambridge University Press, 2003)

DeRoover, Raymond, *The Rise and Decline of the Medici Bank, 1397–1494* (Cambridge, MA: Harvard University Press, 1963)

Dillon, John, "Iamblichus' Defence of Theurgy: Some Reflections," *The International Journal of the Platonic Tradition* 1 (2007), 30–41
 "Iamblichus of Chalcis (circa 240-325AD)," *Aufstieg und Niedergang der römischen Welt*," 36.2 (1988), 862–909

Dionisotti, Carlo, *Scritti sul Bembo*, ed. Claudio Vela (Turin: Einaudi, 2002)
 Aldo Manuzio: umanista e editore (Milan: Polifilo, 1995)

Dorez, Léon and Louis Thuasne, *Pic de la Mirandole en France (1485–1488)* (Paris: Leroux, 1897)

Doucet, Victorin, *Supplément au Répertoire de M. Frédéric Stegmüller* (Florence: Collegium S. Bonaventurae ad Claras Aquas, 1954)

Dougherty, M.V., "Introduction," in Dougherty, ed., *Pico della Mirandola: New Essays*, 1–12

ed., *Pico della Mirandola: New Essays* (Cambridge: Cambridge University Press, 2008)

Duff, J. Wight, *A Literary History of Rome in the Silver Age* (London: Unwin, 1927)

Duffy, Eamon, *Saints and Sinners: A History of the Popes* (New Haven, CT: Yale University Press, 1997)

Edelheit, Amos, *Ficino, Pico, and Savonarola: The Evolution of Humanist Theology 1461/2–1498* (Leiden and Boston: Brill, 2008)

Edwards, Mark, *Printing, Propaganda, and Martin Luther* (Berkeley: University of California Press, 1994)

Edwards, Mark J., "Two Images of Pythagoras: Iamblichus and Porphyry," in Blumenthal and Clark, *The Divine Iamblichus*, 159–72

Eire, Carlos M.N., *Reformations: The Early Modern World, 1450–1650* (New Haven: Yale University Press, 2016)

Eisenstein, Elizabeth, "An Unacknowledged Revolution Revisited," *American Historical Review*, 107 (2002), 87–105

The Printing Press as an Agent of Change (Cambridge: Cambridge University Press, 1980)

Eisner, Martin, "In the Labyrinth of the Library: Petrarch's Cicero, Dante's Virgil, and the Historiography of the Renaissance," *Renaissance Quarterly* 67 (2014), 755–90

Boccaccio and the Invention of Italian Literature: Petrarch, Cavalcanti, and the Authority of the Vernacular (Cambridge: Cambridge University Press, 2013)

Erasmus, *On Free Will*, in *Controversies: De libero arbitrio / Hyperaspites* 1, ed. and tr. Charles Trinkaus, *Collected Works of Erasmus*, 76 (Toronto: University of Toronto Press 1997)

Ciceronianus, tr. Betty I. Knott, in *Collected Works of Erasmus* (Toronto: University of Toronto Press, 1974), v. 27, pp. 337–448

Opus epistolarum Des. Erasmi Roterodami, ed. P.S. Allen (Oxford: Clarendon Press, 1906–58)

Novum instrumentum omne, diligenter ab Erasmo Roterodamo recognitum et emendatum (Basel: Froben, 1516)

Faithfull, R. Glynn, "The Concept of 'Living Language' in Cinquecento Vernacular Philology," *Modern Language Review* 48 (1953), 278–92

Falco, Benedetto di, *Rimario* (Naples, 1535)

Farmer, Stephen A., *Syncretism in the West: Pico's 900 Theses (1486): The Evolution of Traditional Religious and Philosophical Systems* (Tempe: MRTS, 1998)

Farris, Giovanni, *Eloquenza e teologia nel "Proemium in librum primum sententiarum" di Paolo Cortese*, Quaderni di civiltà letteraria (Savona: Sabatelli, 1972)

Fava, Domenico, *La Biblioteca Estense nel suo sviluppo storico* (Modena: G.T. Vincenzi e Nipoti di D. Cavalotti,1925)

Febvre, Lucien and Henri-Jean Martin, *The Coming of the Book: The Impact of Printing, 1450–1800*, 3rd ed. (New York: Verso, 2010)

Fera, Vincenzo and Mario Martelli, eds., *Agnolo Poliziano: Poeta, scrittore, filologo* (Florence: Le Lettere, 1998)

Festugières, Jean, "Dante et Marsile Ficin," *Bulletin du Jubilé* 5 (1922), 535–43

Ficino, Marsilio, *Commentaries on Plato*, ed. and tr. Michael J.B. Allen (Cambridge, MA: Harvard University Press, 2008)

Commentaire / Commentarium = Marsilio Ficino, *Commentaire sur le Banquet de Platon, De l'amour / Commentarium in convivium Platonis, De amore*, ed. and tr. P. Laurens (Paris: Belles Lettres, 2002)

Le divine lettere del gran Marsilio Ficino, 2 vols., ed. Felice Figliucci (Rome: Edizioni di Storia e Letteratura, 2001)

Platonic Theology, 6 vols., ed. and tr. Michael J.B. Allen and James Hankins (Cambridge, MA: Harvard University Press, 2001–06)

De triplici vita, ed. and tr. Carol Kaske and John R. Clark (Tempe: MRTS, 1998)

Über die Liebe oder Platons Gastmahl, ed. Paul Richard Blum (Hamburg: Meiner, 1994)

Letters, tr. by the Language Department of the School of Economic Science, 10 vols. to date (London: Shepheard-Walwyn, 1975–2015)

Opera Omnia (Basel, 1576)

Theologia platonica de immortalitate animae (Florence: Antonio Miscomini, 1482)

Libro di Marsilio Ficino della Cristiana Religione (Florence: Niccolò di Lorenzo, undated but before March 25, 1475)

Field, Arthur, *The Origins of the Platonic Academy of Florence.* (Princeton: Princeton University Press, 1988)

Fiorelli, Piero, "Pour l'interprétation de l'ordonnance de Villers-Cotterêts," *Le Français moderne* 18 (1950), 277–88

Flavio, Biondo, *Italy Illuminated*, ed. and tr. J. White (Cambridge, MA, Harvard University Press: 2005)

Historiarum ab inclinatione Romanorum imperii decades (Venice, 1483)

Fossati, Felice, "Francesco Sforza e la pace di Lodi," *Archivio Veneto*, 5th series, 60–61 (1957), 15–34

Franklin, Carmela Vircillo, "'Pro communi doctorum virorum comodo': The Vatican Library and its Service to Scholarship," *Proceedings of the American Philosophical Society* 146 (2002), 363–84

Freedberg, David, *The Eye of the Lynx: Galileo, His Friends, and the Beginnings of Modern Natural History* (Chicago: University of Chicago Press, 2002)

Fried, Johannes, *Donation of Constantine and Constitutum Constantini: The Misinterpretation of a Fiction and Its Original Meaning* (Berlin and New York: de Gruyter, 2007)

Frier, Bruce W., general editor, *The Codex of Justinian*, 3 vols. (Cambridge: Cambridge University Press, 2016)

Fubini, Riccardo, *Politica e pensiero politico nell'Italia del Rinascimento: dallo stato territoriale al Machiavelli* (Florence: Edifir, 2009)

"Contributo per l'interpretazione della *Dialectica* di Lorenzo Valla," in Graziella F. Vescovini, ed., *Filosofia e scienza classica, arabo-latina medievale e l'età moderna*, (Louvain-la-Neuve: Fédération Internationale des Instituts d'Études Médiévales, 1999)

Quattrocento fiorentino: politica, diplomazia, cultura (Pisa: Pacini, 1996)

Italia quattrocentesca: politica e diplomazia nell'età di Lorenzo il Magnifico (Milan: FrancoAngeli, 1994)

"All'uscita della scolastica medievale: Salutati, Bruni, e i *Dialogi ad Petrum Histrum*," *Archivio storico italiano* 150 (1992), 1065–103

Umanesimo e secolarizzazzione da Petrarca a Valla (Rome: Bulzoni, 1990)

"Biondo Flavio," in *Dizionario biografico degli italiani* 10 (Rome, 1968), 548–51

Galilei, Galileo, *Il saggiatore*, ed. Ottavio Besomi and Mario Helbing (Rome: Antenore, 2005)

Gardet, Louis, *La pensée religieuse d'Avicenne* (Paris: Vrin, 1951)

Garfagnini, Gian Carlo, ed., *Convegno internazionale di studi*, 2 vols. (Florence: Olschki, 1997)

Gargan, Luciano, "Gli umanisti e la biblioteca pubblica," in Cavallo, ed., *Le biblioteche nel mondo antico e medievale*, 163–86

Garin, Eugenio, *Rinascite e rivoluzioni: movimenti culturali dal XIV al XVIII secolo* (Rome: Laterza, 2007)

    Umanesimo e secolarizzazzione da Petrarca a Valla (Rome: Bulzoni, 1990)

    La cultura filosofica del Rinascimento italiano (Florence: Sansoni, 1961)

    Studi sul Platonismo medievale (Florence: Le Monnier, 1958)

    ed., *Prosatori latini del Quattrocento* (Milan: Ricciardi, 1952)

    "*Endelecheia* e *Entelecheia* nelle discussioni umanistiche," *Atene e roma* 5 (1937), 177–87

    Giovanni Pico della Mirandola: Vita e dottrina (Florence: Le Monnier, 1937)

Gee, Emma, "Cicero's Poetry," in Catherine Steel, ed., *The Cambridge Companion to Cicero* (Cambridge and New York: Cambridge University Press, 2012), 88–106

Gellius, Aulus, *The Attic Nights*, ed. and tr. John C. Rolfe (Cambridge, MA: Harvard University press, 1947)

Gentile, Sebastiano, "Il ritorno di Platone, dei platonici e del 'corpus' ermetico. Filosofia, teologia e astrologia nell'opera di Marsilio Ficino," in C. Vasoli, ed., *Le filosofie del Rinascimento* (Milan: Mondadori), 193–228

    "Sulle prime traduzioni dal Greco di Marsilio Ficino," *Rinascimento*, 2nd series 30 (1990), 57–104

    "Intorno a Proemio XIII," in Landino, *Comento*, 114–18

    S. Niccoli, and Paolo Viti, *Marsilio Ficino e il ritorno di Platone: Mostra di manoscritti, stampe, a documenti* (Florence: Le Lettere, 1984)

Gerl, Hanna-Barbara, *Rhetorik als Philosophie: Lorenzo Valla* (Munich: Fink, 1974)

Gersh, Stephen, *Middle Platonism and Neoplatonism: The Latin Tradition* (Notre Dame: University of Notre Dame Press, 1986)

Gerson, Lloyd P., *Aristotle and Other Platonists* (Ithaca: Cornell University Press, 2005)

    "What Is Platonism?" *Journal of the History of Philosophy* 43 (2005), 253–76

    ed., *The Cambridge Companion to Plotinus* (Cambridge: Cambridge University Press, 1996)

    Plotinus (London: Routledge, 1994)

Gigante, Marcello, "Ambrogio Traversari interprete di Diogene Laerzio," in Gian Carlo Garfagnini, ed., *Ambrogio Traversari nel VI centenario della nascita* (Florence: Olschki, 1988), 367–459

Gill, Joseph, *The Council of Florence* (Cambridge: Cambridge University Press, 1959)

    Personalities of the Council of Florence (Oxford: Oxford University Press, 1964)

Gilson, Simon, *Dante and Renaissance Florence* (Cambridge: Cambridge University Press, 2005)

Gingerich, Owen, *The Eye of Heaven: Ptolemy, Copernicus, Kepler* (New York: American Institute of Physics, 1993)

Glomski, Jacqueline, "*Incunabula Typographiae*: Seventeenth-Century Views on Early Printing," *Library* 2 (2001), 336–48

Godman, Peter, *From Poliziano to Machiavelli: Florentine Humanism in the High Renaissance* (Princeton: Princeton University Press, 1998)

Goodman, Lenn, *Avicenna* (London: Routledge, 1992)

Goldthwaite, Richard, *The Economy of Renaissance Florence* (Baltimore: Johns Hopkins University Press, 2009)

Gordan, Phyllis W.G., *Two Renaissance Book Hunters* (New York: Columbia University Press, 1991)

Gorni, Guglielmo, "Storia del Certame coronario," *Rinascimento* n.s. 12 (1972), 135–81

Gouwens, Kenneth, "Erasmus, 'Apes of Cicero,' and Conceptual Blending," *Journal of the History of Ideas* 71:4 (October, 2010), 523–45

Gracia, Jorge, "The Transcendentals in the Middle Ages: An Introduction," *Topoi* 11 (1992), 113–20

Grafton, Anthony, "How Revolutionary Was the Print Revolution?" *American Historical Review* 107 (2002), 84–87

    Leon Battista Alberti: Master Builder of the Italian Renaissance (New York: Hill and Wang, 2000)

    ed., *Rome Reborn: The Vatican Library and Renaissance Culture* (New Haven: Yale University Press, 1993)

    "The Importance of Being Printed," *Journal of Interdisciplinary History* 11 (1980), 265–86

    "Conflict and Harmony in the Collegium Gellianum," in *The Worlds of Aulus Gellius*, 318–42

    and Eugene F. Rice Jr., *The Foundations of Early Modern Europe, 1460–1559* (New York: Norton, 1994)

Gregory, Tullio, *Platonismo medievale: studi e ricerche* (Rome: Istituto storico italiano per il medioevo, 1958)

Greenblatt, Stephen, *The Swerve: How the World Became Modern* (New York: Norton, 2012)

Grendler, Paul F., *Schooling in Renaissance Italy: Literacy and Learning, 1300–1600* (Baltimore: Johns Hopkins University Press, 1989)

Gutas, Dimitri, *Avicenna and the Aristotelian Tradition* (Leiden: Brill, 1988)

Hadot, Pierre, *What Is Ancient Philosophy?* (Cambridge, MA: Harvard University Press, 2004)

    Philosophy as a Way of Life, ed. Arnold I. Davidson, tr. M. Chase (Oxford and New York: Blackwell, 1995)

    Plotinus, or, the Simplicity of Vision, tr. Michael Chase (Chicago: University of Chicago Press, 1993)

Hall, Robert A., *The Italian Questione della lingua: An Interpretive Essay* (Chapel Hill: University of North Carolina Press, 1942)

Haller, Hermann, *The Other Italy: The Literary Canon in Dialect* (Toronto: University of Toronto Press, 1999)

Hankins, James, "The Virtue Politics of the Italian Humanists," in Patrick Baker, Johannes Helmrath, and Craig Kallendorf, eds., *Beyond Reception: Renaissance Humanism and the Transformation of Classical Antiquity*, forthcoming

    "Teaching Civil Prudence in Leonardo Bruni's *History of the Florentine People*," in Sabrina Ebbersmeyer and Eckhard Kessler, eds., *Ethik – Wissenschaft oder Lebenskunst? Modelle der Normenbegründung von der Antike bis zur frühen Neuzeit* (Berlin, 2007), pp. 143–57

ed., *The Cambridge Companion to Renaissance Philosophy* (Cambridge: Cambridge University Press, 2007)

Humanism and Platonism in the Italian Renaissance, 2 vols. (Rome: Edizioni di storia e letteratura, 2003)

ed., *Renaissance Civic Humanism: Reappraisals and Reflections* (Cambridge: Cambridge University Press, 2000)

Repertorium Brunianum: A Critical Guide to the Writings of Leonardo Bruni (Rome: Edizioni di Storia e Letteratura, 1997)

Plato in the Italian Renaissance, 2 vols. (Leiden: Brill, 1990)

Harkness, Deborah, *The Jewel House: Elizabethan London and the Scientific Revolution* (New Haven and London: Yale University Press, 2007)

Hay, Denys, *Flavio Biondo and the Italian Middle Ages* (Oxford: Oxford University Press, 1959)

Helmrath, Johannes, "Streitkultur. Die 'Invektive' bei den italienischen Humanisten," in Marc Laureys, ed., *Die Kunst des Streitens. Inszenierung, Formen und Funktionen öffentlichen Streits in historischer Perspektive* (Göttingen, 2010), 259–93

Das Basler Konzil, 1431–1449: Forschungsstand und Probleme (Cologne: Böhlau, 1987)

Hesiod, *Theogony. Works and Days. Testimonia*, ed. and tr. Glenn Most (Cambridge, MA: Harvard University Press, 2007)

Hexter, Ralph, "Aldus, Greek, and the Shape of the Classical Corpus," in Zeidberg, ed., *Aldus Manutius and Renaissance Culture*, 143–60

Hiatt, Alfred, *The Making of Medieval Forgeries: False Documents in Fifteenth-Century England* (Cambridge: Cambridge University Press, 2004)

Hill, Julia Cotton, "Death and Politian," *Durham University Journal* 46 (1953–54), 96–105

Hirai, Hiroshi "Concepts of Seeds and Nature in the Work of Marsilio Ficino," in Allen and Rees, *Marsilio Ficino*, 257–84

Hladky, Vojtech, *The Philosophy of Gemistos Plethon: Platonism in Late Byzantium, between Hellenism and Orthodoxy* (Aldershot: Ashgate, 2014)

Hobbins, Daniel, *Authorship and Publicity before Print: Jean Gerson and the Transformation of Late Medieval Learning* (Philadelphia: University of Pennsylvania Press, 2009)

"The Schoolman as Public Intellectual: Jean Gerson and the Late Medieval Tract," *The American Historical Review* 108 (2003), 1308–37

Hoffmann, Walther von, *Forschungen zur Geschichte der Kurialen Behörden*, 2 vols. (Rome: Loescher, 1914)

Holford-Strevens, Leofranc, *Aulus Gellius: An Antonine Scholar and His Achievement* (Oxford: Oxford University Press, 2003)

and Amiel Vardi, eds., *The Worlds of Aulus Gellius* (Oxford: Oxford University Press, 2004)

Holmes, George, *The Florentine Enlightenment, 1400–50* (London: Weidenfeld and Nicolson, 1969)

Horace, *Satires, Epistles and Ars Poetica*, ed. and tr. H. Rushton Fairclough (Cambridge, MA, Harvard University Press, 1991)

Houston, Daniel S., *The Aldine Lascaris: A Greek Textbook in the Italian Renaissance*, unpublished PhD dissertation, Johns Hopkins University, 2015

Huizinga, Johann, *Erasmus and the Age of Reformation* (Princeton: Princeton University Press, 1984)

Hunt, Jonathan, *Politian and Scholastic Logic: An Unknown Dialogue by a Dominican Friar* (Leiden: Brill, 1995)

Iamblichus, *On the Pythagorean Life*, tr. with notes and an introduction by Gillian Clark (Liverpool: Liverpool University Press, 1989)

De mysteriis, ed. Edouard des Places (Paris: Les Belles Lettres, 1966)

De vita pythagorica, ed. L. Deubner (Leipzig: Teubner, 1937)

In Nicomachi Arithmeticam introductionem, ed. Ermenegildo Pistelli (Stuttgart: Teubner, 1894)

De communi mathematica scientia, ed. Nicola Festa (Stuttgart: Teubner, 1891)

Protrepticus, ed. Ermenegildo Pistelli (Stuttgart: Teubner, 1888)

Idel, Moshe, *La Cabbalà in Italia* (Florence: Giuntina, 2007)

Ilardi, Vincent, *Studies in Italian Renaissance Diplomatic History* (Aldershot: Ashgate, 1986)

Imber, Colin, *The Ottoman Empire*, 2nd ed. (New York: Palgrave Macmillan, 2009)

Institut d'Études Médiévales, ed., *Les genres littéraires dans les sources théologiques et philosophiques médiévales: définition, critique, et exploitation* (Louvain-la-Neuve: Université catholique de Louvain, 1982)

Isidore of Seville, *Etymologiae*, 2 vols., ed. W.M. Lindsay (Oxford: Oxford University Press, 1911, reprint 1971)

Jenkyns, Richard, "Silver Latin Poetry and the Latin Novel," in John Boardman, Jasper Griffin, and Oswyn Murray, *The Oxford History of the Classical World* (Oxford: Oxford University Press, 1986), 677–97

Jerome, Saint, "Praefatio in Evangelio," in Robertus Weber and Roger Gryson, eds., *Biblia sacra iuxta vulgatam versionem* (Stuttgart: Deutsche Bibelgesellschaft, 1994), 1515–16

Select Letters of St. Jerome, ed. and tr. F.A. Wright (Cambridge, MA: Harvard University Press, 1991)

De optimo genere interpretandi (Epistula 57), ed. G.J.M. Bartelink (Leiden: Brill, 1980)

Johns, Adrian, *Piracy: The Intellectual Property Wars from Gutenberg to Gates* (Chicago: University of Chicago Press, 2009)

The Nature of the Book: Print and Knowledge in the Making (Chicago: University of Chicago, 1998)

"The Coming of Print to Europe," in Leslie Howsam, ed., *The Cambridge Companion to the History of the Book* (Cambridge: Cambridge University Press, 2014), 107–24

"How to Acknowledge a Revolution," *American Historical Review*, 107 (2002), 106–28

Jolivet, Jean, *Abélard en son temps* (Paris: Les Belles Lettres, 1981)

Jones, Philip, *The Italian City-State: From Commune to Signoria* (Oxford: Clarendon, 1997)

Jonge, H.J. de, "Novum testamentum a nobis versum," *Journal of Theological Studies* 35 (1984), 394–413

Jordan, Constance, *Pulci's* Morgante: *Poetry and History in Fifteenth-Century Florence* (Washington, DC: The Folger Shakespeare Library, 1986)

Kent, Dale, *Cosimo de' Medici and the Florentine Renaissance: The Patron's Oeuvre* (New Haven: Yale University Press, 2000)

The Rise of the Medici: Faction in Florence 1426–1434 (Oxford: Oxford University Press, 1978)

Kent, William Francis, *Lorenzo de' Medici and the Art of Magnificence* (Baltimore: Johns Hopkins University Press, 2004)

Kessler, Eckhard, "Die Transformation des aristotelischen Organon durch Lorenzo Valla," in Kessler, ed., *Aristotelismus und Renaissance*, 53–74

"The Intellective Soul," in Schmitt and Skinner, eds., *The Cambridge History of Renaissance Philosophy*, 485–534

ed., *Aristotelismus und Renaissance: In memoriam Charles B. Schmitt* (Wiesbaden: Harrasowitz, 1988)

Kidwell, Carol, *Pietro Bembo: Lover, Linguist, Cardinal* (Montreal: McGill-Queen's University Press, 2004)

Kircher, Timothy, "Landino, Alberti, and the Invention of the Neo-Vernacular," *Albertiana*, 19 (2016), 29–48

Living Well in Renaissance Italy: The Virtues of Humanism and the Irony of Leon Battista Alberti (Tempe: MRTS, 2012)

Klibansky, Raymond, *Plato's Parmenides in the Middle Ages and the Renaissance: A Chapter in the History of Platonic Studies* (Toronto: University of Toronto Libraries, 2011)

ed., *Plato Latinus* (London: The Warburg Institute, 1940)

The Continuity of the Platonic Tradition during the Middle Ages, together with Plato's Parmenides in the Middle Ages and the Renaissance (London: The Warburg Institute, 1939)

Kirkham, Victoria, "Le tre corone e l'iconografia di Boccaccio," in Michelangiola Marchiaro and Stefano Zamponi, eds., *Boccaccio letterato* (Florence: Accademia della Crusca, 2015), 453–84

Kohl, Benjamin J., "The Changing Concept of the *Studia Humanitatis* in the Early Renaissance," *Renaissance Studies* 6 (1992), 185–209

and Ronald G. Witt, eds., *The Earthly Republic* (Philadelphia: University of Pennsylvania Press, 1978)

Kraye, Jill, "Lorenzo Valla and Changing Perceptions of Renaissance Humanism," *Comparative Criticism*, 23 (2001), 37–55

"Ficino in the Firing Line," in Michael J.B. Allen and Valery Rees, eds., *Marsilio Ficino: His Theology, His Philosophy, His Legacy* (Leiden: Brill, 2001), 377–97

"Cicero, Stoicism, and Textual Criticism: Poliziano on *katorthoma*," *Rinascimento* 2nd series, 23 (1983), 79–110

Kretzmann, Norman, Anthony Kenny, and Jan Pinborg, eds., *The Cambridge History of Later Medieval Philosophy* (Cambridge: Cambridge University Press, 1982)

Kristeller, Paul Oskar, *Il pensiero filosofico di Marsilio Ficino* (Florence: Le Lettere, 1988)

Renaissance Thought and Its Sources (New York: Columbia University Press, 1979)

Medieval Aspects of Renaissance Learning, ed. and tr. Edward P. Mahoney (Durham, NC: Duke University Press, 1974)

Le Thomisme et la pensée italienne de la Renaissance (Paris: Vrin, 1967)

Studies in Renaissance Thought and Letters, 4 vols. (Rome: Edizioni di storia e letteratura, 1956–96)

The Philosophy of Marsilio Ficino (New York: Columbia University Press, 1943)

Supplementum ficinianum, 2 vols. (Florence: Olschki, 1938)

Labowsky, Lotte, *Bessarion's Library and the Biblioteca Marciana: Six Early Inventories* (Rome: Edizioni di storia e letteratura, 1979)

Laertius, Diogenes, *Lives of Eminent Philosophers*, 2 vols., ed. and tr. R.D. Hicks (Cambridge, MA: Harvard University Press, 2000–05)

Laffranchi, Marco, *Dialettica e filosofia in Lorenzo Valla* (Milan: Vita e Pensiero, 1999)

Landino, Cristoforo, *Comento sopra la Comedia*, 4 vols., ed. Paolo Procaccioli (Rome: Salerno, 2001)

De vera nobilitate, ed. Maria Teresa Liaci (Florence: Olschki, 1970)

"Orazione fatta per Cristofano da Pratovecchio quando cominciò a leggere i sonetti di messere Francesco Petrarca in istudio (1467–70)," in Cardini, *La critica del Landino*, 342–54

Laurens, Florence Vuilleimier, *La raison des figures symboliques à la Renaissance et à l'âge classique* (Geneva: Droz, 2000)

Laurens, Pierre, "Introduction," in Ficino, *Commentaire / Commentarium*, IX–LXIX

Lea, Henry Charles, *A History of Auricular Confession and Indulgences in the Latin Church*, 3 vols. (Philadelphia: Lea Bros.: 1896)

Lèbano, Edoardo A., "Introduction," in Pulci, *Morgante: The Epic Adventures*, xi–xxxiii

LeGoff, Jacques, *The Birth of Purgatory* (Chicago: University of Chicago Press, 1984)

Lelli, Fabrizio, ed., *Pico e la cabbalà* (Mirandola: Centro internazionale di cultura, 2014)

Leonhardt, Jürgen, *Latin: Story of a World Language*, tr. Kenneth Kronenberg (Cambridge, MA: Harvard University Press, 2013)

Leppin, Volker, *Martin Luther*, 2nd ed. (Darmstadt: Primus, 2010)

Lepschy, Giulio, *Mother Tongues and Other Reflections on the Italian Language* (Toronto: University of Toronto Press, 2002)

Les genres littéraires dans les sources théologiques et philosophiques médiévales: définition, critique, et exploitation (see Institut d'Études Médiévales)

Lesaffer, Randall, "Peace Treaties from Lodi to Westphalia," in Randall Lesaffer, ed., *Peace Treaties and International Law in European History: From the Late Middle Ages to World War One* (Cambridge: Cambridge University Press, 2004), 9–44

Libera, Alain de, *Penser au Moyen Age* (Peris: Editions du Seuil, 1991)

Liebeschütz, Hans, *Medieval Humanism in the Life and Writings of John of Salisbury* (London: University of London, 1950)

Lines, David, "Beyond Latin in Renaissance Philosophy: A Plea for New Critical Perspectives," *Intellectual History Review* 25 (2015), 373–89

　"Aristotle's Ethics in the Renaissance," in Jon Miller, ed., *The Reception of Aristotle's "Ethics"* (Cambridge: Cambridge University Press, 2012), 171–93

　"Humanism and the Italian Universities," in Celenza and Gouwens, eds., *Humanism and Creativity: Essays in Honor of Ronald G. Witt*, 323–42

Lloyd, G.E.R., *Aristotle: The Growth and Structure of His Thought* (Cambridge: Cambridge University Press, 1968)

Lombard, Peter, *Sententiae in IV libris distinctae*, 2 vols., ed. Victorin Doucet (Grottaferrata: Collegium S. Bonaventurae ad Claras Aquas, 1971–81)

Long, A.A., *Hellenistic Philosophy: Stoics, Epicureans, Sceptics*, 2nd ed. (Berkeley: University of California Press, 1986)

Long, Pamela, *Openness, Secrecy, Authorship: Technical Arts and the Culture of Knowledge from Antiquity to the Renaissance* (Baltimore: Johns Hopkins University Press, 2001)

Lowry, Martin, *The World of Aldus Manutius* (Ithaca: Cornell University Press, 1979)

Luiso, Francesco Paolo, *Studi su l'Epistolario di Leonardo Bruni*, ed. Lucia Gualdo Rosa (Rome: Istituto storico per il medioevo, 1980)

Luther, Martin, *Werke. Kritische Gesamtausgabe,* part 4, *Briefwechsel*, vol. 2, ed. Johannes Ficker (Weimar: H. Böhlaus Nachfolger, 1931)

　Werke. Kritische Gesamtausgabe, 58 vols. (Weimar: Böhlau, 1883–1948)

　De servo arbitrio, in Luther, *Werke. Kritische Gesamtausgabe*, vol.18, pp. 551–787

Maccarrone, Michele, *Vicarius Christi: Storia del titolo papale* (Rome: Facultas Theologica Pontificii Athenaei Lateranensis, 1952)

Machiavelli, Niccolò, *Il principe*, ed. G. Inglese (Turin: Einaudi, 1995)

　Opere, 3 vols., ed. Corrado Vivanti (Turin: Einaudi-Galimard, 1997–2005)

MacCormack, Sabine, *The Shadows of Poetry: Virgil in the Mind of Augustine* (Berkeley: University of California Press, 1998)

Mack, Peter, *Renaissance Argument: Valla and Agricola in the Traditions of Rhetoric and Dialectic* (Leiden: Brill, 1993)

MacMullen, Ramsey, *Paganism in the Roman Empire* (New Haven: Yale University Press, 1981)

Maïer, Ida, *Ange Politien: La formation d'un poète humaniste (1469–1480)* (Geneva: Droz, 1966)

Mancini, Girolamo, *Vita di Lorenzo Valla* (Florence: Sansoni, 1891)

Marcozzi, Luca, "Making the Rerum vulgarium fragmenta," in Ascoli and Falkeid, *The Cambridge Companion to Petrarch*, 51–62

Marenbon, John, *Aristotelian Logic, Platonism and the Context of Early Medieval Philosophy in the West* (Aldershot: Ashgate, 2000)

   The Philosophy of Peter Abelard (Cambridge: Cambridge University Press, 1997)

   Later Medieval Philosophy (1150–1350): An Introduction (London: Routledge, 1987)

Marmo, Costantino, *Semiotica e linguaggio nella scolastica: Parigi, Bologna, Erfurt, 1270–1330* (Rome: Istituto Storico Italiano per il Medioevo, 1994)

Marsh, David, *The Quattrocento Dialogue: Classical Tradition and Humanist Innovation* (Cambridge, MA: Harvard University Press, 1980)

   "Grammar, Method, and Polemic in Valla's 'Elegantiae,'" *Rinascimento*, n.s. 19 (1979), 91–116

Martines, Lauro, *April Blood: Florence and the Conspiracy Against the Medici* (Oxford: Oxford University Press, 2003)

   Strong Words: Writing and Social Strain in the Italian Renaissance (Baltimore: Johns Hopkins University Press, 2001)

   Power and Imagination: City-States in Renaissance Italy (Baltimore: Johns Hopkins University Press, 1988)

   The Social World of the Florentine Humanists, 1390–1460 (Princeton: Princeton University Press, 1963)

Masai, Francois, *Pléthon et le platonisme de Mistra* (Paris: Les belles lettres, 1956)

Mattingly, Garrett, *Renaissance Diplomacy* (Boston: Houghton Mifflin, 1955; Baltimore: Penguin, 1964)

Mauramuro, Guglielmo, *Expositione sopra l' "Inferno" di Dante Alighieri*, eds. Pier Giacomo Pisoni and Saverio Bellomo (Padua: Antenore, 1998)

Maxson, Brian, *The Humanist World of Renaissance Florence* (Cambridge: Cambridge University Press, 2013)

Mazzocco, Angelo, *Linguistic Theories in Dante and the Humanists: Studies of Language and Intellectual History in Late Medieval and Renaissance Italy* (Leiden: Brill, 1993)

   and Marc Laureys, eds., *A New Sense of the Past: The Scholarship of Biondo Flavio (1392–1463)* (Leuven: Leuven University Press, 2015)

Mazzotta, Giuseppe, *The Worlds of Petrarch* (Durham, NC: Duke University Press, 1993)

McCahill, Elizabeth M., *Reviving the Eternal City: Rome and the Papal Court 1420–1447* (Cambridge, MA: Harvard University Press, 2013)

McLaughlin, Martin, *Leon Battista Alberti: La vita, l'umanesimo, le opere letterarie* (Florence: Olschki, 2016)

   "Petrarch and Cicero: Adulation and Critical Distance," in William H.F. Altman, ed., *Brill's Companion to the Reception of Cicero* (Leiden: Brill, 2015), 19–38

"Humanist Criticism of Latin and Vernacular Prose," in Alastair Minnis and Ian Johnson, eds., *The Cambridge History of Literary Criticism*, v. 2 (Cambridge: Cambridge University Press, 2005), 648–55

Literary Imitation in the Italian Renaissance (Oxford and New York: Oxford University Press, 1995)

Medici, Lorenzo de', *Opere*, ed. Tiziano Zanato (Turin: Einaudi, 1992)

Menn, Stephen, "The *Discourse on the Method* and the Tradition of Intellectual Autobiography," in Jon Miller and Brad Inwood, eds., *Hellenistic and Early Modern Philosophy* (Cambridge: Cambridge University Press, 2003), 141–91

Meserve, Margaret, *Empires of Islam in Renaissance Historical Thought* (Cambridge, MA: Cambridge University Press, 2008)

Migliorini, Bruno, *Storia della lingua italiana* (Milan: Bompiani, 1998)

Monfasani, John, *Bessarion Scholasticus: A Study of Cardinal Bessarion's Latin Library* (Turnhout: Brepols, 2011)

Greeks and Latins in Renaissance Italy: Studies on Humanism and Philosophy in the Fifteenth Century (Aldershot: Ashgate, 2004)

"The Ciceronian Controversy," in Glyn P. Norton, ed., *The Cambridge History of Literary Criticism, vol. 3, The Renaissance* (Cambridge: Cambridge University Press, 1999), 395–401

Byzantine Scholars in Renaissance Italy: Cardinal Bessarion and Other Emigrés (Aldershot: Ashgate, 1995)

Language and Learning in Renaissance Italy (Aldershot: Ashgate, 1994)

"Was Lorenzo Valla an Ordinary Language Philosopher?" *Journal of the History of Philosophy* 50 (1989), 309–23, repr. with same pagination in Monfasani, *Language and Learning*

"Pseudo-Dionysius the Areopagite in mid-Quattrocento Rome," in J. Hankins, J. Monfasani, and F. Purnell Jr., eds., *Supplementum Festivum: Studies in Honor of Paul Oskar Kristeller* (Binghamton: MRTS, 1987), 189–219, repr. with the same pagination as essay IX in Monfasani, *Language and Learning*

Monnerjahn, Engelbert, *Giovanni Pico della Mirandola: Ein Beitrag zur philosophischen Theologie des italienischen Humanismus* (Wiesbaden: Franz Steiner, 1960)

Moraux, Paul, *Der Aristotelismus bei den Griechen: von Andronikos bis Alexander von Aphrodisias*, 2 vols. (New York: De Gruyter, 1973–84)

Mormondo, Franco, *The Preacher's Demons: Bernardino of Siena and the Social Underworld of Early Renaissance Italy* (Chicago: University of Chicago Press, 1999)

Moss, Ann, *Renaissance Truth and the Latin Language Turn* (Oxford: Oxford University Press, 2003)

Müllner, Karl, ed., *Reden und Briefen italienischer Humanisten* (Munich: Fink, 1970)

Müntz, Eugene and Paul Fabre, *La Bibliothèque du Vatican au XVe siècle, d'après des documents inédits*, Bibliothèque des écoles françaises d'Athènes et de Rome, 48 (Paris: Thorin, 1887)

Muscetta, Carlo and Daniele Ponchiroli, eds., *Poesia del Quattrocento e del cinquecento* (Turin: Einaudi, 1959)

Najemy, John, *A History of Florence, 1200–1575* (London: Wiley-Blackwell, 2008)

Nauta, Lodi, *In Defense of Common Sense: Lorenzo Valla's Humanist Critique of Scholastic Philosophy* (Cambridge, MA: Harvard University Press, 2009)

Nifo, Agostino, *Libri duo, De pulchro primus, De amore secundus* (Leiden, 1549)

Nigro, Salvatore, *Pulce e la cultura medicea* (Rome: Laterza, 1978)

Nisard, Charles, *Les gladiateurs de la république des lettres aux XVe, XVIe, et XVIIe siècles* (Paris: Levy, 1860)

Novikoff, Alex. J., *The Medieval Culture of Disputation* (Philadelphia: University of Pennsylvania Press, 2013)

Oberman, Heiko, *Luther: Man Between God and the Devil*, tr. Eileen Walliser-Schwarzbart (New Haven: Yale University Press, 1989)

O'Brien, Emily, *The "Commentaries" of Pope Pius II (1458–1464) and the Crisis of the Fifteenth-Century Papacy* (Toronto: University of Toronto Press, 2015)

Olympiodorus, *Commentary on Plato's Gorgias*, tr. Robin Jackson, Kimon Lycos, and Harold Tarrant (Brill: Leiden, 1998)

O'Malley, John W., *Trent: What Happened at the Council* (Cambridge, MA: Harvard University Press, 2013)

    Trent and All That: Renaming Catholicism in the Early Modern Era (Cambridge, MA: Harvard University Press, 2002)

    "The Feast of Thomas Aquinas in Renaissance Rome: A Neglected Document and Its Import," *Rivista di storia della Chiesa in Italia* 35 (1981), 1–27

    "Some Renaissance Panegyrics of Aquinas," *Renaissance Quarterly* 27 (1974), 174–92

O'Meara, Dominic J., *Plotinus: An Introduction to the Enneads* (Oxford: Oxford University Press, 1993)

    Pythagoras Revived: Mathematics and Philosophy in Late Antiquity (Oxford: Oxford University Press, 1989)

    "Ordonnance de Villers-Cotterêts," in *Recueil général des anciennes lois françaises*, 29 vols. (Paris: Belin-Le-Priers, 1821–33), vol. 12, part 2

Pade, Marianne, *The Reception of Plutarch's Lives in Fifteenth-Century Italy*, 2 vols. (Copenhagen: University of Copenhagen, 2007)

    ed., *On Renaissance Academies* (Rome: Quasar, 2011)

Palmer, Ada, *Reading Lucretius in the Renaissance* (Cambridge, MA: Harvard University Press, 2014)

Papio, Michael, "Introduction: Boccaccio as Lector Dantis," in Giovanni Boccaccio, *Boccaccio's Expositions on Dante's Comedy*, 3–38

Park, Katherine, "The Organic Soul," in Schmitt and Skinner, eds., *The Cambridge History of Renaissance Philosophy*, 464–84

    and Eckhard Kessler, "The Concept of Psychology," in Schmitt and Skinner, eds., *The Cambridge History of Renaissance Philosophy*, 455–63

Parodi, Severina, *Quattro secoli di Crusca: 1583–1983* (Florence: Accademia della Crusca, 1983)

Passanante, Gerard, *The Lucretian Renaissance: Philology and the Afterlife of Tradition* (Chicago: University of Chicago Press, 2011)

Perreiah, Alan, "Humanist Critiques of Scholastic Dialectic," *Sixteenth-Century Journal* 13 (1982), 3–22

Pertusi, Agostino, ed., *La Caduta di Costantinopoli*, 2 vols. (Milan: Mondadori, 1997)

    ed. *Testi inediti e poco noti sulla caduta di Costantinopoli*, Il Mondo medievale: sezione di storia bizantina e slava 4. (Bologna: Pàtron Editore 1983)

Petrarch (Francesco Petrarca), *Sine nomine*, ed. Ugo Dotti (Turin, 2010)

    Res Seniles: Libri V–VIII, ed. Silvia Rizzo (Florence: Le Lettere, 2009)

    Letters of Old Age, 2 vols., tr. Aldo Bernardo (New York: Italica, 2005)

De insigni obedientia et fide uxoria: Il Codice Riccardiano 991, ed. Gabriella Albanese (Alessandria: Edizioni dell'Orso, 1998)

Lettera ai Posteri, ed. and trans. Gianni Villani (Rome: Salerno, 1990)

Opere di Francesco Petrarca, ed. Emilio Bigi (Milan, 1963)

"Testament," in Theodore Mommsen, ed., *Petrarch's Testament* (Ithaca, NY: Cornell University Press, 1957), 68–93

Prose, ed. Giuseppe Martellotti (Milan: Ricciardi, 1955)

Le familiari, ed. Vittorio Rossi, 4 vols. (Florence: Sansoni, 1933–68; reedition, Florence, Le lettere, 1997)

Epistolae de rebus familiaribus et Variae, 3 vols., ed. G. Fracasetti (Florence: Le Monnier, 1859–63)

Opera Latina (Venice, 1503)

Petrucci, Armando, *Writers and Readers in Medieval Italy: Studies in the History of Written Culture*, ed. and tr. Charles M. Radding (New Haven: Yale University Press, 1995)

Pettegree, Andrew, *The Book in the Renaissance* (New Haven: Yale University Press, 2010)

Piché, David, ed., *La condemnation parisienne de 1277*, in *Texte latin, traduction, introduction et commentaire* (Paris: Vrin, 1999)

Pico della Mirandola, *Oration on the Dignity of Man: A New Translation and Commentary*, eds. Francesco Borghesi, Michael Papio, and Massimo Riva (Cambridge: Cambridge University Press, 2012)

De ente et uno, ed. Raphael Ebgi and Franco Bacchelli (Milan: Bompiani, 2010)

Opera Omnia (Turin: Bottega d'Erasmo, 1971), a facsimile of Pico della Mirandola, *Opera Omnia* (Basel, 1572), with extra material

De hominis dignitate, Heptaplus, De ente et uno, e scritti vari, ed. Eugenio Garin (Florence: Vallecchi, 1942)

Pigman, G.W. III, "Versions of Imitation in the Renaissance," *Renaissance Quarterly* 33 (1980), 1–32

Pillinini, Giovanni, *Il sistema degli stati italiani, 1454–94* (Venice: Universitaria editrice, 1970)

Pinborg, Jan, *Die Entwicklung der Sprachtheorie im Mittelalter* (Münster: Aschendorff, 1967)

"Speculative Grammar," in Kretzmann, Kenny, and Pinborg, eds., *The Cambridge History of Later Medieval Philosophy*, 254–69

Pine, Martin, *Pietro Pomponazzi: Radical Philosopher of the Italian Renaissance* (Padua: Antenore, 1986)

Plato, *Euthyphro, Apology, Crito, Phaedo, Phaedrus*, ed. and tr. Harold N. Fowler (Cambridge, MA: Harvard University Press, 2014)

The Symposium, tr. Christopher Gill (London: Penguin, 1999)

The Complete Works of Plato, ed. John M. Cooper (Indianapolis: Hackett, 1997)

Opera, 5 vols. (Oxford: Clarendon, 1995)

Phaedrus, tr. Alexander Nehamas and Paul Woodruff (Indianapolis: Hackett, 1995)

Plotinus, *Enneads*, 7 vols., ed. and tr. A.H. Armstrong (Cambridge, MA: Harvard University Press, 1966–88)

Poliziano, Angelo, *Coniurationis commentarium / Commentario della congiura dei Pazzi*, ed. Leandro Perini (Florence: Firenze University Press, 2012)

Silvae, ed. and tr. Charles Fantazzi (Cambridge, MA: Harvard University Press, 2004)

Due poemetti latini, ed. Francesco Bausi (Rome: Salerno, 2003)

The Stanze of Angelo Poliziano, tr. David Quint (University Park: Pennsylvania State University Press, 1993)

Stanze, Fabula di Orfeo, ed. Stefano Carrai (Milan: Mursia, 1988)

Lamia: Praelectio in priora Aristotelis analytica, ed. Ari Wesseling (Leiden: Brill, 1986)

Commento inedito alle Selve di Stazio, ed. Lucia Cesarini Martinelli (Florence: Sansoni, 1978)

Miscellaneorum centuria secunda, eds. Vittore Branca and Manlio Pastore Stocchi (Florence: Olschki, 1978)

Della congiura dei Pazzi: Coniurationis commentarium, ed. Alessandro Perosa (Padua: Antenore, 1958)

Opera Omnia (Venice: Aldus Manutius, 1498)

Lamia, in Celenza, *Poliziano's Lamia*, 191–253

Porphyry, "Life of Plotinus," in Plotinus, Enneads, vol. 1, 2–87

Porter, James I., "What Is 'Classical' about Classical Antiquity?" in *The Classical Traditions of Greece and Rome*, ed. James I. Porter (Princeton: Princeton University Press, 2006), 1–65

Proclus, *Theologia platonica*, 6 vols. ed. and tr. Henri D. Saffrey and Leendert Westerink (Paris: Les Belles Lettres, 1968–97)

Pulci, Luigi, *Morgante*, 2 vols., ed. Giuliano Dego (Milan: Rizzoli)

   Morgante: The Epic Adventures of Orlando and His Giant Friend Morgante, tr. Joseph Tusiani, introduction and notes by Edoardo A. Lèbano (Bloomington: University of Indiana Press, 1998)

Purnell, Frederick, "The Theme of Philosophic Concord and the Sources of Ficino's Platonism," in Garfagnini, ed., *Marsilio Ficino e il ritorno di Platone*, 2: 397–415

Quaglioni, Diego, *Politica e diritto nel Trecento italiano: il "De tyranno" di Bartolo da Sassoferrato* (Florence: Olschki, 1983)

Quaquarelli, Leonardo, "Moglio, Pietro da," *Dizionario biografico degli italiani* 75 (2011), 267–73

Quint, David, "Humanism and Modernity: A Reconsideration of Bruni's *Dialogues*," *Renaissance Quarterly* 38 (1985), 423–45

Quintilian, *The Orator's Education*, 5 vols., ed. and tr. Donald A. Russell (Cambridge, MA: Harvard University Press, 2001)

Rabil, Albert, ed., *Knowledge, Goodness, and Power: The Debate over Nobility among Quattrocento Italian Humanists* (Binghamton: MRTS, 1991)

Rao, Ennio, *Curmudgeons in High Dudgeon: 101 Years of Invectives (1352–1453)* (Messina: EDAS, 2007)

Refini, Eugenio, "Aristotile in parlare materno," *I Tatti Studies* (2013), 311–41

Regoliosi, Mariangela, *Nel cantiere del Valla: Elaborazione e montaggio delle "Elegantiae"* (Rome: Bulzoni, 1993)

   ed., *Pubblicare il Valla* (Florence: Polistampa, 2008)

   Lorenzo Valla e l'umanesimo toscano: Traversari, Bruni, Marsuppini (Florence: Polistampa, 2009)

   Lorenzo Valla: La riforma della lingua e della logica, 2 vols. (Firenze: Polistampa, 2010)

Reynolds, L.G. and N.G. Wilson, *Scribes and Scholars: A Guide to the Transmission of Greek and Latin Literature*, 4th ed. (Oxford: Oxford University Press, 2013)

Ricciardi, Roberto, "Cortesi, Paolo," *Dizionario biografico degli italiani*, 29 (1983), 766–70

Richardson, Brian, *Printing, Writers, and Readers in Renaissance Italy* (Cambridge: Cambridge University Press, 1999)

Rist, John, *Plotinus: The Road to Reality* (Cambridge: Cambridge University Press, 1967)

"Plotinus and Christian Philosophy," in Gerson, ed., *the Cambridge Companion to Plotinus*, 386–413

Rizzi, Andrea and Eva del Soldato, "Latin and Vernacular in Quattrocento Florence and Beyond: An Introduction," *I Tatti Studies*, 16 (2013), 231–42

Rizzo, Silvia, "I latini dell'umanesimo," in Giorgio Bernardi Perini, ed., *Il latino nell'età dell'umanesimo* (Florence: Olschki, 2004), 51–95

Ricerche sul latino umanistico (Rome: Edizioni di storia e letteratura, 2002)

Il lessico filologico degli umanisti (Rome: Edizioni di storia e letteratura, 1984)

"Il Latino di Poliziano," in Fera and Martelli, eds., *Agnolo Poliziano: Poeta, scrittore, filologo*, 83–125

Robin, Diana, *Publishing Women: Salons, the Presses, and the Counter-Reformation in Sixteenth-Century Italy* (Chicago: University of Chicago Press, 2007)

Roller, Matthew, "The Exemplary Past in Roman Historiography and Culture," in Andrew Feldherr, ed., *The Cambridge Companion to the Roman Historians* (Cambridge: Cambridge University Press, 2009), 214–30

"Exemplarity in Roman Culture: The Cases of Horatius Cocles and Cloelia," *Classical Philology* 99 (2004), 1–56

Rollo-Koster, Joëlle, *Avignon and Its Papacy, 1309–1417* (Lanham, MD: Rowman and Littlefield, 2015)

Rosier, Irène, *La grammaire spéculative des Modistes* (Paris: PUF, 1983)

Ross, David, *Aristotle* (London: Methuen, 1923)

Rossi, Filippo de, ed., *Sonetti di Matteo Franco e di Luigi Pulci* (Lucca, 1759)

Rubenstein, Nicolai, *The Government of Florence under the Medici (1434–1494)*, 2nd ed. (Oxford: Clarendon, 1998)

Rubini, Rocco, *The Other Renaissance: Italian Humanism between Hegel and Heidegger* (Chicago: University of Chicago Press, 2014)

Ruggiero, Guido, *The Renaissance in Italy: A Social and Cultural History of the Rinascimento* (Cambridge: Cambridge University Press, 2015)

Rummel, Erika, *Erasmus' Annotations On the New Testament: From Philologist to Theologian* (Toronto: University of Toronto Press, 1986)

Desiderius Erasmus (London: Continuum, 2004)

Runciman, Steven, *The Fall of Constantinople* (Cambridge: Cambridge University Press, 1965)

Rundle, David and Martin McLaughlin, "Introduction," *Renaissance Studies* 17 (2003), 1–8

Rutherford, David, *Early Renaissance Invective and the Controversies of Antionio da Rho* (Tempe: Arizona Center for Medieval and Renaissance Studies, 2005)

Sabbadini, Remigio, *Le scoperte dei codici latini e greci ne' secoli XIV e XV*, 2 vols. (Florence: Sansoni, 1905–14; reprint edited by Eugenio Garin, Florence: Sansoni, 1967)

Saffrey, Henri, "Florence, 1492: The Reappearance of Plotinus," *Renaissance Quarterly* 49 (1996), 488–508

Salutati, Coluccio, *De tyranno*, in Salutati, *Political Writings*, ed. Stefano Ugo Baldassarri, tr. Rolf Bagemihl (Cambridge, MA: Harvard University Press, 2014)

On the World and Religious Life, ed. and tr. Tina Marshall (Cambridge, MA: Harvard University Press, 2014)

De fato et fortuna, ed. Concetta Bianca (Florence, Olschki, 1985)

Epistolario, ed. F. Novati, 4 vols., Fonti per la storia d'Italia, 15–18 (Rome: Istituto storico italiano per il medioevo, 1891–1911)

Salviati, Lionardo, *Regole della Toscana favella*, ed. Anna Antonini Renieri (Florence: Accademia della Crusca, 1991)

Santangelo, Giorgio, ed., *De imitatione: Le epistole "De imitatione" di Giovanfrancesco Pico della Mirandola e di Pietro Bembo* (Florence: Olschki, 1954)

Santini, Emilio, *Leonardo Bruni e i suoi* Historiarum Florentini populi libri XII*: Contributo allo studio della storiografia umanistica fiorentina* (Pisa: Scuola Normale Superiore, 1910)

Schmitt, Charles B. and Quentin Skinner, eds., *The Cambridge History of Renaissance Philosophy* (Cambridge: Cambridge University Press, 1988)

Schucan, Luzi, *Das Nachleben von Basilius Magnus* Ad Adolescentes*: Ein Beitrag zur Geschichte des christlichen Humanismus* (Geneva: Droz, 1973)

Schuster, Britt-Marie, *Die Verständlichkeit von frühreformatorischen Flugschriften: eine Studie zu kommunikationswirksamen Faktoren der Textgestaltung* (Hildesheim: Olms, 2001)

Segoloni, Danilo, ed., *Bartolo da Sassoferrato: studi e documenti per il VI centenario*, 2 vols. (Milan: Giuffrè: 1962)

Serene, Eileen F., "Demonstrative Science," in Kretzmann, Kenny, and Pinborg, eds., *The Cambridge History of Later Medieval Philosophy*, 496–517

Setz, Wolfram, *Lorenzo Vallas Schrift gegen die Konstantinische Schenkung* De falsa credita et ementita Constantini donatione*: Zur Interpretation und Wirkungsgeschichte*. Bibliothek des Deutschen Historischen Instituts in Rom, 44 (Tübingen: Niemeyer, 1975)

Sforza, Giovanni, *La patria, la famiglia, e la giovinezza di Papa Niccolò V: Ricerche storiche*, Atti della Reale Accademia lucchese di scienze, lettere ed arti, 23 (Lucca: Giusti, 1884)

Shaw, Gregory, *Theurgy and the Soul: The Neoplatonism of Iamblichus* (University Park,: Pennsylvania State University Press, 1995)

"Theurgy: Rituals of Unification in the Neoplatonism of Iamblichus," *Traditio*, 41 (1985), 1–28

Simonetta, Marcello, *The Montefeltro Conspiracy: A Renaissance Mystery Decoded* (New York: Doubleday, 2008)

Federico da Montefeltro and his Library (Vatican City: Biblioteca apostolica vaticana, 2007)

Sinisgalli, Rocco, *Il nuovo "De pictura" di Leon Battista Alberti – The New "De pictura" of Leon Battista Alberti* (Rome: Kappa, 2006)

Smalley, Beryl, *The Study of the Bible in the Middle Ages*, 3rd. ed. (Oxford: Blackwell, 1983)

Smith, Pamela, *The Body of the Artisan: Art and Experience in the Scientific Revolution* (Chicago: University of Chicago Press, 2004)

Soranzo, Giovanni, *La lega italica (1454–55)* (Milan: Vita e pensiero, 1924)

Soudek, Josef, "A Fifteenth-Century Humanistic Bestseller: The Manuscript Diffusion of Leonardo Bruni's Annotated Latin Version of the ps.-Aristotelian Economics," in E. P. Mahoney, ed., *Philosophy and Humanism: Renaissance Essays in Honor of Paul Oskar Kristeller* (Leiden: Brill, 1976), 129–43

"Leonardo Bruni and His Public: A Statistical and Interpretative Study of His Annotated Latin Version of the ps.-Aristotelian *Economics*," *Studies in Medieval and Renaissance History* 5 (1968): 49–136

Statius, *Silvae*, ed. and tr. D.R. Shackleton Bailey, with corrections by Christopher A. Parrott (Cambridge, MA: Harvard University Press, 2015)

Stegmüller, Friedrich, ed., *Repertorium Biblicum Medii Aevi*, 11 vols. (Madrid: Consejo Superior de Investigaciones Cientificas, 1950–80)

ed., *Repertorium commentariorum in Sententias Petri Lombardi*, 2 vols. (Würzburg: Schöning, 1947)

Steinberg, Justin, "Dante *Estravagante*, Petrarca *Disperso*, and the Spectre of the Other Woman," in Zygmunt G. Baranski and Theodore J. Cachey Jr., *Petrarch and Dante: Anti-Dantism, Metaphysics, Tradition* (Notre Dame: University of Notre Dame Press, 2009), 263–89

Stinger, Charles M., *Humanism and the Church Fathers: Ambrogio Traversari (1386–1439) and Christian Antiquity in the Italian Renaissance* (Albany: State University of New York Press, 1977)

Stump, Phillip H., *The Reforms of the Council of Constance, 1414–1418* (Leiden: Brill, 1994)

Tambrun, Brigitte, *Pléthon: Le retour de Platon* (Paris: Vrin, 2006)

Tavoni, Mirko, *Latino, grammatica, volgare: Storia di una questione umanistica* (Padua: Antenore, 1984)

Tennyson, Lord Alfred, *Selected Poetry*, ed. Norman Page (London: Routledge, 1995)

Torre, Arnaldo della, *Storia dell'Accademia platonica di Firenze* (Florence: Carnesecchi, 1902)

Toussaint, Stéphane, *L'esprit du Quattrocento: Pic de la Mirandole: Le De ente et uno et Réponses à Antonio Cittadini* (Paris: Honoré Champion, 1995)

Tracy, James D., *Erasmus of the Low Countries* (Berkeley: University of California Press, 1996)

Twemlow, J.A., ed., *Calendar of Entries in the Papal Registers Relating to Great Britain and Ireland. Papal Letters, v.7, AD 1417–1431* (London: Mackie and co., 1906)

Ullman, Berthold L., *Studies in the Italian Renaissance* (Rome: Edizioni di Storia e letteratura, 1973)

and Philip A. Stadter, *The Public Library of Renaissance Florence: Niccolò Niccoli, Cosimo de' Medici and the Library of San Marco* (Padua: Antenore, 1972)

The Origin and Development of Humanist Script (Rome: Edizioni di storia e letteratura, 1960)

Valcke, Louis and Roland Galibois, *Le périple intellectuel de Jean Pic de la Mirandole* (Québec: Les Presses de l'Université Laval, 1994)

Valla, Lorenzo, *Correspondence*, ed. and tr. Brendan Cook (Cambridge, MA: Harvard University Press, 2014)

Dialectical Disputations, 2 vols., ed. and tr. Brian Copenhaver and Lodi Nauta (Cambridge, MA: Harvard University Press, 2012)

Ad Alfonsum regem Epistola de duobus Tarquiniis [and] Confutationes in Benedictum Morandum, ed. Francesco Lo Monaco (Florence: Polistampa, 2009)

Laurentii Valle Emendationes quorundam locorum ex Alexandro ad Alfonsum primum Aragonum regem, ed. Clementina Marsico (Florence: Polistampa, 2009)

Laurentii Valle Encomion Sancti Thome Aquinatis, ed. Stefano Cartei (Florence: Polistampa, 2008)

On the Donation of Constantine, ed. and tr. Glenn Bowersock (Cambridge, MA: Harvard University Press, 2007)

Raudensiane note, ed. Gian Matteo Corrias (Florence: Polistampa, 2007)

Orazione per l'inaugurazione dell'anno accademico 1455–1456: Atti di un seminario di filologia umanistica, ed. Silvia Rizzo (Rome: Roma nel Rinascimento, 1994)

Antidotum Primum: La prima apologia contro Poggio Bracciolini, ed. Ari Wesseling (Van Gorcum: Assen, 1978)

De vero falsoque bono, ed. and tr. Maristella Lorch (New York: Abaris, 1977)

De falso credita et ementita Constantini donatione, ed. Wolfram Setz, in the *Monumenta Germaniae historica*, 10 (Weimar: Böhlau, 1976)

"Dialogue on Free Will," tr. Charles E. Trinkaus Jr., in Ernst Cassirer, Paul Oskar
    Kristeller, and John Herman Randall Jr., *The Renaissance Philosophy of Man* (Chicago:
    University of Chicago Press, 1948), 155–82
Elegantiae linguae latinae (Venice, 1496)
"Encomium of St. Thomas," tr. Patrick Baker, in Salvatore I. Camporeale, *Christianity,
    Latinity, and Culture: Two Studies on Lorenzo Valla*, 297–315
Varro, *On the Latin Language*, 2 vols., ed. and tr. Roland G. Kent (Cambridge, MA:
    Harvard University Press, 1951)
Vasoli, Cesare, "*Il De christiana religione* di Marsilio Ficino," *Bruniana et Campanelliana*, 13
    (2007), 403–28
    "La biblioteca progettata da un Papa: Niccolò V e il 'suo canone,'" *Babel: Littératures
    plurielles* 6 (2002), 219–39
    ed., *Le filosofie del Rinascimento* (Milan: Mondadori, 2002)
    Quasi sit Deus: Studi su Marsilio Ficino (Lecce: Conte, 1999)
Verde, Armando, *Lo studio fiorentino, 1473–1503*, 5 vols. (Florence: Olschki, 1973–94)
    "Domenico di Fiandra: intransigente tomista non gradito nello studio fiorentino,"
    Memorie dominicane 7 (1976), 304–21
Verger, Jacques, "Patterns," in H. De Ridder-Symoens, *A History of the University in
    Europe*, 2 vols. to date (Cambridge: Cambridge University Press, 1992–96), 1:
    35–67
Vianello, Nereo, "I libri di Petrarca e la prima idea di una pubblica biblioteca a Venezia,"
    in *Miscellanea marciana di studi bessareonei (a coronamento del V Centenario della donazione
    nicena)* (Padua, 1976), pp. 435–51
Vidal, Fernando, "Brains, Bodies, Selves, and Science: Anthropologies of Identity and the
    Resurrection of the Body," *Critical Inquiry* 28 (2002), 930–74
Virgil, *Aeneid*, tr. with notes by Frederick Ahl (Oxford: Oxford University Press, 2007)
    Eclogues, Georgics, Aeneid, 2 vols., ed. and tr. H. Rushton Fairclough and G.P. Goold
    (Cambridge, MA: Harvard University Press, 1999)
Vitale, Maurizio, *La questione della lingua* (Palermo: Palumbo, 1964)
Viti, Paolo, ed., *Firenze e il Concilio del 1439*, 2 vols. (Florence: Olschki, 1994)
    ed., *Pico, Poliziano, e l'umanesimo di fine Quattrocento* (Florence: Olschki, 1994)
Volpi, Guglielmo, "Un cortigiano di Lorenzo il Magnifico ed alcune sue lettere," *Giornale
    storico della letteratura italiana* 17 (1891), 229–76
Volz, Hanz, *Martin Luthers deutsche Bibel: Entstehung und Geschichte der Lutherbibel*, ed.
    Henning Wendland (Hamburg: Wittig, 1978)
Wacquet, Francoise, *Latin: Or, the Empire of a Sign*, tr. John Howe (London and New
    York: Verso, 2001)
Waley, Daniel and Trevor Dean, *The Italian City Republics* (London: Routledge, 2009)
Walser, Ernst, *Poggius Florentinus: Leben und Werke* (Leipzig: Teubner, 1914)
Wesseling, Ari, "Commentary," in Angelo Poliziano, *Lamia: Praelectio in priora Aristotelis
    analytica*, 21–115
Whitford, David M., "The Papal Antichrist: Martin Luther and the Underappreciated
    Influence of Lorenzo Valla," *Renaissance Quarterly* 61 (2008),26–52
Wilks, Michael, ed., *The World of John of Salisbury* (Oxford: Blackwell, 1984)
Williams, Gordon W., *Change and Decline: Roman Literature in the Early Empire* (Berkeley:
    University of California Press, 1978)

Wippel, John F., "The Condemnation of 1270 and 1277 at Paris," *The Journal of Medieval and Renaissance Studies* 7 (1977), 169–201

Wirszubski, Chaim, *Pico della Mirandola's Encounter with Jewish Mysticism* (Cambridge, MA: Harvard University Press, 1989)

Witt, Ronald G., *In the Footsteps of the Ancients: The Origins of Humanism from Lovato to Bruni* (Leiden: Brill, 2000)

"What Did Giovanni Read and Write? Literacy in Early Renaissance Florence," *I Tatti Studies* 6 (1995), 83–114

Hercules at the Crossroads: The Life, Works, and Thought of Coluccio Salutati (Durham, NC: Duke University Press, 1983)

"Introduction," in Salutati, *On the World and Religious Life*, vii–xvii

Woodhouse, C.M., *George Gemistos Plethon: The Last of the Hellenes* (Oxford: Oxford University Press, 1986)

Woolfson, Jonathan, ed., *Palgrave Advances in Renaissance Historiography* (New York: Palgrave, 2004)

Wyatt, Michael, ed., *The Cambridge Companion to the Italian Renaissance* (Cambridge: Cambridge University Press, 2014)

Zanato, Tiziano, *Saggio sul Comento di Lorenzo de' Medici* (Florence: Olschki, 1979)

Zeidberg, David, ed., *Aldus Manutius and Renaissance Culture* (Florence: Olschki, 1998)

Zippel, Giuseppe, *Storia e cultura del Rinascimento italiano* (Padua: Antenore, 1979)

Zorzi, Marino, *La libreria di San Marco: Libri, lettori, societa nella Venezia dei Dogi* (Milan: Mondadori, 1987)

INDEX